Store Wars
Shopkeepers and the Culture of M

C000277238

Historians have traditionally argued that economic change before the Second World War destroyed the world of the independent storekeeper, and have consequently interpreted protest by the independents as a desperate counter-attack against the emergence of a society based on mass production and mass consumption. In *Store Wars* David Monod counters that myth by showing that the rate of small-business growth in retailing remained relatively constant into the 1930s despite rising competition by the mass marketers.

Monod finds that independent retailing, rather than being destroyed by modernity, was transformed by it, as the success of small-business people came to depend on the store owners' ability to adapt to the demands of an economy increasingly predicated on 'bigness.' Shopkeepers had to modernize their stores, improve their accounting, retreat from open-book credit, develop closer relations with their suppliers, and depend more on manufacturers for advertising, pricing, and promotion. Monod describes the profound impact of this adaptation on retail unity, on small-business values, and on shopkeepers' political and associational activities, and reveals how trade associations were used by 'progressive' merchants to fight for trade reforms that hurt marginal competitors.

By emphasizing the differences among shopkeepers and by exploring the apparent dissonance between trade practice and small-business ideals, *Store Wars* contributes to the ongoing debate regarding the existence and the unity of the 'lower-middle class.' It also provides new interpretations of both the reform process and the Reconstruction campaign of 1934–5.

DAVID MONOD is an assistant professor in the Department of History at Wilfrid Laurier University.

DAVID MONOD

Store Wars
Shopkeepers and the
Culture of Mass Marketing
1890–1939

UNIVERSITY OF TORONTO PRESS
Toronto Buffalo London

© University of Toronto Press Incorporated 1996
Toronto Buffalo London
Printed in Canada

ISBN 0-8020-0650-7 (cloth)
ISBN 0-8020-7604-1 (paper)

Printed on acid-free paper

Canadian Cataloguing in Publication Data

Monod, David L., 1960–
  Store wars : shopkeepers and the culture of mass
  marketing, 1890–1939

  Includes bibliographical references and index.
  ISBN 0-8020-0650-7 (bound)
  ISBN 0-8020-7604-1 (pbk.)

  1. Retail trade – Canada – History. 2. Small
  business – Canada – History. 3. Canada – Economic
  conditions – 1867–1918.* 4. Canada – Economic
  conditions – 1918–1945. I. Title.

  HF5429.6.C3M6 1996 381.1'0971 C95-933024-0

Cover illustrations: (Front) Grocery department in Liesemer & Studer's
Didsbury, Alberta, general store, 1915, featuring expensive glass-topped
'silent salesmen,' prominently displayed brand-name goods, and high-priced
storage bins behind counter. Items in front of counter were moved there for
the sake of the photo, to emphasize richness of stock. (Glenbow Archives,
NA-703-8)

(Back) 'Interior of Jewish store, Calgary,' c. 1920. This shoestring operation
has one relatively inexpensive glass display case, but the rest of the fixtures
are plain wood. Some attention has been given to organization of stock, but
the effect remains chaotic. (Glenbow Archives, NA-2916-2)

University of Toronto Press acknowledges the financial assistance to its
publishing program of the Canada Council and the Ontario Arts Council.

Contents

ACKNOWLEDGMENTS / vii

ABBREVIATIONS USED IN THE TEXT / ix

Introduction: The Shopkeeper, the Historian, and the Petite Bourgeoisie / 3

1 Shopkeeping's Divided World / 17

2 The Folklore of Retailing / 54

3 The Development of the Mass Market, 1870–1930 / 99

4 Progressive Retailing / 149

5 The Survival of the Fittest / 195

6 Resale Price Maintenance / 230

7 The Politics of Folklore / 286

A Closing Balance / 340

TABLES / 351

NOTES / 363

INDEX / 427

Acknowledgments

Any effort to understand social behaviour involves problems of identity, culture, ideology, economics, business, social activism, and politics. To myriad historians and social thinkers who have worked in these fields, I am indebted for insight and guidance in ways which endnotes cannot express. I am particularly grateful to my teachers and dissertation committee at the University of Toronto and especially to Carl Berger, who suffered my enthusiasms with patience and wry humour. My studies at the time were supported by doctoral fellowships from the Social Sciences and Humanities Research Council and the Fonds FCAC. Research funding from Wilfrid Laurier University, as well as a course-relief grant, made subsequent research and writing much less effortful.

Colleagues in the History Department at Wilfrid Laurier have been unfailingly generous and encouraging; they make it a singularly lively and stimulating place to work. I sent a copy of the manuscript to Mark Cox, a historian whom I hardly know but whose dissertation covers a similar topic, and he responded with twenty pages of extraordinarily helpful, closely argued analysis. I thank him again for his kindness and for the uncommon generosity of his scholarship. I wish I could also thank the late Ian Drummond for his helpful uncovering of errors and omissions. At the University of Toronto Press, Rob Ferguson was unfailingly helpful, and Elizabeth Hulse, who copyedited the manuscript with startling efficiency and precision, made the final process an almost pleasant experience. Several friends and colleagues – Terry Copp, John Ingham, Keith Walden, Cynthia Comacchio, Suzanne Zeller, and Craig Heron – also read drafts or parts of drafts of this manuscript, and as some of them remind me, I am heavily indebted to them. But I know that they will understand when I single out three dear friends for their contributions: Enrico Cumbo, Nicholas Terpstra, and George Urbaniak. At different stages in the progress of this work they offered camaraderie, commentary, and conversation and, in their singular ways, inspiration. They will, in turn, understand why this book is for Michaela Milde. For more than a decade she has lived closely with it and always maintained its worth. I know that we will both now delight in turning it over to Adam, a little boy who knows that every book must be judged by the strength of its binding.

Funding problems almost prevented this manuscript from appearing; that it has been published is attributable to the support and advocacy of Gerry Hallowell of the University of Toronto Press. I am also deeply grateful to Terry Copp, who, as chair of the History Department, supported my efforts, and to the Office of the Vice President Academic at Wilfrid Laurier University for generously contributing to the costs of publication. I only hope that the book lives up to the confidence that was placed in it.

A condensed version of chapters 1 and 2 appeared in the *Journal of Social History*, spring 1995; an extended version of the first part of chapter 5 appeared in the *Journal of the Canadian Historical Association*, 1993.

Abbreviations Used in the Text

CMA	Canadian Manufacturers' Association
CPhA	Canadian Pharmaceutical Association and its provincial chapters: PEIPhA, NSPhA, NBPhA, QPhA, MPhA, SPhA, APhA, BCPhA
FMA	Furniture Manufacturers' Association
FTL	Fair Trade League
ISA	Industrial Standards Act
NFTC	National Fair Trade Council
NIRA	National Industrial Recovery Administration
NRA	National Recovery Act
OCP	Ontario College of Pharmacy
ORDA	Ontario Retail Druggists' Association
ORGA	Ontario Retail Grocers' Association
ORHA	Ontario Retail Hardware Association
PATA	Proprietary Articles Trading Association
RMA	Retail Merchants' Association of Canada and its provincial chapters: PEI RMA, NS RMA, NB RMA, QRMA, ORMA, MRMA, SRMA, ARMA, BC RMA
RMAC(S)	Retail Merchants' Association of Canada (Saskatchewan)
rpm	resale price maintenance
SCO	Supreme Court of Ontario
WDA	Wholesale Druggists' Association
WGA	Wholesale Grocers' Association

STORE WARS

Introduction

The Shopkeeper, the Historian, and the Petite Bourgeoisie

'Who am I?,' asks a Retail Merchants' Association flysheet from the mid-1920s:

Je rampe comme le dragon de l'Apocalypse, à travers les vallées,
   les montagnes et les plaines.
Je ne constuis pas des villes.
Je ne développe pas des fermes.
Je n'érige pas des bâtisses.
...
Je viens pour prendre, non pour donner ou aider.
Je coup les dépenses, je ne fais pas livraison ni de crédit.
Je n'encourage aucune industrie locale.

The answer: 'Je suis chain store. Propriété des étrangers.'[1] Such naïve verse, bristling with hostility to what has become so ordinary, sounds almost quaint today. Were people really moved by these self-serving words? Could the mass merchandisers have been seriously considered such marauding and unnatural intruders? Doggerel then, but does that make it any less significant? Propaganda such as this was, after all, pretty common fare in the early decades of the twentieth century. Thousands of people were involved in anti-chain and anti-department store protests, and they produced, in their efforts, an immense amount of paper. Throughout the early twentieth century, aggrieved shopkeepers lobbied governments, spattered the press with demands for protection, and bombarded the public with flyers. Currency alone does not, of course, denote value, and the poetry itself is pretty bad. But reflect a moment on the ideas themselves: imagine the emotions that must have motivated the shop owners' complaint, sense the panic behind the rhyme, and then recoil from its nativism and narrowness. There is, after all, something uncomfortably alive about this faded, dated protest.

What gives our reading of the retailers' words a special resonance is the collective memory of the 1930s. Emotions such as those expressed here – xenophobia, traditionalism, a fear of bigness, and a suspicion of modernity – have often been associated with movements of right-wing protest. This is because retailers (who together with artisans and farmers are generally thought to form the petite bourgeoisie or lower middle class) were prominent members and electors of Italian and German fascist parties, and their yearnings, resentments, and loyalties have been widely considered to have supplied the emotional energy for both movements. As early as the mid-1930s, social scientists were proposing that fascism was itself a manifestation of the 'psychic derangement' experienced by traditional business people confronting the modern age.[2]

Intellectually cramped and stilted, trapped in their petty concerns and unable to see past their own front doors, independent shopkeepers are thought to have entered the twentieth century psychologically hamstrung. Having sacrificed art, learning, imagination – curiosity, even – in the pursuit of their petty business interests, they are depicted as being incapable of accepting the challenge of progress. Big business and big labour appeared to them as threats: monster interests crushing cozy neighbourhoods and time-honoured work practices in their remorseless advance. As class lines sharpened and big corporations emerged in the last decades of the nineteenth century, members of the petite bourgeoisie panicked. And because of certain psychic predispositions, independent retailers and other self-employed people turned for relief to demagogic politicians who promised to punish those disrupting their world. It did not matter whether small shopkeeping was really being undermined by big-business competition; what mattered was that independent retailers thought they were suffering. And such a belief was as much a result of the store owners' antediluvian mentality as it was of any real insecurities.

As Svend Ranulf explained in his 1938 monograph *Moral Indignation and Middle Class Psychology*, the peculiar mentality of lower-middle-class people – the 'puritanism' born of the long 'frustration of their natural desires' – led shopkeepers to seek relief from anxiety in 'the punishing of others.' As a result, they chose to lash out at the symbols of economic progress and change: foreigners and outsiders (Jews especially), communists, trade unions, liberated women, jazz music, and big businesses –

anything that represented a threat to their own narrow conception of the social order. Change threatened the mental security of the petite bourgeoisie, creating 'status anxieties,' 'cultural despair,' and 'emotional crisis.' It was this 'psychic' breakdown – the exaggerated, pathological response to social transformation – that explained the rise of right-wing mass movements in the twentieth century. For some analysts, this hatred of innovation and fear of disorder served as the tap root of all that was nasty in the modern world. As the great American sociologist Harold Lasswell observed, 'a disinterested tendency to inflict punishment practically does not exist in communities where the lower middle class is of little significance.' There is nothing innocuous, then, in the Canadian retailers' versifying against the mass market; the quaint anti–chain store flysheet can be read as a proto-fascist tract, and the desperate protests of a group suffering the impact of competition can be seen as a foretaste of genocide.[3]

Ideas such as these became part of Canada's intellectual inheritance with the rise of sociological history in the years after the Second World War. Before the fifties, when economists dominated Canadian studies, retail protest was largely interpreted as a simple form of business atavism. Progress, the economists reasoned, was bound to involve an increasing centralization of economic activity, and while Judgment Day might not be as swift or as clean as the independent retailers imagined, they were at least right in sensing its coming. Railways and automobiles and economies of scale had made mass distribution inevitable, and traditional retailing was only so much grist for modernity's mill. 'The chain stores have made and will continue to make inroads on the unit store,' observed a government analyst in 1926, and 'they have found the progress easy because of the slackness and inefficiency of many small merchants. Naturally, such inefficiency, in the face of keen competition, has been responsible for business failures. From the viewpoint of the public interest, this should not be regarded as an evil ... but as the beginning of the solution.' In other words, the problem lay not with the mass merchandisers, who were bearers of efficiency, but with those traditional shop owners who were unable to accept the accelerated pace of contemporary business life. Consequently, while independent retailers might be deserving of some sympathy, they were hardly worthy of analysis. Proprietary enterprise, Lloyd Reynolds noted in 1940, was quite simply 'archaic,' making twentieth-century small-business protest no more interesting than 'the smashing of machines by hand workers during the Industrial Revolution.'[4]

It was only in the fifties that Canadian scholars accepted the European idea that small-business protest was produced by a peculiar and dangerous 'lower-middle-class psychology.' Despite a reluctance in these early Cold War days to engage in class analysis, Canadian authors did quietly adopt the idea that economic change generated a group-specific psychosis. John Irving, in his classic study of Social Credit in Alberta, saw 'resentment,' 'insecurity,' and 'hate' behind the 'mass psychology' of social unrest. Social Credit, like other movements of right-wing protest, arose, he explained, 'when primary, or even derived, needs are frustrated.' 'Right-wing populism,' Irving explained, was 'a rural and small town' phenomenon, backed by members of 'a puritanical lower middle class' tortured by visions of 'social disintegration' and driven by fear towards 'a strong-willed, dauntless leader who would take them out of the wilderness.' Similarly, William Mann, in his treatment of religious dissent in western Canada, found evangelical 'non-conformists' to have been primarily members of the lower middle class who, he noted cryptically, were 'inclined to neurosis and neurasthenia.' A few years earlier, Everett Hughes, in his study of Drummondville, made the same connection in tracing anti-Semitism, nationalism, xenophobia, and sympathy for Naziism largely to the 'aggressions,' 'insecurities,' and 'resentments' of the 'French Canadian small businessman.'[5]

In fact, it was in Quebec that the idea of a lower-middle-class psychosis proved most influential. Quebec's postwar intellectuals, pumped up on European culture, discovered in the petite bourgeoisie the symbol of everything that they found backward, trivial, and weak. To their widely opened eyes, the traditional lower middle class appeared the bulwark of archaic nationalism, the mainstay of Quebec's parochialism, and the source of Duplessis's power. By the early 1960s, social critics such as Trudeau began to use the term 'petit bourgeois' in the way that many French intellectuals did – as a form of abuse. For those who thought the rebellion of 1837–8 a nationalist fiasco, the petite bourgeoisie was to blame; for those who disliked ultramontanism, there was a petit bourgeois ideology; for those who thought pre–Second World War Quebec nationalists excessively conservative, there was a 'petit bourgeois mentality' at work; for those who abhorred Quebec anti-Semitism, it was a petit bourgeois aberration; for those opposed to Abbé Groulx and the Action française, it was a manifestation of petit bourgeois anti-modernism; and for those who thought that the Quiet Revolution provided a clean sweep, there was a new middle class seizing power from the old.[6]

Ironically, outside Quebec, interest in the petite bourgeoisie declined in the 1960s just as class as an historical concept began to enjoy increased acceptance. This change was in large measure a result of the growth of a Marxist consensus within social studies and the ascendance of working-class history. For those engaged in studying the proletariat's struggle, the lower middle class must have seemed a dead skin that needed to be discarded. Not one of the two real classes within modern capitalism, the petite bourgeoisie was intriguing only in the degree of its proletarianization. Artisans continued to attract attention, but only because interest shifted from studying them as part of a small-business grouping to their role as members of a working class carving out its identity. Little space within this emerging perspective was accorded to those engaged in retailing, an occupation which, to working-class historians, offered nothing more than the distressing possibility of *embourgeoisement*. Consequently while occasional Lasswellian comments continued to fleck the works of some Canadian historians – most notably, the business histories of Michael Bliss and his students – by the 1970s independent retailers had all but disappeared from view.[7]

This has not been the case in Europe or, to a lesser extent, in the United States. Since the 1970s, a certain disaffection with economic growth has come to characterize social and economic theory, and this discontent has helped to spin the historiographic compass in new directions. Among European historians, the main focus of the revisionism has been the idea that lower-middle-class people have a psychological predisposition to irrational and reactionary behaviour. Instead, two theories have been advanced to explain petit bourgeois extremism. According to some historians, the rightward drift of small-business politics in the 1880s and 1890s was a result not of latent reactionary tendencies, but of the manipulations of conservative politicians seeking to fragment the left-leaning petit bourgeois–proletarian alliance of the mid-nineteenth century. Orleanist industrialists and landowners in France, Junkers and 'feudalized' capitalists in Germany, Catholic Party strategists in Belgium – these are now seen as the puppet-masters of petit bourgeois protest. As for the independent proprietors, their susceptibility to manipulation is still most often explained in terms of psychological factors: the trauma of military humiliation in France and Germany, the isolation produced by the leftward march of the trade union movement, the resentments caused by economic marginalization. Though this interpretation accepts the psychic instability of the petite bourgeoisie, it breaks from the older approach in portraying small business people as victims rather than as villains.[8]

An alternate, though not necessarily contradictory, view is to emphasize the petite bourgeoisie's real, rather than 'ideological' or ideational,
problems. Where this interpretation differs from the preceding is in the
way that some historians present the stratum's economic and social
problems as producing extremist behaviour. From this angle, the lower
middle class was not pulled to the radical right by self-serving politicians or driven there by left-leaning workers; it grew reactionary of its
own accord. Modernization attacked the small-business community: it
spawned low-priced big-business competitors; it undermined customer
loyalty; it drove down profits and narrowed opportunities. Quite logically, small business people protested against these changes using time-
honoured associations, experiences, and mutualisms. Voluntary organizations – shooting clubs, religious associations, gymnastics groups –
promoted the sort of small-town values (apoliticism, thrift, enterprise,
and xenophobia) which lay at the heart of twentieth-century *völkish* ideologies. Similarly, petit bourgeois theatre, with its anti-Semitism, nostalgia, and anti-establishmentarianism, legitimized an extremist response
to social change. Economic distress served, in this interpretation, to
politicize the class culture of the petite bourgeoisie and to transform
once-local associations into movements of mass protest. Once again,
however, there was nothing intrinsically irrational or psychotic about
the lower middle class; desperate times simply produced a call for
extreme solutions.[9]

Like their European counterparts, students of small-business protest
in America have worked recently to dispel the image of the irrational
lower middle class. They write, in this regard, in the shadow of Richard
Hofstadter, whose searing indictment of American populism as a pre-
cursor of McCarthyism (and McCarthyism as a kind of American fascism) owed so much to the writings of Lasswell, Ranulf, and Reich. But
unlike European historians, American scholars have generally shied
away from class analysis and have instead used generalized terms like
'the middle class,' 'the small business community,' and even 'the people'
to describe a group that in Europe would be considered thoroughly petit
bourgeois. Thus Robert Weibe never refers to a lower middle class in his
discussion of the 'status anxieties' and desperate protests of late-nineteenth-century small business people and farmers confronting the emer-
gent mass society. Still, in spite of this tracing of consensus history,
American analysts have followed the main trends of the European histo-
riography: in the 1950s and 1960s they associated anti-trust activism,
populism, and McCarthyism with the unreasoned fears and irrational

resentments of small business people; in the 1970s and 1980s they treated anti-monopolism as an insurgency grounded in traditional community values and work cultures; they saw Bryanite Democrats and white supremacists as luring the populists to the right; they questioned the 'reactionary nature' of the 'old middle class'; and they redefined McCarthyism as a conspiracy of the Republican establishment.[10] The main difference is that American historians have generally gone further than their European counterparts in their redemptive efforts. By rooting what in Europe is regarded as small-business jacobinism in a Jeffersonian tradition, American scholars have depicted nineteenth-century petit bourgeois values as viable and even admirable. Indeed, they suggest that community-centredness, independent entrepreneurship, and participatory democracy all represent the basis of a new idealism; one struggled over by left and right, it is true, but a positive force none the less. The ideas of a declining stratum driven to unreason by modernization have become, in the eyes of many interpreters, the hope for America's future.[11]

The new work being done on the social history of the lower middle class has helped restore a much-maligned stratum to its senses, but certain difficulties remain. Underlying much of the scholarship, new and old, is the idea that retailers and other petits bourgeois constituted a premodern fragment – a traditional group set adrift (whether psychologically or materially) on the waves of economic and social change. Their response, which most agree involved battening down the hatches and awaiting a political saviour, might well have been understandable, perhaps even logical, but it was none the less desperate. Even if they were motivated by positive community-oriented traditions, lower-middle-class activism still seems to carry the pathetic features of a lost cause.

The trouble with this characterization is that even as social historians have been busily rethinking petit bourgeois politics, a few enterprising business and economic historians have been reconceiving the dynamics of modernization. And while their ideas have yet really to challenge the institutional, big-business bias of so much of the literature, the idea is spreading that small might not be merely beautiful but efficient and enterprising as well. Proprietary manufacturing in the developing world has undoubtedly been the greatest beneficiary of the new interest in the economics of small business, but attention is now also being paid to independent retailing. The reappraisal began when economic historians took a fresh look at the nineteenth-century French economy and realized that it enjoyed significant growth despite its domination by small firms.

Proprietary enterprise, it seemed, was not by definition unproductive or unimportant. Armed with this knowledge, researchers in England and America began to investigate petty entrepreneurship's contribution to the development of countries whose economic histories had long been dominated by the study of the large firm. While Marxist historians started negotiating the concept of 'combined and uneven development' – implying the continuing relevance of earlier forms of enterprise within a subsequent economic formation – conservative business analysts chortled over the evidence of entrepreneurial opportunities. According to Philip Scranton, it all serves to show that small business should be considered in its own right and not as a 'peripheral' element in an economy shaped by bigness. Seen this way, 'proprietary capitalism' represented 'a different version of industrial development,' in no way inferior to the managerial route simply because its advocates 'followed a different path to profit, prominence and accumulation than did the mass-production corporate giants.'[12] Long thought a doomed element in the modern economy, small-scale property is now emerging as a viable and even necessary contributor to business development.

This rediscovery of small property is having a profound effect on the business history of the self-employed. At its furthest extreme, it has led a number of neo-conservative historians, inspired by the discovery that large-scale capitalism did not eliminate small-scale opportunity, to denounce optimistically the whole theory of petit bourgeois decline. By showing, for example, that the number of independent artisans actually increased at the very moment when factory producers were supposedly blotting them out, these historians have demonstrated that small enterprise remained a functioning element within nineteenth-century industrial capitalism. Though ultimately, artisanal and retail labour may have changed, it did not disappear; rather, it found a new home in the manufactory and convenience store. Adaptation is therefore perceived to be the key, for far from languishing in backwardness, small business people were competitive and alert to changing techniques. Big businesses certainly existed, but independent enterprise preserved its vitality by charting a separate route to modernity. Eschewing the image of the trembling economic reactionaries, the new conservatives have recast the petty proprietors as resourceful entrepreneurs brimming with business initiative.[13]

These different perspectives – the social and the economic – have yet to be fully joined. If small business people were capable of adapting to the demands of the modern economy, how is their politicking to be understood? Can social historians continue to root political extremism in traditional work practices and relationships if those activities and inter- actions were changing in conformity with new market forces? What makes these questions so difficult to answer is the wall of assumptions obstructing the view. Revolutions, pasts and presents, traditions and modernities – these terms of disjunction provide the framework for our understanding of the emergence of the modern world. Old and new confront each other in history books as irreconcilables – the antithesis destroying its thesis – to such an extent that when a 'tradition' persists we wonder at its 'survival.' The hermeneutic postulate that all acts are reinterpretations and that nothing that happened can ever be re-created has attracted the interest of few historians of the lower middle class. But it is precisely this concept that the literature on small-business adapta- tion forces us to consider. Just because proprietary enterprise was a con- tinuation of a nineteenth-century form does not mean that it remained the same. And if business practices were continually remaking them- selves, by what right do we assume that ideas were not?

Unfortunately, those historians who have recently confronted the issue of economic adaptation directly have been reluctant to consider the possibility that the ideologies of the petits bourgeois may have been as adaptive as their business practices. As a result, they have accepted a separation of the material and the cultural and have resorted to older psychological explanations for petit bourgeois attitudes and values. In Philip Nord's elegant treatment of late-nineteenth-century Paris shop- keeping, independent retailers are presented as progressive business people and reactionary thinkers. The point, Nord suggests, is that Pari- sian retailers were unable to modify their social expectations as quickly as they changed their business practices. Even as they adapted to meet the competition of the department stores, they were confronted by the destruction of the world in which their class culture had been formed. Urban renewal churned up old neighbourhoods, new boulevards sliced through established shopping areas, and the severe depression of the 1880s drove down profits. These factors created a crisis of confidence which pushed shopkeepers towards the political right. But it was socio- cultural change rather than economic distress which best explains the development of their lower-middle-class resentments.[14]

Ironically, this line of argument lands Nord uncomfortably close to the 'psychic derangement' school even as he seeks to rehabilitate the shopkeepers by presenting them – like E.P. Thompson's handloom workers or Lawrence Goodwyn's populists – as defenders of an older communitarian value system. Attitudes and values that grew in a certain historical context are depicted as becoming petrified, enduring long after the disappearance of the environment that nurtured them. Despite Nord's efforts to reconstruct the retailers' world sympathetically, he detaches ideas from material realities and in so doing raises the possibility that retailers were simply too parochial, stubborn, and unreasoning to adjust their expectations as quickly as they changed their selling practices. But how else can one rationalize business adaptability with apparent political and social conservatism?

It is a problem that Thomas McCraw, in his award-winning study of the regulatory impulse in the United States, also fails to resolve. As with many American historians, McCraw sees the turn-of-the-century anti-monopoly or anti-trust movement as a small-business protest. Confused by the emergence of a mass market, worried by the development of large industrial and marketing enterprises, battered by the economic depression of the 1890s, American petits bourgeois lobbied for regulation. Their aim was to use the power of the state to destroy the large combinations. Their demands were not, however, motivated by real economic problems. As McCraw explains it, the American economy at the turn of the century was structured like a big doughnut made up of 'central' (big) and 'peripheral' (small) businesses organized into industries which themselves 'assume either a centre or peripheral configuration and ... maintain that configuration over a long period of time.' In other words, small businesses and large were 'fundamentally different' and more complementary than antagonistic.[15]

Having adopted this perspective McCraw, not surprisingly, finds petit bourgeois protest unjustified. Because peripheral business people lacked the 'necessary vocabulary' to conceptualize economic growth, they believed that all industries were about to be taken over by trusts. But in this belief they were mistaken: though big businesses may have been destroying 'the atomistic commonwealth' of the petit bourgeois imagination, they posed no threat to competition, opportunity, or small-business survival. McCraw's interpretation becomes even more critical when he illustrates this thesis with a biography of the trust-busting lawyer Louis Brandeis and the small shopkeepers whose cause he represented. Suddenly the absence of a 'necessary vocabulary' becomes a boneheaded preference for old-fashioned things. The words that McCraw employs in his description of Brandeis whisper 'psychic derangement' to anyone familiar with the writings of Lasswell, Ranulf, and Reich: Brandeis, we learn, disliked wealthy people; he was 'profoundly disturbed by ostentatious consumption'; he 'loathed such modern devices as automobiles and telephones'; he had a 'hatred of advertising'; he was overfond of things 'that had served him well in the past.' In addition – and here McCraw's use of the term 'petit bourgeois' takes on an even-darker cast – the regulations that Brandeis and the retailers endorsed 'required nothing short of authoritarian action by the state.' Though ostensibly profiling a single individual, and one who could hardly be called petit bourgeois, McCraw indicts an entire social stratum.[16] Like Nord, he resolves the conflict of tradition and modernity by implying that retailers had a split personality. Rather than opening new dimensions of analysis, the notion of peripheral firms in this instance serves only to refurbish a moth-eaten interpretation.

It is the goal of this study to present a more-coherent account of business adaptation and shopkeeper activism using the Canadian example. At its centre lies a single interpretive problem: were independent shopkeepers in the late nineteenth and early twentieth centuries able to adapt – culturally, politically, and economically – to the demands of the emerging mass market? A simple question, but answering it necessitates a rethinking of small-business 'culture' and 'action.' This rethinking is doubly important because of the thick coating of assumptions that now encrusts the study of the petite bourgeoisie. What, after all, do we mean by 'adaptation'? What do we mean by 'culture'? What does political participation or even activism involve? What are the implications of the word 'shopkeeper'? It is not my intention to sound obtuse; these questions need to be asked if we are to gain real insight into the independent retailers' history. Moreover, because this study offers a critical exploration of an interpretation that has become an axiom (the idea that lower-middle-class people were spiteful conservatives unable to adjust to the modern world either in reality or belief), these questions need to be asked.

Some will probably find the approach that has been chosen an unwelcome plunge into unfamiliar waters. Not only are the issues foreign to many Canadian historians, but the idea of using historical evidence to reinterpret a theory will strike many as overly deductive. The fact that we do not yet have a clear idea of shopkeeping's history will only compound the problem. This work does not pretend to offer a comprehensive treatment of Canadian retailing; it is not organized as a chronology; it does not give due treatment to all those who owned shops or all places or regions where trading was practised. Instead, it focuses on that group of shopkeepers who joined organizations and lobbied politically, and it assesses their ideas and businesses practices. Although this segment of the shopkeeping population constituted a minority, it was the group which has most often been referred to in discussions of petit bourgeois values and actions. In trying to understand whether historians have successfully interpreted lower-middle-class behaviour, we must therefore necessary focus on this group.

But theoretical problems determined more than just the subject of this study; they also tailored its form. The work is divided into three sections, each of which questions a different aspect of the orthodox approach. The first section (the first two chapters) offers a profile of retailing, a composite picture of the retail activists who form the subject of this book, and a discussion of their 'ideology.' The key issue is whether historians are correct in suggesting that there was a single, definable 'retail' response (whether 'deranged' or not) to economic change. The point of the first chapter is to show that there was no structurally unified retailing lower middle class confronting the mass market and that Canadian shopkeepers were deeply divided amongst themselves. The problem then becomes one of explaining the common culture that many historians believe united small business people despite their many differences. Chapter 2 draws on semiotics to account for this phenomenon. By distinguishing between symbolic forms, whose generalized acceptance served to unite retailers, and the actualities of speech, which worked to divide them, the chapter suggests that while historians are right in seeing retailers as possessing a single cultural inheritance, they have greatly exaggerated the bonding powers of the ideals that shopkeepers shared. Since a lower middle class as a material or cultural unity did not exist in Canada, the idea of a 'petit bourgeois psychology' or, indeed, of a 'small-business actor' is clearly compromised.

The second section (chapters 3 through 5) explores another major theme of the literature: the economic transformation affecting retailing in the late nineteenth and early twentieth centuries. The initial argument is that the growth of the mass market should be conceived not in terms of the rise of a few big stores but as a shift in power within distribution away from merchants and towards manufacturers and consumers. The implication of this suggestion for business adaptation and profitability forms the subject of the succeeding two chapters. This section raises questions about several previous approaches: first, that the type of independent proprietors who joined associations were 'traditional' in their business practices; second, that small business manifested an entrepreneurial ideal; third, that 'peripheral enterprise' offered 'an alternative route' to capital accumulation. This section shows that the divisions within the retail sector widened over time and that the people who were most heavily involved in protesting the costs of modernization were themselves busily modernizing.

The last section looks at retail association and politics in light of the preceding observations. The goal here is to prove that retail activists were as 'modern' in their political demands as they were in their business practices. Chapter 6 focuses on the major organizational struggle of the trade associations in the early twentieth century – the campaign for resale price maintenance (rpm) – and argues that the goal of the protest was a closer integration of independent retailing with large-scale production. Though the association members clearly embraced rpm because they were worried about their ability to compete with the chains and department stores, the solution they proposed was 'progressive' not 'reactionary.' The final chapter looks at retail-oriented political activism in the 1930s, and it deals with both the federal Reconstruction movement and the major provincial protests. Building on the work of European historians who see small business people 'seduced' by rightwing politicians, this chapter proposes that shopkeepers exerted little more than a symbolic influence over the right-wing demagogues of the thirties. Faced with the presumed failure of big business in the Depression, politicians such as Harry Stevens and William Aberhart called for the restoration of a small-business utopia, something which in practical terms was quite impossible for the modernizing shop owners.

Clearly, though questions arising out of the idea of a 'lower middle class' dominate and inspire the discussion, the activities of Canada's retailers can only be understood against a backdrop of economic change. And encased within the treatment of independent retailing's adaptation and fragmentation is an interpretation of Canadian social, political, and economic development that stands at odds with much of the literature. In essence, the suggestion is that a mass market emerged in Canada between 1870 and 1930, with 1919–21 serving many Canadians as a kind of epiphanic moment. This revolutionary transformation took the form not just of an expansion in consumer spending but of a new attitude to the making, selling, buying, and regulating of goods. It was to this transformation – so enormous in its reach and so subtle in its grasp – that modernizing retailers adapted. This part of the analysis should have remained in the background, but I must admit (as careful readers will doubtless suspect) that as time passed I became increasingly fascinated with the larger process. As a result, the book explores not just the shopkeepers' adaptation to the mass market but also the motivations and contributions of consumers, manufacturers, wholesalers, and politicians. The resulting tension between subject and background will prove, I hope, a matter of interest rather than distraction.

Still, this book in essence remains a critical assessment of the historians' retailers, mainly 'foreign' historians it is true, but not ones whose theories have lacked Canadian application. And it is no wonder. Canada was home to most of the developments and political movements that in other countries have been interpreted in lower-middle-class terms. Like other modern capitalist states, Canada experienced a retailing revolution in the late nineteenth century which saw the emergence of a national market, large-scale production, and mass merchandising. Like other small business people, retailers in Canada joined associations to protect their livelihood. As with independent shopkeepers in the United States and western Europe, merchants in Canada pushed for regulations designed to level the playing-field on which big and small competed. And like those considered petit bourgeois extremists in other places, Canada's shopkeepers in the 1930s supported political parties pledged to the 'restoration' of a small-business utopia. It is the irony of that appeal, rather than its relevance, which this book seeks to demonstrate.

1

Shopkeeping's Divided World

Like all those categorized as petit bourgeois, independent shopkeepers have been victimized by generalizations. Widely considered a subspecies of a larger collection, be it petit bourgeois, middle class, or small business, store owners are assumed to share characteristics common to all their kind. For most analysts, what homogenized the group and gave it its structural unity was the fact of self-employment. 'The one thing they all have,' announce Bechhofer and Elliott, 'the crucial thing[,] is petty productive property, and it is property with which they work themselves. It is their labour and very frequently that of their family and kin, that they mix with this property and though a good many also become employers of hired labour, the scale of that exploitation is typically very small and it is an extension of, rather than a substitute for, their own labour. These are the most fundamental features of what we shall call the petite bourgeoisie and from them flow the stream of [the group's] experience.'[1]

Many interpreters, and particularly those concerned with social structuration and mobility, stop here. The presumption of their work is that while those who own property might be different in many respects, self-employment none the less generates a single approach to social and productive relations. This much of the interpretation is held even by those who believe that the petite bourgeoisie occupies an indefinite position outside the actual class structure. As Marx observed, the unity that lower-middle-class people enjoyed arose out of material similarities rather than social interactions: they 'live in similar conditions but without entering into manifold relations with one another. Their mode of production isolates them from one another instead of bringing them into mutual intercourse.' Consequently, to the extent that they possess a similarity of condition, they form a unity; to the extent that 'the identity of their interests begets no community ... they do not form a class.'[2]

It is on these points that the whole issue turns. How is the small-business or lower-middle-class collectivity to be conceived? By selecting the characteristic 'self-employed' from among all the things which people who owned small businesses did and shared, those who emphasize material commonalities are according primacy to the form of individuals' relations with their own labour power. It is assumed that the mode itself (control over one's labour) creates a single set of conditions and perceptions and a single identity of interest (which Marx would call a self-interest hostile to notions of collectivity). So even though it might be recognized that independent proprietors did not generally 'associate' and actually competed against one another, the structure of their work made them see the world and act upon it in consanguineous (if not collaborative) ways.

The discussion which follows is concerned with exploring the extent to which this fact of self-employment both structurally unified Canadian retailers and generated a common set of experiences and understandings. Distanced by gender and geography, polarized by wealth and experience, multitudinous in their occupational variety, Canada's shopkeepers would appear from the outside to be a group without form. True, all storekeepers did own stock and had customers – bought and sold – and most worked in a shop of some sort, but cohesiveness was here to be found only in the range of difference. Though all traders acquired goods and sold them to someone else, both the goods they sold and the manner in which they sold them were as various as 'all the world and little Billing.' Consequently, the ways in which self-employment manifested itself need to be studied rather than ignored.

Furthermore, the simple fact that independent shopkeepers were not alienated from their labour does not mean that they enjoyed a similarity of condition. Retailing in Canada was a deeply stratified occupation, and an increasingly insurmountable barrier separated the main street shopkeepers from the poorer tradespeople of the backstreets. Though retailers shared a state of self-employment, that condition would appear to have generated different realities for different people. And finally, those who retailed carried into trading prejudices and perceptions which may well have kept them divided. The common reality of small-business ownership cannot be assumed to have homogenized the shopkeepers' gender, ethnic, or class perceptions; rather, retailers could plausibly have shaped their understanding of their mutual relations around values alien to the pursuit of their trade. In short, by what logic can the existence of self-employment be considered to have given tradespeople a commonality of interest or experience? Did forces such as wealth, trade, and gender define the retailers' experience of retailing, or did self-employment transcend the interests and identities which acted upon it?

NINETEENTH-CENTURY RETAILING: DEVELOPMENT AND
FRAGMENTATION

One indication that confusion over retailing's nature was a historical, rather than a purely interpretive, problem is the lack of information about it. If the census can be taken as a sign of popular attitudes, shop-keepers were not even considered a definable grouping until early in the twentieth century. Although an attempt was made to count 'merchants' in the late nineteenth century, the term was applied equally to wholesalers, retailers, brokers, and agents. Only in 1911 did the census enumerators specifically count the number of proprietors in the retail trades, and in 1923 they made a half-hearted stab at a full 'census of retailing.' But it was not really until 1931 that distribution received the kind of attention which had been lavished on manufacturing for over half a century.

This neglect was not simply a result of the conservatism of Canada's statisticians. Occasional press efforts at counting business activity in the late nineteenth century revealed similar biases: wholesalers and retailers were always grouped together as 'merchants,' and no sustained effort was made to distinguish between trades or business types. Nor was the neglect attributable to a shortage of examples. Though they were unevenly distributed and concentrated in towns and cities, there was, in terms of population, probably almost as high a proportion of merchants in 1850 as there would be eighty years later. In fact, in some urban places there was an even higher per capita concentration of shops and warehouses. In Saint John at mid-century, 7 per cent of the population was engaged in mercantile pursuits; in Brantford 3 per cent was self-employed in commercial or service occupations; in Hamilton almost 6 per cent of the population were merchants. By 1871 Darroch and Soltow found 5 per cent of Ontario's population owning business establishments (roughly the same percentage for the country as a whole), and the census for that year suggested that a little over a third of these individuals were engaged in trade. Evidence suggests that the number of retailers grew significantly in the last decades of the nineteenth century, but by 1931, when the census takers began their enumerations, there was no higher a concentration of tradespeople than there had been in the 1850s. In 1931 brokers, wholesalers, and retailers still comprised around 2 per cent of the population, but by this time the urban mercantile population in Saint John, Brantford, and Hamilton stood at a standard 1.5 per cent of the total.[3] In other words, the long delay in retailing's recognition as a distinct occupation had little to do with the actual visibility of its practitioners.

What really explains retailing's ill-defined character throughout much of the nineteenth century was the haphazard style of its pursuit. Most rural general storekeepers – and there were many – were also wholesaling. Though they sold commodities to farmers, the bulk of their business involved the shipping away of their customers' grains and wood. The more affluent general merchants also operated grist, saw, or carding mills in buildings adjacent to their shops.[4] It is, in short, difficult to determine whether these country merchants were manufacturers, brokers, or shopkeepers. In the bigger centres, where custom was large enough to permit specialization, the vast majority of those selling – shoemakers, confectioners, jewellers, butchers, clothiers – were also manufacturing. In the towns there were grocers, booksellers, and hardware and dry goods dealers doing a purely retail trade, but their number remained small. Moreover, they were not really considered to have more in common with each other than with people in other walks of life: the grocer and haberdasher were no more of a kind than were the farmer and the sailor, the lawyer and the priest.

Because they did not consider themselves a group, merchants did not see any reason to associate formally. The wealthiest might mingle at social functions, and artisans in a single trade might occasionally cooperate or even unionize, but there was precious little inter-occupational cooperation. Consequently, when historians collectivize the mid-nineteenth-century small-business sector, they rely on 'objective' criteria that people at the time would not have recognized as unifying. Historians assume that the simple fact of self-employment gave individuals a common status or identity, a twentieth-century notion alien to the wealth- and prestige-conscious Victorians. Indeed, grocers, the one group of self-employed people who did acquire a certain corporate identity, were commonly considered disreputable.[5]

Of course, most tradespeople did not give much thought to their professional credentials. Theirs was an unspecialized and unsystematic enterprise, not only in terms of the stock carried and the work performed, but also in the way the business was conceived. The daybook of Charles Tench, a rural Ontario merchant-miller in the 1840s, is not untypical in making little distinction between his various entrepreneurial activities. Tench's building of a closet, his reports on the weather, the marriages of his friends, the sales in his store, the yield from his farm, the work in his mill, and the wages of his clerks and farm workers cover the pages with sunny abandon.[6] Store owner, miller, farmer, and neighbour – Tench's roles were so closely intertwined as to make their separation inconceivable; his was a world without pigeon-holes.

The business of merchandising reflected this lack of specialization and professionalism. Individuality rather than cash served as the nexus of mid-nineteenth-century trading. In hundreds of country stores, where barter remained at the centre of distribution, a deal was as good as the people striking it. Prevailing market prices would regulate commerce broadly, but store accounts reveal that a modest, though significant, freedom was exercised in the setting of individual exchange values. The worth of an egg or a salted cod varied according to the position, resources, and independence of the producer and the relationship that person enjoyed with the shop owner. Debt, along with poor transportation, kept customers returning to the same stores even if they ended up paying marginally more. The heavily indebted customer could expect a less favourable deal than the one whose account was clear, as merchants quietly put what they could towards the account's carrying costs.

In fact, nothing was more individual than credit. In many stores, accounts were paid, or not paid, at the customers' convenience, and it was not until the 1870s that enough cash entered the economy to allow most buyers to pay their bills monthly, though some paid more frequently and others far less often. Shopkeepers kept track of these credit accounts in journals organized by the name of the purchaser, which meant that most retailers must have known pretty well everyone who came into their shops to buy. And why not? A big country store at mid-century might sell to two or three hundred people a year; many of the smaller ones had a customer pool of around fifty.[7]

The long-standing, but personal, nature of the credit relationship also extended from merchants to their suppliers. In this age before commercial travelling, store owners still made an annual buying pilgrimage to the major wholesaling centres. There they placed orders for the year's goods with their suppliers, were wined and dined, and made arrangements for the marketing of local produce. These contacts were important because so much of the commercial life of the colonies depended on trust: wholesalers would often be paid annually, but sometimes they would continue supplying a retail debtor for years on end.[8] Capital requirements were minimal, stamina rather less so. Even though early-nineteenth-century trading was a slower, less complicated business than it would become, it was in many ways more trying. Long credits might buy a shopkeeper time, but in many cases the result was that one could see trouble approaching from farther off. And there was, in this age, much less that one could do to avoid it.

Not until the last half of the nineteenth century did these practices begin to change and shopkeeping as a 'profession', gradually and painfully to emerge. And as it did so, retailing as a distinct activity established itself in the public perception. It was a complex process marked, on the one hand, by the development of retail specialization and, on the other, by the blurring of trade lines. Work processes and workplaces were transformed; ideas and attitudes revised, and the locus of power shifted. Charting these changes is the subject of the middle chapters of this book, and I will leave their discussion until then. What is important at this juncture is the way that professionalization pulled retailing in contradictory directions. Even as it created a new recognition of merchandising as a distinct and separate occupational category, it widened the gaps among shop owners themselves.

It was the railways that first connected the fragmented landscape of commercial life. The job fell not so much to the great lines ploughing through to Sarnia and Halifax and Vancouver, but to the feeders that linked Mount Forest to Toronto and Swift Current to Winnipeg. By the 1880s railway cars brought Montreal-made shoes and Stratford furniture to communities at a reduced price, and the new business introduced by cheaper travel allowed factories to increase outputs and productivity and to drive prices down further. In this respect, railways unified the market-place, but they also intensified the differences between people and places. The arrival of the railway triggered changes: new products appeared on store shelves, new travelling men arrived with their suitcases of samples and catalogues of wares, new pleasures and comforts became affordable to consumers. But the railways also undermined much of the producer economy, driving a ribbon of steel between the makers and the consumers of goods. For most artisans, the railways brought either increased trade and distant markets or crushing competition and annihilation. In other enterprises the increased volume of goods and trade encouraged specialization, general merchants becoming clothiers or grocers or furniture dealers; in some it demanded a simplification of function. To all trades it brought an equal measure of both insecurity and hope.[9]

Prior to the railway-wrought triumph of the factory-made product, most small-town and urban shopkeepers remained as much artisans as vendors. Made-up clothing continued to be bought from neighbourhood tailors and dressmakers; butchers generally still slaughtered their own meat; apothecaries formulated their own compounds; booksellers still published; even grocers tended to buy in bulk and do their own sorting, mixing, and packaging. The retailing trades were limited to dry goods, some hardware and food lines, and silverware, china, and glass. In the country, where general merchants supplied most of the goods from bins, barrels, and bundles, the retailer acted as both seller of merchandise and buyer of produce. Now, however, small-scale butchers, druggists, shoemakers, and confectioners – people who through most of the nineteenth century had made the goods they sold – were driven out of production and into distribution by cheaper prepared goods.

Clothing provides probably the clearest example. Once the virtual preserve of dressmakers and bespoke tailors, by 1900 it had found its way onto the rack. Ontario in 1881 had almost six times as many independent dressmakers as ready-made women's clothiers; by 1921 off-the-rack clothiers outnumbered dressmakers almost three to one. Similarly, in 1891 there were 1,650 tailors and 190 ready-made clothiers in Ontario; thirty years later there were 700 tailors and over 1,000 retailers of ready-to-wear men's clothing (table 1). Factory production, which by the turn of the century was largely concentrated in a few cities and towns, undercut the market for made-to-measure clothes. The result was a separation of production and sale and a specialization of retail function.

Specialization was everywhere overwhelming generalism. Even in newly opened marketing areas, such as the Prairie provinces, retail specialism had marginalized all-purpose merchandising and much of artisanal retailing by the early twentieth century. It was, in this way, a different frontier from the one pioneered in pre-Confederation Quebec or Ontario. The homesteader of the early twentieth century settled with the promise of attainable urbanity. Not for the western farmer the decades of isolation and deprivation, the log highways, the only occasional neighbourly visits. By the time most of the sod was busted in western Canada, a marketing revolution had placed Coca-Cola within physical reach of almost every family. Organs, breakfast cereals, and, in a few short years, automobiles made this a very different sort of homesteading. One should not minimize the hardship of the initial period of settlement or underestimate the crushing influence of plains flatness, but the Prairies were commercialized even before they were peopled. True, the thinness and relatively recent settlement of the population did allow for the survival of older forms of merchandising well into the twentieth century: rural Saskatchewan in 1931 still boasted 1,600 general country stores. But the small towns and villages by that time also contained 480 groceries, 300 candy stores, 250 drug stores, 270 gas stations, and 640 building-supply shops. Larger towns such as Moose Jaw had no general stores (other than a department store and a five-and-dime), but it boasted 7 men's clothing shops, 5 appliance stores, 47 groceries, and 6 tobacconists.[10]

Yet even as the retail trade segmented along trade lines, the boundaries which divided it started to blur. Pre-packaging and large-scale production did not just raise retailing's lid; they also released its dynamism. It was more than a question of the shoemaker beginning to repair more than to manufacture or the butcher to chop rather than to slaughter and cure; it was also a matter of defining the skills that were now needed. When a medicine had to be made in a back room, it was easier to keep its supply under control; but when Beecham's made the pills, how could an apothecary prevent anyone from selling a box? All of a sudden grocers had to resist the sale of bottled and canned goods by fruiterers and butchers, hatters had to fight to keep stock out of the hands of haberdashers, hardware men had to skirmish with furniture dealers and druggists, and general merchants had to fight a rearguard action against just about everybody. In short, the demise of craft lines which followed from large-scale production and cheap transportation eroded occupational skills and knowledge even as it created the possibility of specialization.

By the mid-1890s, border wars were erupting all through distribution. It was never enough for merchants simply to watch their own trades; the vigilant retailer had also to keep an eye open for competition by outsiders. Overhanging much of the inter-trade rivalry was the hostility which the specialist felt for the dilettante. Pharmacists, in particular, prided themselves on their professional expertise and resented the fact that grocers were encroaching on their territory by selling Epsom salts and potassium nitrate. Hardware merchants similarly felt that they alone had the skill to distribute hammers and screws, and butchers could not understand how grocers could presume to sell an eye of round. While governmental interference might help in some cases (the

Poisons Act and the health laws were used to good effect), retailers generally relied on less-formal measures (such as pressuring wholesalers) when trying to restrict the sale of goods by non-specialists. Fortunately, few merchants carried things to the extremes reached by Charles Fryer, a hardware and lumber dealer in Beisecker, Alberta, who, when competition with the general store across the street really heated up, fired two shots at his rival 'with intent to put him out of business.'[11]

Increased competition became for most tradespeople the embodiment of the marketing revolution. For those looking to set themselves up in trade, the anticipated growth in consumption which price deflation sparked held the promise of tremendous opportunities, while higher incomes provided the capital for store ownership. In the 1880s and 1890s working and farming families discovered that they could just as easily buy a shop as get a mortgage for a house or a lien for machinery, and stores consequently proliferated in Canada's towns and villages. Already by 1889 grocers in many communities were discussing the fact that 'the shopkeeping class has increased at a prodigious rate,' and they were looking for ways of suppressing 'the evil of OverTrading'. As the *Canadian Grocer* explained: 'it would certainly pay two-thirds of the traders of the land to board and lodge the remaining one-third if they would simply get out of business and cease to annoy and impoverish by expensive competition.'[12] The turn of the century found pharmacists, shoe sellers, and clothiers in many different places expressing dismay over the growth in competition and reflecting unhappily on the degree to which conditions had changed for the worse.

Once again, the available statistics allow us no more than to sketch impressionistically the development of retail services. The published decennial census is a poor source for trade statistics prior to 1931, and the information that can be gathered from city assessments, directories, and credit-rating agencies provides us with only imperfect insight into retail developments (these can be found in table 8). According to the census of 1871 there were 25,000 merchants in the country (which was without doubt an underestimation since on the basis of the trade directories, Ian Drummond found that 17,000 were operating in Ontario alone), while the *Monetary Times* in 1880 assessed the number to be 56,000 (the census counted around 40,000 in 1881). We can estimate with relative certainty that in 1911 there were some 81,000 individual managers and proprietors (retail and wholesale) running distribution enterprises and that by 1921 this number had risen to 104,000.[13] From the Ontario trade directories we can add a few heavier brush strokes to this lightly sketched portrait, and we can in particular bring into relief the growth spurts of the food (1870-90), men's clothing (1910-30), hardware (1880-1910), jewellery (1880s), and retail shoe (1880-1900) lines (table 1). Overall, the growth rate was fastest in the 1870s and 1880s, when the number of food and drug stores doubled, furniture retail businesses expanded sixfold, and even general stores and dry goods businesses increased by about 30 per cent.

In terms of store density, the retail sector in Ontario would also appear to have expanded at a significantly faster rate than the population in the 1870s and 1880s (we can estimate that the store-person ratio rose from around 1:95 up to about 1:80 between 1871 and 1891) before contracting in the twenty years preceding the First World War (when the overall ratio fell back to roughly 1:90). Among the different trades, the Ontario example also reveals a general increase in the number of stores per person between 1871 and 1895, followed by a decline in store density between 1895 and 1921. In clothing the ratio changed from 1:680 to 1:312 (1871-95) and back up to 1:680 (1921); in furniture it moved from 1:5,263 (1871) to 1:2,310 (1895) and up to 1:4,458 in 1921. Only in the food, hardware, and drug trades did store density continue to rise over the entire period. These are, of course, provincial averages which tell us nothing about regional or local conditions, and there can be no doubt that in some places the rate of retail expansion dramatically exceeded or lagged behind the general increase.[14]

The question as to whether there could be too many traders has been vexing retailers at least since Adam Smith. On one level, the accessibility of shopkeeping was one of its major attributes, the idea being that distribution was a mirror of the community and that the growth of trading was a simple reflection of the increase in societal wealth. 'It is not true that there is just so much business to be had,' observed the BC *Retailer* typically; 'as a rule, the more tradesmen the more trade.'[15] But this comment implied only an abstract acceptance of competition because in practice the shopkeepers would start complaining about its injustices the moment their turnovers started to be affected. Indeed, the distance between a vague sense of competition as healthy and a pragmatic attack on it as destructive was very quickly travelled. In areas where there were a large number of new stores or, alternatively, where consumer expenditures fell in relation to the number of existing stores, complaints about the increase in 'destabilizing' competition were sure to arise. Because there was no objective measure, concern about overtrading tended to result from value judgments – from the shopkeepers' sense that competition had passed the limits of fairness. And it was this fact which would make the idea of overtrading so much the tool of the store owners' prejudices.

The emergence of a handful of large-scale distributive enterprises in the 1880s and 1890s in this sense only added to the independent proprietors' concerns. Most of the stores that would later dominate the retailing imagination – Eaton's and Simpson's in Toronto, Morgan's, Murphy's, and Dupuis Frères in Montreal, Spencer's in Victoria – grew from relatively modest beginnings in the 1860s and 1870s, but some, such as A.J. Freiman in Ottawa, Woodward's in Vancouver, and Ogilvy's in Montreal, had beginnings closer to the turn of the century. These stores were all characterized by their 'departmental' organization (the separation of display stock, workforces, accounts, and buying by type of goods) and by the centralization of their administration and management. But it was not their form that made them so singular; it was their size. These businesses came to be called 'mass merchandisers' not because they sold 'to the masses,' but because they sold so much. And because of size they were able to buy in volume, price goods more cheaply, and pay for the kind of advertising that gave their lower prices wide currency. It was their method of marketing, a system entirely dependent on volume and scale, that made them so threatening to the increasing number of independent specialty shops.[16]

In order to protect themselves from the competition of big and small alike, retailers in the late nineteenth and early twentieth centuries began to organize. The Toronto Retail Grocers' Association was formed in 1887 and its Kingston counterpart two years later, and a Grocers' Protective Association of Guelph appeared in late 1889. That same year, three hundred small-town and country merchants gathered in Hamilton to create the Ontario Businessmen's Association, while Retail Grocers' Associations appeared in 1890 in Carleton Place, Montreal, and Peterborough. Toronto jewellers first organized occupationally in 1886, Montreal's dry goods merchants formed their first association in 1897, and hardware dealers in Ontario mobilized in 1905.[17] The organizations that retailers created all did similar things: they lobbied municipalities for early-closing by-laws; they demanded higher licensing fees for, and sometimes even prohibitions on, street vendors; they discussed ways of reducing competition. In effect, anxious retailers determined to restrict competition in their trades sought to manipulate early-closing, licensing, and even health and safety regulations in order to impede business growth.

Of all retailers, druggists were unquestionably the most successful regulators of their craft. They enjoyed the earliest start: as early as 1831 the apothecary's practice had been brought under the control of law, and in 1871 the Ontario Pharmacy Act established the provincial College of Pharmacy and provided it with the exclusive right to examine and license druggists. Under this and subsequent acts in other provinces, only 'qualified' druggists could run a pharmacy, which under Ontario's 1889 legislation meant someone who had apprenticed for four years, including two years' residency at the college. Because of their success, the pharmacists served as models for many other shopkeepers. Like the druggists, butchers and fishmongers in the first two decades of the new century used health regulations to control their trades: in Vancouver they obtained municipal by-laws which prevented meat and fish vendors from living on their business premises, while in Montreal they backed regulations prohibiting the outdoor display of meat. Hairdressers, barbers, and watch repairers eventually also tried to emulate pharmacists in getting schools established that alone could license prospective tradespeople, while bakers tried to enforce apprenticeship regulations.[18] In all this activity the established shop owners' goal was to solidify their market niches by defining the boundaries of their trades and ensuring their ability to regulate entry.

By the late 1880s specialized journals also started to appear – in groceries, jewellery, and hardware – which catered to the needs of those carrying on particular trades. The journals served as how-to guides for retailers: they offered advice on bookkeeping, promotion, and display; they helped store owners decide where to buy; and they served them by predicting fashion trends. The journals made their points by example, offering descriptions of successful advertisements and illustrations of proper methods of keeping stock. The trade press therefore followed the example set by legal casebooks and medical school laboratory work. The new professional training of the late nineteenth century emphasized doing over watching, practical over abstract knowledge. Retailing's publicists intended the emphasis on learning to bring a new dignity and professionalism to the merchandiser's craft.

In this goal shopkeepers were successful. By the turn of the century the idea that retailing constituted a distinct sector had begun to emerge. The separation of production from final sale and the streamlining of trade functions gave shopkeeping an appearance of greater homogeneity. Instead of shoemakers who sold and butchers who slaughtered, there were now shoe stores and meat shops doing an almost purely resale business. As cash became more commonplace, barter also gave way, and while many retailers would still operate as agents for whole-saling merchants, buying from the community would be increasingly distinguished from selling to it. Numbers also helped. The rapid increase in the number of shopkeepers in the last decades of the nine-teenth century served to augment distribution's image, as did urban growth and the development of central shopping districts. More and more, retailing seemed to be taking its place alongside manufacturing as a definable and autonomous economic sector.

The paradox of all this change was that the image masked an espe-cially complex reality. Even as people came to recognize merchandising as a certain form of business, shopkeeping itself became increasingly diverse and fragmented. Not only were there many more tradespeople doing many different sorts of things, but there were also, because of licensing and organization, education and place, an increasing division between occupational insiders and outsiders. At the same moment, immigration gave retailing greater ethnic diversity, and in the wake of a loosening of provincial restrictions on female property rights, there was an influx of women into trade. Most importantly, as retailing grew and competition intensified, economic differences among store owners assumed an ever higher profile. By the time the census enumerators began their work in 1930, retailing may have been accepted as a single category, but retailers certainly were not.

MAIN STREET CONFRONTS BACKSTREET

The nineteenth-century world of distribution changed fast in the four decades preceding the Great War. Affluence and expectation led to an increase in competition and rising tensions within retailing. These changes would have been impossible without the development of ready-made, increasingly pre-packaged and manufacturer-advertised goods. The result of centralized large-scale production was both an increase in demand and a condition under which people with less skill or experience were able to take up selling. Consequently, even as pro-ducer-vendors metamorphosed into retailers, they saw their crafts invaded by dilettantes who had never learned how to slaughter a pig or make a cough syrup. Some, such as dry goods merchants, hatters, and tailors, found themselves marginalized by ready-made clothing and off-the-rack clothiers, while still more, including food dealers, looked on in shock as the proliferation of products disrupted trades that restricted consumption had once kept relatively closed.

What especially outraged the more-established merchants in the late nineteenth century was the fact that much of the increased competition seemed to be coming from people who had no business running a store. Retail expansion coincided with increased immigration and with a rise in women's business involvement. Neighbourhood stores, opened by 'wives of respectable artisans,' the *Canadian Grocer* snarled in 1889, were now appearing every day on the backstreets of market towns. 'With a light heart she invests her hard earnings in some back street,' the journal continued, 'with the result that before the short space of six months has elapsed, her husband's wages are mortgaged, as it were, each week to meet her accounts ... her social and pecuniary position is truly pitiable.' Or it would have been if she did not 'steal away' so much of the trade. That was why one Pembroke merchant could declare pointedly that 'laws are needed to place the handling of food into the hands of properly experienced men.'[19]

Economic tensions lurked behind these complaints. Old and well-established urban retailers and affluent general merchants could accept the movement of some of the more prosperous artisans or agents into merchandising, but they were suspicious and resentful of the explosion in retail services. The struggling tailor who decided to open a small men's furnishings shop or the backyard butcher who went into the meat business was a threat to the custom of the old-timers. The need for differentiation which followed from increased competition and the proliferation of goods only added to the established merchant's difficulties. As the old-schooled generalists moved cautiously into specialized trades like groceries or furniture, they felt themselves harassed by a multitude of smaller, newer, poorer businesses buzzing around their trade.

There was, in effect, a pecking order among retailers. By the late nineteenth century, affluent, established traders lent their red-brick and plate-glass dignity to the main streets of the small places and the downtowns of the larger ones, while in newly settled areas, their imposing false fronts and clapboard sides became a feature of every rural crossroad and railway junction. Poorer shops – in some cases little more than crates piled up outside a house – dominated the backstreets. As demand grew and prices fell, working people converted their front parlours into stores, knocking out some street-facing wall to accommodate the larger window that retail selling demanded. In country places, farmers erected crude shacks along dirt tracks or milk sheds and florist shops on the margins of towns. For many more struggling retailers, 'business' consisted of even less: the back of a truck or wagon, a pushcart, or more rarely by this late date, a pedlar's pack.

Affluent merchants complained that the competition of these marginal tradespeople was cutting into their business, but it is impossible to know for sure. In theory, a gain for one vendor is a loss to another, but in real terms there is no way of knowing if small-shop competition actually prevented any main street dealer from attaining a desired volume of sales. Not that it really mattered. What was obvious to everyone was that the number of shops was increasing, and especially during the 1870s and 1880s, when the growth was most pronounced, shopkeepers believed that competition reduced profits. This much can be shown: judging from the directories and credit-rating service listings, it is clear that at least in some trades, marginal shopkeeping was growing fast. In the Toronto grocery business, for example, the size of the shoestring sector (comprising stores capitalized at under $2,000, with sales under $5,000 a year) grew from 58 per cent of the total number of groceries in 1890 to 64 per cent in 1900 and to 75 per cent by 1930 (table 2), while the actual number of small stores more than tripled. Though a big city like Toronto may have been exceptional in these growth rates, other places were also witnessing tremendous increases in the number of their back-street shops. Even though the shoestring sector's share of grocery outlets in five smaller Canadian cities (Kitchener, Windsor, St Catharines, London, and Brantford) remained constant (at roughly 70 per cent) between the late nineteenth century and 1930, the actual number of small shops in these places more than doubled.[20]

Moreover, there is evidence to suggest that smaller stores were coming into more direct competition with larger ones. Table 2 reveals something of this development through a random (12 per cent) sample of grocery shops chosen from the 1902 and 1930 Toronto directories tabulated according to the income levels, population densities, and housing types of the city's residents.[21] The physical distance between rich and poor which the 1902 figures reveal had been widening in Toronto over the course of the late nineteenth century as the city experienced the digging of what Ira Katznelson termed its 'urban trenches.' The main feature of this growing segmentation was the movement of the wealthy into those relatively self-contained communities that lay on the fringes of the old walking city. And from the 1902 sample we can conclude that larger storekeepers were following the richer inhabitants into the Rosedale and High Park areas, the middle class into the Annex and up into the neighbourhoods bordering Yonge Street, and the more affluent blue-collar workers into the areas north of College Street in the west and Danforth in the east.[22]

But the evidence from Toronto further suggests that as the urban market took shape, competition increased for the custom of the affluent workers and well-to-do bourgeois who lived in the newer suburban districts. In the first two decades of the twentieth century, smaller stores began to desert the backstreets of the inner city and move into shopping grounds closer to the now increasingly desirable markets. In 1902 about one-half of all the food shops in the better areas of Toronto had been capitalized at under $2,000; by 1930 front-parlour stores outnumbered the larger by a ratio of two to one. The impression one gets from Toronto is that a few years after the larger shops had located on the main streets adjoining the new neighbourhoods, the smaller ones began to proliferate on the backstreets.

The example is no more than suggestive, but it does illustrate a pattern noted at the time: more-affluent retailers 'pioneered'; poorer ones gravitated to established markets. This pattern makes sense because most small vendors depended for their livelihood on a convenience or corner trade. Too poor to advertise, they needed regular clienteles to make ends meet; too small to afford a large stock, they survived on the 'supplemental' trade. Their sales were made up of the can of fruit here and the cigarette pack there, the newspaper and bunch of flowers, the toy, the bag of sugar, or the bottle of hooch. They needed to be open late and on holidays because it was then that their trade was best, and there had to be many of them because their attraction lay in their proximity to people's homes. Small wonder, then, that main street merchants considered them parasites.[23]

Such was especially the case in areas where credit sales remained the norm. Because many main street traders continued through most of the twentieth century to sell at least part of their stock on credit, they regarded every dollar spent in a rival store as theft. The worker who bought his pack of cigarettes for cash at the backstreet store was spending money that could have been used to pay down his debt. The amounts were admittedly small, but to main street dealers already resentful of the competition, their customers' spending choices were the cause of considerable agitation. Unable to punish their own customers for this 'disloyalty,' they lashed out against the smaller dealers who made it possible. The difference between the main street merchant and the shoestring shopkeeper, stormed the *Retail Merchants' Journal*, 'is the difference between the merchant who is in business when trade is dull as well as when business is good, who helps his customer over their troublesome times by granting them long and short credits and the merchant who jumps here and there where the opportunity is best ... taking away a large part of the trade through a species of manifestly unfair competition from the [main street] merchant who certainly has prior and best right to it.'[24]

Fair enough, but the question remains: did these hostilities actually reveal a structural division in retailing? What difference did the size of one's investment or the volume of one's business really make to the lives of merchandisers? Answering these questions is difficult because of the deficiencies of the pre-Depression statistics; however, an analysis of the evidence available for 1931 and 1941 does show store size to have been the great defining element in retail stratification. The figures suggest that while trading was, like any occupation which cut through the wealth hierarchy, a continuum from the most marginal to the most prominent, there were definable clusters throughout the spectrum.[25] Tables 3 and 4 follow the census categories, but use three different measures of retail enterprise (capitalization, turnover, and size of workforce) in order to expose the patterning of wealth. If quintiles 1, 3, 4 and 5 are thought of as small, mid-sized, and large independent businesses, then 2 and 4 can be treated as transitional, spanning the gap between the largest of one grouping and the smallest of the next. And it is difficult not to be struck by the distance covered by these transitional quintiles.

By the 1930s shoestring stores made up a vast proportion of the retailing stratum (between 30 and 40 per cent depending on the measure), but sold a tiny percentage of the total volume and employed none of retailing's non-familial workforce. By the time a store was turning over $30-40,000 in stock, its owner could afford to employ a few clerks and earn a comfortable return on the dollar. According to the 1941 Canada census, the average income earned by the proprietor of a store with annual sales of under $5,000 (quintile 1) was $439, considerably less than half the average wage earned in manufacturing ($1,200). In contrast, owners of mid-sized stores selling between $30,000 and $100,000 (quintile 3) averaged incomes of $2,100 a year, with a variation either way of around $700.[26]

But store size did not only determine incomes; it also restricted profitability and capital. One rule governed gross profits, and it was that the smaller the business, the higher the mark-up. At a time when the average grocery was selling on a 17 per cent spread, the shoestring dealers were operating on a margin of 40 per cent. Unfortunately for the shoestring storekeepers, the greatest proportion of these gross profits had to be used in their own support, for where the average grocer in 1941 took 6.5 per cent of his turnover in earnings, the smallest was removing 22 per cent. Because the backstreet stores were struggling under the burden of simply supporting their owners, they could not provide enough to maintain non-familial workers.

If it was in part the varying abilities of store owners to derive a living from their business activities that distinguished them, then retailing's connections to the broader workforce become crucial. Where shop owning for the larger merchants was a full-time job, small traders opened the doors to their parlour shops when they came home from work; their wives or children ran the stores when they were away at the factory (or, less frequently, they ran the stores while their wives and children worked); whole families even took to selling goods in the front yard or on the street corner on Sundays and holidays.[27] Larger shop owners recognized that the only thing that allowed the smaller ones to exist was the fact that their owners kept a familial foot in the paid labour force, and they therefore complained vigorously about the unfair nature of the competition. As Joseph Warden, a well-to-do general storekeeper, raged when referring to a tiny shopkeeper who was 'stealing' his business: 'He don't need to work his wife so for it is she who runs the Business[;] he has ... a good steady job.' The rebuke was one often levelled against the smallest traders. Their 'major complaint,' Everett Hughes wrote of the prominent retailers of Cantonville, 'is that they [the small] don't have to make a living from their businesses since members of the family work in industry and so steal custom which rightfully belongs to the merchants who bear the full burden of overhead.'[28]

Small retailers not only had family members working in blue-collar jobs, but they were also more likely to come from working-class backgrounds themselves. The figures in table 5 are not definitive since they were derived from the limited (30 per cent) proportion of insolvents in the 1920s and 1930s who listed their previous occupations in the bankruptcy court records for Ontario, but there are indications that the shopkeepers' ties to the blue-collar workforce decreased as their stores became larger.[29] According to the bankruptcy records, 32 per cent of shoestring dealers in the interwar years came from blue-collar backgrounds, as opposed to only 13 per cent of larger traders, and this figure probably underestimates the proportion because the occupation in which small traders predominated, the grocery business, was under-represented in the sample. Out of a random sample of 148 Toronto backstreet grocers for 1900-30 whose previous occupations could be determined from the directories, almost two-thirds had blue-collar backgrounds and 47 per cent had previously been members of the unskilled or semi-skilled workforce. This is not to suggest that all working-class entrepreneurs opened shoestring shops – according to the bankruptcy reports, around half of them did not and among Toronto grocers 37 per cent acquired larger businesses – but there was a decided concentration of one-time wage-earners among the ranks of shoestring tradespeople (table 5).

Not surprisingly, the backstreet retailers were also more likely to live where they worked. For middle-class people in the nineteenth century, home was perceived as a retreat, a sanctuary from the pressures of working life. And this view made the ability to 'separate the productive tasks from the reproductive' a hallmark of bourgeois respectability.[30] Working-class people did, from the last decades of the nineteenth century, also obviously live away from their work, but they remained in the shadow of the smokestack. Moreover, when they made the financial leap into retailing, they had no choice but to sacrifice their domestic ideals to financial realities. As the Ontario bankruptcy court records show, where 52 per cent of shoestring retailers in the interwar period lived and worked in the same building, just 28 per cent of main street traders did. The residence upstairs or in the backroom came to signal marginality and illegitimacy in the eyes of affluent tradespeople.

By the early twentieth century, store size therefore determined much: it was the great visual indicator of class status in retailing; it defined possibilities in merchandising; and it limited the amount of stock one could put in, the improvements one could make, the type of locations one could choose, the market niche one could exploit, the staff one could hire. While it is unclear whether a similar rift existed in the late nineteenth century, there is no reason to expect that it did not. Certainly, the way main street retailers in the 1890s discussed the backstreet competition implies a deep divide. Of course, many shoestring dealers did reach for the 'shopocracy,' and thousands failed each year. It was a hard life: shoestring store hours were long, trade was generally slow, and returns were minimal. These factors added up to a simple truth: those who began their business life in a small store tended to remain small traders. In the sample of Toronto grocers drawn from the directories between 1900 and 1940, only one in twenty shoestring dealers was ever able to raise his or her credit rating. This reality cut across the other forces of retail differentiation. Ethnicity, for example, gave rise to many conflicts among tradespeople, but store size divided members of immigrant communities just as surely as it did native Canadians. Indeed, while main street English-Canadian merchants often found grounds for agreement with prominent traders in new ethnic communities, when it came to their relations with immigrant shoestring traders, the conflicts had been overdetermined to the point of irreconcilability.

ETHNIC ENTERPRISE

Of course, ethnicity was a major force of division within late-nineteenth- and early-twentieth-century Canadian retailing. By the First World War shop owning had become a highly racially and ethnically stratified occupation, with almost every group in the country boasting its own storekeeping stratum. Though Canadian-born made up 68 per cent of the workforce in 1931, they comprised about 63 per cent of all merchants, while individuals of European (not including British) or Asian birth made up 18 per cent of the total store-owning population and 13 per cent of the workforce generally. When the 'racial origin' of the immigrants was included, the proportion of retailers from continental European and Asian backgrounds grew to about 22 per cent of the total, as compared with 20 per cent of the general workforce.[31]

The scale of immigrant involvement in retailing did, however, vary from group to group. In 1921 retail proprietorship was almost twice as popular among continental European and Asian immigrants as it was among the British-born, and while the gap had closed somewhat by 1931, British migrants were still statistically underrepresented in distribution. Canada's Italian and Asian communities were, in contrast, contributing richly to the shop-owning mass: 4 per cent of all employed Japanese immigrants, 3.8 per cent of all Chinese, and 4.3 per cent of all Italians, as compared with 3.8 per cent of the total workforce, were shopkeepers in 1931. None, however, were more prominently engaged in merchandising than Canada's Jews. A staggering 16 per cent of all gainfully occupied Jews listed themselves as proprietors of retail stores in the 1931 census. Numerically, these merchants were most common in Quebec, Ontario, and Manitoba, provinces with large and established immigrant communities. But Jewish retailers were also remarkable for their willingness to move independently into areas where they were ethnically isolated. Seventy per cent of Nova Scotia's 700 Jews and one-third of Saskatchewan and Alberta's 3,200 were owners of retail stores in 1931. This pattern was in marked contrast to the behaviour of other ethnic middlemen, who tended to cleave to their groups.[32]

Generally speaking, ethnic enterprise enjoyed its great growth spurt in the decade preceding the First World War. By 1911 there were 22,600 foreign-born retailers in Canada; twenty years later the pre-1911 migrants still operated 20,000 stores, or 56 per cent of all first-generation immigrant businesses. With the exception of Asians, the predominance of the pre-war migrants was more than simply a result of the overall decline in immigration in the 1910s and 1920s. Among Italians, for example, 37 per cent of all those gainfully employed in 1931 had entered Canada before 1911, as compared with 57 per cent of the retailers. The same was true of other peoples: 52 per cent of Jewish shop owners in 1931 had migrated before 1911, as compared with only 40 per cent of all workers, while half of all Polish merchants, as compared with 26 per cent of the workforce, had been part of the pre-war immigration. These numbers become even more startling when it is realized that only 7 per cent of the total number of retail stores operating in 1931 had been in existence twenty years before.[33]

This distinctive feature of ethnic retailing arose initially from the poverty of most migrants. Relatively few of those emigrating to Canada came to retail, and the majority had no previous experience in trade. It took time, then, for recent immigrants not only to save enough to begin selling, but also to develop the contacts with suppliers necessary for business start-up. The market niche for this first generation of merchants was the ethnic enclave, the point upon which immigrants focused their community identification. Although centring around churches or meeting places or particular shops, enclaves were less specific places than ideational representations of a past life to people living in a new land. And though the points of reference were often located in neighbourhoods where people of a particular ethnic group lived, the Little Italy and Chinatowns of Canada's urban places did not require a residential ghetto: they were constructions of memory, not geography. Consequently, for shopkeepers, owning an ethnic store in an enclave meant drawing the custom of people more far-flung in terms of residence than might otherwise be expected. Just as Italian or German immigrants might forsake the nearest church in order to travel to the one they associated with their culture, so too would they walk or ride past countless food and clothing stores on their way to the shops that served their memories.[34]

In the early twentieth century the majority of ethnic entrepreneurs played middleman roles for their own group, and they had minimal contact with other consumers. In cities where enclaves appeared, British- and French-Canadian shop owners left immigrant areas, and their vacated stores were taken over by minority business people.[35] In these places the immigrant shopkeepers devoted themselves to providing for their own communities both ethnic goods (such as olive oil, kosher pickles, and thousand-year-old eggs) and services such as banking and labour exchanges. For subsequent generations of immigrant entrepreneurs, the trouble with all this was that the first group of merchants had quickly cornered the market. Those who had, by the First World War entrenched their positions as middlemen to their people were, like all merchants, jealous of their trade and keen to prevent ruinous competition. And because of ethnic suspicions and the barriers to immigrant borrowing, established merchants found it easier to contain potentially challenging business developments.

By the First World War the particular patterning of ethnic distribution ensured that minority retailers in many parts of Canada had developed their own infrastructures of service: they had their own community wholesalers, trucking operations, and channels of credit. In most lines, minority distribution converged with the mainstream only at the top – at the ultimate, and to most retailers invisible, point of supply. The Toronto banana trade in the 1920s was a case in point: the fruit would be shipped green by the United Fruit Company twice a week and bought by Italian jobbers. They would sell the green bananas to Italian wholesalers, who would ripen them (the smaller lots in their homes, the bigger in warehouses) and distribute them to the Italian pedlars and greengrocers. Credit was extended by the fruit company to the jobbers and from the jobbers to the wholesalers and so on down the line to the actual customers.[36] It was a structure so thoroughly Italian that people forgot the Guatemalan plantations and American multinationals that supplied the goods. To most consumers, and to many who retailed, the banana had become an Italian fruit.

Not only did ethnic retailers buy from within their own group, but they also tended to hire people from inside their communities and to raise capital from among fellow immigrants. Chinese tong and hui were in this sense no more than peculiarly formalized expressions of what was otherwise a common practice. The tong was a type of cooperative business enterprise following clan lines which invested its members' money, distributed profits, and controlled competition. The hui was a cooperative credit association – sometimes familial, sometimes not – from which members could borrow for business purposes. Where the tong helped larger clan groupings to extend and entrench their power within the community, the hui allowed people without the necessary personal resources to finance business and property investments. Not surprisingly, the wealthiest Chinese merchants (sometimes working through powerful local Chinese Benevolent Associations) figured prominently in both institutions, engaging in both to buy urban rental property, to increase the number of retail customers linked to them by bonds of debt and loyalty, and to obstruct the activities of rivals. Less formalized, but fulfilling similar functions, were mutual aid societies in other immigrant communities. Based mainly on Old World connections, these fraternal organizations provided death benefits, unemployment relief, and short-term credit to members. The benevolent associations tended to be dominated by shopkeepers and other small businessmen, who used the societies' virtual control over credit resources available to poor immigrants to entrench their positions within the community. Consequently, these societies placed high stock in lending members money to buy houses: thereby guaranteeing shopkeepers a stable market within the neighbourhood.[37]

Clearly, while internal sources of credit enabled many poor immigrants to finance business and residential investments, they also solidified the power of the immigrant élite. Because enclave business people were reluctant to fund those who might enter into competition with their own stores, such credit also helped contain the effects of immigrant business activity and to channel growth outward into the host market. Mike Sule, for example, a Hungarian butcher in the employ of a Hungarian-Jewish retailer in downtown Toronto's immigrant neighbourhood, was supplied with credit and stock by his employer when he decided to go it alone and open his own store. Not surprisingly, he located his store out of competitive distance from his erstwhile employer's business, and he catered to a clientele from beyond the immigrant community. Similarly, Chinese guilds, such as the laundry guild, stipulated that competing businesses must be located a certain distance apart, while the Japanese Shoe Repair Association lent start-up money to prospective members so long as they located in towns where no other Japanese shoe repair shop existed.[38]

Apparently, by the First World War the best opportunities still open to would-be immigrant retailers were those lying outside the enclave. Unfortunately, the ambition for store proprietorship did not decline with the decreasing demand for retail services within the community. Among immigrants, perhaps even more than with English and French Canadians, retailing offered one of the few routes to better incomes and improved status.[39] Because of accent, colour, or culture, many immigrants found themselves denied access to higher-quality education and better-paid jobs. As the ethnic communities grew and became more established, there was therefore increasing pressure placed on the system to expand self-employment opportunities. Much of this pressure was seasonal since large numbers of immigrant workers were unemployed in the winter months. Though peddling or opening a small shop had traditionally been ways in which unemployed men and women survived the hard times, by the Great War the enclaves simply could not provide enough opportunities for all the would-be vendors. The immigrant entrepreneurs first opened new businesses along major arteries near their own settlements, but a few began to move farther afield.[40] As pedlars and backstreet traders started migrating from the city centres, they could increasingly be found selling their wares in the newer middle-class residential districts. More and more, the customers of these immigrant vendors were drawn from a wider section of society. A 1936 petition submitted by three thousand clients of Chinese pedlars in Vancouver reveals that almost all were identifiably Anglo-Saxon and that most were in professional, clerical, and skilled blue-collar occupations. Similarly, Italian fruit vendors in Toronto followed middle-class consumers up Yonge Street, while Jewish and Lebanese clothes pedlars sold to other immigrants and native Canadians across the resource frontier of northern Ontario.[41]

Of course, those entrepreneurs who left their enclaves moved into selected occupations that ethnic stereotyping made acceptable. The Italian fruiterer, Chinese laundryman, and Black barber became fairly common sights in Canada's towns and cities, but the Asian pharmacist, the Greek hardware man, and the Portuguese butcher did not.[42] And it was here, perhaps, that Jews enjoyed a special advantage. Already accepted as the retailing minority of the Old World, they faced a broader range of options when it came to merchandising. Thus Jews opened general stores in frontier districts; they ran shoe, clothing, and furniture shops in small towns; they operated bakeries and grocery stores in large cities. Empowered in this way by cultural stereotyping, they were able to turn retailing into a kind of ethnic vocation.

No matter what the trade, it was the movement of ethnic entrepreneurs into areas of competition with English- and French-Canadian retailers that provided the spur to nativist attacks. In Vancouver, for example, it was the penetration of Chinese merchants into the grocery trade outside the Pender Street enclave that led to the campaign for discriminatory licensing, a fact that explains why the grocery section of the Greater Vancouver Retail Merchants' Association accepted the existence of Asian merchandising, but wanted a licensing law to restrict Asians to 'designated areas.' It was similarly the movement of Jews into areas of French-Canadian settlement that provoked retail hostility in Quebec: 'on les voit d'abord dans les quartiers ouvriers dans les petites épiceries,' wrote one Montreal agitator. The English 'n'est jamais venu faire competition dans l'Est,' wrote another, but 'Nous avons laissé le Juif pénétrer dans l'Est, nous voler nos commerces, nos épiceries, nos boucheries, nos magasins de vêtements, de meubles, de merceries, de chapeaux.' As Everett Hughes observed of Drummondville, 'the Jew' was hated because he 'operates and competes upon the French-Canadian businessman's own level.'[43]

Immigrant business people's efforts to tap non-community sources of credit and supply created similar problems. Forced by poverty to look to the host community for at least some of their capital, immigrant entrepreneurs none the less felt marginalized and alienated from their English- and French-Canadian suppliers. Consequently, they attempted to shape external credit and employment to their own and their group's advantage. Bankruptcy court data, for example, reveal that ethnic traders paid down debts to suppliers and creditors from within their communities before addressing more distant debts to strangers and outsiders. It was a logical and common practice, and the enclave could reward these gestures. When Joseph Surface, a Dundalk general merchant, declared bankruptcy, his Italian creditors all agreed to drop their claims against him, and the Italian Aid and Protective Association discharged his remaining debts at twenty-five cents on the dollar and placed the business back in his hands.[44] But these types of practices were regarded with considerable outrage by French- and Anglo-Canadian merchants, who argued that immigrants were both 'disloyal' to their new country and unfairly advantaged by their ethnicity.[45]

It was these practices which made the competition between immigrant and native shopkeepers so singular. Fuelling the nativism that periodically mobilized English- and French-Canadian merchants was a sense of the differentness of immigrant retailers that had nothing to do with the real business of running a shop. Beyond the enclave, where immigrant shopkeepers catered to a specialized market, ethnic businesses looked and operated much like native stores. Although they continued to carry a certain amount of specialized stock, made greater use of the street for display purposes, and sometimes closed on different days of the week, these were fairly subtle distinctions, not generally associated with the merchants' ethnic background.

Certainly, no one ever commented on aspects that should have been major sources of cultural differentiation, such as the fact that Chinese grocers outside the enclave still made little distinction between sweet and savory in their shelving. Indeed, English- and French-Canadian merchants seemed perplexed that ethnic stores did not appear sufficiently different. Some were even aggrieved by the fact: 'they are great imitators,' one Vancouver retailer noted of his Chinese competitors, 'they dress and speak as we do. They keep their books in English and send out their accounts in English. They are as obliging, courteous as any white man ... it seems and it is sometimes laughable the way they watch us ... If we put some new line in our windows, they copy. If we make a change in our store, they do the same.' Given these similarities, 'what is to prevent them from ousting the whites?' Even the Sunday opening of Jewish and Asian stores, something which caused considerable alarm, was disconnected from issues of cultural difference. There was nothing taboo about opening on Sundays; it was an question of 'fairness.' Allowing Jewish stores to open on Sunday, one critic charged, 'would practically give them a monopoly over other business,' a control that could be prevented only if all the 'other stores remain open ... and thousands of clerks are deprived of their liberty to this day of rest.' If Jewish bakers were not prevented from selling on Sunday, a Vancouver businessman told a Lord's Day Alliance activist, 'it simply means that we would have to protect our own business from any such unfair competition by opening ourselves.' Clearly, the hostility directed at Jews for choosing a different 'Lord's Day' did not arise from Gentile retailers' inability to conceive of doing the same thing.[46]

No, the great gulf between immigrant and native storekeepers lay, not in irreconcilable differences in actual trade practice, but in the name over the door. And to this extent it was prejudice unrelated to the fact of merchandising that kept immigrant and Canadian-born apart and legitimized treating the immigrant as alien and unwelcome. The degeneracy of Orientals, the treachery of Jews, the criminality of Italians – these were considered realities which did not need to be evidenced in actual practice. As a result, native retailers could maintain the position that immigrants must be made to conform to Canada's laws without expecting acceptance into its society. They took for granted the immigrants' cultural inferiority, denied their assimilability, and insisted on their control. Jews could never be made Gentiles or Indians whites, but they could be forced to live according to the dictates of the dominant community, separate but equal in their obedience of its laws.

Still, even though it was ethnic stereotyping that made the immigrant retailers the focus of a particular type of hostility, it was competition that led Canadian store owners to oppose their merchandising. Race and ethnicity were meaningful to retailers, as to most Canadians, but from a purely commercial perspective, they were arbitrary categories. An ethnic stigma would have underlined and coloured one retailer's suspicions of another, but it was the fear of losing business that stoked the fires of nativism. As we have seen, retailers in the late nineteenth and early twentieth centuries were concerned about all forms of competition; ethnicity and race simply legitimized one type of opposition. The retailer who protested that a competitor was undercutting his prices would attract less sympathy than one who claimed to be driven out of business by a Chinese invasion or a Jewish conspiracy.[47] This was one reason why English- and French-Canadian shopkeepers supported the ghettoization of ethnic enterprises: so long as the immigrant entrepreneurs remained in their Little Italy and Chinatowns, the shopkeepers were willing to accept their existence. Racial and ethnic differences would certainly have fragmented retailing, but the isolation of one group from another would not have created such active tensions without competition.

Nativist merchants at the time would doubtless have been oblivious to these distinctions. Few separated the issue of competition from that of ethnicity: it was, they insisted, the racial or ethnic characteristics of their trade rivals that made their competition intolerable. Jews, these retailers were convinced, were by nature dishonest, Chinese unclean, and Italians incompetent and shifty. Competition under these circumstances was not 'legitimate', because the Jew who cheated his customers or the Asian who lived in filth was not having to meet the same standards of conduct as the native Canadian tradesperson. Again, these stereotypes did not have to be borne out by reality to be considered true; their function was too important. It was vital for retailers to be able to place their competitors beyond the pale: it not only made the loss of sales, caused inevitably by competition, somewhat easier to bear, but it also enabled business people, theoretically committed to the idea of freedom of enterprise, to justify their desire to restrict opportunity.

The root of retail nativism fed upon the same problem that drove main street merchants to complain about the proliferation of backstreet shops. Nativism added credence and direction to the hostility, but it did not create the fear of competition. And the two conflicts – the economic rivalry between main street and backstreet and the cultural hostility of native and immigrant – were deeply and inseparably linked. The fight to control minority trading was fought by the same people who campaigned against small-business growth. There is surprise here: because of their relative poverty, most of the merchants who opened stores outside the enclave ran shoestring businesses, the majority being pedlars, backstreet traders, and corner merchants. Their business activities would have been resented no matter who they were, but nativism added distinctive force and character to the complaint.

While elements of separateness – different credit channels, hiring practices, and ways of life – kept retailers apart, they did not generate open and sustained conflict. It was more than simply 'otherness'; it was competition – or the fear of it – that made elements of separateness appear threatening to French- and English-Canadian retailers. And yet, what gave that competition its nativist dimension was prejudice unconnected to actual selling. Because of their preconceptions, English and French Canadian retailers saw individual minority tradespeople as members of a dangerously cohesive block, armed with their own credit, employing their own people, joining their own associations, infiltrating the host society. The separateness that kept retailers apart, that drove immigrants into selected occupations, that nurtured enclave power relationships, also made immigrants feared.

SEX-TYPED MERCHANDISING

Women's place in retailing, while perhaps even more confining than the immigrants', was rather more ambivalent. Female shop owners worked in an industry that not only was scored by sex-typing, but was also witnessing a prioritizing of gender considerations. Because shopping was widely considered a female activity by the turn of the century, retailing became a kind of syncretic occupation: a manly endeavour (entrepreneurship) in the service of a feminine urge (buying). Until the nineteenth century, there had been little need for the overwhelmingly male shopkeeping group to confront this ambiguity; for all but the very rich, consuming was considered a necessity rather than a desire. The words themselves exposed this reality, with 'consumer,' the older word, implying the individual's ultimate use of the item and 'shopper,' the mid-nineteenth-century term, evoking an activity disconnected from its objective (acquisition). Retailing adjusted to this change with its own semantic turn, as the word 'store' (the place where goods were kept prior to consumption) gave way in the late nineteenth century to the more popular 'shop' (where the vendor's autonomy was subsumed by the activity of the buyer). Women, not surprisingly, came to be associated with the developments these words signified, as the cause of both the promise and the insecurity which accompanied the dawn of the marketing age. The feminization of shopping, retailers lamented, had destroyed customer loyalty because while men were believed to 'prefer to shop where things are familiar, women are fickle customers and have to be kept interested.' In short, 'shopping,' the 'feminine' act of seeing and desiring but reserving one's buying, was widely considered the cause of increased competition and high-pressure marketing.[48]

If retail publicists meant what they said, shopkeeping should have become a predominantly female activity; women, after all, might have been expected to know better how to cater to their sisters' needs. But such was not the case. Instead, retailing's masculine image in the late nineteenth and early twentieth centuries was reasserted in two ways: first, through the emergence of a 'science of marketing' and, second, through the continuing emphasis on the store owners' responsibility to the public. Both rationalizations of male pre-eminence rested on the notion that consumer desires had to be channelled and controlled so that women who shopped might be prevented from devouring luxuries and ruining their families. Selling came to involve grave and manly social obligations.

Ultimately, these attitudes served to contain and restrict the spread of female entrepreneurship. In English Canada married women obtained the right to transact business independently of their husbands only in the 1870s and 1880s (in French Canada such authority would come only in the 1930s). These legal changes made it possible for more Canadian women to enter business during a period when opportunities were multiplying, and there is little question that female entrepreneurship increased in the late nineteenth century. In Hamilton the number of businesswomen increased by 50 per cent in the two decades following Confederation; in Victoria Peter Baskerville found a tripling in the number of women owning retail or artisanal retail enterprises between 1881 and 1891 (with some 130 listed in the Vancouver and Victoria directories by the later date); and even in Montreal, if the evidence from Sainte Anne Ward can be considered typical, there was an increase in female shopkeeping between 1861 and 1891. There were four thousand women retailers listed in the census in 1911, the first year for which national statistics became available; ten years later there were a little over six thousand; in 1931 the number was close to twelve thousand. These figures represented a growth of from 5 to 6 to almost 10 per cent of all merchandisers.[49]

Despite these gains, women remained occupationally sex-typed: accepted as, and accepting of, a presence in trades geared to relatively low-cost frivolities – hairdressing, stationery, millinery, and fancy goods – yet all but barred from such big-ticket items as furniture or such sensitive ones as drugs. The only exceptions to this rule were in lines in which women's domestic role was thought to have given them a certain 'natural' proclivity: groceries and women's and children's clothing. It was the constricting influence of the normative that kept all but a few women from moving beyond their accepted sphere. Most people would simply not have thought to undertake something beyond that which they felt was proper and known, and women were not believed to have sufficient 'sense' of what running a hardware or shoe or meat or auto shop involved. This assessment of natural proclivity would have been justified by the feeling that consumers would not trust a female proprietor. Since women did not repair cars or paint walls, they would not have had the experience necessary to advise customers. That these things could be learned, that some women did repair and paint and build, that women probably knew as much about nice furniture as most of the men who sold it, meant little to people at the time. Such was the power of the gender stereotypes.

Like ethnic shopkeepers suffering from, operating within, and profiting out of the stereotyping of their abilities, women made strides in merchandising by exploiting the very values that isolated them. As certain trades came to be considered more 'womanly,' men increasingly moved out of them. In dry goods, for example, 370 of the 4,180 merchants were female in 1911, twenty years later women accounted for 588 of the 2,238 proprietors. In other words, the real number of men selling dry goods declined by 60 per cent, while the number of women increased by roughly the same proportion.[50] Perhaps the saddest aspect of this separation of men's and women's work was the fact that, with the exception of clothing, groceries, and candy, the trades being 'feminized' were declining. While the unexplained classification changes over time make it difficult to offer definitive comparisons between census categories, dry goods was a disappearing trade, as were dressmaking and baking, and the number of book and stationery shops was also decreasing modestly (by 10 per cent). These changes go some way to explaining the 'openness' of these trades to women (sectoral decline made it easier for them to obtain credit and supplies from wholesalers interested in sustaining their businesses), in addition to providing added justification for the lower credit rating most women were assigned (these were higher-risk areas).

These factors were only part of the structural constraint on female entrepreneurship. Though no evidence existed to impute the reliability of female shopkeepers, creditors were reluctant to trust them with too much stock or to fund them in non-traditional areas. Assessment agencies such as R.G. Dun and Company consistently rated even those women it considered 'reliable' at a low level. And though the numbers being assessed grew over the course of the late nineteenth century, there was little change in the actual valuations being assigned. In 1865–70 evidence from Hamilton suggests that only 15 per cent of female retailers were assessed for credit worthiness and just one in ten received a 'good' rating. By 1890 Dun and Company was listing one-third of the female-run businesses, but only one in twenty now received a 'good' or even 'fair' rating. The expansion was a function of Dun's greater efficiency and ability to survey a larger proportion of the retailing population, but little progress is revealed in the perception of women's worth. Indeed, those women who received the highest ratings invariably shared characteristics unrelated to their actual business acumen or potential. Not only were those rated 'good' credit risks older than the norm; they also tended to be either married to shopkeepers or widowed into store ownership. Furthermore, they tended to be clustered in the dry goods trade, which was still, in the late nineteenth century, the most prestigious area of female employment.[51]

That retailing was something of an extension of women's domestic associations is also observable in the singular residential pattern of female shopkeepers. Unlike bourgeois men, who tended to separate their shops and their homes, well-to-do female storekeepers as late as the interwar period were more likely to reside above their businesses. Among the Ontario bankruptcy court sample, 27 per cent of affluent males lived where they worked, while 38 per cent of main street female store owners came home through the shop door. Not surprisingly, the proportion was highest among married and widowed women with children.

The enduring power of this sex-typing through the interwar period prevented women from experiencing much change in their occupational opportunities. In 1911 the only trades where women were statistically overrepresented were groceries and confectioneries (11 per cent), dry goods (10 per cent), and books and stationery (9 per cent). Twenty years later they were still overrepresented in only these same trades, though they had increased their hold on the dry goods business (25 per cent female proprietorship), confectionery (19 per cent), women's clothing (41 per cent), and bookshops (16 per cent). The only new area of female entrepreneurship was the news-stands: 13 per cent of newsstand owners were women in 1931. In other words, while women's participation in retailing increased, it did so only in the sex-typed trades. Despite consumption's emergence as a female activity, and in spite of the enormous changes affecting women's overall image and employment in the early twentieth century, retailing remained rigidly valuated as a male endeavour.[52]

Even within businesses which listed themselves as female owned, gender inequalities served to diminish many women's authority. In all likelihood a large proportion of those listed as female proprietors were only titular owners, sheltering husbands and families from business liabilities. Just 55 per cent of all female shopkeepers who declared bankruptcy in Ontario in the 1920s actually ran their stores themselves, the remainder of the shops being 'managed' by husbands (33 per cent), sons (5 per cent), or other male relatives (7 per cent). Sometimes these women would have had little knowledge of the actual operations of the stores they 'owned,' though much would depend on the families involved. As Ida Caplan, the legal owner of a Sudbury clothing store, rather naïvely declared at her 1924 bankruptcy hearing, 'I didn't mix with the business, I didn't know the business – I didn't say anything because I didn't know anything.' (Recklessness seemed a family trait, for when her husband was asked to rationalize his wife's ostensible financial involvement in the shop with her ignorance of its operations, David Caplan told the judge, 'doesn't a husband handle money for his wife? Every husband – all the time. What do you think?')[53] Ida Caplan's total exclusion from her own business might well have been unusual, but it does point to one extreme that could be covered by a legal title.

The degree to which women engaged in the running of a business would have been as variable as the families themselves. Indeed, for all the women who were kept out of a shop's management, there were others who participated fully in its operation, so much so that one Hungarian women interviewed a half-century later felt the need to apologize for the fact that she had kept working in a factory in the early 1930s rather than helping her husband in his butcher shop. And for every Ida Caplan there was probably an Ida Stone. Stone's father had been a furniture dealer, and while she was a teenager, he had nursed her entrepreneurial instincts by taking her on buying trips and encouraging her to speculate on second-hand furniture sets. By the time she was nineteen she was in business for herself, and she continued to run a store of her own – and keep her own bank account – even after her marriage to a clothier in 1923. In fact, in Stone's case it was her husband who knew nothing about the operations of her business. What is intriguing, however, is that at her bankruptcy hearing Stone's creditors and the court refused to believe that she could have managed a furniture shop without the help and supervision of her husband.[54]

Preconceptions, then, did much to marginalize women, creating a deep rift within retailing. As with ethnicity, prejudices unconnected with the actual business of running a shop invaded and fragmented the store-owning mass, a fact that is in many ways ironic because for all the preoccupation with difference, the profile of female shopkeepers actually bore a striking resemblance to that of men. In the blue-collar workforce, women were generally young, single, and employed in factories for only a short time. None of these conditions pertained to female storekeepers. Women retailers were mature, and their age distribution was similar to that of males. In 1941 only 5 per cent of female storekeepers were under 24 (compared with 3 per cent for males), and 73 per cent were between the ages of 35 and 60 (about 80 per cent of men). Furthermore, they were mostly married or widowed, only one in three being single, roughly the same proportions as within the male population.[55] Still, gender valuations, whether supported or not by experience, constructed the framework of perception and provided the language of expression. No matter who the female shopkeepers were or how they acted, they presented themselves and were presented by men as different. Words that might for some have served to empower and legitimize their entrepreneurship could easily be used to isolate and demean that same activity.

There was, however, one thing other than sex which set male and female retailers apart, and that was the fact that, almost without exception, women ran small corner stores. One traveller in 1920 estimated that there were only about two dozen 'successful' female shoe retailers, while the *Furniture World* placed the number of furniture dealers closer to forty. Though there were many more female food traders, the *Canadian Grocer* never made much of the fact and continued right up to the

Second World War to describe retailing in purely male terms. Affluent female shopkeepers represented a tiny minority: 70 per cent of female-owned grocery stores in Toronto between 1900 and 1940 were assessed at the lowest level possible (under $2,000), and the remainder were rated by the Dun company at $2,000-9,999; only a handful of the stores owned by women would have represented an investment of above $10,000. According to the bankruptcy records, there were significantly more corner shopkeepers (owning assets under $2,000) among the female proprietors (38 per cent of the total) than there were among the men (24 per cent). Women employed fewer workers, they received a lower credit rating, and they took considerably less out of their stores than did their male counterparts; in fact, where only 14 per cent of males paying themselves a regular salary out of their businesses earned under $800 a year in the 1920s, one in three women made below that amount.[56]

It was the fact that petty proprietors earned so little that made small shop trading so much a woman's world. A large proportion of corner shopkeepers were seasonal or part-time business people who used trading as a supplement to familial wage labour. Many would have been like Katherine Florence, who ran a corner grocery on Emerson Street in Toronto. Her husband, George, was a semi-skilled worker, and she had for many years been a tailor in the Eaton's factory. Opening a store was a means of augmenting the family income – George continued working for the Toronto Ignition Company – while at the same time allowing them to escape from the house on Harvie Street in which they both boarded. Store ownership also allowed them to become landlords themselves, for though they rented the building in which they ran their store, they sublet the apartments above it to others. Like sweating, child labour, and boarding-house keeping, store ownership was a way out of poverty for many families; but unlike outworking, it also involved a significant advance in status. For all the insecurities that accompanied its marginal position, the working-class – shop-owning family had a toe-hold in the world of capital.[57]

Class differences therefore underlined the gender divide in retailing. They reinforced the predominant belief that women were only part-time shopkeepers, engaged in trading to support husbands unable to maintain their families. To this extent, the larger merchants' prejudice against small-shop competition reinforced their perception of female retailing as an aberrant by-product of women's domestic obligations. Class prejudices in this way justified regarding women's merchandising as less important by allowing it to be dismissed as a simple and temporary supplement to the family income. It was probably also this intertwining of class and gender assumptions that allowed for some women's differential treatment. Widows, for example, were always a case apart. This was especially so for those surviving affluent merchants, and it accounts for the allowances that were made for them. Not only did widows generally receive the highest credit ratings, but they were also occasionally welcomed into the main street retail associations – which is not to suggest that widows were considered the equal of the men they had married. Though separate from the mass of female backstreet traders, they remained a group apart: respected for their efforts to continue the family business (and therefore the husband's work), but different none the less.

Clearly, gender, though an imaginary difference in retailing, created deep divisions among shopkeepers. It did not matter how much women might have acted like men; they could never be considered the same. These gender preconceptions created and maintained a real structural divide in merchandising: women were limited to specific trades, they received lower credit ratings, and they were expected to work close to home. The fact that they were also overwhelmingly backstreet traders only strengthened the elements of separation. Far from being oppositional constructions, class and gender were intertwined and mutually sustaining. For male main street tradespeople, these differences served to reinforce retailing's masculine character. By marginalizing women, and thereby keeping them outside the mainstream of retailing's occupational imagery, shopkeeping males succeeded in denying the feminization of their work. Faced already with the challenge of female consumption, they could not accept the idea of feminized merchandising. Of course, sex-typing was woven deeply enough into the fabric of this society for women to have assimilated its messages and to have justified their own actions by reference to its code. As we shall see, though they attempted to redefine retailing in light of the female experience, they never challenged the domestic ideology that constrained them. Consequently, even though unprecedented numbers of women penetrated the most sacred of male institutions, the independent enterprise, they remained apart, an all-but-unacknowledged presence. Again, as with immigrant minorities, sex-typing gave women certain advantages – certain avenues of success that were more easily entered and where their sexuality worked for them. But they remained on the psychological margins of enterprise, a sex apart.

A DIVIDED STRATUM

Retail expansion in the last decades of the nineteenth century, coupled with the specialization which competition aroused, produced a new perception of shopkeeping. Where retailers had never been much distinguished from agents or factors or wholesalers, they now began to emerge as members of an occupation with its own character. By the Great War, store owners not only read trade-specific journals, attended specialized classes and seminars, and organized occupationally; they were counted and classified as well. And yet, even as retailing began to assume its own personality, its members increasingly fragmented. The very forces which in the second half of the nineteenth century decimated skills and created the urge to specialize also pulled thousands of shopkeepers of different ethnicities and classes into increasingly direct competition. Trade was pitted against trade as store owners struggled to preserve their stock from prying rivals; main street fought to keep business away from the backstreets; French and English Canadians lobbied to restrict ethnic tradespeople to designated areas; men and women confronted each other as rivals across a chasm carved out by gender assumptions.

Paradoxically, with the exception of wealth and trade, which clearly forced retailers to do their jobs differently, the other elements of separation had only a limited impact on the business of selling. True, enclave retailers did organize their shelves differently, they did stock exotic goods, and the sights and smells of Canada's Chinatowns, Polishtowns, and Little Italy, were certainly distinct and defining. But when immigrant retailers began catering to other ethnic groups – and it was this that made them a problem in the eyes of native merchants – they divested their stores of much of their outward distinctiveness. It was not the fact that ethnic retailers did things differently which made them outsiders; it was ethnic prejudice which made them different even when they behaved like native Canadians. Similarly, what marginalized women in retailing was not the way they organized their stock or advertised their wares, but their sex. No matter what women did, in the eyes of male storekeepers they would always remain women.

Class prejudices – as materialized in the difference between main street and backstreet – played a crucial role in reformulating ethnic or gender prejudices as business differences. Because so many female-run and ethnic shops were small, realities specific to the backstreet could be associated with the whole. All female or immigrant shop owners could be criticized for practices that were specific to the poorest elements. Living and working in the same place, unsanitary or cramped conditions, street trading, late hours of opening, supplementing the family business with industrial wages – these were things which were regarded as making ethnic or female shopkeeping 'unfair.' That they were not cultural preferences so much as financial necessities for many or most minority tradespeople was unimportant. The division of wealth – which supplied the only substantive difference in the actual business of merchandising – was made over into an issue of ethnicity or gender. Ethnic hostilities and sexual concerns thus fed on the structural divisions of wealth, and prejudices irrelevant to the actual business of selling were provided their occupational dimension.

Clearly, then, the assumption of retail solidarity flowing from the condition of self-employment is, in the case of Canada's shopkeepers, misleading and confining. They were a deeply divided grouping, fragmented by the intertwining forces of trade, wealth, class, gender, and ethnicity. A shifting, protean, competitive mass, store owners had little personal contact with each other and wished their businesses had less. Those who did associate tended to share characteristics unrelated to trading, and they most often met in places removed from their stores: fraternal organizations, mutual aid societies, churches, and sports clubs. Trade associations, the only real forum for occupational interaction, were, as we shall see in the next chapter, limited to a small minority of male merchants sharing common class and ethnic characteristics. While historians and sociologists have long asserted that retailing 'straddled' the class divide between workers and bourgeois, they seem to have underestimated the degree to which the sector split under the strain.

2

The Folklore of Retailing

In January 1923 Henry Watters, president of the Standard Drug Company and one-time mayor of Ottawa, spoke before a convention of the Ontario Retail Merchants' Association. 'Our class is not organized,' he announced, 'and organization at the present time is necessary.' He was sounding a familiar call, one that was being echoed by fellow RMA organizers in countless gatherings all across the dominion. 'Class' mobilization was seen by many proprietors as the only method of ensuring the independent shopkeepers' position in an age of increased competition. Not only had Watters's generation experienced increasing competition from within the proprietary sector, but it had also witnessed the emergence of the mass-marketing department stores. In fact, unlike many other retail organizations which were established to control the growth of independent trading, the RMA, since its founding in 1897 by a group of Toronto shopkeepers frightened by the growth of the Eaton's department store, had been leading the organizational struggle against mass marketing. It had done so by keeping in close step with its price-cutting opponent: in 1905, the year that Eaton's opened its first store outside Toronto in Winnipeg, the RMA became a federation and began establishing provincial branches in the west. Soon after Eaton's opened a Montreal store, the association set up offices in Quebec, and as the corporate giant began mail-order deliveries in the Maritimes, the RMA established a New Brunswick branch. 'In recent years department stores have devised schemes whereby each line of trade is used as a jugglery,' the RMA's journal explained in 1906; 'with careless indifference they price staple lines of all kinds of merchandise from candy to gas stoves. Sometimes the prices are up and sometimes the prices are down just according to the manner they think can best attract the common multitude and make the public believe that they are the only people in the retail trade who are able to sell at a low price.' The trouble was that such actions were 'contra to that high and ennobling spirit that is set forth in the "Golden Rule,"' and to prevent them, retail merchants must 'act together ... vote together ... and think together.'[1]

Over time the RMA did, however, become more than simply a counterweight to the mass marketers. The organization was also heavily involved in campaigns to control growth within independent shopkeeping itself. From the outset, the association had lobbied for higher licences on pedlars, had actively fought for early closing and Sunday observance, and had been a key player in the campaign for Oriental exclusion. The RMA had also pressed wholesalers and manufacturers to tighten up on credit, to shorten terms of payment, and to fix prices and control margins. Moreover, it had been involved in efforts to license all traders, to improve in-store bookkeeping and display, to organize cooperative buying ventures and advertising pools, and to have retailing introduced as a university credit. Trade organizers justified these changes by citing the need to professionalize merchandising: to make the work more humane by restricting its hours and to encourage cleanliness and order so that prices might be reduced and services improved. But behind this professional canon lay the reality of hierarchy and caste: retailing was a divided world, and in the name of progress RMA members were seeking to improve their own condition at the expense of those whose trading they considered 'unfair.' In fact, the language of professionalism was shot through with racial, gender, and class prejudice.

In this sense, the RMA seems an organization at odds with itself. On the one hand, it promoted a syncretic image of merchandising, a vision of a united retailing class overcoming the barriers of geography and trade. The apparently inexorable rise of cut-rate mass merchandising was the threat around which the RMA felt that storekeepers could be united. The obstacles to such a campaign were not perceived to be conflicting interests, but rather the logistical difficulties involved in mobilizing a widely dispersed group whose members possessed a false sense of themselves as competitors and not cooperators. Education and a solid organizational structure were therefore seen as the instruments of occupational unity: retailers had to recognize their common interest in fighting the mass-marketing peril.

But even as the association worked to build this national front, it spoke and acted in ways that drove retailers apart. Efforts to restrict competition through licensing or early closing had a direct and threatening appearance to backstreet traders, who could afford neither the high fees nor the loss of 'after hours' custom. Nativist campaigns to control and marginalize ethnic shopkeeping by imposing rigid standards of behaviour served only to alienate immigrant store owners, while the manly professional discourse and the cigar-smoking, euchre-playing club life of RMA gatherings exerted little appeal to women raised in a gender-stratified society.

Still, these two forces – the divisive and the synergetic – should not be seen as opposing poles tugging at the soul of storekeeping; each worked within the context of the other. Those drawn to the RMA conceived of people who retailed as individuals sharing certain interests and objectives, and they regarded those who disagreed as 'illegitimate.' In effect, shoestring traders and women and immigrants were placed by the RMA beyond the word: with few exceptions, they were not 'retailers' and therefore did not belong to the store-owning 'class.' Defining the group in ways which excluded those who did not fit the mould eliminated the contradiction of unity and diversity. The valence of the shopkeeping ideal which the term 'retailer' expressed, and the RMA promoted, was therefore limited by properties outside itself.

This fact has been too seldom recognized by the retailers' historians. Though many accept the idea presented in the previous chapter that retailers never formed a 'structural' or 'material' singularity, most remain loath to abandon the notion of a homogeneous lower middle class. Arno Mayer offered the classic statement of this position when he wrote some twenty years ago that while small business was 'too heterogeneous, indeterminate and polymorphous to be given any single label or to fit into a rigorous conceptual definition,' independent proprietors did have a 'singularly cohesive' belief system 'that is common to all segments of the lower middle class and that justifies treating them as a coherent phenomenon.'[2] In effect, shopkeepers were unified by their 'culture' rather than by any objective measures of wealth or status or gender or ethnicity.

Usually described as a negation – and therefore aptly named 'antimodern' – the peculiar culture of the lower-middle-class or small-business grouping has been thought to consist of a hostility to bigness, xenophobia, a proclivity to panic, and a 'readiness to demonize all forces which threaten the traditional order.' It was this 'culture' which Ranulf, Lasswell, and Reich considered the basis of petit bourgeois meanness and to which Lipset, Fromm, and Hofstadter attributed their irrational status anxieties. Though never disconnected from the fact of self-employment, trade culture is none the less often described as unifying in spite of the differences generated by small business itself. As one of retailing's most perceptive and sympathetic historians observes, if 'from both the economic and the social point of view ... there were profound differences within the group,' culture – and here the reference is to the same 'politicized' consciousness discussed by the 'status anxiety' analysts – 'could then perhaps be best interpreted as compensating for a lack of common interest.' In short, 'behaviour cannot be deduced from a rigid socio-economic framework of analysis'; rather, one should look to 'the words and the discourse of people themselves' and to their 'cultural expression, ways of life, tastes and so on.'[3]

This study resists such a separation of the cultural and the material, the word and the act. In the previous chapter we saw the degree to which Canadian retailing in the late nineteenth and early twentieth centuries was a divided stratum. Now we will explore the ways in which those divisions manifested themselves in trade culture and thereby prevented the emergence of a unified or mobilizable retail grouping. It is not, however, my intention to deny shopkeeping's existence as a set of social idealizations. Unlike Richard Hamilton, who implies that small business people lacked a common language of identification, this chapter will argue that retailers did possess an important, if largely modal, unity. Shopkeeping as an abstraction – as a folkloric image – did exist, and all trading people identified themselves as retailers by reference to the symbols comprising its folkloric memory. The issue was not the existence of reference points; it was that retailers approached those symbolic images from different directions. I will attempt to illustrate this argument primarily by using the example of those people who in the early twentieth century sought to create a retail-movement culture.

At the centre of the discussion which follows is the distinction between ideational structure and action, language and speech. Folklore provided small business people with a series of images to which tradition, culture, and history had granted certain inherent meanings. But symbols could vary in meaning according to their speech usage. This distinction is important because both structure and speech are inevitable components of identification. People identify with groups because they see themselves as embodying an imagined collectivity's symbols. But they individualize the symbols through the very act of reflecting upon them – structure becomes activated through its employment.[4] This process of individualization takes the form of understanding one symbol in the context of the totality of symbols to which the individual is drawn. Since codes have multiple meanings, how we interpret any one will depend to a large extent on how we interpret others. A male retailer would form thought pictures on hearing the word 'businessman' that might be different from those of a woman with her own gender consciousness. Moreover, the individual identities influencing the expression of symbols vary in importance according to time and place: the boisterous, song-singing, cigar-smoking male members of the Canadian Furniture Association became far more genteel when participating in the organization's annual family picnic. Selves cannot therefore be twisted apart like the painted shells of *matrushka* dolls. It is possible to detect in a single idea or action a multiplicity of social constructions, which means that each person's sense of belonging to a group begins with a definition based on his or her understanding of the symbols of the other collectivities with which he or she identifies.

When considering the retailers' identity, then, it is necessary to go beyond the interpretations of historians such as Mayer and to analyse not just the symbols through which store owners defined themselves as independent business people but also the interests that helped them to personalize those ideals. Identity is a point of intersection where different ideas of belonging – different symbolic codes – meet and define each other. A group can be thought to exist only when the reference points of language are narrowing enough to minimize the impact of different readings. This, in the case of retailers, was never the case. Consequently, a 'thick' description of identity is necessary in a study of shopkeeping culture; one that remains sensitive to the interplay of alternative non-occupational code systems. As Mary Ann Clawson observed in a similar vein, identifications 'based upon class, gender, race, and ethnicity may appear as a set of discrete alternatives but more commonly, the density of historical experience intertwines them in intricate and consequential ways.'[5] It is this density which we must now try to unravel.

IMAGES OF A GROUP

For all their differences and hostilities, Canada's retailers did understand their occupation to represent certain things. At the centre of their image of merchandising was the belief that it was a distinct activity with a social valuation above manual labour. As sociologists in the 1940s and 1950s discovered, the great mass of people in blue-collar employment, irrespective of ethnicity, sex, or work, dreamed of one day owning a small business. But what does it mean to say that an occupation has a 'status'? Clearly, it is more than simply identifying shop ownership with a higher income, for as we have seen, a great body of merchants earned barely enough to keep themselves alive, and trading was, for most store owners, a high-risk venture. Rather, status implies a valuation of a type of employment related to, but not dependent upon, the material rewards of its undertaking. It relates to the images which a type of job conveys; it is much more a symbolic than a material category. Consequently, while they often perceived their incomes to have been improved by ownership, most petty proprietors believed that the characteristic which really defined their status was their 'independence.' They were, as they were so fond of saying, 'their own boss.'[6] In this sense, self-employment was less a material reality – as students of the social structure imply – than a perception. It was in ideas that retailing existed and not in the shopkeepers' work habits or political beliefs or incomes.

As an imagined occupation, turn-of-the-century retailing had a hoary lineage. For centuries, merchant publicists had been busily marketing the idea that commerce was a sublime endeavour. According to seventeenth-century propagandists such as the French economist Jules Savary, buying and selling had been ordained by God in order that love and harmony should reign among men, while Richard Rolt, an English publicist writing in the 1750s, thought merchandising to be 'that alone by which our nation keeps up its head.' Early writers on trade were agreed that commerce and social peace were closely intertwined. Trade, they argued, brought people together: it facilitated the exchange of goods, and it created the social bond which engendered community life. Not only would existence be wretched without the material benefits bestowed by commerce, but humanity would lack completeness. Business channelled society's ambitions, and because it rewarded people's fair dealings, it made them good. Here was a line of reasoning that shopkeepers everywhere would find particularly congenial. 'Industry' and 'honesty,' piped Daniel Defoe (himself a dry goods merchant), 'raise credit in trade'; 'he that gets all he can honestly, and saves all he gets,' agreed the bookselling Ben Franklin, 'will certainly become rich'; 'commerce leads to justice, temperance, industry and frugality,' insisted William Temple, a Trowbridge clothier, 'and if it does not encourage a profuse generosity, at least it cultivates an amiable benevolence and humanity.' To the philosophizing shopkeepers, morality was minted in the market-place.[7]

Injunctions to honesty were especially important in an age characterized by long credit lines and minimal opportunities for the personal
assessment of one's business contacts. Constrained by primitive transportation and compelled by the cash shortage to run extended loans,
eighteenth- and early-nineteenth-century merchants had to rely on
informal reputations and familial connections when assessing the worthiness of their clients.[8] Occupational pride and honest living were
highly prized largely because they were thought to be guarantors of
easy credit and good custom. But no matter what its practical deriva-
tion, over the course of time the conception of selling clearly grew
beyond these mundane considerations and assumed an emotional significance in the eyes of its practitioners. Business, the shopkeeper came
to believe, depended on sobriety, honesty, and service, and one's success in trade was simply a reflection of one's ability to defend the interests of customers and creditors. This moral correctness and social
responsibility in turn found its expression in group activities such as the
celebration of feast-days and the performance of confraternity rituals.
Trade became an ethical and social good, and in its workings could be
seen the natural reflections of the proper order of things.

Clearly, retailers in the late nineteenth and early twentieth centuries
did not live in the world of Defoe or do things in the way described by
Savary. But just as words such as 'soldier' or 'woman' or 'nation' were
constructions of time and power whose meanings were recognized even
by those who did not themselves belong to the groups described, 'merchant' carried a socially and historically determined message. It had a
symbolic existence that had evolved over centuries and that would
change only slowly. It was, in short, a 'social memory.' Taken as a
whole, the idealism reflected in the construction formed a central feature of the European work tradition, and while subject to myriad variations, it remained distinct enough to transcend political, geographical,
and ethnic boundaries. Carried to North America by French and English
alike, the folklore of commerce drove thick roots into the fertile soil of
the coastal frontier, and here, as in Europe, it flourished and fractured,
folding itself through concepts such as self-help and moral uplift into
the broader bourgeois ethos of the nineteenth century and working its
way through anti-monopoly sentiment and the belief in the just price
into the language of popular radicalism.[9] Immigration did little to
diminish the power of this folklore. A good number of those emigrating
to Canada came with experience in small business, and many others
entered shopkeeping because it was one of the few avenues for self-

improvement open to ambitious immigrants. So great was the dream that the reality of far more small businessmen failing in enterprise than succeeding did nothing to inhibit the newcomers' enthusiasm. By the end of the nineteenth century, with the emergence of retailing as a distinct occupation, a shopkeeping variation on the broader proprietary ideal emerged, a complex of symbolic representations that was more value system than description of practice.

This folkloric codification of proprietary work activities had at its centre private property and the 'independence' that it engendered. Owning one's own business signified the shopkeeper's freedom; it was the instrument for achieving upward mobility and social prestige. 'In the individual and in the preservation of his initiative is the germ of the future,' proclaimed the *Retail Merchants' Journal* in 1907, and since the progress of the individual was closely linked in the retail tradition to the success of the whole, 'kill the germ and civilization would die of stagnation.' It was the shopkeepers' ownership of property that made them 'independent,' and 'independence' became one of the crucial symbols in the retailers' self-presentation. Thanks to their autonomy, shopkeepers tended to see themselves and their stores as the axle on which society turned and advanced. Independent property was the key because the traders' importance hinged on their ownership of a business – on their 'having a stake,' as they liked to say. The shop owners had 'their all' invested in their communities, they 'devoted their lives to their business,' and this involvement made them 'the backbone of any city, town or community [in which they lived].'[10]

By the turn of the century this symbolic unity of owner and enterprise – the shop made the shopkeeper 'independent' – was coexisting with another, ostensibly contradictory image, that of the autonomy of the work itself. Under the influence of new ideas of limited liability, retailers began to see their businesses as separate entities. In place of the oneness of shop and owner, the newer retail image held the business to be something in which the retailer must 'engage' or even 'serve.' Nautical images became popular, as did representations of merchandising as a mountain or obstacle that one had to 'climb' for success. 'Are you the man at the helm,' a promotional advertisement asked; 'are you running your ship along the safest and shortest course to success?' The idea of the retailer steering or scaling his trade, with the accompanying implication that one must be robust and bold to undertake it, might have been expected to restrict the image of the store owner as 'independent.' Clearly, the mountain or ship did not make the individual free; they bound the person to a task, with independence in this case arising solely from the fact that one was free not to do it. But such was not the case. Rather, it was the freedom to fail, the notion that the effort to master something other than oneself made one independent, which served to rationalize the two symbols. 'If you fail to land all the business that is at your door,' noted one publicist, 'it is lack of salesmanship on your part ... it is almost invariably the dealer's fault.'[11] Still, both images did exist in an uncertain harmony, with retailers at times implying a complete empathy with their businesses and at others presenting their trades as an obstacle to be overcome. Though they might conceptualize its form differently at different times, the idea of independence remained central to the retailers' occupational imaginings.

Size was also crucial to the shopkeepers' folkloric self-conception. Invariably, they used the words 'small businessmen' to describe themselves, even though some of them were running truly substantial establishments. George Hougham, interwar secretary of the Retail Merchants' Association, told a Senate committee that he took any store with under ten clerks to be 'comparatively small,' a generous estimate by which about 90 per cent of all retail outlets fell into the class of 'small' shops. Words were crucial, however, and 'small,' like 'independent,' carried a powerful psychological charge. Being small was important because it made the retailers seem approachable and unthreatening – like honest yeomen in the market-place. The small independent retailer, a Hamilton merchant hymned, was a 'modest, obliging, good-natured, hard-working individual, simple in his tastes.' In contrast, the manager of 'the big interest' was a 'selfish, grasping, enterprising monopolist, never satisfied, always reaching out for everything in sight, whose god is making money and getting control.' Consequently, only 'small' enterprise could ensure the survival of proprietary capitalism and, as a result, of the democratic society itself.[12]

The retail merchants' belief in the importance of preserving their diminutive independence was closely linked to their image of the healthy society. 'Community' was another key word in shopkeeping's symbolic dictionary, and like a trader's circle, it was thought to be built on trust and on the interdependence of each individual part. Merchants and consumers had to 'co-operate'; they had to 'each day show a spirit of brotherhood' the one towards the other. This cooperation was necessary, explained H.G. Prior, a furniture dealer from Portage la Prairie, because 'men could not live to ourselves alone.' Picturing themselves in their small and neighbourly shops, the retailers visualized the happy community that bustled all about them. Where 'independent distribution' prevailed, George Hougham intoned, local institutions 'built around the family' thrive; 'there is an atmosphere subtle and refreshing which characterizes the relationship between the proprietor and his sales people, and between the store and its patrons.' The neighbourhood shop, agreed a merchant from the Maritimes, 'is the place where the community problems are discussed. If the storekeeper and his store were to be eliminated the public welfare would certainly suffer.'[13]

In the late nineteenth century, as images of the consumer soured somewhat, retailers did begin to discuss community in nostalgic terms. Increasingly, they regarded their customers as unreliable, demanding, and selfish, and they depended on gendered images to describe shoppers' increasing fickleness. 'The modern merchant can't afford to turn his nose up at catch penny tricks when the public desire them,' observed a retailer writing in the *Dry Goods Review*; 'it is astonishing what will attract the customer.' Try, for example, using 'odd prices' to draw trade: 'it is surprising how the public is attracted to a twenty-two cent article that sold rather slowly at twenty cents.' Here was the image of the child-like consumer, fascinated by some 'oddity' or 'trifle'; merchandising in this way was a matter of grabbing someone's attention. Good display similarly came to be seen as 'crucial,' for 'no woman will walk by without looking to left and right to see the goods on display ... and people now-a-days buy pretty much from what they see.'[14] But these ideas of the fickle and naïve buyer, presented with veiled contempt by retailer after retailer, rested on their opposite. Behind the sense of 'what is' lay the 'what was' of distribution – the image of what trading should be, the feeling that a community of loyal customers should exist – and it was this sense that gave the new formulation its power.

The notion of the folkloric community also remained firmly entrenched in images of the relationship that was supposed to exist between shopkeepers and their clerks. In the retail tradition, clerks were portrayed as proprietors in training – 'The Clerk of To-day is the Merchant of Tomorrow,' one headline proclaimed – and it was the 'duty' of merchants to 'instruct' their salespeople in the arts of keeping shop. The ideal retailer took his clerks 'into his confidence' and encouraged them to 'feel a personal responsibility in the welfare of the business.' The ambitious clerk, in return, thought only of 'how he can increase his worth to his employer,' and he gave 'his whole mind to business ... [being prepared] to work early and late, and what he does he does well and quickly.' Since commercial folklore treated the workplace, the community, and the family as inseparable spheres, it followed that it was the shopkeepers' duty to take their clerks' education in hand. Storekeepers had to look after their employees' physical well-being by steering them away from corruption and encouraging them 'to take part in healthful amusements.' Moreover, workers had to be taught the importance of community service, and they had to be shown the benefits of thrift and enterprise.[15]

'Service' was in many ways the natural companion to the values associated with community support and employee training. An intricate symbol which was used to characterize the entire relationship of mutual dependence between retailer and customer, service embodied 'le contact direct et permanent de marchands à clients, le credit, la livraison à domicile.' Like all retail symbols, however, it did not just denote functions; it also expressed the spirit which filled them. Just as they conceived of their workers as children in need of education, so too did retailers feel that they had a duty to teach and uplift their customers. To cite one shoe dealer, the good trader had to 'educate our customers to buy proper footwear.' Service meant preventing shoppers from buying recklessly, and it necessitated the store owner's advising his or her buyers as to what best suited their needs. 'I would not sell a woman tea in a thirty pound box,' a Toronto grocer declared rather heroically, because 'that thirty pound box would last her more than two years and by that time the tea will have lost considerable of its strength and flavour.'[16] Like community, then, service represented both the concept of serving (and with it, dependence) and also that of knowing (and with it, superiority).

Credit, though unavoidable in a cash-strapped economy, was undoubtedly the most important component of the retailers' service ideal. Sometimes portrayed as a 'support' which retailers provided to the public – as in a statement such as 'I would not like to be the one to suggest that the retail store is a philanthropic unit of distribution, although it sometimes amounts to that' – it was also depicted as something which the consumers ruthlessly exploited. Credit was a term loaded with mutually sustaining contradictions. Like all forms of philanthropy, it involved not just social responsibility but also conceit, and because of this fact, it was a duty which had a way of bestowing distinction. 'The average farmer regards the retailer in his own town as one upon whom he can lean,' the *Canadian Grocer* observed in mixed pride and exasperation; 'the retailer is expected to carry the farmer from crop to crop.' Credit was not, however, merely a service to the poor; it was also the exchange method of preference for the rich. As one Toronto shop owner pointed out; 'Cash stores carry cheap goods ... I mean by this low grade ... It's doubtful to my mind if a strictly first-class grocery store catering only to the finest class trade can be carried according to the modern cash idea.'[17]

Real credit was itself many things – a convenience to the rich and a necessity for the poor – and the ambivalent nature of the service was in large measure a result of the one flavouring the other. A hint of moral superiority penetrated the retailers' depiction of even those who were buying on time by choice rather than out of necessity, while store owners felt a certain pride at being the ones to whom the insecure had to turn for support. Ultimately, it was the fact that credit gave retailers the power to mete out rewards and punishments to rich and poor alike which best explains its complex character. To this extent, service became a symbol of the retailers' folkloric responsibilities and duties, and also of their authority. In time, retailers would abandon credit, but the mind-set would remain. It would reveal itself in the sustained use of the service symbol, in the continued employment, long after most retailers had retreated from open-book credit, of expressions such as 'the public leans on the retailer for support,' and 'credit is the life-blood of the community.' Moreover, it would continue to influence the shopkeepers' sense of themselves, its subtleties finding reflection in the belief that it was the store owners who had access to something (knowledge or goods) which the public wanted and in the self-effacement which they felt they had to display in order to make their customers feel that it was they, the customers, who dictated the terms of the exchange relationship.

Ultimately, of course, the object of all this concern was money, but this did not mean that profit would be any less idealized than service. As Michael Bliss has shown, the word 'profit' signified the reasonable return for work done and investment risked. 'We as retailers,' proclaimed the Retail Merchants' Association, 'must have fair wages – improperly called by some profits.' Money was something earned not taken, and it was therefore as much a duty for retailers to accept as wages were for them to pay. There was, however, always a distinction that had to be made between good money and bad. To small business people, capitalism was not neutral or objective or divorced from morality. 'All nature has taught, and the operations of man have taught for many centuries[,] that every honest endeavour is entitled to a legitimate reward,' observed a Vancouver retailer. 'Anything in nature that does not produce and pay a profit is considered useless.' 'Profit' was here being treated, as it was when used as a retail symbol, as something which generated goodness: 'well organized and directed money is a boon and a benediction,' a trader explained. Profit as moral capital, not profit as lucre, was therefore the goal of enterprise. 'Dans le commerce, il y a le côté matériel, mais les éléments philosophiques, moraux, et psychologiques y sont de la plus haute importance,' said Zephrin Hébert, one of the founders of the Quebec branch of the Retail Merchants' Association. Indeed, 'when the masters of money lose sight of a high and true concept of its use ... it smirches and has a degenerating tendency.'[18]

Not surprisingly, then, while shop symbols were used to venerate the successful pursuit of profit, the retail tradition repudiated those who had made money by unethical means. The bad business people could be recognized by their sales practices: they cut prices, sold short weights and false goods, and used misleading advertising. And these immoral dealers, with their unfair practices, were capable of spoiling the trade for everyone. The distinction between ethical and unethical merchandising was the key to the store owners' concept of competition. Indeed, business folklore held that competition was the only true source of growth: it encouraged initiative and pluck, and thereby led to the discovery of new ways of satisfying society's wants. 'Competition is the mainspring that forces us toward higher ideals,' explained the Toronto jeweller E.M. Trowern; 'this is true of every position in life.' But what the retailers valued was not destructive competition – not that 'evil thing' which hides 'beneath a comely exterior the worst forms of economic and social vice.' Rather, what they valued was the kind of competition that 'uplifts' and 'improves.' 'Legitimate' competition was not 'selfish'; it 'receives no special privileges and does not undertake to take advantage of its position.' This was the sort of competition that existed between sporting chums; it was friendly, spirited, and ultimately good for body and soul. 'Don't knock your competition,' the BC Retailer urged; 'be a good sport. Play the game. Keep good natured.'[19]

One important corollary of this vision was that in order to remain competitive, retailers had to be artisans of 'progress'; words like 'up-to-date,' 'live,' 'modern,' and 'scientific' were as much a part of the trading vocabulary as were 'independent' and 'small.' If the retailer 'balks at the hilt of progress he falls into the one-idea rut which will sooner or later relegate him to the class of has-beens,' said the trade press, and most readers would have agreed. As one storekeeper exclaimed, 'the motto of every successful enterprise to-day should be, and is, to a great extent, "Be Progressive."'[20]

Taken together these ideas – service, community, the living profit, fair competition, independence, smallness, progress, and the morality of enterprise – constituted retailing's folkloric memory. These words were representational, to the extent that there was an intrinsic relationship between the signifier (say, independence) and the signified (the condition of being self-employed), and there can be little doubt that retailers did many of the things, such as joining voluntary organizations and supporting local charities, that folklore encapsulated. But the sense of the words transcended their particular applications. It did not matter whether an individual retailer provided 'services' or not; he or she was in a 'service' occupation, and the word 'service' expressed an entire relationship. Similarly, it did not matter if a retailer employed no clerks; 'small business' as a symbol still implied a certain relationship which, if the shop owner did have employees, he or she would have regarded as an ideal. The fact that many, if not most, employers did not live up to the image was similarly irrelevant and did nothing to diminish its power. Note how many store owners in the late nineteenth and early twentieth centuries found themselves denounced for running 'brutal sweat shops,' powerful evidence of an image of how workers should be treated, and note how often those employers protested that they would do more for their workers if only they could. Clearly, like metaphors which exist both as things represented and as non-contiguous values, retailing's symbols did not just approximate realities; they also encoded judgments.

The symbols that comprised shopkeeping's folklore were the stock of the group's historical experiences congealed and stored as memories. People were able to identify themselves as merchants because they saw themselves in relation to, and as embodiments of, its remembered symbols.[21] They knew that retailers were people who were independent, who provided neighbourhood services, who were small- and not large-scale entrepreneurs, who made reasonable profits, who bought and sold on behalf of their communities; and it was in reflecting on themselves doing these things that shopkeepers were able to conceive of their membership in a collectivity of individuals who did likewise. In this way, the symbols gave rise to the store owners' thoughts of belonging; by placing their own work within the context of folklore, they were able to experience their connectedness with retailers past and present. Symbols unified their experiences and gave them coherent form.

SYMBOLS INTERPRETED

But to understand retail identities we still have to ask, What did tradespeople make of their symbolic inheritance? Or, to maintain our metaphor, How did they understand the cultural grammar that was folklore and how did they use it? These are not easy questions to answer, in large measure because the silence of most shopkeepers has obliterated so much of their history. Only the wealthiest store owners wrote about their experiences – even to the extent of preparing advertising copy – and the vast majority of merchants joined no organization which could claim to embody their opinions. The trade press, while exposing the architectural design of the retailers' symbolic inheritance, does not show how those symbols were invoked. Fortunately, one of the most revealing avenues into the proprietary mind that was opened in the 1920s remains available today: the case files of the Supreme Court of Ontario's Bankruptcy Office. These documents – brutally democratic in their coverage of small and great, men and women, immigrants and native-born – contain the only recorded statements of thousands of ordinary tradespeople about their businesses and themselves. Prepared in moments of crisis by those who had failed, they offer a rare glimpse into retailing's symbolic world. Since the pressing need for most bankrupt store owners was to explain and absolve their failures, the statements they made were designed to reveal their expectations and ideals. That their words are stilted – uttered no doubt in self-justification, sometimes even in a blatant effort to deceive their creditors – only adds to their importance because in their explanations, self-delusions, and lies, these ordinary shopkeepers drew solidarity and strength from the folklore of their trade. And in their ability to manipulate folkloric symbols to mitigate their circumstances lay the very essence of retailing's ideational existence.

This fact was nowhere more clear than in the bankrupts' attitude to the earning power of their investments. Ostensibly in business to make money, failed shopkeepers were continually denying the profitability of their own enterprises. Unlike executives of larger businesses who were proud of their dividends, store owners clung to the folkloric dictum that good retailers were ordinary persons not plutocrats, entrepreneurs content with the merest frosting of money. Of course, what motivated these assertions was the desire to prove that their shops had not failed because they had squandered the profits, but the words chosen to express that idea remain telling. 'I made nothing more than absolute necessities,' explained the Lebanese owner of a backstreet men's furnishings shop in a northern Ontario mining town; 'I took just enough to keep our families alive,' noted a partner in a corner grocery from Markham; 'I took a salary for services rendered,' said a main-street men's clothier from Toronto; 'made as little as possible,' announced an Italian fruiterer, exceeding all the others in his humility. For a Franco-Ontarian general merchant, his store generated nothing more than the 'strick necessary for living,' while a substantial meat-shop owner in St Catharines felt that he made no 'profit, just bare living expenses.' Another – this time a Jewish proprietor of a large Toronto clothes shop – after claiming to have paid himself a salary of $45 a week from his business, explained, when asked about an additional $40 a week that seemed to have disappeared from the till; 'I took that to cover expenses: I had to move out of my apartment [he roomed with his partner and left when the partnership dissolved] and the place I got was more expensive in rent.' The idea behind all these statements is that stores did not generate profits; they ensured subsistence. Merchants drew a distinction between living expenses and profits, and the latter, they argued, came only after the former had been comfortably provided. That the law might treat any surplus as profit was so incomprehensible to them that they could not understand the lawyers' questionings or their creditors' hostility. 'This money you paid yourself belonged to your creditors,' one lawyer snapped; to which the confused retailer could only reply, 'no, it was my money, made honestly.'[22]

A large number of folkloric assumptions underpin these statements: the unity of shop and owner; the image of the independent business person as servant not boss; the sense that a store should produce a return commensurate with the work expended in its operation. But there is more. Lurking behind the shop owners' unpretending manner was the smugness of smallness, the quiet insistence that retailers were little people who deserved better. 'I have never had a car in my life,' one trader asserted, 'and never had a radio and these are little things: that others in poorer circumstances have and we have been very, very economical.' There is an unmistakable arrogance to assertions such as these, a sense of a sacrifice known and endured for the good of the business. This pride in vulnerability was central to retailing's folklore; it was the emotional heartbeat of smallness and service. 'Lily,' a well-to-do clothier recalled telling his wife, 'have patience and hope we will receive.'[23] It was a quintessentially small-business observation.

Failed ethnic retailers were particularly fond of emphasizing their vulnerability and innocent suffering. In so doing they drew upon another powerful folkloric tradition, the immigrant myth. Here one symbolic construct – the ordinary shopkeeper struggling to maintain his or her bearings on storm-tossed waters – was conveniently aligned with another folkloric image – the simple peasant struggling to maintain his or her bearings in a foreign land. In both mythic universes the villains were the same: unfeeling officials, big business people, heartless bureaucrats; and in both it was the innocence and powerlessness of the retailer-immigrant that was emphasized. Consider this fascinating exchange; a wholesaler asked his Jewish customer about certain heavily secured bank loans: 'You know, Mr. Raport, I suppose, that when you went to the bank to obtain a line of credit, you signed an agreement? I suppose you signed whatever was put in front of you?' 'That was the trouble,' replied the debtor; 'I did sign a lot of papers and I asked the new Manager what it was and he said, just a mere form, that is nothing ... I don't know what I signed.' Not unexpectedly, what he had signed was a chattel mortgage prioritizing the bank's investment in case of bankruptcy. But what is remarkable here is the mutually agreed-upon infantilization of the retailer. Whether true or not, the idea of the gulled immigrant, reading little English, dovetailed so nicely with the notion of the innocent retailer, a well-meaning ingenue victimized by scheming creditors, as to make an appeal to it almost involuntary. The wholesaler knew, even before asking, what had happened and with good reason: it was such a common defence. When questioned about a chattel mortgage that she had signed, a female trader responded, 'I could not read English, after the children came in and the children read it and they said to me that is a paper from the business – but I don't know nothing.' That this signing of unread papers could become such a powerfully convincing excuse was possible only because retailers were not considered to be street-wise in their business dealings. The fast-talking travelling salesman simply 'brought it in and laid it down and pointed to where I was to sign my name,' declared another bankrupt; 'I signed without reading it over.' And then there was the element of trust: 'he said we had an agreement whereby I could now obtain this line of credit ... [and] he was a good fellow and his company had been good to me ... I guess I trusted them.' That this retailer was a retired farmer and should have known the meaning of a chattel mortgage was not lost on his creditors' lawyer.[24] Though it is entirely possible that these things happened, we must recognize that shopkeepers were seeking to be absolved from blame by emphasizing their naïvety. Their goal was not simply to explain, it was to excuse. And in this sense it was the proprietary myth that served to transform their actions into justifications.

The failed retailers' sense of helplessness did not, however, preclude a fierce pride in their stores. 'From a small beginning I built this little business up,' explained a Jewish immigrant who had begun as a pedlar and after twenty years owned a large Queen Street shop in Toronto; 'everything I had went into that store.' As for his bankruptcy, three chains stores did him in 'with tremendous sales and they were underselling me and my sales dropped to a very small amount.' Here were all of retailing's symbols encapsulated: the smallness, the proprietorship, the vulnerability, the feelings of sacrifice, the unity of owner and enterprise. Shopkeepers presented their businesses as extensions of themselves, appendages whose actions they did not always control but suffered from none the less. Consider this brief exchange between another Jewish retailer and a lawyer enquiring into a personal loan:

Q. You borrowed it for yourself?
A. I borrowed it to move ... to move the business, to fix up the store.
Q. You say it was for the business?
A. I didn't have any cash at the time and I needed it.
Q. When you say you needed it, do you mean the business needed it?
A. The business needed it.[25]

In these questions and answers can be seen the conflict of business cultures: the lawyer, spokesman for limited liability and the separation of individual and property, and the retailer, unable to fully separate his subjectivity from its object. Was the store he or he the store? Seen this way, limited liability was less a legal form than a state of mind.

The aroma of the folkloric community wafted through the bankruptcy court whenever a retailer appeared. Once again, the folkloric image was exposed through its opposite: the idea that failure could be explained by the disappearance of natural community loyalties. When explicating his bankruptcy in Oshawa, one shop owner noted that 'the neighbourhood has gone down terribly ... there is a big foreign element there now and they are labourers and often out of work.' For another, business trailed away 'because of trade with worthless itinerant customers.' A clientele such as his did not have 'loyalty,' a third shop owner observed, 'with them it was just fighting tooth and nail to get the sale.' 'You can ask anybody in Town, the Banks or anyone,' a rural merchant complained, placing a bitter twist on the notion of community; 'business has been cut down by forty per cent since the Town went dry. Not that all farmers are boozers necessarily, but human nature is the same all over. They will always go with the crowd. I found that out.' These retailers seemed to believe in the organic connection of shop and consumer; in the idea that they were owed custom by the sheer fact of their being in business. Failure came when imbalance entered the equation, when the buying public failed to appreciate the service which the shopkeeper was rendering. To most retailers it was the ingratitude of the buyer that was to blame, but occasionally a merchant adopted a sadder tone. As one female merchant observed in explaining her bankruptcy, 'people were strangers to us.'[26]

Trade folklore was a language that retailers activated through speech. As a sign system it generated meanings which retailers could use to contextualize their situations. In fact, for bankrupt merchants, the employment of the folkloric image – whether community, independence, smallness, or the living profit – eliminated the necessity of explanation. Because the emotional import of the signs was widely understood, shopkeepers could account for their situations simply by referring to a symbolic ideal. It was this shared ability to conceive that gave retailers their sense of belonging to a small-business collectivity. The meanings of the symbols had a certain fixity bequeathed by time and practice, and this is what made their employment so effective. A retailer could tap into an entire symbolic value system simply by mentioning the 'loyalty' of his customers or the leanness of her profits. Reference to these symbols was intended to unname the individual, to exculpate an act by showing that bankruptcy was part of an eternal and unyielding system. It was not anything the shopkeepers did; it was their 'community' that was at fault or their natural naïvety that was taken as a matter of course. What made retailing exist as a cultural form – ideas about the independence of its proprietors, the smallness of their investment, the interdependence they maintained with their customers, the simplicity of their business practices – could be summoned by simple word use to account for the ability of individuals to succeed in it as a business reality.

Sign systems are not, however, mere structural abstractions. They exist through usage, and they are subject to the continuous variation of individual speech and intent. Signification has a practical, ideological purpose for the people producing it, meaning that individuals engaged in different social interactions will employ symbolic codes to express particular interests. Through speech, codes are personalized and interpreted, and the impressions conveyed, while dependent on the general acceptance of the symbol's importance, will also be situationally dependent. We noted something of this process in observing the alignment of an immigrant myth with a retailing symbol. In that case, the ethnic entrepreneurs were attempting to reinforce the one idea (that retailers were simple people who could not be expected to know the intricacies of finance management) with another myth (that language problems made recent immigrants susceptible to exploitation). This process of reinforcement actually served to give the retail symbol an immigrant spin, and by individualizing the style of its expression, the ethnic shopkeepers were announcing their differentness from other, non-immigrant store owners. The individuality of the 'acting subject,' as Umberto Eco called the sender of the message, could be 'read,' and the method that was used in 'self-construction' could be determined, through an analysis of the style of sign conveyance.

This process can also be seen in the way that female retailers 'feminized' their expression of retailing myths. What should have been clear from the preceding description is that shopkeeping's folkloric inheritance was fundamentally masculine. That was only to be expected, given the age in which the occupational imagery evolved and the status of women at the time, but it compelled female shopkeepers in subsequent generations to find their own ways of imagining their place in business. According to Lucy Eldersveld Murphy, women were distinguished by their ability to harmonize a 'female culture' with 'male' entrepreneurial values. Their advertisements were more 'friendly' (if in a 'prudish' way); their shops were more easily depicted as 'women's gathering places'; their sensibilities were more 'aesthetic.' Male observers in the late nineteenth century supported these judgments, commenting regularly on the tasteful interiors, attractive window displays, and 'womanly virtues' of female proprietors.[27] Obviously, we should be careful about pressing this argument on the basis of the evidence available. The intentions of male contemporaries were different from those of today's historians, and one must be cautious about accepting their views – whether upright or turned on their head – as indicators of tangible difference. The words of self-definition available to women were, after all, 'populated with the intentions of others.' Attractive window designing was not, for instance, a peculiarly female skill, and its 'feminization' in the late nineteenth century resulted from the extension of an oppressive ideology of separateness into retail work.

Still, the fragmentary evidence does suggest that women interpreted the folklore of self-representation in light of their experiences as women. The way in which language is used – speech – is always a consequence of practice, and to this extent, it is reflective of divergent understandings. Perhaps it was the insecurity associated with their crossing into a male sphere; perhaps it was the often-noted 'empathy' to which women were socialized. Whatever the cause, women did justify and present their actions as shopkeepers in ways different from men. Where men promoted their actions with reference to tests ('We have found,' announced one male phonograph dealer, 'that people who come to buy generally have an ear. The voice of a huckster or hot-dog barker is incongruous in selling music. Our clerks [therefore] practice to develop a well-modulated, firm voice ... they make as few motions as possible ... they are trained to be graceful when they place the record upon the turntable') or entrepreneurial initiative ('when the retailer balks at the hilt of progress he falls into the one-idea rut which will sooner or later relegate him to the class of has-beens'), women often referred back to their empathetic relationship with their customers. 'I had always been an enthusiastic customer of the T. Eaton Company,' a retail consultant remembered, 'and as a woman I had reason to know the value of their style policy. As a businesswomen I appreciated their system and service.' Or in a similar way: 'I did the buying for the store, because as a woman I knew what customers like.' Or again, and this time from a male whose daughter worked in his drug store: 'business was good when she was in toiletries ... the young people liked her because she was one of them ... After my daughter was married [and left], business slipped.'[28]

Behind these statements lay a fundamental difference of perspective. Where men serving a female clientele needed to study and scheme, to 'hunt for trade' and 'entice people into the store,' women announced their reliance on their empathy with their customers. Where men considered themselves outsiders who needed to 'educate' as much as 'exploit' their market, women projected themselves as 'providers' whose superior knowledge came from their greater sensitivity to consumers' needs. Though these rationalizations had no measurable impact on success rates in merchandising or the actual look or operation of stores, they do reveal the mutual nature of the gender divide in retailing. Women were not simply marginalized by men; they propagandized their own distinctiveness. These different constructions of retail knowledge, of the relationship between shopkeeper and community, and of identification between owner and enterprise were gendered variations on the folkloric form. Women read the symbol – say, service – in light of sex-typing, and where men saw service as an educational process, women perceived it to be a quasi-familial duty.

The same tracings of domesticity can also be found imprinted on ideals of proprietorship, smallness, and the living profit. Women in bankruptcy court consistently made the point that they retailed in order to fulfil familial obligations. 'My husband was severely burned in the Haileybury fire,' Margaret Killoran, a northern Ontario grocer, explained. 'We had nine children. But I had no experience in business and should never have gone into it.' Presented in a staccato style, this testimony is instructive for what it leaves unsaid. Killoran forces the reader to become an active agent at her defence and to conclude, on her behalf, that because her husband was incapacitated and there was a family to support, she had been forced to open a business. But who knows? That Killoran could rely upon a domestic ideal to fill in the blanks at a time when her business behaviour was being assessed demonstrates the extent to which non-trade values could transform the understanding of retailing's nature. Even when women employed myths of ownership, they did so in ways which emphasized their particular vulnerability and domestic responsibility. 'I have been putting everything I had into the business, even what my husband gave me, in order to make it go,' a Toronto dry goods dealer declared, placing a feminine spin on the concept of 'giving your all.' And when it came to explaining the returns on their investment, the living profit took on a literal meaning. 'I took only groceries for the Home,' noted one merchant; 'enough to support five children,' announced another; 'no profit. I looked after my house,' stated a third cryptically. Over and over, failed female retailers drew attention to their homes, their husbands, and their children. Needless to say, few men made mention of their wives' contributions or even of their familial responsibilities in their testimonies. There were, of course, some radicals. Ida Stone, for example, made no bones about the fact that she enjoyed making money and knew how to invest it. One of her few public regrets was that she lent money to a husband who subsequently filed for bankruptcy, 'and I did not get a cent back.' But from the evidence available, she was, in this regard, in an absolute minority.[29]

The point here is simply that shopkeepers interpreted the folklore of retailing and shaped it to reflect the individual circumstances of their lives. Men and women both accepted the code system – the idea of independence, the notion of service, the importance of community, the pride in ownership – and also implicitly acknowledged retailing's male sex-typing. In order to be retailers, women therefore had to find individual ways of reading the symbols; they had to reassert their own femininity and redefine the folkloric code in ways reflective of dominant ideals of womanhood. As with ethnicity, one symbolic system was being interpreted in light of another.

A female interpretation of folklore was only possible because the codes had certain intrinsic meanings, a recognized relevance upon which all retailers could draw, and to this extent, historians who emphasize the cohesiveness of small-business culture are correct. Trade folklore transformed a collection of individuals doing similar things into a group of business people with a basis for mutual identification. Moreover, the images they used were extremely old; ideas such as progress, community, and service figured as prominently in the writings of Defoe and Franklin as they did in the advice literature of such twentieth-century experts as Paul Nystrom and Frank Stockdale. But just because they employed a traditional symbolic code did not mean that Canada's retailers were all of one mind. Every symbol creates understanding through an interpretive act, and a traditional image might be used to express a very different message. After all, the word 'service' was not being used the same way by the seventeenth-century shop owner and the proprietor of a modern 'self-serve' grocery.

This simple truth also affects the idea that trade folklore served to unify the small-business community. Those who have argued that shopkeepers were united in their ideological conservatism tend to confuse words and meanings. The individual retailer did not approach folklore as a disinterested spectator; rather, he or she appropriated and individualized the ideal. This was also true of retailing's organizations. Individuals joined groups when they felt that they shared enough similarities to speak to each other in the same way. Leaders and promoters of organizations then endeavoured to forge those commonalities of speech into a single and unifying reading of the collectivity's symbolic essence. But because symbols were invariably subject to individualization, group speech was as much exclusive as inclusive. By establishing single readings, the discourse of unity served to exclude all those who did not feel drawn to that way of speaking. To this extent, the simple employment of a folkloric image cannot be taken to indicate a commonality of interest. Because groups, like individuals, read folklore in particular ways, each act of interpretation could be a declaration of separateness.

THE RMA: VOICE OF MAIN STREET

Anyone seeking to join a trade organization in early-twentieth-century Canada confronted an embarrassment of riches. They could sign into local groups, such as the Businessmen's Association of Parkdale or the Guelph Grocers' Association, that were limited to a few streets in a single community, or take out a membership in provincial or national associations such as the Canadian Pharmaceutical Association or the Retail Merchants' Association. It is impossible to know how many tradespeople were associating at any one time, since support for the smaller organizations cannot be documented and even the larger refused to publicize their membership. What can be said is that in the late-twenties the RMA, which was the largest of the country's trade associations, claimed to have the paid-up support of 20 per cent of general merchants, 16 per cent of hardware dealers, 10 per cent of shoe retailers, and 8 per cent of grocers, with membership before the Second World War peaking at 10 per cent of the shopkeeping total. The other national organization, the CPhA, insisted that it represented nine in ten druggists. In the same years, the Ontario Retail Hardware Association numbered 60 per cent of the members of that trade in the province, and the Ontario Retail Grocers' Association involved 5 per cent of all the food retailers.[30] Given that much of the membership was overlapping, it is likely that associational support in the best years numbered between one-fifth and one-quarter of the proprietary stratum.

Choice there may have been, but the decision to join an organization remained a complex matter. All groups possess a character which they foster through interaction and boundary maintenance – through a process of honouring those activities in which the group engages and ritualizing those features which divide the collectivity from others. The role of propaganda and leadership is to help in the demarcation of those boundaries by encouraging the sense of differentness that emerges naturally out of the shared ideals and activities which first drew members together. Groups therefore develop a character that might be no more than embryonic at the time of their origin. Consequently, an understanding of associational activity requires a locating of the basic reference points of the mature group's collective identity, as well as a determination of the limits that it managed to establish.

The Retail Merchants' Association promoted itself as a trade organization without boundaries. It was, declared one manifesto, 'the one organization under which all retail merchants can rally, no matter how poor, or what their creed, their religion or their race might be.' According to early organizers, occupational unity was the association's reason for being; its aim was 'to direct the attention of all retail merchants to the necessity of having a united retail trade.' Such collective action was deemed necessary because of the great threat confronting independent shopkeeping in the late nineteenth and early twentieth centuries. It was

the competition of the mass merchandisers – department stores beginning in the 1890s, mail-order houses in the second decade of the new
century, and chains in the 1920s – that led the retailers to heap high their
defences. What the big stores were doing, independent entrepreneurs
insisted, was 'to say the least, metaphorically commercial murder.'[31]
To many at the time, chains, departmentals, and mail-order houses
appeared bent upon trade monopoly, and they seemed to be using
every means at their disposal to drive their competitors out of business.
'We are face to face today with a foe,' said Norman Ratz, a Waterloo
grocer, 'whose onslaughts ... are most merciless; they are wielding
sledge-hammer blows at our existence.' For many shopkeepers, mass
distribution and traditional retailing were fundamental opposites.
Where the independent store owners liked to see themselves as
engaged in the business of community philanthropy, the corporate
retailers were portrayed as 'soulless distributing machines geared by
volume, screaming for net profits.' While the community shops served
with restraint, the success of the big stores was believed to rest on their
ability constantly to increase their market shares to the detriment of
everyone else's. According to small-business activists, the corporate
merchandisers could 'never relax' in their 'intense drive for volume,'
and distribution was being tarnished by 'the almost shrieking hysteria'
of the big stores' advertisements, which 'clothed in the language of the
advertising copyist, the pandemonium of barkers on a circus midway.'
In short, the mass merchandisers threatened the folkloric ideal of retailing and, in so doing, promised to destroy the distinctiveness of trade
itself. As the RMA's George Hougham expressed it, in the hands of the
mass marketers retailing 'ceases to be a dignified service and becomes a
mad scramble for an ever increasing share of the consumers' dollar,
aided by modern witch-doctors skilled in the art of appealing to mob
psychology.'[32]
The struggle to unify retailers against mass merchandising was therefore portrayed as a conflict between dream worlds. RMA activists seldom talked about what retailers did or how departmental or chain store
competition affected actual sales practices; instead, trade spokesmen
presented the struggle as one of ideals in collision. In justifying legislative controls on big-business competition, E.M. Trowern, the founder of
the RMA, declared in 1908, Was not the retailer 'the well-spring of the
healthy community[?] ... no businessman has as much influence among
every family ... every door is open to him with a cordial welcome.' It
was he 'who has been most interested in the community life, in the con-

struction of good roads, in the building of schools, hospitals and churches.' A quarter-century later, W.L. McQuarrie, secretary of the Saskatchewan RMA, made the same point in the same way: 'in the matter of the building and maintaining of our churches, it is the retail merchant who took the leading part as he did also in sports and entertainment, hockey teams, baseball teams, schools, public libraries, swimming pool, skating rink, agricultural society and practically every effort that goes to make up the social and recreational life of the society.' In both cases the interior message was the same: should the mass marketers succeed in establishing their control over distribution, the foundation of the entire Canadian community would be lost. Again and again the retailers warned that the mass merchandisers were a 'drain' on the national lifeblood. 'It was the individual businessman who very largely built our communities,' George Hougham announced in the mid-1930s; 'around him and through him grew up standards of living and contentment which made Canada the envy of the world.' If the big stores succeeded in their attempt to destroy independent shopkeeping, another observed in 1915, 'the Canadian nation will collapse.'[33]

The heart of the retailers' protest ideology therefore lay in the same folklore of trading that served all those conceiving themselves to be shopkeepers. Trade activists concentrated their efforts on the defence of an abstraction, on the set of codes that expressed retailing's imagined essence rather than its trade realities. That this remarkable situation developed was entirely due to shopkeeping's social, geographic, and economic fragmentation. RMA officials and members used folkloric symbols because they were the only mechanism by which a retail collective could be conceived; it was only by reference to these symbols that shopkeepers could be imagined as a united group. And such unity, even the pretence of such unity, was extremely important to the RMA because it was fundamentally a lobby group. Its key demands – buy at home, resale price maintenance, discriminatory taxation – all depended on the actions of others, whether manufacturers and wholesalers or politicians and judges. In order to achieve its goals the organization had therefore to sound as though shopkeepers were united and mobilized behind it; which is one reason why the association never publicized its membership. So great was the power of folklore, so widespread its acceptance, that it alone was considered necessary to establish the organization's representativeness.

Of course, images can deceive. As a point of convergence, retailing's symbolic inheritance was essential to those interested in occupational mobilization. By emphasizing issues such as independence, smallness, community, the living profit, and service, RMA activists could ostensibly give all merchants a sense that the organization was working for them. The problem with trade folklore was that its symbols were read by individuals with disparate identifications and motivations. And the moment one moved from the abstract notion of identity to the actual process of identification, one raised the possibility of conflict.

Though the RMA attempted to demonstrate its inclusiveness by defending the folkloric ideal, its members actually read the symbols in a unique and sectarian way. This was not done consciously or maliciously: those who joined the association simply believed that their definition of retailing's symbolic core was the real one. The key concept here was 'legitimacy.' Even in its initial manifesto, the RMA stipulated that membership was 'confined ... to the legitimate retailer.' Those who did not accept the RMA members' approach to folklore were by definition 'illegitimate' and therefore not real retailers. As a result, the notion of legitimacy did not necessitate a questioning of the inclusiveness of the folkloric inheritance. As not-retailers, the illegitimate were alienated from the symbolic memory. This distinction is important because the establishment of group boundaries did not provoke self-analysis. Those who failed to fit the definition were simply excluded from the imagined collective; there was no need to ask whether the group itself was being too narrowly defined. Consequently, organizers of the RMA were not being flippant in boasting of their association's accessibility even as they narrowed its appeal. As they saw it, the only conditions that they placed on membership were that one be a 'legitimate' owner of a retail business and that one pay the $10 annual fee. The RMA activists would have seen no confusion of their ideas; they would undoubtedly have argued that anyone was free to enter the organization so long as he or she agreed to live by the Golden Rule.[34] What they failed to mention was that the rule measured only those who conformed to standards that were sexist, nativist, and class defined. Small wonder that the RMA found its membership limited to only a fraction of the retail population; it developed into an exclusive movement that was antithetical to the interests of thousands of traders.

The character of the Retail Merchants' Association was established through the act of interpreting the folkloric code. In the first place, the words that association members used to characterize legitimate retailing were heavy with class meanings. The philosophy of the store owner, one writer advised, should be to 'look prosperous ... There is nothing which wreaks greater injury to the retailers' business than to permit the impression that he is not thriving.' The reason for this was simple enough – 'The cheap appearing store means cheap patrons' – but the method for appearing affluent was more complicated. Retailers were advised to use a distinct and stylish letterhead, to keep their stores bright and attractive, to hang eye-catching signs over their doors, to put up attractive window displays, and to keep their clerks well turned out. As their businesses served as symbols of their neighbourhoods, the store proprietors had a duty to make them look successful and efficient, for 'the store is a window on the community.' And besides, public confidence was good for sales, which was why J.A. Gagnon of Verdun believed the secret to his success was that he tried to be 'one of the leaders' in his city. Mix 'in all things to better your home town,' he advised his retailing brethren, 'if you want to succeed ... Spread your personality and that of your store.'[35]

These snippets of advice, offered unreflectively by writers on trade, prominent merchants, and business association executives, all reflect the activists' moyen bourgeois sense of the importance of their stores. Legitimate merchants, joiners instinctively felt, were persons of substance, employers of clerks, keepers of books, contributors to charities, members of voluntary organizations, founts of community wisdom. They were the ones who had a special obligation to defend their trades, to uphold the standards of their craft, to enjoy the maximum benefits of their markets. Small capitalist traders were not mere penny operators; they were masters of capital and labour, and this was revealed in the ways that they spoke about their stores. The modern retail store had to be 'like a well-regulated, well attended engine – everything running smoothly and the engineer, that is the boss, walking around calmly, always serene, while the cogs and wheels – the clerks – do the work, sputter and whirr.'[36] The assumptions that organized retailers made about the interests of all shop owners tell us a good deal about those who were joining associations. When they spoke before trade gatherings or wrote articles in business journals, they took it for granted that the audience they were addressing was made up of important people in their communities with large investments in their stores. This was how they saw themselves and this was how they chose to see all 'legitimate' retailers. And these selfsame presumptions can also be found shingling their use of such symbols as work and community and progress.

'Work,' Daniel Rodgers observed, 'was the gospel of the bourgeoisie.' The middle class developed its work utopianism in the nineteenth cen-

tury from a stiff compound of older proprietary values and contemporary ideas concerning moral education and spiritual uplift. In this rich
formulation, work came to be prized for more than just its results; its
merits were now thought to lie in the toil it involved. Everything, bourgeois moralists argued, came from effort: health grew from strain, salvation out of pain, success through exertion. 'A man coins himself into his
labor,' Emerson wrote, 'turns his day, his strength, his thoughts, his
affection into some product which remains a visible sign of his power.'
Small capitalist shopkeepers were among work's most fervent idolaters,
and everywhere they could be found affirming its articles of faith. 'Luck
has very little to do with [success],' one retailer concluded a speech on
the food business to a rapt group of Brantford RMA members, 'and I'll
venture to say that the grocers [who did well] had no more capital than
many others who quit or were forced out. The secret of their success has
been courage, initiative and a willingness to adapt themselves to changing conditions.'[37]

These ideas of work as uplift shaped the more-affluent retailers' reading of symbols such as the living profit, independence, and service.
Legitimate success came from discipline and self-repression, from the
ability to control the innate desire to have fun and from the channelling
of one's human energies into labour. And discipline was a habit that
had to be cultivated. The retailers who today are 'barely earning a living,' a pharmacist noted, 'as boys did not look upon every errand as a
chance to be polite, prompt, energetic; on every lesson in school as a
foundation stone in their success structure. They did not think that the
demoralizing hours of indolence and shiftliness [sic] which they were
weaving into the web of their lives would mar the fabric forever, and
reproach them for all time.' The living profit was therefore not simply a
matter of subsistence; it was a symbol of enterprise. In work dwelt uplift
and in perseverance lay salvation for the individual and for humanity
because it was through labour and the discipline it entailed that people
gained 'independence and the right to be called men.'[38]

As anxious as other members of the bourgeoisie to justify their social
leadership in terms other than money, activists and joiners placed heavy
emphasis on education as an architect of uplift. In fact, as changes in the
nature of distribution made it harder for people to justify their conviction that work alone created success, bourgeois thinkers increasingly
stressed the value of a professional or scientific training. Work unin-
formed by knowledge came increasingly to appear as energy squandered. 'Distinction in pharmacy,' a prominent druggist declared before

a Vancouver convention of the BCPhA in 1912, 'requires an adequate training in the sciences of physics, chemistry and botany,' as well as 'neatness, precision, truthfulness, system, patience, [and] analysis.' And this emphasis on knowledge was not limited to quasi-professional lines such as pharmacy. 'There is no more room in the grocery trade for the slovenly, the unskilled, the charlatan,' announced a trade activist. 'Knowledge of palate and eye, backed up by the knowledge and practice of a thousand and more technical details, will be indispensable qualifications to the man' who would be grocer.[39]

This effort to shore up their claim to privilege through an emphasis on the superiority of their knowledge also led affluent retailers, as it did other middle-class people, to attempt to establish professional standards for their trades. The retail associations and the trade press took it upon themselves to lead the shopkeepers in their fight to professionalize. The trade organizations offered designs for 'model stores,' gave instructions on 'commercial window dressing,' and provided guides to 'the scientific use of display.' At its grandest, this kind of support took the form of trade shows, such as the one at the Toronto Armoury hosted by the Ontario Retail Hardware Association, where 150 booths were set up to demonstrate to all comers the advantages of a proper use of window space and display shelving. Similarly, 'model retailers,' such as Clayton Ironside of Kintore, Ontario's, found themselves profiled in the trade journals and celebrated for their scientific approach to selling: 'his investment is small,' the *General Merchant* reported, 'his stock turns rapidly and at a good profit, the business is strictly cash and the lines he stocks lend themselves readily to display.'[40] The press ran innumerable articles each year on window designing, proper store layouts, advanced bookkeeping, up-to-date management, improved labour relations, and suggestive advertising. Retail experts wrote an endless stream of advice columns and travelled the country giving lectures on modern merchandising. Literally hundreds of books were published, especially in the 1920s, offering advice on how to succeed in distribution. The Retail Merchants' Association was especially active in advancing the cause of progressive shopkeeping. It was the force behind the introduction of courses in retail management at three major Canadian universities, it set up model stores and organized group advertising, and the Saskatchewan RMA even imported Frank Stockdale, its own American 'retail commercialist,' to spread the gospel of store modernization.[41]

The desire to professionalize has most often been presented as part of a panicky middle-class response to a late-nineteenth-century crisis of authority, and there was certainly an element of such a response in the retailers' thinking. Professionalization offered psychological support to traders under threat from increased competition and economic change. But anxiety propelled people only part of the way into professionalism; what pushed them over the top was the realization that it was also status enhancing. Bourgeois merchants saw their professional neighbours developing occupational pretensions in the late nineteenth and early twentieth centuries, and they sought to share in the action. It was not just a matter of preserving what they once were; they wanted professionalism in order to enhance their role in the community. 'In these modern days salesmanship has justly been classed as a profession, and has developed along scientific lines,' one trader remarked proudly, if perhaps prematurely, 'until it ranks equally as high as law, medicine and kindred sciences, and requires equally as much study, thought and training.'[42] Here was the retailer on a par with other members of the modern bourgeoisie: well educated, cultured, and technologically proficient. No mere huckster this or victim of status anxieties. The small capitalist joiner was interested neither in standing still in a moving world nor in continuing to link his name to that of the marginal, front-parlour dealers.

And underlying all these forms of self-affirmations was their negation. The RMA declared its purpose 'to have the retail trade of cities, towns and villages restricted, as far as possible, to the legitimate retailer,' but it failed actually to define 'legitimacy.' To its members fell the role of supplying the symbolic juxtaposition of moral and immoral with practical content. Retailing's small capitalist traders took the legitimate to be the professional (not the 'cheap jack'), the well educated (not the 'mossbacked'), and the prominent (not the 'shoestring'). By employing folkloric symbols such as service, success, independence, and legitimacy, members effectively drew a boundary around themselves and excluded those who failed to measure up. Contrasting the moral with the immoral, the legitimate with the charlatan, and the retailer committed to his community with the interloper committed only to himself served to distinguish main street from backstreet, rich from poor. And small capitalist joiners added to their quiver of opposites such powerful ideas as the difference between the clean and the unclean, the honest and the crooked, the light and the dark. These images allowed the retailers to bypass the moral question of whether they had the right to try to limit opportunities in merchandising and to redefine their protest as a struggle to promote ethical retailing and healthy progress.

Little shops that stayed open late or on Sunday became particular targets because they were seen to be flouting professional standards and corrupting the morals of the people. One small grocer in Belfountain, Ontario, for example, was criticized for providing 'anything he is asked for,' meaning that 'youngsters from 12 to 14–15' were being 'pedled cigarettes.' Another, in Cedarvale, who kept his shop open late on Saturday had it described suggestively as 'a meeting place for all the undesirables in the district ... [He] has a bunch of young girls and boys hanging around and their language is such that it makes a respectable person feel ashamed to pass.' Similarly, small shops were generally condemned for transgressing the laws of health and hygiene by remaining dark and dirty. As one Burnaby retailer remarked of the owner of a 'small store on the outskirts,' 'he kept his bins [for bulk goods] so dirty, you could hardly see what they contained.' When asked about them, the grocer thought his business was being complimented on its fixtures and responded proudly, 'Yes ... you've got to have these nowadays, or the rats will eat everything up. We are worried to death with them.' An apocryphal tale, no doubt, but one that exposes the more affluent traders' preconceptions none the less surely.[43]

Those who could not afford to rise to the standards that association members erected were simply held to be unworthy – deficient in that basic industriousness needed to make a success of one's life . Indeed, the 'immoral' proprietors did not even deserve the designation 'merchant.' Shoestring traders were 'hucksters,' individuals of limited ambition and ability. To association members, the trade disrupters were sordid, immoral individuals, people content to 'get a bare living or run behind.' Their stores were disgraceful: untidy, dirty, and filled up with outdated stock; their credit was worthless, their experience minimal. They had no stamina, no ability to bear up under the strain of competition. 'Every year in Canada, there are almost innumerable dealers setting up retail stores on a "shoe string" as the saying goes. They carry on the struggle for a while, but have so little financial stamina that they are put out of pain by the first real jolt they get.' And because they had no professional standards, these shopkeepers were actually harming retailing by the very fact of their pitiful existence. As Walter Ing, a prominent Vancouver grocer, sneered, the 'would-be retailers in business today can only be regarded as a hindrance and an obstacle to building up the retail trade to the status and respect which is its due.'[44]

Licensing, which the RMA promoted with enormous vigour throughout the early twentieth century, was in reality a not-so-veiled attempt to eliminate backstreet competition. 'Applicants for licenses will have to furnish reasonable assurance that they are competent as retail merchants,' one retailer explained, relying on assumptions of legitimacy to explain his point. According to others, licensing should take the form of a law requiring a standard of training or apprenticeship, for as one Keene, Ontario, RMA member quipped, 'a merchant without training spoils business for everyone.' For a St Catharines businessman, licensing 'will prevent all kinds of people from starting hole-in-the-wall stores and improve the situation of the shopkeeper ... It takes three years to make a grocer, and no man should be permitted to run a business unless he knows it.' Reducing competition, explained George Champaigne of Niagara Falls, would ultimately improve profits because 'the more stores, the cheaper the goods.'[45]

Class values, which reflected not only the shopkeepers' material conditions, but also their sense of themselves as business people were central to the associational experience. Originally, the RMA cast a fairly wide net and attracted a reasonable balance of the retail population. Over time, however, its dominant character emerged, and the organization came to represent a distinct minority of tradespeople. As can be seen from table 7, one feature that clearly came to distinguish the RMA's members was capital. Though the organizations began life with a sizeable representation of small shopkeepers, by the First World War the Retail Merchants' Association was made up almost entirely of individuals running mid-sized and larger independent stores, and it seemed to have had little appeal to those outside the ranks of retailing's gentry. Half of the membership was drawn from the richest 20 per cent of retailers, and the very largest independents showed up in the association's lists with four times the frequency with which they appeared in the market-place (compare with tables 3 and 4). The 'typical' RMA of the interwar years was the owner of a store capitalized at roughly $6,000–30,000, a man likely to employ two to eight full-time workers and to have an annual turnover averaging $30,000–120,000. George Hougham once described the average association member as the owner of a 'neighbourhood department store,' a telling comment on the RMA's self-perception.[46]

As the RMA developed and grew, association members consolidated the boundary round their class by singling out as unethical traders (price cutters and merchants open late at night and on Sundays) exactly that group which had been excluded from membership. But class, while central to the organizational experience, did not preclude other forms of identification. Joiners were more than just rich tradespeople; they were also liable to be English or French Canadian, and they were almost invariably male. And when members of the trade organizations used the folkloric codes, they did not do so simply in class ways; they also revealed their ethnic and gender biases. These groupings, with their different boundaries and their different criteria for inclusion and exclusion, therefore worked with class prejudices to define the small capitalist shopkeepers' sense of who they were and with whom they wanted to associate.

In fact, the entire discourse of independence, service, and profit, in its 'professional' guise, was loaded with gendered assumptions. It was not just that trade activists and publicists continually referred to 'men' in their speeches and writings; the actual values they associated with legitimacy contained a masculine valuation. The validity of the notion of the professional depended on acceptance of the superiority that came from specialized knowledge, experience, or long-term success. From the late nineteenth century, professionalism implied both a full-time status and an extended commitment to the work involved. Thus it was incompatible with the dominant construction of the feminine, which ascribed women's 'proper' commitment to homes and families. Women were expected to be full-time women, and this role implied keeping a house, raising a family, and caring for the weak. Unfortunately, in the zero-sum game of life, the engagement in work demanded of 'professionals' meant a sacrifice of the nurturing vocation expected of women.

It was not, however, the time commitment alone which sex-typed professionalism. The development of the concept of the 'business profession' was in many ways an effort to leaven the entrepreneurial ideal of the 'masculine achiever' with a pinch of gentlemanly conduct.[47] As the business climate became increasingly competitive and volatile in the late nineteenth century, retailers found themselves engaged in a more vigorous struggle for success. This contest served not only to divide shopkeepers further; it also threatened to reconfigure their folklore by increasing the acceptability of unrestrained competition. If store owners were fighting for their very survival, then distribution became a primeval struggle for supremacy. In this context, any act was justified if it meant increasing one's market share. But the entrepreneur as predator was also the individual who broke free of tradition and order; he was, in symbolic terms, the creative destroyer. Professionalism blunted the challenge which this notion of competition posed to community by reinvigorating the folkloric ideal of healthy and uplifting rivalry. A profession was perceived to be a 'brotherhood,' and its members revealed their mutual 'respect' by following 'professional rules of conduct.' The business professional therefore embraced the life in trade but rejected the dishonesty, selfishness, and greed of the unrestrained market-place. In this way, professionalism reasserted the folkloric ideal of gentlemanly competition – the image of business as sport.

The fact that the ideal professional was supposed to be a Boy Scout in the 'real' world again raised barriers to women. Females attempting to cross over into a profession were already perceived to have sacrificed their proper natures, but they could not look to the notion of professionalism for an alternate image construction. Barred from the brotherhood that underlay the professional ethos, well-to-do women were adrift in the liminal space. Those who attempted to assimilate came to be regarded as strange and monstrous hybrids, unnaturally aggressive and overbearing individuals who had crossed over into a world where they did not belong. Ruth Hamilton, a one-time manager for Eaton's who later became a retail consultant, was described by George Hougham of the RMA as 'unusually outspoken.' Similarly, the manager of Montreal's Pharmacie Moderne, a Madame Charbonneau, was portrayed by her male competitors as 'formidable,' a sort of Amazonian aberration who was 'not to be trifled with.'[48]

The only way for women to avoid the stigma that followed their entry into the male professional space was for them to continually assert their femininity, in effect, to deny their desire for professional status. Most did so simply by undervaluing their successes. Anne Simpson of Innisfail, Saskatchewan, for example, who became the first woman delegate to a CPhA convention, when interviewed in the *Canadian Pharmaceutical Journal*, seemed anxious to explain that she was still Miss Simpson, the rose-cheeked country girl. Drawn into science, she explained, because she was a lover of plants, she had turned to pharmacy because (offering a female spin on the retail myth and not, I think, an early statement of the feminist) it offered one 'the glorious privilege of being independent.' But though now a professional, Simpson continued to love womanly things. While the men joined clubs and went fishing, 'I dote on cooking, and all other kinds of housework. I practice at every opportunity, even to washing dishes.'[49] Simpson could well have been saying only what was expected of her, but her refusal to confront the sexism of the proprietary-professional myth was a testament to its authority even over those that it harmed.

Professionalism was, however, only one of the ways in which retail propagandists and joiners attempted to masculinize legitimacy. Association members had a battery of beliefs that could be used to keep the females at bay. Women were continually treated in associational folk speech as helpmates: they were part of the proprietor's support network and not independent agents ('in every retail grocery or general merchandise store of any size,' the RMA-backed *Retail Grocers' Review* explained, 'there should be a young lady in the office'). While the shopkeeper of tradition would have been expected to have had a wife to help him around the store – the termagant behind the counter being something of a stock character in popular culture – the 'small business' was unquestionably a patriarchy. It was a matter of pride. One main-street retailer, whose wife participated with him in the management of a women's clothing store, made plain the shopkeepers' sensitivity to suggestions of their own entrepreneurial impotence: 'she did most of the buying ... [but] I don't know [if] you would call it her ... responsibility ... I don't know where the responsibility would come in ... we both decided what she would buy.'[50]

Traditional gender differences also account for the uneasiness that small capitalist retailers experienced when they began hiring women in the 1880s, misgivings they expressed through patronizing remarks and discriminatory actions. Sam Peps, for example, the shopkeeping sage of Pepsville, Nova Scotia, always made a point of distinguishing between his male clerks and 'the girl Sally' he employed in the women's wear department. This was a common response because women were generally considered 'unskilled' workers with no long-term prospect in retailing. Where male clerks might one day become retailers in their own right, females were regarded as cheap labour best suited to tasks requiring little imagination or selling ability. It was apparently vital that men and women be kept at least psychologically segregated in this way, ostensibly because their 'natures' demanded it. In this manner, window-dressing was thought to be an appropriate 'women's business' because it 'appeals to the artistic temperament ... and it demands a certain knowledge of psychology as well as taste, a sense of colour and proportion, a realization of timeliness.' Elevator operating was not: as the systems officer at Eaton's observed, 'more attention would be paid to women operators by customers ... which might result in proper attention not being given to the running of the elevators.' Space itself thereby came to be gendered; store windows were described as 'the eyes of the store,' which ought 'to be kept as bright as a bride adorned for her wedding,' while the selling area 'must be all bone and sinew.' Not surprisingly, men who crossed into this female space had somehow to affirm their masculinity, which is why male drug-store clerks who worked the cosmetic counter in the 1920s were nicknamed 'sheiks' and affectionately satirized for their virility.[51]

Accompanying the main-street retailers' disparaging attitude to the female shop worker was the shadowed contempt they felt for the modern consumer. Late-nineteenth- and early-twentieth-century shoppers were invariably portrayed as women, and this assumption seemed to justify the independent proprietors' opinion that the public was easily victimized. The view fitted in well with the notion of women's seduction by men: departmental and chain store advertisers 'tempted' female shoppers with their low prices, and once they had them, 'kept them returning for more.' Similarly, pedlars were attacked for 'preying' on women while their husbands were off at work. 'Many timid housewives complain of these house-to-house peddlers,' an RMA brochure affirmed, 'total strangers who persist in entering their houses to show merchandise without permission [of the husband?]. Records show this is a dangerous practice, for it is very hard for the unsuspecting housewife to determine the good from the bad.' It was not, however, all the dealers' fault. The ambivalence of the Victorian approach to femininity also found voice in the well-to-do retailers' discussions because women were thought to invite the attentions which ensnared them. 'Here is a woman,' the *Canadian Grocer* explained, 'whose complexion is her pride. But how is she to maintain it?' The advertisers provided no more than 'an answer to her question with soaps and cosmetics.' Pedlars, hucksters, and mass merchandisers, in short, offered 'an answer to her desires.'[52] Both sides of the image were important elements in the retail imagination because they justified the organized retailers in their belief that only the legitimate shopkeeper could be relied upon to serve the consumers' needs without exploiting them. 'Ethical trading' in this sense meant a man's ability to trust another with his wife, daughter, or lover.

This ingrained sexism provided a major obstacle to the entry of women into the trade organizations. None of the 400 association members whose names were drawn from the trade press were women, and of the names on a list of grocers prepared by the RMA, only 13 of 563 were female. Moreover, out of the 13, all but 2 were widows of once-prominent merchants who were continuing to operate family stores after the deaths of their husbands (another was the daughter of a deceased merchant). These attitudes also manifested themselves in the ways that the trade associations structured their activities. Trade meetings often featured poker or euchre, drinking, and cigar smoking, activities from which women were excluded. Picnics were often exclusively male, including the annual CPhA picnic in Hamilton, which was supposedly open to 'all the city's druggists.' The trade associations also contained secret fraternal societies open only to men, such as the Yellow Dogs or the Prairie Wolves, groups whose activities included late-night prowls after conventions and whose rituals involved howling at the moon and eating mock dog biscuits.

In short, gender and class worked together to define the association members' notion of legitimacy. Because of their natures, women could not be professionals, they could not be expected to manage a 'real' store, and they could not be womanly and still participate in the RMA's male-affirming rituals. That most female shopkeepers were poor only served to confirm the small capitalist male retailers' perceptions. It was obvious to main-street tradespeople that with few exceptions, women did not belong in retailing. Since success came only to those who struggled, it must have been their feminine natures that prevented women from becoming successful proprietors. Joiners were therefore able to fill folkloric images with a multitude of assumptions and prejudices. Symbols such as independence or competition could be used as vehicles for the retailers' other identities. Folklore brought together what appeared to be discrete points of reference – gender and class – and intertwined them in mutually sustaining ways. They could, of course, be separated as needs arose – shoestring males were as unwelcome in the organization as front-parlour female traders – but the points of reference none the less often worked to reinforce each other. The thick padding of identification could be thinned at will without damage to their folkloric container.

Of course, ideas such as professionalism and legitimacy were barriers not simply to women. Anyone who could be ascribed a character in conflict with the joiners' values could be excluded from the group. Jews, for example, were traditionally stereotyped as competitive and devious and unpleasantly greedy. This image made them unlikely professionals because to be a professional one had to be a Christian gentleman. The Jews, explained one trade association member, 'possess no business ethics'; the goal of each one of them, he argued, was to be 'top dog.' To another retailer, business practices could only be 'cleaned up' if something were done to control 'the greedy grasping Jews,' while yet another felt that 'Jews are only interested in making money.' The connection between Jews and greed was, of course, etched in the psyche of early-twentieth-century Gentiles just as surely as the image of the rootless outsider, surviving by quick wits and entrepreneurship, was cherished in the memories of Jews.[53] Particular embodiments of the competitiveness and individualism of the new world of marketing, Jews were deemed singularly dishonourable and untrustworthy. Though a handful did join the trade associations, their acceptance was muted by a general distrust of their motives.

Driven by fear of competition to attempt to control all those they rated illegitimate, the retail associations occupied the forefront of Canada's ethnic purity campaigns. In Quebec the Achat chez nous movement, which the RMA sponsored, was one of the main instruments of anti-Semitism in the province, while in British Columbia and Alberta the retail association was closely affiliated to the Oriental Exclusion League. Shopkeeper nativism was not, of course, limited to these three provinces or organizations: there is some evidence that retailers were prominent in movements such as the Ku Klux Klan and the Deutscher Bund. In Winnipeg retailers who tried to enforce early-closing laws singled out the Jewish shopkeepers in the north end as early as 1891–3. The Manitoba RMA became involved in an attempt in 1921–2 to regulate Sunday shopping which brought it into direct and often slanderous conflict with the predominantly Jewish Small Stores Association. And as late as 1936 in Toronto, Jewish stores were targeted by a Sunday-closing alliance in such a way as to provoke among RMA members 'the most unfortunate anti-Semitic feeling.' Vitriolic assaults on minorities were neither unusual in the years surrounding the First World War nor directed only at the Jews. Italians and other southern Europeans were also frequent, if uncoordinated, targets of attack by RMA members and other nativist retailers.[54] But unlike Achat chez nous and the anti-Oriental lobby, none of these episodes were organized and none involved the merchants' association in its official capacity. Nativist slurs might frequently be made and acts of malice perpetrated, but these involved individual proprietors and not the retailers as an organized body.

Still, nativism formed another basis of the association members' identification, and they loaded retailing's symbols with racialist messages. When the grocers' section of the RMA failed to get a proposed early-closing by-law passed in Vancouver in 1922, it evoked the community-interloper image by blaming the failure on the 'the invasion of Orientals and foreigners into our field.' In much the same way as small retailers were described as having no 'skill,' the west-coast Chinese were criticized for their lack of expertise. 'Ask any of the type past referred to what is the difference between All Spice and Pastry Spice; what is Cream of Tartar; what is Pure Jam, etc., etc.!' And like the petty retailers, the ethnic entrepreneurs were condemned for the impurity of their stores ('why should grocery stores be stores during the day and bunk houses at night') and the cleanliness of their proprietors ('We must *condemn* the practice ... of storing groceries to be consumed by the public in the bedroom of the possibly and probably none too clean owners'). As E.R. McTaggart, president of the Greater Vancouver section of the RMA, observed with respect to the rising trade competition, 'if ... the laws regarding building restrictions were enforced so that the Oriental was not permitted to live in a "piano box" minus sanitation, you would see some difference.'[55]

Much the same was said in Quebec about the Jews. Like the Chinese, the Jewish retailer was generally considered 'malhonnête' and 'déloyale ... il n'y a pas que cela pour expliquer son succès.' But unlike those who vilified Asians, anti-Semites tended to emphasize the dishonesty and malevolence of their victims, rather than their impurity and strangeness. The goal of the Achat chez nous movement, for example, was to convince consumers that they must boycott Jewish stores because to do otherwise was unpatriotic. Jews, Achat chez nous propagandists declared, were growing rich while French Canadians suffered, a fact that was kept hidden behind a façade of poverty. Moreover, Jewish merchants were not prospering honestly: 'rouerie, perfidie, fraude, fausse représentation, mensonge, crapulerie, absence d'éthique et de sentiment d'honneur, telles sont les portes d'entrée et de sortie de la grande majorité des Juifs dans notre vie économique.' Like the Chinese, Jews were depicted as an invading force: 'on les voit d'abord dans les quartiers ouvriers dans les petits épiceries, où l'on trouve tout ce q'on veut; ouverts jour et nuit, sur dimanche comme sur semaine, ils esquivent la loi de fermeture à bon heure.' And their actions resulted in 'une concurrence ruineuse à tous nos petits magasins, qui disparaissent peu à peu.'[56] Though different in some ways from its rampage against the Chinese in western Canada, the RMA's Achat chez nous campaign manipulated the same folkloric images. Disloyalty, illegitimacy, an absence of professional ethics, an interest in profit over service – these were the images used to convey the immigrant's otherness.

Paradoxically, the isolation of ethnic communities appears to have provided a basis for much of the suspicion that existed between Canada's retailing groups and fostered a sense that foreigners were trying to remain isolated. When the English- and French-Canadian shop owners hired their own, it was seen as natural and normal, whereas when immigrants did the same thing, it appeared as though they were insulating themselves from the host society. As the RMA's official organ snarled in 1938, 'because they make use of their families to evade Minimum Wage Laws, the average merchant cannot compete with the Oriental.' The perceived differentness of the minority retailers became a special problem when certain ethnic traders began to seek markets among the native-born because it raised fears of a unified foreign grouping preying off an unsuspecting indigenous population. To French and English retailers, the immigrant entrepreneurs came to appear a subversive, secretive, and united block, while their mostly female customers seemed ignorant of the ways in which foreigners were 'violating' their trust. Asian merchants on the west coast were thought to be members of a conspiratorial group, while in Montreal the shop owners felt that they were competing against 'un seul race étrangère: Les Juifs,' who, unlike Canadians, 'forment comme ailleurs un bloc solide.'[57]

While some immigrant retailers did join the RMA, as with the handful of women members, they were continually defending their culture and attempting to build on the commonalities of class. Of the four hundred members whose names were recorded, 85 per cent were identifiably English or French in origin; the bulk of the remainder were German. And no wonder: any rich Jewish or Chinese traders who wanted to join the RMA had to accept the organization's history of nativism. As Nathan Pollock, a Jewish shopkeeper from Kinistino, explained when he joined the organization, his goal was to fight the belief that 'Jewish traders are to blame [for hard times] more than any other merchant.' Within a given context, an individual's identification with ethnic or class groupings might loom dominant without his or her becoming a Jekyll and Hyde. In this instance, Pollock seems to have been hoping that the economic interests he shared with other RMA members would counterbalance the ethnic difference. He did not, however, stop identifying with his own culture: as he noted, he felt that 'the prejudice of generations' against the Jews was 'becom[ing] ever more acute.'[58]

Doubtless, many retailers joined organizations such as the RMA in order to attack immigrant shopkeeping. The British Columbia chapter, for example, had only been created in 1918, but by 1922 it numbered almost 1,200 members. This tremendous growth was attributable to a resurgence of anti-Asian feeling in western Canada, especially in those smaller centres where Asians were few in number but large in psychological import. In many places the newly formed RMA chapters were little more than vigilante groups created to harass Asian retailers and to 'keep this a White Man's country.' Success, however, proved hard for the provincial section to bear, and by early 1923, with the Oriental Exclusion Bill moving through Parliament, the issue began to fade and with it much of the membership. At the BC RMA's 1923 convention, held shortly after the passage of the Exclusion Act, the association admitted that it was running a deficit, that 60 per cent of its members had failed to pay their dues, and that 15 per cent had not renewed. Those who remained RMA supporters now slipped into apathy: out of 150 questionnaires sent out to members late in 1923 asking for ways to revitalize the organization, only 15 were returned.[59] Clearly, it was the race issue, rather than the problem of controlling mass merchandising, that largely accounted for the membership surge in British Columbia.

But because they used the same symbols to conceive of their hostility to mass marketing and ethnic retailing, joiners did enjoy a sense of belonging to a broad and sympathetic collectivity. Whether members for years or only for a matter of months, those associating with the RMA had a sense that the organization represented their interests. It was actually immaterial whether individuals were drawn to association because they wanted to control shoestring trading or because they were living in areas where immigrants appeared the major problem: the commonalities of speech allowed each to recognize the moral justice of the others' position. This was why RMA members in PEI could support the cause of Oriental exclusion even though the nearest Chinese retailer was a lone grocer hundreds of miles distant in Saint John. The Island traders believed that they understood the issues raised a continent away because they had a folkloric concept of 'unethical' and 'demoralizing' competition. Class and ethnic prejudices worked – sometimes together, sometimes separately – to create the associational predisposition, and practice made them mutually affirming.

As a result, the established character of the organization was exceptionally important. Though some traders associated simply to express their nativist prejudices, they also knew that the groups they joined were representative of the shopocracy. Even in BC, poor white merchants did not tend to participate in the RMA, even though many of them shared the wealthier retailers' racist views. The problem with retailers was that even those who shared common attributes of class or race or gender remained isolated from and competitive with each other. Main-street merchants might agree on their hostility to someone else, but they were none the less suspicious of each other's motives. After all, main-street storekeepers had as much to fear from each other as they did from the backstreet. Consequently, well-to-do English- and French-Canadian merchants mobilized when some issue rose above their individual rivalries, but they were unwilling to sustain active membership. The trade associations, which served as touchstones of moyen bourgeois attitudes, ultimately failed to solidify the identity of even a minority of tradespeople. The associations helped to broadcast, refine, and legitimize the shopocracy's sense of itself, but they did not transform the main-street traders into a group *for itself*. Certainly, the organizations developed a character and, because of this, a constituency. But the latency failed to develop into consistent activation. Even the affluent traders only associated together when an issue demanded their attention. That they did so quite readily is a revelation of their sense of commonality; that they did so sporadically is a reflection of their undiminished individualism.

Legitimacy in retailing was therefore not a static thing: shopkeepers were at one and the same time business rivals and members of classes, ethnic groups, occupations, and trades. The ranking and relationship of people's identities cannot be simplified or made overly consistent; shopkeepers, like the retail associations that represented them, developed a character, not a mechanical function. The organizations shifted and flexed with the changing interests of their members: sometimes, as during the First World War the great issue would be rationing; at others it was Chinese exclusion; at still others, licensing or Sunday observance. Clearly, all of these issues affected the membership in their business capacity, otherwise they would not have moved together down the occupational channel. But it would be wrong indeed to limit joiners to a single motivation or interest. They were people who shared a series of overlapping loyalties, and as they changed in response to their world, their numbers expanded and contracted – always within a certain field, of course, and one laid out by the commonalities of class and ethnicity and gender – but it was movement all the same.

CULTURE WITHOUT CLASS

Clearly, the bonding properties of a small-business culture can be defended only if the differences which that ideology expressed are ignored. The Canadian evidence suggests that those advancing the idea of a homogenizing petit bourgeois ideology are exaggerating the influence of the shopkeepers' occupational symbols. Because they tend to abstract the ideas from the individuals expressing them, 'idealist' inter-preters read the words and not the meanings they encoded. All retailers may have been committed to notions of smallness, independence, ser-vice, and locality, but they did not use these words in the same way. The contention offered here is that people identified with each other because they filled abstract notions of the group with their own subjectivity. Shopkeepers had a sense of what a retailer was because they could see their own activities in light of standards bequeathed them by history. Folklore thus operated as a shared resource, a collective memory out of which identity could be fashioned. But that does not mean there is only one form of identity. People do not simply measure themselves against a fixed image; they also reconceptualize the ideal in conformity with their own experience and understandings. Symbols have a range of characteristics which bracket their definition, allowing all people who embody those ideals to share a certain basic empathy, but they are not self-determining. All symbols are interpreted. Shoestring shopkeepers did not consider themselves any less 'retailers' than the main-street traders, which they would have done had they been simply measuring themselves against the shopocracy's definition of merchandising. Both groups could appropriate the symbolism of distribution and make it their own.

The myths of retailing therefore formed a framework of identification by whose reference people who retailed could position themselves as shopkeepers. But ideals and realities were not synonymous. When retailers articulated their occupational identity, they said actual things to and about each other. And the moment they turned from the 'ideality of the [symbol's] meaning' to the 'reality of the thing' which they addressed and described, they broke the closure of folklore and the sin-gularity of their cultural inheritance.[60] The occupational commonalities that independent store owners enjoyed on an abstract level disappeared as soon as they listened to what they were saying. Retailing was a divided world, and those divisions could not be subsumed by a shared symbolism.

Consequently, though retailers traced their singularity to their folk-lore, they cannot be treated as a collectivity. They were an unstable col-lection of mutually suspicious individuals whose abilities to work together depended on the capacity of an issue to awaken the commonal-ities that their myriad interests had given them. It took such factors as class and nativist prejudices and gender attitudes to structure their understandings of trade symbols in such ways as to encourage even a minority of them to work together. Because retailing itself involved symbols but not fixed readings, the shop owners' identification with each other was a product of interests carried into trading from outside. A retail issue may have triggered their actions – such as the BC retailers' fear of Asian competition – but it was their common sense of themselves as 'whites' which turned their folkloric inheritance into an instrument of group action. It was the combination of a collection of mutualisms unconnected to the business of trading with a set of suspicions flowing from business competition which made retailers such an unstable group of joiners. Folklore served to channel their myriad identities and give them a retailing shape, but it could not turn competitive individualists into cooperators. As soon as an issue was resolved, main-street shopkeepers simply returned to the business of stealing each other's trade. The symbolic language of retailing – service, community, smallness, independence – provided shopkeepers with a structure of identification, but the fluidity of identity is perceptible in the ways that language was nuanced into discourse.

3

The Development of the Mass Market, 1870–1930

So far, this study has been concerned with challenging the idea that retailers should be treated as members of a homogeneous petit bourgeois grouping. Whereas older works suggest that shopkeepers were united by the sheer fact of self-employment and newer ones insist that despite their material differences store owners possessed a collectivizing 'culture,' I argued that the economic and social divisions among retailers undercut the unifying power of their occupational memories. This interpretation was grounded in the distinction between language and speech and in a discussion of the ways in which the common properties of the one could be distorted by the individual inflections of the other. The subsection of the retailing mass which, because it tended to join associations and express its opinions through the press, has most often been considered representative of the whole was in fact a group narrowed by commonalities of sex, race, and class. With these points offered, I would now like to shift gears and run at a second major theme in the historical and sociological literature: the notion that economic change threatened the survival of 'small business' as a whole.

That the maturation of the industrial economy involved the destruction of the personal enterprise is an axiom for many business and economic historians. In fact, Edith Penrose noted that the disappearance of the individual firm has 'often been treated as almost a law of nature' by economists. In the classic formulation, probably most familiar to contemporary historians in its Chandlerian guise, big business is seen as adaptive, market sensitive, and cost efficient, while independent enterprise is defined as resistant to innovation and unresponsive to changing conditions. The 'survival' of proprietary business is therefore usually perceived to be incidental to the main current of economic development, and those who discuss it generally explain its existence away as a result of 'imperfections' in the competitive system. Big business therefore offers students of the firm their most logical field of study, with petty property attracting interest largely because of its nagging habits of persistence.[1]

In the academic literature, the fortunes of the independent proprietors have improved significantly over the last three decades. Rediscovered as something beautiful and distinct by alternative economists and social thinkers in the 1970s, 'small business' rode the crest of the 'authentic lifestyle' wave; consumers, it seemed, no longer trusted the mass-produced article. As big ideas in little packages proliferated and the dream of founding the next Apple Computer Company flitted through entrepreneurial heads, 'small business' as a topic of inquiry enjoyed its nascence. Though still marginalized by traditionalists in the field, petty enterprise no longer lacks for champions. Many of today's scholars see independent business as more innovative, dynamic, and entrepreneurial than large-scale enterprise; they emphasize the closer relations that exist between owner and worker and the improved morale that results; and they stress the flexibility that unharnesses smaller firms with lower fixed costs. Though still regarded as different from big business, proprietary enterprise is now widely deemed to be better.

The following three chapters investigate the early-twentieth-century persistence of independent property as a form of investment in Canadian retailing. The central argument is simple: independent retailing did not disappear with the coming of the mass market and many shopkeepers did very well. This was because some sectors of the store-owning stratum were able to adapt to changing market demands. What most distinguished those who profited was the fact that they were running medium- to large-sized independent firms; as chapter 5 will suggest, shoestring tradespeople suffered increasing failure rates as mid-century approached. While this did mean that retailers classified in other ways – women, ethnics, urban or rural tradespeople – experienced new market conditions in disparate ways, they did not do so primarily because they were women or immigrants. Adaptability to changing demands was undoubtedly affected by gender or culture, but this study suggests that it was one's ability to afford innovation that made the real difference. As will be shown, the vast majority of retailers were aware of changing approaches to floor layouts, the need for account books, and new forms of packaging, and almost everyone experienced the growing pressure for cash payment. Because all but the most isolated retailers felt the shifts in consumer preference and supplier need and because almost all were aware of the departmental and chain store methods, they all knew what 'successful' forms of merchandising looked like in the early twentieth century. Everything depended on how many of the new business approaches they felt they needed or could afford to implement. And while cultural preference bracketed and influenced this adaptation to the mass market, revenue was what made it possible.

This approach hinges on a different way of conceiving success in proprietary retailing. For most who have investigated the topic, independent property was a distinct form – 'small business' was different from big because it was small – which generated its own variety of entrepreneurship. This view of independent enterprise derives from the Schumpeterian notion of success as a function of creativity: the entrepreneur who prospers is by definition an innovator. The interpretation offered here is different. This study argues that most of the proprietors who did well in the early twentieth century did so through emulation. Big businesses – manufacturers, department stores and chain stores, even mail-order catalogues – pioneered new ways of merchandising which consumers found appealing and sought to encourage. The mass merchandisers set higher standards for marketing behaviour, consumers demanded that all shops conform to new styles and price levels, and manufacturers pushed retailers to operate more efficiently. Pressured by the price competition, by the insistence of their suppliers and customers on modernization, and by their own commitment to success, large numbers of independent proprietors adjusted to the new business environment. But their success came to depend not so much on their ability to preserve the traditional forms of retailing as on their skill at catering to the demands of an economy now predicated on bigness. Increasingly, store owners were finding that to survive they had to keep pace with the fast-changing demands of an economy geared to mass production, national marketing, and brand identification. It was therefore largely a matter of finance rather than culture: everyone could see what the bigger businesses were doing; not everyone could afford to copy them.

I have divided this topic by cause and effect. The chapter which follows looks at the forces creating the mass market – an improved standard of living and mass consumption, production, and distribution – and discusses the impact of these new agencies on the way that people approached the distributive system. Chapter 4 then explores the adaptation of the main-street independent retailers to the new demands of the market-place. The final chapter in this section measures the success of their efforts in relation to their competitors: the backstreet traders and the mass merchandisers. Throughout, I have tried to maintain the view that the mass market was less a set of economic conditions than a way of seeing and doing. Though improved standards of living and new technologies were clearly an important part of the story, the consumer society was revealed not in a set of statistics but in people's spending and selling choices.

A QUESTION OF DEMAND

Given the importance of the subject, it is surprising how little we know about the movement of goods. Somehow, for all the ink that European and American historians have poured onto it, the contours of demand remain mussy and ill-defined. Much of the literature quite simply confounds, with the British being particularly obsessed with identifying a 'consumer revolution' and then relegating it to as distant a past as possible. To cite David Levine, 'historians are forever using and then debasing their own coinage, and so we now have consumer societies and even consumer revolutions, dating from 1780, 1760, 1700, and even 1560.'[2] Part of the problem is that historians have been so convinced of the existence of a sharp division between the 'self-sufficient producer economy' and the 'consumer economy' that the discovery of any store-bought commodities in the pre-industrial world has been taken as a sign of a revolution in spending. The truth is that people have always bought and sold goods and they have always wanted more than they could produce for themselves – which is really a way of saying that the prominence assigned to issues such as the standard of living might well be misplaced. People will generally spend more money when they have it, and even in old-regime societies cyclical variations resulted in changes in consumption. How then can we justify seeing any one of those periodic upswings as tangibly different from the others?

Recognizing the problem, many historians of consumption have shifted attention away from the amount of spending and onto issues such as consumer attitude and the availability of goods. The original novelty underpinning the consumer society, notes Neil McKendrick, lay not in the spending power but in the 'desire' and 'ability' to consume, and this enabling was in part a result of 'changes in commercial technique and promotional skill.'[3] Naturally, innovations in marketing did not happen without the stimulus of demand, but the correlation is not necessarily a perfect one. A small shift in consumer preference might lead to major adjustments in business practices, and these in turn can serve to work far-reaching changes in the way that consumers perceive goods. Though the relationship between market and marketers is reciprocal, historical productions need not find their origin in forces of equal magnitude.

In Canada marketing practices began to change decisively only in the 1870s and 1880s. Demand had been growing steadily, if not uninterruptedly, since at least the beginning of the century, but the gradual expansion of consumption had been easily encompassed within an existing system of trading; all that was needed was an increase in the number of shops.[4] Consequently, the early-nineteenth-century growth in the market was not only slow enough for few commentators to have notice it, but it was also gradual enough for many to have become mesmerized by its short-term fluctuations. Only in the 1850s did the pace of economic life begin to quicken noticeably. As railways, population growth, and larger manufacturing establishments developed, marketing patterns started to shift.[5] Established firms managed for a time to adjust their practices to accommodate the changes, but the system could expand only so far. By the 1880s and 1890s, the major structural changes accompanying modern distribution – the development of direct marketing, private branding, and manufacturer-controlled advertising, a rapid growth in retail services, and mass merchandising – were beginning to make their presence felt. Increasing demand had sparked a revolutionary transformation in supply, and it was this change in the nature of distribution that made the 'mass market' such a singular phenomenon.

These changes will be discussed below at greater length, but before we move on, it is important that we deal briefly with the issue of consumer spending because it remains such an important and contentious one. Though I would suggest an acceleration rather than transformation of spending, the standard works on the subject argue that consumption actually declined between 1870 and 1923. Not only do some writers see Canada as suffering from a prolonged depression between 1873 and 1896, but many believe that its people were struggling simply to keep themselves alive. Apparently, the situation did not improve over-much in the succeeding decades: while exports recovered in the early twentieth century, inflation chewed into real wages and led to an actual deterioration in an already-sorry situation.[6] Without putting too fine a point on things, it was hardly a favourable environment in which to achieve a revolution in merchandising.

Sadly, very little marketing evidence survives from the late nineteenth century against which to test these assertions. Figures on retail sales were not collected until 1923, and they remained imprecise for another decade (see table 9). One must therefore fall back upon less-satisfactory measures such as gross domestic disappearance in order to get some idea of what and how much people were buying. But even here there are problems: though figures are available for many grocery items – which did make up the single largest category of purchase for all non-farm Canadians – food is generally considered an inelastic commodity.[7] And yet the domestic disappearance figures do suggest a rise in the consumption of most food products, with the exception of beef and mutton. The average Canadian ate about six ounces of meat a day in 1891 and seven ounces by the early 1920s; tea and coffee use increased from one cup a day in 1881 to four cups by 1910, while sugar consumption rose by half between 1900 and 1920 (table 10). New types of fruit and vegetables were also becoming part of the Canadian diet: by 1900 the average individual's annual pound and a half of currants and two bushels of apples were being supplemented by imports of bananas and pineapples and by the domestic manufacture of tinned pears and prunes.

This expansion in food consumption was also reflected in the steady increase in the number of grocery stores. Figures for Ontario, while hardly incontrovertible, none the less suggest a doubling in the number of specialized food shops between 1871 and 1891, followed by a further 60 per cent growth over the next forty years (table 1). The relative steadiness of this rise in food distribution and consumption would suggest that the average Canadian was enjoying a gradually improving diet. From the grocery store numbers, it also appears as though the greatest expansion came in the 1870s and 1880s, though the domestic disappearance statistics do not allow us to corroborate these findings (the rapid rise in beef consumption during these decades may, however, be significant).

If there was an acceleration in food provisioning and consumption in the late nineteenth century, what doubtless lay behind it was the long deflation in prices that lasted until the turn of the century, the effect of which was, as the *Canadian Grocer* noted, to 'rob the word luxuries of their old-time significance.' According to Michel, food prices (wholesale) moved erratically downward after the late 1860s, falling as much as a quarter by the mid-1890s. We know little about farm incomes, but wages remained far stickier than prices, meaning that working people in the urban centres were enjoying increased purchasing power during at least the 1870s and 1880s. Prices did begin to rise again in the first decade of the new century, and by the First World War they had reached a level not seen since the 1850s, but there are few indications that buying actually slowed. In fact, the inflation appears to have affected store-bought goods less than it did wages (one exception being beef, which accounts for the move to pork after 1900).[8] And while the rate of food-store expansion slowed between 1891 and 1911, the figures on domestic disappearance question whether this slow-down was accompanied by any decline in consumption.

All of this change relates solely to food, which, while revealing something felicitous about people's diet, does not prove increased spending. As Lévy-Leboyer and Bourguignon have argued, money expended on calories might well obstruct, rather than reflect, a general growth in the sale of other products.[9] Again, we do not have the necessary statistics to test this theory, but estimates of spending based on production figures for the period (table 11) do not suggest that the expansion in food processing was occurring at the expense of other consumer goods manufacturing. Between 1871 and 1891, outputs of non-food goods actually increased more rapidly than food items, with entertainment-related products enjoying the most significant increases. Each sector enjoyed its own growth spurt: household goods in the 1870s, clothing and entertainment in the 1880s, food in the 1890s. Though these figures are only a rough guide – since the census enumerators were counting the production of manufacturing establishments and not of farms, butcher shops, and backyard stills – they do not support the view that the production of non-food goods suffered from the effects of an improved diet.

We should not, however, write off the great depression of the late nineteenth century. People did feel that business was performing poorly, and their convictions demand our respect. Doubtless, part of the reason for their belief lay in the slow growth of international trade, part in the recurring financial crises of the period and in the consequent contraction of credit, and part in the way business people traditionally calculated profitability, but not all. In 1879 the directors of the Eastern Townships Bank, while deploring the dullness of the export trade and the 'continued gigantic crisis' in finance, observed that 'the savings habits of all classes, the greater energy thrown into the work of the farm, the cheapened cost of all manufactured products, all seem to tend to better returns.' Over the next decade, however, the directors found domestic trade 'dull' and noted often that 'manufacturers' stocks of merchandise are accumulating in their hands.'[10] All that one can suggest is that while real incomes were clearly improving and consumption increasing, there remained a sense that the expansion in domestic demand was falling short of expectations. Or, to put it another way, for all the increase in demand, industrialists realized that they had the ability to produce far more than they were selling.

One possible explanation is that the affluence of the late nineteenth century was not sufficiently widespread to generate the kind of growth that people anticipated or were prepared to satisfy. Heightened consumption among a relatively small segment of the population could mask the continuing poverty of the majority and could lead one to exaggerate the size of the market. Fortunately, we can test this thesis, at least for Ontario's working class, through the statistics compiled by the Bureau of Industries from 1885 to 1889. Because the bureau was not particularly refined in its approach to the cost of living, it did not measure people against an imposed standard, but simply asked them to indicate how much they earned and how much it cost them to live.[11] And the results indicate a fairly broadly based prosperity. According to the bureau, the 'average' worker in Ontario enjoyed a small surplus of income over expenditure, with the cost of food and clothing ranging from $300 to $335 for a family of five between 1884 and 1889 and with family earnings over the same period averaging $386–425 a year.[12] The 'typical' male worker in the late 1880s was able to 'save' something between $15 and $40 a year, or between 5 and 10 per cent of his income. But averages provide us with false harmonies to which few workers conformed: sex, marital status, housing condition, type of employment, and place all intruded discordantly to shatter the overall impression. All told, the bureau found that one in four workers were running a deficit between 1884 and 1889, while a further quarter spent all that they earned on subsistence. For those with a surplus, about a third (17 per cent of the total) had an excess of income over self-defined necessities of more than $100 a year. It did not seem to matter much if one had a family or not; what really counted was that one was male, that one earned over $500 a year (moulders, machinists, boilermakers, and, thanks to the building boom, stonecutters, plumbers, and plasterers), and that one lived in one's own house. Single women with dependents (0.5 per cent of the total) unquestionably had the hardest life: they worked more days than anyone else, they spent half as much (their cost of living was one-third less than that of males with the same sized families), and they still consistently spent more than they made.[13]

The bureau's findings confirm the view of many historians that gender was the great differentiator among wage-earners, but they also show that within the male workforce it was housing. Because of escalating rental costs in the late nineteenth century, those who succeeded in buying were able to devote more of their income to acquiring other things: those who owned earned on average 5 per cent more than tenants, but they could afford to spend 11 per cent more on clothing and 7 per cent more on food. Despite these higher expenditures, the cost of living for owners was 20 per cent less than it was for tenants, meaning that home-owners even had a sizeable surplus that they could save or spend on non-essentials. And homes offered other advantages: against them one could borrow, and rooms in them could be rented. By the First World War second mortgages had become – alongside borrowing on insurance policies – the single largest 'institutional' source of capital for working people seeking to go into business for themselves. The advantages enjoyed by home-owners might also help account for the relative poverty of Montreal's working people. Montreal was a city of tenants.

The statistics assembled by the Bureau of Industries provide us with no more than a snapshot of a few thousand urban consumers in one province, but they do suggest that the consumption of non-essentials among the working class was a possibility for about half the Ontario wage-earning population and that one in five enjoyed a substantial surplus income. The trouble is that even if these proportions can be considered typical of the country, it is hard to judge whether the poor would have sufficiently limited the mass market since we lack a standard for measuring the significance of the figures. Were more working people able to consume a greater amount in 1885 than they had been in 1865? Much of the evidence would suggest so, though that does not answer the question as to whether a labouring population which was still 50 per cent impoverished was sufficient to deflate expectations of economic growth. What is possible, however, is that if there was an economic brake, it was applied not so much by a narrow base of consumption as by people's spending choices. Let us recall the comments of the bankers of the Eastern Townships: it was 'the savings habits of all classes' that they applauded and not the 'spending habits.' Could the perceived sluggishness of the domestic economy have been caused not by a shortage of consumers but by the reluctance of people to spend the money they were earning?

While it seems clear that the 1870s and 1880s witnessed a significant expansion in consumer goods manufacturing, that expansion may have been slower than was hoped, in part because people were still restrained in their spending. This characteristic would make sense in an economy emerging out of scarcity: accustomed to thinking in terms of crushing periodic downturns and seasonal unemployment, those workers who were enjoying relatively high real wages for perhaps the first time were choosing to buy houses, rent larger apartments, or take out life insurance policies rather than acquire more clothes or furniture or luxuries. It would help to explain the ferocious growth of the insurance industry, which at 11 per cent per annum between 1870 and 1900 outstripped all the other financial intermediaries combined and the GNP. It would also make sense of the often-noted explosion in the domestic construction industry during the 1880s.[14] Ironically, it may well have been only when land and housing prices began to soar in the late 1880s that well-to-do working people turned to a more energetic acquisition of goods. The resultant increased demand would in turn have contributed to the inflation of the early twentieth century.

This interpretation would fit with what we know of developments in the countryside. In both Ontario and Quebec the last three decades of the nineteenth century witnessed a general shift away from wheat production to livestock and fodder crops, with the number of milch cows in Ontario increasing 60 per cent between 1871 and 1901 and with the number of other cattle and hogs close to doubling. In Quebec the average number of dairy cows per farm rose from three to five and of other cattle from three to four. Similarly, in Ontario there were tremendous increases in both the size of the average farm and the amount of improved acreage per farm, the latter rising from an average of 51 acres to 65 between 1871 and 1901. And though the rapid expansion of agricultural settlement in the 1870s and 1880s and its subsequent contraction in the following decade led to some fluctuations in the Quebec statistics, the average farm in the province still grew from 93 to 104 acres over the last three decades of the century. Contemporaries also suggested a rapid increase in expenditures on farm machinery, and while general figures are unavailable, in Ontario the average farmer owned 34 per cent more machinery (as measured in current dollars) in 1901 than he had twenty years before. Only in the Maritimes, where there had been no significant change in agricultural acreage and no large-scale investment in farm machinery, did agriculture fail to register a major transformation in the last decades of the century.[15]

Farmers were apparently spending a terrific amount of money on farm improvements. Buying cattle, planting feed crops, and acquiring machinery and land all took capital, money that was not being spent on other goods. This did not mean that farmers, any more than home-owning workers, were living poorly – as a cattle buyer in Chatham noted in the late 1880s, 'Their way of living, keeping house, their mode of coming to town, their dress and the dress of their families, the furniture of their houses, and all that sort of thing, have immensely improved' – but they were still spending less than expected despite the relatively low cost of living because they were investing heavily in capital assets.[16] Long-term security appears to have ranked higher in their personal calculation than short-term comfort. Still, as with more-affluent working people, there are reasons to suspect that the farmers' consumption of non-agricultural goods increased moderately in the late nineteenth century.

Of course, there remained a large number of poor people living in the countryside, just as there were in the cities, though that poverty might itself be a sign of rising affluence.[17] As country retailers in Ontario realized, the growth in spending power, the expansion of commercial farming, and the out-migration of poorer farmers were all closely intertwined: 'one man now operates more acres,' a shop owner noted, 'he has fewer competitors ... and consequently he is in a vastly improved financial position.' Shopkeepers believed that it was in their interest to extend these changes, and they were actively involved in the promotion of agricultural education and farm improvement.[18] Still, it is vital to remember that the prosperity of rural Canadians was subsidized in large part by the out-migration of hundreds of thousands of others (largely to the United States). In effect, though many farmers in the late nineteenth century were enjoying higher incomes, the rich harvest was none the less growing in the furrows marked out for it by the class structure in the countryside.

Though consumption in the last three decades of the nineteenth century was not rising as quickly as business people had hoped, demand does seem to have been increasing. Much of the talk of economic hardship was possibly the result of the sluggishness of international trade and of the fact that working and farming people were channelling a good portion of their surplus income into land and housing. This pattern of spending particularly aggrieved Canadian manufacturers, who knew that wages in the 1870s and 1880s were high and prices falling. Their workers' spending choices seemed to them to be restraining economic expansion. It was in part to overcome this resistance that increasing numbers of manufacturers began to involve themselves in the direct marketing of their products. If retailers and wholesalers could not be relied upon to release the spending potential they knew existed, manufacturers would have to take matters into their own hands. In effect, the last three decades of the nineteenth century laid the social foundations and created the business incentives for mass marketing.

Those possibilities found realization soon enough. In the first three decades of the new century the consumer society truly revealed itself to shoppers and business people alike. New forms of distribution were created, advertising became infinitely more refined and important, channels of trade were simplified, and the beat of marketing life quickened. None of this change would have occurred without the presence of demand. And yet once again, much of the data on the standard of living tells a more ambiguous story. Though wages continued to increase until 1921, many analysts hold that prices rose even more quickly, thereby reducing living standards. Piva and Copp have suggested that the real wages of working people in Toronto and Montreal were declining in the early twentieth century, though it might be noted that national indices, such as Bertram and Percy's, show that labour incomes rose slightly more quickly than prices until 1913 and after 1920, allowing at least the possibility of increased consumption.[19] Much depends on whom one chooses to study. Certain occupations – most notably the building trades – were highly volatile, especially given the rapid rise in housing prices before the First World War. Other workers were suffering the impact of de-skilling or unemployment at the hands of new technologies and work processes. Migration also complicated an already-complex picture by pouring a relatively steady stream of jobless people into the workforce. Between 1902 and 1929 Canada was the destination for 4.4 million migrants and the departure point for probably upwards of 3 million. This staggering turnover – with as much as a tenth of the population on the move in the heaviest years – obviously distorts estimates of long-term changes in the overall standard of living. The impact would have been bad enough were not the economy itself also subject to the complicating influence of a string of escalating economic crises in 1907–9, 1913–15, and 1920–5, the first two of which were accompanied not by deflation, as in the late nineteenth century, but by bursts of inflation, while the third involved a wage and price collapse.

And yet, though we will probably never be sure about just what was happening to the standard of living, it is hard to resist the idea that habits of spending did grow. The available consumption indicators do continue to point to an increasing domestic absorption of goods: we have already noted the rise in per capita food consumption up to the First World War, and there are no signs of a subsequent decline before the

Depression. The average Canadian ate 7 ounces of meat a day in 1922 and 7.4 ounces after 1925, with the amount falling to 6.7 ounces in 1930; by 1928 this typical individual also consumed annually 10.5 pounds of store-bought biscuits, 29 pounds of butter, 13 pounds of candy, and a gallon of dairy-made ice cream. The average Canadian adult male bought three shirts a year every year from 1923 to 1929, one to two pairs of overalls, a collar, and either a set of suspenders or a pair of garters, while the average Canadian adult woman in 1927 spent $80–100 on her own ready-made clothing (not including footwear or furs), almost half of which went to dresses and suits. This latter sum might not sound like much, but a mid-quality dress in the mid-1920s cost $12–15, so our 'typical' woman could afford a modest wardrobe each year.[20]

Even on the newly settled prairies, consumer spending appears to have risen rapidly to match Canadian norms. Though 1930 was not a good year for western farmers, as the collapse of grain prices and regional drought led to mass migration and terrible suffering, figures on commodity consumption show that Prairie families were still spending close to the national average on basic consumer goods. The average Canadian male (all these averages include individuals over ten years of age) in 1930 spent $33.50 on men's and boy's clothing, while the average woman purchased goods worth $50.40; together, $10 was spent on shoes, $6.30 on household furniture, and $2.30 on toiletries. In the Prairies males spent on average $29.50 and women $46.20 on clothing; together, $9.90 was used for shoes, and $4.10 was spent on household furniture and $2.00 on toiletries.[21] Given the unusual circumstances of the time, the closeness of western spending to national averages would support the view that little separated spending habits in the west from those prevailing elsewhere in the country.

Moreover, during the 1920s people of moderate means began to buy such big-ticket consumer items as automobiles and furniture sets, often on delayed-payment plans. Consider a random survey of southern Ontario farms in the early twenties which found that while only 30 per cent of those questioned felt they were doing well economically, 63 per cent had automobiles, 41 per cent owned an organ or a piano, and all bought packaged breakfast cereal. Consider also a near-contemporaneous study of 300 homes on 'moderately sized' (under three-quarters of a section) farms in Manitoba which found that while over half had no running water and three-quarters were not wired for electricity, 80 per cent of their owners had automobiles and 84 per cent owned a piano, an organ, or a gramophone. Consider, finally, a 1932 study of two hundred

Montreal workers of whom close to 40 per cent were either living on credit or barely scraping by and only 20 per cent were enjoying relatively comfortable and stable incomes, but 30 per cent owned a radio, 40 per cent had a gramophone, and one in four possessed a 'living room suite.'[22]

As time passed those working people who had acquired a little property or capital in the last decades of the nineteenth century seem to have lost some of their sense of vulnerability and begun to demand more things – a chesterfield, a silk shirt, some cosmetics, a pair of dress shoes – while the wealthier continued to seek out a range of different goods – refrigerators, vacuum cleaners, expensive cars, and fur coats. If taste was not expanding in this way, how can one explain the extraordinary variety and volume of new goods hurtling down upon consumers in the early decades of the century? 'To-day we have a demand for articles that few ever thought of buying twenty-five years ago,' wrote a Winnipeg grocer in 1913; 'take the biscuit for example. We carry a large assortment of fancy biscuits and some of them are very expensive, but there is an immense demand for them. Yet I remember when soda biscuits, fruit biscuits and hard-tack practically comprised a grocers' business stock.' The *Shoe and Leather Journal* nodded in agreement: 'the mania for novelty and an insatiable pursuit of variety have brought about [many] unnatural demands.'[23] Comments such as these point less, perhaps, to the standard of living than to changes in consumer preference. Where modestly affluent people in the 1870s and 1880s had apparently chosen to save rather than spend – a reflection of their nineteenth-century mind-set – they now appear to have wanted to see the fruits of their labours manifested in new goods. The suggestion is that individuals who once would have lived with few luxuries started to expect an ongoing improvement in their lifestyles. They began shaping their spending choices, perhaps even sacrificing food quality or living space, in order to buy new things. This change did not necessitate any dramatic increase in actual spending power; what it did involve was a dramatic shift in priorities.

It was a process that migration served to advance rather than slow. Think of the rapid transformation in dress and the necessary expenditure on household furnishing that followed the immigrant's arrival at a Canadian port. English and French Canadians commented often and unfavourably on the strange clothing of the early-twentieth-century newcomers – the sheepskin vests, baggy trousers, coolie hats, pull-on boots, and coloured headscarves – but most of those symbols of differentness were quickly discarded. As Andrew Heinze observes, a trip to the photographer in a newly acquired suit of ready-made 'American' clothes was almost a rite of passage for immigrants. Buying a jacket or a shirtwaist and skirt, a brimmed hat, and a pair of lace-up shoes was a statement of the transformation from peasantry to promise, from impoverishment to prosperity. Photographers augmented these images of material assimilation by keeping tie-pins, jewellery, watches, and feathered hats just in case the recent migrant had not yet acquired them. Though many would have struggled to afford the change of clothes, the perceived necessity of material assimilation and the desire to represent the new self in terms of goods signalled the immigrants' absorption into North America's consuming culture. For those marginalized within society, goods became a statement of acceptability and success, the measure of distance from the peasant lifestyle so many of the immigrants had travelled to escape. For Irish women dignity came with 'lace curtains' in the windows; for Jews it meant a piano in the parlour; and while each group's image of respectability was undoubtedly defined by homeland experiences with gentility, the goods they were buying were decidedly North American.[24]

It was in large degree the desire of ordinary people to know what was fashionably acceptable that made the shop-girl such a symbol of the new age. For working and farming families, the daughter serving behind the counter in the downtown store was more than just a breadwinner; she was a bell-wether of style. Women were the fastest growing element in the paid workforce (their share increased from 13 per cent in 1911 to almost 17 per cent by 1931), and of the occupations they entered, few were more rapidly feminizing than retail sales work. Women made up 22 per cent of the sales force in 1901, 32 per cent in 1921, and 44 per cent a decade later. These shop workers were young – 60 per cent of them were under 25 in 1931, as compared with 32 per cent of males – and they were overwhelmingly single. Not surprisingly, given the nature and location of their work, they spent a significant portion of their incomes on clothing. In fact, even shopkeepers fretted over the spending habits of their clerks. In one morality tale published in a trade journal's 'clerk's page,' a retailer despaired over one of his workers, a fashionable 'good time girl' who spent all her money on clothes and dated lots of men, and he wished that she was more like his second salesgirl, who dressed simply, worked hard, and ultimately found a husband of promising affluence. For Victorian moralists, such as the members of Toronto's Social Survey Commission, the clerical worker's

fashion preferences led inevitably to prostitution, since even 'the virtu-
ous girl, earning a scanty living by honest toil,' was continually tempted
by the 'finery and luxury' which could only be obtained 'by relaxing the
vigilant struggle to maintain her self respect.'[25]

But the young wage-earning woman was only the most salient feature of a feminization of shopping that was thought to be occurring in
the late nineteenth and early twentieth centuries. Though women had
always bought goods, and there is no way of knowing whether men
were actually shopping less, the perception at the time was that buying was increasingly becoming a female activity. The ever-rising number of urban working women provides part of the explanation for this
impression, but not all. There were, quite simply, still too few wage-
earning women earning too little for their actions to account fully for
the new definition of buying. In fact, married women who did not
work outside the home made up the bulk of the 'new' shoppers, and it
was they who attracted the retailers' keenest attentions. It is not, however, entirely clear why this should have been so. One possibility is that
the development of alternative leisure activities undermined Saturday
as the family shopping day and shifted buying activities to weekdays,
when wage-earning husbands were working. Another is that public
transportation systems, road resurfacing, and policing may have
added to female mobility, allowing them to occupy downtown streets
that might once have been considered the terrain of employed men and
the underclass. But the most probable explanation was the expansion of
retailing itself. When the number of shops was limited, customers
were known and the women shopping would have been identified by
their local butcher or shoe seller with their homes and husbands. It
was, after all, the male wage which determined credit worthiness, and
it was the man who was ultimately held responsible for the bills. The
collapse of the traditional customer pool which followed the expansion
of merchandising undermined all that. Suddenly, retailers were dealing
with women whose families, homes, and characters were unknown;
moreover, they were increasingly coping with the anonymity of the
cash payment. This last factor, more than anything else, would have
created the impression that women did the buying alone, because more
than simply shopping, they now seemed free from domestic constraints.

No matter what inspired it, the feminization of consumption transformed the nature of shopping. Selling became increasingly sexualized
as commodities were designed and promoted to appeal to what was

now seen to be an independent and mobile female clientele. Matching the sex of the clerk to that of the shopper was only one way in which retail practices were altered to accommodate the new situation. Male and female goods were also carefully segregated, advertising was increasingly aimed at showing women how their bodies should properly look, and shop floors were rearranged to encapsulate ideas about the female temperament (with 'impulse items' at the front and staples at the rear).[26] These changes reveal a new approach to consumers and, by corollary, a new attitude to consumption, a change noted by moralists, such as those on the Social Survey Commission, which implicitly drew attention to the growing temptations of goods. In effect, the early twentieth century witnessed a revolution in the perception of the buying experience. As women became consumers, shopping was reconstructed to accommodate its new sexual identity. Instead of aiming to establish familial loyalty through small talk and credit, retailers found themselves 'courting' their female customers. This led to the redefinition of consumer activity as vicarious promiscuity (shopping around), sensual gratification (sampling or trying on), and seduction (most commonly through advertising and layout). These images were not created by a handful of patriarchal advertising agents and department store executives; they were a product of the reciprocal relationship between buyer and seller that lay at the heart of a consumer society.

To accommodate the new, aggressive, and – because thinking about it was gendered – 'unpredictable' mass which they now began to call 'consumers,' business people designed marketing strategies and created innovative business forms. They also adjusted their attitudes to selling. These changes are further signals of the transformation in the nature of consumption, which, while linked to the rise in spending, contradicts the assumptions that flow most readily from the falling-standard-of-living argument. Inflation doubtless made life more difficult for ordinary Canadians, but it did not destroy the promise of material acquisition which the long deflation of the nineteenth century had encouraged. To facilitate the desires of shoppers, retailing developed and grew; there was a steady expansion in the number of independent stores throughout the period, and vast new merchandising businesses were created. These national marketers owed their existence to the gradual emergence of a mass market and to the business changes which that development encouraged. To this extent, they became the particular symbols of the emerging and newly feminized 'consumer society.'

MASS MERCHANDISING

They had begun innocently enough in the late 1870s with the expansion of a few dry goods stores in downtown Toronto, but they soon assumed a more dramatic aspect. By 1900 the department stores had come to be regarded by main-street shopkeepers as 'a curse on the community,' 'the root and factor of the most injurious conditions that surround us to-day.' As their historians have shown, the department stores were the pioneers of modern marketing: they were the first big establishments to offer the public a wide range of popularly advertised goods sold on cash terms and at fixed prices. Unlike the 'traditional' service shops, where goods were kept hidden behind counters and clerks interceded between the customers and the products, anyone could enter a department store, look about, and leave without having to purchase anything or talk to anyone.[27] In allowing the public access to their stock, the department stores were, in the eyes of many merchants, threatening the retailers' traditional role as arbiters and guardians of community taste. The departmentals thus come to appear the very symbols of the feminization of consumption and the separation of home and spending, something they advertised by loading their counters with such a fantastic array of items. By selling goods 'from candy to gas stoves' with 'careless indifference,' they ignored the folkloric injunction that the trader must know intimately each of the products being sold (Eaton's was not alone in countering that it took responsibility for the goods marketed and would provide refunds for any purchasers who were not satisfied). Moreover, by laying their goods out in garish, low-priced displays, the department stores were tempting consumers to their destruction. In other words, they were the very manifestation of the breakdown of customer 'loyalties' and the desire to acquire which underlay the development of mass consumption.[28]

As early critics from Émile Zola to Theodore Dreiser observed, the department stores were also the ultimate symbols of the feminized market. 'C'était la femme que les magasins se disputaient par la concurrence, la femme qu'ils prenaient au continuel piège de leurs occasions, après l'avoir étourdie devant leurs étalages. Ils avaient éveillé dans sa chair de nouveaux désirs, ils étaient une tentation immense, où elle succombait fatalement, cédant d'abord à des achats de bonne ménagère, plus gagnée par la coquetterie, puis dévorée. En décuplant la vente, en démocratisant le luxe, ils devenaient un terrible agent de dépense, ravagaient les ménages, travaillaient au coup de folie de la mode, toujours plus chère.' It was this power which made them the targets of so much moralistic abuse. They became the corporate 'seducers,' preying upon women's vulnerabilities. The goods they sold were thought to 'call' to women – '"My dear," said the lace collar ... "don't give me up." "Ah, such little feet," said the leather of the soft new shoes, "how effectively I cover them"' – and the easy access was believed to render appeals such as these irresistible.[29] The cash-only policy which the big stores for years maintained and the anonymity of a sales relationship in which the owner was a distant presence perfectly suited the departmentals to the developing anonymity of shopping. Consequently, the anxieties that men felt at the liberation of women through consumption came down upon the department stores' heads. And though the departmentals struggled to turn themselves into 'cultural oases' with their reading rooms and concerts and restaurants, it took them some time to shake off the Lothario image.

Obviously, the department stores were not alone in becoming female spaces. Most main-street shops felt the same pressures and attempted to attract the same market captivated by the departmentals. But the great stores stood out all the same. And what made them particular symbols of unlimbered desire was, of course, their size. The sheer dimensions of the stores allowed them to offer their customers the kind of one-stop shopping provided by traditional general stores without involving them in any sacrifice of selection or any sense of awkwardness if they did not know the owner. Moreover, size allowed the departmentals to manipulate what one prophetic commentator called 'the psychology of the crowd.' Merchandise was laid out in such a way that customers were forced to pass among counters filled with attractively displayed luxury goods on their way to buy staples such as food and shoes. So great was the value of 'impulse buying' that when the departmentals introduced telephone ordering in the early twentieth century they stipulated that staples were not available to telephone customers. To further exploit their size, the department stores put in restaurants and circulating libraries, the one to keep customers in the store, the other to keep them returning.[30] Theirs was a stylish and powerful method of selling, and it tended to feed on itself: some of the departmentals, most important merchandising innovations arose out of the discoveries that a crowd tended to attract a crowd and that frenetic buying among some tended to induce frenetic buying among many.

The department stores were monuments of display, and they towered over their competitors: where a good-sized independent store in Canada in 1919 would occupy roughly 3,000 square feet, Eaton's Toronto branch boasted 1.1 million square feet of shopping space; where the average shop in Canada in 1924 was capitalized at well under $15,000, the investment represented by Simpson's Toronto store was almost $18 million.[31] The department stores were vast in conception and in design, though Canada's stores never attempted to mimic the *fin de siècle* opulence of Paris's Au Printemps or Au Bon Marché. Of Toronto's two greatest stores, Simpson's was certainly the grander, with its brownstone Romanesque exterior, high ceilings, and dark oak showcases. The store featured high-priced British imports and catered primarily to Toronto's fashionable society. Simpson's was not alone in this: though they undersold their competitors in lines such as groceries and notions, before the First World War most department stores were up-market shopping bazaars. In Montreal W.H. Scoggie, Ogilvy's, John Murphy and Company, and Dupuis Frères were all 'high priced' stores, and the most successful of the city's departmentals, Henry Morgan and Company, was known for 'charging the highest prices in the city.' Morgan's was a stately, reddish brown, six-storey building filled with extraordinarily expensive fixtures; the company even went so far as to make an advertising feature of an Italian mirror in its millinery department which had cost the business over $3,000 in 1899.[32]

Unlike most of its competitors, Eaton's began life as a bargain shop, though by the mid-1880s it was actively trying to cast off its rather common beginnings. Timothy Eaton had initially specialized in staple goods and notions, meaning that customers in the 1870s rarely came in to make purchases totalling more than one dollar. While this fact does not prove that the store catered exclusively to a poorer clientele, it does imply that people perceived Eaton's to be a place where they could buy small staples: buttons, gloves, bonnets, underwear, flannels, and cheap cottons. It seems most likely that from the outset the store had served as a source of cheap staples to the more affluent workers' wives and of simple notions to the middle-class shoppers.[33] Growth, however, apparently depended on the store's ability to obtain a larger share of the middle-income earners' purse, and as Eaton's developed from a mid-sized dry goods business into a departmentalized giant, it became steadily more fashionable and up-market. By the First World War, the inexpensive lines and farm goods had worked their way down into the basement, and departments featuring French lingerie, embroidered linens from Madeira, fine porcelains, and tailor-made shirts had come to occupy the upper storeys. Eventually, the company would even go so far as to remove most of the cheaper lines and pack them off to a separate 'annex' store. Within departments, mid-priced and expensive stock was kept separate. Clothing, for example, was neatly segregated, with fashionable Paris imports separated from less costly copies of New York ready-mades by the liberal use of art glass. Doormen were hired to assist those arriving in carriages and to clear the crowds from the display windows, and the store's advertisements were soon advising the public that the sales force would try not to discomfort the poorer customers.[34] The family's aristocratic pretensions grew apace: there was the old founder who relished his nickname 'the Governor,' the family that to insiders became known as 'the Court,' the son who was hailed and mourned like some crown prince, the homes that all came to bear gentrified names. It appeared as though the Eatons were lifting their store's image on the back of their own rising social prestige.

But perhaps intentionally, the store never quite sheared away all signs of its plebeian past. Many women continued to see Eaton's as a low-priced staples store, and the catalogue in particular was criticized by middle-class consumers for its fixation with 'things [that] are rather cheap.' Unlike Simpson's, the Eaton's outlet in Toronto remained functional and subdued, never aiming above the modestly bourgeois; a shop offering fashionable and expensive goods at reduced prices to those who yearned for French fashions and imported bibelots but who lacked the resources for a European tour. The store made it its particular mission to bring the world of distinction to a mid-western city: 'lessons' in golf, 'lessons' in embroidery, 'demonstrations' in table etiquette, 'lectures' on interior decorating, concerts by Schnabel and Pons – such were the special attractions offered by this greatest of Canada's department stores. In all this, the store's appeal was quintessentially provincial: it provided goods and uplift to a society that was thirsting after worldly culture, and yet because of its vast size, it was able to do so without having to sacrifice the trade in shovels and cheap prints and caps.[35]

Arguably, over time the emphasis on class over gender probably did help to relieve some of the moralists' dismay at the departmentals' heady rise. Certainly, by the 1920s few commented on the corrupting influence of the great stores, and many even welcomed their genteel cultural influence. But to my mind, what really created this change was the gradual acceptance of the new consumer economy. What attracted a panicked reaction in the 1890s had become a commonplace in the years after the First World War; 'profligate' female shoppers and consumer excess were even celebrated as symbols of the roaring new age and its new women.[36] The point is important since it lends further credence to the idea that consumer attitudes and expectations had been transformed. The feminization of shopping and the 'consumerization' of demand had become accepted realities. And of all stores, Eaton's best encapsulated that passage as it moved from crass renegade to become 'Canada's retailer.'

By the First World War Eaton's had become far and away Canada's leading retail business. Its Toronto store was immense, an industrial-retail complex linked together by walkways and underground tunnels. In Winnipeg eight spacious and imposing storeys enclosed twenty-one verdant shopping acres and featured, by 1925, twenty-nine elevators and an eighteen-hole miniature golf course on the seventh floor. The success of the business dazzled competitors and foreign visitors alike. Eaton's was 'the first merchant in the land,' according to an envious Hudson's Bay Company official; its influence was 'unparalleled anywhere else in the world,' in the eyes of an English tourist; 'no matter how early the hour the store is busy,' commented an awed American journalist in 1923. By 1930 Eaton's was receiving one dollar out of every two spent in department stores across the country, and this ratio gave the company a staggering 7 per cent share of all retail sales. Its rise to these heights had been spectacular: total sales (including mail-order) had increased from $1.6 million in 1891 to $53 million by 1914 and up to $225 million in 1929. Eaton's assets had grown apace, from $885,000 on incorporation in 1885 to almost $108 million within forty years.[37]

Eaton's made it company policy seriously to underprice its competitors on all standard lines carried in its stores, while superior style was relied upon to sell the most expensive goods. As R.Y. Eaton, who masterminded the company's development in the first half of the twentieth century, specified, 'on regular lines the original prices [at Eaton's] should be noticeably lower than cash prices in other stores.' Indeed, prices on most goods were kept low enough that from the early 1890s through to the early 1920s the company shied away from price cutting. 'Sales' were regarded as bad for the company's image because they gave 'the Public less confidence in our Regular Prices as being the lowest obtainable and encourage waiting for reduced prices.' Reductions on regular lines therefore came only occasionally during the year, generally in the two weeks preceding stocktakings (the January white and the July green tag sales). Rather than dropping prices on regular stock, buyers were instructed to search out special 'leaders' that could be featured at a lower mark-up (5–15 per cent, or 'just enough profit to pay for the work of handling'), and merchandise managers were advised to mark these goods 'special values' rather than 'reduced' so as not to give the customers any wrong ideas. For greater effect, the store massed these special values and unleashed them on the public one day a week, Friday being the traditional day, with the advertising bombardment beginning on Thursday. And to keep its low prices before the public, Eaton's relied upon newspaper advertising. In this promotion, as in all else, immensity characterized the company's dealings: R.Y. Eaton estimated that for a special sale in the early twentieth century the company might buy twice as many columns of advertising in the Toronto *Star* as there were columns of text, and another observer calculated that by the early thirties Eaton's was running an average of two pages of advertising in each of the Toronto evening newspapers every day of the year.[38]

The mass merchandisers were able to offer such low prices in large measure because of the power they wielded over their suppliers. This is not to say that the departmentals had not achieved certain economies; they produced some of their more popular lines of merchandise in their own factories, they established buying offices in foreign markets, and they bought as often as possible from the manufacturer so as to avoid wholesalers' charges. But these economies were, after 1900, much less significant than they might once have been. As the department stores grew larger, their overheads rose dramatically, and by the time that people started collecting the relevant data, the departmentals' operating costs were far higher than those of the main-street independents. Moreover, the economies achieved by direct buying were far less significant than they might appear because big stores which did not buy through wholesalers obviously had to operate their own warehouses and employ their own teams of buyers. Similarly, though manufacturing was for a time a cost saver, by the end of the First World War the department stores were finding that they could buy goods from outside sources cheaper than they could produce them themselves. It was not that there were no savings exacted, but the modest chiselling that was achieved through vertical and horizontal expansion simply did not have lasting cost-related value.

Where the big stores made real savings was in their buying. Bulk buying was standard practice for all merchants, and every retailer expected to get a better price on the placing of a bigger order, but the mass merchandisers were always able to wring out more. The largest stores received advertising allowances, rebates, special premiums, and placing discounts, as well as additional buying concessions on their biggest purchases. Even where discounts should have been standardized, the largest retailers received more because of the huge orders they were able to generate. The placing discount, for example, was given by clothing and footwear manufacturers to customers making early orders: the standard rubber footwear discount in the 1930s was 7 plus 2, 7 per cent for the early order and 2 per cent for cash payment (which for rubber footwear always meant thirty days). The rule of thumb, however, was that the bigger one was the bigger one's discount was going to be, for while large wholesalers such as York Trading Company were offered $7\frac{1}{2}$ plus 2, Simpson's received 15 plus 1 and Eaton's obtained 15 plus 2.[39] In other words, everyone might profit somewhat from the discounting system, but the bigger one's order the more one obtained. Size, then, was in itself a guarantee of low prices.

Size was everything to the department stores; it was their greatest attraction and the chief source of their low prices. This fact explains why it took some time for the departmentals to begin really to unbalance urban trading. Though many of them had existed since the late 1870s, it was only in the 1890s that the departmentals grew large enough for the power of their size to become manifest. By 1894, however, retailers in Montreal had begun to agitate against the Scoggie store, and a year later W.A. Murray's and Eaton's in Toronto became the targets of abuse. The real problem was that the big just kept getting bigger. In 1904 Simpson's pressed into the Montreal market with the purchase of the John Murphy store, and in the next year Eaton's opened its massive Winnipeg branch.[40] But the biggest department stores were not only acquiring new outlets; they were also, through their mail-order catalogues, extending their influence far beyond the cities that contained them. Mail-order buying had originally been introduced in the 1870s by ordinary retailers despatching goods on demand to regular customers, and this 'informal' type of enterprise remained common at least until the Second World War.[41] But Eaton's quickly institutionalized the practice, issuing its first catalogue – a thirty-four-page unillustrated buyer's list appropriately titled The Wishing Book – to visitors at the Toronto Exhibition of 1884. Ten years later, Simpson's moved into the mail-order business as well.

Before 1910 the mail-order system remained in its infancy, though it was, as the *Canadian Grocer* quipped (emphasizing the sexual element), 'a pretty lusty infancy.' As was its wont, Eaton's moved with considerable caution into the mail-order business, and until 1909 the service was restrained by the company's reluctance to detach its catalogue operations from its over-the-counter operations. Things did improve, of course; under its first system, when orders were received, clerks went in person to the appropriate department in the store and picked out what had been requested, 'paying' with an internal cheque issued against the mail-order division. The change came in 1903; a separate mail-order shipping office was created, and a new system was put into place whereby requests were despatched by pneumatic tube to the appropriate department and then shipped out to the packaging department. But even so the procedure remained slow and expensive. Only in 1909 did Eaton's finally separate the mail-order division and move it into its own building in downtown Toronto. In the new mail-order warehouse, goods were departmentalized and stored on site. When orders were received, a numbered form was sent to the appropriate storage department, which affixed the ticket to the item and sent it by conveyor belt down to the packaging division. There the orders were boxed and then transferred to the postal department for mailing. The system was sleek and efficient, and the optimum turn-around time was reduced from six hours to two.[42]

Possibly Eaton's beefed up its mail-order department in anticipation of the tremendous increase in business that was likely to follow the much-discussed inauguration of a parcel post service in Canada. Finally launched in 1914, the parcel post broke a psychological barrier by bringing goods right up to the door rather than dropping them off at the railway freight office. The year it was introduced, Simpson's moved its mail-order division out of the store and down to a separate warehouse on Front Street, and in 1916 Eaton's experimented with the first 'mail order extension house.' By 1920 Simpson's was selling $13.1 million by mail, while Eaton's was turning about $60 million in catalogue sales. In effect, these two companies were making somewhere around 3 per cent of the total volume of retail sales by post.[43]

In the decades surrounding the First World War, the activities of the department stores and mail-order houses served to heighten appreciably the level of retail competition and to intensify the marketing effort. Because of the departmentals and their catalogues, selling came to appear as a struggle for the consumer's soul. Independent stores were forced to plead and cajole and advertise and merchandise to win back to themselves customers who had now been freed from traditional shopping loyalties. The competition for the female consumer therefore sharpened the marketing atmosphere in the early twentieth century and made advertising and promotion an everyday reality. Wherever they went, whether in small towns or big cities, buyers were bombarded with messages to spend here rather than elsewhere. This was something new and exciting, and it added to the allure of the goods themselves. No wonder people began to want more and to feel themselves empowered by their ability to buy. Incredibly enough, after 1920 the intensity of the competition increased even more with the arrival of the chain stores. They were unlike the big department stores, which used amenities and catalogues and a wide selection of goods to draw customers to their sumptuous downtown locations. The chains did not attempt to attract customer to the store; they carried their stores directly to the customers. In order to draw the business, they even more than the departmentals, used low prices as their particular selling instrument, and they were ruthless in their determination to undersell their competitors.[44] And their success terrified main-street shopkeepers and department store managers alike. By 1925 the chains had cornered a share of the market as large as that of the departmental and mail-order houses combined (table 9). What had taken the other mass merchandisers forty years to accomplish, the chains had done in five.

The chains were the fastest growing retail organizations in early-twentieth-century Canada (tables 8 and 9), but their rise had not been without interruption. Discounting the Hudson's Bay Company's shops, their first appearance in Canada shortly preceded the century's turn. Manufacturers and wholesalers opened the first modern chains as distributing branches for their products; the fish wholesaler Robin, Page and Whitman moved into the outport supply business in the mid-nineteenth century, and the William Davies meat stores and P.T. Legaré buggy and carriage shops were both founded in the 1880s. The Hamilton groceries of William Carroll claimed the honours as the country's first autonomous retail chain; founded in 1893, Carroll's by 1906 had six outlets in operation. Other openings followed in rapid succession: T.P. Loblaw opened his first store in 1910 and his third in 1912, Dowler's St Thomas clothing stores also began expanding in 1912, and Overwaitea's of Vancouver opened in 1915. But their growth was, on the whole, sluggish; by 1919 Loblaw's included nineteen stores, Dowler's four, and Carroll's only thirteen.[45]

Not until the economic crisis of the immediate postwar years was the ginger really provided to chain store expansion. The chains capitalized on the arousal of consumer interest in low prices that accompanied the inflationary 1919–21 years and the subsequent depression. They kept their prices down when everyone else's were being inflated, they put goods on sale before anyone else did, and they continued to devalue their stocks in advance of the general wholesale price index. As T.P. Loblaw explained in 1925, the chains 'provided a new channel for distribution ... [they have] succeeded in putting goods on the consumer's table at a lower price than the wholesaler can buy them for.'[46]

Between 1919 and 1921 the number of Dominion grocery stores multiplied sixfold, and they then doubled again over the next two years. Dominion's sales rose from $2.4 million in 1920 to over $12 million by 1925, an increase of 400 per cent. It was the industry leader in the grocery field; the creation of W.J. Pentland (a one-time executive with the A&P) and R. Jackson, who together bought out the tiny T.P. Loblaw grocery chain in 1919 for $115,000, Dominion in 1929 recorded a net profit of $640,000 on sales of over $24 million.[47] For his own part, Theodore Pringle Loblaw, after a brief stint as manager of the never-very-successful United Farmers of Ontario retail cooperative, opened a new chain in Toronto in 1920. Like the Dominion chain, Loblaw's did extremely well in the depression of the early twenties, and in 1925 the company had sales of $8 million.[48] The two other large grocery chains – Safeway's in the west and the A & P in Quebec and Ontario – were both American-owned corporations which expanded into Canada in the later twenties. By 1931, the Great Atlantic and Pacific Company was running 300 stores, while Safeway, which had begun Canadian operations in 1929, had 140.[49] By 1930 there were chain stores in every province, though they were not evenly distributed. The chains enjoyed their largest market shares in Ontario, Saskatchewan, Alberta, and British Columbia, with BC leading the rest. Prince Edward Island, in contrast, had fewer chain outlets than many city blocks in Toronto or Vancouver.

Where they were established, the chains targeted the same market as the main-street independents. Unlike the shoestring shops, which tucked themselves into the backstreets, the chains picked locations of prominence. City directories reveal that in Toronto four out of every ten chain store outlets were located on Yonge Street north of Bloor Street, in the wealthy neighbourhoods bordering Forest Hill, and along Bloor and Roncesvalles in the High Park area (places accounting for 25 per cent of the population), while a further 22 per cent were located in the skilled Anglo-Saxon working-class district between the Danforth and Gerrard Street (which accounted for 17 per cent of the population). They appealed not to the poor (who could have most profited from their lower prices), but to workers and bourgeois of moderate income (table 2). According to a 1935 study of the cheese-buying habits of 3,200 families in Oshawa, Quebec City, and Calgary, while families of all income levels bought some cheese in all types of stores, it was people with incomes of $1,000–2,000 a year (roughly the average wage of salaried employees and securely employed skilled workers) who were most likely to buy all or part of their supplies from chain stores (department stores were by this time most popular for food goods among those with incomes of over $2,000 a year).[50]

Outside the grocery field, chain store development, while increasingly important in the 1920s, was less impressive. In the clothing business there were, by 1930, 63 chain store companies operating 372 stores and representing about a 12 per cent market share, while in the furniture and dry goods trades the chains were almost non-existent. Only in the area of shoes and drugs and in 5¢ and 10¢ varieties did the chains exert a strong influence. In the drug business the chains transacted 20 per cent of all sales in 1930, while in the five-and-dime trade they held a virtual monopoly. In many cases, in particular in the shoe, clothing, and drug businesses, chain growth was the result of the forward integration of manufacturing concerns. The G. Tamblyn Company, Toronto's most important drug chain-store firm, was a subsidiary of Imperial Tobacco, and among the clothiers, D'Aillard's, Alexander Furs, Tip Top Tailors, and Robinson's were all manufacturer-operated chains. In shoes the chain movement was pioneered by Agnew-Surpass, a big Brantford shoe manufacturer, but by the late twenties even small producers such as Invictus, Natural Tread, Dack's, and Slater had entered the business.[51]

Variety stores were the line most fully under the control of the independently owned chains. S.H. Knox, a cousin and sometime partner of Frank Woolworth, opened Canada's first 5¢ and 10¢ store in Toronto in 1897. A few years later E.P. Charlton, the Yankee variety store magnate, moved his chain into Montreal, and by 1912 his firm was operating 18 stores in Quebec and the Maritimes. The Woolworth red-fronts first appeared in Canada in the wake of 'the great $65 million merger' of 1912, when Knox's 108 stores in the United States and Canada and Charlton's 48 were swallowed into Woolworth's expanding nickel-and-dime empire.[52] The company developed rapidly in Canada, but like all chains it expanded fastest during the depression of the early twenties: Woolworth's sales, which stood at $3 million at the time of the merger, multiplied to $15 million by 1924. Its main rivals, before Kresge's expanded northward in 1928, were Metropolitan Stores and United Stores, but Woolworth's star outshone them all. In 1930 the Diamond W's $20 million turnover represented over half of all variety store sales.[53]

'On the streets of our cities,' one druggist warned in 1929, 'the independent merchant is being very largely replaced by the chain units.' And so it must have seemed. The Bureau of Statistics estimates of 1924 had shown that there were about 1,200 chain outlets in Canada; within six years there were over 8,000. They were, for the independent storekeepers, a national pestilence. Every province by the middle 1920s had its share of chain stores, and retailers across the dominion were feeling the sting of their competition. The very opening of a chain outlet in a town was enough to set the merchants panicking. In fact, everyone except the rural retailers saw the chains as a far greater threat to their existence than the department stores or mail-order houses had ever been. The chains seemed so formidable in part because when they did enter a place, they did so in a swarm. Toronto alone had more chain store outlets in 1930 than many provinces, and it had twice as many as in all the Maritime provinces combined. In cities with populations of over 30,000 in 1931, chain stores controlled 33 per cent of the grocery trade and 30 per cent of the drug business. For retailers trading within these cities, the chain presence was strongly felt, but those outside were not immune. The chains were a new phenomenon, and they seemed to have taken over with frightening speed. Retailers everywhere worried that once the chains had completed their monopolization of the big-city trade, they would be moving out into their own little markets. 'Whether the chain store has invaded his field or not,' one Swift Current retailer observed, 'the independent merchant must prepare for the day when it will attempt to do so.'[54]

But fear of the chains' growth rate was only one of the ways in which their influence preceded their arrival. Even more important than their actual presence was their psychological impact. The chains, with their stylish outlets and unquestionable price appeal, captured the public mood and left their competitors scrambling to keep up. Their growth was based on their highly destabilizing skill at undercutting their competitors. 'We give you made to measure clothes that you will be proud of for the low price of $17.50,' one chain store boasted, and 'they are equally as good as can be obtained for $25 to $30 elsewhere.' By the second decade of the twentieth century, consumer tastes had been aroused by these dramatic appeals to the pocketbook. Not only the independents but even the department store giants watched the growth of the chains with envy and alarm. Everyone was feeling the pressure to emulate their methods. Even in small communities which had no chains, shoppers were aware of the low prices that the chain merchandisers were making possible and were demanding that their local storekeepers meet them. 'The thing that surprised me,' wrote Sam Peps after he had visited a chain store in a nearby town, 'was the buying atmosphere. In this the modern chain is a dangerous competitor.'[55]

The growth of the mass merchandisers provides further evidence of the emergence of a new culture of spending. Because of increased competition, consumers now had the power to shop around, to compare prices, to buy what fit best or looked nicest. The ability of independent retailers to control consumption in traditional ways – by personal connections to their customers – quite simply disappeared. Shoppers adjusted to these changes in the early twentieth century with a new approach to their own influence as consumers. They now expected to be able to buy what they liked where they liked, and they fought fairly vigorously to defend that privilege. The most aggressive retailers also adjusted, creating vast new marketing agencies designed to harness the tremendous potential that consumerism represented. But for most independent retailers, the changes were none the less challenging and disorienting. Already struggling to cope with the growth in competition from within their own ranks, they now had to contend with the low prices and unlimited selections offered by the marketing giants. Along the main arteries of major towns and cities, chain stores threatened them from every side, while the departmentals pulled customers towards downtown with their own peculiar gravity. And thanks to the catalogues, there was no escape for rural merchants because even the most isolated shoppers could now buy with abandon. The same breakdown of customer loyalty, the same detachment of the shopper from the valuation of her home that troubled urban retailers, had come to the countryside.

THE CONSUMER IS BORN

To return then to Neil McKendrick's proposition, the emergence of a consumer society might be found not in standard-of-living figures but in attitudes and options. Clearly, business people believed that their ground was shifting, but shoppers, I feel, shared the sense of novelty. The major indicator of this is that people came to regard themselves as 'consumers' in a very modern way during the first three decades of the twentieth century. As they experimented with the empowerment which their ability to 'shop around' engendered, consumers forced changes in business attitudes and approaches. The mass merchandisers were a preliminary response to the independence of the female shopper, as was brand-name advertising and direct marketing. Ultimately, perhaps, the counter-offensive of a business community anxious to restore stability to the market-place may well have subdued consumers. But for a brief moment it seemed, at least to many business people, that shoppers were massing themselves into a force more powerful and dangerous than any they had faced on their shop-floors. And this returns us, ironically, to a major issue for cost-of-living analysts – the rise in the price of goods.

By today's standards, the inflation that came after 1896 was not especially severe, but it did become extremely painful to ordinary people at the time. Retail prices rose modestly between 1896 and 1905, jumped dramatically in 1906–7, and then stabilized again before resuming a somewhat more rapid upward course in 1909.[56] Overall, between 1896 and 1915 the inflation in store-bought goods averaged about 6 per cent per annum, a rate which was not high enough to concern most people on a day-by-day basis but which over the long term pushed prices considerably higher. What was most disconcerting was that although the price increases before the First World War did not fully eliminate the gains made during the great deflation, they were pushing in that direction. When, in 1910, the *Canadian Grocer* first covered the rising cost of living in depth, it found that while meat and cheese were the only widely consumed food goods that were more expensive in 1910 than they had been in 1870 (almost double), most prices had increased significantly over the preceding eight years. The evidence, as we have already noted, is contradictory as to just how severely this price rise affected actual spending, as late as 1913 the *Grocer* and other trade sources were arguing that there had been little slackening in demand and that 'for all the talk of financial stringency, it doesn't appear people were much less flush with their money than usual.' None the less, that same year the federal government was evidently concerned enough about the economy to appoint an inquiry into the rising cost of living.

Once again, much probably depended on who one was, where one lived, and what one liked to buy. People in the bigger cities were generally more severely affected than those in smaller towns, though things were not everywhere equal since food prices in Montreal apparently rose more slowly than they did in Halifax or Toronto. People with fewer buying options would also have been more adversely affected: Jewish shoppers, for example, picketed and vandalized kosher butcher shops in the eastern United States in 1902 and 1907, though there does not seem to be any evidence of a similar Canadian agitation before 1917.[57]

But it was workers who were unable to negotiate higher salaries and wages, people in rented accommodation, the seasonally employed, and the majority of single working women – those people who had entered the twentieth century in a disadvantaged position – who undoubtedly suffered most from the inflation. And, of course, when unemployment soared in 1907–8 and 1913–14, thousands of other working people joined them in experiencing the terrible pain of a rising cost of goods.

Paradoxically, the most vocal complainants against the high cost of living were not those who probably suffered the most. The primary organizational response to rising prices, the Consumer's League (which moved north from the United States in 1912), was a white-collar organization.[58] Similarly, the Civil Servants Association was one of the earliest and most outspoken proponents of the indexing of salaries to prices, and the most consistent blue-collar interest in consumer issues was to be found within the Trades and Labor Congress. The main support for consumer cooperatives came from uniformed workers, miners, clerks, civil servants, and more-prosperous farmers. In other words, the great agitation for action on consumer issues came largely from the ranks of relatively well-to-do labour, from within the salaried office workforce, and from the commercial farming population. It is not therefore implausible to suggest that the high cost of living stirred the greatest resentment among people who were of modest to moderate means, people who had enjoyed a margin of comfort in the late nineteenth and early twentieth centuries and who now worried that inflation was going to drive them down into the ranks of the poor. To this extent what was at stake was the level of comfort – the range of consumer possibilities – not the basic ability to subsist, clothe, and shelter oneself. In other words, inflation set off such a powerful explosion because it affected people who were increasingly accepting of a consumerist frame of mind.

The scope of the public protest against high prices grew in tandem with inflation after 1907, but during the First World War the scale of the unrest changed dramatically. The cause lay almost entirely in the surging prices of the war years. During the war the general rise in commodity prices exceeded 13 per cent, and in some lines the increases were even larger: a 1916 *Hardware and Metal* survey found that in one year the price of bolts and rivets had risen 130 per cent, aluminum was up 300 per cent, and there had been a doubling in the cost of nails. Not surprisingly, it was the rise in food prices that was of greatest concern to ordinary Canadians. While the price of carrots, cabbages, onions, potatoes, and plums remained stable between 1914 and 1918, the cost of meat and poultry, flour, butter, and eggs doubled, and tea, coffee, lard, and rice almost tripled in price, while the cost of peas and beans went up 350 per cent. Canadian consumers were understandably enraged: 'last year we paid twenty-five, twenty-six and twenty-eight cents a dozen for eggs or thirty cents a dozen,' one worker complained, 'and this time you cannot buy them or you would reach down and give a chunk of your wages for them and the same with butter. Stuff that is produced right under your nose, you cannot get ahold of.' The *Canadian Grocer* felicitously suggested that if people would just change their consumption habits they could still eat cheaply: 'it would entail ... a recurrence of cabbage soup and the frequent appearance of corn-meal mush and the total absence of such aristocratic items as butter and eggs. But it could be done.'[59] Realistically, of course, it could not. Consumers – even those of relatively modest means – could no more return to a mid-nineteenth-century diet of thin soup and bread than they could go back to making their own clothes or cooking on a log fire. Mass consumption ('pampered palates' to its critics) was here to stay.

The inflation brought by the war easily fired the miscellaneous protests of the pre-war years into a consumer agitation, the kind of unrest that derived less from insecurities than from expectations and that transcended, without escaping, class and regional boundaries. Though worker and bourgeois, farmer and urbanite, might have acted separately, and in fact oppositionally, all were consumers motivated by a similar desire to continue accumulating goods. While expectations differed (one train conductor, a man of modest means, illustrated what the rising cost of living meant to him by saying that 'forty years ago ... I could buy a nice little pig for $5.00, and today you would have to pay very nearly that for a good roast,' while an Ottawa bourgeoise, equally concerned with increasing prices, observed, 'I am not complaining about the high price of foodstuffs as much as about the high price of luxuries ... I may say that I am asked $35 for a very simple hat'), people of all types, in their own way, were talking about expectations. That was why individuals on different sides in the class struggle might appear to agree on consumer-related issues: during the Winnipeg strike of 1919, for example, it was not only the workers who were on the streets protesting against declining real incomes. As one anti-strike banner read, 'We Will Maintain Constituted Authority, Law & Order! Down with the High Cost of Living ... To Hell With the Alien Enemy ... God Save the King.'[60]

The possibility of increased consumption, thrown up in the late nineteenth century, led many people to expect their lifestyles to improve continuously and their shopping horizons to expand steadily; the great tragedy of the inflation was that it forced almost everyone to do without what they had come to believe was necessary or desirable. In other words, even if inflation led to a decline in real wages, it did nothing to limit the desire to own. The peculiar combination of high pay and relative job security with frustrated aspirations helped radicalize the insurgency of the war years. 'Men and women have been magically awakened,' a Prairie socialist explained, 'and are now, everywhere, enquiring and pressing for better homes, more comforts, more complete education, higher culture ... the comforts enjoyed by the few, must be enjoyed by the many.' But the trauma of inflation should not be taken lightly. Though perhaps less life-threatening than the periods of scarcity that had occurred in the early and mid-nineteenth century, the inflation was no less painful for the dreams it could shatter. One worker speaking before the 1919 royal commission on industrial relations made this fact clear when he said that although he had hoped that his daughter might be able to stay in school and eventually become a teacher, rising expenses had pushed her into a factory. Here was the human impact of a spiralling cost of living.[61]

During the early twentieth century, theories abounded concerning just who was to blame for the inflation. According to most economic experts, the high cost of living resulted from inflexible and inviolable economic laws: rising prices occurred when demand outstripped the capacity of society to produce. This unhappy state could arise from several causes, but the most likely culprits were excessive wages (which allowed for over-consumption) or inefficient production (which caused underproduction). Thus the Victorian moralists who authored the government's 1915 report on the cost of living could suggest that while 'the wants of the people had multiplied on every side ... in this Dominion we are proportionately working fewer hours than ever before, and we have a greater number of idle in our midst'; in this interpretation, the only solution to inflation was more labour and restrained spending.[62]

Many manufacturers in the inflationary years before the armistice agreed, and they felt they had the facts to prove it. They could show that most industries were running at maximum effort, and they were willing to credit the public with practising real restraint. The cause of inflation therefore had to lie in excessive wages. High wages, they reasoned, drove up production costs and thereby prices, which meant that working people were themselves largely to blame for their own problems.

Working-class consumers, however, did their maths and began to raise questions: wages, they figured, had increased only 33 per cent between 1915 and 1919, but prices had almost doubled (these were the numbers most commonly used at the time). How then could one claim that higher wages were the cause of higher prices? Relying upon traditional notions that human actions and not impersonal forces controlled the market-place, many consumers laid the blame for the high cost of living squarely on the self-seeking profiteers. The average citizen, remarked a saddened cost-of-living commissioner in 1919, 'knows little or nothing of the [cause of high] prices ... [and] he is prone to assume that the increased prices spring from the exorbitant profits of those manufacturing or dealing in them.'[63]

Many people, in particular those who were active in the retail cooperative movement, pointed the accusing finger at independent shopkeepers, who, whether from inefficiency or malice, were thought to be grossly inflating their margins. 'You see the merchant and his family take trips to the seashore,' ran one advertisement for a Windsor co-op, 'ride around in automobiles, and wear diamonds on the profits. You can readily see that they could not afford those luxuries if they did not double their money on every article they sell.' Because they were the most visible of all business people, shop owners were regularly vilified by their customers and by the press. Sam Peps of the *Maritime Merchant* must have touched a nerve when he described how one shopper attacked him for his high prices. 'It was no wonder some people got rich,' the customer stormed, 'for they were grinding the faces of the poor. She was sure the dress the girl Sally had sold her cost not more than a quarter of the price she paid, and that there ought to be a law to send extortioners to jail.'[64]

But while the majority of people probably felt that the retailers were making too much money, most of them were hunting bigger game. When ordinary consumers thought about profiteering, their minds most often turned not to the retailer but to the 'combine.' In the years surrounding the First World War, talk of combines rose from the streets and swirled up through voluntary organizations, business meetings, and newspaper articles and onto the floors of legislatures. Alerted to the 'trust' evil by the writings of the American muckrakers and confirmed in their suspicions by the merger wave of the immediate pre-war years, Canadian consumers came to suspect, when prices shot up or goods became scarce, that the combine was at work. In the words of one working-class Québécois, 'Big firms, manufacturers and other company raised too much profit, on the poor people.'[65]

Like other consumer-related issues, belief in a trust conspiracy was not limited to people of any particular class, region, or education. C.T. Cross, a wealthy Vancouver businessman and chairman of the BC Reconstruction Committee, was sure that the prices of 'all the food stuffs are controlled by two or three firms. The trouble does not lie with the retailer at all, but with those people who have the cold storage plants and the millers.' Mrs W.C. Hughson, a civil servant's wife and member of the Ottawa Consumer's League, was similarly convinced that 'five great companies control [it] all ... they control the land development, stockyard development, terminal and railway facilities of stockyards, banks, packers, machinery and supplies, cold storage warehouses and miscellaneous things.' Likewise, the secretary of the Montreal TLC thought that 'there is a great superabundance of food to feed Canadians well but those who get control of it produce an artificial shortage by sending it to the four corners of the globe where they secure high prices for it often creating famine prices in the very country which is the base of production ... The cold storage plant is the convenient medium through which the operation is made possible.' Even Mackenzie King, campaigning in Berlin (Kitchener) in 1911, felt inspired to lash out against the 'combines [that] enhance prices and control supply.' Federal government efforts to diffuse the public's agitation over combines, through an investigation into meat packing and an inquiry into cold storage facilities, met with little success; predictably, the government succeeded only in making itself appear a tool of the trusts.[66]

The rising clamour over combines reflects the growing power and politicization of consumers. Their influence had really first been felt by retailers coping with the feminization of buying, but things had turned more worrying since then. Now there was direct, constant, and even orchestrated complaining, a good deal of agitation in favour of legislation, and during the war years, even widespread demands for a conscription of wealth to end 'the gain of the private profiteer.' The cold storage companies and the meat packers were the ones being criticized most often, but all business people had cause for concern. After all, the agitation against high meat prices had forced the creation of public abattoirs in some of the larger cities, and several governmental investigations had been launched. Few in business liked all the talk of conscripting wealth, and they worried about where the government's involvement might end. Moreover, while the consumers' most powerful weapon, the boycott, remained largely unexplored during the inflationary years, it was nevertheless a dark cloud on the horizon. There were periodic calls for mass consumer resistance to high prices, and as prices kept rising (one independent Toronto study found that between September 1919 and February 1920, white bread rose 10 per cent, sugar increased 32 per cent, and beef shoulder jumped 25 per cent in price), it began to seem only a question of time before the public angrily struck out against inflated prices. As the Associated Clothing Manufacturers nervously remarked in April 1920, 'there is a widespread feeling at the present time that the patience of the public as to high prices is about exhausted. Ways and means to reduce prices are discussed everywhere.'[67]

According to shoe retailers, they were the first to feel the prick of the consumers' lancet. Footwear had been a particular source of public irritation for some time. Prices had risen dramatically during the war: the cost of a pair of ordinary men's shoes had soared from about $3.50–4.50 in 1915 up to $9–12 by 1919, and women's shoes had leapt from $4–6 up to $9–15. Faced with high prices, consumers had been conservative in their buying, and though there had been good years in 1916 and 1919, the domestic shoe trade had generally been poor after 1911. Typically, there was a good deal of talk of a shoe combine, and despite a 1915 investigation into the industry, rumours of a business conspiracy continued. In fact, the shoe industry was the one that Progressive Party leader T.A. Crerar most liked to hate, and the party's platform of 1919 even contained a reference to the 'Plunder on Boots and Shoes.' Catastrophe, however, only struck the industry in May 1920, when the government – showing that peculiar death-wish which characterized the last years of Tory rule – brought in a luxury tax which, among other things, levelled a charge on all shoes selling for over $9. Evidently conceived by someone in the Department of Finance who never went shopping, the tax pinned a 15 per cent surcharge on everything costing more than a pair of summer sandals. The major department stores, which had stocked heavily in the wake of the relatively healthy 1919 season, opted to slash the prices of all shoes in stock 15–25 per cent in order to cushion the impact of the tax. That panicked already edgy retailers: clear-out sales hit every major city, and shoe salesmen desperately tried to dump their summer stock in what the president of the Shoe Dealers' Association called 'an epidemic of panic ... an influenza of commerce.' After three months of wild selling the market stabilized, but the price of shoes had dropped about 50 per cent, and with retailers refusing to stock ahead, the manufacturers had begun to lay off their workers.[68] By the time that the government revoked its tax on luxuries, the industry was already spinning into depression.

What had begun in shoes soon spread to other lines. Again there were precipitating causes: the immense reconstruction contracts that North American business people had anticipated from Europe failed to materialize, manufacturers began to worry about the unused productive capacity that they had built up during the war, the global wheat glut had brought down prices, and in 1920 the Americans had raised emergency tariffs. And then in the fall of 1920 consumer purchases began to drop away. Consumers were responding to the postwar instabilities and their suspicions of profiteering by sharply curtailing their purchasing, and the *Financial Post* estimated that in 1920 buying fell off by 25 per cent. The level-headed blamed the decline in spending on the weather and the wheat crop, but many others in that panicky autumn insisted fearfully that what had happened was that the buying public had finally gone on strike. 'The public,' the rumour spread, 'unquestionably from one cause and another has decided that prices have gone as high as there is any reason for them to go, and with one accord have decided to wait for a change.'[69]

The repercussions from this fantastical rumour immediately rebounded onto the manufacturers, who suddenly found themselves confronting retailers refusing to buy their spring 1921 stocks. Orders which had been avidly placed during the boom years were now cancelled mercilessly. Inventories which had once served to make men rich now ruined them. Prices, the retailers insisted, had to fall, and in order to precipitate that deflation they began to dump their unsold inventories at bargain-basement prices. The stampede then began in earnest: the price of men's suits fell from an average of $45–50 to $30 in the space of six months, nails dropped 50 per cent, and grocery prices dipped one-quarter. Storekeepers placed no orders ahead, bought in small lots, and stocked only for immediate needs, consolidating the general trend towards hand-to-mouth buying. It was a seller's nightmare. 'We are passing through an economic revolution,' one merchant explained referring to the general sentiment, 'and price is now king.'[70]

The early twenties were a confusing and unhappy time for many business people, and the experience led to new questions about the nature of the domestic economy and about the principles upon which mass consumption was being built. 'The fall in prices in 1920,' one manufacturer pondered, 'was not caused by overproduction'; nor was it a result of greater economies since 'manufacturing costs have certainly not decreased, nor is there any immediate prospect that they will.' Indeed, most producers believed their factories to have been run efficiently and their payrolls to have been high (too high, in fact). This left them at a loss to explain the decline in retail sales. 'There is no special reason why trade should be dull,' a puzzled monthly report of the Canadian Bank of Commerce observed, 'when the railways, factories and mercantile establishments are distributing in the form of wages such large sums.' For many business people, the only factor that seemed able to account for the sudden deflation had been the public's decision that prices were too high and that they would buy only what was necessary. 'The public is like a drunken man that has been enjoying a great spree,' reasoned Harry Greenblatt, a Toronto clothing manufacturer, and 'now he is sobering up and coming down to earth.'[71]

It was a hard pill to swallow, in part because the notion of a separation of demand from supply (which the buyers' strike implied) required capitalists to ingest a whole new approach to the economy. It was too much for some, and a large number of business people stoically resisted the concept. But most manufacturers and distributors accepted at least a part of the message of the buyers' strike: demand now appeared to be a quasi-independent variable that would have to be actively nurtured and governed. The long road from female mobility to the buyers' strike had brought business people face to face with the unpredictable power of the consumer.

COMING TO TERMS WITH MASS CONSUMPTION

Through much of the nineteenth century, manufacturers had not been very much concerned about consumption or distribution. Preoccupied with the problems of making goods, they had given little thought to their circulation. In practice, most manufacturers seemed to have subscribed to the principle that 'supply always creates its own demand,' or as one Winnipeg industrialist put it, 'it is an axiom that it is impossible for the world to produce more than it consumes.' Relying upon Adam Smith and J.S. Mill (who, 'in spite of all competitors, never grow old'), Canadian business people generally felt that there was a basic harmony in the economy and that each element in production and consumption, investment and savings, ultimately balanced out the others. At the centre of the business world was manufacturing, the producer of all capital and value in the society and the activity from which all other economic functions took their cue (Mill's idea was that 'demand and supply always rush towards an equilibrium, but the condition of stable equilibrium is when things exchange for each other according to their cost of production').[72] It was a view from a world of scarcity, a world in which relatively little was being produced and in which only a small section of the population was buying much beyond its basic needs, a world in which increasing production was itself the miracle of the age.

There is no doubt that these beliefs made sense in the context of their time. Through most of the nineteenth century, wholesalers not manufacturers were the key players in the distribution process: supply, credit, and product availability were in large measure determined by wholesale merchants, who placed orders with producers and established the terms of sale to the retailers. Manufacturers in effect made goods for the wholesalers, who sold them to the retailers, who in turn tried to sell them to the consumers. And in keeping with the general philosophy that demand looked after itself, all suppliers remained strangely isolated from the consumption process, 'in the past,' wrote one wholesaler, 'the accepted method of distribution involved sending a salesman to cover a given area and trusting to providence that the business was there.' Before the 1870s dynamic changes had, of course, occurred, but in only a few isolated instances had these involved an alteration in the suppliers' attitude to consumption. The rapid increase in the volume of trade in generic goods which accompanied industrial growth had led to commercial specialization and to a virtual disappearance of the general merchant – in place of one wholesaler dealing in a broad spectrum of goods, there were now many jobbers, each of whom specialized in distributing a limited number of product lines – but the increase in production had not fundamentally altered the wholesalers' business; it had only encouraged the division of their labour.[73]

The belief that demand followed supply provided the perfect environment for the development of such Victorian notions of work and spending as thrift and enterprise. According to the economic orthodoxy, real value was created by labour expended in production, and profits were the difference between the amount of wages paid and the prices received. 'The value of a forest tree,' one businessman explained, 'is the value received for the labour expended in hewing it into square timber, sawing it into boards and turning it into an article of furniture.' Because real value did not depend upon demand but rather upon the process of production, it followed that prices were a reflection of wages and that steadily rising prices would suggest an improvement in popular wealth. 'It is a well known fact,' observed *Industrial Canada* in 1903, 'that throughout the nineteenth century there were alternate periods of prosperity and depression ... and that the good times were as invariably attended by high prices as the bad times were by low prices.' A 'twenty-five per cent rise in the cost of living,' the *Financial Post* announced cheerfully in 1910; 'nothing gives the economist greater satisfaction.' People were, of course, complaining, but 'so long as prices are rising, profits are rising and wages are advancing.' Indeed, it could be observed even of the wartime inflation that while it 'contributed to diminish the standard of comfort of certain groups of the working class, and of a large proportion of the middle class, yet the increase itself is after all rather a sign of prosperity than of the reverse ... [An] advance in the price of the means of subsistence is a usual phase in a society, which is growing rapidly in numbers, and which is enjoying the benefits of increased production.'[74]

Sticking by these traditional values, business people therefore not only welcomed the inflation that began in the 1890s, but they also actively resisted efforts to raise wages 'more quickly' than prices through such 'artificial' means as union action. Because rapid inflation was believed to be caused by some 'unnatural' disequilibration, such as over-consumption or declining productivity, more production was needed to make goods affordable. And responsible manufacturers had an obligation to keep wages in check during such periods because restraint was needed to restore normalcy to the market. Because goods were the embodiment of the labour expended in their production, it was only logical that wages could not be increased without a concomitant increase in output. 'Wage scales,' the association of men's wear manufactures insisted, could not be set 'on the basis of the cost of living ... scales of wages are governed by production.' The Victorian manufacturers' fondness for inflationary periods and their belief that piece wages were truest make sense only if it is realized that business people at the turn of the century were operating in an intellectual world still governed by the concept of scarcity. They hinged their approach to the economy on the assumption that demand had to adapt itself to supply. Thus employers in the early twentieth century tended to argue that workers whose earnings were not keeping pace with inflation were actually consuming too much and that they had to reduce their purchases in order to bring their needs in line with the amount that was being produced.[75]

Actions, however, were coming into conflict with ideas such as these, and it was the dust raised by continuous production itself that first sullied the pristine face of the traditional approach. It was easier for manufacturers to think in terms of equilibriums, real values, and ready demand in an age before declining prices seemed chronic. But the long deflation of the late nineteenth century, the increased levels of competition, and the feminization of shopping forced some business people to think more about the need to harness and coax demand. As early as the 1890s, a few Canadian business people were discussing the issue of 'overproduction,' which they felt was becoming a systemic problem within industrial societies. While most business people still believed that declining prices were the result of supply-side factors and none indicated an awareness of the demand-oriented economic theories then developing in Europe, some none the less felt that flooded markets might need special cultivation. The growth of private branding was one symptom of the change in thinking about consumption – an indication of some manufacturers' interest in distinguishing their product from their rivals'. It was no surprise that trade-marked goods should make their first major appearance in food and drugs – in the two lines where consumer concerns over price and quality were most pronounced – nor was it any wonder that it was manufacturers in these lines who first developed advertising aimed at convincing the public of the merits of their wares. Rapid reinflation, which the manufacturers so welcomed, actually only served to augment those concerns. As a result, by the turn of the century, 'greater stress is being laid upon the stability of the manufacturer than ever before ... [the consumer] is not only buying more and more trade marked merchandise, but he wants to know who and what is behind the trade-mark.'[76]

Packaging became more and more important as shoppers grew increasingly sensitive to the way things looked. J.M. Schneider, the Berlin sausage manufacturer, found retailers refusing to stock his wieners until he had succeeded in producing them in a standard size. Druggists faced similar packaging problems, for as one of them observed, 'people are want to judge a good deal by outside appearances, and when you present to them a remedy, however good, with a poorly printed badly trimmed label or a certain carton funereal in its sombreness, it will take considerable persuasion to induce them to purchase it.' In a short time, noted the advertising journal *Printer's Ink*, 'consumer confidence' had become 'the first and most important step in almost every manufacturer's merchandising programme.' As some businessmen experimented with package shapes that would instil 'confidence,' others signed their labels and offered 'personal guarantees' of quality to their customers. It was a move applauded by ordinary consumers everywhere; as one shopper wrote in the *Woman's Home Companion*, poor quality goods could best be avoided by careful housewives sticking to one trusted brand; 'this,' the author observed, 'is the safest way to trade at any store.'[77]

The new stress being placed on packaging and promotion would lead some manufacturers to question their traditional neglect of consumption and to accept the fact that demand had to be stimulated. Advertising and packaging could accomplish some of this goal, but by the turn of the century many brand-name manufacturers realized that they had to move even closer to the consumers and find out what the retailers were doing. 'Can the present-day manufacturer get by if he merely makes a good mouse-trap or a good watch or a good food product?' asked the *Printer's Ink*, 'Yes – to a certain degree, but never will he become a dominant factor in his particular line ... He must go a step further if he wants to gain the right kind of public confidence, and make people feel that he knows more about "watchology" than anyone in the field.' To accomplish this goal, many manufacturers felt that they had to gain greater influence over the people who actually sold their products. 'The first and most important step in almost every manufacturer's merchandising programme has been to win the dealer's confidence': he had to 'educate' the retailer about his products, and he had to 'foster the family idea between the manufacturer and *his* dealers.'[78]

During the early years of the century, a growing number of manufacturers increased their contacts with retailers through direct marketing. These industrialists realized that only by doing the distributing themselves could they ensure that their goods were promoted over their rivals' and that the public was getting the message of their advertising. Moreover, direct marketing gave brand-name manufacturers an added price edge in an inflationary period by allowing them to avoid the jobbers' profits and to reduce their prices to consumers.[79] But in moving to absorb the wholesalers' function, manufacturers effected a revolution in the distribution process. By the time people began collecting figures on these things (in 1930), they found that wholesalers were playing a relatively small role in the distribution of domestically manufactured goods. In Ontario, clothing manufacturers and meat packers were selling about 2–3 per cent of their stock through independent wholesalers; furniture makers were distributing around 5 per cent; makers of pickles, cotton yarns, and hats shipped 10–12 per cent; and shoe manufacturer and makers of woollens were selling approximately 25 per cent. In food one 1925 study estimated about 30–40 per cent of the retail grocer's stock was bought from jobbers. Overall, the wholesalers still handled 46 per cent of the total volume of goods sold, but this was because they distributed most imports and bulk goods (they marketed two-thirds of the fruit and vegetables). Without doubt, where manufacturers could deal direct, they had made the decisive choice to do so.[80]

So long as the manufacturers had made generic goods more or less to the wholesalers' order, they had had little reason to think in terms of demand. The job of the producers was to make things; it was up to the wholesalers to circulate and the retailers to sell them. But the development of pre-packaging, brand-name advertising, and direct marketing was changing all that; now the manufacturers had to think about consumption and the ways that they might influence it.

To rationalize demand with supply what was needed, many business people felt, was an 'engineering of consumption' to match the production engineers' achievements in industry. Advertising, the 'institution of abundance,' as David Potter called it, was, by the turn of the century, one already well-known, but as yet under-travelled avenue. In the inflationary years surrounding the Great War many manufacturers began experimenting with direct advertising in order to win 'consumer confidence' and build sales. Candy manufacturers, for example, were, by the outbreak of the war, extremely concerned about 'the gross libel on sweet meats' perpetrated by health reformers intent on proving 'that candy is injurious to health, that it causes early and rapid decay of teeth, that it impairs digestion and so forth.' Launching a major promotional campaign, the chocolate manufacturers under the leadership of Harold Lowney began a marketing blitz aimed at selling 'Chocolate as Food': 'it is a matter of actual scientific demonstration,' announced one advertisement, 'that one pound of chocolate produces the same amount of body-building nutriment as six eggs, a pint of milk or one pound of steak.' Lowney was delighted with the results of his campaign, and as chocolate sales rose, he beamed that the 'old bogey of the disintegrating tooth' had not only been given 'a solar-plexus,' but the idea that chocolate 'was but a luxury' had been changed into a 'favourable appreciation of chocolate as food.'[81] Similar campaigns were initiated during and just after the war by shoe makers, meat packers, drug manufacturers, furniture producers, and myriad others, all aimed at pacifying 'the subtle aggressions' of the buying public.

While there was nothing new in high-powered advertising, and while brand-name promotion had been growing since the 1880s, the temper of the literature was undeniably changing. The increasing use after 1912 of 'psychological advertising' has often been noticed by historians, but for our purposes its significance rests in the fact that in trying to manipulate what was now perceived to be a disinterested or even hostile mass of shoppers, the new form of advertising evidenced an increasing awareness on the part of manufacturers of the active and autonomous power of the consuming public.[82]

It was, however, the 'buyer's strike' and the consequent discovery of the consumer that ultimately fractured the Victorian consensus concerning the nature of the economy. The classical view that demand followed supply had been unravelling for some time, but few industrialists had retied the intellectual knots. Now, however, a large number of manufacturers were provoked into revising their attitudes to progress and shifting the emphasis away from production and onto consumption. Rather than worrying about increasing outputs to raise the standard of living, these industrialists suggested – in the midst of the postwar deflation – that the income issue had to come first. As they saw it, Canada did not suffer from a 'dearth of goods ... on the contrary, we are yearly growing richer in goods,' and as a result, it was not the issue of production that had to be addressed. What had really caused the wild inflation of the early twentieth century had not been inadequate supplies or immigration but excessively low wages: people just did not have the money to buy all the products that were in the system. Why, then, had prices risen and not fallen? The problem, these critics suggested – using the classic language of engineering – lay in the resultant oversupply of goods and the consequent wasteful duplication of services. As O.D. Street, the general manager of Canadian Westinghouse, explained in 1922, the whole economy had fallen in upon itself because 'we find ourselves confronted with a situation where the capacity to produce in most countries vastly exceeds the country's capacity to absorb.' Instead of lowering prices, increased production had encouraged them to go higher because the multiplication in the number of producers that followed from increased outputs had led to a duplication of services (including advertising costs), and this had served to push up overheads. 'Competing factories,' Street charged, 'do not produce at lower cost, in fact, the tendency is for production costs to rise because this [competing] production cuts into the business held by other factories.' Over time, this 'overproduction' forced businesses to price still higher to compensate for declining marketshares, with the result that the cost of goods outstripped wages. The result was not so much a buyer's strike as a surrender – consumers could not afford to keep buying.[83]

This view was going to gain widespread support during the early

1920s and again in the 1930s, two sharply deflationary periods, when consumer spending dropped away dramatically. The new approach rested on two pillars, one that manufacturing suffered from restricted demand resulting in overproduction and the other that the average Canadian's standard of living was too low. And converts to this consumer-centred overproduction thesis offered two primary solutions: first, that there had to be a 'weeding out of the undesirable manufacturers' through some form of price-fixing or production controls and, second, that wages had to be increased so that people would have the money to buy more highly priced goods. '[We] must deal ... with human beings as the paramount factor in the problem,' one manufacturer explained, and work towards 'the definite improvement of the conditions of the many, for the giving to them of greater purchasing power to enjoy the products of agriculture and industry.' Business people also offered two suggestions as to how the goal might be accomplished: in the more-stable price periods, they tended to argue that increased efficiency could reduce overheads without affecting wages, and they looked particularly at the savings that could be achieved through direct marketing. In the more disruptively deflationary periods, however, such as in the early twenties and early thirties, many of them were tempted to throw caution to the wind and argue that 'increased prices are needed' because only inflation 'would enable us to pay more to our workmen and our clerks.'[84] In some ways, these overproduction theorists in their fondness for inflation, were remaining true to an element of Canada's late-Victorian orthodoxy, but in suggesting that the solution to falling prices lay in higher wages and restricted outputs, these manufacturers were proposing something quite heretical.

The majority of Canadian manufacturers did not see things their way. Unlike the believers in a demand-driven economy, most makers of consumer goods in Canada continued to trust in the production-centred view that incomes had to follow outputs. However, the discovery of consumption also led these manufacturers to break with the nineteenth-century view to the extent that they began to argue that it was inflation which had caused the price collapse of the early 1920s and that deflation was good for business. 'A falling price level brings higher purchasing power,' one businessman now exclaimed, 'by giving an increase of real wages – a rising price level will have the opposite effect.' Instead of diagnosing the cause of depression as lying in low wages, these business people insisted that economic downturns resulted from the high prices flowing from inadequate production or inefficient distribution.

Consequently, the remedy to insufficient consumption 'is not to restrict production ... but to increase production, thereby reducing costs and prices, with the result that sales are increased and more employment can be given.' Since these manufacturers still believed that labour was the source of values, it followed that incomes could not go up without prices rising; hence 'an increase in wages would prove to be a reduction of wages and would lead not to increased employment but to an increase of unemployment.'[85]

In the 1920s this vision was to become the basis of what one historian has called 'the ethos of mass production': the view that constantly increasing the supply of goods would assure economic prosperity and social peace; that mass production itself might offer 'a panacea for the industrial and business ills of all nations.' And there could be no risk of saturation, for, as a National City Company newsletter announced in 1926, 'There can be no such thing as general overproduction so long as human wants remain unsatisfied ... There is not a family in a four-room apartment that would not like to have a six-room apartment ... there is not a family without a motor-car that would not like to have one, and most of the families having one would like to have another. The great problem of the world is so to organize and co-ordinate the resources and industries of the world to secure the greatest possible production and distribution of all the things that minister to the comfort and welfare of the population. That is the great appeal.'[86]

Though they differed in myriad ways, one thing still united 'inflationists' and advocates of deflationary 'mass production' in the 1920s. For both, attention for the first time shifted from the mundane concerns of production to the more-flamboyant preoccupations of distribution. As Stephen Fox has observed, in the 1920s 'distribution and marketing replac[ed] production as the natural limit on industrial activity.'[87] Where 'overproductionists' focused their attention on the need to encourage demand through high wages and controlled distribution, believers in mass production felt they needed to eliminate the 'bottlenecks' that inhibited the market's equilibrating tendencies. Both therefore looked to distribution as a way of solving industry's problems. But what needs to be emphasized is that this change had not been produced by impersonal economic forces. The discovery of marketing came because of real decisions made by real individuals living in dynamic business circumstances. In fact, the new concern with marketing was a direct result of the manufacturers' unpleasant confrontation with consumers in the years surrounding the First World War. It was a discovery forced on business people by the actions of Canadian shoppers; marketing came of age only after a perceived consumer revolt forced the business world to rethink its approach to the economy. It was a change of tremendous significance, and it was to have a dramatic and revolutionary impact on the independent retailers, who suddenly found themselves in the front line of a new entrepreneurial offensive.

THE MARKETING AGE

'In the last generation,' B.T. Huston, editor of the *Canadian Grocer*, observed, 'the methods of business have entirely changed. Transportation systems have annihilated distances; catalogues have supplemented samples, and the facilities for doing every kind of business have increased enormously.'[88] He might well have gone on, adding to his list the growth of the department stores, the revolution in packaging, the improvement in shop layouts, the development of national advertising, the growth and diversification of retailing, and the gradual decline in the wholesalers' influence. It was the speed and scope of these changes that more than anything else attested to the dramatic transformation which had affected consumption, production, and distribution in the late nineteenth and early twentieth centuries. The whole complexion of the domestic economy was irrevocably changing: where once demand had been small, it was now large; where once products had been few in number, the choice was now overwhelming. What lay behind all this was the manufacturers' expanded capacity to produce on a large scale and the public's deepening desire to consume. Large-scale production and falling prices had made increased consumption possible, and for all the hardship that would accompany the return of inflation, the mass market was here to stay. No one was more aware of this fact than the established shop owners, who, despite all their fears about the destabilization that had resulted from the coming of mass consumption, found that there was little they could do about it. Competition and the pressures exerted by both buyers and sellers were inexorable forces of change.

And as the inflation puffed up prices, the scope of these consumer expectations expanded. With consumption endangered by double-digit inflation, people took to the streets to demand the continuation of abundance and a guarantee of their power to spend. By the end of the First World War, customers had emerged as tangible things – no longer workers or farmers or bourgeois, but people whose goal it was to buy and whose power lay in their control over their disposable income. So great was the influence of this newly conceived grouping that when the postwar economic collapse finally came, business people were ready to blame it all on a buyer's strike. The recognition, not of consumption, but of the consumer shook business people out of their lingering belief in the producer society and opened their eyes to what practice had already in large measure revealed. Manufacturers now talked less about thrift and sacrifice and more about spending; they thought less about labour as a source of value and more about demand as a source of profits. Advertising and marketing in the 1920s became the business élite's response to its new constituency, and the logistics and preconceptions of salesmanship came to dictate the ways in which the consumer society was to be understood. The mixture of contempt and fear, the desire to pacify and soothe, the need to dismantle desires and then reintegrate them in acceptable ways – all these were objectives in part shaped by the manner in which the consumers were revealed and the oppositional relationship that underpinned their discovery.

Retailers were among the first business people to experience the mass market, and they were certainly the first to sense the power of the consumer agitans. As with other business people, their knee-jerk response to buyer unrest was to try to deflect the criticism away by stepping up their folkloric appeals for community cohesion and by denouncing the evil influences of trusts, combines, and price-chopping departmentals. Unfortunately, even as they complained about what was happening, they felt pressured to adapt. The real trouble with mass consumption was that it provoked an unpleasant kind of expertise among shoppers; store owners found their prices coming under unending scrutiny, and they discovered their shops continuously being criticized for not looking as clean or bright as Eaton's or Woolworth's. No matter how much their preferences might lead them to distance themselves from the mass merchandisers, consumer demands were foisting incessant price and display competition upon them. The need to meet the big stores on the questions of price and shopper convenience was not something that independent merchants could avoid. Adaptation was a process that could not be halted, and as fast as changes were instituted, new demands arose.

The manufacturers and wholesalers added to the retailers' worries, especially after the buyer's strike of 1920. Convinced as they were of the inefficiency of distribution, suppliers determined that they had to teach the shop owners how to sell. Retail stores, the brand-name producers now argued (and the jobbers agreed), were little other than showcases for products that had been packaged, advertised, and, to all intents, sold before the customer ever walked in. Essentially, what the manufacturers and wholesalers decided they had to do was to try to make the independent retailers adopt the strategies pioneered by bigger businesses: they wanted shopkeepers to begin cost accounting, to practise hand-to-mouth buying and cash selling, to departmentalize their stock, and to undertake suggestive marketing. As with the consumers, their models for much of this new approach were the chains and department stores, for as J.S. McLean of Canada Packers told a gathering of the Retail Merchants' Association, 'you've got to do business better than the chains ... You have got to do it by selling better goods and better service, by operating a cleaner shop ... the chains cannot compete with the individual retailer if the latter looks after his business in the right way.' A Montreal biscuit manufacturer concurred: 'only modern business systems and activities can stand out against a great concentrated industry ... the best way of meeting the competition of present trade, is to meet them on an equal footing.'[89] During the early twentieth century, both suppliers and consumers actively pressured retailers to adapt to the world of corporate capitalism. In the new business age, standing still became a luxury that no one could afford.

4

Progressive Retailing

The transformation of merchandising was a complicated process. It was shaped by the growth in consumer tastes, by the gendering of shopping, by trade competition, by shifts in manufacturer attitudes, and by the collapse in wholesaler authority. In demanding better goods, cheaper prices, and more attractive displays, shoppers were offering modernizing shopkeepers the carrot of increased sales, an offer which, in light of the stick of monopoly wielded by the mass merchandisers, shop owners refused at their peril. Indeed, while trade association members reacted with hostility to the growth in competition and the disintegration of traditional trade relationships, they did not long believe they could insulate themselves against the mass market's influence. After all, the customers who were picking up their underwear at Eaton's were buying their borax in the main-street store. Shoppers did not suspend their tastes just because they moved from a chain store to an independent: they still wanted to find cleanliness, attractiveness, and price competitiveness. Similarly, the independent retailers' suppliers did not want to provide significantly more services or longer credits to their independent customers than they were offering the corporate giants. As a result the independents had to compete directly with the mass merchandisers and to try, without the teams of buyers and scores of managers, to offer comparable selections of goods and values. Doing so doubtless placed a heavy burden on store proprietors, intensifying their business worries and driving still deeper the competitive wedge that divided them from their neighbours. But it also forced them to emulate, as far as possible, the methods that were being pioneered by larger enterprises.

At heart it was a question of power. To what extent could retailers afford to ignore changes that were, by all accounts, reflecting and enhancing the tastes of their customers and the desires of their suppliers? As wholesalers and manufacturers came to accept the realities of the consumer economy, most of them retreated from the idea that demand was a simple function of production and acknowledged that consumer spending had to be fostered and directed. This realization pushed certain manufacturers first to expand their interest in advertising and direct marketing and later to increase their involvement in distribution, while it led others to press store modernization as an instrument for reducing prices. Wholesalers in the meantime, spurred to action by a sense of their declining importance, also moved to secure their remaining influence over merchandising by organizing retail buying groups and by altering credit relations. Through their sales promotional material and in the preconditions they established for buyers wanting to handle their products, suppliers charted the course of retail change. They urged independent shopkeepers to abandon service and move to cash or some form of instalment selling; they pressured them to give up their traditional ad hoc methods of accounting and adopt more 'scientific' bookkeeping; they helped them to modernize their fixtures and departmentalize their stock; and they even encouraged them to experiment with such chain store marketing practices as high-turnover selling and self-service.

In this way, the transformation of nineteenth-century merchandising involved not only the development of the mass merchandisers but also the modernization of independent retailing. If proprietary capitalism was to survive in the consumer economy, it could do so only by changing. It had to accept the more complete domination of large-scale capital and adjust to the selling practices of its most-hated competitors. Essentially, independent enterprise had to evolve into a relationship of complementarity with big business. For all that folklorically minded proprietary businessmen continued to protest their opposition to consolidated capital and their independence from it, they were unable to keep themselves apart. The process of change did not, however, affect all business people equally or at the same time: the first to adapt appear to have been those who were most affected by the competition of the mass merchandisers and those who, because of their size, attracted the scrutiny of their price-conscious customers and their market-sensitive suppliers. Adaptation therefore served at once to push the small capitalist independents into an emulation of large-scale business and also to exacerbate the tensions between the more 'progressive' merchants and those shoestring traders who could not afford to modernize.

MODERNIZING THE SHOP-FLOOR

The typical store of yesteryear, the *Canadian Grocer* observed in 1900, was 'untidy – floor soiled, windows dirty, stock poorly arranged, counters and scales sticky, and everywhere a manifest lack of order and system.'[1] Gloomy, dank, low-ceilinged, its air heavy with the smells of putrefying food and mouldering cloth, the real mid-nineteenth-century shop seems inseparable now from its Dickensian stereotype. Though the image was almost certainly an exaggeration (many of the better-class urban stores were already bright and clean and nicely arranged by the late eighteenth century), there remained enough truth to it for the modernizing retailers to have had little trouble convincing themselves of their own radical break with the past. Part of what had made mid-nineteenth-century stores appear so shoddy and disorganized was the lack of balance and order in their displays. There was, however, little that could be done about this problem. Because almost everything that the merchants sold arrived at their stores in bulk, whatever packaging was done had to take place on the premises. Moreover, because of the limits of transportation and communication, retailers had to carry fairly extensive stocks.

Storage and display were serious problems for mid-nineteenth-century retailers: currants and raisins came in barrels, packed so tight they had to be cut out with a knife before being washed and separated; sugar arrived in one-ton hogsheads and had to be dug out with a shovel (the hard crystals on the top to be mixed in a sugar grinder with the molasses at the bottom); butter came in barrels or sometimes in blocks, and it therefore had to be scooped out or cut; dried fruit had to have the stones removed; flour, cereals, and biscuits all came in huge five-foot barrels; eggs were shipped in large crates packed in straw or else pickled in enormous jugs. All these goods had to be weighed and packaged in home-made cartons or bags made of blue graph paper and marked in pencil as to their contents. Meat – generally bacon in a grocery store – was kept hanging with muslin drawn over it at night; where fruit was stocked, it had to be hung up for ripening and then displayed in wicker baskets or else placed in the sun on the window-sills. Jam was most often supplied in casks, and people would bring their own jars to be filled. Butchers had to have their own brine tanks and long salting trays. Clothing and shoes also had no containers, and they were kept rolled or folded on shelves or loose in large boxes; notions, hosiery, and small goods had to be stored behind or on top of counters or in small bins on the floor. Heavier goods – tools, buckets, brooms, chairs, and tables – were often hung from the ceiling because of the problem of space. Only stores that sold small, intrinsically attractive goods, such as jewellery, toys, high-priced cloth, hats, china, and millinery, or else those that carried goods which lent themselves to bottling or placement in jars – drugs and confectionery – could ever hope to present an appearance of cleanliness and symmetry.

The problems involved in storage and display led shopkeepers to present their wares in what now seems a peculiar way. The standard shop of the mid-nineteenth century was rectangularly shaped with counters running along three sides. Behind these closed wood counters were floor-to-ceiling shelves on which the bagged, bundled, or boxed goods were stored and displayed. In most shops the central floor space was kept as empty as possible (because of space constraints, larger barrels or furnishings sometimes had to be kept there), though better-class businesses such as millinery, drapery, and jewellery stores would generally have stools or chairs on the customer side of the counter to allow greater comfort during the viewing of samples. Almost invariable clerks – whom customers could see only from the waist up – would take from the shelves every item the buyer wanted to see. Without specifically asking to inspect an item, shoppers would be able to see the goods they bought only from a distance of a couple of metres. The lack of product standardization, especially in fresh foods, was a further encouragement to this labour-intensive form of merchandising. As one trade expert noted, if customers were allowed to choose their own fruit and vegetables, the first in the store 'would skin over everything, taking the cream and leaving the rest skim milk.'[2]

It was the proliferation of pre-packaged goods after 1870 that first allowed shopkeepers to revolutionize their displays. Once jams and preserves became obtainable in small jars and tins, cereals and biscuits in boxes, and fruit and vegetables in cans, a new kind of order was possible even in that most disorderly of shops, the grocery. In a short time, stores became shrines to the pre-packaged product. Like so many Imhoteps, retailers could be found constructing enormous pyramids of goods, stacking the tins of Gilett's Lye and Royal Baking Soda and Vinola tomatoes on the countertops and shelves, building up the levels until the mountain of cans towered over the counters, over the customers, over the store interiors. Behind their silent salesmen they lined up their boxes and jars, neatly and harmoniously arranging the shelves to best complement each size, colour, and type. By the 1890s shoe retailers were also overhauling their shops, as the arrival of cardboard boxes banished the bins and crates and opened up the central floor space. Though the lack of a standard size made their constructions somewhat unsteady, shoe merchants began stacking the cartons up the walls from floor to ceiling, giving their shops the look of having being built out of boxes. For the clothing merchant, the rise of ready-mades and alongside them the increasing use of the clothes hanger and horse (called a mantle-hanger until the 1890s, an indication of its limited use) served to sweep jackets, dresses, skirts, and coats off the counters and out of their storage chests (strangely, blouses and shirts remained folded rather than hung).[3]

If new packaging helped organize many of the stores that dealt in smaller goods, more rapid deliveries speeded the transformation of those that handled the larger items. Furniture and appliances posed the greatest display and storage difficulties for retailers because of the enormous amount of space they occupied, and traditionally tradesmen had gotten around this problem by piling up their stock, cramming it into basements and attics and suspending as much as they could from the rafters. The problems of shipping and stocking were so severe that until the 1880s most furniture stores were located within easy reach of the factory, and with the notable exception of the big Jacques and Hay works in Toronto, few manufacturers had to make use of long-distance transportation. Improvements in travel and communication in the late nineteenth century not only opened regional and even national markets; they also allowed for more-frequent buying and reduced the merchants' need to carry such heavy stocks. Contact between manufacturers and retailers stepped up as catalogues began to be used, and annual furniture shows were established to draw more far-flung distributers into closer relationships. The furniture and appliance manufacturers became avid promoters of every new communication and transport technology – mail orders, automobiles, telephones – anything that might sensitize them to their local markets (buy a telephone, one trade booster urged the retailers, and 'connect up with nationally advertised goods at any time'). One sure sign of the increasing frequency of ordering is that manufacturers began in the 1910s to revise their catalogue price-lists every six months rather than every year. In fact, by the late 1920s some appliance manufacturers had even worked out a system whereby their smaller 'agents' kept only one sample of each model or just a brochure in the shop, and customers wanting to purchase an item had the product shipped to them direct from the warehouse.[4]

The acceleration of shipping and communication ultimately allowed for less stock to be kept on hand, and like pre-packaging, this change facilitated the transformation of store layouts. Eaton's (copying Wanna-maker's in Philadelphia) first experimented around the turn of the century with uncrowding the furniture display and laying out the stock in such a way as to simulate a real room. The great advantage of the authentic display, the manager of Eaton's furniture department explained, was that 'it will often cause a person to buy more than they originally intended to. They are looking, probably, at a living room suite, but the other decorations and goods are shown up so well that they think they would like to have them also.' The new showroom appearance of the furniture store had thus ushered in the age of the 'ensemble': the display in which complementary cushions, lamps, carpets, and bric-à-brac were featured in order to tempt the consumer into buying a package. By the 1920s some manufacturers had begun producing goods and fabrics to complement their furniture and had started hiring professional decorators who could direct merchants in the arrangement of their ensembles.[5] The new furniture store had therefore bridged the chasms that separated home and shop and factory, and who now would think of hanging their dining-room sets from the ceiling?

The new space available to storekeepers did, however, create its own demands, and as retailers tidied up their stores, they acquired a whole range of new fixtures designed to enhance the appearance of their stock. Silent salesmen found a place in every up-to-date business (these appropriately named fixtures were large glass-fronted and -topped cases with glass shelves), as did smaller glass 'bins' that could be stood on the floor or stacked. Praised as 'sanitary and dust-proof' and far more appealing than 'the unsightly barrels which have been a time-honoured feature of the general store,' these new glass fixtures protected the stock while at the same time inviting the customer's inquiry. Keep this observation in mind: 'quality goods and poor fixtures are like diamonds in a poor setting.' But it was not just a matter of having the right cases; the fixtures also had to be placed in such a way as to create 'a buying atmosphere.' When customers entered a modern store, it was crucial that 'the desired suggestions would be born right in the[ir] mind[s].' Because retailers had preconceptions about their female customers' behaviour, they were convinced that they made decision on impulse rather than reason. Consequently, in store layout, it was 'all impression – all appearance – of course, but its effect is quite apparent on the mind. And, after all, this is the very desideratum wanted, for unless one is in the proper mind one does not buy.'[6]

As customers became more price and quality conscious and began to exploit the advantage latent in pre-packaging (the ability to 'shop around'), storekeepers grew increasingly sensitive to the need to attract women into their shops. As every modern proprietor knew, 'You've got to hustle for trade these days, it doesn't always walk into your store without a pressing invitation.' To a large degree the job of attracting customers to shop involved, the marketing experts argued, updating the appearance of the store in order to excite an innately female desire to spend. The new store had to be bright and sterile: all high centre fixtures had to be removed, counters shifted away from shelves to give customers a clearer view, shelves lowered and the highest goods brought down to around eye-level, and display cases moved to the centre like islands around which the customers might surge and flow. Butcher shops should install refrigerators to keep goods cool, and large fans should be set whirring overhead to 'eliminate fly pests.' Out of the drug store must go the traditional globes of green, yellow, and red, the sponges, glass counters, trusses, and artificial limbs. General storekeepers were instructed: 'Do not spread sawdust all over the floor, sawdust and modern hosiery are not on friendly terms with each other ... Do not permit men and boys to lounge in the store ... Housewives hate to walk into a store that is crowded with loafers who stare at her blankly as she makes her purchases.' Cleanliness improved all things, no matter how homely: 'even a pound of lard is a thing of beauty when it is fresh, and sweet, and clean.' Lighting bright, floors of linoleum, prices clearly marked, groceries at rear and dry goods at front, 'impulse items' where the shopper could not miss them – such was the look of the modern store. In the past few years 'the conditions of trading have changed so rapidly that it has been almost bewildering,' a Jarvis store owner of fifty-seven years complained in 1928; 'even the old-time smells have been banished by ventilation.'[7]

Shopkeepers knew that the ways in which goods were displayed were becoming almost as important as the products themselves. Concern over the unclean had been progressively growing over the course of the nineteenth century as people dug sewers, drained swamps, and paved streets in order to purify and deodorize their environment. As anxieties over pollution had increased, European scientists had turned their attention to product quality. Food was the primary target of their inquiries: in 1820 Accum had published his *Treatise on Adulterations of*

Food and Culinary Poisons, which disclosed that almost everything people ate and drank was more or less poisonous ('There is Death in the
Pot,' read the cover of the first edition of Accum's book); and in 1850 Dr
Hassall provoked a parliamentary investigation in England with his
announcement in the *Lancet* that it was impossible to find pure food
anywhere in London.[8] Significantly, politicians in Canada awoke to the
problem of adulteration only in the mid-1870s, when the federal government authorized the testing of flour, liquor, meat, and petroleum moving between provinces and into or out of the country. Temperance, the
Victorian bourgeoisie's first, knee-jerk moral response to the developing
mass market (give the people money and they will drink it away), was
the engine that drove this first legislative intervention into the market-
place, but things would not stop there. Larger municipalities soon followed the federal initiative by appointing their own milk, meat, and
water inspectors, and a decade later, in 1884, Macdonald's Conservatives, under prodding from the medical and scientific establishments,
pushed forward a bill which would have allowed for the federal supervision of all retailed foods. Rumours of ergot in rye, meat cut from dis-
eased cattle, milk laced with pulverized horse brains, coffee mixed with
sawdust, green tea coloured with copper sulphate, and liquor tainted
with sulphuric acid and oil had excited the fears of the scientifically
informed: 'the germs of death are scattered all around us,' exclaimed Dr
C.A. Lesage in the House of Commons, and 'they are [being] sold under
the cover of incognito.'[9]

As medical propaganda concerning cleanliness and purity filtered
through society, it blended with, rather than destroyed, the popular
demand for goods, and instead of leading people to buy fewer, more-
reputable products, it induced consumers to demand a rise in qualities
but not prices. What began with the moralizing middle class's concern
over the effects of consumerism on product quality and consumer self-
discipline quickly became a popular demand for greater standardization. There is little doubt that one of the results of the broad attack on
product quality was that people of moderate means – civil servants,
clerks, skilled workers – came to accept new standards of cleanliness as
necessary and grew increasingly suspicious of cheap foods and drugs.
As one semi-skilled employee of International Harvester explained in
1919, the worker who wants to be 'a respectable citizen ... must have a
respectable environment and live in that manner too, by having everything up-to-date, both with regard to sanitary arrangements in his
house, cleanliness of his house, and the appearance of himself and his

children too, both in the respectability of clothing and also the necessities of life.'[10]

What the desire for pure goods translated into was not a decrease in consumption but rather an increasing emphasis on packaging. When the National Council of Women debated the issue of shoddy goods, its members proposed the labelling of products with their contents and the standardizing of tins and bottles to prevent false weights and measures; when the Trades and Labor Congress discussed the adulteration of canned goods, its solution was the marking of all products with their contents and the dating of containers. Not surprisingly, cleanliness became a major concern for shopkeepers: floors had to be swept, counters dusted, scales and scoops kept free of grease, and everything ventilated to prevent the accumulation of 'rancid and disagreeable odours ... greasy barrels and tubs should be placed so that they will not come into contact with women's skirts.' As stores all over the country switched their names to 'The Pure Food Grocery' or 'The Temple of Purity' or even 'The Clean Shop,' retailers were clearly taking note of the fact that 'the clean store impresses her [the customer] at once with the idea that what she buys is clean and good.' The clean store, in short, built 'confidence and custom.'[11]

Flies became particular targets of the retail merchants' brush and broom. Once thought to be almost useful 'as purifiers of the air ... and in consuming solid matter that would otherwise decay into elements that would circulate offensively,' they were transformed by the Pasteurian revolution into the agents of sickness and death. 'In its search for food it goes from one place to another,' a school text warned; 'it may feed on the waste material from our digestive system or on the secretions from the mouth or nose, if these are not properly disposed of, and its next feeding place may be the sugar bowl or the milk jug.' The house fly carried death on its hairy feet – typhoid, diphtheria, consumption, influenza, pneumonia, erysipelas. The fly, observed one eminent microbiologist, 'is the universal distributor of filth and disease.'[12]

War on the fly necessitated dramatic preparations: grocers were urged to put in ceiling fans to keep the air moving, butchers were advised to shelter their meat behind glass, and fruiterers were told to throw mesh over their wares; bins and buckets proliferated, products were moved off the streets, and tarpaulins were stretched over delivery wagons. 'Stop the fly in his mad careers,' North America's biggest manufacturer of sticky fly-paper cheered as the retailers sprayed and swatted; 'we must destroy the flies, not [just] drive them from place to place.'

The shopkeeper of tomorrow, predicted one columnist in 1910, 'will be an expert in the art of ventilation ... the shop, the counter, the scales, will all be kept as clean as the operating room and the instruments in an hospital ... A generation ago, the fixation with cleanliness would have been regarded as insane fastidiousness ... Today, the people demand it.'[13]

The transformation of the shopkeepers' physical world served to alter more than just its olfactory impact. In the traditional store, where boxes and barrels and home-made blue bags had predominated, the customer who wanted to see something had to be shown it by the owner or his clerks. Silent salesmen, glass bins, and lowered shelving did not entirely eliminate this aspect of service – shelves were still kept safely behind counters, and glass bins and silent salesmen could be opened only from behind – but they did allow the shopper an unobstructed view of the goods they were considering. The 'progressive' store of the early twentieth century served as a way station between the traditional shop and the self-serve showroom. In fact, even as store modernization approached its maturity, some retailers began flirting with its heir apparent. In January 1914 the first self-service shoe store opened in Toronto, and four years later, H.M. Jenkins set up the first Canadian self-serve grocery.[14]

The process of simplifying the selling method and increasing the flow of goods and money also had an impact on shop labour, for as the *Canadian Grocer* explained, the goal of modernization 'was to enable the clerks to wait on a greater number of customers in a given time.' The point should not be taken too literally since 'efficiency' was a relative term and until self-service began to cut into the workforce, most stores still employed an extraordinary number of clerks (a big urban grocery store with an annual turnover of $200,000 in 1918–20 could employ up to twenty-five workers, a pharmacy of similar size as many as twenty, a clothing shop perhaps fifteen). And yet modernization was intended to increase the number of customers without significantly adding to the payroll, thus allowing for more money to be made. In fact, the whole trend in retail labour management, though very irregular, was towards greater output, increased specialization, and a finer division of labour.[15]

Sales clerks who might once have not only sold goods in various parts of the store but also assisted in price marking, preparing bulk goods, wrapping, stocktaking, and decorating were increasingly being made responsible only for selling in a limited number of departments.[16] For the owner-manager, store modernization brought greater responsibilities for publicity, finance, accounts, and control and a reduction in the amount of time actually spent with the customers. Where one salesperson might now be responsible for dressing the windows and arranging the displays, another would have the duty of stocktaking and merchandise receiving. This process of specialization had a significant impact on gender balances and also on retail ideologies. Since dispensing packets and ready-made wares required comparatively little expertise, the 'prestige' of both shop worker and shop necessarily suffered.

Outside women's clothing and dry goods – where females occupied almost all the clerical positions – retail workplaces remained carefully segregated according to sex. Though a fast-increasing segment of the workforce, the shop-girl was regarded rather disdainfully by employers as a symbol of retailing's de-skilling. In grocery stores women were hired largely to work cash registers; in shoe businesses they sold stockings and incidentals; in pharmacies they handled the cosmetic trade. According to the shop custom, they were erratic and unreliable, best suited to those branches of trade where 'dress and pleasant manners are really more necessary than mental ability.' Never regarded as capable of 'salesmanship' (the gendering of the term was no accident), female clerks were hired because retail selling had been 'reduced' to 'handing out packets of tea from eight to five.' Some shopkeepers even candidly admitted that they believed the girls 'should be at school or at home playing with their dolls' rather than working in a shop.[17]

The drift of all this should be clear: modernization was transforming the retail shop into a showcase for goods, and it was the orderly displaying of products that was becoming its primary function. But the goods that retailers were exhibiting were no longer identified with them; rather, they were now associated with their manufacturer. This, undoubtedly, was the greatest change brought on by pre-packaging, for in the new world of boxes and brands, when one bought Post's Grape-Nuts from a retailer, there was no doubt that it was *Post's* Grape-Nuts that one was buying. How much different would it have been to have bought an unspecified cereal packaged in a hand-folded blue paper bag: would it not then have seemed the *shopkeeper's* Grape-Nuts and not Post's, even if Mr Post's factory had made it? The implied marginalization of retailers in the minds of the consumers and the changing nature of their shops began the process of making distribution itself into a kind of promotional mechanism, a sort of free-standing corollary to the newspaper ad and the sales catalogue. And like those other forms of promotion, the real onus on the retail outlet would gradually become that of projecting the right image and presenting someone else's products in

the clearest possible way. This obligation in turn compelled shopkeepers to watch more closely each other's successes and, in the early twentieth century, to make the departmentals and chains into models to be
emulated.

UP-TO-DATE MANAGEMENT

Pre-packaging, more rapid deliveries, and improved selling also
changed the terms under which goods were sold. Instead of having to
rely upon the wholesaler to supply the qualities and quantities appropriate to their clientele, the retailers could, by dealing directly with the
producers, more easily determine for themselves the goods that would
fill their shelves. They could, thanks to the expansion of the rail system
and later the growth of the trucking industry, order more frequently,
receive goods more rapidly, and stock less heavily. One Sudbury clothing retailer reported how he always went to Toronto himself, bought his
stock from the factories, and shipped the goods up to his store. He made
the trip at irregular intervals – whenever his stock ran down – paying
cash as he earned it, but he guessed that he was in Toronto every couple
of weeks. By the mid-1920s a Napanee general-store owner also boasted
about the speed of shipping, insisting that with the development of
trucking he could telephone Belleville for goods one day and have them
delivered the next. Ordering 'hand to mouth,' as it had come to be
known, enabled shopkeepers to buy only what goods they needed,
thereby reducing their insurance costs and lowering the risks of over-
stocking. As the Canadian Grocer pointed out as early as 1900, 'it pays
best to trade on the hand to mouth system, whatever your neighbour
may think of you [for carrying such light stocks]. In these days of fierce
competition, you need buy only what is required for immediate use, for
even the best firms appreciate the very smallest orders.'[18]

By the First World War, store owners were generally buying more frequently and in smaller lots. F.A. Edwards, a Bayfield, Ontario, general-
store owner, usually placed orders twice monthly, buying on average
ninety separate lines from his major dry goods supplier, Gordon
Mackay and Company, each month. In addition, from 1927 to 1938
Edwards dealt with eighty-seven other wholesalers and manufacturers.
This profligacy was typical: Cairncross and Lawrence, a London drug
store, in an average month in the late twenties placed orders to sixty different suppliers; Nathan Fine, a family clothier in Peterborough had
seventy-two different suppliers; a furniture dealer in Sudbury had

forty-four; a grocer in Bronte, Ontario, had forty-seven. These suppliers were also widely spread all across the country: James Mulholland, a men's clothier in Picton, Ontario, was buying from manufacturers in seventeen different places ranging from Truro, Nova Scotia, to Rock Island, Illinois. And while the individual size of the orders would vary according to trade, the shipments received from each supplier for the business just cited averaged around $40.[19] It was all a far cry from the traditional domination of the individual wholesale merchant over all the supplies going out to his flotilla of retail outlets.

But the retailers purchased their increased ability to gear supply to demand at a high price, for what the growing use of private branding and hand-to-hand buying really produced was a tightening of the supplier's relations with the retailers. One of the most significant indicators of this development was the increased stringency being applied to the credit offered to retailers on their purchases. In the nineteenth century, wholesalers had not only provided store owners with goods; they had also supplied them with almost all of their non-familial short-term credit. As the century progressed and as the speed of commercial transactions increased, the terms of that credit became shorter.[20] In the 1870s and 1880s credit of 120 days had been considered reasonable, and some wholesalers had even offered handsome discounts on goods paid in six months. The 'cash' discount generally referred to payment within 30 days, though even Timothy Eaton in 1894 found one supplier willing to give a cash discount on 60 days. By the First World War, however, the cash terms offered by manufacturers and wholesalers in dry goods, clothing, groceries, and hardware had fallen fairly dramatically to 10 days, and few could expect any reduction in price if their notes were payable in over 30.[21]

The pressure in favour of shortened terms placed many retailers in a precarious position; it meant that in order to pay their suppliers or to qualify for discounts, they had to collect on their own customer accounts fairly rapidly. Doing so could prove a significant problem, particularly for those shopkeepers serving a clientele whose income was insecure. Where an account was questionable or where the debtor was unable to pay on time, the retailer might find himself cornered. The problem for storekeepers was that they lacked the legal recourse which their suppliers used against them. Shop owners found unpaid customer accounts of under $20 virtually impossible to collect. Special collection agencies refused to follow up on small accounts, and solicitors' fees were too high to justify their being hired to press recalcitrant debtors. In contrast, failing to pay even small debts to a supplier could be fatal to the independent storekeeper since 'the day the suit against him is reported in Dun's or Bradstreet's sheet he is placed on a cash basis [by all his suppliers] and the circulation of his merchandise becomes C.O.D. only.'[22]

'Service' retailing had been pre–First World War Canada's most characteristic form of distribution. Essential in many cash-starved communities, store credit was 'expected to carry the farmer from crop to crop' and worker from pay-day to pay-day. Generally the credit that shoppers obtained was unsecured by a lien or mortgage of any kind, though merchants in resource communities, such as in the Maritime outports, often managed to work their customers into a relationship of real debt dependency.[23] Similarly, where large expensive products were involved, security could be required: farm implement companies, for example, in the pre-war period when selling machinery obtained chattel mortgages under which farmers pledged a certain number of acres of a specified crop to the vendor, agreeing to deliver the harvested produce to a designated elevator and making out the ticket of sale in the name of the creditor. But these iniquitous arrangements did not govern the purchase of most goods in the majority of places. Indeed, the great bulk of book credit was handled in a very haphazard manner, and the terms for repayment were remarkably flexible. In places where only one cash crop was grown, farmers would pay their bill for the year at harvest time; in other regions they amortized their debts more gradually. Often farmers sold eggs or milk to the retailer, and occasionally shopkeepers themselves employed their own customers and retained their wages in order to pay off previously acquired debts.[24]

There was no rule governing the length of time it took to clear away the proverbial tick. Thirty per cent of the accounts of Alexander Davidson, an Ennotville, Ontario, shoe dealer in the 1890s who catered to the farm trade, were outstanding for over one year and a further third were paid in between two and twelve months. At Stepler's drug store in Strathroy in the early 1920s, customers were usually expected to make payments on credit accounts twice yearly, and they were generally required to discharge annual accounts in full before they were granted further accommodation. However, people tended to set their own terms: most made bimonthly payments (61 per cent); others paid twice a year (23 per cent); some redeemed accounts in full but did so only once a year (15 per cent); a few, however, never paid at all. In May 1926 William Moore, a Carradoe farmer, made purchases at Stepler's drug store valued at $13.75. Four years later, with the account still unsettled, Stepler imposed a one-dollar interest charge on the debt, and the store continued to add one more dollar per annum to the account by way of interest until the account was finally dropped from the books in 1935 as uncollectable. As the dominion statistician observed in 1933, though individual book accounts were invariably small – 'hand-to-mouth debts as it were' – they totalled enormous amounts. Indeed, 'few farmers can cultivate their farms without some credit from either a bank or store, and if no credit were extended, they could neither purchase nor produce anything.'[25]

In Canada's larger towns and cities, credit was also a major element in the distribution system at least until the 1920s, though most stores had also been selling for cash from the 1870s. In fact, while many stores in the poorest areas had to offer credit to their customers and while the rich thought it demeaning to pay on delivery, consumers of moderate means were paying up front in most of the shops that had opened in their neighbourhoods by the 1910s. Stuart Harris, a Toronto butcher, might not be considered untypical of those relatively affluent retailers serving a well-to-do working-class neighbourhood. His store was largely 'cash and carry,' for while he employed one delivery boy two days a week and offered some credit, in 1919 his credit sales accounted for about 28 per cent of his annual turnover. As female consumers of comfortable means increasingly went after the best price for the goods they desired, they broke the credit connection that bound the family to the neighbourhood shop. It was therefore among the consumers who had been newly empowered by the mass market that cash made its first inroads and not among the haute bourgeoisie. Indeed, most affluent people were far more indebted to the local shopkeepers than were the poor.[26]

Consumer actions, preferences, and price competition had already, by the First World War, helped move ambitious retailers away from the open book, but the final retreat was sounded by the shopkeepers' creditors, not their customers. The merchant who collected on his accounts only once or twice a year had to buy goods on similar terms from his suppliers. Although most retailers before the First World War resisted the total abandonment of credit in order to keep at least a core of regular customers, they could not afford the same luxury with their suppliers. The tightening of mercantile credit was one of the strongest forces pushing retailers away from traditional forms of credit. 'In the past,' one grocer wrote to a debtor concerning his outstanding account, 'jobbers allowed us 30 days credit on our purchases which made it possible for us to be accordingly lenient with our accounts. However, these jobbers now insist upon all accounts being paid each week. You can see what this does to us when our customers do not pay us accordingly.'[27] A Roland for an Oliver, the retailers might say: they had less time to pay, and so their customers would have to be more efficient as well. Simple perhaps, but it was the beginning of the end for the open book.

Unfortunately, switching completely to cash was a hazardous business – retailers could easily offend good customers, and they risked encouraging comparative shopping – and so, not surprisingly, the vast majority of retailers initially preferred improving the credit system to forsaking it. In order to lower prices without abandoning all their credit, storekeepers began experimenting with mechanisms for reducing the chances of default. Some had customers fill out personal information forms at the shop, and they fixed maximums on the credit allowed and billed monthly. In other communities retailers tried to expand on this idea by establishing vast customer-rating; services: these were centralized banks of information where the names of delinquent shoppers could be registered. Another solution was to improve the chances of collecting on a bad account, and since court actions were difficult and unpopular, this meant working out some way of frightening people into paying their bills. It was to accomplish this end that business people organized cooperative creditors' associations to chase down their customers. Evidently, credit was coming more and more into question even among those who did not feel they could live without it. In fact, the 'credit evil' was the major topic of discussion at the founding meeting of the western RMA in 1905, and shop owners seemed unanimous in their belief that while they had no idea how it could be introduced into the countryside, a cash system should be collectively adopted as soon as possible.[28]

In those trades where customer credit could not be sacrificed or restricted, new forms of lending gradually rose in prominence. During the interwar years, there had been a dramatic increase in the use of instalment selling by retailers, who saw hire purchase as a substitute for the less-secure form of open-book credit. Under the terms of a hire-purchase sale, the customer agreed to pay the merchant according to a pre-arranged schedule, with interest calculated according to the length of time between delivery of the article and the final payment. Furniture companies in the 1880s were the first to use instalment selling on a large scale, and they were soon followed by sewing machine, piano, and harmonium dealers. In the 1920s retailers of automobiles and radios also adopted the hire-purchase method. During the Depression, when wholesale credit tightened further and debts became increasingly difficult to collect, storekeepers in many different trades began to sell on instalment. In 1930 instalment sales made up 21.5 per cent of all retail credit sales. Ten years later a full 37.5 percent of credit sales took the form of hire-purchase arrangements. Selling on instalment became popular in almost every trade in the twenties and thirties except for those which dealt in consumables. Few small grocers, pharmacists, or general merchants could sell through a hire-purchase plan, but more and more automotive dealers, furniture salesmen, and appliance retailers did; the instalment bug now even bit the clothing trade, and by 1940 over 50 per cent of all the ready-made apparel being sold on credit was coming under a regular monthly payment plan. Time sales also accounted for 20 per cent of the heating fuels being sold to consumers and a quarter of all the hardware sold.[29]

The philosophy behind the instalment method was, however, very different from that underlying the open book. Unlike the relationship with the traditional service retailer, whose control over his accounts was largely personal and familial, the bond between customer and merchant under the instalment plan was entirely legal. In contrast to the retailer who liked to think of interest as a moral punishment inflicted upon those who intended to defraud, the instalment seller treated it as an intrinsic part of the commodity's price. He or she did so because the customer was generally unknown to the creditor except through a contractual agreement. Once believed to be the paramount expression of the community's moral worth, credit was here being used as the measure of its business sense. It had become the weapon of a legal system that had already shed its pre-capitalist commitment to regulating the substantive fairness of economic exchanges. Store credit was making its fundamental twentieth-century transition from a quasi-communitarian to a purely commercial exchange.

This increasing institutionalization of the credit system led naturally to the rise of the independent sales-financing companies and their growing domination over the system of hire-purchase selling. Under a sales-financing agreement, the retailer, in a single transaction, sold an article on a deferred payment plan to a customer and at the same time sold the credit contract to a second company. The dealer often made out the sales agreement on forms provided by the finance company and imposed interest according to a predetermined schedule. Perversely enough, the store owner had become an intermediary between the financial institution and a potential borrower (or as one retailer complained, the finance company treated him 'as a manager and not as a proprietor'). In some cases the retailer remained responsible, as the finance company's 'agent,' for collecting the instalments; in others the company that held the paper collected the money. The most common practice by the 1920s was for the shop owner to discount the lien he had received with the manufacturer (for, say, 80 per cent of face value) and for the manufacturer then to discount the note with a sales finance company (at 90 per cent).[30] Not surprisingly, the bulk of sales financing concerned the purchase of the larger consumer durables: passenger cars made up one-third of the intermediaries' business, and electrical appliances and radios comprised 10 per cent. According to Professor E.P. Neufeld, the growth of the sales intermediaries had been startling: corporate assets, which in 1926 had stood at $24 million, had risen by 1929 to $55 million, and in 1940 they stood at $72 million. The development of the sales finance companies is something of a barometer of open-book credit's declining fortunes; of the eighty-two companies in operation in 1940, twenty-five had opened between 1925 and 1929 and twenty-one between 1935 and 1939.[31]

This centralization of consumer credit was also manifested in the sudden interest taken by large financial organizations in funding consumer borrowing. Until the 1920s individuals who needed personal loans had had few real options; if a retailer would not credit them with the desired goods, then there had remained only family or friends or an advance from a moneylender or pawnbroker. It would have been virtually impossible for anyone to obtain a bank loan for consumer purposes, and there were no independent consumer finance companies. In the late 1920s, however, large-scale capital became involved for the first time in the business of consumer lending. In 1928 the first consumer loan company, Central Finance Corporation (later Household Finance), was incorporated, and in the mid-thirties the Canadian Bank of Commerce opened the dominion's first personal loans division. During the 1930s a hierarchy of lending swiftly emerged in the rapidly developing consumer finance sector; the least-attractive customers continuing to ply the traditional credit channels, while the most secure borrowers turned to the Commerce.

It was the personal loan companies which, by assuming many of the responsibilities once shouldered by the storekeeper, made the greatest impact on retailing. These intermediaries served the type of customers

Monod, David. Store Wars. Shopkeepers &
the Culture of Mass Marketing
(1890-1939) (Canada) (1996)

Parallels = US retailers:

"progress" "modern" — retailers see ?
in early 2012 c. — extended businesses
to be "progressive"   P 66

General Sts of statements ~88 - 89
controlled price stores obvious dismal like
large ? — or weekly quota   P 89

Autonomy / retailing P 102 - 7 in Canada
of Chain stores schedule — 1870s + 1880s slow
Quickened pace — 1900 - 1930   P 110
Canadian ? — workers state. P 113
Diminish of earnings — changing value of shopping
— result in ? in ? consumer rolls —

Eaton's marketing book y end P113-19

Sie & cost P120-21   Main Canadian s/w

Stephen Leg. to see themselves as consumers Pro

who could not satisfy the bank's rigorous requirements and who did not have anything they wanted to pawn. 'All he has got,' explained one expert, 'is a reputation in the community for meeting his debts when he can, paying his bills, and who has reasonable prospects of employment.' In other words, the individuals who borrowed from the consumer finance companies had once been the service retailers' preferred customers. The storekeepers and the finance companies therefore struck up a close relationship; indeed, personal lending in many ways became the credit arm for retailers, who, because of the growing use of cash and the faster rate of exchanges, could no longer afford to shoulder their customers' accounts. When storekeepers found a credit account that could not be collected, they would 'call in the fellow who is slow to pay and say "now you owe me $100; if you can give me $50, I will square this off. You can go somewhere and get $50."' This was the most common use of personal finance in the interwar years; according to Household Finance, the largest of the lending companies, a full 65 per cent of its loans were given to amortize retail debts.[32] For the store owners, personal finance meant an acceleration in their own ability to collect on debts, but in the long term it also implied a further contraction of their credit function. Gradually they were to learn that instead of selling on credit to their customers and having the personal-finance companies reimburse them, it was easier to eliminate the store credit altogether and let the customers pay cash with the borrowed money.

Though credit had not disappeared by 1940 (almost 60 per cent of all retailers in 1940 were still using some kind or degree), the nature of that credit had altered irrevocably. Two-thirds of grocery stores were selling either entirely or largely on a cash basis, and roughly half of all the clothes stores in Canada were cash stores, with the bulk of the remainder having credit accounts that totalled less than 30 per cent of their total turnovers. Overall, one-third of all stores were offering no credit, and another third recorded open-book accounts worth less than a third of their total sales.[33] Not surprisingly, credit selling was being most extensively used by automotive, furniture, and appliance dealers and by rural general storekeepers. But for all except the last of these, true open-book credit had already been largely superseded by more rigorous types of instalment plans.

Competition had undoubtedly been one of the main agents of the change, but we should not exaggerate the influence of the chains and department stores. For while they acted – as they had for those improving their displays – as reference points for retailers, their own retreat from credit had been much more a symptom of change than its cause. What was working most powerfully to undermine the open account was the increasing speed of commercial exchanges and the growing need for a secure method of collection. The departmentals made the move to cash because they realized that manufacturers would give them better terms for prompt payments. This fact was something that all dealers understood, but it was only when competition publicized the savings which the cash stores were offering that ordinary retailers decided it was worth their while attempting to close the book. Moreover, it was not being left up to them alone: as the twentieth century progressed, manufacturers and wholesalers were unilaterally shortening their terms and closing the gap between cash and credit. Ultimately, what these various changes achieved was to make prices more important than service, even in many high-class independent stores that had long regarded credit as essential to their success.

Change would not therefore be contained to the showroom floor. The growth of the mass market was transforming methods of supply and display, and it was revolutionizing traditional sales practices. Stores now looked different, were staffed by a new type of clerk, and sold under altered terms. And watching over all these changes was modern accounting, the natural corollary of the new stress being laid upon orderly display, faster supply, and more-impersonal forms of selling. Most larger stores had kept accounts in the late nineteenth century, and after the creation of an income tax in 1917, retailers making over $1,200 were required to keep at least a minimum record of their stock, sales, and profits. But the older system of bookkeeping had relied on the daybook (which described daily transactions), the monthly journal (which reorganized the daybook to reveal debits and credits), and the ledger (which summarized accounts). During the early twentieth century, however, the old-style daybook began to give way before the receipt, and the functions of the journal were in turn assumed by the self-journalizing invoice and the indexed credit account drawer. The ledger similarly fell victim to rationalization, and instead of the original one-volume account, separate ledgers were increasingly being kept for accounts receivable and payable and for store expenses.[34]

The increasing sophistication of store books is significant not only because it became so complicated that accountants had to be hired but also because, just as with the changing shop layouts, it was a reflection of new attitudes to business. One of the most important features of the traditional proprietary enterprise – and one that retail folklore continued to reflect – was the way that stores were treated as extensions of the household. Where books had been kept, daily sales and receipts would be entered as they occurred alongside withdrawals of cash or goods for household or staff purposes. This sleight-of-hand style of bookkeeping became much more difficult under a fully rationalized method. Indeed, many of the new prefabricated bookkeeping systems, such as the popular McCaskey System or the pre-columned set of books offered by the National Cash Register Company, would not allow for these entries unless they were listed as a sale or a cash withdrawal – which then meant accounting for them in the 'Cash in drawer' column. Stocktaking also raised the difficulty of accounting for the family's consumption of goods if no record had been kept. And in any case, improvements in bookkeeping, especially when experts were hired to make up the books, probably made businessmen more conscious of the formal nature of their accounts. This new awareness would explain why personal information tended to disappear from the more up-to-date records. As with modern store fixtures, the new method itself was creating the new meaning.

The impact of 'scientific bookkeeping' cannot be minimized, because it involved more than just a new way of counting. Improved record keeping systematized a whole slew of haphazard procedures and imposed a new uniformity on modernizing shops. Retail experts, for example, urged merchants to go further than just maintaining cleaner books and to reproduce in their accounts the physical divisions that they were introducing into their stores. In this way, storekeepers would keep separate purchase and sales records for each section or 'department' (such as millinery, furniture, or fruit). The advantage of this approach would be that a store owner would be able to determine quickly which departments were paying and which were not. 'Sound merchandising,' retailers were informed, 'frowns on season to season carryovers,' and departmental organization enabled owners to pinpoint slower-moving items 'and force them out.' The retail experts' enthusiasm for departmentalization reveals the invisible current driving store modernization. In urging retailers to departmentalize, the experts were asking them to apply to their businesses the 'functionally' based organizational systems already prevalent in manufacturing and larger-scale distribution. The proprietary shops should become, in effect, miniature replicas of Eaton's or the A & P or Parke Davis.[35]

The crucial thing was that by permitting comparisons, modern accounting encouraged merchants to contrast their own activities with those they now regarded as the retail norm. Unfortunately, because of the paucity of Canadian statistics, the measure of retail success in the 1920s became the Harvard Business School's annual publication of retail store practices, supplemented in the 1930s by surveys carried out by the major American trade associations, the National Cash Register Company, and the U.S. Department of Commerce.[36] The way in which these reports were used by zealous accountants and modernizing shopkeepers to measure efficiency can be seen in the 1930s correspondence between J.M. Thomson, an Owen Sound furniture dealer, and his accountant, F.H. Rabnett. The accountant was continually urging Thomson to change his trade practices and bring his store into line with the accepted averages. 'The normal percentage [for advertising],' Rabnett wrote in 1933, 'is over 5.5% ... [and] we would suggest you plan to increase your outlay in this respect immediately,' 'According to the Harvard Survey,' he wrote a few months later, 'the average rate of stock turn for a Furniture Store is 3 times per year, and your rate figures at once per year [sic], for the last five months.' And there were more authorities in the quiver in 1935: 'The latest figures published by the National Cash Register Company show the average rate of stock turn for Furniture Stores to be two times per year ... [your] rate now figures at 1.25,' The National Cash Register Company also had something to say about advertising in 1937: its 'latest figure ... is 7.2% of sales and this being an average, the better businesses must be spending a lot more.' Sometimes, of course, comparative statistics could be used to cheer a despondent retailer (as in Rabnett's assurance that Thomson's falling sales in 1938 were 'quite in keeping with the percentages in retail businesses shown in government reports'), but more often than not the statistics served to chastise and worry. Little thought appears to have been given to the applicability of the national (and generally foreign) averages to individual cases or to the question of relative store resources or to the issue of different community needs and potentials. In fact, modernizers such as Rabnett even felt comfortable contacting up-market big-city retailers such as Ridpath's in Toronto for advice as to what a mid-sized town business such as Thomson's should be doing.[37]

Looking back, then, we can see that 'modernization' involved a kind of homogenization of twentieth-century business, though few merchants at the time would have thought in these terms. For most progressive store owners, what they were doing was systematizing and rationalizing inefficient practices and eliminating those contradictions that had restricted profitability. Money was for them at the centre of it all. New fixtures and displays improved the appearance of stores, but that result was always secondary to the profits that could be made from intensifying the 'buying atmosphere.' But in systematizing their businesses, the shopkeepers were following the advice of suppliers and retail experts who had become convinced that mass manufacturing and marketing should serve as models for merchandising. Retailers were being encouraged to think of themselves as on a par with big businesses, and in so doing they were being led to conform to the demands of the great transformation that had accompanied mass production.

THE WORD FROM THEIR SPONSORS

By the interwar years, however, the manufacturers, wholesalers, and trade experts who promoted modernization were not always agreed on what course retailing should take. Though they mostly accepted the importance of improving the appearance of the shop and they generally asserted the centrality of departmentalized cost accounting, on issues of pricing and promotion there were clear differences. As we have seen, opinion within early-twentieth-century manufacturing was divided between those who advocated low-priced, high-volume selling and those who believed in higher fixed prices and controlled consumption. For the apostles of mass production, the best retail store was the one that sold the most at the cheapest price, while for the price fixers, the model shop was the one that emphasized high unit profits, selective price reductions, and quality service. It was a controversy that was to have a major impact on the direction of retail modernization and trade politics.

The dispute between what we might call inflationists and deflationists was grounded to a certain extent in the nature of the work being done. Though individual disciples of mass production and of output restriction could be found in every trade, the former did seem to predominate in those industries producing more generic-type goods where brand-name identifications were weakest. This distinction made sense. Before the Second World War a lot of brand-name products carried high prices and were promoted for their superior taste or quality. This was especially the case with food, drugs, and toiletries, but it was also true of such things as nationally advertised appliances, musical instruments, and watches. As the ads proclaimed: 'People Whispered: Husbands always ate in town. Tasteless "bargain bread" was to blame ... Hurry your husband home [with] Wonder Bread,' 'Listerine – the Dentifrice of the rich – Results not price the deciding factor,' 'All of the rich, tonic

goodness. All of the famous tomato healthfulness ... Men with the suc-
cess-habit eat wisely and well. They enjoy Campbell's Tomato Soup regularly,' 'We all had dull white teeth simply because our toothbrushes
turned limp when wet ... [But] Today an entirely new brush has been
perfected – a brush that cannot get soggy when wet. It is made of the
world's costliest bristles, hand selected. And each of the bristles is
water-proofed. Dr. West's famous Water-proofed toothbrush.' The
stress in national advertising such as this tended to fall on issues related
to reliability, truthfulness, and the uplift that would come from the use
of an expensive, but superior product. Many brand-name manufacturers were therefore predisposed to favour stability in their pricing as a
confirmation of their products' quality. And because they linked higher
prices to issues of quality, health, and uplift, defenders of the manufacturers' right to fix prices could argue that 'a serious result of the [price]
cutting of branded or proprietary articles ... is the lowering of moral
standards.'[38] Fixed prices tended to accompany products aimed at
'quality' markets, goods promoted for their trustworthiness; items
whose producers wanted the consumers to identify with the manufacturer and not with the dealers who carried their wares.

Not surprisingly, the manufacturers' divergent perceptions regarding
prosperity and pricing would influence their understanding of distribution. For the disciples of mass production – believers in the primacy of
manufacture and the need to open the floodgates of spending – retailing
was almost by definition an uneconomic expense. Distribution was
nothing more than a way of getting goods from the factory to the consumer, and the best retailing system was the one that made goods available in the quickest, most systematic, and cheapest possible way. Mass
producers therefore had little time for talk of 'community' or 'service';
they wanted order and efficiency. In the cost-cutting industrialists'
view, there were simply too many shopkeepers, they were too spread
out, they were not efficient enough in their marketing, they added too
high a mark-up, and they tended to know too little about the goods they
sold. Mass production, James Malcolm, the minister of trade and commerce in the late twenties and a prominent furniture manufacturer, told
a Canadian Manufacturers' Association dinner in Guelph, 'is continually driving manufacturing costs down, but retail prices stay stubbornly
up.' In fact, 'innumerable cases can be found where the retail price is ten
to fifty times the manufacturing price.' Thus, 'reducing the costs of distribution' became for these manufacturers 'one of the major problems
facing industry to-day.' For Malcolm, the power of science and order

were going to have to be mobilized against wasteful retailing. 'Capital and science between them have achieved mass production. National advertising and growing prosperity have provided mass consumption ... in between ... was the narrow neck of the hour glass, restricting the free flow of goods.'[39]

During the 1920s industrial critics of independent retailing tended to regard the chains and department stores as the best hope for a scientific system of distribution. As one Toronto clothing manufacturer remarked, 'the small dealer is doomed unless he will wake up and learn to merchandise in ways and at prices somewhat comparable to those of the chain and department stores.' Manufacturers liked the way that the big stores sold in huge quantities, and they appreciated the enormous orders they were able to place. Yes, an increasing number of them were disturbed by the fact that in order to offer such low prices the mass merchandisers shaved down the manufacturers' profits, but so long as sales remained good, they kept most of their complaining to themselves. And whatever misgivings they may have had concerning the merchandising giants were certainly not being translated into greater support for the independents. Independent retailers, one manufacturer remarked with typical contempt, were 'incompetent, blindly ignorant, biased, lazy, and even a trifle unscrupulous,' and 'they stood between them [the manufacturers] and the expansion of demand for their goods.'[40]

What little interest the mass producers showed in proprietary retailing was conditioned by a single thought and that was the need to get its cost down. In pursuit of this goal, manufacturers of mass-produced generic lines in the early 1920s took up the task of fostering what they called 'commercial intelligence.' Commercial intelligence rested on the belief that 'if techniques of tests, standards and specifications were in operation, much of the selling effort would inevitably collapse, margins would come down to reasonable levels, and the actual [retailers'] profits would probably be steadier if not larger.' Therefore, in trade after trade, organizations staffed by producers and their representatives began to appear – organizations whose chief object was the elimination of 'disorderly marketing.' The clothing business alone in the mid-1920s had a Cotton Textile Institute, a Hosiery Retail Dry Goods Association, a Wool Institute, and a Wholesale Dry Goods Institute, all devoted to applying to retailing 'the measuring stick and the micrometer.' Furniture manufacturers set up the Home Furnishings Bureau, whose catchy slogan was 'Better Furnished Homes Mean Greater Happiness,' while soap and glycerine producers established the delectably titled Cleanliness Institute. The Canadian Manufacturers' Association formed its own branch, the Commercial Intelligence Department, in the mid-twenties, whose aim was to discover the answer to that most pressing question: 'What Does it Cost to Distribute?'[41]

According to the advocates of mass production, retailers' sales had to be 'stimulated,' and 'turnover' had to be made the first and last word in marketing. This approach might just seem common sense, for retailers had, after all, always been concerned about their sales volumes and especially during deflationary periods had tended to try to increase their turnovers by keeping smaller stocks and pricing more closely. But the object of this strategy had simply been to avoid being caught with large volumes of goods when their prices were falling, and a higher turnover was seen as a way for retailers to clear their shelves more quickly. In general, then, business people at the turn of the century had thought not in terms of volumes but in terms of unit profits. 'There is little satisfaction in turning over a lot of goods, but doing it at little or no profit,' the *Furniture World* advised; a good profit had to be made on every sale, for while 'it is all right to aim at big volumes,' it was insanity 'to sacrifice profit to secure it.'[42]

In keeping with this philosophy, prices would be set in such a way as to use demand to the advantage of profit: margins would be made higher on goods that turned more often, and they would be lower on more-slow-moving items in order to stimulate their sale. Ultimately, this practice of higher unit profits on demand goods would pay off in the form of larger net earnings, since the 'grocer who sells his lettuce at $2\frac{1}{2}$¢ per bunch may have a somewhat larger trade than his neighbour ... [But] I doubt if his aggregate profits will be near that of his neighbour who charges $3\frac{1}{3}$ for the same goods.' As a general rule, the traditionalists went on, it 'is a poor policy to sell twice the amount of goods at one half the amount of profit,' and those that believed 'that more can be sold if the price is low' were simply being 'senseless.' Before the First World War the only people who pursued turnover were the trade demoralizers – departmentals and cut-priced independents – 'cheap men' whose aim it was 'to unsettle the course of trade.'[43]

The turnover approach to selling, which the experts began to promote during the inflationary war years, was based on radically different principles from those that had underlain the traditional profit-oriented method. Those manufacturers and business experts who advocated a high-turnover strategy began with a calculation of costs and worked forward towards profits. They argued that it was better to sell ten items for $1.00 each than to sell one item for $10.00 because fixed charges per unit marketed were lower when stock was turned more frequently and less capital was tied up at any one time in storing the goods. But what made the turnover recipe really piquant was the suggestion that the greater the volume sold the lower the unit price might be – meaning, in practice, that goods which were in higher demand should carry a lower mark-up than those which sold more slowly.

The issue of store turnover had first been brought to the attention of promoters and manufacturers during the price explosion of the war and immediate postwar years. During the worst years of the inflation, the manufacturers and trade experts began to pressure shop owners to mark their goods more closely, and later, when consumer purchasing came to a standstill and prices declined, they added to their advice the footnote that it was not enough for unit production costs to come down if retail prices remained high. At the centre of their argument was a belief that the shopkeepers' activities had to be harmonized with those of the manufacturers, since only by augmenting the volume of the retailers' business could the producers increase their own. Traditionally, when retailers had faced periods of crisis, they had cut wages and advertising expenses; a practice that scientific managers now warned was 'unwise' because of its impact on earnings. 'The better way' of coping with deflation, the experts suggested, was 'to decrease overhead by decreasing its percentage proportion by increasing the volume of business.' There was, in short, 'a great necessity for turnover ... a necessity that becomes more pressing in view of the falling market ... For the time being volume of customers is more important ... than consideration of profits.'[44]

During the deflation of the early twenties, most independent retailers did not need much prodding. With the chains and department stores slashing prices on every side, the shop owners had little choice but to follow suit and try to make up in turnover what they were losing on lower unit prices. Moreover, shortened credit terms from their suppliers forced them to work on increasing their cash flow. Consequently, retailers had to admit that 'de tous les facteurs qui contribuent au succès ou à la faillité dans le commerce du détail, il n'y en a pas de plus important que celui du virement.' Turnover became the golden elixir of retailing. Did the shopkeeper have problems with expenses? 'The best way to decrease overhead is by decreasing its percentage proportion by increasing volumes.' Were the merchants not making enough? '[I]t is not the amount of profit but the rapidity of turnover that counts in the long run.' Were the dealers running short of ready cash? 'The thief in the night ... is the "idle dollar" – the dollar that, for some reason or other, is invested in goods that do not move.' As one commentator observed: 'The turn-over bug has bitten the retail merchant. They have read so much about turn-over that many of them believe that if they turn-over their stock often enough they will arrive in the millionaire class in no time.'[45]

The irony of the turnover theory is that it was again based on a model lifted from continuous-process manufacturing and first perfected in mass merchandising. Turnover, in its productive variant, had been the idea that had given birth to mass production: the progressive decrease in unit cost as output rose. It was, however, an odd philosophy for retailers to ingest. After all, one would not expect the average shop-keeper, with his minimal investment in relatively long-lasting fixtures and his low capitalization, to be particularly concerned with the prob-lems of a poor floating-to-fixed-capital ratio. Most proprietary business people believed themselves to be earning a living on their sales, not accumulating a return on their investments. None the less, they were informed by the marketing experts that 'invested money is the source of profit ... and it is evident that to double the turnover comes to the same thing as doubling the amount of stock without increasing the invest-ment. Or, vice versa, one half of as many turnovers results in doubling the amount of money invested for the same quantity of goods.' The rhet-oric of the assembly line permeated the discussion of turnover in the 1920s, for as one instructor on remodelling improbably enough advised, be sure to put high turnover items at the back of the shop 'to draw the customer,' but ensure also that they are within easy reach of the clerks so as to 'cut out lost motion and keep down expense.'[46]

In contrast to the disciples of mass production, the brand-name man-ufacturers who favoured price stabilization had a more benign, if ulti-mately even more interventionist, view of retailing. Like the mass producers, they saw a need to reform the independent channel (in order to shift merchandising expenditures over to wages), but unlike the deflationists – whose primary interest was cost – the price fixers were looking to turn the independents into a real alternative to the mass mar-keters. What these manufacturers especially desired was to find a way of countering the merchandising giants' habit of using their products as bargain bait. (Any departmental or chain store managers worth their salt knew that they could draw a bigger crowd by cutting the prices of nationally advertised and price-protected items than they could by putting a house brand or generic item on sale.) Through much of the early twentieth century the manufacturers would try to persuade the mass marketers to respect their fixed prices, but they only intermittently felt strong enough actually to refuse to supply those bulk buyers who ignored their wishes. Better from their perspective would be to weld the independents into a docile and efficient group who could be used as a counterweight to the aggressive mass merchandisers. Price fixers therefore also became involved in counselling independent shop owners, remodelling their stores, organizing their displays, and moulding their advertising, but they went further than the mass producers in trying to fix their prices. Obviously interested in making retailing cheap so as to allow manufacturing to become more expensive, they also recognized that independent shops were not going to be able to mount a successful challenge to the mass merchandisers until they were able to compete in terms of image, style, layout, service, and – within prescribed limits – price. But while tolerating selective cutting, these manufacturers were always careful about not letting the independents play games with the prices of their own products. 'The public,' a brand-name clothing manufacturer explained helpfully, 'is definitely brand conscious ... the sale is half made when one offers brands like Cook's Clothing, Stanfield's Underwear, Harvey Woods Holeproof Hosiery or GWG Work Garments. Retailers should not try to compete with big stores when they cut prices on these lines because they can't – rely on service, quality, value for money and attractive displays.'[47] Such a view was all very well, but it should not blind us to the fact that the manufacturers' long-term objective was to strengthen the hand of independent retailing by restricting its independence.

Brand-name manufacturers were generally unhappy with the increasing popularity of the turnover idea in the 1920s. Many brand-name producers, together with most wholesalers, were actually anxious to prevent the spread of the turnover approach because it threatened both to lower prices and to require retailers to keep smaller stocks, thereby transferring more of the cost of warehousing onto the already financially strapped middlemen. Moreover, wholesalers by the interwar years were struggling to control direct marketing by providing greater liberality in their credit terms. If turnover made independent shops more efficient and gave them the cash to pay on delivery, there was even less need for the wholesalers' services. T. Johnson Stewart, a Vancouver wholesaler, found the idea so offensive that he went before a convention of RMA grocers to urge them back to their senses. The doctrine of turnover,' Stewart pleaded, 'is insidious when applied as the average grocer is being taught to apply it. If he continues to apply it – to depend on it ... he's bound to fail. For the very simple reason that his business is not big enough in dollars and cents to depend on "Turnover" for anything like the ratio he depends on it to make a profit.' Shaving prices and relying on turnover was, to Stewart, no solution: the shopkeeper had to make a good profit on all lines and on all sales.[48]

Industrialists interested in price stabilization were also threatened by turnover because it encouraged the independents to take the initiative in lowering prices. What they tended to argue was that retailers should forget price, accept lower sales, and concentrate on providing quality service. Stores that followed the low-price – high-turnover approach, a representative of a pharmaceutical manufacturers' association explained, were nothing more than 'cheap jack establishments ... Pharmacy is a profession [not a trade]. What would happen if signs read "J. Smith, cut-rate doctor" or "J. Brown, cut-rate lawyer"? Such a sign would lower the professional prestige of these men and bring them into contempt.' And so too with the retailer. In fact, the model retailer should 'be content to build his business on better service and better merchandising methods and to limit his inducements for price appeal to articles on which the manufacturer does not attempt to maintain prices.' Leave the customer who bought 'on a purely price' basis to the chains, a high-quality men's clothier agreed; 'it is a fatal mistake for the individual clothier to attempt to meet the chains store offerings on a price basis ... The big goal for the clothier should be to buy his clothes on a quality basis and teach his customers the importance of quality in clothes.' It was a view that price stabilizers subtly promoted in their advertising: as E.R. Squibb, the price-fixing pharmaceutical firm, explained, the point of its national advertising campaign was 'increasing the prestige of the druggist who carries the Squibb line,' which it thought could be achieved by emphasizing the pharmacist's knowledge and training and his pivotal role in the community. Between the lines one can easily read Squibb's intention to dichotomize quality and price, knowledge and ignorance.[49]

It is impossible to know how many retailers followed one course or the other. Certainly, the trade press contains many true confessions by shop owners preferring to sell at a high mark-up and in lower quantities rather than going after volume. The weakness of the turnover approach, they generally agreed, was that it was destructive of 'personality' and ultimately of profits. With shop owners and their clerks working to maximize sales, business people were not taking the time to deal with consumers as human beings. As a result, shoppers saw no advantage to buying at a proprietary store and went off to shop at one of the departmental or chain outlets. Only by maintaining their skill and marketing their personality, these storekeepers suggested, could their businesses really compete. Undoubtedly, many of those following a high-mark-up strategy were either too small or too inefficient to sell in large volumes, or else they were serving communities or carrying the type of stock where price was less of a concern. But many of them – including druggists and automobile, appliance, and piano dealers – were also operating in businesses where price-fixing was the norm. Of course, I am presenting the high-turnover and high-margin approaches as opposites simply for the sake of clarity: in practice even the most service-oriented dealer ran sales, periodically cut prices, and lowered margins on high-demand lines. Moreover, because most shops stocked goods with strong brand-name identification as well as those of more generic quality, they could maintain prices on some lines and cut them on others. But what we are dealing with here are tendencies, and from this perspective there can be no doubt that there were two different philosophies at work in retailing.

This is the crucial point, for whether coming in the guise of a high-turnover or a high-margin approach, progressive pricing strategies (just as much as cost accounting, departmentalization, and systematic stock keeping) represented an application to independent retailing of systems that had been designed outside the proprietary sector. Though a traditional symbolic language was used to promote the high-margin approach (the emphasis being placed on values such as personality, independence, community, and quality), the goal of price maintenance was little different from that of high turnover: it aimed at making the proprietary shop into an extension of the manufacturing plant. The only difference was that in the case of the 'service-minded' manufacturers, the goal was to have the retailers sell their goods at higher prices and to maintain the image of product reliability. In fact, the control exercised by the manufacturers promoting 'independence' and 'quality' through higher prices was far greater than that of the producers urging shopkeepers to adopt a high-turnover approach. For where the advocate of high stock turnover recognized the shopkeepers' right to set their own mark-ups according to their sales, the high-margin promoter believed that the merchants' job was to 'protect' prices pre-set by the manufacturer.

Leading price fixers, such as the makers of household appliances and cars, began in the 1920s rigidly to police the marketing and pricing of their products. The Kelvinator Company, for example, referred to its dealers as its 'resale team,' and it established fixed retail prices for its refrigerators. The company further regulated the traders' profits by increasing the margins as sales rose: a vendor received a 30 per cent gross margin on his first $1,200 sold, 35 per cent on his next $1,200, and 40 per cent on all sales over $2,400. Kelvinator also required biannual reports of its agents, 'sales effort' – in effect, a list of the number, names, and addresses of all the prospects, interviewees, and purchasers. As one marketing executive remarked, 'manufacturers realize that it is not enough to put their merchandise on the dealer's shelves and then forget it. They must do everything in their power to break down sales resistance – to create a demand for their products – to help the dealer sell them.' Sometimes manufacturers could become quite tyrannical in their pursuit of this goal. One such, the Imperial Tobacco company, allowed the retailer little freedom in the merchandising of its products. The company had its own teams of window trimmers, who unilaterally made up all the retail displays featuring Imperial products; it frequently pressured shop owners to remove rival tobaccos that were being featured too prominently; and so severely did it police its prices that when in the 1930s one Montreal retailer gave away a few packets of Imperial cigarettes to unemployed workers, the company cut him from its preferred supply list.[50] Imperial was somewhat notorious for its highhanded practices, but the extent of its control does point to the underside of the price fixers, insistence on quality and service.

Like the price-fixing manufacturers, but for different reasons, the wholesalers who advocated high-margin selling also adopted an interventionist policy with respect to retailing. And as with the trade experts' and manufacturers' involvement, the wholesalers' program of reform involved fostering the dependency of the 'independent' distributors while at the same time promoting the retail sector's reliance on a big-business model. For wholesale merchants, the growth of the mass market had been especially painful, and '[d]irect selling to retailers' had led many 'to predict the doom of the wholesaler.' The pessimists were not far wrong, for the triumph of mass production had strewn Bradstreet's sheet with the names of dismembered mercantile establishments. The first to fall had been the dry goods wholesalers, the most princely of all the merchant princes, who were trampled almost inadvertently in the onward rush of the ready-made clothing industry. In 1875 Toronto

alone had boasted of some twenty-five substantial dry goods wholesalers; fifty years later only two remained. Wholesaling in groceries and
hardware survived longer, but direct selling and price competition
began to take their toll around the First World War. Eleven Ontario grocery wholesalers disappeared between 1910 and 1925, and of the ten
largest food wholesalers in Toronto in 1917, only five were still in operation ten years later. In the hardware trade, the mergers, failures, and
take-overs began in 1923 and continued to gain momentum until they
culminated in the huge Cochrane-Dunlop Hardware Company merger
of fifteen major businesses in 1927. It is difficult to be certain, but somewhere around twenty-six major hardware wholesalers seem to have disappeared between 1923 and 1929.[51]

Merger was not, however, a sufficient survival strategy, for while it
helped eliminate competition among wholesalers, it did little to resolve
the problem of the jobbers' increasing economic irrelevance. In response
to this challenge, wholesalers decided upon a bold counter-offensive
and began to advance into retailing, opening their own chains or linking
up with their customers in 'voluntary pooling' arrangements. Under
pooling contracts, retailers agreed to buy a majority (if not all) of their
stock from one supplier, to use the pool's advertising, and to sell at
prices fixed by the pool. In return, members were able to buy and sell
and advertise at less cost than could full independents. Their growth
was relatively limited outside the grocery, hardware, and drug trades in
the twenties and thirties, but voluntary pools – or voluntary chains, as
they were more accurately called – none the less became one of the most
important forms of distribution in post–Second World War Canada.

Louis K. Liggett's United Drug Company, established in Boston in
1903, was the first nationally successful voluntary chain. Liggett had
chanced upon the idea of establishing exclusive retail agencies while
working as a salesman for Virol tonic (a mixture of sherry and cod-liver
oil). In principle, the agency would provide the merchant with exclusive
distribution rights to the product in his community, thereby allowing
him a competitive advantage. The manufacturer or wholesaler would in
turn obtain a secure outlet for his merchandise. The UDC was the natural extrapolation from this agency concept. It was a wholesale house
(later a manufacturing concern as well), which supplied the retailers
who subscribed to it with most of their stock and all of their advertising,
as well as with a house brand, the famous Rexall line. The retailers joining United would purchase shares in the wholesale firm and would
agree to buy their merchandise only from that company. In return, they

were promised low prices on the goods they purchased, as well as a dividend at the end of each year. In 1909 Rexall moved north, and by 1934 there were almost a thousand independent UDC druggists operating in Canada.[52]

The first Canadian voluntary chain was a local group, the Drug Trading Company, formed by retailers who established their own wholesaling house in Toronto around 1900; on a provincial scale, the Superior Stores organized in 1918, and Merchants' Consolidated was established in Winnipeg at about the same time. The latter two companies were grocery pools modelled on the UDC. To join, storekeepers had to buy two shares in the pool (Superior's cost $100 per share) and had to purchase all their stock through the cooperatively owned wholesale house. The merchant further agreed to honour group advertising and pre-set price levels and to run 'specials' only on those lines that were being featured at the time in all the stores in the pool.[53]

In theory, the members controlled the chains by electing the administrative board, which determined the group's advertising and sales policy. But almost from the start it was clear that the widely dispersed shopkeepers, preoccupied with their own businesses, could not themselves manage the wholesale operations, and so the supply function was detached from the retailers' control. Consequently, though the independent wholesalers had initially condemned the pools as simply bodies of shopkeepers 'who were trying to cut out the wholesale trade,' in time their attitude mellowed. Like the wheat pools, the retail cooperatives became more powerful than the sum of their parts, with the wholesale departments exercising a degree of control over their distributors that made them the envy of the private trade. Not surprisingly, the pooling idea soon began to appeal to wholesalers threatened by the manufacturers' increasing penetration. The Toronto jobber John Sloan and Company organized the Red and White chain in 1924 (549 outlets in 1930); Adanac stores (150 outlets in 1930) was run by the James Lumbers Company; Laporte Martin Ltée in Montreal set up Victoria Independent Grocers (605 stores in 1930). By the Depression, two-thirds of voluntary food businesses, representing perhaps 15 per cent of the grocery trade, were agency-style operations directed by private wholesalers.[54] Altogether, by 1931 one in five independent food retailers and one-quarter of the drug stores were members of one of the voluntary chains.

The appeal of the voluntary chains for the independent trade was that they promised to make the proprietors more competitive with the bulk-buying mass merchandisers. One of the chief ways that they could challenge the corporate giants, the wholesalers argued, would be for them to buy goods at the same low prices as the big stores. To do this, they had to begin mass marketing for themselves. But survival cost the cooperators dearly: they had to follow fixed guidelines on advertising and selling, they had to submit to group window-dressing and displays, and they increasingly had to pay high royalties to the wholesalers for the privilege of selling the house brands. Rapidly, it was becoming the case that the retailers could do only what their wholesaler allowed them to do, making the pools into something like independently operated replicas of the corporate chains. The bond tying the independent to the pool was certainly less close than that linking the branch manager to his chain's head office, but in practice the difference was more one of degree than of kind. As the Montreal wholesaler Joseph Laporte explained, the wholesaler had to 'organize his group of retailers on the same principles of a chain of stores, such retailers giving him all their business. The wholesaler with such a group of selected retailers should establish short terms, sell his customers no more than requirements, and have each contribute a small sum for an advertising fund, adopt an identification slogan so that customers will know the stores, and finally, give merchandising service to the group of stores. In such cases the travellers become trained as supervisors.'[55]

As the pools were already so much like the chains, it became feasible for many of the cooperative wholesalers to make the small adjustments necessary in their operations and get into the chain business for themselves. As early as 1916 the United Drug Company had opened Liggett's Drug Stores, a fully owned chain subsidiary, while the York Trading Company, Superior's wholesaler, was by the early thirties running shoe and hardware store chains. Macdonald's Consolidated, a Winnipeg-based wholesaler that was supplying a voluntary chain, was taken over in 1929 by Safeway, which continued to provide stock and advertising to the independent stores in the pool. Though it operated its pool in competition with its own business, Safeway treated the voluntary chain as simply another element in its growing retail empire.[56]

Together, but each for their own reasons, manufacturers and wholesalers pushed store improvement, offered advice and money to retailers wanting to remodel their stores, and became increasingly involved in promoting, displaying, and advertising their products. Forsyth Shirt Company, for example, ran its own newspaper advertisements in the early twenties and then urged retailers to use them to increase sales: 'endeavour to stimulate the interest of the ladies in buying shirts for

Christmas gifts,' the company advised one retailer curtly; 'clip the advertisement from the paper and put it in your window.' Other manufacturers made it their practice to dictate to their retailers the type of goods they stock. 'We suggest,' the Comfort Kimona Manufacturing Company informed the London dry goods retailer W.L. Mara, 'that you place the quantity you require and leave it to us to select your assortment. There is no doubt you will be entirely satisfied with the selection.' Occasionally the retailers resisted (one grocer recalled how he had to fight off his wholesaler's attempt to get him to sell shirts in his store), but more often they complied passively, especially when the supplier accepted responsibility for any loss its intrusions might cause.[57]

For the manufacturers and wholesalers, 'store modernization' and more direct control over marketing were masterful solutions to the problems raised by the birth of the consumer. Some felt that by reducing retail prices, modernization promised to make goods more affordable without affecting incomes, while others saw it as a means of maintaining prices and restricting competition. For wholesalers, store modernization seemed vital to their continued existence. It was this new formulation, and the hopes aroused by it, that was in large measure responsible for making the business environment of the later 1920s appear so robust and zestful. The manufacturers' had come even more slowly than the public to accept the realities of the consumer economy, for while their involvement in marketing had grown dramatically over the course of the late nineteenth century, their willingness to integrate the changing economic realities into the structure of their business values and practices had been somewhat delayed. The jobbers, in turn, had continued to resist manufacturer domination in some trades up until the early 1920s. As a result, something definite separated the world of 1928 from that of 1918. The 1920s were indeed 'the marketing decade' – an era marked by a new consensus on the importance of distribution – and they had all the appearance, then and since, of an entrepreneurial golden age.

For retailers, the paradox of modernization was that the process of becoming more competitive was pulling the independent stores into a more symbiotic relationship with their suppliers and into a more imitative one with their chain and departmental competitors. Though not expropriated by big business, proprietary capital was being drawn into its orbit, assuming its values, and adopting its methods of organization and merchandising. 'The retailers' interests,' one marketing specialist wrote in 1927, 'are identical with those of the manufacturer.' The producer, retailers were advised to think, was 'now a partner in [the] store,' and as such, he was to be held 'equally responsible in so far as a merchandising profit is concerned ... [The manufacturer's] job only begins when he places his line in your department. His real job is to help us move out his line and to do so not only at a profit but in a way that will cause more women to buy more regularly from us.' Advertising, the brand-name good, the crisis of wholesaling, and the manufacturers' growing marketing interests had brought suppliers right into the market-place, and now it was they, not the retailers, who appeared to be the people most in contact with consumers. On this level, it did not really matter whether the wholesalers or manufacturers endorsed high-turnover or high-margin merchandising; their message was the same. Retailers had to serve the interests and needs of the people who were supplying them, and they had to adjust their own selling strategies to the practices of their mass-merchandising competitors. Modernization therefore brought with it an ever-increasing dependency: shopkeepers were being forged into just another link in the chain that bound manufacturers to consumers. Did you, Mr Retailer, a Toronto *Globe* article asked, ever consider how many of the things you sold 'were nine-tenths sold to your customers before you even buy them from the manufacturer?' Breakfast food, soap, syrup, shoes – all were being pre-packaged and pre-marketed to the consumer. 'Twenty-five years ago a man had to be a grocer to run a grocery store ... To-day he only needs to have the physical strength to pull a package off the shelf and sell it over the counter.'[58]

PROGRESSIVE RETAILING'S DIVISIVE IMPACT

Just as pre-packaged goods and national advertising were transforming the shop into a quasi-autonomous marketing branch for brand-name manufacturers, the centralization of credit was turning the retailer into something of an agent for finance capitalism. Undoubtedly, these changes brought tremendous benefits to consumers, and they helped independent merchants to accommodate, in the short term at least, the threats posed by mass merchandising and consumption. But the overall direction of the process itself remains significant. There was more to the 'rise of big business' than merely the growth of the gigantic corporations. Managerial capitalism developed through the reproduction of its forms and through a reconstruction of popular images and ideas in conformity with its technical and organizational imperatives. The concept of space, for example, was transformed by the interaction of existing notions of the locality with the new realities of national transportation, just as the idea of ownership was changed through the democratization of possession. Similarly, economic structures and ideas were altered by the new standards of business practice; we have seen how bookkeeping was updated, floor layouts and storage arrangements revised, relations with workers reformed, and the personal-credit nexus broken. Modernization brought with it changes that, in being transmitted, modified, translated, and popularized, rebounded off existing practices, altering their characters. For independent retailers, the birth of the mass society involved not a destruction of proprietary capitalism but a growing 'symbiosis' of big and small capital.

The effect was most profoundly felt by the type of retailers who were already being drawn into groups like the RMA. The evidence suggests that the main-street shop owners felt most sensitized to the competition of both the shoestring retailers and the mass merchandisers and that they were, as a result, particularly vulnerable to the price and product demands of their customers. Modernization would therefore have offered them a particularly important competitive edge. By the early twentieth century, systematic shopkeeping was coming to be seen by small capitalist merchants as the secret not only to success but possibly also to survival. 'It is apparent that if the community retailer is to survive,' the RMA secretary, George Hougham, told a gathering of shop owners, 'he must not lie down on his job, but he must be up and doing, using methods of the big fellow to stimulate and increase his turnover.' In fact, 'if a storekeeper is feeling the pressure of modern conditions, he probably needs to go modern himself.'[59]

To one degree or another, store modernization did change the way that all retailers sold goods. The cash system, in particular, seems to have been adopted not only by the vast majority of urban merchants but also by a large proportion of rural shopkeepers. Indeed, while the published census returns are stubbornly uninformative, they do at least reveal the widespread use of cash in the interwar years. Even among country general stores and groceries – both of which would have been most likely to follow the open-book method – only 7 per cent were selling over three-quarters of their stock in the traditional manner by 1931.[60] Similarly, the universalization of pre-packaged products, like the tightening of credit, brought changes to all retail businesses. As the new standardized goods found their way onto shelves across the country, new methods of display and storage were introduced into corner shops and main-street emporia alike. In this respect, modernization seemed to be narrowing the divide between retailing's rich and poor.

But the changes brought by modernization, while reformulating the differences between shops, did nothing to lessen them; in retailing it remained easy to judge the book by its cover. The well-to-do stores continued to look different from the poorer: their fixtures were nicer; their displays were more aesthetically pleasing; their stock was richer. Moreover, the bigger stores were able to keep abreast of fashion – from the sombre extravagance of the 1890s to the seamless lines of the 1920s – while the smallest could remodel only infrequently. This fact would have served to fossilize the smaller shops, making them look like throwbacks to now-embarrassing unfashionable styles. Moreover, while modern fixtures were relatively inexpensive – $300–400 could outfit a corner store and much could be acquired second-hand or built oneself – products at this price looked inferior. For fixtures, one expert advised, cherry or mahogany was essential; 'under no consideration think of pine, whitewood or ash, as it is impossible to make them look anything but cheap.' Given that thousands of shoestring merchants went into business with far less than the $300-400 considered necessary for even these low-priced woods (10 per cent of all small shops in the 1920s were opened on under $100, and 30 per cent involved an investment of under $300), it is obvious that many of the smaller shops must have continued to look very cheap indeed.[61]

Unfortunately, because so few records have survived for the corner stores, it is impossible precisely to document the impact of modernization on the whole retail sector. But perhaps this very difficulty can offer us some valuable insights. In the early twentieth century most retailers did not keep what the experts considered to be adequate accounts; one government official in 1919 observed that most tradesman 'are unfortunately ignorant about their own concerns.' This made bookkeeping one of the true measures of progressive shopkeeping.[62] Standards, the trade boosters insisted, had risen dramatically, and 'the guess-work' had to be removed from merchandising. Those retailers who did not keep books of the modern type were merely declaring their own inefficiency and archaism. It was a view that dominated the press, the advice circulars of the manufacturers, and – to judge from the opinions they expressed at meetings and in interviews – the minds of the main-street shopkeepers as well. It was also a view that impregnated the records of the bankruptcy court – one of our few statistical windows on Canadian retailing – and spawned the three progressively more-revealing questions that were asked of insolvent shopkeepers concerning their accounts: Did they keep a daybook? Did they maintain a stock book? Did they make up an annual balance? The point was clear: for the court, the more advanced the bookkeeping, the more inexplicable the failure.

Given the latitude generally applied to the term 'daybook' (the Board of Commerce in 1920 discovered that among retailers the 'accounting systems in use – when there were any – differed so widely that they gave no basis for comparison'), it is impossible to tell just what the retailers who answered yes to the bankruptcy court's first question had in mind (at least one who thought he had a daybook produced his bank deposit slips instead).[63] But the possession of a daybook can be considered as evidence of at least a minimum of record keeping. Stocktaking was perceived to have been a much more sophisticated and progressive form of accounting, and the composition of an annual balance was the real test of modernity. The application of these assumptions can be seen in table 12, which divides retail stores according to their capital as in tables 3 and 4. Clearly, while almost all businesses kept some variety of account, the proportion keeping more up-to-date books rose markedly as the store's size increased. Almost twice as many mid-sized shopkeepers (stores capitalized at $2,000–35,000) kept daybooks and ledgers (or their equivalents) as shoestring dealers, three times as many took stock, and four times the number balanced their books. A clear correlation therefore existed between enterprise size and the degree of system involved in the shop's management.

No such clear correlation existed between sex and bookkeeping, though ethnicity does seem to have exerted some influence. All told, 66 per cent of bankrupt male retailers in Ontario kept a daybook in the interwar period and 61 per cent of females; 41 per cent of males took stock and 28 per cent balanced their books; among women the figures were 37 per cent and 15 per cent. That a lower proportion of women kept accounts was, however, largely attributable to the fact that very few of them were running large retail establishments; indeed, female shoestring traders were marginally more likely to keep books than their male counterparts (a consequence, no doubt, of the tendency of rating agencies to undervalue the credit worthiness of female-owned stores). Among immigrant tradespeople, Jews were far and away the most likely to keep records: 80 per cent of those declaring bankruptcy in Ontario kept some form of ledger, 40 per cent took stock, and a surprising 30 per cent balanced their books at least once a year. By way of contrast, 33 per cent of Italians kept no books at all, and one in four held a stocktaking and balanced accounts. Still, within each group, wealth remained the major determinant of accounting. Where 17 per cent of Jewish-run shoestring shops took stock and 12 per cent made up a balance, 60 per cent of main-street stores were stocktaking and one in two was posting a balance. Among the sample of backstreet Italian shop owners, none engaged in any form of sophisticated accounting, while 40 per cent of the more affluent were taking stock and balancing accounts. In short, though cultural background affected one's openness to up-to-date bookkeeping techniques, wealth and class controlled implementation.

Arguably, then, income and size of investment were the crucial determinants of modernization, at least when it came to accounting. Unfortunately, we have no way of knowing if other aspects of modernization – self-service, cash sales, store refurbishment, turnover selling – were more common to one ethnic group or another. Nor is it possible to say whether gender influenced adaptation: the documents simply do not exist for a significant enough sample. Unlike wealth, which clearly determined retailers' ability to buy new fixtures or advertise their wares, cultural predispositions exercised a more-subtle, less-determinate influence. Still, because modernization helped to define 'professionalism' and 'legitimacy' in the eyes of trade boosters, there is no question about its culture-typing. As main-street retailing modernized after 1900, store management and careers became increasingly associated with men and the lower-status sales work with women. Similarly, the ethnic exclusiveness of the retail organizations and the blindness of the trade press to issues of ethnicity served to redefine professionalism as the prerogative of 'native' Canadians. In this respect, modernization, even if undertaken by men and women of diverse backgrounds, was publicly associated with male main-street traders. Like other issues that determined legitimacy, adaptation was a weapon in the hands of the shopocracy.

It would be wrong, however, to assume that the main-street traders' appropriation of the modernizing discourse meant that they knew what they were doing. Testimonials in the trade journals would suggest that the majority of substantial merchants were busily adopting advanced accounting, but the court records qualify that conclusion. Not only were a high proportion of them keeping only partial records, but a large number had pretty peculiar ideas about the books they were maintaining. Adrien Pommier, for example, a mid-sized jeweller in Timmins with a store capitalized at $12,000, once tried to explain the problems he faced when discussing his margin of profit with his supplier. Pommier's usual method had been to double the wholesale price of all the jewellery he sold, but he was not sure what percentage this increase represented: 'once I was saying 50% but I misunderstood the 50% and 100% markup. I said 50% for the reason that we received catalogues from wholesalers and most of the prices were marked 50% deduction, and that meant an article marked $1 would cost 50¢, and I thought it was the same thing when an article was marked $2 to sell it for $1 and that would be a 50% deduction, but they [the wholesaler] told me that would be 100%.' The unfortunate Pommier, taking this good advice, happily announced a 100-per-cent-off sale and soon found himself in bankruptcy court. It was not an uncommon problem. Progressive retailers were told to calculate mark-up on the basis of the selling price, but a great number of merchants could not understand why. 'As an illustration, rather homely,' a Saskatchewan furniture dealer wrote to an accounting expert, 'if in 1912 I had two boys and in 1916 I had four boys, according to your method of figuring my increase would be only 50 per cent, but I hardly think you could make my wife believe it.' A small survey of twenty-five prominent grocers in 1915 confirmed this confusion when nine of them wrote back explaining that they figured margins on invoice costs, while sixteen calculated them on selling prices.[64] It would be wrong, therefore, to suggest that just because retailers kept books, they knew how to use them.

This does not mean that modernization was an illusion. Scientific merchandising was a distinct goal for small capitalist merchants, and methods that were deemed progressive were being widely adopted in the early twentieth century. I present the qualifications simply to show that the rate of change was uneven: some retailers were putting in new windows and lights, others refurbishing their displays, still others advertising more or making up annual balance sheets, and some were doing all these things and more. Overall, the more competitive retailers were certainly trying to appear more responsible in their merchandising and bookkeeping, but even the large merchants were making mistakes. That fact only serves to underline the point suggested earlier: modernization represented a change of form, a new criteria for business-like behaviour. Merchants did not turn to systematic bookkeeping or brighter lighting because the need for it emerged organically out of their own business practices. Progressive accounting, like cash selling and modern decorating, was something that they adopted because it seemed necessary in order to stay up to date. The ambitions and methods came first; the understanding followed rather more slowly.

But while many modernizing retailers may not have understand the full complexity of systematic bookkeeping, thousands of them were nevertheless ardently embracing the new methods. The same can be said of those shopkeepers who joined the voluntary pools: for all that the buying groups restricted their 'independence,' the retailers who joined them were not victims; they were enthusiasts. Rather than appealing to the weakest and most dependent shopkeepers, pooling, like up-to-date bookkeeping, attracted the support of the most important proprietors. Merchants' Consolidated, for example, was not unusual in only accepting subscribers who ran 'standard stores,' which it defined as those with 'a competent man running it and clerks.' The average shop in the Merchants' chain carried a 'well-assorted respectable stock' and turned at least $20,000–25,000 a year in 1919 (this turnover would give the merchant assets of perhaps $8,000–10,000) Only one of the twenty major grocery pools operating in Canada in the late 1920s, the Courvette Sauriol chain in Montreal, had members whose turnovers averaged under $20,000. The typical pool member would have been an individual not unlike Jerry Burns, a Toronto grocer in the Superior chain. Burns's store had annual sales of $27,000–28,000 and employed one full-time and one part-time clerk in 1919. He estimated that his personal income was about $1,500, but he supplemented this salary by taking what groceries he needed out of his stock. As with most of the other modernizers, Burns saw himself as a 'small grocer in a neighbourhood ... in a moderate residential district of working people.'[65] And while he believed himself to be operating a smaller store than many of his fellow cooperators, it was considerably bigger than the average shop of its day. The pools seem to have overwhelmingly represented the same constituency as that being drawn into the RMA and as that busily adopting up-to-date bookkeeping and modern store fixtures.

Though gender or ethnic background may have affected the pace of modernization, the different capital resources available to shop owners unquestionably played a major role in determining its pattern. Given the cost of store decorating and the need to have stocks and turnovers that were large enough to make anything more than rudimentary bookkeeping worthwhile, it was only to be expected that the richer merchants should be the ones in the best position to undertake 'progressive' renovations. Moreover, as we have seen, larger store owners and petty proprietors often came from different backgrounds, and they seem to have brought different skills with them into retailing. The trader who followed his father into merchandising or who had worked for some

ℬ

years as a clerk would likely be more predisposed to pursue marketing trends than the working-class wife who opened a small clothing shop in her front room. Modernization became part of the small capitalist retailers' professional ethic: it justified their alienation from the smallest dealers and supported their claim for inclusion in the modern middle class. In this way, the process of modernization served to increase the differences between traders rather than to unite the retailing stratum. And this widening gap found its expression in small capitalist retailing's folkloric speech.

Could the merchant 'with small capital succeed?' asked one trade journal in 1912, and the answer it received from its readership was resounding: without at least $1,000 in cash and $2,000 in credit, it 'would be impossible to start in business nowadays.' 'Impossible' is not usually thought of as a relative term, but with more than half of all retailers opening their stores on less than $1,000, the journal's readers were clearly interpreting reality rather loosely. What they meant, of course, was that it cost a lot to open the type of store they considered 'legitimate,' and they had a point: when the *Canadian Grocer* listed the essential features of a 'small grocery business,' it counted off 80 square metres of selling space, a large plate-glass window, sanitary bins, silent salesmen, good wooden shelving, an adding machine, a coffee grinder, a meat chopper, a computing scale, a cheese cutter, a cash register, and a typewriter. By equating legitimacy with progressive merchandising, the small capitalist retailers were adding powerful new accents to their already non-inclusive speech. They were justifying their antipathy for the shoestring traders by labelling them 'old fashioned,' and they were implying that only those who had no interest in serving their customers would resist going modern. The penny retailer (generally a 'foreigner with a scatter-gun conscience') was portrayed as having 'no fixed principles in doing business,' meaning that he or she was really in retailing merely to make money. As a result, the smallest did not invest more than the minimum in their stores, they did not pay attention to what their customers wanted, and they survived not through effort but 'at the expense of creditors and legitimate dealers.' For all these reasons, one shoe trader declared, 'I say at the first intimation they should be squelched.'[66]

But in addition to the visible distinctions which modernization made even more apparent, systematic shopkeeping widened the psychological gulf between rich and poor. The progressive retailers saw themselves as people whose stores were 'inviting, stock bright, service courteous, accurate, prompt,' and they considered the backstreet shop to be run by 'the fellow with the Fly-bitten stock, whose Long Whiskered Methods somehow survived the Ark, whose Motto yet runs – "Because Feyther [sic] did."' The modern moss-backed distinction reinforced the affluent storekeepers in their determination to limit opportunities in distribution. It helped to justify licensing and apprenticeship regulations by convincing merchants that retailing was a difficult undertaking for which training was essential. Moreover, system raised the retail store's status, making it more seriously a place of business and less a local hang-out. It was therefore no longer appropriate for shops to be 'stores during the day and bunk houses at night.' In fact, modern storekeepers in rural areas were even urged 'not to permit boys and men to lounge in the store discussing politics, batting averages of baseball teams or who they had out on a date the night before. I would tactfully remind the loungers that I owned a public store and not a social club.' Finally, retail modernization allowed shopkeepers to draw their inspiration from other fields of enterprise and to place their stores on an equal level with factories or offices. The 'unfit' in manufacturing, transportation, and banking had already disappeared, the *Shoe and Leather Journal* observed, and 'if we eliminate the unfit in one category we must do the same in the others. Such is the law of business.'[67]

Here again we can see how words were being used to mediate between folkloric structures and non-trade interests, how they were serving to infuse such traditional values as progress and competition with class-heavy meanings. Historians have tended to notice only the symbolic continuities within the merchants' speech and have consequently underestimated the retailers' ability to adapt to changing circumstances. The truth is, of course, that small capitalist merchants never saw progress as incompatible with their own survival and were fully capable of adapting their businesses to the demands of the mass market. Such adaptation did, however, generally require them to bend their symbols to the needs of contemporary speech. But there was no resultant psychic derangement; instead, modernization reinforced affluent dealers in their self-perceptions, confirming them in their belief that they were as clear headed and entrepreneurial as big business people, without challenging their sense that in being independent and in daily contact with their customers, they were better than the best of their corporate rivals.

Theirs was, admittedly, a self-serving understanding of change, and it did stop well short of explaining the totality underlying the rise of the mass market. They conveniently drew a distinction between business form and meaning, and in so doing they were able to praise modernization without welcoming consolidation. Naturally, they also remained largely silent on the other dimension of modern merchandising: centralization. It was not that they were incapable of recognizing this process – as we shall see, many retailers were critical of the growing power of the manufacturers – but they did not know what they could do about it. Most retailers were keenly aware of their dependence on their suppliers, and they regarded the strengthening of those ties as necessary for their continuing prosperity. Moreover, in much the same way as they avoided confronting modernization's challenge to their own independence, the shopkeepers ignored the fact that they were participating – through curtailing credit and service – in dismantling the very society that they claimed they were specially qualified to protect. The community that turned to its small businessmen for guidance, that depended upon their moral evaluations of its worth, that perceived white-collar workers as owners in training, was fast disappearing even from myth, and the retailers were playing a major role in its destruction. They were, however, for the moment enjoying enough success in their efforts to avoid questioning their time-honoured values. The mass market was for them full of entrepreneurial possibilities. All that concerned them was that they should be given the chance to capitalize on its potential.

5

The Survival of the Fittest

'Of the small shopkeepers, some grew larger, others smaller, some disappeared before your eyes. But to be "in business for oneself" was a hallmark of respectability.' More than half a century after leaving his childhood home in Barrie, A.R.M. Lower could still warm his memories at the pot-bellied stove of the folkloric store. His thoughts about the congruence of work and worth, his trust in the values of 'independence' and 'respectability,' his belief in the superiority of a society based on 'social and economic solidarities,' his sense that every proprietor was a 'small businessman' – all these attest to the lingering influences of his roots in trade. Here were Canada's shopkeepers as they liked to see themselves: united and influential, 'the town's most representative class,' the backbone of the turn-of-the-century locality. How differently would Fredelle Bruser Maynard remember her childhood in the Prairies in the 1920s and 1930s. Her father flitted from place to place, victimized by anti-Semitism and selfishness, driven from one failure to another by his customers' refusal to pay their bills and by the ferocious competition of the chain stores. Her father's businesses, according to her recollections, grew progressively more oppressive, the work more degrading. 'Papa's last store was in Grandview,' Bruser Maynard recalled; 'the building – store and dwelling combined, an arrangement I had come to dread – was, if anything, more depressing than the last, a great box sheathed in corrugated metal that clattered hideously in bad weather. The house smelled of sour milk, the store of sweat and cheese ... [In the store] the fabric on the bolts was faded, the puffed wheat chocolate bars had worms. The shallow glass display boxes fronting the grocery counter contained substances so ancient, so close to total disintegration, that barley was scarcely distinguished from coffee beans.' Here worked the shopkeeper as outsider, a victim of his own dreams of profit, an aspiring community paragon ('substantial though not rich') degraded by having 'dealt in money.'[1]

We might see the contrasts between these two images as consequences of different places and people, but retail propagandists in the early twentieth century would have found in them a broader significance. Between 1900 and 1930, they would argue, retailing had been changed: failure had superseded success; despondency had supplanted pride; exclusion had displaced belonging. The comforting ebb and flow of late-Victorian business life had given way before the fratricidal slaughter of modern competition. Stores that had once seemed the very symbols of community strength were now appearing and disappearing with film-reel speed. Shop owners would ascribe much of the blame to the mass merchandisers, whose 'monopolizing ambitions' had so 'demoralized independent business,' but not all of it. Though the total sales volume had grown, the sad truth was that in trade after trade the number of independent storekeepers had itself outstripped demand. As the editor of the Shoe and Leather Journal sighed, 'there is not enough business to go around ... We may kid ourselves with the idea that people are barefoot or hiding shoe sins with galoshes, and that the money is there to spend on shoes when the need becomes apparent, but the fact remains that there are three people working to meet this need where formerly there was one.'[2] Was it any wonder that the shop owner should no longer seem the image of stability?

It is important to remember that modernization took place amid such increasing competition and uncertainty. The mass market brought sharpened competition, shortened credit terms, and more-rapid style changes, and it was accompanied by population movements, new transportation technologies, and shifts in income. All of these things made the store owners' job more difficult: they had to market more aggressively, operate on tighter margins, anticipate public taste, and respond to demographic changes. The excitement brought by mass consumption and feminized shopping was tempered by doubt and worry. Operating on a narrower margin of error, with less time and more competition, main-street retailers were at once elated and fearful. Market adaptation promised much, but what if one misjudged the market, gambled on unsaleable stock, or spent too much on fixtures that did nothing for sales? It was a trying time.

The shock waves of uncertainty can still be felt in the records of the bankruptcy courts. The mass market suggested great things, but opportunities were all too easily transformed into obstacles and promises into pitfalls. Rapid fashion change in popularly priced clothing and foot-wear, for example, was a development which offered shopkeepers a mechanism for increased sales: 'good styles,' observed a men's wear journal, 'are those which when seen make the old lines look out of date ... [Annual style change] seems to be the one important method that will stimulate business and create opportunity.' But fashion could also prove the ruin of many retailers since seasonal lines, if not sold, were likely to depreciate by 30 to 50 per cent. Claude Ives, a clerk in a Bowmanville shoe store, was not alone in feeling the cutting edge of style. In 1921 he bought the stock and fixtures of the store in which he had worked for $5,000 cash and agreed to pay his former boss, Fred Foley, a further $8,500 plus $2,000 in interest over the next five years. Unfortunately, Ives had mortgaged his flexibility and committed his cash savings, meaning that he could not respond to the dramatic summer style change of 1922, which saw high-backed women's shoes give way to low-backed ones. Unable to dump the old goods because of his debts and too cash-poor to restock with the newer shoes, he watched help-lessly as his business dwindled. To make matters worse, he had to con-tinue to pay capital and interest to Foley 'on stock which could not be turned over and which remained on my shelves as a handicap to me.' Desperate and demoralized, he sold the store at forty cents on the dollar and returned to clerking; five years later Foley had him in court for fail-ing to pay the remains of his debt.[3]

The mass market placed edged tools in the hands of retailers wanting to stay competitive. The instruments of success which it provided – expanded markets, higher volumes, psychological advertising, improved display, hand-to-mouth buying – not only involved what were often expensive risks, but they also demanded a keen eye and a sharp pencil. And store owners were operating on an ever-narrowing margin of error. Hand-to-mouth buying and reduced terms of borrow-ing gave shopkeepers the flexibility to move with demand, but they also thinned the credit cushion. Where nineteenth-century wholesaler credit had extended the life of even struggling businesses for years, debts in the twentieth century were measured in months, sometimes even in weeks. Flushed with money made during the war, James Barter, a farmer in Middlesex County, Ontario, decided on an easier life in distri-bution. With $8,000 he bought a large shoe store in London in 1918, and within three years he had done well enough to afford the move to larger premises. It was an unwise time to undertake expansion: the market contraction caught Barter with unmanageable overhead and soaring debts. Sensibly enough, he cut back on his buying and began disposing of his stock at reduced prices in order to meet his outstanding liabilities; his creditors' response was to make all future orders COD. Barter then asked his main supplier, Dupont et Frère of Montreal, to extend his credit and allow him to put in new goods. Although unwilling to see their own shoes used to pay off their competitors' bills, the manufacturer agreed to extended terms, but only on the condition that Barter sign a $4,000 chattel mortgage to the company. The one-time farmer, for whom the chattel mortgage must have been a familiar purchasing device, willingly signed, but retail was not agriculture and shoes were not farm implements. News of the paper quickly circulated, and Barter's other suppliers promptly demanded payment on all outstanding debts. He was forced to make an assignment late in the summer of 1922; the entire spiral had taken less than ten months.[4]

Of all the mass market's changes, however, none was more easily grasped or more feared than the intensification of price competition. Independent shopkeepers realized that though they might price closely and market energetically, the biggest shops could still undersell them because they bought for less. As one Saskatchewan RMA official explained, 'It is impossible for any merchant to remain in business, do what he may, if his competitor through certain means can buy for 80 cents or 90 cents the same goods for which that merchant has to pay one dollar.' Not surprisingly, many retailers therefore blamed their suppliers both for the lower prices offered by the chains and for the demoralizing price cutting. 'Most of the suppliers took advantage of his inexperience ... and sold him goods at greater prices than prevailing market prices,' a Preston clothier charged, 'making it impossible for him to compete and as a result he sold a considerable quantity of goods below cost.' It was a common problem because the sales necessary to meet the mass merchandisers could easily turn close prices into losses. 'We marked goods up 30%,' a Toronto men's wear dealer informed his bankruptcy hearing, but 'we never got it, in the sense that we would have to very often hold a little sale that would practically take it all away.' 'I had to run a line,' another explained, 'I had to use specials and in some cases sell under cost.' And those specials could often serve as a drain on profits in that 'they had to be advertised, I sent out five or six or seven thousand circulars ... every week ... the overhead was killing me.' The modern retailer – high-pressure marketer, vigorous advertiser, competitive seller – was lacking in elbow-room.[5]

There was sense, then, in the main-street shopkeepers' belief that business life had grown more brutal. Thousands of well-placed and modernizing dealers failed in retailing every year, and thousands more tiptoed carefully round bankruptcy's rim. Still, the problems are easily exaggerated. Though many shopkeepers and most of their historians have described the twentieth century as a period of unrelenting decline for independent enterprise, there is evidence to suggest that the reality was far less bleak. The pain of those who failed should not be ignored, but it can be placed in perspective. Independent retailing did not follow a descending trajectory; rather, like all functioning sectors in the economy, it weathered good times as well as bad. As we have seen, while the number of retail stores grew more rapidly than the population in the late nineteenth century, rapid population growth between 1890 and 1910 meant that store density declined in the first two decades of the twentieth. Furthermore, inflation was very good for profits since retailers were able to mark up stock on a rising market far in excess of the purchase price. These factors alone would suggest a reduction in price competition in the decade preceding the First World War, an idea reinforced by diminished associational activity between 1907 and 1919. Conditions do seem to have changed in the 1920s. During the first part of this period, prices fell precipitously – a horrific situation for tradespeople – and then stabilized at a relatively low level, providing incentive to price warfare. The number of independent stores was also again increasing more rapidly than the population (though the actual *rate* of increase was slower than it had been between 1900 and 1920). And in the 1920s the chains enjoying their initial growth surge, greatly increasing the pressure on the margins of their rivals. Paradoxically, these adverse conditions appear to have been somewhat relieved during the 1930s, because while prices fell again in the early years, competition, measured in terms of store density, also decreased, and the mass merchandisers, as we shall see, found themselves hoist with the petard of their own fixed costs.

These cycles were reflected in both business longevity figures and store failure rates. According to *Dun's Review*, the number of commercial failures – which had increased more than threefold between 1919 and 1929 to equal 18,630 (only slightly less than the total number failing over the previous two decades) – actually declined in the 1930s to 12,521. Similarly, the statistics on bankruptcies for the interwar years show that while there were about 2,200 retail bankruptcies every five years in Ontario between 1920 and 1935, the number dropped sharply to around 800 between 1935 and 1939. The most painful year for Ontario shopkeeping between the wars was 1924 (1,000 retail bankruptcies), with 1932 running a distant second (550 stores). The overall pattern, then, is that after a long period of minimal change in the annual number of business failures (with 1914 and 1915 standing out as exceptionally bad years), disaster struck in the twenties (with troughs in 1921–4 and in the early thirties), and the situation then stabilized again in the five years preceding the Second World War. The information on business longevity provided by the census supports these conclusions, with about 28 per cent of retail businesses in 1920 having survived the decade and with 40 per cent of those opened before 1930 remaining in business eleven years later.[6]

Something interesting was happening to retailing in the years between the wars. In the first place, distribution's growth rate (in terms of store numbers) slowed dramatically from a 65 per cent increase between 1911 and 1921 to 20 per cent in the twenties and down to a 9 per cent expansion over the course of the thirties. Moreover, this deceleration was coming at the expense of new stores, not old. The census returns for 1931 and 1941 offer snapshots of the age distribution of retail businesses, and these show that while the proportion of young enterprises failing did not appreciably change, the life expectancy of those that made it through their initial years was lengthening. This characteristic means not only that the decline in retail expansion was largely attributable to a drop in the number of business starts but also that competition was at least physically diminishing.[7]

There is also reason to believe that much of the burden of failure was carried by the more-marginal businesses. Though shopkeeping remained an accessible form of enterprise throughout the interwar years, interest in penny trading appears to have been declining, especially during the 1930s. Between 1931 and 1941 the number of shoestring enterprises fell from 13,600 to 11,800, despite an overall growth of 9 per cent in the distributive sector. Even in the grocery business, that most open of all trades, the proportion of backstreet stores fell from 27 to 22 per cent of all shops over the course of the Depression decade. This decline does not, however, seem to have been simply a product of immediate economic hardship. There are indications of rising instability within the shoestring sector even during the 1920s, a period when the number of little shops increased prodigiously.

The grocery trade is the best bell-wether of changes in opportunities for penny entrepreneurs, and figures drawn from Dun's reference books for Ontario show a declining life expectancy among the smallest businesses over the course of the early twentieth century. Even eliminating the fly-by-night stores from the calculation leaves one feeling that conditions were worsening from at least 1920. Among backstreet stores opened between 1910 and 1914 and trading in 1915, the median life expectancy was eighteen years, as compared with twenty-one years for the larger businesses. For those opening between 1916 and 1919 and still in business in 1920, the median store now survived seventeen years, with the life expectancy of main-street enterprises moving upward slightly to twenty-two years. But backstreet stores opened between 1921 and 1924 and in business in 1925 had a median longevity of fourteen years, while the largest could still expect to remain open nineteen years. In other words, there is evidence to suggest that some of the hardships experienced by shoestring stores in the 1930s can be traced back to the 1920s. Furthermore, if the smallest stores were bearing a disproportionate share of retailing's failure rate, then the position of main-street trading was probably more stable even than the census figures indicate.[8]

Some of small-shop trading's weakness doubtless derived from the push and pull factors of the labour market. According to the bankruptcy records, 38 per cent of shoestring dealers in the 1920s came from blue-collar backgrounds as opposed to only 15 per cent of larger traders, and the data presented in table 6 suggest that the numbers of working people opening grocery stores in Toronto tended to rise during periods of depression. It is not clear whether it was increasing unemployment or price deflation (and the consequent inflation in the value of savings) that led to the increase in blue-collar business starts during the early twenties and early thirties, but in either case, the decline in the penny shop's life expectancy might have been caused by improving employment conditions and reinflation in the later twenties and the later thirties. The proportion of groceries run by women mirrored these trends: in the early twenties annual rates of opening grew from 7 per cent to 9 per cent and then jumped again in the early thirties from 9 to 13 per cent (stabilizing at 12 per cent through the later thirties). Clearly, Toronto's women, like its men, were more likely to move into grocery trading when times were hardest and options most limited. Much the same could be said of shops run by merchants of non-English backgrounds. In the bad times about 46 per cent of all grocery start-ups were initiated by minority merchants; in the better years the proportion dropped to 35 per cent. Once again, however, controlling for store capitalization reduces these rates of change dramatically. Opportunities and incentives for female and immigrant entrepreneurship remained largely a function of the vicissitudes of the shoestring sector.

Though there can be no doubt that these figures are partially measuring labour-market forces, the overall trend implies that working people, particularly unskilled and semi-skilled men, were growing progressively less inclined to open stores. And in this regard, it is notable that there was an overall decline in both blue-collar business openings and small-shop longevity for the period as a whole. In fact, taking the better years alone, the proportion of male working-class grocers in Toronto decreased steadily from 50 per cent in 1910–19 to 43 per cent for 1925–30 and to 27 per cent from 1935 to 1940, with the greatest change again coming in the later thirties. At the same time, the number of female grocers rose steadily from 6 to 9 per cent. And while working-class storekeeping may have been increasingly feminized in the interwar years, it was still declining. Between the First and Second World Wars, the number of blue-collar shopkeepers dropped by almost 40 per cent.

Still, job-market cycles probably do not fully account for the vicissitudes of penny shopkeeping. Shoestring trading was itself becoming more difficult, and the image of distribution was hardening. And behind both this real and this perceived shift in retailing's character was store modernization. As we have seen, one of the great changes in terms of business practice in the early twentieth century was the shortening of credit and the consequent acceleration of account payments. This development probably affected tiny stores later than it did larger ones because the former still tended to rely on one supplier (a wholesaler in the case of grocers, dry goods dealers, dressmakers, and tailors; a manufacturer in the case of tobacconists, shoe retailers, and ready-made clothiers) for the bulk of their stock. But as life became more difficult for food wholesalers in the 1920s and for manufacturers in the 1930s, the cashflow problem grew in importance. As a result, a 'lack of capital' increasingly became the smallest retailers' major complaint. In 1924 only 7 per cent of Ontario's insolvent penny traders cited a shortage of working capital as the reason for their bankruptcies, as opposed to 10 per cent of those with over $2,000 invested; by 1937 30 per cent of shoestring traders explained their failure in this way, as opposed to 18 per cent of larger stores.[9]

Back at the turn of the century it had been possible to open a store with a few hundred dollars borrowed from a friend or relative, and because merchandise creditors could easily be delayed for a year or more, one could feasibly pay for one's starting stock with profits spread over two or more turnovers. When, however, credit was cut back to a month or three, stock had to be paid for before it was entirely sold. The corner retailers might get along for a while paying small amounts against their debts, but as time passed their accounts simply accumulated, burying them beneath their invoices. In 1933, when Martin Kinkhammer acquired his hardware business in Dublin, Ontario, he had no more capital than a good reputation. Having promised to pay the previous owner's widow in instalments, he worked hard to cut costs – living at his mother-in-laws, taking only $20 a month in wages – so that he might put $800 a year towards meeting his debt to the estate. The problem was finding additional money to pay for the stock he had to buy. He struggled on for a remarkable four years, subsidized by his wife's wages and his mother-in-law's food, but he could never achieve solvency: 'paying that first stock without capital to start with,' he observed, 'is the reason for the bankruptcy. When that first stock was sold it had to be replaced and without surplus capital I see it cannot be done, next thing to impossible.' It was the same story from countless small traders, even those that felt they might otherwise have been able to make a go of it. A London men's wear merchant who opened his store with $150 borrowed from his sister-in-law felt that his business was improving over the course of its fourteen months in operation: 'there was an increase all the time I was there, but I started with so little and it was so small.' The problem was again a shortage of cash. 'My capital was dwindling faster than it was built up. If I had had another two or three years I would have made money, but I did not have the finances to carry on.'[10]

The cash-flow problem probably served as a stimulant to backstreet retailing's feminization. Historians have often emphasized how a shop could help a working family weather economic cycles, subsidizing the low paid and supporting the unemployed.[11] Ironically, contemporary commentators most often described small business as a drain on the family income, a reckless waste of hard-earned money. And while the growing number of women in retailing during bad times would tend to support the former assertion, it is good to remember that at least during the start-up period, when most businesses failed, a store cost more than it earned. Families remembering the golden days of rapid retail expansion in the late nineteenth century may have hoped that the store would carry them through, but the reality of merchandising in the interwar period was somewhat different.

The failure of shoestring traders who once would have survived could only have helped to darken distribution's image as a place to invest. Hard-working and honest people were failing in retailing simply because they did not have enough money to begin with. It must have seemed confirmation both of the small capitalist traders' vigorous predictions concerning independent retailing's demise and of the experts' assertions regarding the need for commercial education and scientific method. In a way, independent merchandising was being made to appear the preserve of the professional masochist.

One sign that all the publicity surrounding the importance of bookkeeping, scientific merchandising, and modern display was having an effect can be seen in the small retailers' apologetic response to questions relating to their own business practices. 'I had to make up a bookkeeping system of my own,' one corner retailer who had earlier worked as an embalmer explained. 'I had no experience in that business and I did my best to keep books so I could figure up at the end of the year what I was doing.' Somehow, this retailer had absorbed the modernizer's cant regarding the need for books, as had the penny trader who noted in his statement of insolvency that he was 'of Finnish nationality and could not keep proper records.' Another small vendor, this time in Peterborough, declared proudly at his bankruptcy hearing that he kept a full set of accounts, though he confessed that he was not sure how much of what he had entered in them was really meaningful. Time and again, penny retailers felt compelled to apologize for failing to adopt the business practices that they believed successful enterprises were employing even when they had good reasons for rejecting them. 'I am interested in the departmental system,' a Pickering shop owner told an inquiring journalist, 'but till the present it has appeared too expensive to adopt, and not only expensive, but cumbersome. If I adopted an adequate system I would need a bookkeeper for the purpose and business does not warrant that.'[12] The use of expressions such as 'I had to make up,' 'I am interested,' 'I could not,' 'I did my best,' 'till the present,' and 'if I adopted' reveal the smaller retailers' discomfort over their own limitations. What is ironic is that for centuries people like these had taken it for granted that account books were not required in their enterprises.

Retailing's folklore, with its reverence for the up-to-date, placed merchants under constant pressure to modernize and in so doing to help in the creation of the kinds of infrastructures necessary to accommodate their new business practices. Cash selling and shortened times on purchases were not imposed on shopkeepers; they were accepted reforms judged as making their businesses more profitable. What is important is that by promoting scientific retailing as the true formula for success (and even survival), shopkeepers were erecting psychological barriers to the entry of the untrained. And because an inclination towards such things as bookkeeping was not evenly distributed through the workforce (table 13), the emphasis on 'system' had the indirect effect of making retailing seem to business 'outsiders' a most forbidding endeavour. All these factors would go some way towards explaining another trend observable in the data on previous occupations, which is that the proportion of people entering retailing with clerical experiences was steadily rising. Though paradoxical in view of the retailers' own belief that shop clerking was becoming less and less an owner's apprenticeship, the change makes sense, given the professionalization of store management practices.

The doorway to retail enterprise therefore appears to have been gradually closing for working-class people, and while the fears of more-affluent store owners concerning the economy's growing inhospitality probably had little truth to them, those of their shoestring competitors almost certainly had. Given the decline in the number of front-parlour shops revealed in the census, the drop in the proportion of working-class entrants into Ontario retailing revealed in the bankruptcy court data and the grocery statistics from the Toronto case-study, which reveal a rising attrition rate among the smallest businesses, there are solid reasons to believe that penny shopkeeping was contracting in the 1930s after suffering increased instability in the 1920s. It was an age when, in terms of independent retailing, bigger was better. Though front-parlour shops may have continued to supply people with the needs of the moment, consumers were choosing to walk a little farther when making their major purchases. What drew them to the larger stores was probably the closer pricing which many small capitalist independents had instituted in response to chain and departmental competition. In the first two decades of the twentieth century, more affluent trades people had complained about the shoestring stores' ability to undercut them, but those fears subsided somewhat during the interwar period. Thanks to store modernization and big-business competition, the pattern was emerging, even among independents, for prices to fall as the scale of enterprise grew.

Consequently, though main-street shopkeepers kept insisting that conditions were worsening, their fears say little about their ability to cope. The mass market complicated trading and made business more aggressive, but thousands of merchants successfully adjusted to the acceleration. As early as 1900, when the *Dry Goods Review* surveyed clothing retailers in downtown Toronto about the impact of the department stores, it found a surprising number adapting to the level of competition. 'So far as his business was concerned,' the journal reported of one Parliament Street trader, 'he would not know they existed'; 'at one time they stole away a good deal of his trade,' it noted of another, but 'now he has the local custom well in hand'; 'we can undersell them on all but what they give away,' boasted a Spadina shop owner, 'and still make a fair profit.' Some months later a still-sceptical journal questioned retailers in the outlying towns and concluded that it was now 'pretty well-founded opinion that the big city department stores do not interfere with the trade of the out-of-town merchants to the extent formerly experienced.'[13] Though many main-street retailers were clearly struggling in the early years of the century, not all were suffering equally. Even as mass production, departmental competition, and the explosion in backstreet merchandising undermined the shopocracy's confidence in the superiority of craft, professionalization through modernization offered its members a new claim on prominence. The complacent Victorian tradesmen who inhabited Arthur Lower's Barrie might have evolved, but they had not disappeared.

A deeper understanding of the larger traders' strategies for survival can be gained only from the records of individual businesses. Like the bankruptcy files, these documents need to be used carefully since they spotlight only the entrepreneurial extreme – those successful enough to leave accounts – but they at least illuminate the range of possibility. One of Windsor's premier dry goods shops, Bartlett, MacDonald and Gow, for example, provides insight into the adaptability of many main-street stores. Its ownership history was typical of that of older community businesses, with each of its owners since its founding in 1860 having worked in the store for a number of years prior to entering the partnership. George Bartlett sixteen years was the accountant for the store's founder, Donald Cameron, while Colin MacDonald was a long-serving department manager, and Alex Gow was for more than a decade Bartlett's replacement in the financial office. Despite sales that grew from around $120,000 a year in the early 1890s to over $300,000 by 1915, the business remained a simple partnership for its first half-century. It never changed location, and what expansion of the main store occurred was accomplished through the acquisition of adjacent properties. There is also something delightfully antique about the way the business paid the mortgages and utility costs on its owners' homes and provided money to every conceivable community organization from the Maccabees to the Ursuline Sisters, from the St Andrew's Society to the Co-operative Commonwealth Federation. Many would see further confirmation of its anti-modern approach in its owners' long-standing membership in the Retail Merchants' Association.[14]

If Bartlett's typified the patrician community store in its overt deference to traditions, it also seemed to conform to the image of the independent business adrift on adversity. Once located at a prestigious location, by the 1920s the store was in downtown Windsor's most troubled sector. The building of a tunnel to Detroit and the declining fortunes of the ferry that ran from the bottom of Sandwich Street (the ferry finally discontinued operations in 1938) cut into the passing trade. Automobiles further altered the urban landscape, as families moved away and Sandwich Street developed – because of the relative sparsity of crosswalks and street lights – into the city's major throughway. The Depression deepened these problems; the collapse of Windsor's automobile economy drove 25 per cent of the workforce onto relief by the summer of 1931, making it the most unemployed city in eastern Canada. But Bartlett's reacted energetically to these changes. Belying its stodgy image, the company moved in the mid-twenties into the branch-store business, opening three specialty clothing shops for men, women, and boys in the blocks adjacent to the tunnel entrance. When the street railway routes were moved and the automobile became king, Bartlett's put in a free parking lot to draw the motor trade. It also countered the Depression by refurbishing the store, putting in a new lighting system, replacing the display counters, altering the floor layout, and increasing its expenditure on advertising.[15] In effect, though the company seemed to evidence the view that small business was traditional and inflexible, Bartlett's refused to succumb to change. Rather, the aging owners responded with lively imagination to the demographic and market shifts that affected their trade.

This idea of building upon strengths – selective adaptation – also ran through the store's business practices. Like many larger dry goods businesses, Bartlett's first innovation had come in the form of direct European buying (George Bartlett had begun the purchasing trips to Scotland in 1885, and Colin MacDonald took over the task in 1890). And Bartlett's great triumph remained its inventory control. Between 1910 and 1940 store sales fluctuated between $250,000 and $600,000, but inventories moved only slightly from $200,000 to $270,000. This phenomenal stock control does speak to the owners' conservative approach to their business; to their willingness to sacrifice a growth in market share to a sound return on the dollar. And yet an investment rather than a market-driven approach should not be confused with immobility, because the product mix in the store changed considerably. Between 1923 and 1936, for example, the value of millinery stock was clipped from $12,000 to $1,000, the dress goods line was trimmed by half, and a dozen new departments were added, including those specializing in furs, toys, toiletries, sweaters, window shades, shoes, and lamps. In effect, while the owners kept tight reins on their annual investment, they were not insensitive to public tastes. Nor were they wary of selling close to keep their inventories moving. All departments between the wars set their opening margins at between 55 and 60 per cent on cost, but the store never grossed anything like this amount. Gross profits earned varied considerably over the years, but they peaked at 49 per cent (in 1918), and in the year of closest pricing they dipped as low as 23 per cent (in 1921).[16]

That is not to make Bartlett's over into a model of entrepreneurial imagination. The company did many things poorly, and the business lost a good deal of money during the 1930s; moreover, in certain respects the company continued to follow a conservative marketing approach. As with so many large stores in the interwar years, the source of trouble at Bartlett's was rising overhead. As one trade expert noted in 1928, 'The most important problem confronting the retailer to-day is that of keeping down the percentage cost of doing business.' At Bartlett's overhead rose steadily throughout the 1920s from 15 per cent of sales in 1918 to 22 per cent by 1927 to 30 per cent by 1936. The branch stores, opened to draw the cross-border trade, were major contributors to the problem, and the men's shop was eventually closed because of poor sales, but even the main store faced soaring expenses. Inventory control and increased turnover were, in the 1920s, the most widely recommended means of confronting rising costs, and Bartlett's pursued both strategies. Turnover was never startling, but the company did increase it from 1.4 to 1.8 between 1918 and 1927, and even during the 1930s Bartlett's careful inventory control kept the goods moving at the accelerated rate of 2.1 turnovers per year. Except deep crisis years – 1921–3 and 1930–3 – the company did not, however, follow the classic turnover approach to the extent of tying margins to stock flow. In fact, the business in more stable periods seemed fairly haphazard regarding gross profits, allowing competition and overhead to dictate the mark-up. This hand-to-mouth approach again suggests the store owners' reluctance to earn lower profits in order to increase sales, a policy which may have reduced store sales in the short term, but which was vindicated during the Depression. From 1930 to 1936 Bartlett's registered big losses and only weathered the storm because of the huge reserves it had packed away during the profit-rich teens and twenties. In other words, both its successes and its failures were products of management decisions, and its owners did their best to change with the times without surrendering the things that worked. These conclusions point to the fact that, while Bartlett's was generally treated more as an investment than a store geared to market share, its owners were willing to adapt to the changing demands of consumers. They experimented with expansion, never allowed their business to moulder, and kept abreast of fashion, and if success is the measure of enterprise, they proved their acumen with an average net profit of 7.5 per cent on volumes (7 per cent on invested capital) for the years their store was in the black (1917–29 and 1936–9).[17]

Unfortunately, in the absence of Canadian trade statistics, it is impossible to judge Bartlett's typicality. On the other hand, even this case makes the point that independent storekeepers were not prisoners of tradition. Some of the decisions its owners made were faulty, but as we shall see, the mass merchandisers were doing many of the same things. And while Bartlett's followed one route to profit, other independent stores were trying different approaches. Hoffmeister Electric, for instance, a mid-sized Vancouver business, aggressively followed the most up-to-date marketing theories. Those associated with the store, like those at Bartlett's, used the language of folkloric remembrance to describe their enterprise, making much of the way the business 'caters to civic pride,' emphasizing how the credit offered 'carries' the customers, and boasting of the attractiveness of the fixtures and the propriety of the 'main street' location. But Hoffmeister was a systems enthusiast: in the 1920s he employed the turnover model, raising the store's stock flow from 1.5 to 3.9 between 1923 and 1929 and rolling back its mark-up by 20 per cent over the same period. When sales collapsed in the early thirties, he remained wedded to turnover by keeping his stock down and reducing his margin still further. Where Bartlett's wanted profits, Hoffmeister pursued market share, and both businesses made money for their owners. In contrast, Bertram Souch, a prescription druggist in Medicine Hat, completely rejected the modernizers' advice. In the worst years of the Depression he increased his inventory and saw his turnover collapse (from twice in the late twenties to less than once by 1933), but thanks to a fixed mark-up of 60 per cent on cost and reduced expenditures on staff, he maintained a net profit of 20 per cent on sales throughout the thirties.[18] There was no formula, no single independent business experience. Different proprietors sold different types of goods to different types of people, and they adjusted their methods to suit the needs of their own markets and contexts. But a very large number of them continued to make good money well into the middle years of the century.

The quantifiable evidence therefore lends little support to the urban small capitalists' opinion that their security was evaporating. Business conditions certainly quickened and hardened in the decade surrounding the First World War, and merchandising grew more difficult, but thousands succeeded in their efforts to master the market. There were periods when things grew worse – the early twenties and early thirties were undoubtedly very trying for business people – but objectively speaking, affluent urban merchants had greater chances of success in 1939 than they had had in 1919. Conditions may have been different in some country places, and general storekeepers were certainly finding life harder from the mid-twenties on than they had two decades before. But these changes mostly involved new buying habits and population movements, and even general storekeepers were not suffering from terminal ill health. It must have bothered rural store owners that the countryside was losing out to the towns, and it doubtless concerned them that there was a gradual thinning out of businesses in their villages, but the majority were witnessing these things, not closing up because of them. In the countryside, as in the cities, it was the new stores that suffered from the relative fall in population, not the older enterprises.[19]

The rise in competition, undoubtedly coupled with trade contractions in certain localities, probably explains much of the small capitalist shop owners' anxieties, but what is important is that while many affluent retailers were complaining about business conditions, a growing proportion were winning their struggle for survival. In fact, standing back a bit and taking in the whole picture, we see a small capitalist sector that was not only modernizing but also apparently becoming more stable. Our conclusion must surely be that the larger stores, far from disappearing into the maw of progress, were being successfully attuned to the mass market. Of course, this does not necessarily mean that the shopocracy was as rich as it once had been, or as prominent, as secure, or as 'independent.' All I have wanted to emphasize is that there is little evidence to support the argument that the actual failure rate of small capitalist stores was increasing. To be honest, if anyone suffered from the revolutionary changes that rocked distribution in the early twentieth century, it was the shoestring merchant.

MASS MERCHANDISING IN THE RED

Of course, the flip side of the stability of small capitalist retailing in the interwar period was the failure of the mass merchandisers to wreak the kind of havoc that was expected of them. If the independent shopkeepers' propaganda was to be believed, department stores should have been found ruining inner-city retailing, chains decimating the main-street competition, and mail-order companies laying waste to the countryside. What the evidence presented above suggests is that while the mass marketers may have been formidable institutions which obtained a large slice of the consumers' spending, their rise was not as destructive as the independents imagined. Both the departmentals and the chains enjoyed tremendous initial growth surges, which for the former had occurred before the First World War and for the latter in the early to mid-1920s, but thereafter their expansion slowed dramatically. Overall, the mass marketers' sales percentage after the mid-twenties did not slip below 28 per cent or rise above 33 per cent (table 9). That this was not from any want of trying is made clear from the eagerness with which the mass merchandisers opened new stores in the later twenties. Unfortunately, their investments would not only fail to reap immediate rewards, but they would leave the big stores heavily debt-burdened and dangerously overextended at a time when credit contracted and operating profits plummeted.

Unquestionably, the least-successful form of national marketing in Canada after the First World War was mail-order selling. Between 1924 and 1930 catalogue sales declined by a quarter, a sorry contrast with the 50 per cent increase in the departmentals' over-the-counter trade (table 9). Even Eaton's mail-order business, the nation's leader, was having difficulty holding its own. Eaton's catalogue trade had grown steadily through the first two decades of the century to peak in 1919–20 at around $63 million, but in the midst of the postwar depression, sales slid by about $6 million, and they only touched the $60 million mark again in the boom year of 1929. The golden age of the mail-order catalogue had indeed been short-lived, and the depression of 1921–4 had signalled its quietus. The difficulty was that a system of selling based on biannual catalogues worked best during periods of relative price stability. Inflationary periods were good for mail-order volumes since people were eager to take advantage of the catalogue's lower list prices, but the companies had to be careful to keep their costs from rising faster than their shrinking gross margins. Deflation, however, was invariably crippling. Not only did a fall in prices suspend the catalogues in mid-flight, but it also exposed the mail-order firms to the negative advertising of sharp retailers quick to expose the excessive prices listed by their mail-order competitors. The success of the mail-order business, a chastened R.Y. Eaton reminded his department heads in late 1921, derived from its ability to market in such ways 'as to allow this business to undersell competition, and we must make all haste to get back these conditions if we are to hold our ground.'[20]

There was, however, more to the mail-order companies' troubles than simply two cycles of price deflation. In the 1920s the number of cars in the countryside more than doubled, and by 1931 42 per cent of Canada's farmers owned an automobile. In Ontario in that year seven out of ten farm operators had a car or truck, and in the Prairies the average was one in two. The automobile did much to liberate country people: it allowed them to travel farther, faster, and more frequently, and it gave them the opportunity to shop when their work was done and not on a separate day.[21] This was good news for stores in local centres, which profited from the increased mobility. Thousands of market-town shopkeepers had learnt by hard experience that they had to meet the mail-order catalogues in price and selection, and they were therefore transforming their stores into neat counterfeits of their big-city competitors. Thanks to the automobile, and to their own efforts to improve the appearance of their stores and the range of their stock, these urban retailers would net good profits in the postwar decade. Times were harder for crossroads merchants, who were forced back on the convenience trade as business migrated to the small towns. Paradoxically, many of them would try to win back some of the trade the automobile had cost them by opening gas bars and service stations.

But if the onward rush of the motor car terrorized hundreds of crossroads storekeepers, it was almost equally frightening to the mail-order executives. And though they did their best to make their businesses competitive with the car, there was less they could do to minimize its impact. Initially, the catalogue companies felt that success might lie in matching the automobile's speed, and they therefore decentralized their facilities in an effort to bring their operations into closer proximity with their customers. Eaton's opened warehouses in Saskatoon, Regina, Moncton, and Edmonton, while Simpson's began shipping orders out of

Regina and Halifax. When this expansion failed to produce the desired result, each company then concluded that the problem was that farmers wanted to go out to shop instead of buying at home, and in order to accommodate this desire, they launched into the agency business. This decision brought the highway's victims into partnership as the departmentals offered agency contracts to crossroads and suffering village shopkeepers. By 1930 Eaton's was running some forty mail-order offices across the country in addition to seventy-two located inside its stores; Simpson's similarly had fifteen large mail-order bureaux, as well as thirty-five smaller agencies. Then, unsatisfied with simply distributing catalogues, the mail-order houses attempted personal solicitation. Generally, the big companies entrusted this task to their local 'agents,' people such as Charles Mills, a general storekeeper in Grenfell, Saskatchewan, who in his spare time travelled around the countryside soliciting orders for Simpson's and then forwarding the purchase forms to the company's Regina mail-order warehouse. But for the smaller mail-order companies, such as Neal Brothers of Winnipeg, peddling orders from door to door would eventually come to replace the catalogue as the primary sales device.[22]

Unfortunately, bringing the store closer to the customer seemed to have little impact on the declining rate of sales. Simpson's eastern mail-order business lost money every year but three in the twenties, the Toronto mail-order operation lost money three years out of six, and the most profitable branch of the operation, Simpson's western, which had seen its sales grow 30 per cent from 1924 to 1929, failed to net more than a modest profit of 4 per cent on volumes. Eaton's, in the meantime, enjoyed a slight increase in its Ontario mail-order sales between 1924 and 1929, but suffered a 70 per cent drop in net profits, while the western operation, which increased its volume by 3 per cent over the same period, saw its profits none the less frozen. These results left government investigators in 1934 puzzling over how such 'astute business concern[s] would continue to operate all these years at such losses.' In fact, there were continuous efforts to revive the mail-order business through innovation, but few of them succeeded. The most highly promoted effort to speed processing, the fully automated Montreal mail-order division opened by Eaton's in 1928, was forced to shut down unceremoniously within three years. Similarly conceived outlets were closed in the later twenties in all regions of the country. Eaton's tried to compensate for these losses by plunging into the chain store business, opening dozens of grocery and general trading outlets in rural areas in an effort to maintain the sales being lost by the catalogues.[23] But in the grim context of the early thirties there was little immediate prospect of a turn-around.

The mail-order companies strained the resources of the departmentals, forcing both Eaton's and Simpson's to rely on their big city stores to convoy the fleet through the storm. Fortunately, operating profits of roughly $1 million at each of the Yonge Street stores were large enough to pull both companies into the black. But though business remained good, there was still no getting around the fact that conditions were changing for the biggest department stores, and each of them was having to experiment with ways of coping with a more-difficult retailing environment. The problem for all of the departmentals seemed to be a relative hardening of their arteries as they reached middle age, though they selected different remedies for the problem. The program at Eaton's and the Hudson's Bay Company was a vigorous (and for the latter, near-fatal) regimen, while Simpson's chose to behave a little more self-indulgently.

Overall, the T. Eaton Company Ltd, which directed the entire retail operation, did very well in the interwar period: gross sales dropped rather dramatically in the early twenties from a high of $150 million in 1920 to $130 million two years later, but they began to recover quickly in 1925 and reached $225 million by 1929, (a 60 per cent increase in sales between 1924 and 1929) and the company remained hugely profitable. When we look more closely at Eaton's business operations, however, some clouds can be found looming on the horizon. One difficulty was the slow growth of the business in its traditional market area. At the Toronto store, sales grew by 20 per cent between 1924 and 1929 in Winnipeg (mail order and store) volumes rose under 10 per cent, and the central Canadian mail order expanded just 4 per cent. Moreover, the real number of customers served in the stores was not increasing: 41.4 million people were served by Eaton's in Toronto in 1924 (77 visits to a cashier per Toronto resident); four years later that number had inched no higher than 43.8 million (74 visits per Torontonian). And as a relative indicator, though Eaton's Toronto store sold twice as much stock in 1929 as Simpson's, its operating profit (before discounts, rentals, depreciation, etc.) was only one-third larger.[24] Indeed, the great increases in Eaton's overall sales were attributable less to increases in the established territories (where sales kept pace with or fell behind population) than to the company's expansion into new areas: the addition of Montreal, Hamilton, Regina, Calgary, Edmonton, Moncton, and Halifax stores, the opening of a string of groceterias and the Teco chain, and the purchase of the Canadian Department Stores.[25] In regions where the store was long established, its growth was levelling off, and the company was compensating for this stagnation with a fierce expansion into new areas. Ultimately, this sales-driven philosophy would also be applied at home when, in an effort to boost Toronto sales, the company launched its highly touted and rather unfortunate College Street expansion.

While Eaton's struggled to keep stiffness away through some energetic stretching, the Hudson's Bay Company tried to diet off its middle-age paunch. The Bay had never been a terribly successful department store – it had had an unfortunate habit of treating its outlets like overgrown fur-trade posts – but in the early twenties all that changed. What the company decided to do was to go after the bargain trade by slashing its prices, cutting its operating expenses, systematizing everything, and making its fortune on increased turnovers. It scored some notable successes, particularly in its smaller British Columbia and Prairie stores, where average stock turns per year increased from roughly three to four and where expenses rose only 10 per cent in the process. But bargain prices were bad for profits, and though sales more than doubled between 1924 and 1929, the company lost four times as much money in 1929 as it had five years before. The situation was at its worst in Edmonton and Winnipeg, where the Bay had its biggest stores. At Winnipeg the company lost $110,000 in 1925 and $447,000 in 1929 despite a rise in stock turn from 2.9 to 3.2 per year. Or perhaps the sentence should read 'because of a rise in stock turn,' for increased turnovers had been accomplished at the cost of runaway expenses (gross margins had risen from 23 per cent to 26 per cent of sales) and a preposterously high percentage of mark-downs (11 per cent of sales). The Bay was paying for its decision not 'to permit Eaton's branches to quote lower prices on any particular line' by sacrificing its profits.[26]

Simpson's followed a very different route from the other two national department stores.[27] Where they tried expanding their sales volumes, Simpson's concentrated on improving its profitability. In fact, by the 1920s the once stylishly up-market Simpson's had slipped into a kind of sober conservatism. Possibly because its three aging owners, H.H. Fudger, J. Flavelle, and H.C. Cox, were not professional retailers, it was operated more with an eye to annual dividends than to such traditional departmental concerns as market shares and trade volumes. As a result, Simpson's expanded very slowly by department store standards, increasing its capital assets from $6 to $13 million between 1920 and 1929, at a time when Eaton's and the Bay grew threefold (Simpson's increased its fixed capital at about the same pace as much smaller businesses such as David Spencer's in BC). Moreover, instead of spending money on opening new stores, Simpson's pumped money into the Toronto business (Simpson's Company Ltd), with $5 million of the $7 million in new capital expenditures going to extending the Queen Street operation. The management was rewarded with a relatively slow, but healthy growth in volumes and greater stability in profits, for though total sales at Simpson's Toronto store rose modestly from $21 million in 1920 to $23 million in 1924 and $31 million in 1929, operating profits remained at a consistently satisfying 7.5 per cent on volume (which was identical to Bartlett's). In direct contrast with its main rival, the company was putting all its eggs in its Toronto basket. And while Eaton's was more or less stagnating in the traditional centres and expanding outside, Simpson's was quietly growing in the city, but suffering everywhere else. Beyond the borders of Toronto, Simpson's had average operating profits of just 3 per cent on sales, a disappointing performance given the booming marketing climate of the later twenties. The mail-order business was a dead weight, and while Montreal was still profitable, it was really just paying its way.

There were other concerns: Simpson's Company Ltd by 1929 was carrying a very high burden of debt: $1.7 million in 5 per cent first mortgage bonds, a $236,000 mortgage on its Mutual Street property, and $4 million in 6 per cent cumulative preference shares (issued to finance a 1928 building extension), on top of the regular capital stock of $23 million. And there was not much cash in the bank – around $50,000 in 1929 for a company valued at $22 million – to meet an operational downturn.[28] Fortunately, Toronto had a manager in C.L. Burton who had developed a winning formula: between 1924 and 1929 he had increased stock flow from 4.6 to 4.9 and pressed down expenses from 89 to 86 per cent of gross margins, yielding higher net profits. And while expenses had risen relative to sales from 20.6 to 21.6 per cent, higher profits had been assured through increased mark-ups (from 29 to 31 per cent on sales). In his unexciting way, Burton was selling more and making more on each sale, and he was thereby ensuring that the big dividends could continue to be paid. The question was whether he could also work his magic with the other branches of the business.

Burton, backed by money from J.H. Gundy and Herbert Holt, acquired control of the entire Simpson's operation in 1929 and immediately set about trying to revive hitherto comatose sections of the business, beginning with the mail-order division. Convinced that the problem lay in the biannual catalogue approach, he decided to issue a new catalogue every sixty days and to handle the anticipated increase in business by dramatically enlarging the Toronto mail-order warehouse. It was a costly mistake. As prices plummeted in 1930, so too did the mail-order trade: down $1 million in 1930–1, $2 million the next year, and $3 million the year after. In 1933 Simpson's mail-order division distributed one-half as much as it had in 1929, and it lost a packet – it was costing the company thirteen dollars to sell every twelve. Retrenchment now seemed the best strategy. Dozens of catalogue outlets were closed, and in 1933 Simpson's proposed eliminating the entire mail-order division. Though the decision was postponed, it was a sign of the severity of the crisis. The store was proposing a full-scale retreat to Toronto, with only its outlet in Montreal left to defend Ontario's perimeter. The company, the president announced, intended 'to leave the local trade to local people, we have no intention of engaging in the branch store business,' or at least not until the business climate had improved.[29]

The Depression served as a kind of corporate endurance test, taxing the super healthy and exposing the frailties of the weak. So while Simpson's mail-order trade collapsed, the big losses at Eaton's were suffered by the Toronto store and by its Canadian and groceteria chains. Operating profits at Eaton's fell dramatically (Montreal's, for example, declined from $1.1 million in 1929 to $111,000 in 1933), but most of the branches managed to hobble it out. Toronto, however, already showing signs of trouble in the twenties, lost close to $2 million between January 1931 and December 1933. Similarly, the Canadian Department Stores chain, which through the late twenties had added some $5–9 million to Eaton's sales volumes every year, had only managed to pay a dividend because Eaton's had surreptitiously pumped around $200,000 a year into the company. Again, the Depression exacerbated the problem, and as the losses grew, so too did the transfers: by 1931 Eaton's was subsidizing Canadian to the tune of half a million dollars, or 5 per cent of its total overhead. No department store, however, did as badly as the Hudson's Bay Company. Operating losses at the Bay grew from $182,000 in 1929 to just over $2 million in 1931. In fact, so desperate did the London shareholders become that in 1936 they offered to sell the entire chain to Simpson's. Apparently, C.L. Burton did not feel that his store could afford the expansion.[30]

'The big stores are not making the profits expected of them,' the *Cana-*

dian Grocer reported gleefully. In fact, competition, which had for so
long been battering the independent merchants, seemed finally to be
levelling the giants. 'The Large organizations are fighting for their own
existence,' the trade press giggled; 'the big stores are jealously watching
each other in order that they won't lose out on a single play and every
effort is being made to keep pace with the speed of the other.'[31] At the
heart of the departmentals' difficulties was not a decline in business –
Eaton's Montreal clerks served more customers per year in the early
1930s than they had in the twenties, and at Winnipeg and Toronto the
company's customer pool remained above 1926–8 levels until 1933 – nor
was it the drop in volumes, since lower sales had more to do with the
deflation in prices than with an actual fall in trade. On the contrary the
problem originated with expenses, not with merchandising. Somehow,
though the dollar value of department store sales declined sharply, costs
remained unconscionably high. In 1925 expenses at Eaton's Toronto
store amounted to 21.5 per cent of retail sales; in 1930 that figure had
risen to almost 24 per cent, and three years later it amounted to a staggering 30 per cent.

At Eaton's, as at the other stores, the managers counter-attacked
aggressively. They increased their expenditures on advertising 23 per
cent to accelerate turnovers, cut their selling staff by 15 per cent, and
pushed down the average sales clerk's wages by one-fifth (one-third in
the case of female staff). They also experimented with greater stock control, with incentives to shoppers to carry home their own purchases, and
with assigning each department manager a fixed budget above which
he or she could not spend. But it was not easy to bring down expenses.
Wages represented just one element in the departmentals' overhead, at
Eaton's accounting for only about a third of total costs.[32] Apart from
wages, each department in a store had to pay its share of taxes, advertising, sundry costs (such as ventilation, donations, doormen, gas, water,
telephones, and uniforms), general office expenses (accounting, audit-
ing, general statistics), delivery, buying-office overhead, and workroom
expenses (alterations and repairs). Moreover, each department was
charged rent and interest on the stock it held (5–6 per cent of the value
of merchandise at cost). Most of the department stores owned the property on which they were situated, but rent was a relatively inflexible
expense since it was calculated simply to cover building maintenance
and operating costs as well as to yield a fairly conservative 4 per cent
profit to the 'rental department.' Similarly, while most operating deficits
would have been eliminated if the stores had simply not been charged 6

per cent on their inventories, that expense represented a real cost on money invested, and the amount had remained fixed since the early days of departmental selling. In fact, it was this 6 per cent, paid by the individual stores to their parent companies, that generally covered the dividends on the stock. Still, it was the inflexibility of these expenses, rather than wage costs, that now most hurt the departmentals. They were big institutions with heavy administrative, delivery, warehousing, and maintenance costs, and they found it next to impossible to deflate their general expenses in tandem with the fall in prices.

The department stores' uncertainty concerning their mark-ups only served to aggravate their problems with overhead. That fixed expenses decline as turnovers increase was a maxim etched in the stone of the departmentals' walls. As a result, the managers believed that there was only one way to reduce overhead, and that was to cut prices and thereby stimulate sales. Tight margins inherited from the twenties were therefore squeezed further: the Bay in Vancouver dropped its mark-ups as a percentage of sales from 31.2 per cent in 1928 to 28.1 in 1932, and even Simpson's in Toronto, which had rejected the low-margin-high-turnover approach, was panicked into conformity, slicing its mark-ups from 31.1 to 30.6 in the first three years of the crisis. Only the most desperate businesses – Canadian Department Stores, Eaton's Toronto, and certain divisions of the mail-order trade – could not afford to carry lower prices and held their margins firm. To compensate, Eaton's became extremely aggressive in its buying and used its huge muscle to force the cuts it could not endure back on the manufacturers who supplied it. Contrary to expectations, however, lower prices did nothing actually to increase sales (though they might have kept customers from going elsewhere), but they did take a great toll on profits. It was this realization that led the departmentals, beginning in 1934, to start raising their prices. By 1939 the Bay's Vancouver store would be marking up goods 32.3 per cent and Simpson's in Toronto would be at 31.1. This change of direction had a bountiful affect on profits.

The great departmentals would therefore survive the Depression years. But they would emerge chastened – less eager to cut prices, less anxious to bare-fist it with their competitors. They were now more willing to behave like yesterday's heroes: giants that moved a little more slowly, saw a little less clearly, and were having trouble keeping up with the wild enthusiasms of their younger rivals.[33] Astute observers had seen the change coming in the twenties, but the department store executives had apparently been reluctant to act with the dignity demanded of their age. Apart from Simpson's, which had behaved with restraint in the postwar decade and only briefly lost its composure in the early thirties, the department stores continued to believe that they could lead the way in retailing. They might have saved themselves the effort because the interwar years belonged to the chain stores.

While the big departmentals had faltered, the chains had rushed madly ahead. Tamblyn Drugs had almost tripled its sales between 1921 and 1929, Dominion had increased its tenfold, and Loblaw's had multiplied its by twenty-two, and there were almost daily openings of new stores – Dominion alone opened an average of one store a week between 1919 and 1929. But we should not be misled: this was an expensive business. Expansion was essential for the chains because they needed huge volumes to cover the costs of their buying and warehousing operations, as well as to give them the power to secure big discounts. But rapid growth entailed heavy fixed costs as shops had to be fitted, rent paid, and stock acquired. Between 1919 and 1933 Dominion increased its capital investment from $20,000 to over $4 million, Loblaw's expanded its from $129 thousand to $5.6 million, and S.S. Kresge doubled its investment in the four years after its 1928 incorporation. This expansion had to be undertaken in anticipation of business – business that often took many years to establish. The A&P, for example, felt that to make its Canadian operations pay it would need to saturate the market.[34]

Launched in Montreal in 1926, the A&P grew quickly from 40 stores to 250 in just four years, but in so doing it saddled itself with oppressive costs. In 1929 the Canadian operation registered a deficit of $1.5 million, and the next year three-quarters of its outlets recorded annual operating losses; all of which led one government investigator to ask, when confronted by the A&P's balance sheet, whether 'all the increasing outlets are just for fun ... why were they making or increasing the outlets as they were if they were not making any money?' The A&P's Quebec divisional manager, attributed it to goodwill: 'a large amount of our losses,' L.W. Beebe explained, 'are so-called paper losses. In the set-up for a new company you have necessarily to invest a tremendous amount of money to get the proper set-up and until you run the proper term of years you must continue to take losses.' Fortunately, American subsidiaries such as this one could lean on their parents for support: the debt of the Canadian A&P to the American company stood at $1.5 million in 1929, while the Diamond W funded its operations in Canada to the tune of $9 million.[35]

Once the chains reached their natural limits – the point at which their volumes were large enough to justify their established infrastructures – they settled down to make some money. For the oldest businesses, this moment had been reached by 1927, and the chains therefore slowed their growth rates in the later twenties. Dominion Stores, which averaged a 47 per cent annual increase in the number of its outlets and a 40 per cent rise in its sales per annum during the period 1920–5, cut its yearly growth rate to 6.7 per cent in stores and 14 per cent in sales over the next quinquennium. It was not, of course, entirely a matter of choice. As one Dominion executive declared in early 1929, the chain was not expanding its operations further 'due to the very strong increasing competition,' and the same explanation was offered one year later when the company began actually to shut down stores. Loblaw's, Dominion's smaller, but ultimately more successful, rival in the Ontario market, was also slowing down in the late twenties. Sales per store had risen for Loblaw's by 83 per cent between 1921 and 1925, but by 1929 they had actually fallen by 4 per cent. Perhaps it was the feeling that the market could not support such a large number of heavily cost-burdened, aggressive competitors that led Loblaw's to discuss a merger with Dominion in 1929 and Carroll's to consider selling out to the A&P.[36] Certainly, the A&P could have used the stability enjoyed by Carroll's southern Ontario chain.

Many companies went beyond talking. Unable to make good on their initial investments, a number sought relief from the heavy weight of their chains in the great merger wave of the late twenties. In 1926 Mailloux and Parent's Quebec grocery stores bought up A.O. Phillip's meat and grocery business and the small Scott Brothers chain. One year later Arnold Brothers acquired Martin Stores from the William Davies Company and then itself merged with Pure Food Stores to form Consolidated Food Products Limited; shortly thereafter, Consolidated bought Piggly Wiggly's Quebec operations. But Consolidated itself swiftly ran into trouble and in 1929 declared a loss of $122,000. That same year Safeway Stores pressed into Canada from the United States, sweeping up the Kirkham chain and MacDonald's Consolidated in its advance; Noad's sold out to Superior Stores; and Tip Top merged with Berger's Tailoring. As one retail analyst observed in 1928, competition seemed to be 'no longer between the chains and the independent but rather between the chains themselves.'[37] In fact, like the industrial merger movement of the late 1890s, high fixed costs accrued by expansion during a business recession were returning to haunt the recovery.

It was in the midst of this adjustment that the market broke. The timing was, from the chains' perspective, doubly unfortunate: those that had just bought up other people's businesses were struggling to adjust their operations to the new volumes, while many of the remainder were preoccupied with downsizing. The Depression made these tasks more difficult because the chains, like the department stores, found costs far stickier than prices. At Dominion total operating expenses rose steadily upward in the early thirties from 17 per cent of sales to 22 per cent by 1933, with the percentage of this taken by wages growing from 33 to 36 per cent. Despite its self-serve approach, Loblaw's was similarly hindered by operating costs that rose precipitously from 11 to 15 per cent of turnover. Tamblyn, the drug chain, had its costs grow from 24 to 27 per cent, while Woolworth's increased from 26 to 28 per cent of sales. 'The trouble with the chain store system,' one government investigator observed, 'is that the operating expenses ... have been too rigid and cannot adjust themselves to the level of commodities.' Wages were the single largest factor in operating costs, accounting for a little under half of all expenses at the variety and drug chains and for about a third of the grocery stores' overhead, but they were not the only expense. As they tended to locate on busy streets, the chains had heavy rental costs (about 25 per cent of their overhead), and they had high maintenance and advertising expenses. On top of these costs the chain outlets had to pay for the centralized bureaucracy – for the buyers, accountants, managers, warehouse operations, and delivery expenses – all of which consumed a quarter to a third of their total overhead.[38]

Ultimately, the chains proved no more immune to the falling rate of profit than the department stores. In some trades, such as grocery retailing, where the large number of competing chains made for keen price competition, profitability was exceedingly low. Net operating profits as a percentage of sales declined at Dominion (still one of the most successful chains) from 2.2 per cent in 1928 to 1.5 per cent in 1933. At Hamilton's William Carroll chain, net operating profitability fell from 3.2 per cent of sales in 1928 to a loss of 2.2 per cent five years later. Times were even harder for the A & P; of the company's 244 Canadian stores, 191 were in the red on their operations in 1930. Overall, the A & P lost $260,000 in 1929 and $82,000 in 1934, even after the addition of huge cash loans from the U.S. parent totalling $1.5 million in 1929 and $2.9 million in 1934. But the grocery chains were not alone: Louis K. Liggett's drug chain lost money on its operations every year, with the exception of two, from 1924 to 1933, and Metropolitan Stores, a Canadian five-and-dime, failed to make any profit between 1930 and 1934.[39]

Like the departmentals, the chains tried to get around their problems by cutting wages and slashing allowances. Wages had never been high for those working in chains, but during the Depression they were reduced to appalling levels. Male workers at Dominion earned $6 for an average work week of sixty-two hours, a paltry sum even in 1934, but one that seems munificent compared with the $3 earned by delivery boys on their feet for the same number of hours. When federal investigators began their price spreads inquiry in 1933, the company hastily adjusted its payroll, inflating male workers to an average weekly wage of $12 and delivery boys to $5.50, a telling comment on how low the company itself considered its previous wages. However, Dominion was not by any means alone in trying to reduce overheads by lowering wages. United Cigar Stores dropped one female clerk's wages steadily from an initial pay of $8 for a sixty-two-hour week to a wage of $6.30 after five years' employment; in the words of the price spreads commission's lawyer, 'if she is there another ten years she will be working for pleasure.' To circumvent the provincial minimum-wage laws, chain stores also relied more heavily on part-time workers. Fully two-thirds of Metropolitan's clerks were part-time, and their average salary was only $4.30 a week. Wages for part-time workers regularly ran from about 9¢ to 20¢ an hour. Unquestionably, however, delivery boys were by far the lowest paid, earning $3 a week at Stop and Shop and between $1.50 and $3.00 at Thrift. Often the stores employed boys from the charity homes and worked them ruthlessly: from 8:00 a.m. to 7:30 p.m. five days a week and from 9:00 a.m. to 10 p.m. on Saturdays. According to one orphanage director, the delivery boy 'goes out to work early in the morning and comes in at night after the rest of the boys are in bed. He is simply existing, that is all – no recreation, no training for the future. He is simply a slave.'[40]

The chains, however, protested that they had little choice but to pay low wages. 'We could not really afford to increase our help there,' the treasurer for Metropolitan Stores explained of the wages paid, 'or else we would be out of business. We have been fighting for the last three years simply to keep in business.' J.G. Johnston, the secretary of the newly formed Canadian Chain Store Association, concurred, though he tried to sound more optimistic: 'for a long time now we have had a very difficult time in every business; profits have almost disappeared in the great majority of businesses, and when commodity prices begin to rise again and the buying power of the public increases the situation will improve.'[41]

But wages were not the only area exposed to the executives' knives, for the price spreads' investigation also made the horrible discovery that the corporate chains had been attempting to reduce overheads by giving their customers short weights. Nothing could have been more pleasing to the independent shopkeepers or more damaging to the reputations of the chains than the realization that every day in tiny ways, the consumers were being cheated. Some of the methods used to deceive the public seem in retrospect amateurish and niggling; one of the most common tricks was to attach three-quarters of an ounce of fat to the beam under the weighing-scale's plate, thus offsetting the scale and giving short weights on meat. Another was for the butcher simply to rest a thumb on the scale when meat was being weighed. Bulk goods, such as sugar, were also regularly sold short. As a rule, sugar was shipped to the individual chain outlets in hundred-pound bags. The individual store then had to repackage the sugar into one-pound bags, and a fixed price had to be charged for each. Unfortunately, the chain head office made no provisions for spillage, meaning that the manager was responsible for the impossible task of turning one hundred-pound bag into one hundred one-pound bags. The result was that each bag tended to be sold short to the consumer. Said one Thrift Store manager, 'we specialize in short weights ... instead of weighing bulk goods sixteen ounces we would weigh an ounce or two less; in some cases more.' Small though the gains might be on each sale, the excess profits made from this type of chiselling did make a difference to many stores. One Dominion butcher admitted that the 28 per cent gross profit the company expected from its meat department was impossible, given the prices at which meat was being sold. The department, he confessed, would yield a margin of about 22 per cent, but since Dominion Stores demanded more, the difference had to be made up 'by gypping the public.'[42]

This cheating was made necessary by the regular chain practice of holding its store managers responsible for obtaining a fixed percentage of profit on sales. Managers bought almost all their stock from their company warehouses, and they sold at prices dictated by their firms' head office. On weekly sales they were required to make a fixed profit in each department: canned goods and fresh fruits, for example, were expected to yield a 33 per cent margin, while baked goods were sold at 32 per cent gross profit on the selling price. When a manager failed to make the required amount – and many complained that they could not, given the prices they were being required to charge – the difference was taken out of their salaries. In order to ensure compliance with these hard rules, some firms, such as Stop and Shop, required managers to deposit $250 annually with the company, which would be used to defray the costs of any losses on profits.[43] There could have been few more-powerful incentives to cheat the consumer than this practice.

In their desperate effort to make their stores pay, the chains were under pressure to reduce expenses wherever possible, but they were also being forced to increase their mark-ups. Unlike the department stores, which were generally reluctant to increase price spreads until 1934, the chains began inflating their mark-ups in the first year of the Depression. Loblaw's raised margins as a percentage of sales from 16.5 to 21.8 between 1929 and 1933, and Woolworth's jacked its mark-ups over the same period from 40 to 42 per cent. All of the chains did this (including Eaton's groceteria), and they did it with such zeal that by 1934 chain store mark-ups were higher on average than those added by the small capitalist independents. Where the average main-street men's wear store was marking up 29 per cent (on sales), the chain was adding 32 per cent; where the typical small capitalist furniture dealer was making 32.8 per cent on sales, the chain was making 39.3. Only in the grocery line were chain margins slightly lower (16 per cent as opposed to 16.5), and even that differential was eliminated by 1937.

Obviously, if the chains were to remain price competitive, they would have to buy more advantageously than the independents and thereby subsidize their higher mark-ups with savings at the supply end. Therefore, as high fixed and sticky operating expenses chewed away at store margins, chain buyers fought to drive down wholesale prices. In 1929 Dominion paid 81¢ to its suppliers out of every $1 it sold; by 1933 it had reduced the suppliers' share to 76¢. Woolworth's in the meantime cut supplier prices from 60¢ to 57¢ on the dollar, Kresge's from 68¢ to 63¢, and Carroll's from 87¢ to 82¢. On top of these lower prices, chain stores demanded discounts, allowances, and rebates from manufacturers whose products they featured in their advertising. The big stores were always reluctant to divulge the extent of these concessions, but some shadowy figures do emerge from the early thirties. Dominion received $500 a month from Weston Bakeries in 1933, and that same year another manufacturer admitted paying Loblaw's $13,000 in special allowances. In fact, Loblaw's, with an advertising budget of $110,000, acknowledged receiving $120,000 in advertising allowances (out of total rebates amounting to $197,000).[44]

In the early years of the Depression, these allowances went a long way towards making chain selling profitable: in 1933 the A & P's operating loss was reduced from a whopping $266,000 to a more manageable $73,000 because of manufacturer allowances, and the generosity of Thrift Stores' suppliers turned an operating deficit of $54,000 into a profit of $72,000. Though ostensibly for use in promoting the manufacturers' products, the discounts and allowances were really a 'blind allotment.' As most suppliers exercised no control over how the allowances were used, they amounted to 'nothing more than an extra discount' – a bonus central to the profitability of many struggling chains. Most manufacturers disliked paying these discounts, but in the context of the early thirties they felt that there was little they could individually do to stop the practice.[45] Ultimately, however, the intensity of the mass merchandisers' buying blitz would agitate manufacturers to such an extent that they would actually seek government help in restricting the bonuses they paid.

During the twenties the managers of most chains and departmentals had been tempted to rush the fences, and in so doing they had severely handicapped their stores. True, they had generated a good deal of adrenalin in the effort (and nail-biting tension among their competitors), but their 'sense of urgency' had ultimately proven misplaced. I don't want to exaggerate: mass merchandising was not fatally flawed or on the verge of collapse, but decisions had been made in the optimism of the postwar decade that would have a deleterious impact on profits in the depression years which followed (tables 8 and 9). Moreover, mass merchandising had failed to live up to expectations. In the twenties the Filenes and the Loblaws had predicted that they would sweep away the independent traders and provide every consumer with the lowest priced goods in the most efficient manner. But the mass merchandisers had instead found it seriously taxing just to stay the course. Independent retailing, far from being overwhelmed, had adapted most efficiently to the new market conditions and had, by the 1930s, come to operate more cost effectively than its great rival. But this outcome was not something about which the shopocracy cared to boast. Thousands of small capitalist traders apparently still felt that conditions in retailing had deteriorated, that bankruptcies had multiplied, and that profits had evaporated. So it came as cold comfort to learn that they were doing relatively better than many of their corporate competitors. 'It is poor consolation to the merchant who has been put out of business by such competition,' a Saskatchewan dealer explained sensibly, 'to know that he is a better merchant than he was before the competition started.'[46] Unfortunately, it is far from clear just how many retailers were actually put out of business by the mass marketers; though everyone knew it had happened, no one could really say to whom.

ACCOMMODATING THE NEW WORLD

Thus we come to the question of motivation. This chapter has argued that small capitalist retailers held certain misperceptions concerning the changes affecting distribution in the early twentieth century. They were convinced that business was becoming progressively less stable, that they were having difficulty making ends meet, and that competition was intensifying. Though there was some truth to these beliefs – competition was unquestionably increasing, and without the tools to measure individual store profitability, we can take the merchants at their word – the available data suggest that they were not being undermined by the changes. Trade became bumpier for owners of main-street independent shops early in the new century, but thereafter it was carried forward at a fast pace. Though new shopkeepers found it harder to establish themselves (with the worst years coming in the early twenties and early thirties), owners whose stores made it through their infancy could look forward to a long life in business. Of course, a rising failure rate among new enterprises would have created the impression of increased instability, but that is not the same thing as saying that the well-to-do traders were themselves in trouble. Nor does the evidence justify the belief – at least for the interwar period – that the competition was ruining them; there was no significant rise in the number of small capitalist failures despite the expansion of mass merchandising and the growth in the number of independent shops. Indeed, it seems to have been the people about whom the affluent traders were complaining – the shoestring storekeepers – who were suffering the greatest hardship in the age of mass marketing.

There were, however, good reasons why affluent tradespeople would have perceived competitive conditions to be worsening. Without access to government statistics and lacking the time or desire to collate the available evidence, they would have acted on what they were able to see. And what they would have observed was a growing number of independent stores, an increasing number of chains, and an intensification of price competition. Furthermore, they would have seen a large turnover in newly opened shops, and they would have been more aware (thanks to the trade press) of the failures of older, more-established businesses (they would have been especially shocked by the disappearance of so many of their old wholesalers in the 1910s and 1920s. Crossroads merchants would have added to these images a perception that the countryside was changing, that their little market centres were slowly dying, and that the younger generation was leaving the farm. And while their own stores may have continued to do all right, that would not have diminished their sadness over the declining prestige of rural life.

In addition, modernization carried risks. Canada's small capitalist retailers were clearly experiencing rapid change, and they were watching rather impotently as vast bridges were built between their own 'island communities' and those of their competitors. The process may not have been putting them out of business, but it was forcing them to adjust to new relations and ever-accelerating demands. And though they were adapting to the changes, they were doing so apprehensively, uncertain as to the success of their efforts. Store refurbishment, hand-to-mouth buying, cash selling, voluntary pooling – all were risky ventures demanding a good deal of money and threatening established custom, and margins in the early twentieth century were considerably tighter, giving even successful merchants a narrowed channel in which to manoeuvre. As George Hougham observed sympathetically, the average retailer 'is afraid to part with the past and afraid to face the future. He realizes that the methods of the last decade are not suitable to the next decade. Yet he is afraid to experiment.'[47]

The uncertainties of the well-to-do retailers sound suspiciously like status anxieties. According to many sociologists and psychologists, small business people were so disoriented by change that a mass persecution complex developed among them which predisposed them to extremism. 'Materially speaking,' Harold Lasswell wrote, 'it is not necessary to assume that the small shopkeepers, teachers, preachers, lawyers, doctors, farmers and craftsmen were worse off at the end than they had been in the middle of the [nineteenth] century. Psychologically speaking, however, the lower middle class was increasingly overshadowed ... The psychological impoverishment of the lower middle class precipitated emotional insecurities within the personalities of its members, thus fertilizing the ground for the various movements of mass protest through which the middle classes might revenge themselves.'[48] Such a conclusion is plausible enough, but it has limits.

Status anxiety does not sum up the retailing mind, and Lasswell is no Cocker. The 'insecurity complex' idea is a crude and inflexible instrument which rests on false premises (that all lower-middle-class people are alike and united) and primitive theorizings concerning the latency of psychological maladjustment among social groups. Though retailers may have been apprehensive, it was not so much fear that drove their actions as ambition. For all that they may have been concerned about the future, progressive shopkeepers saw scientific retailing as trade and status enhancing. They were not simply trying to defend what they had once been; through professionalization they were hoping to improve their standing, just as they were seeking to make their businesses more profitable by adopting modern sales practices. Similarly, though they caricatured and de-legitimized their trade rivals, they did not do so because they viewed the mass marketers and the shoestring shop owners as their superiors. Implicit within the decision to alienate their competitors in discourse was a moral judgment: in denouncing the chains, departmentals, and penny storekeepers as foreigners, hucksters, and business demoralizers, the small capitalist merchants were at once distancing and belittling them. So while progressive tradespeople were suffering the increased tension of modern business life, they were not looking backward. What they wanted – and what they thought they deserved – was greater security and increased profits in the here and now. In this sense, to understand the shopkeepers we must come to grips, not with their worries, but with their ambitions.

6

Resale Price Maintenance

We come at last to the issue of retail activism, a topic which has, for many interpreters, posed hardly a problem at all. Traditionally, historians regarded shopkeeper protest as a knee-jerk response to the degradation of the 'small business sector' in the modern age. Their minds poisoned by the experience of economic decline, shopkeepers are presented as having sought security in chauvinism, anti-modernism, and demagoguery. In informal alliance with small manufacturers and farmers, the retailers are seen to have fought an irrational and hopeless struggle to restore their marginal economic and social positions. From entrenched positions on the political right, they launched populist attacks on the emerging corporate order. Poincarism and Poujadism in France, Reconstruction, Duplessisism, and Social Credit in Canada, populism and McCarthyism in the United States, Naziism in Germany – all have been seen as the political reverberations of the declining stratum's *cri de cœur*.

In recent years historians have effectively challenged aspects of this interpretation. By evoking images of 'debt peonage,' American historians have associated populist protest more closely with traditional European peasant unrest than with reactionary twentieth-century petit bourgeois protests. In Belgium and Germany right-wing politicians have been blamed for manipulating small-business fears and have been held responsible for the reactionary character of retail dissent; and in France and Italy shopkeeper activism has been linked to the erosion of traditional social cohesions rather than with the challenge of big-business competition. Still, even revisionist historians tend to describe storekeeper activists as 'traditional' and 'declining,' and those who do not believe that big business was proletarianizing them none the less suggest that fear of impoverishment led store owners to suffer a politicizing set of status anxieties.

The problem is therefore one of conceiving Canadian retail activism and political unrest in light of main-street shopkeeping's adaptation and stability. What drove retailers to associate if it was not fear for their continued survival, and what is to be made of their ostensibly anti-modern demands? The argument offered here is that trade organization in Canada was less about survival than about controlling competition and increasing profits. Modernization involved tremendous costs and risks, and main-street retailers were anxious not only to defend what they had but to make their efforts pay. Mass merchandisers and backstreet shop owners were each perceived to have possessed 'unfair' competitive advantages which retailers wanted to eliminate: where chains and departmentals used their buying power to 'browbeat' suppliers into giving them large discounts and their advertising to 'seduce' consumers into buying their wares, shoestring shops had the advantage of being small enough to break the laws on early closing and Sunday observance without detection. Similarly, where immigrant shopkeepers were thought to be 'unfairly' supported by their communities, women were believed to be 'subsidized' by their husbands. In short, retailers protesting 'illegitimate' competition were attempting to 'level the field' of competition. They were firmly convinced that by controlling what they defined as 'abuses' they could eliminate the competition that constricted their profits and aggravated their uncertainties.

As we have seen, this approach to competition was shaped by the modernizing shop owners' non-business identities. Though trade warfare was an undeniable business reality, the main-street storekeepers who joined the retail associations and fought to solidify their competitive positions, employed non-occupational measures of legitimacy and illegitimacy. Because they shared gender, class, and ethnic assumptions, they did not perceive any of their own number to be 'destabilizing' opponents, even though they were in competition among themselves. 'Illegitimacy' was reserved for those who, because they were outsiders to the shopocracy, did not fit élite definitions of professionalism and for those who, because of their size and aggression, had turned themselves into irresponsible combines intent on monopolizing trade. If it was the insecurities experienced by those adjusting to rapid change that motivated organization, it was none the less something beyond retailing that led them to define who was and who was not to be controlled.

And yet, even though the peculiarities of their social positioning structured the oppositions within retailing, main-street shop owners shaped their response to the mass market amid circumstances beyond their control. Up-to-date accounting, turnover selling, self-service, cash merchandising, psychological advertising, hire-purchase contracts, bulk buying – these were approaches developed in bigger businesses and grafted onto shopkeeping. The Retail Merchants' Association and the other major trade organizations promoted and encouraged retailing's modernization, but this was not the only way in which the power relationship implied by adaptation – the assimilation of main-street shopkeeping into corporate culture – was materialized in associational activity. Shopkeeper activism was in many ways a further manifestation of small capitalist retailing's accommodation to the mass market.

This chapter will bring together the three themes explored so far – the importance of folklore as a medium for translating sociocultural preconceptions into organizational objectives; the influence of the centralization of power over distribution into the hands of manufacturers; and the modernization of retailing practices – and will demonstrate how they together served to define shopkeeper protest. It was a process that took time. Market adaptation changed main-street retailers' ideas and attitudes and altered the focus of their protests over the course of several decades. There is no question that the shopocracy's first response to the growth of the mass market had been resistance, but as store owners modernized, they gradually accepted the need for assimilation. Ironically, because they continued to employ a relatively static folkloric imagery when expressing their goals, it is easy to misread their demands and overlook the adaptation within the stasis.

This theme is explored below through a discussion of the most important tactic for 'levelling' the field of competition, the struggle for the legalization of resale price maintenance (rpm). According to traditional interpreters, resale price maintenance – a condition under which a supplier fixed the retail price for a product and prevented sellers from reducing that price – was the clearest manifestation of the shopkeepers' anti-modernist ambitions.[1] The trouble with this interpretation is that it derives from a single definition of the economically 'modern.' For those who believe that mass production must lead to the progressive reduction of consumer costs, any effort to fix or maintain prices is by definition repressive and regressive. However, as we have seen, price-fixing was as 'modern' a belief as the deflationary mass-production ethos: both emerged out of the collapse of the Victorian economic consensus. In fact,

rpm not antimodern as traditionally believed, but instead a modern, systematic impulse the idea that rpm was a 'modern' response to mass consumption flows naturally from the argument that modernization involved the increasing 'administration' of the 'flow of a high volume of goods from the suppliers of the raw materials through the processes of distribution to the retailer or ultimate consumer.' Understood in this way, the fixing of resale prices becomes yet another example of the manufacturers' attempt to coordinate the movement of goods. Like brand-name advertising, which manifested the producers' desire to influence consumption, price maintenance was an effort to systematize distribution. And from the retailers' perspective, what more powerful symbol of their acceptance of business modernization could there be than their willingness to surrender control over their prices and profits?[2]

RESISTING THE MASS MARKET

Walking to work one morning in 1909, G.A. McCann, a thirty-five-year veteran of competition in the Toronto drug trade, reflected on the changes that were transforming his craft. When he began in business, he recalled, 'the druggist compounded his prescriptions, made his pills, plasters, suppositories, et all [sic]' and earned 'more than a good living.' But all that had changed. Now advertisers pushed mass-produced 'patent' medicines 'with the sole object of getting the people's money. The real virtue of the medicine, or its intrinsic merit does not enter ... at all.' With the proliferation of these mass-produced 'proprietary' or brand-name medicines in the 1880s and 1890s, price competition grew more serious, and with the loss of the manufacturing function to the 'patent medicine men,' pharmacists became mere vendors 'whose job it is to simply hand out the packaged product.' McCann's solution to the changes brought by the mass market was simple: resistance. 'Put up a line of family remedies yourself,' he advised. 'You will make more on them; you will control them, and if they have merit ... every sale will be an advertisement for your personality.' And as for the patents, 'make light of them to your customers; keep everlastingly knocking them.'[3]

Retail associations developed out of just such hostility to the emerging mass market. In the 1880s, when increased amounts of cash in the economy, more efficient transportation, and intensifying competition ripped apart the dependencies that had linked consumers to their neighbourhood stores, established shopkeepers began to worry. What particularly concerned them were those aspects of the new merchandising which they believed flowed from shopping's feminization: browsing, rapid style changes, and the emphasis being placed on cleanliness and purity. To main-street store owners of the late nineteenth century, the 'modern shopper' was little more than a 'gambler' whose 'speculations' led her to 'prowl around the stores' looking for bargains. Unfortunately, this type of customer 'makes or mars the success of the store. What she wants, in the way of weaves, colours and other details, is the great question.' The problem for merchandisers was that they had increasingly to cope with a market in which goods were 'only temporarily in vogue,' and the only way to do so was to 'find out what that woman at the counter is going to want, [satisfy the demand, and] ... then promptly drop it and go on to something else.'[4]

Pre-packaging by manufacturers and the private branding of their goods were a crucial preconditions for this type of shopping. For price and style comparison to make sense, consumers had to be able to compare similar goods in different stores. The products themselves therefore became targets of the established retailers' hostility and confusion. For many late-Victorian retailers, the variety of goods available was quite simply 'bewildering.' Today's store, a grocer remarked in 1900, 'includes an almost innumerable aggregation of dainties and luxuries;' 'the taste of the public is becoming more and more critical, and not only must the palate be gratified, but the eye must be pleased as well.' Moreover, pre-packaging, as G.A. McCann observed, was a destroyer of skills. Another retailer observed that 'almost everything nowadays is handed over the counter in packets, and fewer and fewer things every year are weighed and measured from bulk ... The grocer who loves his trade may well look with regret at this inevitable tendency, as it takes his expert knowledge and the art of salesmanship out of his life, and makes the man behind the counter little better than an automatic machine, which hands out packets when money is put in the slot.'[5]

The retailers' worries therefore came to centre on the products themselves, and in the 1880s and 1890s they began to protest loudly, if impotently, against the proliferation of 'cheap goods.' 'There has been a perfect frenzy the last ten years for cheap goods. It has taken almost entire possession of the female sex; and the men are a good second,' one clothier announced. The goods came in all shapes and sizes, wherever one found 'low priced trash rather than the meretricious articles.' But worst of all, declared a house wares dealer, were the 'ugly short-lived furniture, the useless Japanese rugs, and other similar abominations.' To the *Canadian Grocer* at the turn of the century, there was a 'senseless, vicious – yes, criminal – tendency to cheap goods,' and the press noted, with more optimism than truth, that 'the men who have become conspicuously successful grocers – in the vast majority of instances – never descended to that sort of tactic [selling cheap goods] nor seldom practiced price cutting.'[6]

The only trouble was that competition made resistance to mass-produced goods almost impossible. Shoestring traders, with their convenient locations and after-hours services, were not about to stock space-consuming pickle barrels and cracker crates. Because of low turnovers and minimal liquidity, their livelihood depended on the type of pre-packaged articles they could buy in small quantities and dispose of quickly. Moreover, the department stores, with their aggressive advertising and close pricing, were the very glorification of mass production's achievements and main-street retailing's demoralization. 'Competition is becoming daily more destructive,' lamented a Toronto shop owner. 'In fact, you have gotten beyond competition, you are dangerously nearing – so far as profits are concerned – annihilation.' And '[w]hat is the cause of this demoralization? Low priced, commonly called cheap goods! Whoever has encouraged these paltry imitations has assisted in this common depression.' The culprit was not really hard to find; to most conservative retailers, the popularity of 'cheap goods' was 'traceable directly to the pernicious department store methods.'[7]

Though ordinary consumers might feel that the departmentals had improved their quality of life by making goods more affordable, main-street retailers had a deeper vision. In the long run, they maintained, the department stores would impoverish the working public because the only way they could offer cut-priced goods was by forcing the manufacturers to supply them with ever-cheaper stock. 'These big stores with their large capital are against the working tradesman ... they crowd the manufacturers down in price, and he in turn tries to reduce the cost by reducing wages, putting in inferior goods, or getting machines that will do the work cheaper.' As John Hargreaves, one of the RMA's early presidents, declared, the department stores 'have destroyed the confidence which should exist in a business community by educating the public to believe that all kinds of deceptions are necessary to successfully retail merchandise over the counter. They have reduced the value of labour, and have destroyed the purchasing power of many classes, thereby affecting all other classes.' And not only are they 'lowering moral standards ... but they are attempting to concentrate the business of the Province into one city.'[8]

In the eyes of many retailers, a malevolent intellect was therefore at work. Indeed, for mass merchandisers to do what they did, 'all kinds of deception[s]' were necessary. The big stores advertised 'deceptively,' they 'slaughtered' prices, and they sold 'adulterated' and 'cheap' goods as quality items. How often did one see products advertised in the daily newspapers at prices which were baldly stated to be as much as one-half of the selling prices asked by competitors, and how often did investigation 'by an expert' show that 'the assertion is false, the goods being only cheap imitations of the high priced goods they are intended to be compared with'? Such misleading advertising was believed to be a common practice of the mass marketers, and it revealed that their secret ambition was not competition but the breaking down of consumer confidence in the independent trade.

Main-street shopkeepers therefore accused the department stores of using high-powered marketing gimmickry: 'schemes' that were 'devised' to 'lure' shoppers. Loss-leaders – 'bait,' in the eyes of the horrified retailers – were dangled before the public in order to draw them in. This was done to the detriment of the shopper since the loss-leaders worked the customer 'into such a state of mental fatuity that he or she does not know whether the full price is paid or not because, in a long list, a few bargains loom up so large, and the profit of the transaction is taken on the rest of the purchase.' The giant stores sold too much, too loudly, and too well, and they were therefore 'contra to that high and ennobling spirit that is set forth in the "Golden Rule."'⁹

In the mid-1890s retailers began to conflate their suspicions of the developing mass market with the departmentals that made the goods so dangerous. In a very real way, they failed to distinguish between the department store as a system of selling and the mass market as an emerging reality of business life. And this was one of the hallmarks of the anti-modernist impulse: the confusion of cause and effect and the desperate thrashing against all aspects of destabilizing change.

Protest in North America began in 1895, when Chicago merchants formed the Cook County Business Man's Association and lobbied for a law to prevent any urban retailer from selling more than one 'class' of goods (they organized trading into ten classes, including groceries, butchering, furniture, tobacco, dry goods, clothing, shoes, flowers and birds, jewellery, and all other lines). Though the Illinois bill was defeated in the State senate, a copy of it passed in Missouri, and by early 1897 several midwestern states were debating the concept. Stimulated by this activity south of the border, Canadian trade periodicals started to reprint muckraking American articles on the departmentals, while small-town papers such as the Orangeville *Advertiser* railed against the 'centralization' of trading which the big city stores represented.

With retailers, the rising chorus of anti-departmental sentiment found its loudest voice among the grocers, who were disturbed by the fact that the department stores had recently begun to offer staples such as flour, sugar, and tea as loss-leaders. In January 1897 the Montreal Retail Grocers' Association set up a committee to lobby wholesalers not to sell food to the departmentals, and the Toronto Retail Grocers' Association took up the cause a couple of months later. So great was the stir this action caused that one Ontario MLA, J.T. Middleton of Hamilton, succumbed to the pressure and agreed to introduce a bill similar to the Illinois one in the Legislature. The bill was soon shelved, but interestingly enough, most MLAs, including the premier, spoke favourably of the proposal, noting that its passage only awaited a greater display of public support.[10]

The presumptuously titled Retail Merchants' Association of Canada was actually founded one month after the introduction of the Middleton bill with just such an objective in mind. Its twin goals were to build public support for an anti-departmental crusade and to unify all retailers into a single powerful organization. In both these objectives the RMA was to prove an utter failure. The new outfit attracted little attention at its inception, and small wonder: though membership figures are unavailable, it probably numbered fewer than one hundred members.[11] Efforts to expand the organization outside Toronto failed, and by mid-1898, with only a London affiliate and snubs both from newly formed retail associations in Ottawa and Peterborough and from the venerable Retail Grocers' Association, the RMA was quietly downgraded and its name changed to the Toronto Retail Merchants' Association. No greater luck was had in the organization's effort to win public support for the Middleton bill, and a key bid to obtain the endorsement of organized labour came crashing down when the Trades and Labor Congress passed a resolution that not only supported the department stores but also welcomed the speedy demise of the higher-priced independents.[12]

The RMA might well have quietly disappeared had not its secretary, E.M. Trowern, hit upon a splendid idea. Acting on his own initiative in the summer of 1898, Trowern (a Toronto jeweller) took Eaton's to court over a deceptive advertisement in which the company had falsely presented a cheap tea set as expensive quadruple plate. The success of his suit was seen as a major victory for the independent trade, and suddenly the RMA began to grow (it also changed its name back to the Retail Merchants' Association of Canada). In 1902 the association had five branches in southern Ontario,and within three years it had sixty-five (around 2,000 members), making it the largest retail organization in the country. Its development would continue to match that of its merchandising nemesis: in 1905, the year that Eaton's opened its first branch store, the RMA became a federation and began establishing provincial branches in the west; when Eaton's moved into the Maritimes, the RMA was not far behind.[13]

What initially motivated the main-street retailers who joined the RMA was outright hostility to the mass market. It was not simply that goods were being pre-packaged and manufacturer-advertised; it was not only that styles were changing more rapidly; it was not just that competition was intensifying; it was the whole idea of mass consumption that disturbed them. Like other bourgeois moralists in late-Victorian Canada, affluent retailers did not believe that working people should be buying mass-produced 'luxuries.' Raised in a world of scarcity and hardship, they perceived the consumption of non-essentials as intemperate: a feminine vice no less harmful to families than the waste of meagre resources which followed from male drinking or gambling. Their concerns were therefore rooted in their bourgeois value structure and reflected their class and gender prejudices. Convinced of the need for 'restraint' and 'enterprise,' they regarded working-class and farm consumption as 'an encouragement to extravagance and a discouragement to thrift and economy.'[14] But because most of their customers were now women, they found it difficult to ascribe to them independence of thought and desire. It was true that womanly weaknesses made shoppers vulnerable, but there could be no doubt that female consumers were being 'enticed to their ruin.' These gender- and class-constructed insights were then transferred to retailing and supplied business relevance through folkloric speech.

Because the legitimate 'small' shopkeeper was driven to be of 'service' to his 'community,' and was after a 'living profit' rather than riches, he would never try to sell his customers something that was bad for them. Illegitimate retailers, in contrast, were 'selfish ... and any scheme whereby some money will roll into their coffers would be gladly taken up.' It was these merchants – the 'cheap jack corner dealer' as well as the departmentalized giant – who were responsible for distribution's demoralization and the consumers' corruption. What was so magnificent about this folklorically constructed critique was that it allowed association members to caricature and align individuals and businesses of daunting diversity and complexity. Through folklore they could denounce the whole process of economic change while at the same time targeting a single 'demoralizer.'

Consequently, department stores, like other 'combines', were regularly attacked for their lack of contact with the community; they were described as an alien presence whose loyalty was to 'nameless investors' rather than to 'the public they served.' The mass merchandisers, announced one small-town critic, 'do not put their money into the local community ... of what value is their money if it goes out to Toronto on the nine o'clock train tomorrow morning?' Ironically, this folkloric juxtaposing of the good citizen and the interloper, the community and the corporation, could be equally applied to more marginal businesses. In fact, immigrant loyalties to an homeland community could be denounced in exactly the same terms. As one delegate asked an RMA convention in Calgary: 'What do they do with their profits? Unquestionably some of it goes back to China. Thousands of dollars leave Alberta alone, for China, each year.'[15]

Retail symbols allowed association members to restructure class, gender, and ethnic prejudices into explanations of business differences. Through the binary oppositions at the centre of retailing's collective memory, male concerns about female entrepreneurship, nativist fears of immigration, and bourgeois hostilities to popular consumption were reconceived as a single issue of occupational legitimacy – which is not the same as saying that the messages carried were as unchanging as the medium. Though their protests were folklorically structured and therefore ostensibly 'timeless,' they represented the concerns of a distinct group of people at a particular juncture in their history. Confronted by destabilizing business conditions, main-street shop owners dreamed of eliminating both the mass-produced good and the frenzied seeker of cheap goods. The only problem was that their resistance could not last. Even as they piled the folkloric barricades around the mass market, they began to adapt to its demands. Resistance – the initial response of a relatively powerful group exposed to rapid and destabilizing change – could succeed only if the shopocracy successfully insulated itself against modernity's influence. This was the point made by G.A. McCann when he called on the druggists to turn back the tide of change. But how many among them, as time passed and the mass market grew, could really afford to heed his advice?

PHARMACY AT THE CROSSROADS

Within the retail organizations, the drift from anti-modern resistance to adaptation and compromise can be charted in the ideas and actions of a remarkable Toronto druggist, John Hargreaves. Like so many prominent shopkeepers, Hargreaves first became active in a trade association when Eaton's began cutting prices after the opening of its pharmaceuticals department in 1896. A number of the city's leading pharmacists responded to this threat by forming the Ontario Retail Druggists' Association, through which they lobbied manufacturers and wholesalers to refuse stock to the departmental. The inability of the ORDA to prevent a patent-medicine price war in the late nineties led Hargreaves, along with his brother and six downtown pharmacists, to organize the Druggists' Syndicate, the country's first buying group. By massing their orders, syndicate members were able to purchase direct from the manufacturers and secure the larger discounts set aside for wholesalers and department stores. Convinced that they had found the means of 'fighting the Devil with fire,' the members of the syndicate became ferocious competitors; in fact, these druggists – 'among the most prosperous in the city' – kept pace with the departmentals' prices by maintaining 'a campaign of active cutting and advertising.'[16]

Bulk buying and competitive merchandising were, however, only two aspects of Hargreaves's modernizing ambitions. In pharmacy, adaptation to the mass market involved a shift from manufacture to retail: from the preparation of medicines to the marketing of patent drugs, toiletries, and stationery. Though a knowledegable chemist (he was the author of the first Canadian formulary), Hargreaves recognized that the pharmacist was becoming more and more the retailer and less and less the scientist. 'The druggist who claims to be a professional man only, is certainly behind the times,' an article in the *Pharmaceutical Journal* explained, 'for the druggist of the twentieth century is not only a prescriptionist, but a merchant as well.' For the syndicate, patent medicines, rather than prescriptions or generalized remedies compounded by the individual pharmacists, were the cornerstone of the drug business. That was why they focused on competing with the departmentals for the proprietary medicine trade: as Hargreaves realized, it was Pear's soap and Beacham's pills that would draw the custom, not in-house cough syrups and tinctures.[17]

It was not a view shared by most leading pharmacists in the late 1890s, many of whom still derived their most profitable business from their prescriptions and personalized remedies. For 'professional,' as opposed to 'commercial,' druggists, what Hargreaves and the syndicate advocated was nothing more than 'Yellow Pharmacy.' For conservatives such as G.A. McCann, the benchmark of trade distinction remained the training they had received at the provincial colleges of pharmacy, institutions devoted to the production of scientists, not entrepreneurs. These bastions of Victorian certitude believed that the profession could be insulated against the mass market's influences by teaching young druggists 'how best to make money as a pharmacist rather than as a dealer in medicines.' In effect, the 'scientific' druggists who dominated the councils of trade felt that the pharmacists' own cold remedies, dyspepsia pills, tonics, and lotions must form the basis of their enterprise. Mass-produced 'proprietaries' should be stocked in limited quantities, with their prices kept higher than the druggist's private lines so as to encourage customers to buy the profit-producing house brands. It was a head-in-the-sand approach that drew on the druggists' intellectual pretensions and was sustained by their college affiliations. Indeed, until the turn of the century the colleges were the focus of collective identification in the drug trade, with the pharmaceutical associations in most provinces being little more than glorified alumni organizations.[18]

Forced to promote their 'business' vision of pharmacy outside the established channels, Hargreaves and other members of what their critics called 'Toronto's cutting establishment' abandoned the ORDA (which had become the provincial pharmaceutical association) and formed a drug section of the RMA in 1900, a purely 'commercial' body that was to have no official connection with the colleges' alumni network. The one hundred and fifty druggists who by 1903 had joined the RMA druggists' section were all wealthy businessmen committed to the idea of improving the shopkeepers' competitiveness by lowering the costs of the national brands.[19] If the independent merchants could be induced to bypass the wholesalers and buy direct as the departmentals did, they would be better placed to compete on a price basis. In other words, the aim was to have the RMA light the torch for a national buying pool.

For pioneer modernizers such as Hargreaves, the department stores were at once evil and worthy of emulation. Even though they cut prices and exploited a vulnerable public, they represented much that was new and exciting in merchandising. In fact, retailers wanting to know how to improve their selling were advised to study the department store, as 'a day or two could be profitably given to the gathering of ideas on store management and accounting.' 'The man who is standing still is going backwards,' a syndicate member noted; 'every age in the world's history has possessed its distinctive characteristic ... and I should unhesitatingly name this the "marketing age."' The great achievement of early modernizers such as these was the separation of the mass marketer from the mass market. They accepted the changes transforming business but wanted the profits to flow through their own cash registers. It was something that their anti-modernist opponents could neither accept nor comprehend. To them, the progressive merchants were not adapting to change so much as encouraging a problem that needed suppressing. The modernizers, one critic mocked, 'are remaining up nights to find out about Eaton's ... they just dote on him – such a friend you know.'[20]

There can be no doubt that it was his experiences with the syndicate which educated Hargreaves to the potential for retail-manufacturer cooperation. And it was Hargreaves who initiated the process of moving the trade associations away from simple resistance to the mass market and towards a new policy based on the retailers' ideological and organizational integration into the emerging producer-driven economy. Progressive merchandising was showing the way, and not only for the members of the syndicate. Though they were not all rushing to join the pool, druggists across Canada were beginning to price more competitively, to replace their store-made nostrums with proprietary goods, and to accept the manufacturers' advertising and advice. In late 1902 Hargreaves and a committee from the new RMA drug section made the connection explicit by negotiating an agreement with the Ozone Company (manufacturer of Powley's Liquified Ozone, an antiseptic and germicide) to fix retail prices.[21]

Under the Ozone plan, the retailer signed a contract with the producer agreeing not to sell Liquified Ozone below a manufacturer-specified price at risk of being denied further stock. Moreover, so as not to affect Ozone's sales, the company announced that it would fix the consumer price below the one currently pertaining, even though both manufacturer and retailer were able to raise their margins. This trick was accomplished by copying the syndicate's method. Hargreaves was no believer in wholesalers, and the contract he negotiated with Ozone set the price direct to the trade so low that it made it uneconomical for jobbers to handle the product. In fact, retailers were able to buy Ozone direct at only a few cents more than the wholesalers had done, thus allowing consumer prices to fall at a cost to no one but the middleman. As G.E. Gibbard, another of the RMA drug section's founders and the editor of the *Cana-*

dian Pharmaceutical Journal, explained, economic change revealed 'the retailer and manufacturer occupying the strategic positions, with the jobber on the defensive.' The only question, Gibbard continued, was whether retailers and manufacturers were actively to speed the process along by becoming 'the upper and nether millstones to pulverize the jobber.'[22]

And therein lay the difficulty. The powerful Wholesale Druggists' Association, which represented almost every jobbing house in the country, officially denounced the plan and resolved to test the contract in court. Remarkably enough, the Kingston judge upheld the Ozone contract, and much to the dismay of the wholesalers, many other manufacturers suddenly began to sign on with the RMA's drug section. By June 1903 nine small manufacturers had adopted resale price maintenance plans, as had the country's two largest pharmaceutical firms, H.K. Wampole and Parke Davis and Company, and together these firms established the Proprietary Articles Trading Association to coordinate their efforts. As the manager of Wampole declared, his company had 2,400 retail accounts, and 'their good-will is of more importance to me than is the money I would get from Eaton's or Simpson's or Burgess-Powell or Karn's [the two latter were wholesalers].'[23]

But jobber resistance was greater than the manufacturers and retailers had anticipated, and closing ranks, the WDA decided immediately to stop handling all the goods produced by manufacturers using the Ozone plan. This move caught the manufacturers before they had prepared their own direct sales services, curtailing the distribution of all their goods and not just those that had been price protected. As shipments plummeted by about 50 per cent, the smaller manufacturers broke ranks, and even the Ozone Company decided to tear up its contract. Big firms, such as Wampole, that were prepared to continue direct marketing then decided it was useless going on alone. 'I was disgusted and dropped out,' the company's president later declared, and in his annoyance he began 'selling my goods to anybody.'[24]

The drug wholesalers realized, however, that the Ozone contract was more a portent than an abberation. They also knew that modernizing retailers would attempt to revive resale price-fixing, and they understood that the growth of direct marketing would ultimately make their resistance irrelevant. They had momentarily slapped back the manufacturers' hand, but they needed to ensure that those grasping fingers remained away. To accomplish this, the jobbers countered Ozone's plan with their own scheme, one based on a contract devised by a wholesaling firm in England in the late 1890s and declared legal by the British courts in 1901. Under their so-called Elliman plan, the wholesalers agreed themselves to protect the resale prices that manufacturers desired on the condition that the producers sold strictly through a wholesale house. Ironically, the Elliman plan would therefore serve to freeze the business clock, preserving the jobber's influence and trading off price stability for direct marketing.[25]

The Elliman plan brought the struggle between manufacturer and wholesaler, retailer and scientist, into the open. The wholesalers did not negotiate with the RMA, but with the QPhA and with the ORDA. The chief negotiator for the retailers was Henry Watters, an Ottawa druggist, one-time mayor, chair of the council of the college, and declared opponent of resale price maintenance. It is not clear why the traditionalists had suddenly embraced price-fixing, but it likely had something to do with margins. Whereas the Ozone plan would have reduced the cost of the brand-name pharmaceuticals by direct marketing from manufacturer to retailer, Elliman promised to keep them high enough to pay the wholesalers' costs and profit, thereby containing their challenge to store-made remedies. In this sense, Elliman not only supported a declining trade channel, but it also helped to reduce the price appeal of mass-produced goods.

What opposition the RMA might have mounted to this challenge was ended when a matchbox *coup d'état* removed Hargreaves and 'his little band of determined workers' from the leadership of the drug section and placed the hero of earlier days, E.M. Trowern, in control. The dream of a great national buying pool was broken, and the RMA now signed onto a contract which specified that no manufacturer would supply 'any syndicate of retailers ... [who] did an injustice to the legitimate wholesalers' by purchasing direct from the factory. The Elliman plan therefore threatened to destroy not just Hargreaves' syndicate but all other cooperative buying pools that sought to bypass the jobber. And in exchange for this concession, the wholesalers genuflected before the old anti-modernist totem by announcing that they would make a 'determined effort' to cut the supply of goods to the department stores (a pretty hollow promise, given that the mass marketers bought most of their goods direct).[26]

Unlike the retailers, the manufacturers put up a determined resistance to this wholesaler-led counter-revolution. Not to be outdone by the jobbing interests, the PATA reorganized and decided it would challenge Elliman in court, claiming that where the law had given them the right individually to set the prices of the goods they manufactured, what the wholesalers proposed was collusion. The judge agreed, and in early 1905 the Quebec Superior Court ruled in *Wampole v. Lyons* that while a manufacturer could sell at a fixed price to a buyer and could require a buyer in turn to sell at a contracted price, prices could not be fixed on goods bought through a third party (a wholesaler). The second blow came one year later when, in *Wampole v. Karn*, a Toronto judge declared the Elliman contract illegal because it had been drawn up, not by the manufacturers of the goods, but by a committee of wholesalers and retailers. This, Judge Clute announced, was collusion in restraint of trade.[27]

To their credit, the wholesalers realized that they were standing at a juncture in business history. Though still strong enough to hinder those seeking to eliminate them, they had failed to restore their nineteenth-century monopoly. Ozone, not Elliman, had been declared a legal form of price maintenance, and the WDA members understood that they would have to negotiate for their survival. In the late summer of 1905 the drug jobbers moved to strengthen their hand through a great merger, which, when it was announced in November, eliminated all but five of the nation's wholesaling firms. Though largely a paper shuffle which resulted in only minimal streamlining, the creation of the National Drug and Chemical Company was designed to give the wholesalers a stronger influence in their discussions with manufacturers. And to an extent it worked – the wholesalers did survive – but their more-limited influence was revealed by the agreements that National reached with the manufacturers in 1908 whereby the combine accepted the right of companies such as Dodds, Moyers Chemical, and W.A. Chase and Company to market direct, but wrung out from the manufacturers an agreement that they would not undercut wholesalers handling their products in direct sales to retailers. The agreement thereby affected prices from the manufacturer to the wholesaler and the wholesaler to the retailer, but no mention was made of consumer prices – resale price maintenance was now the manufacturer's prerogative. Deals such as this ensured National's existence, but only with the manufacturers' cooperation. By 1910 the power of the drug wholesalers had been decisively broken.[28]

Ironically, the retail organizations initially refused to follow the wholesalers into the twentieth century. The anti-modernists who had seized the initiative from Hargreaves and the syndicate were not likely now to capitulate to the patent-medicine manufacturers and their modernizing allies. Consequently, both the RMA and the pharmaceutical associations responded to the Elliman débâcle like forsaken lovers – desolate yet determined upon self-sufficiency. And none were more bitter in their public rejection of modernization than the druggists. The reaction had begun at the OCP as early as 1906 when the college's council decided that it was time to restructure the program in order to educate students even better on 'how best to make money as a pharmacist rather than as a dealer in medicines.' This goal would be achieved by instructing prospective pharmacists in how to equip a laboratory, by showing them 'the most profitable pharmaceutical and galenicals to manufacture,' and by educating them on 'the best methods of building up the prescription trade.' This same spirit of reaction inspired the organization in 1907 of the Canadian Pharmaceutical Association, a federation designed to give national prominence to the various provincial associations and colleges. Pharmacists were no longer going to be content to work as '"hewers of wood and drawers of water" for the proprietary men, feeding on husks while the overlord revels in luxuries.' The road to prosperity was clearly marked: prescriptions and home remedies. In short, the only way for professional pharmacists to regain control over retailing was for them to renounce the mass market.[29]

Thus, after the failure of the Elliman plan, atavism was declared the order of the day as everyone defiantly reclaimed the comfort of their remembered past. But the psychic retreat aroused little enthusiasm; rather, it seems to have been accompanied by a growing apathy. If shopkeepers were simply to carry on as best they might, what use was association? As the RMA suddenly discovered, individualism was now throwing 'insurmountable difficulties' along the path of organization. In mid-1907 lack of support forced the RMA's *Journal* to cease publication; in 1908 the association reported paid-up memberships to have dropped 15 per cent in one year; in 1911 the furniture section disappeared; a year later the drug section was abolished; in 1914 the entire BC provincial section disbanded; and by 1918, even by the RMA's own optimistic account, membership in central Canada had shrunk by one-quarter over the preceding decade (the organization grew overall, but only because of new associations forming in western and Atlantic Canada; (see table 14). Nor did the pharmaceutical associations do much better: though they maintained their membership by automatically enrolling all college graduates, active involvement dropped away, and in 1912 the CPhA suspended all conventions until further notice.[30] It was the first appearance of what would become a typical pattern: trade mobilization hinged upon the development of an issue on which interests could focus; once the issue was resolved (either in victory or defeat), the organizational effort collapsed. Without any active occupational identification, the retailers could not sustain united action.

The problems of summoning enthusiasm for what was clearly a major defeat were compounded by economic circumstances. Not only did the retreat into reverie follow the Ozone-Elliman disaster, but after 1907 the retailers suddenly found themselves better placed to afford going it alone. As inflation began to take hold, rpm threatened to become more of a burden to retail profits than a boon. Manufacturer-fixed prices, especially when marked on the package, were disliked by retailers during inflationary periods because they hindered the rapid increase of prices. As a shoe dealer explained, resale price maintenance in a rising market made him feel 'that pretty soon I would be working for the manufacturer.' Now, 'if a sale goes wrong [because a product is priced too high] the loss is mine. But I generally make the sale. No sir: in future I work for myself and make my own terms. The boot is on the other leg now.'[31] Fortunately, inflation also reduced the incentive for store owners to cut prices in order to draw custom. This was especially true during the First World War, when the shortage of things to buy turned distribution into a seller's market. Even the department stores found their underselling restricted because scarcity limited their ability to bargain down suppliers' prices. In this way, what helped the retailers maintain a position of defiance to the mass market and what enabled them to congratulate themselves on having restabilized commerce were circumstances beyond their control. Thus, while the trade leadership's anti-modernist retreat was received sympathetically by retailers, few felt sufficiently inspired actually to pay a membership fee and act on their opinions.

The point is crucial because while the policies of the business organizations were vaguely in tune with attitudes among the trade, the two were not synonymous. Retailers could feel a certain antipathy for fixed prices during inflationary periods, and the professional organizers might therefore assert the need for retailers to fight for their independence, but that does not mean that ordinary business people were returning to the sales practices of their ancestors. That the retailers were not, by 1910, atavistic enough actually to participate in an organizational struggle against mass consumption tells us something important about the depth of their commitment. They were eager to get back to business, and if one thing was clear to them, it was that they did not want to waste their money and time with association.

This realization should remind us of the importance of penetrating the rhetoric and recognizing that though the affluent traders may have sought psychological relief by submerging themselves in the past, they were continuing to do business in ever more modern ways. The inflationary years around the First World War were actually marked by significant advances in progressive merchandising as retailers channelled their increased profits into store refurbishment. Even the trade organizations were compelled to temper anti-modernism with practical advice to the modernizing tradesperson. In the west, for example, where the RMA championed the cause of reaction in the guise of a 'Buy at Home' campaign, the association continued to promote modern marketing and to devise schemes for the elimination of credit and the promotion of cooperative buying. At the 1913 Regina convention of the SRMA, the delegates not only passed resolutions attacking consumer co-ops and mail-order houses, but they also resolved to set up pools to bulk their own purchases, and numerous workshops were held on up-to-date selling and store redecorating. Similarly, in Nova Scotia, where the RMA was organized in opposition to the mail-order houses, the association also became involved in a scheme to set up a technical school to educate clerks in salesmanship and progressive marketing.[32] In this way, despite the association's avowed loyalty to the 'traditional' wholesalers and antipathy for the 'unreliable' manufacturers, it was continuing to investigate methods of modernizing distribution.

Even the pharmacists were living in a fantasy world when they proposed to drive out the branded lines with their own home-made curatives. Estimates for 1913 suggested that in the typical drug store, prescriptions and home-made remedies represented only 15 per cent of the total trade; more than a third of what was sold was made up of branded proprietaries, and 45 per cent was accounted for by sundries and non-proprietary drugs (such as bromide, iodine, and ammonia). Privately branded goods and sundries were coming to form the core of every retailer's stock in trade, and increasing numbers of trade-marked goods were arriving with their prices fixed. One cannot exaggerate the degree to which these new proprietaries rained down on the retail pharmacists: in 1880 the Wholesale Druggists' Association listed 4,200 branded drugs; by 1912 the number had grown to 39,000. In truth, the CPhA was actually having a good deal of trouble defending its reactionary approach to the mass market, and when someone at a Vancouver meeting proposed putting the organization's support behind a line of store-made pharmaceuticals based on the formulary, the motion was defeated in large measure because of the back-room opposition of the patent manufacturers.[33]

But this was not the only irony. More peculiar still was the fact that despite the retailers' official opposition to manufacturer domination, the restabilization of trade and a change in the political climate during the war actually allowed for the quiet progress of resale price maintenance (after all, where Elliman had been found illegal, Ozone had not). Though the consumer prices of most goods continued to be set by the retailers, there can be no doubt that by 1920 many hundreds of products were being controlled by their manufacturers. It was a solution to price instability that was becoming increasingly popular among specialized producers who manufactured a prominent and nationally advertised brand – Arrow shirts, Hurlbut shoes, Gillett's Lye, Colgate and Euthymol toothpastes, Slocum Psychine, Curol, Castoria, the Sutherland Sisters' Hair Grower, all Nyal products, Canada Sauce and Vinegar, Cream of Wheat, and Mathieu's Syrup of Tar – all the products of companies which sold the bulk of their goods direct to the retail trade. Consequently, though profit-hungry shopkeepers continued to complain about rpm, the spreading influence of the brand-name manufacturers could not be checked.

The first struggle for resale price maintenance had therefore left an uncertain legacy. Two sharply antithetical options had presented themselves to the shopkeepers: anti-modernist resistance to the mass market through appeals to sentiment and a wholesaler-backed campaign against branded goods, or acceptance of progressive merchandising and of the manufacturers dominant position. Both strategies aimed at eliminating the price-cutting department stores' advantages, but the methods and meanings of each were different, for where one sought to present shoppers with clear choices, the other aimed at obliterating the distinctions between big and small and at shortening the distance between manufacturers and consumers. Ostensibly, the cause of tradition and independence won out in 1905–7, with the syndicate broken and reconstituted as the rather less contentious Drug Trading Company, the Ozone plan defeated, and the retailers apparently committed to raising margins and discouraging the private brands. But the issue was not so simple, for no matter what the trade associations might say or do, the current of business change remained irreversible. As the popularity of the private brands continued to grow, the retailers had quietly to accept the manufacturers' increased influence over advertising and pricing. By the First World War, despite the rise in margins and the continuing insistence of the retailers that they would be their own masters, manufacturer dominance and progressive merchandising had come to stay.

TRADITIONALISM ABANDONED

The patent-medicine companies were in the forefront of the revolution in distribution; they had been among the first consumer goods manufacturers to attempt vertical integration and direct marketing, and they had early experimented with price maintenance. Because of direct marketing, the drug wholesalers' influence had been in decline since the 1890s, and their attempted counter-attack in the early twentieth century had ended in legal defeat, merger, and marginalization. But while the drug manufacturers led the assault on nineteenth-century distribution, others were not far behind. In the new consumer industries – ready-made clothing and factory shoe and furniture manufacturing – direct marketing had grown alongside sales; in dry goods, among the oldest of the trades, the jobber's influence had shrivelled amid the rise in ready-to-wear. By the First World War, the wholesaler continued to lead only in the grocery and hardware lines. Unfortunately, where the struggle in the drug industry had been played out between price-fixing manufacturers and equally restrictionist wholesalers, the triumph of direct marketing in the food business coincided with the development of a new approach to distribution. While price-maintaining manufacturers and wholesalers struggled for control over retailing, consumer resistance was pushing mass producers and politicians towards a reassessment of the whole principle of restricted distribution. By the time that price-fixing merchants and manufacturers had resolved their difficulties, the intellectual and legislative framework in which merchandising operated had changed.

Though the situation in groceries was complicated by the fact that new brand-name manufacturers, such as jam and sauce producers, manufacturers of starches, breakfast foods, and prepared meats, tended to market their own products, food wholesalers in the pre-war years continued to handle most of the bulk goods and perishables. Guarding the jobbers' position was the venerable Wholesale Grocers' Guild, an organization which traced its lineage back to an 1884 agreement which stipulated that sugar refiners would sell at a special discount to members of what was then called the Grocers' Guild, in exchange for which the wholesalers would maintain a fixed price to the retail trade (unlike the WDA during its Elliman period, the guild did not try to police the prices that retailers charged consumers). The agreement had further maintained that refiners would offer only one price to the jobbing trade (discounted for guild members) and that they would not undersell the wholesalers in any direct dealings with retailers. By the First World War the guild, which reconstituted itself as an association in 1916, had similar agreements covering matches, pickles, spices, vinegar, flour, and starch and had worked out contracts with such brand-name manufacturers as Heinz, Kellogg, and E.W. Gillett whereby producers agreed to sell to wholesalers at a lower price than they sold to retailers.[34]

The success of the WGA should not, however, be taken as an indication that nothing had changed in the food business. By 1920 most mainstreet grocery stores bought between a half and three-quarters of their stock direct from the manufacturers – tea, meat, milk, bread, and most non-food items – relying on wholesalers to supply their fresh fruit and vegetables, almost all their imported wares, some of their brand-name stock, and a majority of their bulk goods. Moreover, the association's success came from its decision to serve the manufacturers rather than defy them. The wholesale grocers, unlike WDA members, never tried to control resale prices; rather, they maintained any price determined by the producer. Moreover, the WGA did not try to prevent manufacturers from selling direct; it simply arranged that the factory price to retailers would be no lower than the wholesalers' price. In effect, as the National Drug members would discover, the grocery jobbers could survive if they could stomach the manufacturers' resale price authority and convince the producers to accommodate their margins.

It was a solution to the problem of direct marketing that received manufacturer and judicial approval. As early as 1888, an investigation into the guild's activities had prompted the passage of Canada's first Combines Act, and it would be investigated again under Mackenzie King's revisions to the law in 1910. But the act left supervision over business to the courts, and they interpreted trade collusion in light of a 1900 Criminal Code amendment that declared illegal only those combinations which unduly restrained competition to the detriment of the public. This section of the code had in turn been interpreted by judges as a sanction for the manufacturers' price-fixing powers and as grounds for the criminalization of retail and wholesale consumer-price collusion. Happily, as the grocers knew and the druggists would discover, this meant that a combination of wholesalers established to protect prices fixed by the manufacturer to the retail trade was entirely legal. On this verdant ground the WGA flourished, to the point that by 1920 it had grown to involve 239 member houses. Conditions, however, were about to change. Between 1919 and 1923 the politicians, under pressure from a public suddenly obsessed with combines, introduced new ground rules for determining the legality of price-fixing.

For the last few years G.B. Nichols, the chairman of Parliament's Special Committee to Inquire into the Cost of Living, observed in 1919 that 'the clamour throughout the country [has been] against present prices.' The government, he went on, was under intense pressure to 'do something ... that should have the effect of reducing the price by legislation.' It was a problem with which the politicians had been grappling since the outbreak of war. As early as 1915 the Tories had been trying to understand the cause of higher prices in the hopes of finding some method of either bringing them down or else pacifying the consumers. But the first governmental inquiry, while firmly rejecting the popular idea that some conspiracy of meat packers, sugar refiners, millers, and cold storage operators was arbitrarily raising prices, was hardly likely to placate the aggrieved public with its conclusion that high prices were caused by 'lazy' and 'supercilious' people working fewer hours, producing less, and spending 'improvidently'.[35]

Worried about the impact of the growing unrest on morale, reassured by the British example, and convinced of the need to bring the war home to a self-indulgent Canadian public, the Borden government then decided to launch an unprecedented experiment in business regulation. In 1917 the Tories established food and coal boards to compel consumer restraint, created a Cost of Living Commission to investigate profiteering, and set up a Fair Prices Board, and in 1919 expanded the Cost of Living Commission into a Board of Commerce in a further effort to 'ease the agitation' over high prices. The idea powering these agencies remained moralistic, for the government's administrators continued to believe, like good Victorians, that prices would fall only if the public's appetite was restrained. As one government pamphlet announced rather crassly, the Food Board 'want[s you] to do more towards economizing our food supply ... Food *must* be conserved: the Government *must* have our money; women *must* sacrifice their vanity, their mean self-indulgence and criminal selfishness on the altar of their country's safety.'[36]

It did not work, of course. Though patriotic Canadians reduced their spending, sacrificing their Saturday roasts and cutting back on their heating, prices still went up. Even beef, whose domestic consumption was almost cut in half during the last years of the war, grew every day more expensive. It was this failure of Victorian restraint that first led the administrators to search out alternatives. But to arrive at the logical solution – some form of governmental or business intervention actually to force prices down – the economic experts had to overcome a major conceptual roadblock. As J.R. McFall, the cost of living commissioner, mused in a private memorandum, the difficulty was that to control inflation 'we must have cheap production ... but how can we promote production than by the highest possible prices for the product.' Here was the central dilemma: like the business community around them, the bureaucrats were finding themselves trapped between the necessity for cheaper goods and their nineteenth-century abhorrence of deflation. They needed to find a mechanism for at one and the same time encouraging investment (through high profits) and reducing prices, but 'how can we have a lowered cost of living and relatively high prices for our products at the same time?'[37]

The answer arrived at after a public inquiry into the cost of living was the same as the one being reached by hundreds of manufacturers: harmonizing high factory with low resale prices 'would be impossible but by cheapening of our system of distribution.' Manufacturers could be guaranteed high prices and consumers lower ones if somehow the cost of merchandising could be reduced. Confident now that they could lick the problem of inflation by attacking the 'cupiditous' merchants, the federal government created a Board of Commerce charged with the duty of exposing the villainous retail profiteers, encouraging production, and bringing down high prices.

But things began to go awry almost immediately. The man whom the government charged with drafting the legislation creating the Board of Commerce, W.F. O'Connor, a maverick and megalomaniac Nova Scotia lawyer, did not support the government's goal of reducing the cost of distribution. 'It is obviously impossible,' he observed, 'as anybody can see, taking the retailer first, to strike off ten percent off his price and have him bear the whole weight of ten percent if the wholesaler is going to charge him just as much as ever. It will reduce it [prices] for a little while, it will reduce it as long as the retailer is possibly able to stand it, and then the retailer will go broke.' The only real solution to high prices, O'Connor went on, was 'if everybody gets together, if the consumer, the retailer, the wholesaler, the manufacturer and very likely the producer all get together and agree that the time has come for a general reduction in prices.' O'Connor was not supporting inflation, to the extent that he believed business inefficiency had made prices too high, but he was convinced that once 'reasonable' profit and price levels had been determined for a product, they should be fixed. He was therefore no advocate of 'mass production' and retail price deflation; rather, he thought that the board should become an agency for enforcing agreements that would fix prices and profits on specific products right through the system.[38]

The sweeping act creating the Board of Commerce gave O'Connor the power to realize his dream of comprehensive price-fixing, but his legal skill could not convince the government to give him the tools to finish the job. What he wanted would have required dozens of clerks and accountants to pore over the books of hundreds of firms to assess the 'reasonableness' of their profits. Moreover, what O'Connor wanted was to have private meetings arranged with business people in which they could discuss price maintenance, but what the government wanted was a public witch-hunt to pacify the consumers. Finally, where O'Connor needed time to make contacts and gather information – primarily through the questionnaires on business profitability – the Tories, ever mindful of the upcoming election, demanded quick solutions. Ultimately, these differences would tear the board to shreds.[39]

The board did, however, transform government attitudes to distribution, if only by bad example. For almost a year O'Connor managed to keep the agency running at odds with official policy, and in so doing he successfully enraged the public, annoyed the politicians, and, to make matters worse, infuriated most business people. Though the board was generally kind to those manufacturers with whom it had dealings (insofar as its policy was to guarantee them steady profits by pegging factory prices to the cost of raw materials), most producers none the less resented the agency's intrusions. Unaware of the differences between the government and O'Connor, business people were asked to fill out forms listing their profits for an organization that was officially engaged in the pursuit of profiteers. Moreover, as Mark Cox has shown, the conservative business minds in the Canadian Manufacturers' Association opposed the bureaucrats' invasion of the managerial sphere and disliked the paperwork that the board's activities required. For while those manufacturers who actually had their prices fixed appreciated the board's generosity, there could be no guarantee that once the administrators gained real knowledge of how their businesses worked, they would remain quite so considerate.[40]

Ordinary retailers had additional reasons for disliking the board. Like the manufacturers, they were suspicious of government investigation, and they were particularly fearful that O'Connor's fact finding might end in charges of profiteering. They had, in fact, few reasons to believe the assistant chairman when he told them he was interested only in maintaining established prices. Under pressure from the government to act on the cost of living, O'Connor felt compelled to produce a pound of profiteering flesh, and the shopkeepers' looked the plumpest. Consequently, under the board's first major order fixing the price of sugar, manufacturers' profits were pegged to the cost of raw sugar, and wholesale margins were fixed as a percentage of prices, but retail mark-ups were set at cents per pound.[41] In other words, if the price of raw sugar rose, the manufacturer's and wholesaler's profits increased, but the retailer's mark-up declined proportionately.

Shopkeepers were therefore even more hostile than manufacturers to O'Connor's interfering, and they revealed that opposition in their refusal to cooperate with the board's fact-finding endeavours. The assistant chairman believed that in order for reasonable fixed prices to be established, he needed data, but few retailers were willing to volunteer information concerning their mark-ups. From the storekeepers' perspective, there were several problems with the government questionnaires they received: they were considered too complicated, merchants were suspicious that they were being investigated as profiteers, people who received the forms wondered why their competitors had been exempted, and many shop owners felt the questions asked were inappropriate to their businesses. O'Connor later maintained that he had been attacked simply for trying to bring system to retailing and that the shopkeepers had resisted his efforts to modernize their businesses by refusing to keep proper records, but he was exercising the bureaucrat's prerogative of blaming someone else for his own mistakes. Ultimately, the board managed to collect a few hundred of its monthly forms, and about two-thirds of the retailers to whom the questionnaires were sent simply refused to cooperate.[42]

The only business people who actually supported the board's activities were the wholesalers. As the first sugar order revealed, O'Connor had a profound empathy for the wholesale merchants, and he did what he could to promote their interests. The connection had deep and personal roots. At a time when the Canadian Manufacturers' Association was still moodily shifting in its indecision over whether to support or condemn the board, the Wholesale Grocers' Association had gone out of its way to laud O'Connor's efforts. In fact, the WGA had lobbied for the board's creation, and its extraordinarily affable leaders – H.C. Beckett, A.G. Pryke, and J.T. Gillard – did as much as was humanly possible to sell the agency among their myriad business contacts. As Beckett declared, the creation of the board had been the 'the most outstanding statesmanlike move since Confederation,' and he thought O'Connor 'is entitled to the highest praise that man can have.'[43] The board returned the favour, and O'Connor's initial order actually discouraged business rationalization by stipulating that all sugar shipments had to pass through the 'established distribution channel,' which the board defined as 'from the refiner to jobber to retailer.'[44]

The love affair continued to blossom throughout the board's brief existence. Late in 1919 O'Connor rebuffed an effort by the newly formed York Trading Company (a retail buying pool modelled on the Druggists' Syndicate) to crack open the grocery wholesale business, and he dismissed the complaints of cooperatives to whom the WGA was refusing to sell. And in addition to endorsing the actions of the association by duplicating its contract, O'Connor ordered manufacturers to follow the WGA's dictates even so far as paying its members a 'loyalty' discount for handling their goods. It was after one such ruling – when the board ordered Dominion Canners to deal only through WGA members – that the new United Farmers government in Ontario, under pressure from several disgruntled businessmen, asked the board, in its capacity as combines investigator, to rule on the WGA as an organization in restraint of trade. Not surprisingly, after a brief inquiry, O'Connor, the chief investigator, found in the WGA's favour, praising its even-handedness and actually denouncing the Drury government for trying to stir up trouble.[45]

Obviously, the behaviour of the Board of Commerce placed the Retail Merchants' Association in a difficult position. On the one hand, mainstreet retailers were becoming increasingly hostile to the board and resentful both of its pricing decisions and of its efforts to determine the profitability of their businesses. On the other hand, the traditionalists who dominate the RMA after Hargreaves's forced departure remained anxious to preserve the traditional lines of distribution. So close had the RMA's relationship with the wholesaler associations become that it had even joined the WGA and the WDA in lobbying for the board, and it had enthusiastically greeted O'Connor's appointment. But the first sugar order soured the relationship for most RMA members by revealing that the WGA would do little to help ordinary grocers and that the RMA's leadership was too weak to influence the decisions.

And it was not just the grocers who were annoyed by the association's weakness. Soon after the first sugar order, the board moved to control the inflation in clothing prices, and O'Connor asked the RMA clothiers' section what margin should be allowed retailers under the upcoming order. The trouble was that the clothing section was made up of only a dozen or so of Toronto's most affluent merchants, and the margins they suggested – 26 per cent on cheaper lines and $33\frac{1}{3}$ per cent on clothes costing over $30 – were a hardship to many of their smaller competitors, even to those cutters who used staggeringly high mark-ups on some lines to compensate for the losses they sustained on others. This was undoubtedly the result anticipated by the RMA, for as Frank Stollery, one of Toronto's most prestigious clothiers and an RMA member, explained, under the ruling 'the stronger men will live, the weaker ones will die.' What the association members did not expect was the mass protests that the ruling would provoke. The order was designed to suit conditions in one city, and its framers had given little thought to the needs of even large clothiers in London, Edmonton, or Moncton. Nor had they considered the reactions of the great numbers of small capital-ist Toronto retailers who sold less than the $50,000 considered necessary to make ends meet using the board's mark-up. Caught out by the explo-sion of hostility that greeted the clothing order, the RMA was forced quickly to reverse itself and – forgetting that it had drafted the price fix-ing order – to announce 'that the whole policy of fixing prices or profits for Retail Merchants is wrong.' It was a reversal to the conservative line of 1908, and it did little to convince even main-street retailers that the RMA knew what it was doing.[46]

The association's alienation from its own potential small capitalist supporters was made even more obvious during the fiasco over the questionnaires. Initially, it believed an investigation into the cost of mar-keting would show that retailers were making fair profits, and it sup-plied the board with the names of retailers to whom it could send its forms. Unfortunately, most store owners bitterly resented the board's inquiries and refused to cooperate, wondering why they had been sin-gled out. Once again, the RMA executive was forced to reverse itself and in mid-summer 1920 to admit that the agency's rulings had 'resulted in a great deal of disturbance ... and uncertainty.' A few days later it took the decisive step of asking the government to 'suspend' the board's fact-finding operations.[47]

The opposition to the board's activities that was developing among shopkeepers had a crushing impact on the RMA. The perception that the organization was somehow working with the agency led to a sharp decline in its already small membership: between June 1919 and June

1920 almost every provincial association outside the Maritimes lost supporters (table 14). It was becoming increasingly clear that either the RMA would have to change its policies, renounce its connection to the wholesalers, and remove its aging leadership or it would disappear. As one angry Guelph retailer stormed, 'I have been paying ten dollars a year to that bunch in Toronto but I fail to see where I have secured one cent's worth in return.'[48]

By the winter of 1919 the entire government-sponsored price-fixing experiment was coming undone. The CMA finally came out against the board, and in January alone the cabinet was forced to deal with separate protests from textile manufacturers, meat packers and flour millers, department stores, and hundreds of independent retailers against the board's questionnaires. In addition, federal authority was being challenged by a combines bill which Attorney General Raney in Ontario had brought forward in his anger over O'Connor's investigation. On top of all these aggravations was the enormous cost of the data processing and the board's stubborn refusal to submit to the regulations of the Civil Service Act. It now seemed to the minister of trade and commerce that O'Connor was a 'lunatic' and its official chairman 'a weakling.' The writing was on the wall, and the cabinet began to pressure O'Connor and his associates to step down. They held out for a remarkably long time, but in June 1920 the board's executive officers finally gave in and tendered their resignations.[49] Determined, however, not to waste what still seemed a sound pre-election idea, the Tories chose simply to return the board to the course they had charted for it all along: the prosecution of profiteering middlemen.

Few people realized, amidst all the jubilation over the board's demise, that something dramatic had just happened in Ottawa. As William White, the new chairman made clear, the reconstituted Board of Commerce would hold itself primarily responsible to the consumers. This position flew in the face of the judicial tradition and of the board's previous activities. Up until now bureaucrats and judges had maintained the view that businesses could collude together, maintain prices, and divide territories so long as they did not, in the words of Judge Falconbridge, 'intend ... maliciously to injure any persons, firms, or corporations, nor to compass any restraint of trade unconnected with their own business relations.' In other words, judicial precedent held that so long as business people acted 'in good faith' and were 'actuated by a bona fide desire to protect their own interests' and those of others in like businesses, they could commit no crime.[50]

The reconstructed Board of Commerce cared little for these niceties. It judged consumption to be the measure of legality and felt that any action which raised prices was a potential restraint of trade. The consumer had become as an active element in the economic calculation. Of course, we will never know how far the board would have gone with this view, because it was dissolved less than four months after White's appointment, but the fact that the agency was thinking of investigating illegal combinations in textiles, builders' and plumbers' supplies, rubber footwear, and canning provides a glimmer of the agency's future.[51] It was not, however, to be. Amid the rain and cold of that unhappy autumn of 1920, as retail sales slowed and rumours of a buyer's strike raced through the business community, prices fell, bankruptcies doubled, and the unemployment rate reached towards 12 per cent, the government deemed it inappropriate to keep harassing the business community, and it abolished the board. The agency had, however, been an augury of things to come, and the dream of a reconstituted Board of Commerce continued to live in the minds of the politicians.

In fact, the ideas embodied in the second Board of Commerce resurfaced two years later when the new Liberal government introduced a revised Combines Bill. 'This legislation,' Prime Minister King explained, 'does not seek to restrict just combinations ... but it does seek to protect the public against the possible ill effects of these combinations.' The legislation empowered a combines investigator to look into businesses accused of profiteering and to prosecute those combinations that operated 'against the interests of the public.' And in keeping with their newly minted commitment to cheap goods, the Liberals defined a combine as a business which was 'enhancing the price of commodities or restricting their sale in a manner detrimental to the public.' Though the government did not intend to use the act to harm private enterprise (the prime minister made that fact quite clear), it was employing low prices and ample supplies as standards for measuring 'bad' businesses and 'good' ones. And like other advocates of what was coming to be called 'mass production,' the Liberals defended their new law by arguing that manufacturing's capacity to produce cheap goods in unlimited quantities had given big business the power to foster human harmony and social contentment.[52]

The combines act of 1923 owed a good deal to the changes inadvertently wrought by the Board of Commerce. It rejected the price-fixing which O'Connor cherished, held consumers not manufacturers and wholesalers to be the judges of legality, and shifted responsibility over business from the judiciary to a federal agency. Under the 1910 combines Act a judge had had to order an investigation by the government; under the new act a permanent combines investigator was created who would advise the government on the advisability of prosecution under section 498 of the Criminal Code. Somehow, the war, inflation, and consumer protest had pushed the state into not only increasing its influence over commerce but also reshaping its approach to collusion. From the way in which the act was described and from the way in which it was used during the interwar period, it is clear that the law was primarily designed to discourage combination in distribution. Though it did not rule out the investigation of mergers, the act targeted price-fixing agreements between individual firms, and it held up public exposure as the surest deterrent. Moreover, the combines law enshrined a low price as the measure of a fair practice, and its administrators praised innovations designed to increase the flow of goods. It was this aspect of the law that so worried price fixers, for as the *Financial Post* editorialized, the new combines legislation seemed 'to be drafted from the point of view that [price-fixing] trade combinations are necessarily and invariably bad and that machinery should be set up to put a stop to them.' Indeed, the supporters of the combines bill had originally proposed making illegal any contract or agreement 'which has or is designed to have the effect of fixing a common price or a resale price.'[53]

The Combines Investigation Act, like the second Board of Commerce, was prescriptive legislation. It was addressed to a problem that had as yet only indirectly manifested itself, and like so many curatives, it had unanticipated side-effects. The politicians were responding to the culture of consumption by repudiating Victorian restraint; like many manufacturers in mass-production industries, they were applying to consumer unrest the solutions of technology and system. Consumer dissatisfaction, King's Liberals believed, could be cured at no cost to wages through increased production, unfettered distribution, and reduced prices. Ironically, in presenting one vision of modernity as superior to all others, the government implicitly rejected the idea of resale price maintenance as a 'modern' economic strategy. It did not do so directly, of course – King maintained that the law did not prevent manufacturers from determining the resale prices of their products – but by using low prices as the measure of legality rather than high wages or stable employment, the law was narrowing the range of options.

A threshold had been crossed in the years between 1919 and 1923. Still-embryonic ideas had assumed form in both government policy and business practice, and a new orthodoxy was emerging from the discredit of the old. Paradoxically, in helping to destroy the Board of Commerce the retailers may have simply avoided the maw of Scylla for the whirlpool of Charybdis. But at least they fared better than the wholesalers.

More than any other group, the WGA had supported the ideas encapsulated in the first board, and the wholesalers had pinned their hopes for survival on a legalization of contracts which guaranteed their right to a 'fair' profit. But the WGA investigation, the aborted Raney combines bill in Ontario, and the subsequent passage of the federal Combines Investigation Act all cast a shadow over the legality of the association's activities. They came at a bad moment for food wholesalers. The WGA, the strongest and oldest of the country's trade organizations, could not survive the combined attacks of direct marketing, hand-to-mouth buying, and governmental investigation in the midst of a collapsing consumer economy.

A business tragedy began to unfold in food distribution, but it was one that public hostility prevented most people from seeing. The economic implosion of 1920–1 hit the wholesalers perhaps hardest of all: they were carrying the heaviest stocks, they were cash starved thanks to the long credits that chained them to the retail trade, and they were the people most affected by the storekeepers' decision to buy hand to mouth. For forty-odd years the wholesale associations had insulated jobbers against direct buying and price competition, but the combination could not survive the breakneck deflation and legal mud-slinging of the postwar collapse. As prices fell and stocks were devalued, markets were thrown open and manufacturers began to bypass association members. The Quebec branch of the WGA was the first to collapse in April 1922, and Ontario soon followed.[54] With the price-fixing arrangements suddenly abrogated, the wholesalers began to compete with each other for the retailers' business, and their long-standing territorial divisions were cast aside. By mid-1924 the entire grocery wholesale field was littered with the corpses of failed firms and the tottering figures of its now-diminished warriors.

Naturally, as the WGA dissolved, the survivors began talking about amalgamation, and when the 'great Woolnough merger,' which created National Grocers was complete, twenty-five of the country's most important wholesalers, including such one-time giants as Eby-Blain, Thomas Kinnear, Marland Woolnough, and W.H. Gillard, had disappeared from sight. Ultimately, between 1920 and 1926 nine of Canada's fourteen largest jobbing firms failed, and thirty-seven others joined in the National Grocers merger. By 1927 the *Canadian Grocer* was estimating wholesalers to be supplying no more than a third of the grocery retailers' stock, and it was predicting that the jobbers would survive only if they adopted voluntary pooling.[55]

The immediate postwar years were therefore witnessing the same transformation in the wholesaling of food that had affected the pharmaceutical sector two decades before. Like the National Drug merger, the creation of National Grocers was accompanied by a division of territory between the different wholesalers and the closure of a number of the smallest houses. And like the drug wholesalers who remained outside the combine, the independent grocers who survived did so by moving forward into retailing and establishing their own quasi-independent chains. By the mid-twenties Lumbers, Sloan, Hudon-Hébert-Chaput, Laporte Martin, MacDonald's Consolidated, York Trading, and Western Grocers' were all jobbing exclusively or mostly to their own buying groups. By 1927 National Grocers was the only firm operating along traditional lines, though it too would move into retailing in 1928 with the purchase of the Leader and Ontario-based Red and White chains.

During the early twenties, the power of the wholesalers to resist direct marketing was shattered. In dry goods, hardware, and shoes, wholesalers had simply been outmoded. In other lines, such as drugs and groceries, trades where the jobbers had fought vigorously against direct marketing, the leadership of the wholesalers had disappeared in the public arena. Ironically, the wholesalers had played their hand at the wrong moment. Aware of their declining influence in the real business world, they had tried to solidify their position through regulation. In this attempt they had been supported by a small and ineffective retail leadership still committed to an anti-modernist defence of the traditional channels of trade. But neither manufacturer nor main-street retailer was prepared to play along. Though most well-to-do shopkeepers resisted the intrusions of the Board of Commerce for reasons other than its defence of wholesaling, they contributed no less surely to the defeat of the anti-modernist position. Never again would the wholesalers try to control merchandising. Indeed, the governmental rejection of the atavistic principle on which O'Connor's board had rested threatened price maintenance in all its forms.

THE TRIUMPH OF MODERN MARKETING: PRICE MAINTENANCE IN THE 1920S

It was time to reassemble the fragments. Shards of confidence in the power of production, splinters of scientific enthusiasm, remnants of a democratic ethos – fitted and glued – were necessary now as a container for public desire. Mass production could alone satisfy consumer demand. The convergence of business and political opinion around mass production in the immediate postwar years signalled the triumph of a new orthodoxy. The older Victorian belief in the restrained and self-regulating market-place had smashed against war, inflation, and consumer unrest. Public debate on the matter had ended with the dissolution of the Board of Commerce, and while a belief in the efficacy of a high-priced, high-paid, systematically ordered market-place would survive among politicians and manufacturers, it would do so as a minority opinion. Ironically, it was at this moment that prominent retailers again started to find the idea appealing. Once rejected as too 'commercial' and 'modern,' price maintenance enjoyed renewed popularity among modernizing retailers in the financially troubled years between the wars. Unfortunately, Canada's lawmakers were no longer willing to cooperate.

The postwar depression found the retail associations recovering from a decade of disarray. Membership in all branches of the RMA outside the Maritimes had plummeted in 1919–20 as a result, in large measure, of the association's ill-conceived support for the Board of Commerce (table 14). It was, however, becoming increasingly clear to main-street retailers that they needed some kind of political voice. The passage of the luxury tax, the support that consumer cooperatives were receiving from the fast-rising Progressives, the attempted passage of a combines bill in Ontario, and the subsequent federal act all supplied proof that the voice of the professional shopkeeper needed to be heard. The RMA was still the only national retail federation, and for all the bad publicity, it had achieved some success. In May 1920 Trowern was able to lead a delegation of two hundred to Ottawa to protest Finance Minister Drayton's imposition of a sales tax on luxuries. When prices fell and the tax was withdrawn late in the summer, the RMA boastfully claimed responsibility.[56]

The campaign to kill the luxury tax gave the association some much-needed publicity, and retailers cautiously responded: early in 1920 a Furniture Dealers' Association was formed, and by 1924 the tiny Shoe Retailers' Association (with about three hundred paid-up members) had affiliated with the RMA. In late 1920 the RMA's drug section was resuscitated, though it made little headway against a CPhA that had been reactivated one year earlier (the RMA drug section in Ontario, for example, had only 50 members in 1921 as compared to 1,300 in the Ontario Retail Druggists' Association). But the RMA's gathering energy, while undeniable, was to all appearances unanticipated and unsolicited.

According to one bemused organizer, the association was displaying signs of life 'out of all proportion to the capital invested in it.' The trouble was that the RMA itself was pathetically undecided on what direction it should take. 'A mere membership increase is not necessarily an indication of real progress', the organizer went on; in fact, 'there is ample evidence that members have joined this organization without the faintest understanding of what they were doing.'[57]

Everything depended on the association's ability to adjust to the modernizing retailers' concerns. And it was British Columbia that pioneered the new course. The provincial chapter was lucky in having discovered an extraordinarily adept secretary and organizer in George Hougham, a Cranbrook grocer, and even luckier in having adopted an unsavoury cause. The immediate postwar years saw the re-emergence of virulent racism in the west as retailers complained that their customers were being 'pressed by the high cost of living [to] trade with the Oriental on account of price'. Unified in their small-town whiteness, prominent merchants in BC turned the RMA into a vehicle for ethnic intolerance. By 1922 the association had 1,200 members, most of them in those small places where the Chinese competition was fairly limited and nativism boiled high. Invigorated now by the nastiness flowing through it, the BC RMA became more concerned with maintaining white supremacy than it was with retail competition. In fact, the passage of the Oriental Exclusion Act – which stopped immigration but did nothing to control trade competition – was greeted by retailers as a victory, and BC membership in the RMA fell significantly (table 14).[58]

The anti-Asian lobby did, however, create a new organization in BC with a new executive, and while the cause quickly faded, its dynamism survived. The membership loss occurred in the smaller towns, where the race issue supplied the associational link: in Vancouver, RMA membership actually increased by 30 per cent between 1922 and 1924. It was not that Vancouver merchants were any less racist than those outside; they too had been drawn together by their skin colour. But in Vancouver the triumph of exclusion had been followed by the emergence of other equally pressing concerns. Outside the city, retailers were largely preoccupied with the prospect of racial survival; inside they were becoming worried anew about the mass merchandisers.

Like other urban traders, Vancouver merchants were hard hit by the deflation of 1920; a blow to profits made even more severe because of the competition of the fast-growing chain stores. And none were more anxious than the city's druggists; they were witnesses to the extraordinary price-cutting expansion of three different pharmaceutical chains, a growth which one commentator suggested was resulting in 'an orgy of slashing prices.'[59] In response to the new competition, the drug section of the BC RMA in 1922 came up with a limited price-maintenance agreement designed to curb chain store competition. The section's newly elected president, Joseph T. Crowder, had achieved this by shrewdly manipulating the retailers' combined advertising power. Under the BC plan, each member-druggist would, in the same week, present a window display featuring the same product, the logic being that the public, bombarded on every side by an identical visual stimulus, would instinctively buy more of the article being advertised. The crux of the plan was that the druggists would all advertise the product at the same price and would put on display only articles made by manufacturers who agreed to enforce price maintenance.[60] Like the Ozone scheme that had preceded it, the BC 'window plan' was an effort to make the independent stores perform like mass merchandisers. But where Hargreaves's idea had democratized the departmentals' buying ability and brought the price of goods down to the levels enjoyed by the biggest stores, Crowder's scheme sought to reproduce the mass-merchandising power of the chains. It was perhaps logical that Crowder was himself a manager of Cunningham Drug Stores, a local Vancouver chain, and someone well versed in the techniques of mass marketing.[61]

The BC window scheme was a qualified success: though it failed to attract more than a handful of manufacturers – Pepsodent being the most important – it did successfully arrest the price cutting of all the articles featured. But more importantly, the window scheme charted the direction of change and breathed new life into the moribund national RMA executive. The plan attracted a good deal of attention among druggists outside the association and the province. In a surprising show of solidarity, the newly organized BC Pharmaceutical Association decided to participate with the RMA in the window-dressing agreement, and it even elected Crowder to its own presidency. Not long afterwards, the border cities section of the ORDA also began to investigate price-fixing and invited George Hougham, secretary of the BC RMA, to explain the window scheme to its annual convention. Shortly thereafter, the ORDA announced that it would follow BC by 'co-operating' with the RMA and loosening its connection to the CPhA. Simultaneously, the Nova Scotia branch of the CPhA declared that it would adopt the BC plan.[62]

The aging conservatives who still dominated the executives of most of the older pharmaceutical associations resisted this pressure. They denounced the window scheme as a failure, suggesting that the manufacturers were insufficiently interested in price maintenance to make it work. They made little effort, however, to explore the validity of this theory. It was true that John Tremble, a founder of the QPhA, had tested the waters at a meeting of the Montreal section of the PATA as early as May 1920. His expressed goal was to turn the Canadian PATA into a replica of its British namesake, probably the most successful cooperative price-fixing organization in the world; the British PATA was a huge organization made up of 436 manufacturers, 61 wholesalers, and 8,000 retailers pledged to maintain the prices of over 2,000 proprietary articles and to boycott any enterprise which endeavoured to sell cut-rate. But Tremble, whose fashionable Montreal store did the vast bulk of its business in prescriptions, had chosen to work through the National Drug and Chemical Company (the wholesale combine) rather than the patent-medicine manufacturers. Out of Tremble's initiative emerged a joint committee headed by C.W. Tinling, the president of National, which was charged with drawing up a price-maintenance plan that would be acceptable to manufacturers and retailers. But the discussions swiftly collapsed when Tinling renewed the WDA's old call for the right to control the trade channel and demanded a guaranteed 15 per cent profit margin and when the conservative retailers insisted that patent medicines should carry a minimum 50 per cent mark-up.[63]

At heart, many members of the executive of the CPhA, with their close connections to the colleges of pharmacy, still saw rpm as a sacrifice of the professional to the commercial. Opposed as they were to bulk buying, store modernization, and the subordination of the retailer to the manufacturer, the association's leaders had done little to cultivate relations with the patent-medicine makers, and they derided the very advertising which the BC druggists had used to such effect.[64] Accepting price maintenance meant destroying what many leading pharmacists still believed to be a vestige of retail autonomy, and it was a trade-off that a powerful minority of more scientifically inclined druggists were still unwilling to accept.

But the depression hammered away at the anti-modernists' remaining resolve. During the inflationary years, the average line of patents, sundries, and toiletries promised the retailer a 40 per cent margin, but by 1922, druggists complained, they were 'lucky' if they could get 25 per cent. While the élite professionals in the trade might remain immune to these price shifts, a younger generation of more 'commercial' druggists were suffering. Initiative therefore remained with the RMA drug sections and their affiliates, and at the same meeting where George Hougham spoke on the BC window scheme, the ORDA resolved to bring the manufacturers of the PATA and members of the BC and Quebec pharmaceutical Associations, the CPhA, and the Wholesale Druggists' Association together at an all-Canadian drug convention to discuss rpm. Held in Toronto in early July 1923, the convention proved a phenomenal success. Its participants decided not only to support price maintenance, but also to invite Sir William Glyn-Jones, the founder of the British PATA, to explain the logistics of industry-wide price-fixing.[65]

Everywhere the anti-modernist resistance of retailing's organizational élite now began to crumble. In January 1924 a stormy annual convention of the RMA expressed its displeasure with the existing administration by appointing the ORMA secretary and George Hougham's friend, N.B. Douglas, as business manager (to 'manage' E.M. Trowern, the aged dominion secretary). A few months later, a rather spiteful Trowern tendered his resignation and was replaced by Hougham as secretary and Joseph Crowder as dominion president, a clear indication of the new course that was being adopted by the association. At the CPhA, in the meantime, the ground swell of support for rpm was also forcing a change in attitudes. Shortly after the all-Canadian convention the association had created its own 'commercial interest committee' (the name betraying a lingering confidence in the distinction between professional and commercial merchandising) to investigate price maintenance. The job of the retail drug trade, the committee's chairman observed, would be to 'bring pressure to bear on the manufacturer so that he will feel the need of something being done'; for the shopkeepers, the manufacturer had again become 'the key man.'[66]

Glyn-Jones delayed his Canadian visit until the spring of 1925, but if the druggists' support for rpm had subsided at all in the interval, it swiftly recovered. Glyn-Jones's one-month speaking tour took him to every major city in the country and to every province except PEI. Everywhere he went he invoked the spirit of the British PATA, 'whipping the druggists into a white heat' and putting and carrying resolutions 'with no opposition.' His influence, one drug store owner confessed, 'seemed little short of mesmeric.' His message was simple: 'relief through "gentlemen's agreements" with individual manufacturers ... has proved to be a delusion'. The drug business 'has been tyrannized long enough ...

and it is time that tyranny be used ... to make the minority [the price cut-ters] use methods of pure and straightforward dealing.' In early May Glyn-Jones convened a meeting of manufacturers, wholesalers, and retailers in Montreal and, allowing no debate, established a 'Provisional Committee to organize an association for the prevention of price cutting of proprietary articles.'[67] With a new Canadian PATA thus launched, Glyn-Jones returned to London.

Enthusiasm for a retail-wholesale-manufacturer PATA refused to wane even after Glyn-Jones's departure: 600 members attended the CPhA's June convention and came out unanimously in support of the PATA approach to price-fixing. Within four months of the founding of the new PATA, 2,700 retail druggists, representing about 77 per cent of the trade, had paid the membership fee and joined the price-fixing asso-ciation. The PATA was now large and broadly based; retailers sub-scribed in vast numbers in every region of the country, and the only province which did not have a majority in support was the one in which Glyn-Jones had failed to speak. Critics charged that the PATA subscrib-ers were small-town druggists reacting against the urban competition for their rural custom, but such was clearly not the case. If anything, the PATA derived greater support from the cities than from the country-side: while 87 per cent of city druggists joined, only 76 per cent of small-town retailers did, which indicates that the price-fixing organization did not represent some rural backlash against 'progressive' retailing.[68] In fact, while size was a factor in determining who would support the PATA, business attitudes were not.

In 1927 the government looked into the books of eight Montreal drug retailers on either side of the PATA issue. Two of the three businesses opposing the price-fixing plan were mass merchandisers – Pharmacie Moderne and Tamblyn's – while the third was a large independent with annual sales of over $200,000. The five PATA supporters were smaller: they averaged turnovers of $55,700 and employed an average of seven clerks; they therefore came from the same stratum of small capitalist shop owners who had traditionally dominated the retail organizations. The degree to which these five were up-to-date retailers is harder to measure from the reports of the government investigators (who clearly sought to portray them as inefficient), but certain evidence can be offered. Three of the five retailers were members of the Rexall voluntary chain; three admitted to having regularly cut prices to meet their com-petitors; all bought the bulk of their stock direct from the manufacturer; and while only two kept what the Labour Department's auditors thought were a complete set of books, all kept some records, and three took stock and made out annual balance sheets. Significantly, although two of the five did large prescription businesses (the two that did not keep completely 'up-to-date' accounts), all did more than half of their business, and three did around 80 per cent, in sundries and proprietaries. In short, the PATA, while it included a number of what could be described as 'professional' pharmacies, cannot be considered a simple counter-attack against the modern economy.[69]

The real message of the PATA was that despite the CPhA's sustained criticism of commercial pharmacy, the majority of Canadian druggists had become progressive retailers. The druggists' uniquely powerful professional traditions and the continuing presence of a number of old-style prescription pharmacists may well have hindered their ideological acceptance of that reality, but in the face of depression and organizational disintegration, the CPhA had given way. Glyn-Jones made it clear that if price-fixing was to succeed in Canada it would only do so if the manufacturer controlled the PATA and modern merchandising governed its practices. According to the PATA council, 'the object of the Association is to secure for manufacturers unfettered distribution to the public through trade channels.' Consequently, manufacturers dominated the association's activities from the first meeting. Among those attending were four of the biggest producers: Blair from Centaur Company (maker of Castoria), Weiss of Sterling Products, Samuel Colgate, and Ritchie from J.C. Eno (all Americans). The two largest Canadian wholesalers, Tinling from National and Arthur Lyman (both of which manufactured about 10 per cent of their stock themselves) were there, – as well as nine representatives from the major American wholesale houses. Ultimately, almost all of Canada's drug manufacturers – 157 of them – would join the PATA and experiment with the price-fixing of over six hundred trade-marked products.[70]

The minutes of the founding meeting of the enlarged PATA reveal that the jobbers deferred to the manufacturers and that the retailers offered no input (none spoke); there was even some confusion as to who should be appointed to the founding committee to represent the shopkeepers.[71] Ultimately, R.B.J. Stanbury was selected, an interesting choice given the fact that he had never owned a shop. Stanbury had run an advertising firm in the early twentieth century (his biggest customer had been the Drug Trading Company, the successor to Hargreaves's syndicate), and he had written the advertising column in the *Canadian Pharmaceutical Journal* before becoming its editor in the late 1910s.

Though undoubtedly knowledgeable and well connected, he had been chosen because he was a promoter of modernization. The retailers were there to provide the numbers, but the manufacturers were to control the operations.

That up-to-date retailing was to be the PATA's governing principle was revealed in the price practices and selling methods the organization endorsed. Manufacturers joining the PATA had to submit the prices of their products to a committee, which ensured that a minimum fixed margin of 33⅓ per cent was allowed to retailers and 15 per cent to wholesalers. There was no discussion of manufacturers' profits. As Glyn-Jones explained, 'I have never dared to ask a manufacturer what his profits are. That is his business.' As for the retailer, 'all ... [he] has to take responsibility for is the profit allowed him.' And while there is no question that the PATA allowed the up-to-date retailer a good mark-up, it was were not grotesquely out of line with current practice. During the mid-1920s, margins were sharply reduced because of the bad economic conditions, but the PATA supported gross profits closer to the levels prevailing during the depression than to those of the prewar and war-time booms. Individual store accounts and Dominion Bureau of Statistics figures for 1924 reveal that while big chain stores such as Tamblyn's were operating on a gross profit of roughly 27 per cent, independents were averaging anywhere from 25 per cent on proprietaries and sundries among the largest traders to 40 per cent among the smallest ones. In this sense, while the PATA modestly raised margins for some of the more-substantial main-street retailers, it did make life more difficult for the corner druggists. But this outcome was central to the PATA strategy: far from protecting the 'inefficient small merchants' (as Reynolds and others have suggested), the association favoured those larger independents who were able to exploit the most up-to-date trade opportunities.[72]

Another sure sign of the PATA's progressive intent was the way that it leaned heavily on the jobbers: Glyn-Jones had initially suggested that a margin of 12⅓ per cent (a figure 2 percentage points below existing mark-ups) be permitted the wholesalers, and it took considerable pressure to force the allowed margin up to 15. But even this figure gave the merchants little protection. The PATA agreement did not compel retailers to use the jobbing channel, and it allowed those shopkeepers who wanted to buy direct to do so at the same prices that wholesalers were obtaining. Moreover, under the PATA agreement, wholesalers had to cover the freight, while retailers did not. Finally, the PATA system fixed a sliding scale of maximum jobbing cash discounts, though many manufacturers went even further and slashed their discounts to well below the approved levels. The end-product was that while the jobbers were guaranteed a slightly higher than average margin, they lost money on discounts and freight, and the fixed-price system guaranteed retailers who bought direct a larger mark-up. Indeed, the only wholesalers who would have profited from the PATA were those operating buying pools where custom was guaranteed and those who were either Canadian importers or foreign exporters whose dealings were with manufacturers beyond the reach of most Canadian retailers. This point explains the strong support the PATA received from National and Lyman's and the fact that so many Americans (twelve of the twenty-six jobbers in the association were dealing out of the United States) endorsed the idea.[73] The truth is that the PATA system was loaded against both the traditional jobbers and the smallest retailers, the two elements that progressive merchants and manufacturers considered the agents of backwardness in distribution.

Ironically, for all the publicity that was accompanying the druggists' moves towards price maintenance, most other trades remained unable to mount similar associational drives. The unusual occupational culture that the college and apprenticeship systems had fostered in the pharmacists, together with the greater involvement of drug manufacturers in the distribution process, had undoubtedly made the difference. Even in those lines where rpm was quite common, such as in the hardware business, price-fixing agreements were generally falling apart under the impact of the prolonged trade depression. Cut-rate selling remained unchallenged in most lines, and in some sectors it was becoming worse as the decade wore on. Though Joseph Crowder stumped the country calling on all retailers to launch a massive price-fixing effort, he was confronted by nothing more than sympathetic inertia.[74]

Only the grocery trade would mount a PATA-style initiative, but as usual, the leadership would come from modernizing interests on the cutting edge of retailing. Late in January 1926 T.H. Clee, the president of Adanac Stores, and F.W. Hall, of Leader (both voluntary pools), together with David W. Clark, probably Toronto's most respected independent grocer and a director of Federated Wholesalers Ltd, set up a 'fair trade provisional committee' to look into the working out of a price-fixing agreement in the grocery field. One month later a convention chaired by Clark but organized under RMA auspices was called to discuss rpm, and out of it emerged a larger steering committee and a name: the Fair

Trade League. The committee was made up of regulars in the Retail Merchants' Association, including Crowder (who was now also on the committee of the PATA), and representatives from the grocery wholesalers. From the beginning, manufacturer enthusiasm was slight; in fact, the Fair Trade League received initial support only from Pepsodent, Nestlé, and Rowntree. Unlike the PATA, which was manufacturer driven, the league was firmly under the control of the pool-operating wholesalers.[75]

The leaders of the FTL were clearly not old-style jobbers. Rather, its founders, Adanac and Leader, were both big buying pools – Adanac was a wholesaler-owned cooperative with 100 stores supplied by Jas. Lumbers and Company and Leader, with 120 stores, a retail cooperative that worked through the York Trading Company – as was the third big Ontario pool to join the FTL, Superior Stores, with 300 outlets. In Quebec the FTL was organized by Hudon-Hébert-Chaput, which ran L'Epicerie Moderne (EM Stores with 380 branches), and Laporte Martin, which operated Victoria Independent Grocers (600 Victory stores). In western Canada the organizers of the FTL were W.H. Malkin, one-time mayor of Vancouver and the city's leading importer, John Horne of Campbell, Wilson and Horne and H.G. Smith – both Prairie jobbers – and S.C. Richards of Western Grocers' owner of the Winnipeg-based Red and White voluntary chain (300 stores).[76]

What must be understood is that it was the biggest and most innovative wholesalers – the businesses that were in the process of creating their own voluntary retail chains – who were behind grocery price maintenance. To this extent, while the FTL and the PATA drew their leadership from different sectors, neither could be described as representing an anti-modern counter-offensive against mass merchandising. In both the PATA and the FTL it was the largest businesses that dominated, and in both it was the most progressive retailers who joined. The organizers of the PATA and the FTL were well aware of these facts. For Glyn-Jones, price maintenance 'undoubtedly gives the manufacturer tremendous power, but we do not apologize for that', while Crowder thought that the FTL was going to be an organization as tightly knit as a chain of stores, in fact, he had visions of 'a big chain – bigger than anything existing in the country to-day.'[77]

The Fair Trade League was officially launched almost one year after the enlarged PATA's foundation in May 1925, but unlike the druggists' association it never proved a great success. There were, it was estimated, about 17,800 grocery retailers in Canada in 1925, as well as some 11,500 country general storekeepers, many of whom sold foodstuffs, and Crowder hoped to enrol at least 10,000 of them in the Fair Trade League. But it did not prove possible: by April 1927 the FTL numbered only 3,700 members, about half of whom came from BC and the Prairies. Though in real numerical terms, this figure made the FTL a larger organization than the PATA, it did not provide the league with the same sort of authority. Although it was difficult to ignore an association that had subscribed over 75 per cent of the retail druggists, it was easy to discount a league which involved only 21 per cent of grocers. It was not just that there were too many grocery retailers; there were also far too many shoestring traders in the food business. Figures for the incomplete census of 1924 and for the national survey of 1931 reflect the structural difference between grocery and pharmacy. Of the 696 drug stores filing returns in 1924, only 5 per cent can properly be called 'shoestring' (sales under $5,000), while in the food trades 26 per cent of the 7,500 stores surveyed were small. The more reliable statistics for 1931 show an even more pronounced difference, with 10 per cent of drug stores and 45 per cent of food stores having sales under $5,000.[78] Given that the ranks of the PATA and the FTL were filled with small capitalist independents and that prices were generally fixed with a margin on which the smallest could not operate, it is hardly surprising that the majority of grocers remained outside the league.

The problem was that numbers were crucial to the success of association-based price-fixing. Like the Ozone plan, both the PATA and FTL experiments sought to empower manufacturers to enforce resale price maintenance by providing them with a supportive and unified market. On one level, then, retail organization was not really necessary to the success of either group: the manufacturers could well have continued to fix prices on their own as they had been doing for twenty years. But the reason that the two organizations had been established was to add to the manufacturers' existing power by providing them with the moral authority and guaranteed support of the retail masses. Had a supplier not had the backing of the PATA or FTL, what assurance would he have had that the merchants would not push items that did not carry a fixed price or that gave them a slightly larger spread? The organizations made sure that retailers not only had the same interest in all price-maintained goods (33.3 per cent), but that with their modestly higher margins they also favoured the fixed over the freely priced products. Moreover, the trade organizations provided manufacturers with a credible excuse as to why they could not sell to a departmental or chain for less, and they provided cheap policing of all pricing contracts. Finally, they shifted legal responsibility away from the producers (shades of profiteering still flitted through the manufacturers' heads) and onto organizations most closely identified with the retailers themselves. Thus numbers were all-important; a group that could enlist the majority stood to gain manufacturer support; a group – no matter how numerically large – that left out the bulk of retailers was too dangerous for the manufacturers to endorse. Consequently, while the PATA obtained the support of almost every major manufacturer in Canada, the FTL was able to enrol only three big and twenty-nine 'peanut concerns.'

Even before the PATA and the FTL had organized their campaigns, the battle over-price had fixing begun. The first shots were fired by Woodward's department store in Vancouver, A.J. Freiman's in Ottawa, and the George Tamblyn chain in Toronto, all of which announced their intention to challenge the legality of the PATA. As proof of this resolve, Tamblyn began to cut prices on every product whose manufacturer enrolled in the association. When Beecham's joined the PATA in July 1926, Tamblyn cut the price of the famous pills from 50¢ to 39¢, and when Dodd's enrolled, the Toronto chain slashed the prices of that manufacturer's products by half. George Tamblyn, preparing for a prolonged siege, had already filled his storerooms with supplies to subvert the boycott he knew would come (action which encouraged the press to roar with delight, 'pills to right of him. Pills to the left of him. Pills all around him').

Tamblyn's assault caught the price fixers off guard, and with the PATA still in its fetal state, the manufacturers began to waiver, dismayed by 'the fusillade of pills with which Toronto the good is being covered.' Only the reappearance of Glyn-Jones, who accepted the position of chairman of the Canadian PATA, averted a recurrence of the Ozone débâcle. 'Some manufacturers have timorously asked me if this proposition is going to be permanent', Sir William declared at his first meeting as head of the PATA; 'if I have to pawn my shirt and live in apartments in Montreal, this movement is going on.' Confidence restored, the administrative committee continued to assemble its price-list, and on 28 August 1926 the PATA began operations. That same day Tamblyn announced the largest sale in the chain's history. 'It is a War,' Glyn-Jones announced melodramatically, as he placed Tamblyn stores on the PATA's 'stop list.' The chain owner responded by demanding an investigation of the PATA as a conspiracy under the Combines Investigation Act of 1923.[79]

None of this activity took anyone by surprise and the retail price fixers clearly had their own ideas about what to say in their defence. Glyn-Jones, who among his other talents was a trained barrister, was sensible enough to recognize that the key issue in the Liberals' combine legislation was the question of detriment to the public; under Canadian law, only such price-fixing associations as 'unduly' or 'unreasonably' enhanced prices were illegal. What Glyn-Jones and his lawyers argued before the registrar conducting the preliminary enquiry to determine whether the PATA warranted investigation under the Combines Act was that it was the price cutter, 'the Cheap Jack or Gutter Merchant with his tawdry wares,' that was the real detriment to the public in that he was responsible for 'the lowering of moral standards of business as a whole.' To this extent, 'we are not establishing a monopoly, we are fighting conditions under which if cut price merchants succeed in eliminating the small distributors, they will have the field to themselves and be able to indicate their own terms.' J.T. Crowder chose a parallel tack: 'price maintenance is not the same as price fixing,' he explained; 'in the principle of price maintenance, the manufacturer of a pair of shoes or a bottle of catsup or of any branded commodity establishes a selling price to the customer. Any other manufacturer of a similar article can establish a higher or lower price just as motor cars have their prices established to-day.'[80]

The registrar, F.A. McGregor, and his assistant, the young W.A. Mackintosh, were not convinced, and the preliminary report they submitted in September 1926 was a simple restatement of the mass-production thesis. According to the registrar, the cost of distribution had grown far out of proportion to its value as a result of duplications of service arising from 'the large number of druggists in the business.' Mass production had lowered the prices of goods, but the public was not enjoying the full benefits of industrial centralization because of the intervening cost of independent storekeeping. Only mass merchandising, by dint of its greater efficiency, could reduce the costs of distribution and initiate 'the needed adjustment and ... better proportionment of distribution and production costs.' While it was evident that 'the chain stores have made and will continue to make inroads on the unit stores; they have found progress easy because of the slackness and inefficiency of the small merchants ... From the viewpoint of the public interest, this should be regarded not necessarily as an evil ... but as a beginning in the solution of the problem of the excessive number of drug stores.' In view of this conclusion, the PATA could not be anything but a combination in restraint of trade. It was protecting the inefficient at the expense of the consumers and 'prevent[ing] the public securing full advantage of such improved methods of distribution as have developed.' It was, Tamblyn declared, 'A Great Victory', and he immediately ran a full-page advertisement in the Toronto press inviting the public to savour the fruits at his chain's 'Great Victory Sale.'[81]

The preliminary report raised the druggists' blood pressure, but it did not actually terminate the PATA's operations. The final decision as to whether the association should be prosecuted under the Criminal Code had to await the report of the combines investigator appointed on the recommendation of Registrar McGregor in December 1926. In the interval, the PATA persevered in nervous expectation, an effort made only slightly easier by Tamblyn's agreement to abide by the price-list while his stores rebuilt their depleted stocks. Unfortunately, the investigation into the PATA, headed by L.V. O'Connor, a retired solicitor for the CPR, was no more sympathetic to the druggists' cause than had been the registrar's. In crucial testimony heard in January 1927, W.J. Fraser, an executive with the manufacturing firm of Northrop and Lyman (the manufacturing branch of Arthur Lyman's wholesaling house), admitted that before the price-list had been issued, his firm had allowed Tamblyn to sell Dr Thomas' Electric Oil for 28¢ a bottle and that after the PATA came into effect that price had been raised to 38¢. There had, however, been no increase in the cost of manufacturing Dr Thomas' Oil, and the sole rationale for the price hike had been the need 'to bring the chain store into line with the smaller retailer'.[82]

Already scenting victory, Tamblyn opted to 'Kick over the Traces' and use his replenished stock reserves to 'Slash the Prices on 98 PATA Articles.' Again the price-fixing association put him on its stop list, but the struggle was beginning to take its toll. In early August 1927 Glyn-Jones suffered a severe 'nervous collapse' while on tour in Vancouver. 'We have not ceded an inch of ground since we got going with our list ... and we are not going to,' the PATA chairman announced defiantly from his hospital bed. But by 9 September he was dead. The investigation was a foregone conclusion; Tamblyn actually broadcast its findings three weeks before the investigator submitted his report. Leaderless and without further recourse, the PATA wavered for an instant and then discontinued its functions on 31 October. The FTL, which had never even begun operations, quietly dissolved itself. 'It is the biggest thing that has ever happened in the history of the drug trade,' George Tamblyn proclaimed; 'the whole price list is wide open.'[83]

Tamblyn's jaunty optimism was understandable in view of his recent triumph, but he was wrong. In the first place, the legal battle continued all the way to the Privy Council, which heard the PATA's challenge to the combines act in 1930 and ruled it intra vires early in 1931. But price maintenance remained a fixture in the drug business, no matter what the government ruled. In 1928 fifty-five manufacturers decided to resurrect the RMA's window scheme and under Crowder's guidance to organize promotional days for their price-protected products, refusing to sell to stores that cut prices. This collaborative effort was to survive eighteen months before the Depression broke it apart. Thereafter, the manufacturers were again on their own, but price maintenance continued to spread slowly across the trade. Many of the big patent-medicine companies – Colgate-Palmolive, Sterling, Johnson & Johnson, Wingate Chemical, J.C. Eno, Squibb, Dr Chase – were busily, if quietly, maintaining their resale prices. The president of the OCP drew attention to the fact when he noted in 1933 that pharmacy 'is on a firmer and surer foundation than I have known it for many years ... the number of manufacturers who consider that the pharmacist is entitled to some remuneration as a distributor is steadily increasing.' There were so many using rpm, another druggist added, that 'I am not even interested in the manufacturers and manufacturers' agents who choose that their goods should be used as a football.' By 1936 the CPhA was estimating that 25 per cent of the druggists' total stock was being successfully price maintained by the manufacturers.[84] Though Tamblyn and the other mass merchandisers had felt that the death of the PATA would free trade, they had underestimated the brand-name manufacturers' interest. Indeed, as their own sales skidded and profits slipped during the 1930s, they too came to accept the need for rpm. Price-fixing in drugs returned to what it had been before – individual, unspectacular, unnoticed by outsiders – but ever more pervasive.

Outside pharmacy there was also considerable price protection, but its extent is far more difficult to document. Certainly many high-profile manufacturers continued to enforce rpm – all the cigarette, radio, gramophone, large appliance, and rubber footwear manufacturers, as well as Bovril, Nestlé, Heinz, Hurlbut shoes, and Dominion Textiles underwear – but what percentage of the total volume these businesses produced is impossible to judge. Without question, however, the failure of the FTL-PATA experiment had had no serious impact on the growth of price-fixing among brand-name manufacturers. That is not to say that a retailer's whole stock would have come price fixed, but probably between a tenth and a quarter of it would have been, and some dealers, such as those selling books or appliances, would have been carrying mostly price-maintained goods. Sales of these products would still be held, of course, but increasingly these sales would have been to clear ends or at the discretion of the manufacturers, who would have authorized merchants to reduce selectively the prices of their brand-name products.

But while the defeat of the PATA and the FTL failed to deter the progress of resale price maintenance, it broke the organizations that had publicly sponsored them. Once their demise became certain, Crowder and Hougham shifted associational efforts to coordinating the various voluntary pooling schemes and offering guidance and information to retailers interested in buying cooperatively. The RMA also stepped up its information services, providing help in stock control, accounting, and window display to enquiring members. In these ways, the organization sought to 'bring to the aid of the independent retailer the sort of merchandising helps and services which the large scale enterprises are now able to employ.' As Crowder explained it: 'the RMA hopes to place the merchant in a position where he can buy and sell in successful competition with the largest buyers.' Unfortunately, association no longer appealed to the well-to-do merchants. Membership figures for the RMA are not available for the late twenties, but the size of the organization seems to been halved between 1923 and 1929, and there are good reasons to believe that the 1925–7 membership was considerably higher than that in 1923 (table 14). Despondent and directionless, the RMA now slunk towards oblivion. At the 1931 convention, a thoroughly desultory affair, Crowder was not only removed from the RMA executive but apparently asked to leave the association. Hougham in turn resigned his national post and became secretary of the ORMA. The new leader of the national organization was S.E. Desmarais, a one-time Liberal MLA in Quebec and an undertaker by trade. It was a strangely appropriate choice for an organization that in the midst of the Depression would decide to make a reform of the law concerning NSF cheques its chief priority.[85]

Though the membership of the ORDA and the CPhA is also unknown, in intellectual terms the druggists fared little better. As in the past, a few zealots took the opportunity to denounce the whole concept of price maintenance as an RMA scheme to commercialize pharmacy. It was, said one druggist, 'an effort by manufacturers to dominate my business.' 'We must shake off the yoke and be independent', A.R. Farley of Hull agreed, 'we are able to manufacture medicines ... we must go back to the practice of pharmacy.' This time, however, no one was prepared to take the reaction seriously – including the reactionaries. Farley promptly tried to realize his dream by founding a manufacturing firm, which was soon contracted to supply corn remedies and cod-liver oil to a Quebec voluntary pool (Goyer's Retail Druggists Union). And the ORDA, which in 1930 announced its break with the RMA and its decision to work for the restoration of the 'old-time professional pharmacy,' declared that it would achieve this lofty ambition through an advertising campaign promoting the pharmacist's 'professional character.' The campaign would feature cosmetics and soaps and show how 'the druggist was best placed to sell these because of his knowledge of Chemistry,' and it would promote the sale of stationery and writing materials by emphasizing 'the Druggist's better education and higher standard of life.' There was nothing ironic in any of this, R.B.J. Stanbury, the editor of the *Canadian Pharmaceutical Journal*, explained, because the commercial pharmacy could still be a traditional pharmacy; druggists might be selling film, soap, price-maintained proprietaries, magazines, and toilet paper, 'but aside from the fact that the druggist finds it profitable to carry such a vast line of miscellaneous items, he is rendering a real service to the community. His store is the community centre – the place where people like to go.' Moreover, as a Montreal druggist explained, 'business is a science too.' By 1931 the druggists' organizations had sunk into a deep, if self-satisfied torpor.[86]

PRICE-FIXING IN FOLKLORIC DRESS

The collapse of the RMA and the CPhA's stagnation should come as no surprise, given what we have seen of trade identities. Indeed, the experience of the organizations had once again shown that retailers were poor cooperators. The small capitalist retailers who joined the RMA lacked the kind of cohesiveness through which group members remain attuned to their collective interests and conscious of the need to organize themselves. They certainly shared a certain bourgeois class empathy, common gender perceptions, and a racial identification, but the shopkeepers had not developed the kind of occupational unity that could overcome their competitive individualism. Retailers therefore organized only sporadically, as a reaction against particular issues or in response to the encouragement they received from powerful and more unified groups outside retailing. During the mid-1920s they had drawn together because price cutting had aroused their interests as modernizing business people. But the identifications they felt during the struggle for price maintenance were not substantially different from the activated sense of community fleetingly experienced by the white merchants of BC in the early 1920s.

Price maintenance, while clearly a trade issue, was burdened with the modernizing retailers' non-occupational prejudices. Granted, the retailers who supported price fixing-hoped that it would act as a restraint upon the chains, department stores, and shoestring traders. Though small capitalist retailers had come to accept mass marketing as a principle, they continued to oppose much that the mass merchandisers did. As Joseph Crowder pointed out, 'a chain store is not necessarily a bad or dangerous instrument,' but it did need to be regulated. 'Chain stores,' he explained, 'are very much like motor cars ... High powered motor cars, if allowed to run riot in a crowded thoroughfare can do a great deal of damage.' And among those elements which the independents felt needed controlling, none was more important than the price cutting of quality brand-name goods.[87] But while remaining a trade issue, the demand for controlled prices was none the less defined by their concept of legitimacy, by their professionalism, and by their sense of themselves as neither corporate magnates nor 'Cheap Jack' operators.

All store owners felt the sting of competition, but only those sharing certain attitudes sought to control it through rpm. It was more than simply a question of margins: main-street retailers insisted that price competition was not something that they were inclined by their natures to do; instead, it was imposed on them by others. 'As for who is responsible for cut prices,' a critic of the main-street shopkeepers' activities observed, 'there is a marked tendency to "pass the buck," with some blaming the department stores entirely, some the chain stores and others even contending that it is the small man in business who is usually responsible.' Whereas 'price' was the football of the 'cheap man,' 'professional druggists' declared, the 'ethical man' preferred to compete in terms of personality, reliability, and image. 'There are other ways of beating a competitor than by this silly price cutting,' Glyn-Jones declared. 'You can do it by service, by caring for your customers.' Business for the bourgeois merchant was a 'prestigious occupation,' and commerce – even for the pharmacists – was by the mid-1920s generally invested with the status of a 'science' or an 'art.' The 'most evil result' of price cutting, observed Glyn-Jones, 'is the lowering of the moral standard of business as a whole.' In short, behaving like the 'Common Cutter or Gutter Merchant' was demeaning to bourgeois businessmen. Of course, shifting competition from price to service or style made good sense to the modernizing shopkeepers. With their handsome storefronts, attractive displays, and more personal service, they felt confident of their ability to out-merchandise the chains and departmentals. Moreover, the margins that would be set on resale goods would be low enough to eliminate most of their backstreet competitors. But these too were the expectations of men of comfortable means.[88]

The issue was also deeply gendered. In the retail press Glyn-Jones was invariably depicted as a 'hero,' a 'Joshua,' 'a born leader,' a 'drug trade Foch.' Supporting price maintenance – essentially a sacrifice of 'independence' – was therefore portrayed as a manly act 'requiring audacity and courage,' and the PATA's struggle was seen as 'war to the knife.' The entire organizational effort was conceived in military terms. 'The strategy of the anti-Tamblyn High Command,' *Drug Merchandising* observed at the height of the contest, 'is, of course, to starve out the War Lord; make him hungry for pills; break down his morale; and force him to make tracks.' If manliness characterized the PATA's supporters, sex defined their opponents. Main-street retailers in Vancouver first organized to prevent 'a price cutting orgy,' and they used erotic imagery to distance themselves from their mass-merchandising rivals. 'The chain store does not differ in any essential from the common department store,' one critical British Columbian observed. 'I passed one of these stores this noon. An enormous crowd before one of the windows blocked the traffic. An overrouged and underdressed young lady was sitting in the window and demonstrating something about bobbed hair. Inside a crowd at the lunch counter – or soda fountain – [were] gulping their lunches.'[89] The image of the chain or department store as brothel had a rich history – the stores were, from the beginning, palaces of seduction – but there was more to this depiction than texturing. Retailers did not simply employ imagery for effect; they conceived of themselves, their businesses, and their activities in gendered ways. Defending retailing from the price cutters was a manly obligation, and it was this perception which in part facilitated shopkeeper mobilization. It is no wonder that Glyn-Jones's admission into the CPhA was accompanied by his initiation into the Yellow Dogs.

Paradoxically, these elements of unity, expressed as they were through a static folkloric imagery, obscured the real lesson of price-fixing, which was that retailing had been transformed. Store modernization had been undermining traditional distribution for over twenty years, though many pockets of conservatism remained. But when the

CPhA made its evidently painful decision to line itself up behind the manufacturers of the PATA, the last organized resistance to the modern distribution system was effectively broken. The bankruptcy of the traditional wholesalers and the dramatic growth in voluntary pooling were simply further signs of the changes taking place in merchandising. Twenty years before, when the courts had smashed the Elliman plan, there had been reactionaries in every trade to point the way back into independence. That no serious conservative critique emerged in 1929 was itself evidence of the new age.

What had begun as an anti-modernist reaction in the 1890s had become, by the 1920s, a drive to integrate retailing more fully into the modern system of production. The folkloric forms of their speech appears to have blinded people to this reality and led them to see retail protest as static and reactionary. But shopkeeping's symbolism, while unyielding in being the force that made small business people what they were, was always suited to the diversity of identities and the flow of situations. In fact, just as mainstreet joiners used images such as 'moral' and 'small' to reflect their class or gender interests, so too did they load them with their changing sense of themselves as modernizing 'professionals.'

The druggist John Hargreaves, for example, stood at the crossroads of distribution. He vigorously supported the greater integration of manufacturing and retailing, but he remained in many other respects a Victorian moralist. 'Ethical conduct', he told a retail gathering in 1904, 'is now so universally acknowledged and recognized that we almost look upon it as part of our science or education'. But these 'high ethical relations can exist quite as naturally in commercial intercourse and associations as in professional organizations.' This 'ethical conduct,' allied to 'professionalism' rather than 'individualism', was the secret of business success and the cement of community. 'My definition of the fearless man is one who lives so close to the Golden Rule, who so recognizes the existence and rights of others, whose aims and objects are so founded on the lofty ideal of advancing and lifting up himself, with his fellows, that he knows no fear, surely he is the independent man.'[90]

Hargreaves was here sounding the familiar chords: small business as ethical activity; independence as moral good; progress for the one as synonymous with progress for the many. But even this apparently atavistic speech was dense with modernist undertones. Remember that at the time he spoke, Hargreaves was trying to win retail support for the RMA, price-fixing, and cooperative buying, and he was being opposed by druggists defending the pre-eminence of the colleges, scientific education, and the in-house nostrum. The retailer, according to Hargreaves, was a 'professional' in need of 'high education' in the 'science' of 'commercial intercourse.' The words were the same – science, learning, profession – but Hargreaves was thinking of merchandising rather than pharmacology. Moreover, the whole address was a veiled attack on professional 'independence.' 'Selfishness,' he declared, 'is generally allied with individualism.' Real 'independence,' he felt, could be found in 'cooperation'. Living by the Golden Rule did not mean the individual's 'upward advancement towards higher goals'; rather, it implied the struggle for collective improvement. That was why Hargreaves felt the 'best interests of the community' could be achieved through 'commercial associations', or, as a subsequent generation would call them, buying pools.[91]

Hargreaves was a man of his age, a prophet, undoubtedly, of modern merchandising, but still a professional bound by his late-Victorian world-view. Pharmacy remained for him a duality, at once a 'profession and trade,' and he spoke of the need for 'the high and noble ideals of the profession' to infuse 'commercial intercourse.' He remained, for all his promotion of progressive merchandising, as yet unconvinced that commerce was quite as noble as science. Twenty years later modernization had penetrated more fully the main-street retailers' thinking. The folkloric images remained the same – ethics, legitimacy, the living profit, the noble undertaking – but they were applied to commercial life with greater self-assurance. 'Business is a science in itself,' a Montreal activist declared in 1927. ' Modern pharmacy must be commercial to the largest extent ... [so] cast aside all the aesthetic thoughts and ideals of oldfashioned professional pharmacy and instead remember that a moderate and judicial application of commercial ethics can gain for [the druggist] as much prestige and material success.' The businessman, remarked another, was 'entitled to public recognition of the high professional standing and dignity of his calling.' And the retail pharmacist in particular 'legally and morally shares a responsibility as great as the physicians.'[92]

The words sum it all up. Though the druggists of the PATA candidly admitted to themselves that, while 'the proprietor may still exist it is difficult to pick him out from his small army of clerks,' they used phrases that evoked images of the devoted professional living above his store and ready to serve at any hour, the person to whom the community would turn for advice. And while they acknowledged that the 'odor of drugs is for the most part gone, supplanted by the odor of fountain syrups', they still insisted that 'the pharmacist is a professional' for whom the term 'drug store [as opposed to pharmacy] was a disgrace to themselves and their profession.'[93]

And yet there was nothing two-faced about their views. The PATA was designed to prevent the price cutting of proprietaries by giving the manufacturer control over retail margins. But shopkeepers defended this objective by insisting on the importance to the community of the 'traditional' retailer. At issue here were symbols – time-honoured images of enormous emotive force that were being used to convey a modernist message. Doubtless retailers relied upon the folkloric images partly because they evoked public sympathy, but it would be wrong to see the merchants as conniving in their appeals. The symbols of shopkeeping were even more important to their own sense of community than they were to the public's. Folkloric memory was the touchstone of retail identity: it provided scattered and competitive shopkeepers with the tools of discussion and cooperation. Modernizing druggists and grocers used the traditional words because they gave occupational shape to store owners' commonalities as up-to-date small capitalist entrepreneurs.

By the mid-1920s, then, progressive shopkeepers thought of themselves as rivals of the mass merchandisers. They kept insisting that their businesses were not more inefficient or unreliable than the corporate stores and that, all things being equal, their prices were as reasonable as those offered by the chains and departmentals. If the mass marketers cut lower, it was only because they had the unfair advantage of size. In short, for all their reliance on the folkloric symbols, the proprietors did see themselves competing in comparable ways for identical customers. The only difference was that the bigger stores were able to sell quality brand-name goods at lower prices.

There can be no doubt that resale price maintenance aimed, to borrow Joseph Crowder's delightful metaphor, at forcing the mass merchandisers to drive with the handbrake on. But that is not the same thing as suggesting that the small capitalist merchants were attempting to remove the engine from the mass economy. The organized retailers had come to this position after much debate and confusion. The anti-modernist position did not yield easily – in part, because of the entrenched authority of the professional leadership; in part, because of the timing of the inflationary cycles – but by the end of the First World War the lines of defence had broken. The Board of Commerce fiasco had played its part, humiliating the traditionalists and undermining their support among the jobbing interests, but even without this unfortunate episode, the currents of modernization were proving inexorable. Unfortunately, in the long run it did the associations themselves little good. The decision against the PATA again broke the organizational spirit and sent main-street traders reeling back into their shops. As the Depression pressed in, the cause of trade organization appeared to be dead.

7

The Politics of Folklore

It is ironic that a shower of public support should have fallen on the retailers only with the withering of their organizational efforts. But the 1930s were singular in that they provoked, even among normally sober people, a belief that economic reform was necessary if enterprise was to be restored. Building upon popular anti-monopoly traditions, many people argued during the Depression that the economic collapse had been brought about by a failure of big business. Stock market manipulations, the 'terrific concentration of wealth,' 'the overcapitalization of industry,' the imp of 'overproduction' – all were blamed for the sudden economic crisis. Much of the 'system,' if not all of it, now appeared to have gone wrong, making it time, as Prime Minister R.B. Bennett explained, 'to replace in the old system those elements which are worn out, broken down, obsolete, and without further utility, so that the system may work.' Was it surprising, then, as criticism of the mass-production economy mounted over the course of the 1930s, that the profile of small business should have grown correspondingly large? Even the urbane *New York Times Magazine* as early as November 1931 was presenting the secret to recovery in terms of a shift from the 'The Ford Formula for Happiness' to 'The Gandhi Formula for Happiness.' Many people had apparently decided that a revitalized small business sector held the key to renewed prosperity: small, it began to seem, might be beautiful after all.[1]

During the 1930s, thousands of Canadians rallied to the vague programs of populists such as William Aberhart, H.H. Stevens, and Maurice Duplessis, who promised the restoration of a society based on petty property and decentralized authority. Socialists in Saskatchewan and Social Crediters in Alberta could alike be found emphasizing the need to defend that sacred Prairie institution, the family farm, and promising to return agriculture to its mystical roots in independence and self-confidence, while in Quebec the reformist Action libérale nationale would declare its goal to be 'la décentralisation des hommes, de l'argent et des industries.' As the influential economist Esdras Minville would explain, to save capitalism 'nous devrons doubler, tripler le nombre ... des petites et moyennes entreprises.' What all these reformers had in common was a belief that small business was more 'moral' than big and that the protection and advancement of petty enterprise had to be one of the primary goals of government.[2]

It is no surprise, then, that historians should support their theories regarding small-business anti-modernism with descriptions of the populist insurgency of the 1930s. The Union Nationale, for example, is seen to have risen to power on a wave of reactionary petit bourgeois nationalism, its leaders determined 'to take whatever steps were necessary to protect the interests of the small-scale French-Canadian business enterprise engaged in a life and death struggle with the larger and more firmly entrenched English-owned corporations.' Similarly, the Reconstruction Party, even to Stevens's biographer, 'was largely an act of political desperation' which 'championed the cause of the hard-pressed producers, small business owners and thousands of nameless Canadians caught by the depression.' Defeat loomed from the outset in this fight so defiant of the current of history. 'Desperation,' 'unreason,' 'panic' – only words such as these can catch the pathetic ambitions of traditionally minded people caught in the stranglehold of modernity.[3]

It is an interpretation that rests on two assumptions: first, that there was a homogeneous and declining small-business community to lead and, second, that the politicians were in sympathy with the goals of the proprietors. As we shall see, neither assumption is easily maintained. In the case of Canada's retailers – who supposedly lent unqualified support to the populists' cause – it is especially misleading to presume solidarity. Shopkeepers were a divided and contentious group, and the organizations which they formed represented only a minority of their number. Moreover, though many of them were working hard to stay competitive, only the most marginal among them – a stratum in any case alienated from the major trade organizations – were really 'declining.' But these were realities about which the politicians remained silent.

Certainly, right-wing populists talked a lot about the problems of small business people, but they seldom moved much beyond the familiar rhetoric. What made petty enterprise so appealing was its evocation of traditional values and its association with images of community cohesion. At a time of deep social distress and ebbing confidence in the established order, smallness offered a psychic balm. But because the politicians who declared their support for proprietary enterprise did so with little understanding of what small business really was, the support they extended was mostly glitter and gauze. Harry Stevens, for example, who declared himself the saviour of petty enterprise in the 1935 federal election, made vague references to the 'Economics of Christ,' to small-business 'morality,' and to the need to defend the local community, but he offered little that was concrete. Like so many other populists in the thirties, Stevens had mastered the imagery but not its content.

The fact that the reformers seldom acted under the advisement of independent business people only served to amplify this folkloric dissonance. The flurry of discriminatory tax laws that were passed through the provincial legislatures in the mid-thirties, for instance, had been accompanied by loud assertions that they were needed to encourage community businesses and destroy the 'foreign' chains and department stores. But the tax idea had not originated with the retailers; it had first been proposed by cash-starved municipal governments in central and eastern Canada who thought that they could at one and the same time exploit an old strain of small-business protest and make a grab at a new source of revenue. The ORMA's secretary, George Hougham, was not far wrong in suggesting that the tax idea had been concocted by 'quick witted politicians to exploit the popular sentiment for the enrichment of the state treasury.'[4] Stevens also drew little from the retailers beyond their symbolism. In fact, most of his information concerning distribution was provided to him by a small group of manufacturers interested in securing the passage of a Canadian equivalent to Roosevelt's National Industrial Recovery Act.

Part of the reason for the lack of input, at least in the case of the retailers, was that the populists' appropriation of small-business folklore caught them completely by surprise. Especially since the war, they had grown more used to being vilified than praised, and the defeat of the price-maintenance campaign in the 1920s had effectively shattered their own associational efforts. Crowder and Hougham fought for a time to keep the idea of association alive with a buying-pool scheme and an attempted revivification of the PATA, but by 1931 the RMA had again disintegrated, its leadership moribund, its membership falling, and its provincial organizations on the verge of bankruptcy. Moreover, the Depression was cutting a wide swath through retail confidence, reducing still further the numbers that might be drawn into the trade associations.[5] In short, it was not the time for the organized retailers to inspire public interest in their work.

PROSPERITY THROUGH INFLATION

The politicization of domestic distribution actually began when the Depression's ravages forced an unlikely group of manufacturers into reconsidering their approach to marketing. During the 1920s a division had opened between those consumer goods manufacturers who followed a price-fixing policy and those who believed that more production and price deflation offered the surest path to continuous prosperity. Both groups contained promoters of store modernization, but there is no question that the price fixers had far closer connections to the independent trade and worse relations with the mass merchandisers. As a result, the retailers' relations with the manufacturers were most developed in drugs, tobacco, appliances, and book lines, where resale price maintenance was common. The industrial advocates of mass production, in contrast, had in the past often neglected and even occasionally renounced the independent channel, preferring to deal with the mass merchandisers or, like some makers of shoes and clothing, to open their own retail outlets. Thus, while drug, packaged food, and hardware manufacturers were experimenting with PATA-like solutions, their counterparts in the less brand-conscious sectors were quietly opening their own retail chains, adopting Taylorite production systems, and encouraging low-priced mass merchandising.

This strategy made a lot of sense in the boom years of the later twenties. Since 1924 the consumer goods industries had enjoyed remarkably good times, with the value of products made in Canada rising about 40 per cent by 1929. There were some clear winners: in the rubber goods industries, pre-tax net profits rose 67 per cent; in women's clothing, they doubled; among automobile makers, profits more than tripled. What underlay these successes were dramatic increases in outputs coupled with modest savings in the costs of labour (averaging 10 per cent) and raw material (averaging 15 per cent). Thus, though wholesale prices for goods such as clothing and footwear fell slightly in the later twenties (6 per cent over five years), successful consumer goods manufacturers were able to make big money by preventing their overhead from rising quite as quickly as their outputs.[6] It was a strategy the manufacturers hoped might see them through bad times as well as good.

Unfortunately, for makers of consumer goods, the crash of the early 1930s was far worse than the depression of the previous decade had been. The total value of consumer goods manufactured in Canada shrank 45 per cent between 1929 and 1933, and net profits declined by an even more precipitous 48 per cent. The total number of wage workers employed in consumer industries fell from 261,000 to 202,000, and average wages plunged by one-fifth. Leading the way down were retail prices, which for food and clothing declined by about one-third (making workers who kept their jobs during the Depression objectively, if not psychologically, better off), but which for some products dropped much more severely. The price of a mattress was cut in half between 1929 and 1934, tinned salmon fell 68 per cent, and children's washable playsuits became 44 per cent cheaper. And just as in the early twenties, changing habits of consumption dealt a further blow to many producers: in the early thirties, people ate less beef and more pork, more chicken but fewer eggs, while men bought more shirts but far fewer collars and cuffs, and women began their mid-twentieth-century migration from cotton underwear to synthetic fibres (artificial silk or rayon).[7]

Because the depression of the 1930s pulled the economy down more slowly – if ultimately more deeply – than had the collapse of the early 1920s, industrialists had more time to respond. And most initially chose to tinker with their winning formulas. While the brand name manufacturers in drugs and tobacco simply tightened their control over retail pricing, the mass producers' first impulse was to do more of what they had done in the 1920s: to step up their marketing efforts and work to lighten their burden of overhead. As the president of Swift Canada Company made clear, if 'every concern within their own business would follow their costs daily, and make an earnest and reasonable effort to sell their own products at a reasonable profit ... [the] situation would soon work around to a common sense basis.' The Depression could only be ended, agreed *Canadian Woodworker and Furniture Manufacturing*, by 'constructive development of markets; more intensive selling; more advertising; improved products; new lines; complete knowledge of products and their application; latest type of equipment; special attention to waste, including waste of unproductive time; standardization of parts; production in multiples and efficient plant organization and production.'[8]

Not surprisingly, in those industries where brand names were less prominent, the Depression dealt its first blow to the factory floor and not to the sales or administrative office; in clothing, for example, 22 per cent of the tailors, 13 per cent of the machine operators, and even 5 per cent of the foremen had been fired by June 1931, but only ten out of six hundred managerial personnel had lost their jobs. While cutting deeply into wages and workforces and eliminating 22 per cent of the jobs, the consumer goods manufacturers actually expanded their sales and administrative personnel by 6 per cent in the first three years of the Depression.[9]

Sadly, streamlined production and increased promotion did not serve to lift Canadian industry out of the muck. Though the size of the industrial workforce was cut every year and despite the steady reduction in overheads, net profits in the consumer goods sector continued to fall. Some industries did fare better than others between 1930 and 1933: in boots and shoes, where labour was hammered by one thousand lay-offs and a one-third cut in pay and where non-wage overheads were slashed by 31 per cent, profits on outputs did edge upward from 16.4 to 16.6 (from 16.6 to 23.3 on capital). But in furniture, cuts of 50 per cent to the workforce and of 70 per cent in overheads still could not prevent profits from dropping from 26.1 to 25.5 per cent of gross value produced (from 27.5 to 14.1 on capital).[10] While the consumer goods sector as a whole experienced sharply declining sales and a falling rate of profit, we need to remember that a few industries in 1933 could feel that their sales and cost-cutting strategies were working. This fact helps to explain the different levels of despair (from the grim to the hysterical) that prevailed even within the more traditionally minded manufacturing circles as 1933 ground on into 1934.

Among those whose industries were continuing to suffer despite their best cost-cutting efforts, the reason most often cited was the increase in competition. In 1928 there had been 444 women's clothing factories in Canada dividing up a $63-million pie; by 1933 there were 540 of them sharing a market that was now 30 per cent smaller. Similarly, while the volume of furniture sold fell by close to two-thirds between 1929 and 1933, the number of manufacturers increased by 10 per cent, and despite the 30 per cent contraction in sales for the baking industry, the number of bakeries actually increased by one-fifth. In spite of the staggering bankruptcy rate, the deflation ensured that hundreds of entrepreneurs in virtually every sector were willing to take a chance on opening new businesses. People who had some savings from the 1920s discovered that their money was now worth far more than it had been before and that they could use that capital to buy property or open a business. What F.R. Scott and H.M. Cassidy reported of the clothing industry was typical of many others: 'Particularly in time of depression, when the clothing foreman or designer, or skilled worker, loses a regular job, he is tempted to sink what little capital he might have into an independent venture in the hope that it will bring him at least some return ... In every instance their chances of success are exceedingly small, but nevertheless they establish themselves as independent proprietors, partly in hope, partly in desperation, and make the position of those already in the business still more difficult by the intensity of their competition.'[11] It was this expansion in small firms that largely accounted for the growth that took place in the number of manufacturing establishments in the early Depression years and that, according to many industrialists, best explained their own declining profits.

Competition from the smaller firms, larger producers argued, stymied their efforts to market their way out of the Depression. Small shops enjoyed several advantages over their larger rivals: they generally worked to order, they were non-unionized, they had minimal fixed costs, they ignored health and safety regulations, and because they hired for the job, they were not burdened by the need to pay a living wage. Moreover, as contract shops, they enjoyed greater flexibility and were designed to respond more quickly than big manufacturers to changing demands and prices. Marx saw the small shop as little more than an 'outside department of the factory' picking up the industrial overflow, and this was in part the case: most of the larger manufacturers in the clothing sector, for example, had their own 'outside shops' to which they sent special orders. But in the 1930s the contractors became something more: they became the factory's rival. To the big clothing, shoe, tinned food, and furniture manufacturers, the 'vile awful sweatshop,' which had once served their interests, had turned into a prime cause of their distress. In the little businesses, insisted one manufacturer, where 'girls are forced to work as long as 60 hours a week under high pressure for as little as $3 or $4 a week ... can be found some of the dirtiest, filthiest places where disease and vermin are anything but strangers. That's where plenty of the "bargains" and "exceptional values" are made.'[12]

English-Canadian manufacturers liked to point to Quebec, with its less-stringent factory regulations, as the source of much of their trouble. 'Quebec has taken to growing and canning tomatoes,' the chairman of the Ontario Growers' Markets Council explained, 'and because of the low costs of labour in that province and the willingness of people there to work long hours for starvation wages, Quebec canners can lay down prices that are below [our] actual costs of producing and processing.' The Ontario men's clothiers, concurred: competition from Quebec, one of them insisted, 'has created an intolerable situation ... One type of manufacturer paying fair wages and observing the law cannot meet the competition of like manufacturers [who do not pay fair wages or observe the law].' Larger shoe producers, men's and women's clothiers and the big food processors in Montreal, however, all protested that the instability was not their fault, but the result of the appearance of hundreds of contract shops out in the countryside. According to Quebec's Associated Clothing Manufacturers, 'unscrupulous manufacturers' in the countryside 'have a free rein and can sell merchandise at practically any price offered to them and in order to make a profit, all they have to do is to cut their employees' wages.' Montreal's shoe manufacturers likewise asserted that it was the movement of business to the Beauce region that was largely to blame for the low-priced contract-shop competition. Montreal shoemakers charged that while they were paying their female workers the reasonable sum of $12 for a sixty-hour week, girls in the country districts were being employed to work seventy-five-hour weeks at 2¢ an hour.[13]

All of these manufacturers realized that the only thing which kept the sweatshops in existence was the demand for the cheap goods they produced. Consequently, larger factory operators did not believe that they would be in such difficulty were it not for certain 'unscrupulous people' who were willing to 'take advantage of the situation to bring the prices of labor down to the lowest level.'[14] Big buyers – mass retailers with the corporate clout to order from whomever they wished – were thought to be the sinister kingpins manipulating the sweatshop economy. They – the chains in the case of bread and tinned food and the department stores in the case of almost everything else – were profiting from the suffering of the legitimate employers and their workers. Squeezed themselves in the early Depression years, the mass merchandisers had turned to squeezing their suppliers. And the pinch hurt.

Furniture and clothing were undoubtedly in the sorriest state because styles and retail prices in those industries were felt to be under the virtual control of the big-city department stores. In furniture the system was simple: buyers from Eaton's and Simpson's would attend the major trade exhibitions in the United States and import selected samples into Canada. They would then invite the domestic manufacturers to bid against each other for the contract to reproduce the chosen styles. If the prices offered were not low enough, the departmentals would threaten to contract out to the small workshops and would thereby force the sweatshop prices on the factory producers. 'Was in Toronto for a few days,' C.M. Bell, a Southampton, Ontario, furniture maker, observed scornfully, 'and in checking over the values on the [department stores'] floors was amazed to see the merchandise that was being offered ... One can understand bargains on discounted lines, but to find merchandise never shown before at these extremely low prices was appalling.' How, he wondered rhetorically, were manufacturers 'producing these goods at the prices they are receiving for them[?]' N.W. Tolmie, one of Eaton's furniture suppliers, provided the answer: 'we have continued to operate both our plants to almost full capacity, but at prices which leave our balance sheet in none too attractive condition. Whether we would be better or not to refuse unprofitable business, I cannot say, but [we] have tried to balance the cost of shutting down against the cost of operating unprofitably, and on patriotic grounds have decided in favour of the latter course.'[15]

Ironically, in the early years of the Depression, the very merchandisers whom the mass producers had praised for their efficiency had become the primary source of their problems. The reason was simple: it was a buyer's market, and factories were forced to sell at dramatically reduced prices in order to keep business away from the contract shops. The trouble for the manufacturers was that price cutting was a slippery slope. With insufficient orders to keep all the factories going, the manufacturers, 'up against it for business,' went out and 'offered the department stores a price as low or probably lower than what had been offered previously.' Then, said the vice-president of the Brantford Washing Machine Company, 'when we go back to these department stores for repeat orders, we were forced to meet the competitive prices that other manufacturers were offering.' To do so, they had to cut wages in the plant and design even-cheaper products. 'I have to reduce prices on superior articles in order to get the business,' sighed the president of the Model Underwear Company. 'Quality does not count.' Not surprisingly, when the *Furniture World* ran a series of articles on the problems of industry in 1933, it began, under the title 'The Furniture Industry's Greatest Menace,' with an analysis of the department stores.[16]

Not all manufacturers felt this way. Those making hardware, which was largely untroubled by department or chain store buying, or radios, electric appliances, pianos, or drugs, where resale price maintenance had been successfully achieved, or automobiles, which were sold through manufacturer-controlled outlets, had many problems in the early thirties, but they did not worry about contracting out, mass buying, or excessive competition.[17] Nor were those making goods under a well-known brand name particularly aggrieved. Their sales were down and their margins clipped, but so long as advertising kept up their product's image and rpm regulated the price, they were sheltered from the storm. What unified those manufacturers who attacked the pernicious influences of the departmentals and chains was that they came from industries in which simple technologies had made outwork possible and in which the mass merchandisers held a sizeable market share. Moreover, they were producing goods in sectors such as clothing, furniture, baking, and fruit canning where brand-name loyalty was minimal. In effect, it was the very manufacturers who in the early 1920s had rejected rpm and promoted the mass-production ethos who were suffering most from competition, mass buying, and price collapse.

And for these business people, facing a price deflation for the second time in ten years, dogged by chronic excess capacity, and apparently unable to sell or save their way out of the depression, the inevitable questions began to be asked: Was mass production working? Could the whole strategy of mass consumption, efficient distribution, increasing production, and steadily falling prices not have a damning flaw? Had not the creation of the direct marketing channel not shifted too much power to the buyers? And for those who doubted, the answer in 1933 was the same as it had been for sceptics in 1923: what the economy needed was not more production but less; what the business community wanted was not lower prices but higher; what the manufacturers desired was not fewer bigger orders but more smaller ones. 'Increased prices,' J.H. Wyatt, the chairman of the Furniture Manufacturers' Association, declared in 1935, 'are the only solution to our problems and would enable us to pay more to our workmen and our clerks. Each and every one of us must make the move for increased prices.'[18]

In the mass producers' struggle to force prices up and eliminate the causes of cheap goods (bulk-buying chains and departmentals and 'unethical' contract shops), the men's garment manufacturers of Ontario became industrial leaders. Under the aegis of the Ottawa-based Canadian Clothing Manufacturers Association and of Toronto's Associated Garment Manufacturers, the men's clothiers spearheaded the campaign for business regulation in the 1930s. Theirs was a remarkable, if not wholly unanticipated, conversion. Frightened by labour unrest, the men's garment manufacturers in Toronto had once before experimented with such controls as industrial councils, binding arbitration, and regulated wage scales, and they had even, grudgingly, accepted the radical inflationists' idea that wages should be pegged to the cost of living and not to outputs. But the sharp deflation of 1920–1 had put an end to the experiments of 1919 and had witnessed the introduction of Taylorite time sheets and piece rates. 'Scales of wages are governed by production and in looking into the situation,' the manufacturers had declared in a classic statement of mass-production principles in 1920, 'we find that there is no high wage unless they [the manufacturers] have compensating production to take care of it.' During the later 1920s the men's clothiers had remained true to these principles, and they had vigorously resisted union efforts to raise wages and organize the contract shops.[19]

They had proved no more sympathetic to their retail buyers than to their workers. During the 1920s some men's clothing manufacturers had, like other producers, greatly expanded their involvement in marketing: businesses such as Forsyth shirts had begun offering improved advertising and display advice to the retailers, and the Canadian Clothing Manufacturers Association had itself launched a 'Dress Well and Succeed' campaign to convince consumers to buy more of the higher-priced wearing apparel. But while a few men's wear manufacturers had supported schemes which promised to increase store sales, they had resisted efforts either to alter their own methods in the interests of the independent trade or to increase their actual involvement in store management. Thus the Associated Garment Manufacturers had rejected retail efforts to stabilize competition, dismissing such things as the RMA's 'four season buying plan' (which sought to give the independents four different periods to clear seasonal stock and thereby more opportunities to meet the departmentals' bargain days). The clothing factories had also undermined the RMA's attempt in the mid-twenties to introduce the 'Ten Pay Plan,' which offered a mechanism for selling clothing through instalments, by refusing to stagger their own credit or to establish financing subsidiaries. What the clothing makers wanted was simply for the independents to become more like the chains and department stores and lower their prices, and they were not interested in following the radical course of store modernization which was to augment retail efficiency by integrating independent distribution into production. 'The small dealer is doomed', William Johnston, the president of Randall and Johnston in Toronto, remarked coolly, 'unless he will wake up and learn to merchandise in ways and at prices comparable to those of the chain and department stores.'[20]

Convinced that the independent retailers were antiquated and not worth supporting, some clothing manufacturers adopted the shoemakers' solution and in the 1920s began opening their own stores. Berger Tailoring Ltd opened its first Tip Top store in 1911, and within seventeen years it owned thirty-nine; Toronto Utility Clothing Company began selling suits by mail in 1924, and Nash Tailoring followed two years later; and Randall and Johnston opened a large factory-outlet store in Toronto in 1928. The Associated Garment Manufacturers even toyed in 1930 with the idea of launching its own chain of stores. Though the chain proposal was killed by Berger and others (who did not relished the idea of the association competing with their own retail stores), the organization did succeed in creating a cooperative warehousing operation (the Central Supply Warehouse) for supplying relief orders to municipalities in the 1930s. It was an important and, for the retail trade, ominous development, revealing, as it did, that as late as 1931–2 the garment manufacturers were still firmly committed to their traditional mass-production attitudes.[21]

Only in early 1933 did the garment manufacturers finally travel to Canossa. Until then they had believed that the Depression could be ended only by increasing outputs, pegging wages to production, and lowering the costs of distribution through direct marketing. Suddenly, however, the Associated Garment Manufacturers reversed its position on all these things. In what was for the men's clothiers a startling volte-face, Warren Cook, the newly elected president of the Associated, announced in the fall of 1933 that the cause of the Depression lay in the fact that 'the people have no purchasing power.' Instead of wanting more production, the manufacturers now declared that 'men and women, hundreds of them, [were] working long hours on which it is impossible to maintain the expenses of life'; in fact, they felt that 'the fundamental principle back of the whole situation is sociological; the wellbeing of the people.' Up to this moment, Cook explained, 'we have been working on the plan of paying the worker as little as possible as a producer, and at the same time we have expected him or her to be a consumer ... and it simply will not work.'[22]

There was a simple reason for the manufacturers' change of heart and that was the realization that they were facing a long-term shift from a seller's to a buyer's market. Contrary to expectations, the manufacturers had not succeeded in marketing their way out of the Depression, and their great creation, the Central Supply Warehouse, had even run into serious financial difficulty and been unceremoniously closed down by the Ontario government. Moreover, they were losing control over pricing to the departmentals and contract shops. To combat the new threat, the manufacturers therefore reversed their position on unionization and resuscitated the virtually defunct agreement they had reached with Amalgamated Clothing Workers' Union in 1919. The Associated Garment Manufacturers then became promoters of a major union drive in the clothing industry, and they facilitated the organization of many of Toronto's contract shops by refusing to send work out unless the contractors accepted the union. The hope was that if the Amalgamated could force wages in the contract shops up to the level of the factories, then the sweatshops owners' price advantages would be eliminated. In Toronto the manufacturers enjoyed considerable success: only Eaton's, Simpson's, and their suppliers (about one-third of the total number of contract shops in the city) were still resisting unionization by mid-1934.[23] The problem now lay in extending the union-management agreement to cover the whole country.

Under the leadership of Warren Cook, the Associated began to search out a method for restricting the supply of low-priced goods. Their goal was to control the sweatshops and end 'the tremendous exploitation of the manufacturer created through the concentration of buying power in Canada.' Cook's perambulating search for a means of attaining this goal drew him to the United States in mid-1933, and he came back converted. 'It is unquestionably the most advanced and extraordinary movement ever introduced into a democratic country,' he ecstatically announced on his return; it was 'absolute socialism almost bordering on communism,' but it held the solution to all the clothing manufacturers' problems.[24] Cook had been wowed by the spectacular flight of the Blue Eagle.

Passed by the U.S. Congress in June 1933, the National Industrial Recovery Act provided the government with the power to authorize industrial agreements designed to raise the purchasing power of workers through minimum wages, to increase employment through maximum-hours-regulations, to prevent predatory competition through price-fixing and production quotas, and to eliminate 'unfair' competition through lawful cartelization. The act provided for the creation of a National Recovery Administration, but this board was designed simply as a regulatory court supervising the implementation of economic policies that had been formulated within the business community itself. The real author of economic recovery was to be the trade association, and the instrument of reform was to be the code. The NIRA made it legal for business people within an industry to collude together and draw up codes fixing hours, wages, outputs, and prices within their sector. The NRA would then be responsible for ensuring that once a majority of business people in the sector had signed a code, everyone would observe its provisions.

If a national industrial recovery act could be introduced in Canada, Cook declared, and codes arranged 'in every line of business and the codes made law, it is expected that overproduction, child labour, sweat shop conditions and many other practices so pervasive today, will be overcome.'[25] The codes would strike at the heart of the economic instability by eliminating the low-priced manufacturers who were supplying the bulk buyers. Moreover, because they could standardized wages and even prices, the codes promised to undermine the department stores' efforts to play one producer off against another. And besides, it was such a little step for the manufacturers to take: they already had an agreement in their industry which stabilized wages and hours, and they had a central warehouse that was apportioning outputs for at least a part of their production; an NIRA would simply legalize these existing agreements and make them binding over the entire Canadian clothing industry.

Cook was not alone in his enthusiasm for the NIRA. While he was busy winning the clothing manufacturers' support for codification, the furniture makers were meeting in Kitchener to demand their own code law. Like the clothiers, the furniture manufacturers' conversion to price-fixing was not entirely unprecedented. In 1918–19 the Furniture Manufacturers' Association had briefly attempted to fix prices and wages, but the scheme had collapsed during the postwar depression. Returning to the idea in December 1932, the furniture makers established a guild modelled on the PATA, which had cautiously sought to bring 'stabilization through orderly marketing.' The guild was patently inflationary: 'prices must go up,' its charter affirmed, 'and what is equally important they must be maintained! ... No retail outlet should be given the opportunity of underselling other retailers on standard merchandise.' It was a policy specifically directed against the departmentals: 'Manufacturers,' the president of the FMA announced in August 1933, 'by allowing special concessions to large buyers ... have put the buyer definitely in the saddle.' Only by controlled prices, he affirmed, could they be prevented from 'continuing to force the manufacturers into an uncomfortable position.' It was, in fact, the Stratford furniture strike of September-November 1933 that had shifted manufacturers' attention away from price-fixing and towards codification and wage regulation. On 26 September, in the midst of the strike, a meeting of the FMA had been hastily convened, and nervous furniture manufacturers had drawn up a minimum-wage–maximum-hours code for the Kitchener-Stratford-Hamilton triangle. Eight months later the furniture association extended the 'code' to cover its members nationwide, and they also expanded its provisions, fixing a maximum trade discount (5 per cent) and banning all rebates, secret discounts, and false advertisements. The code was voluntarily accepted by the 53 FMA members, as well as by 27 non-affiliated businesses. These were the industry's leading firms, for they together employed 65 per cent of the industrial workers and produced three-quarters of the furniture, but according to a government investigator in 1934, 288 of the smaller producers chose to remain outside of the wage agreement. It was to control these businesses and to ensure the binding authority of the code over its own members that the FMA in March 1934 called for the passage of an NIRA.[26]

There has been some considerable disagreement as to how extensive support for codification really was in the mid-1930s. Some historians have suggested a widespread enthusiasm, especially among big-business leaders, while others have argued that what minimal support there was for a Canadian New Deal was restricted to the small-business sector. The disagreement is understandable, in part because the currents of business opinion in 1933–4 were turbulent and swiftly moving. We can, however, distinguish three strands of thought regarding industrial regulation. First, there were the old price fixers of the 1910s and 1920s, business people working in industries with high levels of brand-name identification who had generally been maintaining resale prices with varying levels of success for some years. The PATA decision had temporarily derailed their efforts, but by the early thirties they had effectively, if quietly, restabilized prices in hundreds of lines. Not surprisingly, industrialists in these sectors, while liking certain aspects of the NIRA, were reluctant to reopen the issue on a political level. On the other hand there was a large group of conservative business people – many of whom tended to belong to the Canadian Manufacturers' Association – that had always opposed resale price maintenance. This business group was the one that fractured in the early 1930s. While many continued to believe that more production and lower prices would eventually spark recovery, in sectors such as furniture making, clothing, canning, building, and baking, a new inflationary–New Deal temperament was coming to hold sway.

One indication of the relative strength of the inflationary-codification position was a 1936 CMA survey which revealed that one-quarter of the organization's membership supported policies such as the shortened work week and the minimum wage. The proportion is surprisingly large, not only because the survey was held in hostile territory (the CMA declared against an NIRA in October 1933), but also because support for what were regarded as inflationary policies still remained so high (a year after the U.S. Supreme Court had invalidated the NRA and in the midst of the economic recovery).[27] Would it be too much to suggest that two years earlier perhaps as many as one-third of the older 'deflationists' might have come to support NRA-style reforms? If so, it would have been a minority, but a sizeable one, even if highly occupationally clustered.

The question of determining the size of the NIRA supporters' businesses is more vexed; the trouble being that there is no legitimate a priori standard for judging whether a business is large or small. It is true that a business such as W.R. Johnston and Company was small in comparison with the CPR or Algoma Steel, but it was one of the country's five biggest men's clothing manufacturers. If a small firm can be defined as one employing less than the average number of workers in that industry, then it is fairly obvious that the smallest businesses (the contract shops) opposed the idea of an NIRA, while the largest supported it.

Unfortunately, though a large number of important manufacturers endorsed codification and though they had much in common, they were still in the absolute minority, and they knew it. What was vital was that they broaden their support to the point that they would be able to convince the federal government to legislate an NIRA, and they did not have much time. With a general election due in 1935 at the very latest, they had to work quickly to convince either the Liberals or the Conservatives to campaign on a New Deal platform. But to do so they needed to show the politicians that they had a winning issue in the NIRA, and it was here that the retailers entered the picture.

TRITON AMONG THE MINNOWS

Back before the First World War, a government agency that could investigate cases of unfair competition and legalize price-stabilizing agreements had been one of the RMA's official demands. But the unfortunate experience of the Board of Commerce had shaken the shop owners' confidence in regulation, leading them to renounced political reform in favour of self-help. Their wounds would continue to smart, however, and during the 1920s the retailers would scrupulously avoid asking for government intervention in the economy and would limit themselves to indirectly challenging the laws through the courts. And after the PATA decision they shied away even from this approach. By 1930 the RMA had adopted voluntary pooling as its major platform, and the most its leaders would now ask of government was the enactment for merchants of the same licensing authority that doctors, lawyers, and pharmacists already enjoyed. Even after the coup which saw Crowder and Hougham deposed from the dominion leadership and the national office returned to Ottawa, there would be no call for state regulation. Though lobbying was restored under Desmarais to its privileged place among association activities, the dominion RMA's major demands in the early thirties would be for more restrictions on peddling, for changes to the Bankruptcy Act, for amendments to the legislation concerning NSF cheques, and for a lowering of the federal sales tax.[28]

Warren Cook was not, therefore, preaching to the converted when he wrote to the provincial RMA offices in October 1933 urging them to support the Associated Garment Manufacturers' proposed 'Bill of Control.' The passage of the NIRA had, of course, already sparked terrific interest in the concept of business 'self-government,' but for tradespeople not all the news had been positive. There had already been a good deal of retail protest against the codes in the United States, and while the furniture section of the ORMA had expressed its approval for an NRA as early as August, the merits of the food code were still in debate late into November, and the organized druggists and hardware dealers were both content to ignore the whole New Deal well into the New Year. Moreover, the retailers could not really sympathize with the manufacturers' worries about sweatshops. Their problem was with the selling of brand-name goods at cut prices, and they were not convinced that this issue could be resolved by controlling competition in manufacturing. But the manufacturers were offering the retailers some powerful and unanticipated inducements, most important among them being a chance for renewal. By 1933 the dominion office of the RMA had closed down, and the organization had fragmented back onto its provincial units. It was an association desperately seeking a cause.[29]

For the manufacturers there were equally good reasons for trying to win the shopkeepers' support: the independents were, by business standards, incredibly numerous, and during the Depression, retailing had been revitalized in its role as symbolic ideal. 'One of the compensations for the depression or readjustment through which the world is passing,' the *Retailer* observed in 1932, 'is that it has brought to the front the value of the small business man as an increasingly important element in the economic structure.' Coming out in support of 'the little guy' and attacking the 'autocracy of dollars,' the 'big interests,' or the 'grip of the twelve,' as so many politicians were discovering, offered a virtual guarantee of public support. And the retailers' importance went far beyond even their folkloric appeal. As they had been insisting for decades, the merchants were leaders in their communities, and that meant they carried real voting power. 'Every retail merchant in Canada can control at least fifty votes,' the RMA propagandists maintained, and in the 1930s people chanced to believe them.[30]

But just because the retailers claimed they pulled a large vote did not mean the manufacturers had actually to listen to them. Consumer goods manufacturers were used to dealing with shopkeepers – used to telling them what to do and to obtaining compliance with their wishes. In building public support for an NRA, Cook told the delegates to the 1934 ORMA convention, the retailers must recognize that the public 'was not interested in whether a manufacturer or retailer made any money.' They could not promote the creation of an NRA simply by telling people how good it would be for them, but shop owners could work with the fact that the public 'realize[d] the necessity of Labour receiving fair treatment.' Instead of concentrating on the evils of low prices or mass buying, Cook went on slyly, retailers should therefore focus their attack on the industrial sweatshops. RMA members had to convince Canadians that the goal of codification was to raise wages and eliminate 'appalling sweat shop conditions.' In doing so, they would be working to control department store competition, because 'in order to sell their finished products at a much lower price ... it must of necessity have been taken out of the workers['] hide.'[31]

While the furniture and clothing manufacturers kept busy convincing the organized shopkeepers that support for their policies would also be good for retailing, Warren Cook began sounding out potential political allies. He found one in Harry Stevens, the minister of trade and commerce and an old acquaintance of the Ottawa men's clothing manufacturer, Percy Sparks. On behalf of the garment manufacturers Cook first approached Stevens in August 1933 with the suggestion of expanding into a full federal inquiry a private investigation which they were sponsoring into the effects of sweatshop conditions on wages and prices. Thanks to Sparks and Tom Learie (the Associated's secretary), the minister was already well aware of working conditions in the industry, and he had already tried, late in 1932, to force a minor improvement in labour standards by giving the Tariff Board the right to investigate working conditions in the clothing factories and refuse tariff protection to any industry not meeting accepted standards. Now, under Cook's influence, he approached Prime Minister Bennett and attempted unsuccessfully to convince him of the need for a full inquiry into sweatshop conditions in Canada. Undeterred by his failure, Stevens one week later urged Bennett to create a permanent investigatory board that could supervise industrial and trade practices. Still unsatisfied, the minister then revived an old cause and recommended that the least the prime minister could do was to amend the Combines Investigation Act to allow manufacturers to collude for the purpose of eliminating the price-cutting evil themselves.[32]

It was no surprise that Bennett should have ignored Stevens: he usually ignored him. As a sixteen-year veteran and self-proclaimed heir to the Meighen tradition, Stevens had been a contender for the Conservative leadership in 1927, and he resented the way in which he had been passed over in favour of the political neophyte Bennett. He had become convinced that he had been snubbed because of his well-publicized failures as a businessman: 'the millionaire group' in the party, he smouldered, had opposed him 'because I am unable to match them – dollar for dollar – in personal wealth.' Stevens had always been consumed with the need to make money and his appetites had already drawn him into a series of dubious ventures: a Vancouver real estate speculation, a failed consumer finance firm, a stock-watered oil company. But none of his efforts had come to much, and they only confirmed his opponents in their belief that he was 'an uneducated cockney with absolutely no knowledge of business or how to conduct it.' Still, Stevens thirsted after more: as minister of commerce he tried to annex the National Development Bureau to his department, he lobbied for control over the National Research Council, and he urged the creation of an internal trade board under his authority, but Bennett seemed intent on containing his ambitions. In fact, in January 1934 the prime minister had even clipped his political wings by attacking his use of patronage and the way in which he had placed so many of his unsavoury business associates in high-paying jobs with the Vancouver Harbour Commission. Small wonder that Bennett should have scorned Stevens's demand for NRA-style reforms. The prime minister was a firm opponent of the inflationary first New Deal, his conviction being that 'the Government which minimizes the importance of maintaining inviolate the open competitive market is standing on quick sand.' Moreover, he believed that 'except in time of war or other national crisis' – which, apparently, the Depression was not

– 'the sole legislative authority that can deal with price fixing is the provincial legislature.'[33]

Stevens clearly felt that he had to re-establish his credentials within the party and to revenge himself on the millionaires, and his opportunity came in what should have been a routine speech to the shoe dealers' section of the ORMA delivered on 15 January 1934, just five days after Bennett had ordered all of Stevens's friends fired from the Harbour Commission. From the start there was nothing routine about it: the media been informed that something was going to be said, and the press was there to cover the speech (no one usually reported on meetings of the shoe dealers' section); someone had even taken the unusual step of having Stevens's address broadcast live over a Toronto radio station. He did not disappoint. After announcing that he had 'no sympathy for radical forces,' Stevens went on to outline the abuses of the system that he felt needed correction. He spoke of four problems: mass marketers destroying independent retailers in Canada's small towns, meat packers giving low prices to farmers, sweatshops in the clothing industry, and a combine in the bread-baking sector. It was a remarkable salmagundi: the portions of his speech dealing with meat packing were lifted from an address he had given in Winnipeg two months before; his views on the baking industry were drawn from a combines investigation of 1931; his ideas on sweatshop conditions and on the evils of mass buying had been supplied by the Associated Garment Manufacturers.[34] What any of it had to do with shoe retailing was anyone's guess.

Apart from his very brief references to department store competition, retailers found little in the speech that directly interested them. As the BC RMA's organ, the *Retailer*, perceptively noted, the address had dealt mainly with the problem of sweatshops and seemed to be suggesting that while 'mass production has been achieved, it is leaving problems which the manufacturer is finding difficult to solve.' For Stevens, however, the speech was a declaration of war. Senator Charles Murphy, one of Ottawa's venerable scandalmongers, could not have been alone in seeing the political manoeuvring that underlay the minister's actions. The Toronto speech, he observed, had been a not-so-veiled attack on Bennett's 'big interest friends' – among them the department store magnate R.Y. Eaton.[35]

It was crucial to ensure that the issue not be allowed to die or to degenerate into a personal feud, and Cook, Sparks, and Learie immediately set about to 'heap coals on the fire.' Within days of the shoe dealers' speech, Cook announced at the ORMA annual convention that the Canadian

Association of Garment Manufacturers (the federal body of which the Associated Garment Manufacturers was the Ontario chapter), together with the Furniture Manufacturers' Association, was sponsoring the creation of a National Fair Trade Council. Warren Cook was to act as council chairman, Percy Sparks and Tom Learie were appointed members of the executive, A.E. Grassby, one of Stevens's former business associates, was to work as treasurer, and George Hougham, now the ORMA secretary, would represent the retailers as secretary of the new organization. Cook hoped the NFTC would transform the retailers and manufacturers into a solid phalanx which could then sell the NRA idea to the nation. He was keenly aware of the importance of publicity: he understood that the NFTC could not succeed if it remained a businessman's association; it had to become a mass movement. As a first step, the Associated began printing copies of Stevens's speech and distributing them to retailers all across Ontario. The initial response was encouraging – Stevens called it 'electrical' – every day, he told one correspondent, 'we receive close to one hundred letters.'[36]

The publicity that followed the shoe dealers' speech forced Bennett's hand. In early February 1934 the prime minister warily announced in the House of Commons that a price spreads committee under Stevens's chairmanship would be appointed to investigate the problems of industry and trade. Bennett made it clear, however, that he did not agree with Stevens on what direction the price spreads inquiry would take. For Bennett, the committee's charge was to investigate 'the causes of the great spread between the cost of commodities to the consumer and the price received by the producer.' In effect, like most business thinkers and politicians of the interwar period, he believed the source of much of the economic instability could be traced to inefficiencies within distribution.[37] As had the Conservatives a decade before, Bennett and his colleagues were hoping to use government power to drive down the costs of independent retailing and to reaffirm the efficiency of mass marketing. But Stevens and his supporters had other plans. They did not think that the problem lay in excessive 'price spreads,' but rather in the cut prices which the department stores were forcing on industry. Moreover, whereas Bennett clearly hoped that the House committee would still the public agitation, Cook and Stevens hoped to use it to foment dissent against the mass merchandisers and 'their' sweatshops.

The hearings themselves opened, logically enough, with the topic that Cook believed would prove most popular: the existence of sweatshops in the garment and footwear industries. The chairman of Ontario's Minimum Wage Board and Harry Cassidy of the University of Toronto both spoke in shocking terms about the degradation of labour, the utter disregard for human comforts, and the foul conditions of work which prevailed in the small workshops. Much of this, Professor Cassidy emphasized, was a direct consequence of the pricing policies of the mass merchandisers: 'the manufacturers complain bitterly that a large buying organization, the department stores mainly, have been setting the pace of the price cutting, which has made it necessary for certain concerns to pass on the cuts to their labour.' It was not a condition which any nineteenth-century cant about the manufacturer's philanthropy or the trickle-down theory could correct. The economic system as it had developed was forcing even well-intentioned business people into reducing wages and forsaking humane working conditions. In fact, 'the burden of the cutthroat competition ... has fallen more heavily upon the firms that have endeavoured to maintain fair conditions of wages and have avoided sharp competitive practices.' Tom Moore, the president of the Trades and Labor Congress, Canada's largest labour federation, agreed with Cassidy that 'in some cases, more up-to-date machine equipment has driven prices down, but I think in general we could say it has been mass buying.' Happily enough for Warren Cook and his friends, both witnesses declared firmly in favour of an NRA. 'The right of combination,' Moore emphasized, must 'be allowed to employers whenever control to prevent exploitation of consumers can be made effective.'[38]

It should be understood, however, that more than one agenda was being followed during the hearings. While the manufacturers wanted bad publicity for the departmentals in order to arouse public opposition to sweating, the retailers had revived their plan to stop the price cutting of brand-name items by chains and department stores, and Stevens wanted revenge. Thus, while the RMA officials who appeared before the Committee played the role that was expected of them – underlining the department stores' depredations, the retailers' centrality to community life, and the moral value of small business – the solutions they proposed to the problems of merchandising were at variance with those of the manufacturers. With the exception of A.E. Grassby, who among his other ventures owned a Winnipeg piano store, all the retailers appearing before the inquiry demanded either resale price maintenance or a law prohibiting secret bulk-buying discounts rather than an NIRA. Ironically, no one seemed to notice the discrepancy.[39]

Perhaps this was because the unofficial leader of the NRA movement was preoccupied with his own interests. The price spreads hearings gave Stevens the national platform he had so long craved, and he feasted on the attention. He gloried in the revelations of big-business infamy. He thrived on the opportunity to bash the corporate magnates and taunt their lawyers. He became so notorious for asking leading questions that even his own committee ultimately moved against him. But he remained unrepentant – vindicated, in a sense, by the hostility. He became a 'Don Quixote' tilting at the corporate windmills, his days, reported an obviously stunned *Financial Post*, 'crowded with adventure ... both in his private and public life he has lived dangerously, scorned safety.' In the midst of the hearings, Stevens, the ostensibly impartial chairman, lashed out against mass merchandising before a meeting of a Conservative Party study club in Ottawa. Thinly veiled in a critique of bulk buying, the speech was part of Stevens's bid to capture his party's leadership, and in it he criticized the financial improprieties of important Bennett supporters such as Joseph Flavelle, R.Y. Eaton, and J.S. McLean. Stevens's statements 'attack directly so many of Bennett's immediate friends that already there is damage beyond repair,' an enthusiastic Mackenzie King reported.[40] But while Bennett for the moment could only rage impotently against his belligerent minister, manufacturers like Cook rejoiced in the publicity being generated.

The price spreads issue was therefore operating on several independent, yet more or less mutually supportive, levels, with everyone involved working hard to conceal the well-rehearsed moves that coordinated their actions. First, the 'impartial experts' set the tone, one after another appearing to document the evils of mass buying and sweating. Joseph Crowder spoke as an 'impartial' investigator into the canning industry; Warren Cook prepared the brief on clothing; Percy Sparks appeared for the drug trade; C.H. Carlisle, the president of B.F. Goodrich and another recent convert to the concept of an NRA, gave testimony concerning the rubber industry; the independent retailers were represented by six different RMA officials; Norman Sommerville, who as the inquiry's counsel directed the questioning, even had prior associations with the shoe dealers' association and had earlier made a name for himself as an opponent of the meat packers. Everyone pointed in a similar direction, but everyone, it seemed, had come to his opinion independently. Only at the end of the inquiry did Sparks let it slip that fifteen of the expert witnesses had been members of the NFTC executive, leaving the Committee with the distinct sensation of being stage-managed. But before anyone could catch his breath, the accountants arrived, their arms laden with the books of the departmentals and chain stores. Their job was to reveal the vast sums of money that the big stores had made while the manufacturers and little retailers had suffered. Then came the former employees; disgruntled workers who spoke of the ways in which the chains cheated the public and the sweatshop owners exploited their labour. After that the managers and owners of the price-cutting big businesses were led in, and the nation watched unsympathetically as they struggled to explain away the months of damning testimony.

It should have worked splendidly, but somehow, for all the brilliance of its conception, the NRA movement ran into difficulties almost from the start. Cook and the National Fair Trade Council quite rightly believed that the campaign's future depended on its success at broadening out; support for a Canadian New Deal had to grow from its roots in the furniture and garment makers' associations; it had to attract proprietary retailers and primary producers, and then it had to enlist the support of working people. But the NFTC was not designed to be a political party; it had no organized bureaucracy, no full-time staff, and no independent source of funds. It was intended to be the propaganda machine that would create such a fervour of support for an NRA that the government would be forced into legislation. Unfortunately, the council failed to clear the first hurdle. The small retailers – the men and women considered by Cook and Stevens to be most likely to endorse the price spreads message – simply did not support the movement in the numbers anticipated.

Though the National Fair Trade Council managed to obtain endorsements from the Retail Merchants' Association, and its affiliates, the Canadian Jewellers' Association and a variety of other small retail organizations, there was little evidence that this institutional support was going to transform itself into a mass following. The most immediate problem was the shortage of funds. The manufacturers had initially hoped that the RMA would pay for the NFTC's operating costs: for its numerous publications, its advertisements, its reprinted speeches, its cross-country lecture tours. But the RMA, itself congenitally cash starved, was unable to contribute to the new organization, leading Grassby to hold the association 'very much to blame' for the council's liquidity problems. The NFTC, Cook complained, 'has had little support from the merchants themselves. An opportunity unparalleled in Canada's history has been provided the retailers of the country to secure some relief from their burden – but they have failed to take advantage of it.'[41]

Harry Stevens concluded that it was yet another sign of public ingratitude. At first he just lamented to George Hougham, 'You know the story in the Scriptures where a feast was laid out and certain people were invited and they did not come ... I fear that is about the position I am in. The feast that I spread for the retail merchants of this country is largely neglected by them and the invitation treated with contempt.' But in time he became more angry. The retailers, he exclaimed, were displaying 'the sort of attitude that makes one wonder if he is not just a plain ordinary fool in trying to help business people out of their troubles.' Hougham could offer only the most painful of apologies: 'this Association with its long history and its set up of directorates, composed of responsible retailers, has found and still finds it difficult to weld retail opinion together for constructive purposes.'[42]

This statement was true, but it was hardly the whole story. As Cook sensed, the real trouble was that a vast number of retailers had been left out of the trade associations. 'If the smaller merchants would only realize that it is their fight and that we are doing everything we can to help then we could get some place,' he observed, 'the opportunity is here and they are not taking advantage of it.' In July 1934, right after the Commons committee prorogued, Cook attempt to encourage broader-based retail participation in the NRA campaign, but the RMA blocked the move and intimated that it might re-evaluate its support. In his desperation to encourage more widespread involvement, Cook then tried to bypass the RMA and its sister associations and organize a separate national retail trade federation in the fall of 1934 which would be entrusted with spreading the NFTC's message. Ultimately, however, only the organized hardware merchants expressed any new interest.[43] Warren Cook was gradually learning that for all their folkloric assertions, the retailers did not speak with one voice.

But there was another aspect to the NFTC's inability to raise the shopkeeping masses beyond simply the divisions among shopkeepers. Even the modernizing merchants – the ones most likely to support Stevens – were reluctant to answer his call with anything more concrete than applause. At issue was the fact that the worst years of the Depression were already over for the main-street trade. Between 1930 and 1933 the total value of independent store transactions had fallen from almost $2 billion, to $1.2 billion and the proprietary sector's market share relative to the mass merchandisers had dipped from 69.4 per cent to 67.9. Nineteen thirty-four was, however, a recovery year – sales volumes went up 10 per cent, and market shares rose again to 69 per cent – and even better times followed in 1935 (table 10). Now that the shopocracy was faced with the promise of prosperity, much of the anxiety it felt in 1933 and early 1934 simply dissipated.

Moreover, the price spreads inquiry, instead of serving as a signal to revolt, acted as a kind of analgesic. Not only were the main-street independents feeling marginally more secure in their businesses, but the inquiry revealed that the mass merchandisers were in serious trouble. Unlike the bad times of the early 1920s, the collapse of the 1930s had not led people into the chains and department stores. It was a period of intense public hostility to bigness: and few big businesses suffered more from the tide of public resentment than the great retail emporia. The corporate giants, according to the manager of the Hudson's Bay Company's Edmonton store, 'lack the good will of the Buying Public,' while the neighbourhood shop had come to be seen as 'the one business organization through which the unfortunate are able to survive the rigours of hard times.' Not only because of their virtual monopoly on sales in places using the relief voucher system, but also because they could still offer, for all their newly achieved modernity, a certain personal warmth, the small stores came to be symbols of security in the midst of depression. The price spreads investigation, the *Maritime Merchant* told its readers, has shown 'that perhaps the small merchant may be coming into his own again ... It seems as if the big mail order and chain systems have at last overreached themselves.' Like the newly published census, the Stevens inquiry 'has confirmed the feeling that the position of the independent merchant has never been threatened by the chain store or mail order firm.' Firm after firm was shown to have lost money in the early years of the Depression, and the independents now realized that modernization had brought their margins down beneath those of the mass marketers. And sensible shopkeepers could easily do the maths: had it not been for the discounts, rebates, and bulk-buying discounts, they would have been able to best the big stores in head-to-head price competition.[44]

What even further buoyed retail spirits was the fact that the inquiry graphically documented the mass marketers' attempts to cut costs and shore up declining profits. Day after day, the inquiry revealed the way that the chains and departmentals had ruthlessly slashed salaries and wages, how they had cancelled spillage and wastage allowances, and how efforts had been made to cheat unknowing customers out of their hard-earned pennies. It was all horribly sordid, and the corporate retailers found they could do little to mollify the public outrage that followed these revelations. They pleaded, rather distastefully, that it was the individual managers and not the stores themselves that were at fault; that, in the words of one disagreeable Dominion supervisor, 'it is the dishonesty of the man [in charge]'; and further, that 'it is against all our instructions.' But this defence was not likely to comfort consumers, and besides, it tended to cast even greater doubts on the big stores' managerial credibility. The Canadian Chain Store Association, which had been hastily formed in mid-1934 to combat the negative publicity, then tried to protest that the chains were not alone in giving short weights. Indeed, an association survey in Toronto found that of 152 packages bought in independent stores, 35 per cent were sold short weight, while only eleven out of sixty-six products bought in chains were actually short. The entire investigation, the chain stores' lawyers argued, was trying to censure the chains for something everyone was doing. 'The evidence which has been produced before the Commission,' raged the counsel for Dominion, 'in all cases is evidence of one sort only, evidence that is detrimental and prejudicial to the corporate chain store ... little or no investigation has been gone into with regards to the policies and activities of the independent stores.'[45]

Many progressive shopkeepers were in a gloating mood. Certainly, they had little to fear from the chain stores' efforts to tar them with their own disreputable brush. They had only to keep their heads down and allow the big stores to self-destruct. The anonymity of numbers was their best defence, and they had no intention of drawing attention to their own situations by intruding upon their opponents' death ritual. When the price spreads investigation, in a spirit of fairness, sent out a questionnaire to 131 independent shop owners asking for information about their business practices, only 36 returned their forms.[46] Perhaps they did not want anyone to know just how like their big-business opponents they had become.

While the independents quietly rejoiced, the chains and departmentals pleaded desperately with their Tory contacts to muzzle Stevens. 'Even the best intentioned and best managed businesses are not free from flaws', an Eaton's representative complained to a friend in the Conservative cabinet, 'and it is of vital importance that a Retail Establishment should not have its popularity unfairly lowered ... a large business like Eaton's so dependent on the Goodwill of the Public, must for its own safety, endeavour to avoid having its well-earned reputation sullied, by allowing one-sided, hurtful statements being broadcast.' But Stevens went on talking, and most big businessmen concluded that the best policy was for each simply to ride out the crisis as best he could, reserving action for the united anonymity of a Board of Trade protest. Few risked speaking out publicly against Stevens, and only C.L. Burton, the president of Simpson's, ever dared to go on the offensive.[47]

It was a dangerous time for the corporate retailers, and a handful of the most financially insecure were even feeling that compromise was necessary to assuage the hostile shoppers. P.A. Chester, the general manager of the Hudson's Bay Company, even believed the big department stores had to 'meet the situation created by the Stevens' Committee and the antagonism of the small merchants' by recanting publicly and agreeing voluntarily to end their 'unsatisfactory practices'. He took the unprecedented step of instructing his store managers to cooperate with the RMA in its efforts to control trade practices. Among the chains, cautious opposition to, rather than compromise with, the independents was also the rule. Morley Smith of Dominion Stores and H.C. Berkstresser, the general manager of the A & P, were the only ones to agree with Chester on the need for passive compliance to avert disaster. Smith and Berkstresser went so far as to write to the price spreads investigator in support of the idea of 'a minimum mark-up' above purchase price in order to eliminate loss-leader selling, but the other food chains countered by quietly declaring their opposition to such a scheme.[48] In reality, the mass merchandisers were all determined to fight governmental intervention, but they did not feel that they were in a position to do so openly. They had to move cautiously because the public was already perceived to be hostile, and the weaker one was, the more careful one had to be. For the moment, the independent merchants appeared to be masters of the situation.

Ironically, unlike the leaders of the RMA, who were delighted with the way the situation was developing, the organizers of the NFTC were dismayed by the low level of trade involvement. They did not fully grasp what was taking place: what they saw were massive turnouts whenever Stevens spoke – 4,000 showed up for an ORMA meeting in November 1934, and one month later 8,000 were on hand at the QRMA convention – but they knew these numbers were not being fully translated into paying supporters. It is a contradiction easily explained, even on the basis of the few figures available to us for the decade. The only sure numbers on RMA membership are for Saskatchewan, where membership grew from 1,500 in 1930 to 3,800 in 1934, and for Quebec, which expanded from 2,000 to 3,000 over the same period.[49] The ORMA probably numbered 4,000 or 5,000 by 1935. All told, then, the RMA may have grown to include 16,000 retailers by 1935, which, given its past record, would translate into perhaps 8,000 paid-up members (see table 14). For the association this was a staggering growth rate – the RMA had more than doubled its size in the space of two years – but outsiders might notice that even at this twentieth-century peak, the organization still represented under 15 per cent of all retailers. Hence the contradiction: the RMA had enrolled more male, main-street merchants than ever before, but it was still hardly representative of all those in trade.

Moreover, as we have already seen, membership in a retail organization did not imply unity of interest. We know next to nothing about the nature of RMA meetings in the thirties, but a rare report from an Eaton's groceteria manager who attended a gathering in Fort William in January 1935 does offer certain insights. The Fort William local, like so many others, had suffered a sharp decline in membership after the collapse of the PATA and had actually allowed its affiliation to the ORMA to lapse through non-payment of annual dues. Price spreads, however, revived interest in organization, and over the winter George Hougham swept through northwestern Ontario in an ORMA-NFTC effort to rebuild support. His mission in Fort William was at once to persuade the local retailers to renew their membership in the association and to convince them to back Stevens. Hougham addressed the thirty assembled shop-keepers on the nature of the price spreads inquiry, and he read them a portion of the brief he had delivered to the committee almost a year before. One of the town's most prominent retailers then spoke about the havoc which mail-order houses had wrought in the community, and he grew so enraged at the thought that he was 'unable to express himself very clearly.' There followed a series of questions to Hougham concerning sweatshops and who was buying from them and why the retailers should be concerned over their existence. Hougham, undoubtedly taking his cue from the previous speaker, announced that the mail-order companies were the chief patrons of the sweatshops. This comment prompted one old grocer, who 'was inclined to be excitable' and remembered earlier battles, to exclaim that the real thing was to go after the combines. So began a long digression into trust busting, which seemed to feature Canada Packers most prominently and which eventually ended in demands for the various participants to sit down and be quiet. Both Hougham and the president of the Fort William local attempted to steer the debate back onto the issue of price spreads, but order could not be restored until a round of the national anthem brought the meeting to a close.[50] The gathering had, however, been a success: membership in the local had been restored to its old levels, and the group had voted to renew its affiliation to the ORMA. But could Hougham really feel confident that he had communicated the message of price spreads? Could Stevens now be assured of the support of the merchants of Fort William?

Events in Ottawa were giving these questions a pressing urgency over the winter of 1934–5. By early November 1934 Stevens's personal discomfort within the party and his rage against Bennett were forcing the situation along a course that neither Cook nor his associates could have anticipated or desired. After a brief recess, the price spreads inquiry had begun sitting again as a royal commission and with Stevens no longer at the helm. On 27 October he had quit both the Bennett cabinet and the chairmanship of the commission in the hope of forcing the party to decide between his leadership and that of the prime minister. He felt his hand was strong: several colleagues had expressed support for him, his election committee was forming in the 'Stevens Clubs' that the National Fair Trade Council was busily organizing, support for him was growing all over the country, and his public exposure was guaranteed in the price spreads hearings. But Bennett, who only a few months before had snarled from between clenched teeth that without Stevens he could not remain as leader, now seemed loath to hand over the crown. Doubtless, by acting boldly, Stevens hoped to duplicate the recent success of the Social Credit movement that had blasted apart the United Farmers government in Alberta from inside. And so immediately after his resignation, all the Stevens Clubs and the RMA members in conservative ridings were instructed by the dominion office to 'wire their member ... insisting on their member demanding your [Stevens's] leadership.' To further intensify the pressure, Stevens gave more and more speeches – as many as three a week throughout November. And everywhere his objective was the same: 'I am going to appeal to you independent merchants to band together ... Alone you are ineffective. United you are irresistible.'[51]

But Bennett called Stevens's bluff. He was determined to remain leader of the Conservative Party if only to deny his one-time minister the opportunity. In a series of carefully orchestrated political manoeuvres, Bennett managed to outflank the party dissidents who might have gone to Stevens and then to unite around his leadership the various factions that had formed within his government. Though Stevens had never had much support even among the back-bench reformers, most of whom supported increased public works spending rather than an NRA, Bennett feared that he did have, and his New Deal broadcasts of January 1935 were designed in part to avert the formation of a cabal. By offering his party a New Deal, the prime minister had put the reformers into the position of either falling into line behind him or joining Stevens in limbo. Similarly, by threatening to turn radical, Bennett had compelled the fiscal conservatives in his party to accept his watered-down reform program as a necessary compromise with the radical faction.[52]

Still, the situation remained fluid. Though Stevens had been isolated, his confidence was not dimmed. Indeed, his enthusiasm grew as Bennett's New Deal legislation began to come down and the reformers in the party started to realize the mistake they had made in believing in the prime minister's belated conversion to their cause. Stevens knew that, with all the other New Deal proposals emasculated, reform hopes would be pinned on the report of the Royal Commission on Price Spreads, which had yet to be tabled. He therefore began to sound defiant, hoping to unite the disgruntled around his own NRA-inspired ideas. He was not, he told the House, going to be 'a mere rubber stamp, if I have views I will express them.' No longer would he feel content with 'general' support for the principles of price spreads. Now, he warned, he would only back the prime minister 'if he comes through 100 per cent.'[53]

Ironically, because he had surrendered the chairmanship and isolated himself on the commission, Stevens played virtually no part in the writing of the report, and its conclusions – which urged a maintenance of the old combines approach, a fairly minor revision to the Criminal Code, and an only half-hearted form of codification – undoubtedly would have disappointed him, had he bothered to study them. But Stevens latched onto the particulars and ignored the general reasoning, and he called for a full implementation of the report's findings as he understood them: revisions to the Companies' Act, creation of a Securities Commission, a redefinition of monopoly in the Combines Investigation Act, minimum-wage and maximum-hours legislation, and the creation of a Trade and Industry Commission that would both oversee industrial trade codes and punish those who offered loss-leaders and obtained secret discounts.[54]

'Are we going ... to drift helplessly and supinely into a Morass of Obsequious Servility to the will of our Over Lords,' Stevens asked a crowd of retailers soon after the release of the report. 'If left uncontrolled [they] will destroy our Democratic Society and replace it with a ruthless Plutocracy under which wealth only would be served ... What is required [to stop them] is "The Will to Do."' The 'Will to Do' – it was typical of the gobbledygook that Stevens was now forced to pronounce when discussing the report (which he still confidently insisted was 'his' report). He did not have much choice. In the first place, the only sections of the report that directly affected distribution – other than the legalization of certain business combinations where competitive circumstances were especially severe – had actually been legislated as part of Bennett's New Deal. The Criminal Code had already been amended in loose accordance with the commission's recommendations: loss-leaders (when 'unreasonable') had been made illegal, as had secret rebates and discounts and territorial price differentials for the purposes of 'destroying' competition. Moreover, the government had renamed the old Tariff Board the Trade and Industry Commission and had placed under its control the administration of the Combines Act.[55]

Furthermore, the NRA, on which Stevens, following the garment and furniture manufacturers, had based his reform hopes, had actually started to look like a political albatross. As early opponents had predicted, the American codes became weapons in the hands of the largest corporations within each sector, which had used their provisions to destroy competition. Moreover, labour had grown unhappy with the wage calculations and the way that employers used the codes to herd employees into company unions.[56] Early in 1935 the courts joined the fray: in January the Supreme Court invalidated the 'hot oil' provisions of the NRA, and in May the axe fell on the whole act. The problem for Stevens therefore lay in convincing the retailers that the report had promised them something more than it had, and he therefore attacked the price spreads legislation that had been passed as a 'repudiation' of the commission's vision of capitalist development.

Bennett, however, had had enough of his annoying colleague, and in a show of strength he took the decisive step and barred Stevens from Caucus. Much to Stevens's dismay, there was no revolt of the back-benchers, and Bennett remained firmly in control. With Stevens now alone and bitter in the wilderness, the NFTC alliance began to come undone. Not only had retail support failed to match expectations, but the manufacturers' enthusiasm also appeared to be cooling. Many industrialists gave up on Stevens when the legality of the NRA came into question, and many more lost interest when Quebec and Ontario began passing legislation that seemed to answer their needs. During the 1934 campaign in Ontario, A.J. Roebuck, soon to be Hepburn's attorney general, had promised the Liberal Party's support for trade codes which would 'see that proper hours and wages are enforced, with the shyster employer put out of business.' At the same moment, the Taschereau government in Quebec, under pressure from the Catholic trade unions and from the the revelations of the price spreads inquiry concerning sweatshops in the province, was putting forward a Collective Agreements Extension Act (popularly known as the Arcand Act) which proposed legalizing and extending voluntary labour agreements. The shoe, clothing, and furniture industries welcomed these initiatives enthusiastically. A strike in Montreal in September 1933 had led to the formation of a Quebec division of the Associated Garment Manufacturers, and it had already established an agreement and arbitration procedure with the Amalgamated Clothing Workers' Union. The passage of the Arcand Act a year later gave the association members precisely what they wanted: an extension of their voluntary agreement to cover the workers employed in non-union shops. The act, observed the Associated, was 'a great forward movement and improvement in the clothing industry – the greatest that has yet happened.'[57]

In Ontario the furniture and clothing manufacturers worked closely with Attorney General Roebuck to define that province's code law, and as in Quebec, they were delighted with the result. Not only did clothing manufacturers extend and legalize the existing Toronto agreement with the Amalgamated, but they also succeeded in modestly reducing the now-binding wage scales to make them conform to those prevailing in Quebec. Ontario's furniture manufacturers, in the meantime, were also working out a code which would widen their own agreement to cover the entire province, and in late July 1935 the first furniture code was approved by an order in council. Under the Industrial Stardards Act the furniture code that was already in voluntary effect in the Stratford-Kitchener-Hamilton triangle was given legal force and extended to the whole province outside Toronto. Though in the long run none of these initiatives would prove satisfactory – the Arcand Act developed too many administrative loopholes, and the furniture code was too rigid and was discarded in 1937 – what was important was that at Stevens's darkest moment, his chief business supporters were seeing their legislative hopes satisfied at the provincial level.[58]

For Stevens events moved with a tragic inexorability. To their credit, most of the leaders of the NFTC did not abandon him, despite the evaporating support. Clearly, the garment manufacturers' terrible handiwork could not be undone, and within two weeks of Stevens's expulsion from the party, the machinery that was to produce the Reconstruction Party had been set in motion. Warren Cook launched a cross-Canada tour to raise enthusiasm for a founding convention, and Stevens set to work drawing up a party platform. The convention never materialized, but on 5 July 1935 thirty-one business and religious leaders gathered at the Royal Connaught Hotel in Hamilton to sign a petition calling on Stevens to form a new party. The next day he accepted their offer, and the Reconstruction Party was launched; only three months remained before the election. At issue, Stevens declared, were the forces of 'concentration' against 'democracy,' 'Youth' against 'Old Age.' In his party platform he promised to implement all the price spreads recommendations, to bring in a job-creation program for 'youth,' to legislate prison reform, to lower mortgage rates and provide higher pensions for veterans, and to spend massively on public works, reforestation, and slum clearance. 'It is neither Socialism nor Fascism', observed the *Financial Post* thoughtfully, 'but it borrows from both philosophies.'[59]

As everybody knew, Harry Stevens was the Reconstruction Party, and he worked like a demon to ensure its success (all that was required was the 'Will to Do'). He began campaigning in the first week of August with a national speaking tour that ran every day for two and a half months. In the meantime, Warren Cook, in his role as party chairman, and T.W. Learie, as treasurer, did their best to build up institutional support. Their aim was to use the network of existing voluntary associations to spread the Reconstruction message, but in this they still met with only mixed success. Money was a large part of the problem, though on-the-spot donations from industrial supporters kept the engine running by fits and starts. More troubling was the fact that the party was having a great deal of difficulty attracting powerful affiliates. The Associated Garment Manufacturers was onside, but the Furniture Manufacturers' Association now refused officially to endorse Reconstruction, as did a surprisingly large number of the other business groupings.[60] Many of them probably felt federal action was no longer necessary given that provincial legislation was in the works which promised to answer their needs at a fraction of the cost of funding a third party.

The Retail Merchants' Association also continued to prove itself a capricious ally. 'There has been a lot of ballyhoo,' observed the *Dry Goods Review*, 'ostensibly representative of retailers' interests, but it has fallen short of the mark.'[61] In fact, the frictions between Stevens and the association were now exploding all around. The association was appearing less and less the unified, representative, docile organization he thought it should be. The Reconstructionists had put their faith in the RMA and still expected that the organization could summon the retailing hordes, but Cook and Stevens were confirmed again and again in their belief that they had received less than they had been promised. Not only were a large number of smaller merchants ambivalent or hostile to the trade association, but many now seemed utterly disinterested in what Stevens himself was trying to accomplish. And the modernizing independents of the RMA were apparently no more interested in broadening their appeal and drawing in the unaffiliated trade elements than they had been a year earlier.

Under intense pressure to sell Reconstruction to Canadians, the RMA began to fragment. Leading Reconstructionists suddenly discovered the looseness of the RMA federation as individual provinces, lacking Dominion coordination, began to go their separate ways. In Quebec both Premier Taschereau and the opposition alliance were promising to legislate against the mass merchandisers, and the QRMA's board was leaning gently towards the Liberals (rumour had it that Rossario Messier, the QRMA secretary, had been promised a place in a Taschereau cabinet). In Saskatchewan and Alberta the provincial branches were also hovering indecisively. The Social Credit party had recently been elected in Alberta and was promising such great things to the retailers that they were anxious not to alienate Aberhart by supporting Stevens. In mid-September, after Aberhart announced that the Party would contest the federal election under its own flag, the Alberta RMA made its choice as well: with only a few weeks remaining in the campaign, the Association decided that it would endorse Aberhart. In Saskatchewan the RMA backed out of politics altogether, and Reconstructionist efforts in the two provinces all but collapsed. The BC RMA, possibly because of its leaders' connections to the provincial Liberals, also dithered about endorsing Reconstruction and only took the half-hearted step late in July in order to prevent 'the costly efforts of the Commission follow[ing] the usual route to oblivion.' But the BC organization lent Stevens little public support and secretly began working with Premier Pattullo on provincial regulations.[62]

It seems ironic, then, that most contemporary observers, and most historians, saw Reconstruction as a shopkeepers' movement. But for all the RMA's weaknesses, the view does have a certain validity. Merchants made up the second largest occupational group contributing candidates (farmers ranked first), though it should be noted that they were outnumbered by both professionals (taken as a whole) and other business people (when grouped together). Furthermore, the RMA was the bulwark of the Stevens campaign on a local level (for all that that support might be worth); as the editor of the *Winnipeg Tribune* noted, 'the Retail Mer-

chants' Association appears to be the nucleus of whatever [party] organization there is.' In most ridings, the RMA local became the Stevens
club, and the shopkeepers arranged for the promotion of candidates and
the distribution of election material. Therefore it was impossible, in
areas such as Alberta and Saskatchewan and much of Quebec, where the
RMA did not lend its support, for Reconstruction organization to pro-
ceed. And yet, though the association provided Stevens with his local
organization, the RMA was not very much involved in the party's strategic direction. The names of the twenty-two people who comprised
Stevens's steering committee are unknown, but the three most important members were in the garment manufacturing business, two others
were publishers, at least two were Protestant ministers, and the publicity director was a journalist. George Hougham and A.E. Grassby are the
only retailers known to have been on the executive committee.[63]

Nor is it clear just how much trade support Stevens received in the
election of 1935. As he himself discovered to his horror, there was a big
difference between obtaining the endorsement of the RMA and winning
the support of the retailers. Ultimately, Reconstruction candidates
polled almost 390,000 votes, or 9 per cent of the total, but given the thin
distribution of party support, only Stevens was elected. The Reconstructionists claimed at the time that this outcome was grotesquely unfair
since 386,000 votes had elected seven CCF candidates and 187,000 had
elected seventeen Social Crediters. But the national Reconstruction vote
was not really disproportionate to the vote received locally, and
Stevens's candidates placed last in the majority of ridings they con-
tested. Unlike both the CCF and the Social Credit parties, which ran for
fewer seats and had strong regional support, the Reconstructionists
received a high vote simply because they ran so many candidates. One
might hypothesize on the basis of this result that the party drew its support from a widely dispersed, but numerically weak, group such as the
retailers, but the evidence is far from conclusive.[64]

Indeed, the occupational group that seems to have most strongly supported the Reconstructionists was not shopkeepers but Atlantic fisher-
men, for the party did best in coastal communities in the Maritimes and
the Gaspésie. Otherwise, Stevens won his greatest support in the Ottawa
Valley and in the mining areas of Quebec and northeastern Ontario; his
candidates ran weakest west of Sault Ste Marie. There is also evidence to
suggest that Reconstruction did better in traditional Tory working-class
ridings, such as the Anglo-Saxon polls in Hamilton East, and least well
in places where there was a large immigrant vote. None the less, when

he later thought about his defeat, Stevens could not help but blame it on the fact that 'the independent merchants were woefully disorganized – in fact disintegrated. There was no co-ordinated effort at all,' and while we should have had their support, most of them were afraid.'[65] He was probably unfair in blaming the RMA exclusively for his defeat: it was not that the organization had failed him, it was only that his advisers had greatly overestimated the association's capabilities. There was simply no homogeneous Canadian *Mittelstand* waiting to be mobilized.

THE REFORM IMPULSE

For the retailers who joined the RMA in 1934–5 and for the thousands who probably voted for Stevens, Reconstruction was a complex experience. To a minority of trade activists it represented the promise of practical legislative reform: perhaps the long-dreamed-of legalization of resale price maintenance, a ban on loss-leader selling, or an end to secret discounting. But to the majority of his retail supporters, Stevens represented something emotional rather than pragmatic. As we have seen, shop owners were not unidimensional people, and they did not generally think or vote in occupational ways. Instead, they brought the wealth of their other identities into their stores and relied on the instrument of folklore to give them their business form. For these merchants, Reconstruction's appeal lay in the fact that their votes were being solicited as never before. If the main-street shopkeepers of Fort William voted for Reconstruction, and we will never know whether they did, it was not because of any direct connection between the party platform and their long-standing organizational demands. Rather, if the RMA members in Fort William voted for Stevens, it was because he propagated the values and invoked on an abstract level the images that small business people cherished. He represented, in effect, retail folklore purged of its content.

Naturally, the leader was unaware of his own lack of meaning. For Stevens, the shopkeepers was the 'little guy', the beleaguered everyman – moral, honest, and all too much neglected. 'Modern efficiency,' he told a Grimsby audience, 'is being bought at too great a price. Namely, the Sacrifice of the personal equation.' And again: 'Destructive competition is uneconomic as well as un-democratic. Democracy postulates the Right to Live.' But unlike the retailers who used words such as these to express their business concerns and transmit their personal prejudices and preferences, Stevens took them at face value. Consequently, even when dealing with the organized retailers' actual demands, he offered only dreams. When explaining, for example, how competition would be regulated, he announced that all that was necessary was for each merchant 'to take a solemn vow that he would not countenance in his own business any of the practices he condemns in others; that he would not buy or distribute goods branded with the stigma of the sweat shops. That he would not accept secret discounts ... that he would not sell goods below cost ... that he would refrain from false and misleading advertising ... If this were done, little need of laws.' What Stevens wanted was to 'inspire the bosses ... to renovate their souls.'[66]

One could, of course, see in these airy proposals a lack of sincerity. Stevens, it could be argued, was not the reformer he appeared; in fact, he was far closer to King and Bennett in doubting the state's ability to control business behaviour than anyone cared to admit. The trouble with this interpretation is that it ignores both Stevens's sincerity and his vapidity. He actually seems to have believed his social gospel and to have felt that he was leading a crusade to rescue Canadians from their own selfishness. Instead of using folklore to express business interests, Stevens had dissolved the realities into the symbolic jelly.

Arguably, his appeals to memory worked. Though the trade leadership and the RMA press were frustrated by Stevens's speeches on 'the Economics of Jesus,' there is evidence to suggest that thousands of shopkeepers were warmed by his attentions. Retailing was a great and heterogeneous occupation, and the associations spoke for only a small fraction of its practitioners. Though main-street shopkeepers, trade experts, analysts, and activists insisted that the real issues were bulk-buying discounts and advertising allowances, the vast majority remained untouched by RMA propaganda. What they liked about Reconstruction was that it made them feel part of a crusade. These shopkeepers were less interested in actual legislation than they were in doing something to end the agony of the Depression. Many of them were inspired by Stevens's religious fervour; many more thought him to be a reformer in the old trust-busting style; others saw him as a means of protesting against the uncaring Tory leadership.

The dozens of letters from retailers that Stevens kept on file reveal the generalized emotions that led merchants to support him. Shopkeepers endorsed Reconstruction because they felt that they were working for social justice. Reconstruction, they felt, was going to 'cleanse the channels of business' and establish an 'ethical business code.' The shopkeepers saw themselves as 'shaking the too powerful off the shoulders of the nation'; they imagined themselves business people for Christ, crusaders against the 'Jews and other Foreigners,' enemies of 'the Juggernaut of modern greed,' and even soldiers of a counter-revolution who were going to 'make the workers, the people, satisfied [that] they are getting a square deal.' For a Burnaby general merchant, the goal was to bring an end to the 'grab and take methods of the day'; there was a 'madness in to-days system that must be got rid of,' he wrote; 'otherwise we are at the mercy of these [big business] hogs.' The mass merchandisers, a Vancouver grocer emphasized, were not just stores; they were creators of a 'system more virulent, wide-spread and degeneratingly soul-destroying than all the servitude of the Black race.' The nation's leaders, this grocer noted, must be made to realize 'the error of an idealism which glorified ... those so-called successful men who have selfishly prospered materially by the savage exploitation of those less effectively endowed with their primitive jungle qualities.' The ideas that people expressed in these letters were varied and confused, but what the letters all convey is the feeling that something big was going to be accomplished, that they were working to change a world. 'Remember Mothers,' one grocer's window sign in support of Stevens read; 'To Forget the Few and Remember the Multitude.'[67]

This sort of response helps to explain why both the RMA's and Stevens' support so quickly slipped away. Having linked itself to Reconstruction's greater idealism, the RMA inevitably suffered its defeat. The hundreds of new members who flocked to the association in the interests of reform would not remain in it once the cause seemed dead. It did not matter that the RMA could be seen to have delivered some practical legislation that would serve the interests of retailers; it had lost the greater struggle for social regeneration. Most of the retailers who had joined the RMA in 1934–5 had not signed on because of their interest in specific occupational legislation. Of course, they had joined the RMA because they were main-street retailers, but the motive for their affiliation had been the way in which Stevens appealed to their reformist aspirations. Like the exclusionist campaign in BC or Achat chez nous in Quebec, Reconstruction had drawn heavily upon identifications unrelated to the real business of managing a store. And here the contrast with the PATA-FTL campaign is significant, because unlike the price-fixing movement (which had used myths to mobilize support for specific business reforms), Reconstruction had subordinated practical change to mnemonic therapeutics. Where folkloric images had served trade ends in the 1920s, progressive retailing in the 1930s had subordinated itself to moral reform's folkloric excesses.

Ironically, the minority of tradespeople who wanted something practical out of Reconstruction seem to have regarded the party with declining enthusiasm. The RMA officials who spoke before the price spreads inquiry had asked for very specific things, such as a ban on secret discounts. In so doing they were careful not to request an abolition of the entire sliding scale; after all, even 'the Government knows that it can purchase large blocks of merchandise at prices considerably less than if small units were taken.' Naturally, the small capitalist trader still wanted large lots to cost less than individual items: main-street had to preserve its advantages over backstreet. But where the independent's business was big enough to warrant the largest discount, why should the department stores be permitted to buy for less by being granted the wholesaler discount, an advertising allowance, or a secret rebate? As C.R. Kneider, owner of a large grocery store in Dunnville, Ontario, advised Stevens, there was nothing wrong with discounting – 'if a person is in the market he is obliged to buy at the best price' – but 'if the price is being forced by some condition which brings about unfair competition' or if 'the mass buyers get... so substantial a rebate or allowance ... as to be able to cut the price so much the small buyer hasn't a chance,' then 'something ought to be done to prevent [it] from existing.' A Saskatoon merchant, encountering W.L. McQuarrie, the SRMA's secretary, as he boarded his train for the price spreads hearings in Ottawa, made the same point: 'the thing I would like to know is whether or not I am getting the last discount.' This was the modernists' message to price spreads: 'if we could get advantage of the buying, the same buying, if we could buy at the same price, there would be no question about competing ... that is the crux of the whole thing.'[68]

For the activists, the main question was not whether Stevens would get elected, but 'whether our Government will enact legislation to regulate [read: prevent] such concerns as Eaton's and Simpson's from being able to purchase their merchandise supplies by unethical practices at a much lower price than the other 125,000 merchants.' These retailers were interested in trade codes not because they symbolized the consensual State but because they wanted to establish resale price maintenance and fixed buying discounts. Similarly, while they acknowledged that licensing would improve business ethics, they were primarily interested in regulation's impact on the backstreet traders. When the retail druggists met in Alberta to debate the benefits of licensing legislation, one delegate cautioned that there would be considerable opposition to it 'from the smaller men.' Another reassured him: 'in Germany they have one store for every six thousand people. Once we get government control of things of that kind all these things will be taken care of.'[69]

The demands of retailers such as these need to be understood as yet another expression of store modernization. Thanks to their continuing efforts to improve their selling, the more-affluent independents felt that they had become as good, if not better, retailers as the managers of the chains and department stores. It was something they felt had been confirmed by the findings of the inquiry into price spreads 'that in the matter of operating costs, the chain stores are most inefficient ... Further, the larger the unit the more inefficient it becomes.' What the commission had 'brought out,' A.S. Whebby of the CPhA agreed, was that 'in the matter of operating costs ... the independents are more efficient.' Clearly, this meant that if the mass merchandisers could only be forced 'to compete on an equal basis,' the small shops would drive them out. Business-oriented joiners consequently wanted to have the discounts, rebates, and allowances given to big buyers limited to no more than 5 per cent below list price, and they sought to have a law passed to make loss-leader selling illegal so that no one would cut 'below the current retail price of these goods in the district.' According to W.L. McQuarrie of the SRMA, 'All that is necessary is that the independent retailer be put on a more equitable basis in relation to the mass buyer in making his purchases, from which point on, fair competition should be unrestrained.'[0] Far from representing a throw-back to the past, the RMA's actual demands closely reflected the shopkeepers' perception of themselves as 'modern,' rather than 'traditional,' merchandisers

Still, as was their wont, the progressive retailers dressed up their demands in dense folkloric flannel. McQuarrie may have been interested in exposing the discount system, but he talked a lot about the decimation wrought by mail-order catalogues on the Prairie community. 'In pressing our views,' he announced, 'we have in mind not only the adverse affect [sic] to the volume and profit of the retailers' business but we have in mind the community life of the settlers throughout the province' – hardy folk, independent people, pioneers, were suffering because the mail-order catalogues were killing the villages that sustained them. As always, George Hougham said it best. In a remarkable presentation, an evocation of all the folkloric spirits, he called for the salvation of community, for the preservation of integrity and independence, for the rights of the small and weak, for an end to selfishness. Mass marketing, he observed, had created a 'cruel' system 'which by its very nature demands volume and still more volume, devastating in its destruction of human values and merciless in its competitive relationships.' No sporting rivalries here, no benign and beneficent commercial relationships. The big stores spewed a 'dominating propaganda appealing solely to the cupidity of the purchasing public, with clever word and pictures that finally persuade Mr. and Mrs. Consumer that massed buying is a virtue and that its high Priests are public benefactors.' But Hougham was not fooled, and he urged the price spreads inquiry to stop 'this mechanism' in its 'predatory career ... For reasons of self preservation? Yes, but also in the interests of the greatest good ... we are all bound together by bonds of economic steel ... what we have to decide is whether we shall all work for the merchandising syndicates or whether opportunity shall be restored to the individual.'[71]

Lovely stuff this. By appealing to folkloric memory; retailing's representatives transformed a crass demand for the standardization of trade discounts into a struggle for the soul of humanity. But in so doing they were not conniving; though they doubtless hoped to stir the public's conscience, they sincerely believed the things that they were saying. The symbolism was what made small business distinct; it supplied merchants with the codes through which they could locate themselves in society and structure their work experiences. Though they used folkloric forms to convey ideas – in this case, the demand for a law to prohibit secret discounts – the importance of the symbols themselves should not be minimized. The structure constrained understanding, creating a logical connectedness between past and future. The shopkeepers concluded that one-sided competition would destroy them and that it would eliminate opportunity and undermine freedom and order. Folkloric memory supplied them with those connections, and they could no more easily detach themselves from its limiting influence than we can remove ourselves from the notion that history is continuous or that democracy is the best form of government.

Unfortunately, when Stevens and his supporters appropriated the imagery, they ignored the messages it expressed. That fact is not terribly surprising given that Reconstruction's agenda was determined elsewhere, by other people, to serve other interests. Unlike resale price maintenance, whose impact on distribution was immediate, the fixing of production quotas and minimum wages for factory workers promised changes indirectly, even hypothetically. There was no guarantee that the manufacturers would stop selling to the mass merchandisers for less, no assurance that they would prevent the chains and departmentals from using their products as loss-leaders. Naturally, the foot-soldiers in the movement could not be expected to fight for nothing, and so Cook and the NFTC leadership had tried to convince them that an NIRA would eliminate the competition that facilitated bulk buying. But it was a hard sell, and most retail organizers remained sceptical and most shopkeepers oblivious. The very rhetoric that appears to have attracted shopkeeping people looking for rebirth in the midst of the Depression alienated others. Though many of those more active in trade associations may well have voted for Stevens, and a few, including Hougham, even ran as candidates, they were much more interested in the practical things which Bennett and the provincial leaders had to offer. For at the very moment when Stevens was sounding the trumpet of salvation, politicians in several key provinces were promising something a good deal more practical.

RETREAT FROM REGULATION

Those seeking tangible reforms rather than nostalgia were much happier with the legislative record of the 1930s than Harry Stevens believed. The defeat of Reconstruction, George Hougham announced, had been only 'seeming ... seeming because I do not believe the defeat was as overwhelming as might appear at first sight.' Indeed, the retail merchants had proven in 1935 how powerful they could be. 'When we requested Ottawa to give us a trade and industry commission it required a Price Spreads Commission to secure it, and it wrecked a government.' Admittedly, the Trade and Industry Commission looked like a toothless wonder, but it did have the power to advertise and supervise voluntary agreements, to study ways of improving commodity standards, product grading, and promotion, and to recommend to the attorney general cases of unfair practices for prosecution. The Weights and Measures Act was tightened, and false advertising, secret rebates, and 'unusual commissions' were made illegal. Moreover, section 498A of the Criminal Code was amended to make it a crime to sell goods at prices so low as to destroy competition, and the Combines Act was altered to include 'substantive monopolies' – enterprises that 'dominated or controlled any class of business' within a given district.[72]

Nor did the Supreme Court rulings, which among other things threw out the section of the Trade and Industry Act relating to codification, have much impact on the effectiveness of the legislation. In fact, the RMA only began consulting the agency after the court's decision, when McQuarrie wrote Chief Commissioner G.H. Sedgewick asking for an investigation of the selling practices of a Safeway store in Prince Albert. To everyone's surprise, Safeway's responded to the commission's letter of inquiry with a promise not to sell products below cost and with a disciplinary action against the branch manager. This remarkable success was then repeated with the Star Department Store in Melfort and a price cutter in Arborfield, all of which led the *Western Retailer* to announce happily in January 1938 that the Trade and Industry Commission was putting a stop to loss leader selling. It was, of course, untrue, but as Mackenzie King had recognized some years before, publicity was a powerful instrument where retailers were concerned. The very threat of exposure for an 'unethical,' if not an expressly illegal, practice was generally sufficient to send merchants big and small scurrying for cover. Even Charles Duquette, the owner of the Pharmacie Moderne (which had led the fight in Montreal against the PATA), bent before the commission's will and agreed to stop the price cutting of Eno's Fruit Salts. As the RMA now realized, it 'did not want Dominion-wide legislation with the attendant bureaucracy and paternalism'; it was happy enough with the legislation in place, though it did want 'clarification' of section 498A to determine how far it could push the prohibition on low pricing for the purposes of destroying competition.[73]

Similarly, in British Columbia, where the RMA scored its greatest successes and actually authored several pieces of legislation, association leaders were content with fairly modest reforms. In addition to an extension of the minimum-wage and maximum-hours laws to cover retail employees, the BC RMA obtained a law to prohibit the retail sale of groceries at below a 5 per cent mark-up and legislation preventing retailers from cutting any resale-price-maintained article. Perhaps with the Trade and Industry Commission in mind, the RMA did not even ask for a mechanism for enforcing the acts. As the BC RMA's secretary, George Matthews, made clear, 'there will be no prosecutions ... with strength of organization [and] co-operation we can deal with 90% of all interested parties.' He may well have been right: the chains all supported the legislation, and every department store except Woodward's ultimately agreed to it, leaving the only mass opposition to come from the shoestring grocers and from the Woodward's-directed Housewives' Leagues.[74]

Consequently, retail activists such as George Hougham appeared to have a good deal to be happy about. But their spirited defence of the RMA's actions masked a more painful reality. Like a brush fire that burned fast and hot on insubstantial fuel, the passage of price spreads legislation had left the retailers' association charred and brittle. If my estimates are correct, membership in the most successful provincial RMAs fell by about 40 per cent from 1935 to 1937, and in Ontario and Quebec the decline was even more severe. 'Our experiences since last October,' Hougham told Stevens in April 1936, 'have been literally heart-breaking. One after another, country branches have dissolved ... in the more remote portions of the province [of Ontario], where branches have not been organized but where we have individual memberships, we get letters ... that leave me stumped.'[75]

The problem was that most of those who joined the association did not do so out of occupational loyalty; rather, their membership was a way of gaining access to the politicians. As a result, many of them gave up on the association as soon as the federal election results became clear. The politics of folklore had drawn them in, but it had failed to harmonize their interests. Once the campaign for societal regeneration had ended in failure, they abandoned the RMA. Unfortunately, the retailers' declining enthusiasm for organizational and political action had a telling effect. As the shopkeepers' ardour for reform diminished, its enemies closed in upon them and the real achievements of their associations were steadily undone.

The reversal began in the provinces. Like their federal counterparts, reform-minded provincial politicians had seen themselves as leaders of a crusade against big-business tyranny and public despair. And for many of them the defence of proprietary retailing – thanks in large part to the price spreads issue – had become something of a *cause juste*. Indeed, one of the tests of reform credibility in 1934–5 seems to have been the willingness of politicians to bash mass merchandising in the name of independence. Duplessis in Quebec, Hepburn in Ontario, Brownlee and Aberhart in Alberta, Dysart in New Brunswick – all were to express their hostility to the chains and departmentals. But all – with the exception of Pattullo in BC, who despite his circumspection was to do more for the retailers than anyone else – were to back away from their commitments soon after the federal election of 1935. The deflation of the Stevens movement would free the air of folklorically inspired reform campaigns all across the country.

During the two euphoric years when the RMA had seemed invincible, many provincial governments were beguiled by its supposed vote-getting influence. The first to move had been Alberta. Over the winter of 1933–4, the provincial RMA, responding to Warren Cook's speech making and to the growing interest in an NRA, joined other organizations in lobbying the provincial government for the authority to draw up business codes. The idea of becoming a Canadian Roosevelt must have looked pretty appealing to John Brownlee, a beleaguered premier about to go on trial for seducing a junior clerk in the attorney general's office at the very moment when his supporters were succumbing to the blandishments of social credit. In February 1934, just days after the price spreads committee began its hearings in Ottawa, Brownlee announced his government's intention to legislate a provincial NIRA, leading the Retail Merchants' Association to begin frantic lobbying for the right to establish codes that might prohibit bulk buying and authorize resale price maintenance agreements. The Trade and Industry Act was passed one month later, and its retail provisions were lifted wholesale from the pages of the RMA's petitions: where 60 per cent of licensed merchants in a trade decided that they wanted a code, a conference would be called by the RMA and a list of regulations compiled and sent to the government. A Bureau of Trade and Commerce was established under the act to administer the regulations and to punish businesses found to be ignoring the codes' provisions.[76]

Brownlee immediately came under intense, though covert, fire for what he had done. The Edmonton and Calgary newspapers, egged on by secret threats from Eaton's and the Hudson's Bay Company, attacked the retail provisions as inflationary. Bennett, acting upon a personal request from R.Y. Eaton, urged the premier not to authorize any retail codes. The farm cooperatives also joined in the chorus of disapproval, as did the Calgary and Edmonton Boards of Trade, through which the mass marketers surreptitiously expressed their opposition. Ultimately, the United Farmers government backed down; as Brownlee informed Eaton's solicitor in Edmonton, 'contrary to the statements made in the Act ... it is not intended to fix codes.' Rather, the premier confided to Bennett, 'we have no intention [of] attempting to regulate prices or wages other than to attempt to establish minimum wages in certain businesses.' For the retailers, all his government would now offer was the establishment of 'minimum prices with respect to certain commodities and services performed ... to remedy conditions arising from ruinous competition ... [The] Bill was not designed to prejudice department or chain stores other than [to] prevent abuses of so called loss-leaders.' It was not such a small 'other' because the government intended to define loss-leaders as selling below cost, which in Eaton's case would have covered about 7 per cent of the groceries and 4 per cent of the drugs it sold in Alberta.[77]

But the increasingly reform-spirited membership of the ARMA was not going to be satisfied with simple loss-leader legislation, and it kept pressuring the government to live up to the full measure of the Trade and Industry Act. When by December 1934 nothing had been done, the association took matters into its own hands and drew up its own retail code to regulate false advertising, 'unfair competition' (which it defined as selling any good at less than a 10 per cent mark-up), enforcement of the Weights and Measures Act and of Alberta's Minimum Wage Act, and a regulation to prevent retailers from obtaining secret discounts. But the time was quickly passing. With the American NRA now in disgrace, the United Farmers of Alberta in utter disarray, and the mass marketers quietly pressuring the government, whatever support for the independent trade had lingered in Edmonton evaporated. 'I have never been at all impressed with the Retail Merchants Association,' observed the author of the Trade and Industry Act late in 1934. Not only could it claim the support of 'no more than a comparatively small percentage of the persons engaged in the business,' but it was motivated solely by the 'self-interest[ed]' desire to 'demolish stronger and better organized concerns.' About a century ago, the deputy minister continued, 'the hand-loom weavers took an exactly similar attitude to the power loom.'[78]

The UFA's apparent betrayal of the Retail Merchants Association threw the organization into the arms of the nascent Social Credit Party. As with Reconstruction, shopkeepers assumed a high profile in the movement without really contributing to its leadership. Aberhart, however, was grateful for their support; he was dismayed by the big-business community's hostility to his theories, and he used the RMA's endorsement to prove that sensible business people could still believe in the ideas he espoused. Moreover, like Stevens, Aberhart projected himself as a leader of the little man, the small proprietor, the honest labourer, and the RMA was as crucial to the party's self-image as was the support of farmers. And besides, the RMA still looked a powerful force in early 1935, so powerful, in fact, that had Bennett not personally intervened, it would have worked out a deal that would have seen a united Social Credit–Reconstruction party contesting the federal election.[79]

In exchange for what he thought to be the organized shopkeepers' considerable backing in the provincial election, Aberhart promised regulations that would eliminate unfair competition and establish 'just prices.' The UFA's Trade and Industry Act, Aberhart said, left the retailers 'in the cold holding the bag,' and what his government promised to do was to give the state the 'power to carry out, and enforce, the regulations you drafted as being helpful to you.' It was indicative of the importance placed on retail matters that Ernest Manning took up the trade and industry portfolio in the new government. In early 1936 Social Credit moved on its promises by introducing legislation aimed at resuscitating the stillborn UFA legislation. But because neither Aberhart nor Manning wanted to anger the farmer-consumers, as Brownlee had done, by threatening inflation, the legislation was an apparent jumble of contradictions. All distributors in the province would now be required to take out a licence, and any retailer refusing to submit to a 'code' would lose his or her right to trade. But in an effort to ensure that just prices did not mean 'unduly enhanced' prices, an amendment to the Trade and Industry Act gave the government the right to appoint a price spreads board with the authority to fix maximum and minimum prices and investigate margins at wholesale and retail levels. The goal, Aberhart explained, was 'to find out a scientific method' of ensuring that all the goods that could be produced 'can be distributed in the most economical and satisfactory manner to the consumer.' None of this argument makes sense unless it is recognized that the act sought to find a way of advancing trade modernization using the independent channel. That was why the RMA was given the responsibility of policing the new legislation and submitting the names of code violators to the board for prosecution.[80]

The big-business community retaliated immediately. 'It is Despotism Triumphant,' the Calgary Chamber of Commerce shouted. For the CMA, the proposals granted 'complete control' over business to the government, while in the eyes of the Calgary and Edmonton Boards of Trade, the act promised 'incredible confusion and paralysis of business.' So angry were the Boards of Trade that they announced even before the laws were passed that they would have the legislation tested in the courts, and dozens of the province's largest businesses advanced the money to fund a challenge. Eaton's also secretly backed the creation of a Consumer's League in Edmonton and ensured that it had the money necessary to mount an advertising blitz against higher prices. But the mass retailers no longer felt the need to limit themselves to covert actions. Eaton's went so far as to make the statement – unthinkable only a short time before – that 'there is nothing to justify the enactment of any legislation ... designed to make a success of a merchant who has previously failed under open and fair competition.' With Mackenzie King now elected and the RMA in accelerating disarray, the mass marketers for the first time openly attacked codification and the licensing laws.

Governments, they insisted, were erring in paying so much attention to the retail association; 'of course they have a perfect right to do on behalf of their own members [what they liked],' observed the secretary of the Calgary Board of Trade, 'but I think the Department of Trade and Industry should understand that there is a large body of retailers outside the Retail Merchants' Association and that [they believe] no code governing retailers should be adopted.'[81]

Never entirely convinced of the merits of the legislation anyway, the Aberhart government retreated before these pressures and the legal challenge. Manning now declared that the price dimensions of the act would be used 'very seldom – maybe not more than six times a year,' and he hastily withdrew the trade bills for revision. Ultimately, they would only be reintroduced in the fall of 1937 after the ideologues in the party revolted against Aberhart's overcautious leadership. But when the rewritten acts respecting licensing and trade codification were finally presented, they had been 'shorn of most of [their] teeth.' The government still had the right to issue licenses, but it could not make regulations setting out conditions for the granting of licences, nor could it rule as to the condition of a licensee's operations or cancel licences for violations. The amended Trade and Industry Act, while allowing codification, made no provisions for the prosecution of code breakers and had no machinery for the administration of any codes drawn up. Furthermore, the government had suspended all price schedules attendant to codes, thereby purging them of their inflationary overtones.[82]

The delay in the passage of the fair trading and licensing laws was a significant reverse for the now-unravelling ARMA, which, in the hopes of reinvigorating its support, had drawn up yet another 'Master Code of Fair Competition and Business Practice for the Retail Trade.' While the government waited, the code remained inoperative, and troubled activists began to wonder what had happened to the reformist government that had once seemed so concerned for their interests. 'You have appointed men who don't care or something, as nothing is enforced,' a retailer wrote to Aberhart in December 1936; 'many have been reported for cutting prices but nothing has been done.' When a druggist active in the RMA asked Manning why the government had failed to enforce the codes, he received a sharp, but succinct reply: 'until the retail trades had agreed on classification amongst themselves it was not intended to confine the merchant.' Relations with the organized shopkeepers continued to worsen when the government, as part of its attempt to implement social credit, proposed establishing state cooperatives that would accept scrip as money. At its 1937 convention the much-diminished, but none the less frustrated, delegates of the Alberta RMA struck out against Aberhart, denouncing his lack of action on codification and declaring their opposition to scrip and cooperatives. Aberhart, an angry Harmatten shopkeeper fumed, should beware; he had underestimated the retailers, for 'we can still beat any government that ever stood in the province of Alberta.'[83] Nobody, of course, believed this claim any more.

The sad experience in Alberta was replicated in other provinces where the RMA had risen to prominence on the shoulders of Stevens. The pattern was everywhere the same. Reform-minded politicians, seeing the RMA as the foundation of a renewed capitalism, promised legislation that would control the mass merchandisers. But even before the legislation could be passed, the defeat of Stevens revealed the association's vulnerability and a big-business counter-attack drained the will from the reformers. This pattern was repeated in Alberta and Manitoba, where the issue concerned trade codes, and in Quebec and the Maritime provinces, where the call was for discriminatory taxation.

Like the NRA scheme, the tax idea was an import from the United States, and like codification, its inspiration had come from people outside retailing. A movement to curb chain store growth through taxation had been developing in the United States since 1922, and by 1931 Georgia, Maryland, North Carolina, Indiana, and Kentucky had all tried their hand at controlling the chains. In Canada the chain tax had grown from the municipality of St Thomas in southwestern Ontario to the Ontario Mayors' Association to municipal councils in Quebec, New Brunswick, and Nova Scotia. But the idea of taxing chains garnished support largely because it was seen as an instrument for raising money, and it was inevitable that Montreal, the city with the largest debt, should have become the centre of the tax movement. In late January 1933 the city of Montreal, with the backing of the QRMA, had requested sweeping changes to the municipal tax law. Included in the proposed Municipalities Bill was a graduated tax on chain stores. It was a similar demand to the one made by the Ontario mayors the year before, and Taschereau, like Ontario premier Henry, had little difficulty killing the proposal in committee by arguing that the chains saved consumers money and that taxing them would raise the cost of living and harm the poor. The RMA and Montreal's municipal officials might keep up the pressure, but for the next two years nothing was done.[84]

As it had for codification, the price spreads issue made the tax on mass merchandising seem politically irresistible. Early in March 1935

Taschereau reversed his earlier position and agreed to support the demand for discriminatory taxation. Two years before, he explained to the bills committee, he had not known how truly wicked the chain stores were, but now that Stevens had shown all, he was bent on their destruction. With a provincial election impending, the opposition jostled with the premier for the right to represent the retailers. 'Cette taxe serait une bonne taxe,' Maurice Duplessis observed of the Montreal proposal; 'elle réparerait plusieurs injustices et procurerait des revenues à la ville.' For the chain stores, he had only scorn: the small retailers were 'the last bulwark of French-Canadian business,' and they had to be protected from the 'foreign capitalists.' The 'tax imposed,' he was reported as saying, 'should be made so high as to force them out of business.' The tax movement now gathered momentum: by early 1936 the towns of Granby, Verdun, Sherbrooke, Lasalle, Lachine, Valleyfield, and Trois-Rivières had all submitted proposals for taxes on mass merchandising, and Duplessis, now premier, agreed to grant them all despite the fact that Montreal's had suddenly come into dispute.[85] Soon after the bills committee approved his tax proposal, Montreal's Mayor Houde – another highly touted friend to all little guys – baulked at the scheme. The newly organized Canadian Chain Store Association, perceiving the city's proposal as the thin edge of destruction, assembled immense forces against it. The association hired a powerhouse legal team in Brooke Claxton and Louis St Laurent and announced it was going to sweep the Houdistes from City Hall at the next election. The mayor initially declared that he would tax the chains to hell, but in late January 1935 he recanted, inviting their representatives to lunch and telling them that he would never implement the tax. In order to raise the needed revenue, he would instead increase the business assessment by a quarter and level a 2 per cent sales tax. Duplessis, however, having thrown his lot in with the independent proprietors, declared during the 1936 provincial election that he would kill Houde's sales tax and extend Montreal's right to tax the chains. The results were outrageous: Duplessis was elected, Houde resigned and was defeated, and Mayor Raynault, his successor, had the chain taxes not only increased but also extended. The sales tax, however, was not repealed, though it was condemned by every consumer and boycotted by over half the retailers in the city.[86]

The QRMA greeted these developments with typical enthusiasm: 'the chain stores have been killing the business of the little merchant in the corner store,' C.-A. Gascon of the grocers' section chortled. 'We don't care whether they are Canadian or American chain organizations, or what their nationality is – we are not narrow minded – but the grocers want to protect themselves.' But the storm that Houde had avoided by renouncing his own tax proposals was about to break over the city. When the new chain taxes were approved, the A&P announced it would eliminate twenty-two stores, Dominion said it would shut eighteen, and Steinberg's (a local Montreal chain) hit on the idea of avoiding the tax entirely by selling its outlets to its managers as franchises for $1 a piece. Thrift Stores, in the meantime, initiated a court action to test the validity of Montreal's new law. Late in the summer of 1937 the chain stores then went fully on the offensive. They launched a major publicity campaign designed to repair their image by showing how many jobs they provided, how many locally made goods they bought, and how many savings they were able to pass on to the consumers. To prove their point by example they simultaneously closed all their stores in Trois-Rivières, the premier's riding, laying off their workers and abandoning their customers. The RMA rejoiced that this move would give trade back to the Québécois, but for the Union Nationale government, things had gone far enough. As a chastened Duplessis now explained to the municipal politicians of Trois-Rivières, 'chain store taxation was not a remedy for [bad] business conditions.' A royal commission was hastily appointed to gauge public opinion, and when it came down against the tax laws, the premier began to act. In May 1939 the taxes in Trois-Rivières were repealed, and the next year the legislature struck down all the other anti–chain store laws. According to Duplessis: 'le temps est venu de juger ce problème froidement et sans démagogie ... cette taxe n'est pas un remède ... après tous c'est le peuple qui est juge. Il peut acheter où ça fait son affaire et où l'on vend meilleur marché. Ces institutions [the chain stores] font un commerce absolument honnête et morale et il faudrait pas porter atteinte á la liberté du commerce.'[87]

There can be no doubt that the RMA had strongly supported the idea of taxes on chains, but as with codification, it had not been the main force behind their legislation. The demand for graduated store taxes came from municipal politicians, who saw chain taxation as a popular form of raising revenue. In some provinces, such as Quebec, the RMA had backed the proposal from the beginning, but in others, including New Brunswick and PEI, it had hardly been involved at all.[88] But the tax movement had none the less everywhere followed the same course as the lobby for a national recovery act. It had profited from the retailers' identification with ordinary Canadians and from the hostility to mass merchandising stirred up by the Stevens committee. Moreover, it was marketed through images drawn from small-business folklore. But as with the price spreads reforms, the tax legislation had suffered a mortal blow after the 1935 election. The collapse of the Stevens movement had raised doubts about the strength and unity of the retail lobby, and within a year the organized shopkeepers' euphoria had given way to despair. Crippled by falling memberships and declining enthusiasm, the trade associations were unable to fight the chain and departmentals' aggressive counter-attacks. And with the economy slowly reviving, political interest now began to shift from punitive reforms to coaxing recovery. Big business started to appear less the villainous destroyer of opportunity and more the benevolent employer of labour. By 1939 almost all the discriminatory legislation that had been passed in the mid-thirties had been either repealed or neutralized.

In a sense, the retailers' traditional dependency – the easy way in which they submitted to others – had cost them severely. For all but a tiny minority, occupational unity was a momentary excursus, a digression with its own importance and subtext, but still secondary to the day-to-day business of running a shop and living a life. Never of central concern even to most main-street retailers, organization had always tended to develop only in response to some immediate need or appeal. There was therefore nothing unusual about the shop owners' political involvements in the mid-thirties. Trade organizations had generally catered to interests beyond retailing, and folkloric memory had always served as the foundation, no matter how weak, of retail activity, binding individual and extra-trade interests to occupational concerns. To be sure, the direction of political reform had been a consequence of a particular conjuncture of circumstances – the Depression, the conversion of the manufacturers to codification, the trend of American reform, the appearance of charismatic leaders – but it had not, for the retailers, been entirely out of keeping with their organizational traditions.

Unfortunately, the politicians who appropriated the retailers' folkloric forms never understood the complexities of trading. They believed in the myths to the extent that they thought that the shopkeepers could deliver on what they promised. Thus, when Duplessis or Stevens referred to the need to protect the 'little tradesmen,' they were operating under the assumption that there was a definable group of 'small' retailers who shared common values and interests. It made sense, in the context of the Depression – when big business had proved its weakness – to appeal to this alternative, countervailing, and as yet politically underexploited tradition. The populists' misperception – both in exaggerating the strength of the independents and in underestimating the economic leverage of the mass merchandisers – led them to propose more than they had the political will to deliver. For many small capitalist retailers, whose mobilization depended on the vitalizing influence of the reformers' folkloric appeals, the inevitable retreat from those promises removed all interest in association or political activism.

A Closing Balance

A.A. Shelley, the first post–Second World War secretary of the dominion board of the Retail Merchants' Association of Canada (Saskatchewan), was typical of the type of businessman who came to dominate the RMA in the interwar period. A Saskatoon grocer, Shelley opened his first store in partnership with his brother in 1920 and ten years later his family firm had grown into a local chain of thirty-six units. In the middle of the Depression the brothers branched off into the voluntary pooling business, and by 1950, in addition to their own stores, they were supplying one hundred independents in the Saskatoon area using the latest in stock control technology. As might be expected, Shelley Brothers also became a missionary of modernization; providing each of its pool members with the services of a 'store engineer' and the advice of a 'retail consultant.' As A.A. Shelley observed, strumming a well worn string, 'Our wholesale policy of supplying the efficient independent at the same uniform cost as we charge our own stores is the only lifeline for the progressively weakening independent.' As secretary of a newly constituted RMAC(S), he proposed extending his business success to the entire retail trade. Price cutting could be prevented, he declared, if any mass merchandiser advertising a loss-leader were forced to sell the product to any retailer requesting a supply of the sale goods (refusal would be made a criminal offence). The independent would then be able to sell the products at the same cut-rate price.[1]

Here in microcosm were reflected the changes that had, since the turn of the century, been transforming independent retailing. Modernization made the small capitalist trader over in the image of the salaried manager; it introduced him to new skills, drew him into chains and pools, and altered the ways in which he thought about selling. The people, the shops, the stock, and even the books that were being kept underwent a major, if subtle, transformation. Store owners who had once debated the ethics of selling brand-name goods were now not only willing to become members of chainlike operations, but they were also ready to accept the mass merchandisers as wholesalers.

In this way, the history of Canadian shopkeeping in the early twentieth reveals something of the process by which innovations in technologies and administrative methods were disseminated through the business system. Though managerial capitalism did not displace traditional retailing as a form of property, it did revolutionize independent business, altering its operational expression and sucking it into the mainstream of economic developments. As late as the 1890s the vast majority of shopkeepers had been little concerned with such things as departmentalization, merchandise control, and commercial design. But under the influence of suppliers and consumers eager to lower retail costs and of corporate competitors skilled in the commercial arts, their interests had changed. In the 'modern' store of the early twentieth century, stock was departmentalized and regularly checked for turnover, staff was divided and retrained to think along functional lines store space was overhauled to give more importance to self-service; and sales were used to push the slow moving lines off the shelf. Thanks to modernization, the more affluent independents succeeded in lowering their overheads, reducing their prices, and making themselves more competitive with their mass-marketing rivals. These modernizers were not business people trapped in the past; they were entrepreneurs acting in ways increasingly congruent with the norms established by big business.

The retailers' suppliers were central to this process of modernization. Struggling themselves to control the incredible volume of goods they now had the power to release, working to determine the proper balance of price and profit, consumption and production, manufacturers came to believe that their own interests were bound up with those of the retailers. Some decided that they had to control resale prices through rpm, while others felt they must force open the floodgates of trade. All, however, were certain of the need to toughen the fibre of independent distribution. Modernization, they thought, should be encouraged so as to stimulate consumption and maximize profits at the expense of retail overheads. And the manufacturers and wholesalers poured a lot of money into 'commercial education', using the leverage given them by their control over discounts and pricing to pressure the independents into conforming with the standards of efficiency that they had set. Sometimes they even entered into the stores themselves, rearranging the fixtures and improving the quality of the displays so as better to feature their products. Through voluntary pools and rpm they controlled retail prices, while national advertising gave them the power to remove much of the dealers' sales function. 'Small' business adaptation had thus come at a cost; while it had surely increased the modernizing shopkeepers' competitiveness, it had also reduced their autonomy. Though the retailers continued to pride themselves on their independence, the process of adjusting to an ideal set by the big firms ensured that their capacity for really autonomous business action was extremely limited.

Adaptation had other costs as well, not the least of them being the increased fragmentation of the retailing population. Storekeeping had always been a polymorphous occupation, but modernization added something new – something which cut across existing conflicts and intensified them. By making progress the criterion for legitimacy – and by allowing modernity to become a function of one's financial resources and training – 'scientific retailing' provided up-to-date merchants with an added moral justification for attacking their proprietary competitors. The ground rules of business were thereby altered; men and women who at one time might have been considered perfectly acceptable traders by their suppliers and creditors were now failing to reach the mark. Where the old divisions of race and gender and income had always indirectly affected an individual's chances for success in trading, modernization ultimately came to determine them. As distribution changed, suppliers began simply to refuse to extend credit to those who did not conform to the standards of the mass merchandisers. Ultimately, this limitation was to have a crippling impact on shoestring trading and, indirectly, on minority trading in general.

The symbiotic relationship that was developing between production and distribution also manifested itself in the shopkeepers' political and associational activities. Price maintenance and the effort to eliminate bulk-buying discounts were not reactionary strategies; rather, they were indicators of the increasing dependence of the small capitalist retailers on their suppliers. Both demands had first been promoted by manufacturers, and both involved an extension of the producers' authority over merchandising. By granting the manufacturers full control over retail prices, rpm allowed them to determine what mark-up the retailers could charge. Gross overheads (including net profits), were thereby made to conform not to the shopkeepers' costs and customs but to the manufacturers' image of how much a modern trader should be allowed to make. The age of independence and enterprise which the proprietors kept insisting they were trying to save depended, they seemed to be asserting, on the intervention of big capital and the greater restriction of petty property's structural autonomy.

Goods lining a shelf, fly-paper on the wall, a carton, and an invoice – all these signs presaged retailing's future. It was a future that modernizing shop owners tended to obscure with their folkloric imagery, but it was one they could not long help embracing. Dreams of resistance proved fleeting because adaptation was at heart an issue of power – power for the progressive shopkeeper, to the extent that only the most affluent could afford its costs, but power also in terms of the trajectory of change. More than simply expanding buying, the mass market altered relationships within the economy, empowering consumers and creating an ascendant corporate culture. Clearly, the triumph of large-scale enterprise did not mean the end of independent property, but it did imply both a constriction of 'independence' and the emergence of a big-business hegemony over techniques and designs.

Folklore has been our golden thread within this maze of change. As much as this book has been about progress, it has also been concerned with identity. Indeed, the two themes have been closely intertwined, for just as folklore clouded the perception of change, it also illuminated the currents of cohesion. It was folklore that provided the code through which individual retailers could understand their group interests, and it was folklore that allowed us to balance both the heterogeneity of merchandising and its subtler forms of unity.

Shopkeepers were an uneasy collection, a group lacking in any real desire for fraternity. Instead, retailers shared a language through which they could express their various occupational ambitions. The commonalities allowed them to understand each other; the diversity of accents kept them apart. So stable, so ostensibly restrictive – the ideal of retailing was still pliant enough to allow its spokespeople to carry the weight of tradition wherever they chose. It was also flexible enough to serve as a vehicle for racism, sexism, privilege, and discriminatory legislation. But most important, by confronting change within a framework of permanence, folkloric forms allowed retailers to preserve the memory of their own importance. It was from this storehouse – from their belief in the superiority of small property – that both the struggle to contain their business opponents and the effort to modernize their stores derived their justification.

THE STRUCTURES OF SHOPKEEPING

The preceding exploration of retail adaption and identification has proposed solutions to major problems arising from the study of the lower middle class. In so doing, it has also offered suggestions for the more-general investigation of groups and their identities. Group and even class formation is treated here as a process by which a collectivity sharing constituent myths struggles for an interpretation. The degree of unity displayed by the collectivity is conceived as a function of agreement over the images embedded in the members' sense of what the group should be. Groups exist through what Patrick Joyce calls a 'master narrative' rather than a 'master identity.'[2] With this concept in mind, I have tried to describe both the images being interpreted and the stories of self that people created to understand them.

The basis of this interpretation is the idea that the imagery, or folklore, of shopkeeping can be considered the symbolic foundation of a social memory. The concept of memory is a valuable one – more accurate than 'culture' or 'ideology' – because it evokes something of the process through which social stereotypes and images are subject to individual recall and articulation. As Luisa Passerini shows in a remarkable study of the recollections of Turin workers in Mussolini's Italy, personal memory is a complex interaction of common narrative forms, cultural stereotypes, and individual experiences. In this way, groups can be seen to share memories of personal experiences – veterans being an especially well considered example – that while heterogeneous, somehow share commonalities. Those commonalities often take the form of things that the individual did not personally experience but are part of the popular traditions of the group or society. Generally, these 'traditions' exist as stereotypes, fixed structures of reminiscence, and even a limiting range of self-presentations. (Passerini documents such formulaic poses as 'the comedian,' the 'irreverent observer,' and the 'rebel'; we might observe the retailers' fondness for self-images like the 'victim,' the 'righteous everyman,' the 'underappreciated social guardian,' and the 'professional.') It is in the common images, forms, and stereotypes that groups may be seen to exist. In an absolute state, social memories would represent the way in which people who consider themselves part of a group or occupation expect to be seen by others. Often the collective memories involve individuals or events, such as the Todpuddle Martyrs or the Holocaust, but they may also be disconnected from specific incidents.[3] The trouble is that collective memories do not, in themselves, express a psychological identity. Instead, they provide the building blocks of group creation, the commonplace notions about oneself, often widespread in society, that can be used in personal reflection and group activation.

Individuals read their collective memories through an interpretive act in which context and prejudice function in defining ways. Those interpretations have here been patterned according to the way in which three non-occupational identifications (gender, class, and ethnicity) shaped the retailers' reading of their collective inheritance. Context is important because it was some immediate experience – in our case, such factors as bankruptcy or competition or supplier lobbying – which led store owners to attempt a more active engagement with each other. But once triggered, the shopkeepers' collective memories were then discussed and defined in terms of the other myths to which they looked for self-understanding. Sometimes retailers came together primarily as white business people, sometimes as men, and sometimes as bourgeois, but each of these different self-referential elements was detectable, to some degree, at all times.

If the unity of a group can be seen to lie in the willingness of its members to articulate and exchange a common understanding of their folkloric inheritance, then association is a crucial condition. And it is here that organizations and organizers play an important role. Through information and debate, activists attempt to build a common definition of the collectivity's nature and purpose. Their goal is to foster a 'movement culture' among those attuned to their interpretation of the points of common reference. Ultimately, what a 'movement culture' achieves is a narrowing of the range of reflection on the group involved. In successful organizations, the movement itself comes to appear a summation of its members' identity. Thus Canadian trade- association leaders worked to unite shopkeepers around a particular perception of 'legitimacy' – an interpretation at once sexist, nativist, bourgeois, and modernist – that they linked to association membership. And it was in this attempt that they failed most conspicuously. Though main-street merchants were sympathetic to the organizers' message, for individual reasons, they never felt the need to sustain an associational effort. They remained competitors with common values, capable, because of shared beliefs and interests, of working together, but never for very long.

This characteristic was undoubtedly what made retailers especially vulnerable to political manipulation. Politicians looking for answers in the 1930s found in the images of proprietary enterprise – lush with cozy and nostalgic implications – a response to the collapse of faith in the mass-production economy. The retail associations, always searching for a counterweight to the independence and competitiveness of the main-street storekeepers, inevitably embraced anyone promising to inspire what they could not themselves create: a real movement culture among store owners. It is doubtful, however, if they could have succeeded. Certainly, the experience of retailers in countries such as Germany, where politicians apparently awakened a 'small-business movement culture' in the 1930s, was that retailing interests were easily sacrificed once power was achieved. Politicians might use the group because of the importance of the myths associated with it, but if the lesson of Naziism is anything to go by, retailers, artisans, and other independent business people were expected to grow fat on slogans alone.[4] And while we should not confuse populist conservatism in Canada with fascism in Europe, politicians in this country who claimed to represent the shop-keepers' interests did little enough for them on achieving power as to warrant comparison.

And yet ever since the 1930s, reactionary populism has been associated with the anxieties and prejudices of small business people. The cruelty of fascism, for example, has been widely considered the toxic detritus of the lower middle class, just as the anti-modernist tone of populist rhetoric has been linked to the psychic anxieties of a disappearing stratum. Out of place in a fast changing world, small-business people are supposed to have fallen victim to a collective paranoia which they expressed through the wholesale repudiation of modernity. Small-business culture in Germany, Shulamit Volkov explained, 'was an expression of undifferentiated hostility, a rejection of all facets of the prevailing social reality.'[5]

Clearly, if the Canadian case can be considered illustrative, we need to think twice before accepting these judgments. So much of what has been written about the lower middle class generally and retailers specifically has been based on relatively superficial readings of their folkloric imagery. Because so little work has been done on the practice and profitability of independent enterprise, arguments have been grounded in the assumption that 'small' business was 'traditional' and therefore declining. The crux of this argument is the belief that folkloric pronouncements can be considered an accurate reflection of the retailers' lifestyle. 'They *were* independent, they *preserved* a close unity between family and business, and they *retained* an organic relationship with the people who served under them. They still *maintained* a sense of community,' writes

Michael Miller in reference to late-nineteenth-century French retailers. And because historians conflate language and reality, they define all those retailers who used traditional symbols as 'backward-looking and fearful.'[6]

This position in turn flows from the presumption that there was a single 'small business' experience and that hardship for one could be taken as indicative of problems for the whole. As we have seen, some segments of the retailing population were 'declining' in the early twentieth century, but others – and they include the people most politicized and organized – were not, we should therefore be wary of generalization about retail behaviour, outlook, or mentality. Instead of accepting folklore as a single and constricting 'anti-modern' perspective inhibiting the shopkeepers' acceptance of the modern world, we should concentrate on the interests people expressed in the words they used.

The result is a different perspective on the opposition between tradition and modernity, stability and change – ideas that in Western thought are most often conceived as antithetical. In most works on the 'declining' lower middle class, actions are routinely described as continuous or discontinuous as though chosen from the table d'hôte of mutually exclusive realities. Tradition is popularly connected to unchangeability; like myth or structure, it is perceived as the ossified antithesis of history – which makes for conceptual neatness, if not for subtlety of analysis. This study has worked from a different presumption: that change was as much an act of reproduction as of destruction. Even as modernizing shopkeepers 'adapted' to the demands of the mass market, they re-created their traditional patterns of ownership and vitalized the folkloric structures of their occupational thought. And because adaptation is a way of giving contemporary relevance to preexisting forms and practices, they ensured independent retailing's survival and function. 'What predominates in all change is the persistence of the old substance,' Saussure wrote; 'disregard for the past is only relative. That is why the principle of change is based on the principle of continuity.'[7]

The effort to present the historical implications of this observation – to capture what Marshall Sahlins calls 'structure in' and 'as' history – shaped both the depiction of folkloric myths in action and the presentation of distribution's transformation.[8] The mass market, research has revealed, did not just appear or even develop through some a priori logic. It lurched into view, a product of the unpredictable interactions of hundreds of thousands of thinking and acting people. Technologies – railways and assembly lines and iceboxes – facilitated the development of the new consumer economy, as did lower prices and shifting preferences and expectations. But those things provided nothing more than the opportunity for mass consumption and production. It was the consumers and producers and retailers – the living people – who gave shape to the possibilities. In this sense, the mass market was not just a system of exchange relationships; it was a state of mind, a way of seeing. This culture of the mass market was formed by the availability and affordability of goods, but people's spending choices and attitudes also determined the goods that were available and the ways in which they were marketed. Consumers, for instance, helped to prod manufacturers into recognizing the need for a new approach to the economy, and manufacturers, by example and influence, pressed their own business methods on the retailers. By disseminating innovations that would have been unimportant without wide currency, independent retailers in turn played as important a role in creating the new economy as did department or chain store executives. The emphasis, then, shifts from mechanistic processes to the ways in which new technologies and buying possibilities opened people to novel interactions and in so doing empowered them in the creation of the mass society.

If the mass market existed in both its idealization and its performance, then it can be conceived as a structural form manifested as a series of sustaining and recreative actions. What forged the structure was the concatenation of the events, and it was the greater form that gave meaning to each individual episode. Though chronologically defined events are minimized, this work therefore remains *événementielle* to the exent that it considers the impact of discrete actions – the purchase of a new display cabinet, the decision to sell for cash, the stratagems of manufacturers wanting to increase their market share – whose cumulative impact was explosive. Where it rejects 'event' history is in its linking of individual decisions back to broader cultural and structural realities and in its reluctance to treat every idea and incident as a unique irruption into unconnected time. Just as folkloric forms ordered and harmonized the retailers' discordant interests, the mass market proved an abstract notion materialized in and lending direction to disparate and individualized desires and behaviours.

Searching for the structure of events led me to emphasize the connectedness of disparate things and to underplay what, from a different position, might appear as differences. In this way, both inflationary price-fixing and deflationary mass production are seen as alternative approaches to a single problem. That some manufacturers could move so easily from one position to the other reveals their essential similarity: both were attempts to solve the problems of coordinating the new instruments of supply with the unpredictability of the growing demand. This interpretation therefore allows both views to exist as different, but equally 'modern,' responses to a set of business problems. Enthusiasts of mass production – and they include such liberal economists and politicians as Mackenzie King – tended to portray supporters of inflation and price-fixing as pernicious reactionaries. Whether manufacturers or retailers in pursuit of resale price maintenance or farmers agitating for parity prices, inflationists had a bad name among Canadian intellectuals and decision makers. But instead of accepting this perspective as 'true' and therefore echoing the biases of contemporaries, Canadian historians should regard mass production as simply one approach (albeit the dominant one) to the problem of development in the machine age. That the 'ethos' of mass production became cultural orthodoxy in interwar Canada should be studied as evidence of its remarkable acceptance as the essence of 'modernity.' And it was not just business people and politicians who felt this way, as the works of Charlie Chaplin, Lewis Mumford, Aldous Huxley, and Diego Rivera reveal.[9]

A multitude of interesting questions related to distribution, production, and consumption in the early twentieth century therefore emerge and are left unanswered. This study, while focusing on the problems implicit in one interpretation of 'small business' development, was never conceived to be definitive. It has simply worked to justify a different way of seeing the process of retail 'modernization' and, in so doing, to challenge certain still-dominant assumptions regarding the people commonly called 'lower middle class.' For Canadian historians, several key points will seem particularly contentious and in need of further discussion – most notably, the timing and extent of the mass market's emergence – and others, such as the feminization of shopping, the character of consumption, and the strategies of business people, still need to be properly investigated. And this is not all that remains to be done.

While gender and ethnicity and class are treated here as important constituents of retail identity, the impact of such factors as region, locality, trade, age, and education still require consideration. Similarly, this work underemphasizes the separate histories of different tradespeople – druggists, florists, bakers, jewellers, grocers, milliners – and all are deserving of proper analysis. We also await business histories of the individual mass merchandisers, and the growing volume of independent store records in archival holdings would now permit meaningful comparative analysis. Furthermore, this discussion has a central Canadian urban focus, and while the evidence suggests a common direction to retail change, regional and local studies will undoubtedly upset many an apple-cart. Backstreet traders, women, and minority shopkeepers also await their interpreters, and here the need is pressing because these groups will only be rescued from obscurity by the oral historian. And so the job is barely begun. Because retailing has attracted so little attention from social, cultural, and business historians, it offers enormous opportunities for inquiry broad and narrow. My hope is that this work has suggested something of its importance, compensation, and appeal as a subject for continued investigation and debate.

TABLES

TABLE 1
Retail stores in Ontario in selected trades, 1871–1931

	1871	1881 (L)	1891 (C)	1895 (M)	1911 (C)	1921 (C)	1931 (C)	1941 (C)
Food stores	3,674(L)	5,845	7,710	8,817	7,997	12,926	12,950	14,019
General/departmental	2,926(L)	1,750	–	3,884	–	2,960	2,789	3,355
Dry goods		729	1,087	646	1,593	–	570	247
	851(L)[a]	–	–	–	–	1,799[a]	–	–
Women's furnishings		551	–	1,189	–	–	646	
Ready-made clothng	118(L)	221	–	214	–	812	1,149	2,802[b]
Dressmaking	473(C)	693	3,851	2,991	–	–	551	
Men's clothing	–	124	182	190	587	884	1,016	1,478[c]
Tailoring	942(C)	408	–	1651	–	–	646	
Shoe (retail)	39(L)	167	389	965	610	1,032	782	788
Shoemakers	1,965(C)	1,335	2,823	1,906	–	–	–	–
Hardware	–	294	–	627	1,429	1,288	1,108	1,117
Furniture (retail)	118(L)	438	283	722	500	658	885	799
Cabinetmakers	190(C)	460	701	208	–	–	–	–
Books and stationery	70(C)	367	299	309	892	608	358	214
Tobacco	–	168	359	–	666	1,290	1,909	–
Drug	463(L)	668	–	844	1,035	1,214	1,464	1,720
Jewellery	90(C)	460	1,068	786	879	868	606	628

SOURCES: 1871: I. Drummond, *Progress without Planning: The Economic History of Ontario from Confederation to the Second World War* (Toronto 1987), 300–8; 1881: *Lovell's Ontario Trade Directory, 1881* (Montreal 1882); *Might's Ontario Business Directory* (Toronto 1895); also *Census of Canada*, 1871, 1881, 1892, 1891; *Census of Canada*, 1921, vol. 4, table 2, 28–9; *Census of Canada*, 1931, vol. 10, table 2, 502–9; *Census of Canada*, 1941, vol. 10, table 9, 275–83.
NOTE: Food stores includes greengrocers, grocers, fruit sellers, meat markets, butchers, biscuit bakers, bakers and confectioners, butter dealers, and fish markets. Women's furnishings includes millinery, hosiery, and lingerie (fancy goods). Ready-made clothing includes women's, girls, and family clothing. Furniture includes appliances, furniture, carpets, and floor coverings. Jewellery includes silver- and goldsmiths, watch and clock sellers, diamond setters, and jewellers.
C = Canada census; L = Lovell's directories; M = Might's directories.
[a] Includes dry goods and women's furnishings.
[b] Includes women's furnishings, ready-made clothing, and dressmaking.
[c] Includes men's clothing and tailoring.

TABLE 2
Toronto independent and chain grocery stores classified according to pecuniary strength and socio-economic rank of neighbourhood, 1902 and 1930 (percentage located within neighbourhoods classified according to status of area)

Pecuniary strength of independent stores	Above average			Average			Below average		
	1902	1930	% Change	1902	1930	% Change	1902	1930	% Change
Under $1,999	9	11	+216	37	47	+228	54	42	+100
$2,000–9,999	17	32	+157	30	42	+85	53	25	–39
Over $10,000	56	50	–40	22	33	0	22	17	–50
Number of chain outlets	–	42		–	38		–	20	
Independents 1902 N = 119 1930 N = 236									
Chains 1930 N = 191									

SOURCES: Stores selected at random from *Might's Toronto Directory*, 1902 and 1930; the pecuniary strength is Dun's credit rating from R.G. Dun & Co., *Mercantile Agency Reference Books*, 1902 and 1930. The quality of neighbourhoods in 1902 was adapted from maps in P.G. Goheen, *Victorian Toronto, 1850–1900* (Chicago 1970), 208–16. For 1930, Toronto's residential neighbourhoods were ranked according to four criteria: concentration of relief recipients (1934), number of houses without amenities (1934) or in 'below standard' condition (1943), number of low-income households (1944), and population density (1930). Only those areas which scored consistently below or above the middle third in any three categories were rated above or below average. The five criteria were derived from Ontario, *The Report of the Lieutenant Governor's Committee on Housing Conditions in Toronto* (Toronto 1934); Toronto, *Report of the City Council's Survey Committee on Housing Conditions in Toronto* (Toronto 1943); City Planning Board, *Annual Report* (Toronto 1944); Toronto, *Annual Report of the City Assessors for Toronto* (Toronto 1930). Grocery chains covered include the A & P, Loblaw's, Stop and Shop, and Dominion.

TABLE 3
Independent stores classified according to their
annual sales, 1931 and 1941

Quintile	Annual sales	1931 %	1941 %
1	under $4,999	38.4	31.6
2	$5,000–29,999	46.5	50.7
3	$30,000–99,999	7.6	14.3
4	$100,000–499,999	7.4	3.1
5	over $500,000	0.2	0.2

SOURCES: *Census of Canada, 1931*, vol. 10, table 6a,
44–55; *Census of Canada*, 1941, vol. 10, table 9, 258–65.

TABLE 4
Canadian retail stores classified according to the number of employees, 1941

Quintile	Employees per store	Stores as % all stores	Sales as % all sales	Employees as % all employees	Avge. store sales ($000)	Avge. no. of employees
1	0	41.4	8.6	0	5.2	0
2	1–3	40.1	26.5	23.6	16.5	1.7
3	4–9	13.8	24.9	26.8	45.0	5.5
4	10–49	4.3	23.5	26.4	136.9	17.6
5	50+	0.3	6.5	23.1	1,269.0	202.2

SOURCES: *Census of Canada, 1941*, vol. 10, table 10, 296–7.

TABLE 5
Previous occupation of bankrupt retailers in Ontario, 1924, 1928, 1932, and 1937 (percentages)

	Capitalization		
	<$2,000	$2,001–10,000	>$10,001
	Quintile		
Previous occupation	1	2	3–5
Pedlar, unskilled	11.3	3.5	2.6
Semi- and skilled	22.7	10.9	12.8
Clerical	34.8	34.6	28.2
Managerial, proprietary	26.2	39.1	46.1
Agricultural	3.5	5.9	2.6
Other	1.4	5.9	7.8
N	141	202	39

SOURCE: AO, RG 22, Supreme Court of Ontario, Bankruptcy Office.
Capitalization based on R.G. Dun credit ratings.

TABLE 6
Last known occupations (held within five years of sample date) of Toronto grocers, 1915–1939 (percentages)

	Date of sample					
	1915	1921	1925	1930	1935	1939
Pedlar	5.9	9.2	2.9	5.0	9.0	0
Unskilled	23.5	18.5	23.3	20.0	23.0	16.7
Semi-skilled	11.6	11.1	10.6	18.3	15.4	5.6
Skilled	14.7	16.7	19.4	8.3	15.4	14.0
Store clerks	13.7	11.1	9.7	15.0	17.3	23.1
Other clerical	14.7	18.5	12.6	16.6	15.6	18.7
Managerial	0	5.5	2.9	1.6	7.7	14.0
Inheritance	8.8	1.8	5.8	5.0	0	2.9
Other retail	5.8	7.4	9.7	10.0	5.8	5.6
Active service	0	0	2.9	0	0	0
N	34	54	103	60	52	36

SOURCE: *Might's Toronto Directories*, annual, 1900–40.

TABLE 7

RMA members and accused trade 'demoralizers' classified according to the capitalization of their stores, 1897–1939

Quintile	Capitalization	RMA members as % N 1897–1910	1919–39	Trade demoralizers as % N 1919–39
1	under $2,000	29.2	2.5	47.9
2	$2,000–10,000	55.1	41.9	40.9
3	$10,000–35,000	12.3	46.9	4.5
4	$35,000–50,000	3.4	4.9	2.3
5	over $50,000	–	3.7	4.5
N		89	81	88

SOURCES: Trade press, 1897–1939; UTL, Lord's Day Alliance Papers; SAB, Saskatchewan Retail Merchants' Association Papers; VCA, Office of the City Clerk's Papers. Pecuniary strength derived from R.G. Dun & Co., *Mercantile Agency Reference Books*, 1897–1939.

TABLE 8

Retail stores in Canada in selected trades, 1921–1941

	1921	1931	1941
Food stores	35,447	44,665	48,468
General and departmental	14,583	12,963	13,506
Dry goods	4,580	1,899	2,205
Men's clothing	2,184	3,956	3,485
Women's clothing	1,711	3,260	4,431
Boot and shoe	2,031	1,623	1,674
Hardware and building supplies	7,720	6,023	5,801
Furniture and appliances	2,405	3,157	3,498
Drugs	3,518	3,594	4,207
Jewellery	1,966	1,532	1,692
Tobacco, newspaper, and gift	1,378	3,249	4,962
Automotive	–	12,846	16,801
Type of operation (all trades)			
Single store independents	–	101,117	117,387
Independent stores in voluntary pools	–	4,988	5,424
Two- and three-store independents	–	4,622	6,029
Chain stores	–	8,476	8,011

SOURCES: *Census of Canada 1921*, vol. 4, 28–9; *Census, 1931*, vol. 10, table 6A, 44–55; *Census, 1941*, vol. 10, table 9, 258–65.

TABLE 9
Canada's retail trade: net sales in Canada, 1923–1940 (in 000s of current dollars)

Year	Total retail sales	Mail-order sales	Department sales	Chain sales	Independent store sales
1923	2,179,398	–	275,681	75,443*	1,828,274
1924	2,138,977	103,785	180,777	–	–
1925	2,303,598	112,086	193,081	–	–
1926	2,568,185	114,163	213,741	–	–
1927	2,783,189	113,125	240,713	–	–
1928	3,035,878	110,011	271,892	–	–
1929	3,157,927	95,481	292,462	–	–
1930	2,755,577	77,838	277,421	487,336	1,912,982
1931	2,319,935	67,460	245,279	434,015	1,573,181
1932	1,914,872	57,081	196,751	360,630	1,300,410
1933	1,775,857	58,119	183,546	328,902	1,205,290
1934	1,941,470	–	254,001	347,186	1,340,283
1935	2,053,699	–	258,653	364,179	1,430,867
1936	2,208,142	–	273,358	394,937	1,539,847
1937	2,453,715	–	288,096	414,133	1,751,486
1938	2,404,756	–	278,536	414,449	1,711,771
1939	2,447,658	–	289,887	432,026	1,725,745
1940	2,736,868	–	324,973	508,554	1,903,341

SOURCES: DBS, *Retail Merchandise Trade in Canada 1930–1940* (Ottawa 1941), tables 2 and 4; DBS, *A Decade of Retail Trade, 1923–1933* (Ottawa 1935), tables 15 and 20; DBS, *Census of Mechandising and Service: Mail Order Business* (Ottawa 1935), tables 1 and 2.
*Derived from *Canadian Grocer*, 40:14 (2 April 1926). Estimate covers grocery chains only.

TABLE 10
Estimated gross domestic disappearance per capita for selected food items, Canada, 1880–1930

	1881	1891	1900	1910	1922	1930
Beef/veal (lbs)	49	80	55	61	73	68
Lamb/mutton (lbs)	15	14	12	9	10	7
Pork (lbs)	–	42	46	67	74	73
Poultry (lbs)	–	–	–	–	6	8
Eggs	–	143	168	204	264	293
Butter (lbs)	20	23	24	28	26	31
Cheese (lbs)	–	–	5	3	3	4
Coffee (lbs)	0.5	–	1	2	2	3
Tea (lbs)	3	–	5	9	8	5
Sugar (lbs)	–	54	60	86	91	93

SOURCES: Meats calculated from slaughter plus import less export; figures can be found in M.C. Urquhart and K.A.H. Buckley, *Historical Statistics of Canada* (Toronto 1965), L-233–42 and L-294–9, and in the annual *Sessional Papers*, Department of Trade and Commerce Reports; for 1900 and 1910, Canada, Board of Inquiry into the Cost of Living, *Report of the Board*, vol. 2 (Ottawa 1915); coffee, tea, and sugar calculated from *Sessional Papers*. Figures for the period after 1922 can be found in DBS, *Estimated Consumption of Meats, Dairy Products and Eggs* (Ottawa 1925 and 1931).
NOTE: The figures for meat are based on pre-1935 DBS calculations. Figures were subsequently revised downward to take account of wastage, but revised numbers are available only to 1926. To make comparison possible, the inflated figures for 1900–30 have been used; the revised numbers may be found in Urquhart and Buckley, L-300–17. Calculations for beef, pork, and mutton consumption pre-1900 based on figures per head at an average dressed weight of pork, 1891: 140 lbs; mutton/lamb, 1881–91: 50 lbs; beef, 1881–91: 600 lbs; and veal, 1881–91: 250 lbs. Ratio of beef to veal was taken as 2:1.

TABLE 11

Constant dollar domestic spending on selected food and non-food goods, 1871–1901 (index 1891 = 100)

	Food	Clothing	Household	Entertainment
1871	54.0	45.9	46.2	37.3
1881	83.4	68.2	110.9	51.6
1891	100	100	100	100
1901	193.7	139.1	97.2	159.3

NOTE: Food consumption was divided into three categories: breads, biscuits, and confectionery; meat; and other goods (starch, pickles and sauces, vinegar, and baking powder). Clothing includes clothes, furnishings, boots and shoes, underwear, and hats. Household goods include furniture, mattresses, wallpaper, soap, ornaments, candles, carpets, mats and rugs, brooms and brushes, clocks, and silverware. Entertainment covers musical instruments, books, liquor, and tobacco. Spending on clothing was weighted using Taylor's export price index (adjusted to 1891 = 100); for bread and meat, Michel's wholesale index was used (again, 1891 = 100); I drew up my own indexes based on imports (in the cases of brooms and brushes, clocks, silverware, and mattresses) and exports in all other cases to cover other food goods, household furnishings, and entertainment expenditures. All figures are based on production values provided in the census and the net balance of foreign trade (I used the *Sessional Papers* of the year ending June of the census year).

TABLE 12

Bookkeeping in the Ontario retail trade in the 1920s tabulated according to store size for bankruptcy years 1924 and 1928

	Stores capitalization			
Type of accounts kept	<$2,000 %	$2,000–10,000 %	>$10,000–35,000 %	>$35,000 %
Daybook/ledger	43.8	77.7	95.6	100
Stock taken	16.5	45.6	78.3	83.3
Balance made	7.4	25.2	65.2	83.3
No accounts	56.2	22.3	4.4	0
N	121	103	23	6

SOURCE: AO, RG 22, Supreme Court of Ontario, Bankruptcy Office files.

TABLE 13

Bookkeeping practices employed in shops owned by bankrupts according to previous occupations of owners, 1924 and 1937 (percentages)

	Daybook		Stock taken		Balance made	
	1924	1937	1924	1937	1924	1937
Pedlar	50	33	25	33	–	33
Unskilled	30	–	–	–	–	–
Semi-skilled	23	50	15	–	8	–
Skilled	53	100	27	33	7	33
Store clerk	72	63	31	50	22	25
Other clerical	60	92	32	62	20	31
Managerial	47	75	33	33	25	25
Inheritance	60	50	60	50	40	50
Other retail	76	60	58	30	27	–
Farmer	71	50	14	50	14	–
Active service	57	–	14	–	14	–
Students	67	–	–	–	–	–

N

1924 = 178

1937 = 52

SOURCE: AO, RG 22, Supreme Court of Ontario, Bankruptcy Office files, 1924, 1927, 1932, 1937.

TABLE 14
Retail Merchants' Association: declared membership by provincial section, 1903–1937

	Total	PEI	NS	NB	Que.	Ont.	Man.	Sask.	Alta	BC
1903	–	–	–	–	–	300[a]	–	–	–	–
1905	–	–	–	–	–	2,200[b]	204[c]	–	–	–
1906	–	–	–	–	–	–	516[c]	–	–	–
1907	5,233[d]	–	–	–	4,300[e]	900[c]	–	–	–	–
1908	4,448[d]	–	–	–	–	–	–	–	–	–
1913	–	–	–	–	–	–	–	600	–	–
1914	–	–	–	–	–	3,000	–	1,500	–	30[f]
1915	–	–	–	1,000	–	–	–	1,500	–	–
1916	–	–	–	–	–	–	800	1,500	–	–
1917	–	–	–	–	–	2,700[b]	–	1,475	–	–
1918	–	–	–	–	–	–	1,050[d]	1,214	627[d]	50[f]
1919	7,619	198[g]		787	637	2,736	748	2,100	413	–
1920	8,128	715[g]		655	1,023	1,982	748	2,316	689	–
1921	–	–	–	735	–	3,995	–	2,157	–	882
1922	–	–	–	–	–	4,116	–	1,800	–	1,176
1923	–	–	–	–	1,500	4,237	–	1,754	–	938
1924	–	–	–	–	–	–	–	1,790	–	965
1927	–	–	–	–	1,011	–	–	–	–	–
1929	6,996	33	339	389	1,098	1,842	628	1,361	906	400
1930	7,781	24	322	303	2,080	1,774	454	1,528	841	453
1934	–	–	–	–	3,000	–	–	3,794[d]	–	–
1935	–	–	–	–	–	–	–	–	800	–
1937	–	–	–	–	–	3,000	–	2,300[d]	–	–

SOURCE: Trade press, 1903–40.
[a] Membership in RMA grocers' section only.
[b] Estimated from paid-up memberships of 1,000 in 1905, 1,263 in 1917, and 3,700 in 1927.
[c] Manitoba and Saskatchewan.
[d] Paid-up members: 2,068 in 1907, 1,789 in 1908, 560 in Manitoba and 376 in Alberta in 1918, 2,300 in Saskatchewan in 1934, and 938 in 1937. The last figure is from D'A. Handy, 'Saskatchewan Merchants in the Great Depression,' *Saskatchewan History*, 43 (winter 1991), note 8.
[e] Estimate for Quebec and Ontario.
[f] Membership in Vancouver's Retail Grocers' Association, a remnant of the BC RMA which disbanded in 1914. It would form the core of a new RMA in 1918.
[g] PEI and Nova Scotia.

Notes

ABBREVIATIONS

ANQ   Archives nationale du Québec
AO   Archives of Ontario
CRHA   Canadian Retail Hardware Association
DBS   Dominion Bureau of Statistics
GAI   Glenbow Alberta Institute
GBCA   George Brown College Archives
HBCA   Hudson's Bay Company Archives
MHSO   Multicultural History Society of Ontario
MMA   Montreal Municipal Archives
MUA   McGill University Archives
NAC   National Archives of Canada
PAA   Public Archives of Alberta
PABC   Public Archives of British Columbia
PAM   Public Archives of Manitoba
RCUWO   Regional Collection, University of Western Ontario
SAB   Saskatchewan Archives Board
SCO   Supreme Court of Ontario
UTA   University of Toronto Archives
UTL   University of Toronto Library
VCA   Vancouver City Archives
WCA   Wellington County Archives

INTRODUCTION: The Shopkeeper, the Historian, and the Petite Bourgeoisie

1 MMA, D36030, Retail Merchants' Association, L'Achat chez nous circular, c. 1925.

2 S. Ranulf, *Moral Indignation and Middle Class Psychology* (New York 1962, orig. pub. 1938); H. Lasswell, 'The Psychology of Hitlerism,' *Political Quarterly*, 4 (1933), 369–76; W. Reich, *The Mass Psychology of Fascism* (New York 1971); D.J. Saposs, 'The Role of the Middle Class in Social Development: Fascism, Populism, Communism, Socialism,' in *Economic Essays in Honour of Wesley Clair Mitchell* (New York 1935), 394–400.

3 Ranulf, *Moral Indignation*, 41–6; Lasswell, 'Psychology of Hitlerism,' 374. This view continued to inform works into the 1960s and 1970s. E. Fromm, *Escape from Freedom* (New York 1971); D. Schoenbaum, *Hitler's Social Revolution: Class and Status in Germany, 1933–1939* (New York 1966); R. Gellately, *The Politics of Economic Despair: Shopkeepers and German Politics, 1890–1914* (London 1974); and S. Volkov, *The Rise of Popular Anti-Modernism in Germany: The Urban Master Artisans, 1873–1896* (Princeton 1978) all stress a 'psychic' crisis and 'status anxieties' in explaining retail protest.

4 Canada, Department of Labour, 'Investigation into the Proprietary Articles Trade Association' (interim report, Ottawa 1926), 17. See also L. Reynolds, *The Control of Competition in Canada* (Cambridge 1940); the quotes are from 114 and 127.

5 J. Irving, *The Social Credit Movement in Alberta* (Toronto 1959), 196, 241–4, and 338–40; W.E. Mann, *Sect, Cult and Church in Alberta* (Toronto 1955), 41; C.B. Macpherson, *Democracy in Alberta: Social Credit and the Party System* (Toronto 1953), ch. 8; E.C. Hughes, *French Canada in Transition* (Chicago 1971, orig. pub. 1943), ch. 19. American historians and sociologists became similarly fascinated by the ideas of fascism's early critics. See R. Hofstadter, *The Age of Reform* (New York 1955), esp. 131–4; V. Ferkiss, 'Populist Influences in American Fascism,' *Western Political Quarterly*, 10 (November 1957), 350–73; and S.M. Lipset, *Political Man* (New York 1959), ch. 5.

6 P.E. Trudeau, *Federalism and the French Canadians* (Toronto 1968; article orig. pub. 1962), 168–9. Though F. Ouellet calls them 'bourgeois,' his French-Canadian 'middle class' is made up of economically insecure shopkeepers, skilled tradesmen, notaries, doctors, and journalists; see 'Les Insurrections de 1837–1838: un phénomène social,' *Histoire sociale/Social History*, 2 (novembre 1968), 72–7; note also the similarities between his description of the anti-capitalist French-Canadian nationalism of the early nineteenth century and portrayals of twentieth-century fascism (right down to its anti-Semitism) in *Lower Canada, 1791–1840: Social Change and Nationalism* (Toronto 1983), esp. part 1. See also D. Monière, *Ideologies in Quebec: The Historical Development* (Toronto 1981), chs. 5–7; J. Levitt, 'Henri Bourassa: The Catholic Social Order and Canada's Mission,' in F. Dumont, *Idéologies au Canada Français, 1900–1929* (Quebec 1973), 200–1; M. Oliver, *The Passionate Debate: The Social and Political Ideas*

of Quebec Nationalism (Montreal 1991), 158–60; G. Bourque, 'Petite Bourgeoisie envahissante et bourgeoisie ténébreuse,' *Les Cahiers du socialisme*, 3 (1979), 112–26; H. Guindon, 'Social Unrest, Social Class and Quebec's Bureaucratic Revolution,' *Queen's Quarterly*, 71 (1964), 150–62.

7 The idea of small business as *embourgeoisement* is most clearly expressed in J. Benson, *Entrepreneurialism in Canada: A History of 'Penny Capitalists'* (Lewiston 1990). Where Benson differs from most other social historians is in his delight over the process. The alternative proposed by some historians of the working class is to obscure the difference between worker and small business operator, the best known instance being P. De Lottinville, 'Joe Beef of Montreal: Working-Class Culture and the Tavern, 1869–1889,' *Labour/Le Travailleur*, 8/9 (1981–2). M. Bliss, 'The Protective Impulse: An Approach to the Social History of Oliver Mowat's Ontario,' in D. Swainson, ed., *Oliver Mowat's Ontario* (Toronto 1972), 186–7; M. Bliss, *Northern Enterprise: Five Centuries of Canadian Business* (Toronto 1987), 425; M. Bliss, *A Canadian Millionaire: The Life and Business Times of Sir Joseph Flavelle, Bart., 1858–1939* (Toronto 1978), 493; J.L. Santink, *Timothy Eaton and the Rise of His Department Store* (Toronto 1990), esp. 205–6. J.F. Wagner's *Brothers beyond the Sea: National Socialism in Canada* (Waterloo 1981), esp. 146–7, and R. Rudin's *In Whose Interest? Quebec's Caisses Populaires, 1900–1945* (Montreal and Kingston 1990) are also heavily influenced by the psychic 'resentment' school.

8 On conservative manipulation in Germany, H.-U. Wehler's 'Bismarck's Imperialism, 1862–1890,' *Past and Present*, 48 (1970), 119–55, provided the model, even though Wehler did not explicitly draw the *Mittelstand* into his analysis until *The German Empire, 1871–1918* (Leamington Spa 1985), 105–13 and 162–3. See also H.A. Winkler, 'From Social Protectionism to National Socialism: The German Small-Business Movement in Comparative Perspective,' *Journal of Modern History*, 48 (1976), 1–18; L. Kettenacker, 'Hitler's Impact on the Lower Middle Class,' in D. Welch, ed., *Nazi Propaganda: The Power and Its Limitations* (London 1983), 10–28. For France, see H. Lebovics, *The Alliance of Iron and Wheat in the Third French Republic, 1866–1914* (Baton Rouge 1988), and W.D. Irvine, *The Boulanger Affair Reconsidered* (New York 1989). Belgium is discussed in P. Delfosse, 'La Petite Bourgeoisie en crise et l'état: le cas belge,' *Le Mouvement sociale*, 114 (janvier-mars 1981), 85–104. The psychic trauma caused by military defeat and a growing socialist movement in Germany is emphasized by P. Fritzsche, *Rehearsals for Fascism: Populism and Political Mobilization in Weimar Germany* (New York 1990), while R. Soucy, *French Fascism: The First Wave, 1924–33* (New Haven 1986), emphasizes the fear of the left.

9 On voluntary associations, see R. Koshar, *Social Life, Local Politics and Nazism:*

Marburg, 1880–1935 (Chapel Hill 1986); on theatre: R.E. Sackett, *Popular Entertainment, Class and Politics in Munich, 1900–1923* (Cambridge 1982). P. Nord's *Paris Shopkeepers and the Politics of Resentment* (Princeton 1986) synthesizes the various interpretations, as does Fritzsche's, *Rehearsals for Fascism*. Both authors suggest that even though retailers were forsaken by the labour movement and seduced by conservatives, their own beliefs remained constant and derived from community and work traditions.

10 R.H. Wiebe, *The Search for Order* (New York 1967). On the communitarian basis of anti-monopoly protest, see M. Cassity, *Defending a Way of Life: An American Community in the Nineteenth Century* (Albany 1989), and S.L. Piott, *The Anti-Monopoly Persuasion: Popular Resistence to Big Business in the Midwest* (Westport 1985); L. Goodwin, *The Populist Moment* (New York 1978), chs. 7–8; R. Griffiths, *The Politics of Fear: Joseph McCarthy and the Senate* (Amherst 1987).

11 In praise of populism are N. Pollack, *The Humane Economy* (New Brunswick 1990); H.C. Boyte, H. Booth, and S. Max, *Citizen Action and the New American Populism* (Philadelphia 1986); R.N. Bellah, 'Populism and Individualism,' in H.C. Boyte and F. Riesman, eds., *The New Populism: The Politics of Empowerment* (Philadelphia 1986), 100–7.

12 On France's 'proprietary road,' see M. Levy-Leboyer, 'Innovation and Business Strategies in Nineteenth and Twentieth Century France,' in E. Carter II et al., eds., *Enterprise and Entrepreneurs in Nineteenth and Twentieth-Century France* (Baltimore 1976), 87–136; R. Roehl, 'French Industrialization: A Reconsideration,' *Explorations in Economic History*, 13 (July 1976), 233–81; P. O'Brien and C. Keyder, *Economic Growth in Britain and France 1780–1914: Two Paths to the Twentieth Century* (London 1978), esp. 146–79; and R. Aminzade, 'Reinterpreting Capitalist Industrialization: A Study of Nineteenth Century France,' *Social History*, 9 (1984), 329–50. For the contribution of small business to American economic development, see J. Attack, 'Firm Size and Industrial Structure in the United States during the Nineteenth Century,' *Journal of Economic History*, 46 (June 1986), 463–75, and 'Industrial Structure and the Emergence of the Modern Industrial Corporation,' *Explorations in Economic History*, 22 (January 1985), 29–52. Petty property in the late nineteenth century is vigorously defended by C. Sabel and J. Zeitlin in 'Historical Alternatives to Mass Production: Politics, Markets and Technology in Nineteenth Century Industrialization,' *Past and Present*, 108 (1985), 133–76, and P. Scranton in *Proprietary Capitalism: The Textile Manufacture at Philadelphia, 1800–1885* (Cambridge 1983); and in the twentieth by M. Piore and C. Sabel in *The Second Industrial Divide: Possibilities for Prosperity* (New York 1984).

13 K.-H. Schmidt, 'Bestimmungsgründe und Formen des Unternehmenswachtums im Handwerk seit der Mitte des 19. Jahrhunderts,' in W. Abel, ed.,

Handwerksgeschichte in neuer Sicht (Göttingen 1978), 241–84; W. Fischer, 'Die Rolle des Kleingewerbes im wirtschaftlichen Wachstumsprozess in Deutschland, 1850–1914,' in *Wirtchaft und Gesellschaft im Zeitalter der Industrialisierung* (Göttingen 1972), 338–48; M.L. Blim, *Made in Italy: Small-Scale Industrialization and Its Consequences* (New York 1990); T.R. Winpenny, *Bending Is Not Breaking: Adaptation and Persistence among 19th Century Lancaster Artisans* (Lanham 1990); S.E. Hirsch, 'From Artisan to Manufacturer: Industrialization and the Small Producer in Newark, 1830–1860,' in S. Bruchey, ed., *Small Business in American Life* (New York 1980), 80–99; J. Christiansen and P. Philips, 'The Transition from Outwork to Factory Production in the Boot and Shoe Industry, 1830–1880,' in S.M. Jacoby, ed., *Masters to Managers: Historical and Comparative Perspectives on American Employers* (New York 1991), 21–42; H. Livesay, 'Entrepreneurial Persistence through the Bureaucratic Age,' *Business History Review*, 51 (Winter 1977), 415–43.

14 Nord, *Paris Shopkeepers*, 82–99, 262–75, and 295–301.

15 T.K. McCraw, *Prophets of Regulation* (Cambridge 1984), 68–79; the quote is from 77.

16 McCraw, *Prophets of Regulation*, 101–9; the quotes are from 106. The finest treatment of small-business political agitation in Canada, M. Cox's 'The Transformation of Regulation: Private Property and the Problem of Government Control in Canada, 1919–1939' (PhD thesis, York University 1990), adopts a similar approach to retail lobbying (see especially ch. 3).

CHAPTER 1 Shopkeeping's Divided World

1 F. Bechhofer and B. Elliott, 'Petty Property: The Survival of a Moral Economy,' in Bechhofer and Elliott, eds., *The Petite Bourgeoisie* (London 1981), 183.

2 R. Berthoff, 'Independence and Enterprise: Small Business in the American Dream,' in S. Bruchey, ed., *Small Business in American Life* (New York 1980), 28–48; D. Burley, *A Particular Condition in Life: Self-Employment and Social Mobility in Mid-Victorian Brantford, Ontario* (Kingston and Montreal 1994); S. Thernstrom, *The Other Bostonians: Poverty and Progress in the American Metropolis, 1880–1970* (Cambridge 1973), ch. 3; T. Kessner, *The Golden Door: Italians and Jewish Immigrant Mobility in New York City, 1880–1915* (New York 1977), chs. 3 and 4; C. Griffen and S. Griffen, *Natives and Newcomers: The Ordering of Opportunity in Mid-Nineteenth Century Poughkeepsie* (Cambridge 1978), 58–68. K. Marx, *Selected Works*, vol. 1 (Moscow 1958), 334.

3 T.W. Acheson, *Saint John: The Making of a Colonial Urban Community* (Toronto 1985), 49; M.B. Katz, *The People of Hamilton, Canada West* (Cambridge 1975), 336; Burley, *A Particular Condition in Life*, 25; G. Darroch and L. Soltow, *Prop-*

erty and Inequality in Victorian Ontario (Toronto 1994), 81; G. Gervais, 'Le Commerce de détail au Canada, 1870–1880,' *Revue d'histoire de l'Amérique française*, 33:4 (1980), 529. Other calculations from the *Census of Canada, 1931*, vol. 10, part 1 (Ottawa 1934), general table 1; New Brunswick provincial table 16; Ontario provincial tables 18 and 28.

4 W.P.J. Millar, 'George P.M. Ball, a Rural Businessman in Upper Canada,' *Ontario History*, 66 (1974), 65–78; S.T. Fisher, *The Merchant Millers of the Humber Valley* (Toronto 1985); B. Wilson, *The Enterprises of Robert Hamilton: A Study of Wealth and Power in Early Upper Canada* (Ottawa 1983); G. Wynn, *Timber Colony: A Historical Geography of Early Nineteenth Century New Brunswick* (Toronto 1981), ch. 5; D. McCalla, 'Rural Credit and Rural Development in Upper Canada, 1790–1850,' in R. Hall, W. Westfall, and L. Sefton McDowell eds., *Patterns of the Past: Interpreting Ontario's History* (Toronto 1988), 41–3. Examples can be found in NAC, J. and S. McEachen papers; AO, D.B. Stevenson Papers, accounts; AO, William and Charles Tench Papers, William Tench's ledger; AO, Marshall N. Stephens & Sons, ledger and letterbooks.

5 Students of the social structure generally treat self-employment as a defining characteristic of the group (see note 2 above). Several important American studies have shown that a middle-class outlook and lifestyle emerged in the mid-nineteenth century, though they have not been concerned with occupational identification. See S.M. Blumin, *The Emergence of the Middle Class: Social Experience in the American City, 1760–1900* (Cambridge 1989), esp. ch. 5; M. Ryan, *Cradle of the Middle Class: The Family in Oneida County* (Cambridge 1981); P.E. Johnson, *A Shopkeeper's Millennium: Society and Revivals in Rochester New York* (New York 1978).

6 AO, William and Charles Tench Papers, daybook for 1852–80; for a similar example from another frontier, see PABC, William Harrison Papers, daybook for 1894–1911.

7 Credit has received a bad press. Among the more sympathetic treatments are G. Carson, *The Old Country Store* (New York 1954), ch. 2; T.D. Clark, *Pills, Petticoats, and Plows: The Southern Country Store* (Norman 1964), ch. 18; L. Atherton, *The Southern Country Store* (Baton Rouge 1949), 47–62; W.T. Baxter, 'Accounting in Colonial Africa,' in A.C. Littleton and B.S. Yamey, eds., *Studies in the History of Accounting* (London 1956), 272–3; D. McCalla, 'Rural Credit and Rural Development,' 43–51; and S. Cadigan. *Hope and Deception in Conception Bay: Merchant-Settler Relations in Newfoundland, 1785–1855* (Toronto 1995). For a selection of articles dealing with the inequities of credit, see R. Ommer, ed., *Merchant Credit & Labour Strategies in Historical Perspective* (Fredericton 1990), and for a good study of the region where credit practices were most oppressive, see S. Hahn, *The Roots of Southern Populism* (New York

1983), 70–7 and ch. 5. Company stores might be seen as similar institutions, though questions are emerging as to how effectively employers controlled their workers' consumption; see P.V. Fishback, 'Did Coal Miners "Owe Their Souls to the Company Store": Theory and Evidence from the Early 1900s,' *Journal of Economic History*, 46:4 (December 1986), 1011–29. Marxist historians have often seen credit as an instrument in the capitalist transformation of the countryside. A good review of this approach to credit is M. Merrill, 'Cash Is Good to Eat: Self-Sufficiency and Exchange in the Rural Economy of the United States,' *Radical History Review*, 3 (1977), 42–71. Figures calculated from rural and small-town account books: AO, G. Stanley, daybook, 1901–3; WCA, Howe, Skelton & Co., journal for 1904–7; WCA, Simon Armstrong, journal 1868–79; WCA, J. McKinnon, daybook, 1888–95; WCA, C.A. Bignell, daybook.

8 *Dry Goods Review*, 6:2 (February 1896); T.M. Doerflinger, 'Commercial Specialization in Philadelphia's Merchant Community,' *Business History Review*, 57:1 (1983), 40; D. McCalla, *The Upper Canadian Trade, 1834–1872: A Study of the Buchanans' Business* (Toronto 1979), 28–40, 150–6; G. Bevin, 'Aperçu sur le commerce et le crédit à Québec, 1820–1830,' *Revue d'histoire de l'Amérique française*, 36:4 (mars 1983), 527–52; Clark, *Pills, Petticoats*, 34–7. An interesting reminiscence of marketing practices in the 1870s can be found in D. Rome, ed., *On Sunday Observance, 1906*, in *Canadian Jewish Archives*, 14 (Montreal 1979), 30–1.

9 B. Forster, 'Finding the Right Size: Markets and Competition in Mid- and Late-Nineteenth Century Ontario,' in Hall, ed., *Patterns of the Past*, 150–73. The impact of the railways on urban development has been most closely studied by western Canadians: M. Foran, 'The CPR and the Urban West, 1881–1930,' in H. Dempsey, ed., *The CPR West* (Vancouver 1984), 89–105; R.A.J. MacDonald, 'Victoria, Vancouver and the Economic Development of British Columbia, 1886–1914,' in P. Ward and R.A.J. MacDonald, eds., *British Columbia: Historical Readings* (Vancouver 1981), 369–95; J.A. Eagle, *The Canadian Pacific Railway and the Development of Western Canada* (Montreal and Kingston 1989), ch. 9; D. Kerr, 'Wholesale Trade on the Canadian Plains in the Late Nineteenth Century: Winnipeg and Its Competition,' in H. Palmer, ed., *The Settlement of the West* (Calgary 1977), 130–52.

10 P. Voisey, *Vulcan: The Making of a Prairie Community* (Toronto 1988), esp. 23–8; R. Loewen, *Family, Church and Market: A Mennonite Community in the Old and the New Worlds, 1850–1930* (Toronto 1993), 153–8 and 208–10; L. Atherton, *Main Street on the Middle Border* (Bloomington 1954), 222–33; D. Boorstin, *The Americans: The Democratic Experience* (New York 1973), 118–29.

11 *Canadian Grocer*, 3:41 (11 October 1889); *Trader*, 21:5 (January 1900); *Dry Goods*

Review, 6:3 (March 1896); *Canadian Pharmaceutical Journal*, 33:2 (September 1899); *Hardware and Metal*, 15:2 (February 1907). Between druggists and grocers the struggles continued: see *Le Devoir*, 3 février 1931, and *Canadian Pharmaceutical Journal*, 63:13 (1 March 1930). For Fryer case, see PAA, Attorney General's Department, Alberta Provincial Police, Annual Report of 'C' Division, 1925; also Beisecker Historical Society, *Beiseker's Golden Heritage* (Calgary 1977), 13 and 205.

12 *Canadian Grocer*, 3:29 (19 July 1889), 3:34 (23 August 1889), and 3:41 (11 October 1889).

13 *Census of Canada, 1871*, vol. 5 (Ottawa 1874), table 1; I. Drummond, *Progress without Planning: The Economic History of Ontario from Confederation to the Second World War* (Toronto 1987), 300–8; Gervais, 'Le commerce de détail,' 531; Canada, *Census of Canada, 1921*, vol. 4 (Ottawa 1924), table 2.

14 Gervais, 'Le Commerce de détail,' 529–31; Drummond, *Progress without Planning*, 300–1; also *Census of Canada, 1921*, vol. 4, 28–9, and *Census of Canada, 1931*, vol. 10, table 6A, 44–55; *Census of Canada, 1941*, vol. 10 (Ottawa 1944), table 9, 258–65.

15 *BC Retailer*, 16:7 (March 1924).

16 That it was size, rather than type, of enterprise which disturbed independent merchants explains why retailers could protest as late as the 1920s that there were three 'trade destabilizing' big stores in Toronto – Eaton's, Simpson's, and Murray-Kay's – even though the last was not, strictly speaking, a department store (Canada, Special Committee on Agricultural Conditions, *Proceedings* [Ottawa 1923], 1563). The best business studies of the department stores are H. Pasdermadjian, *The Department Store: Its Origin, Evolution and Economics* (London 1954), and R.M. Hower, *A History of Macy's of New York, 1858–1919* (Cambridge 1943). Canadian studies include J.L. Santink, *Timothy Eaton and the Rise of His Department Store* (Toronto 1990), and D. Harker, *The Woodwards* (Vancouver 1976).

17 *Canadian Grocer*, 3:25 (21 June 1889), 3:37 (13 September 1889), 3:40 (4 October 1889), 3:34 (23 August 1889), 4:2 (10 January 1890), 4:11 (14 March 1890), 4:27 (4 July 1890); *Dry Goods Review*, 7:8 (August 1897); *Shoe and Leather Journal*, 31:3 (1 February 1918); ORHA, Retail Hardware and Stove Dealers' Association, Minutes, 1905–22.

18 Other pharmacy acts modelled on Ontario's were passed in Quebec (1879), Manitoba (1894), Nova Scotia (1911), Saskatchewan (1913), Alberta (1914), New Brunswick (1922), British Columbia (1944), and PEI (1950). In provinces that did not have colleges, a four-year apprenticeship was followed by an examination administered by the Pharmaceutical Association. See A. Raison, ed., *A Brief History of Pharmacy in Canada* (Toronto 1968); A.M. Martin, *Phar-*

macy in Canada (Vancouver 1955); *Canadian Grocer*, 19:5 (3 February 1905); *Le Prix courant*, 38:34 (21 août 1925); *Retailer*, 13:6 (February 1922). For hairdressers and barbers, see SAB, Saskatchewan Retail Merchants' Association Papers, 166, Minutes of the Hairdressers' Trade Section Meeting, 18 May 1937, and H. Wright to W.L. McQuarrie, 25 March 1937. AO, Department of Labour, Minister's Office, 1935, contains a box of petitions from barbers in the Industrial Standards Act files. Watch repairmen were found in ANQ, Ministre de l'industrie et de commerce, box 62, J.E. Cornellier à M. Duplessis, 17 decembre 1937.

19 *Canadian Grocer*, 3:29 (19 July 1889) and 14:39 (28 September 1900).

20 Information derived from a directory-based study of longevity and mobility in the Toronto grocery business. For this study a 10 per cent sample of city grocers was chosen from *Might's Toronto Directories* at five-year intervals beginning in 1905 (around 1,100 businesses). Only individuals who had not appeared in the previously consulted directory were chosen for inclusion in the sample. The opening date of the business was then traced from the directories, as well as its disappearance date. The previous occupation of the owner was also sought, and any movement in store location was noted. Each business was then traced through R.G. Dun & Co., *Mercantile Agency Reference Books*, to determine the store's capitalization and how it changed over time. A similar study was made of Kitchener (some 150 businesses), and more limited studies for 1910, 1919, and 1928 were made for Windsor, St Catharines, London, and Brantford (300 businesses altogether).

21 Because an optimum store location could be on a poorer street adjoining a good area, I divided the city into broad areas, and those stores falling in the border zone (two blocks each way) were counted separately and then divided equally among the zones they bordered. The other difficulty is that many stores, especially on streets such as Queen and Parliament, targeted the passing trade, with the result that the 'below average' category is unquestionably inflated.

22 P.G. Goheen, *Victorian Toronto, 1850–1900* (Chicago 1970); on the theory see I. Katznelson, *City Trenches: Urban Politics and the Patterning of Class in the United States* (Chicago 1981), ch. 1.

23 The small shop's sale of liquor was a particular target: see *Canadian Pharmaceutical Journal*, 33:3 (October 1899); *Canadian Grocer*, 11:8 (19 February 1897).

24 *Canadian Grocer*, 14:13 (30 March 1900); *Retail Merchants' Journal*, 2:10 (October 1904).

25 For an alternate view, see C.P. Hosgood, 'A "Brave and Daring Folk"?: Shopkeepers and Trade Associational Life in Victorian and Edwardian England,' *Journal of Social History*, 25:2 (1992), 287–9.

26 Calculated from *Census of Canada, 1941*, vol. 7, table 16.
27 AO, RG 22, Supreme Court of Ontario, Bankruptcy Office; see for example, 24:52, R.G. Berman and H.W. Sands file, 5 February 1925, and 24:1182, Ida E. Caplan file, examination, 3 September 1924. M.W. Gregg, 'The Housing Problem in a City Block' (MA thesis, University of Toronto 1916), 111, makes reference to the sale of poultry.
28 UTL, Lord's Day Alliance Papers, box 13, J. Warden to A.I. Terryberry, 4 September 1925; E. Hughes, *French Canada in Transition* (Chicago 1971), 79.
29 The bankruptcy court archive contains the case records of individuals filing for bankruptcy in Ontario. Each file contains various legal documents – list of creditors, notices of motion, petitions, orders, and affidavits – as well as a statement of affairs filled out by the bankrupt. This latter document proved most generally valuable since it contained information on the bankrupt's previous occupation, starting capital, date of opening, assets and liabilities, bookkeeping practices, and explanation for failure. In a minority of cases – about one in thirty – the files also contained a transcript of the court hearing. All of the retailers declaring bankruptcy in 1924, 1928, 1932, and 1937 were studied, and thirty-three variables were derived from the information in their files. This information forms the basis of many of the figures presented in this book. For simplicity, I have noted only those calculations where the source is not clear in the text; where references to individuals are made, case files are cited.
30 For shopkeepers, see C. Hall, *White, Male and Middle Class: Explorations in Feminism and History* (New York 1992), 108–23.
31 *Census of Canada, 1931*, vol. 7 (Ottawa 1934), tables 44 and 49.
32 DBS, *Origin, Birthplace, Nationality and Language of the People: A Census Study* (Ottawa 1929), 204–5; calculated from *Census of Canada, 1931*, vol. 7, table 49. The one partial exception to this rule can be found among Alberta's small Chinese population, more than half of which was engaged in retailing. But even here the Chinese tended to cluster, forming a community of retailers linked closely to the larger BC settlement.
33 *Census of Canada, 1911*, vol. 7 (Ottawa 1914), table 4; *Census of Canada, 1931*, vol. 7, tables, 44, 46, and 49; *Census of Canada, 1941*, vol. 7, tables 11–12 and 26. *Census of Canada, 1921*, vol. 1, table 2; *Census of Canada, 1931*, vol. 7, table 53; *Census of Canada, 1941*, vol. 7, table 5.
34 H.P. Chudacoff, 'A New Look at Ethnic Neighbourhoods: Residential Dispersion and the Concept of Visibility in a Medium-Sized City,' *Journal of American History*, 60 (1973), 76–93; K. Conzen, 'Immigrants, Immigrant Neighbourhoods and Ethnic Identity: Historical Issues,' *Journal of American History*, 66 (1979), 603–15; O. Zunz, *The Changing Face of Inequality: Urbaniza-*

tion, Industrial Development and Immigrants in Detroit, 1880–1930 (Chicago
1982), 78–9; D. Ward, *Poverty, Ethnicity and the American City, 1840–1925*
(Cambridge 1989), 182–9; J. Zucchi, 'Italian Hometown Settlements and the
Development of an Italian Community in Toronto, 1875–1935,' in R.F. Har-
ney, ed., *Gathering Places: Peoples and Neighbourhoods of Toronto, 1834–1945*
(Toronto 1985), 121–46; K. Anderson, *Vancouver s Chinatown: Racial Discourse
in Canada, 1875–1980* (Montreal & Kingston 1991), 75–82; R.B. Aiken, *Montreal
Chinese Property Ownership and Occupational Change, 1881–1981* (New York
1989), 83, 122–3, 135–40.

35 H.A. Gibbard, 'The Means and Modes of Living of European Immigrants in
Montreal' (MA thesis, McGill University 1934), 49–59; Gregg, 'The Housing
Problem in a City Block,' 71–2; D. Brandino, 'The Italians of Hamilton' (MA
thesis, University of Western Ontario 1977), 30–2.

36 MHSO, interview with the Meschino brothers, 22 August 1978. In this
respect, the wholesalers operated as middlemen not only in the distribution
system but also in the ethnic structure. The Italian Trading Company, for
example, bought from seventeen different jobbers of whom only three were
Italian; of its retail customers, however, 80 per cent were Italians; see SCO,
Bankruptcy Office, Italian Trading Company Bankruptcy File, 24:426.

37 B. Wong, *Patronage, Brokerage, Entrepreneurship and the Chinese Community of
New York* (New York 1988), 86–109 and 131–5; P. Yee, 'Business Devices in
Two Worlds: The Chinese in Early Vancouver,' *BC Studies*, 62 (summer 1984),
44–67; E. Bonacich and J. Modell, *The Economic Basis of Ethnic Solidarity: Small
Business in the Japanese American Community* (Berkeley 1980), 56–7; I. Light,
Ethnic Enterprise in America (Berkeley 1972), ch. 2.

38 MHSO, interview with M. Sule, 9 December 1976; Light, *Ethnic Enterprise*, 92
and 69.

39 This was not true of all communities since 'improvement' is to a large extent
culturally defined. Some groups chose not to enter retailing in proportionate
numbers, possibly because of traditional antipathies or else because other
avenues were more open. Thus, while Sicilians might have gone into fruit
retailing in large numbers, the Friulani were more likely to open construction
businesses. See J. Zucchi, 'Italians in Toronto: Development of a National
Identity, 1875–1935' (PhD Thesis, University of Toronto 1983), 128–57. Trans-
planted value structures probably also explain the prominence of Jews and
Chinese in retailing since both were traditional 'middlemen minorities'; see
E. Bonacich, 'A Theory of Middleman Minorities,' *American Sociological
Review*, 38 (1973), 583–94.

40 J. Zucchi traces this movement among Termini fruit sellers in Toronto in
'Occupations, Enterprise and the Migration Chain: The Fruit Traders from

Termini Imerese in Toronto, 1900–1930,' *Studi Emigrazione*, 22:77 (marzo 1985), 72–3. See also Aiken, *Montreal Chinese*, 81–2 and 117.

41 VCA, Office of the City Clerk's Papers, box 206, file 8, Petitions to BC Coast Vegetable Marketing Board, 1936. A study undertaken in Los Angeles in the same year found that 34 per cent of the customers patronizing Japanese food stores were non-Japanese. This was a dramatic increase from the 9 per cent figure for 1915; see C.C. Wong, 'The Continuity of Chinese Grocers in Southern California,' *Journal of Ethnic Studies*, 8:2 (Summer 1980), 71. See also MHSO, interview with the Meschino brothers; Zucchi, 'Occupations, Enterprise,' 72–4; G. Gold, 'A Tale of Two Communities: The Growth and Decline of Small-Town Jewish Communities in Northern Ontario and Southwestern Louisiana,' in M. Rischin, ed., *The Jews of North America* (Detroit 1987), 230–1.

42 V.A. Mah, 'The Bachelor Society: A Look at Toronto's Early Chinese Community from 1878 to 1924' (unpublished research paper, University of Toronto 1978), 21–2; E.K. Francis, *In Search of Utopia: The Mennonites in Manitoba* (Altona 1955), 154–6; L. Schmier, 'For Him the "Schwartzers" Couldn't Do Enough: A Jewish Peddler and His Black Customers Look at Each Other,' *American Jewish History*, 73:1 (September 1983), 44.

43 *BC Retailer*, 12:12 (August 1921); *Canadian Grocer*, 29:13 (26 March 1915); *Le Miroir*, 4:36 (25 décembre 1932); Hughes, *French Canada in Transition*, 218. For a discussion of anti-Oriental feeling among merchants, see P. Roy, 'Protecting their Pocketbooks and Preserving their Race: White Merchants and Oriental Competition,' in A.R. McCormack and I. Macpherson, eds., *Cities in the West* (Ottawa 1975), 116–38; Anderson, *Vancouver's Chinatown*, 118–22. For retail anti-Semitism in Quebec, see I. Abella, 'Antisemitism in Canada in the Interwar Years,' in Rischin, *The Jews of North America*, 238–9; L.-R. Betcherman, *The Swastika and the Maple Leaf* (Toronto 1975), 4, 7, 23, and 33; M. Brown, *Jew or Juif: Jews, French Canadians and Anglo Canadians* (Philadelphia 1987), 182–3; J. Langlais and D. Rome, *Jews and French Quebecers: Two Hundred Years of Shared History* (Waterloo 1991), 96–100; and P. Anctil, *Le Rendez-vous manqué: Les Juifs de Montréal face au Québec de l'entre-deux-guerres* (Montreal 1988), 244–7.

44 SCO, Bankruptcy Office, 28:595, Sam Sussman file, examination of debtor, 7 May 1929; examination of Sam Lipovitch, 8 May 1929; examination of Mrs. A. French, 8 May 1928; ibid., 24:868, Joseph Surface file, report of trustee, 5 January 1925. When Joseph Alessandro's fruit business declared bankruptcy in early 1928, he had twenty-one suppliers, none of whom were Italian. His books revealed, however, that he had cleared all his outstanding debts to fellow Italians in December 1927; see ibid., 28:3, Joseph Alessandro file, 28:3, examination of debtor, 10 April 1928.

45 These accusations were, of course, completely unfair, since English and
French Canadians did exactly the same things. Of the thirty different
employees hired between 1891 and 1918 by the British-Canadian shopkeeper
Lawrence Yeoman whose wage records have survived, five were his children
and all but two of the rest were identifiably Anglo-Saxon. Even big companies such as Eaton's practised discriminatory hiring well into the 1930s: an
internal study of Eaton's employees found that of its 11,000 Toronto workers,
94 per cent were either Canadian-born or British immigrants and over 80 per
cent were Anglican, Presbyterian, or United Church members. By way of
comparison, 61 per cent of Toronto's population belonged to one of the three
main Protestant denominations in 1938. The selectivity employed in hiring is
made even clearer by the fact that of Eaton's non-Canadian, non-British staff,
only 226 out of 562 worked in sales, the rest being employed in the factories;
the store and mail order, however, employed 81 per cent of the total number
of workers. See WCA, Lawrence Yeoman's Drug Store Records, box 3, sales
and expense ledgers, 1891–1907 and 1908–18; AO, T. Eaton Co. Ltd., 181–1,
employee statistics, 11 October 1938.

46 *Canadian Grocer*, 14:32 (10 August 1900) and 29:15 (9 April 1915); UTL, Lord's
Day Alliance Papers, box 12, Secretary's Report on Quebec and the Maritimes, 1921–22; box 17, G.G. Webber to R.H. Pooley, 27 April 1931.

47 At least some shopkeepers were quite crass in their acceptance of this fact:
Joseph Crowder, the president of the BC Retail Merchants' Association, for
example, cautioned Vancouver grocers against agitating on purely competitive grounds. If Chinese traders were 'attacked solely from a retail grocers'
point of view,' he explained, 'the Association [would be] laying itself open to
severe criticism.' It was, after all, 'the public who buy from the Chinese grocer,' and they did so for a reason. Instead, advised the RMA president, grocers should concentrate on matters that were more clearly 'racial' than
'commercial' since these questions could be expected to more clearly attract
the sympathies of consumers. *BC Retailer*, 12:12 (August 1921).

48 *Canadian Grocer*, 16:31 (7 January 1901). The irony, of course, is that social
critics generally see shopping as a symbol of the consumer's imprisonment
in a world of goods – of the erosion of restraint and the commercialization of
self. To retailers, however, the shopper had the power, and the merchandisers had to outbid each other in image and style and in price to attract his or
her custom. This idea is explored in two marvellous books: E.S. Abelson's
*When Ladies Go A-thieving: Middle Class Shoplifters and the Victorian Department
Store* (New York 1989) and G. Reekie's *Temptations: Sex, Selling and the Department Store* (St Leonards 1993).

49 Hamilton information derived from a database prepared from city directo-

ries and R.G. Dun credit manuals by E. Adolphe. I am grateful to Ms Adolphe for providing me access to her fine research. See also P.A. Baskerville, 'She Has Already Hinted at "Board": Enterprising Urban Women in British Columbia, 1863–1896,' *Histoire sociale/Social History*, 26:52 (novembre 1993), 218–19; B. Bradbury, *Working Families: Age, Gender and Daily Survival in Industrializing Montreal* (Toronto 1993), 198 and 245–6.

50 *Census of Canada, 1911*, vol. 4, table 44; *Census of Canada, 1931*, vol. 10, table 1A.

51 Derived from E. Adolphe's database of female entrepreneurship in Hamilton.

52 *Census of Canada, 1911*, vol. 4, table 44; *Census of Canada, 1931*, vol. 10, table 1A.

53 SCO, Bankruptcy Office, 24:1182, Ida Caplan file, examination of Ida Caplan, 3 September 1924, and examination of David Caplan, 3 September 1924.

54 MHSO, interview with H. Sule; information from *Might's Toronto Directories*, 1910–39, and from Toronto city assessment rolls, 1910–39; also SCO, Bankruptcy Office, 24:862, Ida Stone file, examination, 9 November 1924.

55 *Census of Canada, 1941*, vol. 7, table 5; *Census of Canada, 1931*, vol. 10, table 1A.

56 Information based on *Might's Toronto Directories*, 1919–39, and R.G. Dun & Co.'s *Mercantile Agency Reference Books*, also for 1919–39; *Shoe and Leather Journal*, 33:13 (1 July 1920); *Furniture World*, 9:9 (September 1919). The *Canadian Grocer*'s attitude is best reflected in its highly misogynous joke section; for an interpretation of this strand of humour, see J. Snell, 'Marriage Humour and its Social Functions, 1900–1939,' *Atlantis*, spring 1986, 70–85. It is worth noting that the thirteen women who made it onto the RMA's grocers' list were all exceptional in that they were managing big stores; see VCA, Office of the City Clerk's Papers, box 195, file 6, petition re early closing, November 1934.

57 J. Benson, *Penny Capitalism: A study of Nineteenth Century Working Class Entrepreneurs* (Dublin 1983), ch. 10; T. Vigne and A. Howkins, 'The Small Shopkeeper in Industrial and Market Towns,' in G. Crossick, ed., *The Lower Middle Class in Britain* (London 1977), 184–210. Information on individual retailers is derived from Toronto city assessments and *Might's Toronto Directories*.

CHAPTER 2 The Folklore of Retailing

1 *Drug Merchandising*, 3:4 (25 January 1923); *Retail Merchants' Journal*, 4:4 (April 1906) and 2:2 (March 1904).

2 A. Mayer, 'The Lower Middle Class as Historical Problem,' *Journal of Modern History*, 47:3 (September 1975), 423–5 and 436.

3 H.A. Winkler, 'From Social Protectionism to National Socialism: The German

Small-Business Movement in Comparative Perspective,' *Journal of Modern History*, 48 (1976), 15; S. Volkov, *The Rise of Popular Anti-modernism in Germany: The Urban Master Artisans, 1873–1896* (Princeton 1978); H.-G. Haupt, 'The Petite Bourgeoisie in France, 1850–1914: In Search of the Juste Milieu?' in G. Crossick and H.-G. Haupt, eds., *Shopkeepers and Master Artisans in Nineteenth Century Europe* (London 1984), 100 and 112. The 'idealist' approach is also followed by R. Gellately, *The Politics of Economic Despair: Shopkeepers and German Politics, 1890–1914* (London 1974); F. Bechhofer and B. Elliott, 'Petty Property: The Survival of a Moral Economy,' in Bechhofer and Elliott, eds., *The Petite Bourgeoisie* (London 1981), 182–200; H.-G. Haupt, 'La Petite Enterprise et la politique en Europe au XIXe siècle,' *Le Mouvement social*, 114 (1981), 3–10; M. Winstanley, *The Shopkeeper's World, 1830–1914* (Manchester 1983); G. Crossick, 'The Petite Bourgeoisie in Nineteenth Century Britain,' in Crossick and Haupt, *Shopkeepers and Master Artisans*, 80–81; and S.M. Zdatny, *The Politics of Survival: Artisans in Twentieth Century France* (Oxford 1990), 181–2. C.P. Hosgood has amended this perspective in an imaginative way by emphasizing the existence of 'old' and 'new' cultures that for a time coexisted, creating the possibility of an ideological rift within retailing; see 'A "Brave and Daring Folk"? Shopkeepers and Trade Associational Life in Victorian and Edwardian England,' *Journal of Social History*, 24 (1992), 285 and 293.

4 On language and speech, T. Hawkes, *Structuralism and Semiotics* (Berkeley 1977), presents the best introduction. My own thinking on language and speech has been greatly influenced by the hermeneutics of P. Ricoeur, esp. part 1 of *The Conflict of Interpretations* (Evanston, 1974); the influence of C. Lévi-Strauss, especially *Structural Anthropology* (New York 1967), will probably also be detected. T. De Lauretis's *Alice Doesn't: Feminism, Semiotics, Cinema* (Bloomington 1984) erupts with good and inspiring ideas; B. Martin in 'Lesbian Identity, Autobiographical Difference' in B. Brodski and C. Schenk, eds., *Life/Lines: Theorizing Women's Autobiography* (New York, 1988), 77–103, comes to grips with problems of a similar kind and offers insight into their interpretive resolution. Thirty years ago H. Zeigler reached similar conclusions concerning small-business politics in postwar America, without defining them the same way. Zeigler suggested that while independent entrepreneurs lacked 'common interests,' they shared 'common attitudes,' and he worked through the implications of that distinction for political mobilization in his fine study *The Politics of Small Business* (Washington 1961).

5 M.A. Clawson, *Constructing Brotherhood: Class, Gender and Fraternalism* (Princeton 1989), 10 and 251–3.

6 F. Bechhofer, B. Elliott, and M. Rushford, 'The Market Situation of Small Shopkeepers,' *Scottish Journal of Political Economy*, 18 (1971), 161–80; F. Bech-

hofer, B. Elliott, M. Rushford, and R. Bland, 'Small Shopkeepers: Matters of Money and Meaning,' *Sociological Review*, 22:4 (1974), 465–82; R.S. Pepper, *Pressure Groups among Small Business Men* (New York 1973), 7–11; R. Robertson, 'The Small Business Ethic in America,' in D. Carson, ed., *The Vital Majority: Small Business in the American Economy* (Washington 1973), 21–34; R. Berthoff, 'Independence and Enterprise: Small Business in the American Dream,' in S. Bruchey, ed., *Small Business in American Life* (New York 1980), 28–48; M.G. Blackford, *A History of Small Business in America* (New York 1991), 101–3.

7 J. Savary, *Le Parfait Negoçiant* (Paris 1675), 1; R. Rolt, *A New Dictionary of Trade and Commerce* (London 1755), entry for 'Merchant'; D. Defoe, *The Complete English Tradesman* [1725], in *The Novels and Miscellaneous Works of Daniel Defoe*, Vol. 17 (Oxford 1841), 275; B. Franklin, 'Advice to a Young Tradesman, Written by an Old One' (1748), in L.W. Labaree, ed., *The Papers of Benjamin Franklin*, vol. 3 (New Haven 1961), 306; W. Temple, 'A Vindication of Commerce and the Arts' (1758), in J.R. McCulloch, ed., *A Select Collection of Scarce and Valuable Tracts on Commerce* (New York 1966), 545.

8 B.L. Anderson, 'Money and the Structure of Credit in the Eighteenth Century,' *Business History*, 12:2 (1970), 87–100; S. Bruchey, 'Success and Failure Factors: American Merchants in Foreign Trade in the Eighteenth and Nineteenth Centuries,' *Business History Review*, 32 (1958), 272–92; D. Miquelon, 'Havy and Lefebvre of Quebec: A Case Study of Metropolitan Participation in Canadian Trade, 1730–1760,' *Canadian Historical Review*, 56 (1975), 1–24; G. Bevin, 'Aperçu sur le commerce et le crédit à Québec, 1820–1830,' *Revue de l'histoire de l'Amérique française*, 36:4 (mars 1983), 541–4; D. McCalla, *The Upper Canada Trade, 1834–1872: A Study of the Buchanans' Business* (Toronto 1979); J.F. Bosher, *The Canada Merchants, 1713–1763* (Oxford 1987), 30–2.

9 J.E. Crowley, *This Sheba, Self: The Conceptualization of Economic Life in Eighteenth-Century America* (Baltimore 1974); R.J. Morris, 'Samuel Smiles and the Genesis of Self-Help: The Retreat to a Petit-Bourgeois Utopia,' *Historical Journal*, 24 (1981), 89–109. On the radical turn in artisanal proprietary thought, see W.H. Sewell Jr, 'Artisans, Factory Workers and the Formation of the French Working Class, 1789–1848,' in I. Katznelson and A.R. Zolberg, eds., *Working Class Formation* (Princeton 1986), 45–69; J. Breuilly, 'Artisan Economy, Artisan Politics, Artisan Ideology: The Artisan Contribution to the Nineteenth Century Labour Movement,' in C. Elmsley and J. Walvin, eds., *Artisans, Peasants and Proletarians* (London 1985), 187–225; I. Prothero, *Artisans and Politics in Early Nineteenth Century London: John Gast and His Times* (Baton Rouge 1979); C. Johnson, 'Economic Change and Artisan Discontent: The Tailor's History, 1800–1848,' in R. Price, ed., *Revolution and Reaction* (New York 1975), 87–114.

10 *Retail Merchants' Journal,* 5:3 (March 1907) and 4:3 (March 1906).

11 *Canadian Grocer,* 29:6 (5 February 1915) and 29:42 (15 October 1915).

12 Canada, Senate, Special Committee on Unemployment Insurance, *Minutes of Proceedings and Evidence* (Ottawa 1934), D-6; *Canadian Grocer,* 33:5 (30 January 1919) and 42:15 (20 July 1928). J.V. McAree, in his sentimental recollection of retail life before the First World War, *Cabbagetown Store* (Toronto 1953), continuously harps on the fact the family 'store was a small one,' but also lets slip that its owner (his uncle John) employed three store clerks, owned around twelve rental properties in downtown Toronto, and numbered among his immediate family a minister of finance (Sir Thomas White), a mayor of Toronto, and a speaker of the provincial Legislature.

13 *Furniture World and the Undertaker,* 9:9 (September 1919); Canada, Special Committee on Price Spreads and Mass Buying, *Proceedings and Evidence,* vol. 1 (Ottawa 1935), 326; *Canadian Grocer,* 22:21 (22 May 1908); *Maritime Merchant,* 40:19 (17 March 1933).

14 *Dry Goods Review,* 14:3 (March 1904); *Canadian Grocer,* 23:23 (4 June 1915).

15 *Canadian Grocer,* 27:4 (24 January 1913) and 23:39 (24 September 1909); *Dry Goods Review,* 14:1 (January 1904); *Shoe and Leather Journal,* 24:6 (June 1910) and 31:7 (1 September 1918).

16 *Le Prix courant,* 39:3 (15 janvier 1926); *Shoe and Leather Journal,* 26:2 (5 January 1912); *Canadian Grocer,* 28:34 (21 August 1914). Druggists were so much inclined to dispense their professional advice that the Ontario Medical Council felt the need to scare them off by having a group of them charged with violating the Medical Act for diagnosing their customers' complaints and recommending curatives, see *Canadian Pharmaceutical Journal,* 34:7 (February 1901).

17 *Canadian Grocer,* 45:1 (2 January 1931), 33:13 (28 March 1919), and 14:39 (28 September 1900); McAree, *Cabbagetown Store,* 9–12.

18 J.M. Bliss, *A Living Profit* (Toronto 1974), 15–31; *Retail Merchants' Journal,* 1:4 (20 October 1903); *Furniture World and the Undertaker,* 1:5 (January 1912); *Canadian Grocer,* 29:3 (22 January 1915); *Drug Merchandising,* 6:20 (30 September 1925); *Le Prix courant,* 33:27 (2 juillet 1920); *Canadian Pharmaceutical Journal,* 53:10 (May 1920).

19 *Retailer,* 4:7 (September 1918); *Furniture World and the Undertaker,* 10:4 (April 1920); *BC Retailer,* 16:7 (March 1924).

20 *Canadian Grocer,* 16:17 (25 April 1902) and 18:46 (11 November 1904).

21 This approach to identification leans heavily on the early work of Peter Berger; see *An Invitation to Sociology* (Garden City, 1963); with H. Kellner, 'Marriage and the Construction of Reality,' *Diogenes,* 46 (1963), 5–22; with T. Luckman, *The Social Construction of Reality* (London, 1991); and with S. Pull-

berg, 'Reification and the Sociological Critique of Consciousness,' *History and Theory*, 4 (1965), 197–211. There is also profit in returning to the source: G. Mead, *Mind, Self and Society* (Chicago 1934). For a historian's introduction to identity theories, see P. Gleason, 'Identifying Identity: A Semantic History,' *Journal of American History*, 70 (1983), 910–31.

22 AO, RG 22, Supreme Court of Ontario, Bankruptcy Office, 32:507, W. George file, examination of debtor, 7 June 1932; 32:803, F. and H. Thompson file; 32:534, N. Cremer file; examination of debtor, 6 September 1932; 32:535, A. Ponzo file; 32:949, Felix Lavergne File; 32:408, W.F. Foster file; 32:417, S. Hertzman file; examination of debtor, 22 July 1932; 24:1409, R. Michael file, examination of debtor, 3 March 1925.

23 SCO, Bankruptcy Office, 28:82, Leo Danson file, examination of debtor, 20 March 1928; 24:1182, Ida Caplan file, examination of Sydney Caplan, 21 August 1924.

24 SCO, Bankruptcy Office, 24:803, M. Raport file, examination of debtor, 1 November 1923; 24:1182, I. Caplan file, examination of debtor, 21 August 1924; 24:479, J. Barter file, examination of debtor, 11 April 1923.

25 SCO, Bankruptcy Office, 28:364, S. Cohen file, examination of debtor, 17 March 1930; 32:819, M. and P. Friedman file, examination of M. Friedman, 7 January 1933.

26 SCO, Bankruptcy Office, 28:208, W. Brooks file; 28:82, L. Danson file, examination of debtor, 20 March 1928; 37:199, C.A. Heffernan file; 24:337, M. Hodgins File.

27 L. Eldersveld Murphy, 'Business Ladies: Midwestern Women and Enterprise, 1850–1880,' *Journal of Women's History*, 3:1 (1991), 77–80; D. Dodd makes the same point in 'Women in Advertising: The Role of Canadian Women in the Promotion of Domestic Electrical Technology in the Interwar Period,' in M. Gosztony Ainley, ed., *Despite the Odds: Essays on Canadian Women and Science* (Montreal 1990), 148–9.

28 *Furniture World*, 8:4 (April 1918); *Canadian Grocer*, 16:17 (25 April 1902); NAC, RG 33/18, vol. 5, R.A. Hamilton, 'My Experience as a Department Store Executive,' 2 March 1934; SCO, Bankruptcy Office, 32:918, Minden's Ltd file, examination of Mrs L. Minden, 7 April 1932; 37:15, A.L. Kitchen file, examination of debtor, 16 June 1937.

29 SCO, Bankruptcy Office, 24:1214, M. Killoran file; 37:57, A.M. Bowers file; 24:133, M.S. Burgess file; 24:1369, E. Moore file, 32:169, A. Hamilton file; 24:469, G.M. Benson file; 37:106, R. Greenwold file; 24:862, S. Stone file, examination of I. Stone.

30 *BC Retailer*, 23:11 (November 1930); *Drug Merchandising*, 6:20 (30 September 1925); Canadian Retail Hardware Association Archive, Minutes of the

Ontario Retail Hardware and Stove Dealers' Association, minutes of 21st annual convention, 16–19 February 1926; *Canadian Grocer*, 39:19 (8 May 1925).

31 *Retail Merchants' Journal*, 4:10 (October 1906) and 1:1 (July 1903); *Canadian Grocer*, 34:5 (30 January 1920).

32 *BC Retailer*, 13:7 (March 1922); *Canadian Grocer*, 33:10 (7 March 1924); Special Committee on Price Spreads, vol. I, 326.

33 *Canadian Grocer*, 22:21 (22 May 1908); AO, RG 3, Premiers' Papers, box 71, N.B. Douglas, 'Retailing in Canada,' (1925); Special Committee on Price Spreads, vol. 1, 396 and 352, *Canadian Grocer*, 29:6 (5 February 1915).

34 *Retail Merchants' Journal*, 1:1 (20 July 1903).

35 *Canadian Pharmaceutical Journal*, 25:7 (February 1902); *Furniture World and the Undertaker*, 1:8 (April 1912); *Canadian Grocer*, 27:35 (29 August 1913); *Electrical Merchandising*, 3:6 (June 1927).

36 *Canadian Grocer*, 21:15 (12 April 1907).

37 D.T. Rodgers, *The Work Ethic in Industrial America, 1850–1920* (Chicago 1978); the quotes are from 13 and 15. Also on work, see P. Faler, 'Cultural Aspects of the Industrial Revolution: Lynn, Massachusetts, Shoemakers and Industrial Morality,' *Labor History*, 15:4 (1974), 367–94; A.S. Horlick, *Country Boys and Merchant Princes: The Social Control of Young Men in New York* (Lewisburg 1975); P. Joyce, *Work, Society and Politics: The Culture of the Factory in Late Victorian England* (Brighton 1980); K. McClelland, 'Time to Work, Time to Live: Some Aspects of Work and the Re-formulation of Class in Britain, 1850–1880,' in P. Joyce, ed., *The Historical Meanings of Work* (Cambridge 1987), 180–209; *Canadian Grocer*, 27:19 (9 May 1913).

38 *Electrical Merchandising*, 7:1 (January 1931); *Canadian Pharmaceutical Journal*, 35:9 (April 1902) and 38:2 (September 1904).

39 B. Bledstein, *The Culture of Professionalism: The Middle Class and the Development of Higher Education in America* (New York 1976); T. Haskell, *The Emergence of Professional Social Science: The American Social Science Society and the Nineteenth Century Crisis of Authority* (Urbana 1977); D. Noble, *America by Design: Science, Technology and the Rise of Corporate Capitalism* (Oxford 1977); *Canadian Pharmaceutical Journal*, 46:3 (October 1912); *Canadian Grocer*, 24:1 (7 January 1910).

40 *Hardware and Metal*, 31:6 (6 February 1923); *General Merchant of Canada*, 2:1 (5 January 1929).

41 *Dry Goods Review*, 31:6 (June 1919). The Manitoba RMA sponsored courses at the University of Manitoba, and the Ontario chapter did the same at the University of Toronto. Quebec had its own schools in retailing, some of which were funded by the RMA and others by manufacturers. The most

prestigious was St Hyacinthe's École Commerciale Practique Lalime. See *Dry Goods Review*, 31:9 (September 1919); *Canadian Grocer*, 44:2 (17 January 1930); *Le Prix courant*, 33:32 (6 août 1920); *Dry Goods Review*, 34:7 (July 1922).

42 *Shoe and Leather Journal*, 31:4 (15 February 1918).

43 UTL, Lord's Day Alliance Papers, box 13, V. Brown to Lord's Day Alliance, 4 July 1925; anon. to Lord's Day Alliance, 2 October 1925; J.C. Gilder to A.I. Terryberry, 16 March 1925; *Canadian Grocer*, 28:30 (24 July 1914).

44 *Canadian Grocer*, 14:32 (10 August 1900); *Electrical Merchandising*, 1:2 (June 1925); *BC Retailer*, 16:10 (June 1924).

45 *Canadian Grocer*, 32:8 (22 February 1918).

46 Canada, Royal Commission on Dominion-Provincial Relations, *Report of Hearings* (31 May 1938), 9693.

47 The terms are C. Rosenberg's from 'Sexuality, Class and Role in Nineteenth Century America,' in E. Pleck and J.H. Pleck, eds., *The American Man* (Englewood Cliffs, 1980), 219–54. See also R.J. Park, 'Biological Thought, Athletics and the Formation of the Man of Character: 1830–1900,' in J.A. Mangan and J. Walvin, eds., *Manliness and Morality: Middle Class Masculinity in Britain and America, 1800–1940* (New York 1987), 7–34; H. Brod, *The Making of Masculinities* (Boston 1987).

48 NAC, RG 10/33, vol. 27, G. Hougham to H.H. Stevens, 6 February 1934; RG 36/12, 400–42, M.N. Campbell to R. Hay, 1 November 1939.

49 *Canadian Pharmaceutical Journal*, 45:11 (June 1912). The feminization of retail folklore can be traced in R. Goffee and R. Scase, *Women in Charge: The Experiences of Female Entrepreneurs* (London 1985), esp. 81–98.

50 *Retail Grocers' Review*, 1:10 (April 1910); *Dry Goods Review*, 15:1 (January 1905); SCO, Bankruptcy Office, 32:918, Minden's Ltd file, 32:918, examination of L. Minden, 7 April 1932. For a nice example of the mythologization of the retailing wife, see McAree, *Cabbagetown Store*, 3–5.

51 *Canadian Grocer*, 35:4 (28 January 1921); *Canadian Pharmaceutical Journal*, 48:3 (October 1914); AO, T. Eaton Co. Papers, Incoming Notices 1928, signatures authorized, 1928; *Drug Merchandising*, 8:7 (30 March 1927); S. Porter Benson, *Counter Cultures: Saleswomen, Managers and Customers in American Department Stores, 1840–1890* (Urbana 1986), ch. 3, and E.S. Abelson, *When Ladies Go A-thieving: Middle Class Shoplifters and the Victorian Department Store* (New York 1989), chs. 4–5, provides insight into the gendered space of the department stores.

52 *Shoe and Leather Journal*, 31:20 (15 October 1918); *Marketing*, 14:5 (May 1920); *Drug Merchandising*, 6:19 (16 September 1925); *Canadian Grocer*, 19:13 (31 March 1905). On contemporary literary treatments of this theme, see R. Bowlby, *Just Looking: Consumer culture in Dreiser, Gissing and Zola* (New York

1985), and R.G. Saisselin, *The Bourgeois and the Bibelot* (New Brunswick 1984), ch. 3.

53 NAC, RG 33/18, vol. 27, 3, R.L. Baker to H.H. Stevens, 18 January 1934; NAC, H.H. Stevens Papers, vol. 93, 'A Victim' to H.H. Stevens, 5 July 1934.

54 J. Langlais and D. Rome, *Juifs et Québécois français: 200 ans d'histoire commune* (Montréal 1986), 158–62; P. Roy, 'Protecting Their Pocketbooks and Preserving Their Race: White Merchants and Oriental Competition,' in A.R. McCormack and I. Macpherson, eds., *Cities in the West* (Ottawa 1975), 116–38; *Men's Wear Review*, 9:7 (July 1919); K.T. Jackson, *The Ku Klux Klan in the City, 1915–1930* (New York 1967), 119–20; J. Wagner, 'The Deutscher Bund Canada, 1934–1939,' *Canadian Historical Review*, 58:2 (June 1977), 180–1; H.M. Trachtenberg, 'The Old Clo'Move: Anti-Semitism, Politics and the Jews of Winnipeg, 1882–1921' (PhD thesis, York University 1984), 171–3; UTL, Lord's Day Alliance Papers, *Lord's Day Advocate*, 18:11 (November 1922); box 19, G.R. Cormack to G.F. Richards, 11 February 1937; MHSO, interview with Mrs L. Giovannielli, 31 August 1981.

55 *BC Retailer*, 13:6 (February 1922) and 14:5 (January 1923).

56 H. Leroux, 'L'Avenir du petit commerce à Montréal,' *L'Actualité Économique*, 2:3 (1926), 8 and 11; *Le Miroir*, 4:34 (11 decembre 1932) and 4:39 (15 janvier 1933).

57 *Retailer*, 31:5 May 1938; Leroux, 'L'Avenir du petit commerce,' 8.

58 *Western Retailer*, 23:6 (June 1936).

59 *BC Retailer*, 16:10 (June 1923) and 17:6 (February 1924).

60 P. Ricoeur, *Freud and Philosophy: An Essay on Interpretation* (New Haven 1970), 504; Lévi-Strauss, *Structural Anthropology*, 59; Ricoeur, *The Conflict of Interpretations*, 87.

CHAPTER 3 The Development of the Mass Market, 1870–1930

1 E. Penrose, *The Theory of the Growth of the Firm* (Oxford 1980), 153; A.D. Chandler Jr, *The Visible Hand: The Managerial Revolution in American Business* (Cambridge 1977); G. Porter, *The Rise of Big Business, 1860–1910* (Arlington Heights 1973). On 'imperfections,' see W. Averitt, *The Dual Economy: The Dynamics of America's Industrial Economy* (New York 1968), or, indeed, A. Marshall, *Principles of Political Economy* (London 1964), 282–6 and 312–16. Students of retailing have focused on different types of 'imperfections': the lack of price competition, goodwill, geographic dispersal of buyers, ease of entry into business, and swings of fashion. See M. Hall, *Distributive Trading* (London 1949), 160–9, and J. Hood and B.S. Yamey, 'Imperfect Competition in the Retail Trades,' *Economica* 18 (1951), 119–37.

2 D. Levine, 'Production, Reproduction and the Proletarian Family in England, 1500–1851,' in D. Levine, ed., *Proletarianization and Family History* (Orlando 1984), 117. The English literature on consumption is a torment. The daring might begin with J. Thirsk, *Economic Policy and Projects: The Development of a Consumer Society in Early Modern England* (Oxford 1978); N. McKendrick, 'Commercialization and the Economy,' in N. McKendrick et al., *The Birth of the Consumer Society: The Commercialization of Eighteenth Century England* (London 1982), 9–33; McKendrick, 'Home Demand and Economic Growth: A New View of the Role of Women and Children in the Industrial Revolution,' in McKendrick, ed., *Historical Perspectives: Studies in English Thought and Society in Honour of J.H. Plumb* (London 1974), 152–210; L. Weatherill, *Consumer Behaviour and Material Culture in Britain, 1660–1760* (London, 1988); B. Fine and E. Leopold, 'Consumerism and the Industrial Revolution,' *Social History*, 15:2 (May 1990), 151–79.

3 McKendrick, 'The Birth of the Consumer Society,' in McKendrick et al., *The Birth of the Consumer Society*, 2. The best study using this approach is S. Strasser, *Satisfaction Guaranteed: The Making of the American Mass Market* (New York 1989).

4 S. Courville, 'Villages and Agriculture in the Seigneuries of Lower Canada: Conditions of a Comprehensive Study of Rural Quebec in the First Half of the Nineteenth Century,' in D.H. Akenson, ed., *Canadian Papers in Rural History*, 5 (Gananoque 1987), 121–49; D. McCalla, 'The Internal Economy of Upper Canada: New Evidence on Agricultural Marketing before 1850,' *Agricultural History*, 59 (1985), 397–416. A good deal of information concerning consumption in pre-Confederation Canada can be gleaned from W.H. Graham, *Greenbank: Country Matters in Nineteenth Century Ontario* (Peterborough 1988); for housing, see W.R. Wrightman, 'Construction Material in Colonial Ontario, 1831–1861,' in F.H. Armstrong et al., *Aspects of Nineteenth Century Ontario* (Toronto, 1974), 114–34; for consumption of household goods: see A. Greer, *Peasant, Lord and Merchant: Rural Society in Three Quebec Parishes, 1740–1840* (Toronto 1985), 45–7 and 155–60.

5 D. McCalla has treated this change most extensively in *The Upper Canada Trade, 1834–1872: A Study of the Buchanans' Business* (Toronto 1979); see also J. Hamelin and Y. Roby, *Histoire économique du Québec, 1851–1896* (Montréal 1971), 343–53; also of importance is B. Forster, 'Finding the Right Size: Markets and Competition in Mid- and Late-Nineteenth Century Ontario,' in R. Hall, W. Westfall, and L. Sefton MacDowell, eds., *Patterns of the Past: Interpreting Ontario's History* (Toronto 1988), 150–73.

6 The warhorses of this school are T. Copp, *The Anatomy of Poverty: The Condition of the Working Class in Montreal, 1897–1929* (Toronto 1974), and M. Piva,

The Condition of the Working Class in Toronto – 1900–1921 (Ottawa 1979)). B.
Bradbury has also found widespread urban poverty in *Working Families: Age,
Gender and Daily Survival in Industrializing Montreal* (Toronto 1993), though it
might be noted that this work's snapshot approach under-distinguishes
change over time even as it emphasizes life cycles. In fact, some of the evidence presented by Bradbury suggests an overall improvement in incomes;
see especially 71, 125, and 131.

7 G.W. Bertram and M.B. Percy, 'Real Wage Trends in Canada, 1900–1926:
Some Provisional Estimates,' *Canadian Journal of Economics*, 12:2 (May 1979),
299–312; R.G. Allen and A.L. Bowley, *Family Expenditure: A Study of Its Variation* (London 1935), 5; A. Rees, *Real Wages in Manufacturing, 1890–1914* (Princeton 1961), 114; F. Stricker, 'Affluence for Whom? – Another Look at
Prosperity and the Working Classes in the 1920s,' *Labor History*, 24:1 (Winter
1983), 26–9. Food was seen by Engels to be a relatively inelastic commodity
whose percentage share of expenditures would fall as the standard of living
rose. Recent research suggests otherwise: see C. Shammas, 'The Eighteenth
Century English Diet and Economic Change,' *Explorations in Economic History*, 21 (1984), 254–69.

8 *Canadian Grocer*, 3:27 (5 July 1889). The dominion statistician in his 1913 study
of the rising cost of living found that increasing rents, not the rise in retail
prices, was the chief cause of the decline in real wages; see Canada, Board of
Inquiry into the Cost of Living, *Report of the Board*, vol. 3 (Ottawa 1915), 141–
413.

9 M. Lévy-Leboyer and F. Bourguignon, *The French Economy in the Nineteenth
Century: An Essay in Econometric Analysis* (Cambridge 1990), 27–46.

10 I. Drummond, *Progress without Planning: The Economic History of Ontario from
Confederation to the Second World War* (Toronto 1987), 105. Drummond's interpretation has enormously influenced the discussion which follows. Eastern
Townships Bank, *Charter and Annual Reports* (Sherbrooke 1912), 223, 302, and
320.

11 Several problems do limit the value of these statistics: in the first place, the
late 1880s were untypical in that they were among the best years for working
people so far as real wages were concerned (the long deflation was still
pressing down prices and earnings remained relatively high). Furthermore,
the sample group was small, with the bureau after 1885 obtaining anywhere
from 1,100 to 6,800 annual returns, but using only 1,700 or so a year in its
cost-of-living tables (the rest were used in the preparation of tables on wages,
number of dependents, length of employment, etc.). On the other hand, the
reports do have the advantage of covering men and women, young and old,
affluent and impoverished, town and city, and they were also innovative in

that they required workers to indicate 'extra' income earned by dependents. The bureau's statistics were based on the methods developed by Carroll Wright. For a thought-provoking critique of Wright's methodology, see D. Horowitz, *The Morality of Spending: Attitudes towards the Consumer Society in America, 1875–1940* (Baltimore 1985), ch. 2. The discussion that follows is based on Ontario, *Annual Report of the Bureau of Industries for the Province of Ontario*, annually 1886–90. For a general summary of the bureau's findings, see T.J.O. Dick, 'Consumer Behaviour in the Nineteenth Century and Ontario Workers, 1885–1889,' *Journal of Economic History*, 46:2 (June 1986), 477–88.

12 Interestingly enough, a coalminer in Nova Scotia also asserted in 1889 that a family of five needed a minimum of $327; see Canada, Royal Commission into the Relations of Capital and Labour, *Evidence – Nova Scotia* (Ottawa 1891), 469–70.

13 Single females over sixteen (10 per cent of the sample) also earned far less than males without dependents (43 per cent less), but they spent far less (25 per cent less on clothing, 28 per cent less on food and lodging, one-third as much on entertainment), and this allowed them to accumulate small savings (though they saved only one-third as much as single males).

14 E.P. Neufeld, *The Financial System of Canada* (Toronto 1972), 220–77; on housing, see K. Buckley, *Capital Formation in Canada, 1896 1930* (Toronto 1974), and for later developments, O.J. Firestone, *Residential Real Estate* (Toronto 1951). While it is true that the real estate boom of 1901–14 would greatly outstrip that of 1886–92, it is worth noting that the earlier increase in real estate construction occurred in the context of relative population stability and that in terms of housing per capita there was a greater change in the 1880s than there would be in the early years of the new century. There is also no question that houses were more affordable in the late nineteenth century than they would be in the early twentieth. See A.G. Darroch, 'Occupational Specialization, Assessed Wealth and Home-owning during Toronto's Early Industrialization, 1861–1899,' *Histoire sociale/Social History*, 16:32 (novembre 1983), 402–5; M. Doucet and J. Weaver, *Housing the North American City* (Montreal and Kingston 1991), table 7.7; R. Harris, 'Working Class Home Ownership and Housing Affordability across Canada in 1931,' *Histoire sociale/Social History*, 19:37 (mai 1986), 121–38.

15 M.C. Urquhart and K.A.H. Buckley, *Historical Statistics of Canada* (Toronto 1965), L7–42, L167–232; D.A. Lawr, 'The Development of Ontario Farming, 1870–1919,' *Ontario History*, 64:4 (1972), 239–51; R.E. Ankli and W. Millar, 'Ontario Agriculture in Transition: The Shift from Wheat to Cheese,' *Journal of Economic History*, 42:1 (1982), 207–15; M. McInnis, 'The Changing Structure of Canadian Agriculture 1867–1897,' *Journal of Economic History*,

42:1 (1982), 191–8; Hamelin and Roby, *Histoire économique du Québec*, 161–205.

16 Canada, Royal Commission on the Relations of Capital and Labour, *Evidence – Ontario*, 499.

17 N. Séguin, *La Conquête du sol au 19e siècle* (Montréal 1975), deals with agricultural poverty on the forestry frontier; for the poor quality of some farmers' diet, see J.I. Jameson, 'What Did Canadian Pioneers Eat?' cited in B. Light and J. Parr, eds., *Canadian Women on the Move, 1867–1920* (Toronto, 1983), 173. Many farmers had so little money that they had to work off their debts; see WCA, Alexander Davidson, Ennotville, journal, 1880–1; AO, Charles Tench's cash book [1838]–1906; PAA, Henry Oppertshauser & Sons Hardware, Stony Plain, customer account book, 1920–5.

18 *Canadian Grocer*, 22:29 (17 July 1908); H.S. Barron, *Those Who Stayed Behind: Rural Society in Nineteenth Century New England* (Cambridge 1984), 68–76; B. Ramirez, *On the Move: French Canadian and Italian Migrants in the North Atlantic Economy, 1860–1914* (Toronto 1991), esp. ch. 1.

19 Copp, *The Anatomy of Poverty*, ch. 2, suggests a decline throughout the first three decades of the century; Piva, *The Conditions of the Working Class in Toronto*, 27–60, echoes Copp's interpretation but stops at 1921; see also Bertram and Percy, 'Real Wage Trends in Canada,' 299–312. E. Bartlett presents a variation on Piva, suggesting a decline in men's real wages in Vancouver from 1911 to 1919, with improvement in the 1920s; see 'Real Wages and the Standard of Living in Vancouver, 1901–1929,' *BC Studies*, 51 (Autumn 1981), 3–62. These interpretations are based on somewhat suspect data. Under the system adopted by the Department of Labour in 1903, a fixed food basket, a basic wardrobe, and a standard type of accommodation were used to calculate prices, with no concessions being made to changing habits and tastes. The difficulty is that while some commodities, such as beef, mutton, and eggs, increased in price very rapidly in the pre–First World War period, others, such as pork, milk, and sugar, did not. As a result, while the government's commodity list offers a rough guide to prices and a measure of a certain lifestyle, it tells us very little about the overall standard of living. Moreover, there were always difficulties involved in defining the cut or quality of the commodity being purchased. In July 1903, for example, a working man's worsted suit was priced at $3–5 in Trois-Rivières, $5–15 in Hull, $23–26 in Quebec City, $10–15 in Sherbrooke, and $20 in Saint-Hyacinthe (NAC, RG 27, vol. 47, 'Schedule E: Ready Made Clothing, Underwear, Boots and Shoes,' returns for July 1903). Clearly, the investigators were not all talking about the same piece of clothing, and one wonders if averaging the price at $14.20 would really circumvent the trouble. (The problem did not go away

with standardized collection practices in 1910. Coats still noted the problems involved in calculating an index of clothing prices in volume 2 of Canada, Board of Inquiry into the Cost of Living, *Report of the Board*, 130.) Similar inexactitude governed the pricing of food: one reporter noted in 1906 that beef could be bought from anywhere from 5–6¢ to 15–18¢ a pound. Until historians actually go back to the original Department of Labour files and contemporary newspaper advertisements and recalculate the cost of living taking into account place and taste, an accurate appraisal of the impact of early-twentieth-century inflation will continue to elude us.

20 DBS, *Estimated Consumption of Meats, Dairy Products and Eggs* (Ottawa 1925 and 1931); DBS, *Report on the Biscuit, Confectionery, Cocoa and Chocolate Industries* (Ottawa 1930); DBS, *Men's Clothing Industry in Canada* (Ottawa annual, 1921–30); DBS, *Women's Factory Clothing in Canada* (Ottawa 1926–30).

21 Calculated from figures in DBS, *Estimated Retail Sales of Selected Commodities, 1930* (Ottawa 1935).

22 DBS, *Estimated Consumption of Meats, Dairy Products and Eggs*, annual, 1922–30; DBS, *The Men's Furnishing Industry in Canada*, annual, 1922–30 (Ottawa 1923–31), table 2; *Census of Canada, 1931*, vol. 10 (Ottawa 1934), part 1, appendix A, table 5; *Marketing*, 16:8 (15 April 1922); *Dry Goods Review*, 35:8 (July 1923); Canada, Select Committee on Agricultural Conditions, *Evidence*, part 1 (Ottawa 1924), 424–5. A contemporary American researcher also found farmers to have been relatively active consumers; see E.L. Kirkpatrick, *The Farmer's Standard of Living* (New York 1929). K. Jellison's, *Entitled to Power: Farm Women and Technology, 1913–63* (Chapel Hill 1993), esp. ch. 2, provides a useful feminist addition to Kirkpatrick. See also H.A. Gibbard, 'The Means and Modes of Living of European Immigrants in Montreal' (MA thesis, McGill University 1934), passim.

23 *Canadian Grocer*, 37:41 (10 October 1913); *Shoe and Leather Journal*, 31:20 (15 January 1918); Strasser, *Satisfaction Guaranteed*, esp. chs. 2 and 4.

24 A.R. Heinze, *Adapting to Abundance: Jewish Immigrants, Mass Consumption, and the Search for American Identity* (New York 1990), 89–91 and 133–44; E. Morawska, *For Bread with Butter: The Life-Worlds of East Central European Immigrants in Johnstown, Pennsylvania, 1890–1940* (Cambridge 1985), esp. 115–16; H.R. Diner, *Erin's Daughter's in America: Irish Immigrant Women in the Nineteenth Century* (Baltimore 1983), 26–7, 67–9, and 141–2.

25 G.S. Lowe, *Women in the Administrative Revolution* (Toronto 1982), 47–62; *Census of Canada, 1911*, vol. 6 (Ottawa 1914), table 1; DBS, *Origin, Birthplace, Nationality and Language of the People: A Census Study* (Ottawa 1929), 204; *Census of Canada, 1931*, vol. 7, table 40; *Shoe and Leather Journal*, 26:7 (1 April 1912); *Report of the Social Survey Commission of Toronto* (Toronto 1915), 22–3.

For a study of morality campaigns affecting female wage-earners, see C. Strange, 'From Modern Babylon to a City upon a Hill,' in Hall et al., *Patterns of the Past*, 255–77. On the female shop assistant, see T. McBride, 'A Woman's World: Department Stores and the Evolution of Women's Employment, 1870–1920,' *French Historical Studies*, 10:2 (Fall 1978), 664–83; C.E. Adams, *Women Clerks in Wilhelmine Germany: Issues of Class and Gender* (Cambridge 1988); S. Porter Benson, *Counter Cultures: Saleswomen, Managers and Customers in American Department Stores, 1890–1940* (Urbana 1986), 231–40.

26 The best study of this transformation is G. Reekie's *Temptations: Sex, Selling and the Department Store* (St Leonards 1993), esp 63–82. See also Porter Benson, *Counter Cultures*, ch. 3; W. Leach, 'Strategists of Display and the Production of Desire,' in S.J. Bonner, ed., *Consuming Visions: Accumulation and the Display of Goods in America, 1880–1920* (New York 1989); and W. Leach, 'Transformations in a Culture of Consumption: Women and the Department Stores, 1890–1925,' *Journal of American History*, 71:2 (1984), 319–42.

27 *Canadian Grocer*, 14:3 (19 January 1900); 16:37 (12 September 1902). Note how the *Retailer* favourably described old-style counters as 'barriers to the public' (21:7 [July 1928]). Good treatments of the department stores' aura can be found in M.B. Miller, *The Bon Marché: Bourgeois Culture and the Department Store, 1869–1920* (Princeton 1981); R. Williams, *Dream Worlds: Mass Consumption in Late Nineteenth Century France* (Berkeley 1982); and E. Zola's indispensable *Au Bonheur des Dames* (Paris 1971, orig. pub. 1883).

28 *Retail Merchants' Journal*, 4:4 (April 1906).

29 Zola, *Au Bonheur*, 110; T. Dreiser, *Sister Carrie* (Baltimore 1981), 98; C. Wright, 'Feminine Trifles of Vast Importance: Writing Gender into the History of Consumption,' in F. Iacovetta and M. Valverde, eds., *Gender Conflicts: New Essays in Women's History* (Toronto 1992), 234–9.

30 NAC, RG 33/18, Royal Commission on Price Spreads, vol. 150, 'Report on Department Stores,' 19–20.

31 Store size was derived from averaging various floor plans published in the trade press. For Eaton's, see S.H. Ditchett, *Eaton's of Canada: A Unique Institution of Extraordinary Magnitude* (New York 1923), 9. See also DBS, *Census of Trading Establishments, 1924* (Ottawa, 1928), table IV; HBCA, Robert Simpson Co. Papers, box 1, 'Preliminary Balance Sheet,' 4 February 1925.

32 M. Denison, *This Is Simpson's* (Toronto 1947), 3; C.L. Burton, *A Sense of Urgency: Memoirs of a Canadian Merchant* (Toronto 1952), 74–5; *Dry Goods Review*, 11:I (January 1901); McGill University Archives, Henry Morgan & Co. Papers, box 4, Henry Morgan & Co. Ltd, 'The Beginning of the Enterprise' (1945).

33 Eaton's promoted the idea that the store initially catered to the 'working

class' and 'the poor,' but the evidence is suspect. The ease with which the
company became more up-market after its relocation and the large number
of fancy goods featured in early advertisements cast doubt on its claim to
have been a working-class shop. Moreover, there are real problems involved
in the literal interpretation of contemporary words such as 'working class';
Timothy Eaton used the term to refer to farmers, and it would certainly also
have been applied to master artisans, small employers, and other proprietors. For Eaton's claim, see W. Stephenson, *The Store That Timothy Built* (Toronto 1969), 24–6; J.L. Santink takes the owner at his word in *Timothy Eaton
and the Rise of His Department Store* (Toronto 1990), 68–9 and 239–40.

34 Ditchett, *Eaton's of Canada*, ch. 3; AO, T. Eaton Co. Papers, series 61, Notices,
1902–3, 'Duties to Mr. Gregory,' 1 November 1902; Santink, *Timothy Eaton*,
126.

35 AO, T. Eaton Co. Papers, series 117, 'Testimonial Letters,' Mrs W.B. Howell
to T. Eaton Co., 19 October 1932; *Dry Goods Review*, 34:11 (November 1922); T.
Eaton Co., *Golden Jubilee, 1869 1919* (Toronto 1919), 212–21; T. Eaton Co.
Papers, series 61, Incoming Notices 1926, C. Boothe to Heads of Departments, 20 December 1926.

36 V. Strong-Boag, *The New Day Recalled: Lives of Girls and Women in English Canada, 1919–1939* (Toronto 1988), esp. 85–6 and 115–20; P. Fass, *The Damned and
the Beautiful: American Youth in the 1920s* (Oxford 1977), ch. 5; V. Steele, *Fashion and Eroticism: Ideals of Feminine Beauty from the Victorian Era to the Jazz Age*
(New York 1985), 236–42.

37 Eaton, *Golden Jubilee*, 177–8; *Men's Wear Review*, 15:4 (April 1926); HBCA,
Hudson's Bay Company Papers, RG 2, series 6, file 6, A.N. MacDonald to E.
Fitzgerald, 4 July 1921; Canada, Special Committee on Price Spreads and
Mass Buying, *Proceedings and Evidence*, vol. 1 (Ottawa 1934), 325; Ditchett,
Eaton's of Canada, 19; Canada, Special Committee on Price Spreads and Mass
Buying, *Proceedings and Evidence*, vol. 2 (Ottawa 1935), 3055–8.

38 AO, T. Eaton Co. Papers, series 61, R.W. Eaton notices, 1905–9, R.Y. Eaton,
'Leaders and Price Cutting to Get Sales,' January 1909; ibid., Incoming
Notices 1928, Notice Re. April 28th issue of *Eaton's News*, 29 February 1928;
ibid., Incoming Notices 1930, D.E. Startup to Supervisors, Group Managers
and Heads of Departments, 28 April 1930; ibid., R.W. Eaton notices, 1905–9,
R.Y. Eaton, 'No Items Advertised in Next Monday's Paper,' 14 December
1907; Special Committee on Price Spreads, vol. 1, 302.

39 NAC, RG 36/12, 400–35, 'Classified List of E-O Discounts,' 18 April 1938,
and A.R. Kaufman to M.N. Campbell, 5 July 1939.

40 Special Committee on Price Spreads, vol. 3, 2744; HBCA, Robert Simpson
Company Archives, Thompson Manufacturing Co., 'Shareholders Min-

utes,' 28 May 1909; Keen's Manufacturing Co. Ltd, Letters Patent, 3 April 1913.

41 The 'informal' mail-order business is described in T.D. Clark, *Pills, Petticoats, and Plows: The Southern Country Store* (Norman 1964), 61–72; C.B. Robinson, *History of Toronto and the County of York* (Toronto 1885), 452–4; RCUWO, W.L. Mara Papers, correspondence, Mrs J.H. Dorsey to Mara's, 19 November 1923, and Mrs R. Lawrence to Mara's, 6 March 1940.

42 *Canadian Grocer*, 19:9 (3 March 1905); AO, T. Eaton Co. Papers, series 61, R.W. Eaton Notices, 1900–2, 8 November 1901; ibid., Incoming Notices, 1905–9; and 'Sub-Committee on Mail Order Methods,' October 1905; Eaton, *Golden Jubilee*, 155; *Le Prix courant*, 41:24 (15 juin 1928).

43 K. Fells, 'Some Information on the Beginning of Eaton's Catalogue and Mail Order,' 11 September 1963, cited in DBS, *Department Stores, 1923 1976* (Ottawa 1979), 15–16. For Simpson's sales in 1920, see HBCA, Robert Simpson Company Papers, 'Eleven Year Profit and Loss Statement Before Dividends,' 4 February 1925; for 1925 see 'Robert Simpson Company – Mail Order Department: Profit and Loss Statement,' 3 February 1926. For Eaton's, see Special Committee on Price Spreads, vol. 3, 3477–8 and 3385, figures for Winnipeg were calculated on the basis of 1925 sales figures, Moncton sales were derived from AO, T. Eaton Co. Papers, 110–1, Mail Order Stock Sheets.

44 Canada, Royal Commission on Price Spreads, *Minutes of Proceedings and Evidence*, (Ottawa 1935), 1681–725; P. Mathias, *Retailing Revolution* (London 1967), 102–5.

45 Robin, Page and Whitman is discussed in Royal Commission on Price Spreads, 471; for Davies, see M. Bliss, *A Canadian Millionaire: The Life and Business Times of Sir Joseph Flavelle, Bart., 1858–1939* (Toronto 1978), 34–5; *Financial Post*, 21 (19 August 1921) has a brief history of Legaré; Carroll's is referred to in Royal Commission on Price Spreads, 991. See also *Canadian Grocer*, 62:11 (25 March 1925); *Men's Wear Review*, 18:6 (June 1928); and *Canadian Grocer*, 49:18 (1 May 1925). C.H. Cheasley, 'The Chain Store Movement in Canada,' *National Problems of Canada*, 17 (Orillia 1930), 58–63, reviews the early history of chain stores.

46 *Financial Post*, 20 February 1925.

47 *Canadian Grocer*, 40:8 (19 February 1926) and 41:4 (18 February 1927); Royal Commission on Price Spreads, 776.

48 *Canadian Grocer*, 40:15 (16 April 1926). Unlike Dominion, Loblaw's and most of the other chains were few in number but rich in stock. At a time when the average annual sales of a Loblaw's store was $200,000 and of an Arnold's outlet was $134,000, Dominion was selling just $36,000 per unit; see *Canadian Grocer*, 43:2 (18 January 1929). Dominion's model in this was the A & P: see

Progressive Grocers' Magazine, *A & P: Past, Present and Future* (New York 1971), 2–19; and G. Lebhar, *Chain Stores in America, 1859–1962* (New York 1963), 25–30. Thus, while Dominion by the late twenties was operating five hundred outlets, it turned just 40 per cent more stock than Loblaw's did with its sixty-five; based on figures in *Canadian Grocer*, 41:29 (16 September 1927), and DBS, *Retail Merchandise Trade, 1930* (Ottawa 1933), table 4.

49 *Canadian Grocer*, 45:22 (23 October 1931). See also Safeway Stores Inc. Archives, 'The Company Moves into Canada,' typescript dated 2 June 1976.

50 G.P. Boucher and W.C. Hopper, 'An Economic Study of Cheese Consumption in Certain Urban and Rural Districts of Canada,' Canada, Department of Agriculture, *Technical Bulletin*, 22 (Ottawa 1939), 8.

51 DBS, *Retail Merchandise Trade, 1930*, table 4. For Tamblyn, see *Drug Merchandising*, 9:5 (29 February 1928); D'Aillard's is discussed in *Financial Post*, 22 (26 October 1928); manufacturer-controlled chains are referred to in Cheasley, 'Chain Store Movement,' 70; for Tip Top, see *Financial Post*, 22 (27 April 1928), and *Men's Wear Review*, 29:3 (March 1929). A fine study of a manufacturer-controlled chain is A. Wilson, *John Northway: A Blue Serge Canadian* (Toronto 1965); see also *Men's Wear Review*, 18:8 (August 1928). For the growth of shoe chains, see *Shoe and Leather Journal*, 27:3 (15 February 1924).

52 F.W. Woolworth Co., 'Historical Background on Company's Origin' (MS. dated February 1984); F.W. Woolworth Co., *100th Anniversary* (New York, 1979), 19. For a general treatment, see J.K. Winkler, *Five and Ten: The Fabulous Life of F.W. Woolworth* (New York 1957), 149–69.

53 Royal Commission on Price Spreads, 590–763.

54 *Canadian Grocer*, 43:18 (30 August 1929); DBS, *A Decade of Retail Trade, 1923–1933* (Ottawa 1935), table 31; DBS, *Retail Merchandise Trade, 1930*, table 4; *Canadian Grocer*, 34:17 (23 April 1920); *Census, 1931*, vol. 10, part 1, tables 5B and 28; for Toronto, table 31; provincial figures are available in *Retail Merchandise Trade, 1930*, table 3. The exception was Saskatchewan, where fully 72 per cent of the chain outlets were in smaller towns and villages; see *Canadian Grocer*, 44:16 (1 August 1930).

55 Tip Top Tailors Ltd, Advertisement Collection, Clipping dated 8 March 1920; *Maritime Merchant*, 40:16 (4 February 1932).

56 The Department of Labour started investigating the cost of living in 1903 and began systematic calculations in 1910. For the earlier period, we must rely on the findings of the 1915 Board of Inquiry and James Mavor's 1907 study of Toronto prices reprinted in *Financial Post*, 15 February 1908.

57 *Canadian Grocer*, 24:3 (21 January 1910) and 27:27 (4 July 1913). The first large-scale consumer protests hit cities in the northeastern United States in 1907–8;

see *New York Times*, 26 July 1907, 4 October 1907, 2 January 1910, 19 January 1910, 7 April 1910, 12 April 1912, 22 January 1911, 10 February 1911, 16 December 1911. For a treatment of wartime riots; see W. Freiburger, 'War Prosperity and Hunger: The New York Food Riots of 1917,' *Labor History*, 25:2 (Spring 1984), 217–39; for the 1917 Toronto bakery boycott, see S. Speisman, *The Jews of Toronto* (Toronto 1987), 195.

58 The Consumer's League had been founded in New York in 1891 in response to an outcry over the conditions of work in the department stores. Throughout its history, the organization maintained a strong interest in women's work. For American treatments of the consumer's movement, see M. Nathan, *The Story of an Epoch Making Movement* (New York 1926), and J.S. Gilkeson, *Middle-Class Providence, 1820–1940* (Princeton 1986), ch. 8.

59 Calculated on the basis of price indexes in Urquhart and Buckley, *Historical Statistics of Canada*, K8.18; *Hardware and Metal*, 25:48 (30 November 1916); and *Canadian Grocer*, 32:33 (16 August 1918); Canada, Royal Commission on Industrial Relations, 'Evidence' (unpub. 1919), vol. 2, 1106; and *Canadian Grocer*, 30:45 (10 November 1916).

60 Royal Commission on Industrial Relations, vol 4, 2175 and 1963; Canada, Special Committee to Inquire into the Cost of Living, *Minutes of Proceedings and Evidence* (Ottawa 1920), 315–16. The banner can be seen in a photograph reproduced in D. Bercuson, *Fools and Wisemen: The Rise and Fall of the One Big Union* (Toronto 1978), facing 148.

61 Royal Commission on Industrial Relations, vol. 2, 1036–7, and vol. 4, 2223.

62 Board of Inquiry into the Cost of Living, 14–17.

63 NAC, RG 110, vol. 3, Cost of Living Commissioner, memo to Sir Thomas White, 28 May 1919. For American theories concerning the price rise, see Freiburger, 'War Prosperity and Hunger,' 217–18, 229–39.

64 *Canadian Grocer*, 27:11 (14 March 1913); *Maritime Merchant*, 41:6 (15 September 1932).

65 NAC, RG 27, vol. 47, F.X. Chadillon to Minister of Labour, n.d. [1903].

66 Royal Commission on Industrial Relations, vol. 1, 184; Special Committee to Inquire into the Cost of Living, 319–20; Royal Commission on Industrial Relations, vol. V, 3219; NAC, RG 27, vol. 48, W.L. Mackenzie King to R.H. Coats, 12 June 1911.

67 M. Robin, *Radical Politics and Canadian Labour* (Kingston 1968), 130; GBCA, 78–27, Associated Clothing Manufacturers Inc. Papers, box 11, memo, 'Increases and Decreases in Retail Prices in Toronto,' March 1920, and 'Material Presented to the Board of Arbitration,' April 1920.

68 *Shoe and Leather Journal*, 28:1 (February 1915), 3:5 (1 March 1920), 33:12 (15 June 1920), 33:11 (1 June 1920); 33:16 (1 September 1920).

69 *Financial Post*, 14 January 1921; *Men's Wear Review*, 10:9 (September 1920) and
    10:10 (October 1920); *Dry Goods Review*, 32:10 (October 1920); *Marketing*, 14:10
    (15 August 1920) and 14:14 (15 October 1920); D.K. Kirk, 'Retail Merchandis-
    ing in Relation to General Business Conditions,' *Harvard Business Review*, 2
    (1923–4), 37–42.

70 *Men's Wear Review*, 11:7 (July 1921); *Hardware and Metal*, 30:3 (28 January
    1921); *Canadian Grocer*, 35:8 (25 February 1921); *Financial Post*, 15 (11 February
    1921).

71 *Marketing*, 14:14 (15 October 1920); *Men's Wear Review*, 10:9 (9 September
    1920); Canadian Bank of Commerce, *Monthly Commercial Letter*, 98 (January
    1924); *Industrial Canada*, 32:1 (May 1921); *Men's Wear Review*, 10:6 (June
    1920).

72 *Industrial Canada*, 7:1 (August 1906); J.S. Mill, *Principles of Political Economy*
    (London 1920), 149. On the change in marketing thought, see M. Sklar, *The
    Corporate Reconstruction of American Capitalism, 1890–1916* (Cambridge 1988),
    53–78.

73 *Dry Goods Review*, 10:3 (March 1900). For the role of the wholesaler, S.
    Bruchey, *Robert Oliver: Merchant of Baltimore* (Baltimore 1956), and his *The
    Roots of American Growth* (London 1965), 53–63, are the best studies. The most
    informative Canadian work is McCalla, *The Upper Canadian Trade*; other
    glimpses can be gained from G. Wynn, *Timber Colony: A Historical Geography
    of Early Nineteenth Century New Brunswick* (Toronto 1981), 114–16, and H.G.
    Aitken, 'A New Way to Pay Old Debts,' in W. Miller, ed., *Men in Business*
    (New York 1962), 72–82. V.D. Harrington, *The New York Merchant on the Eve of
    the Revolution* (New York 1935), 57–70, describes early cases of specialization.
    H. Woodman, *King Cotton and His Retainers* (Lexington 1968), chs. 2–6, and
    F.M. Jones, *Middlemen in the Domestic Trade of the United States, 1800–1860*
    (Urbana 1937), chs. 1–4, are good studies of later trends.

74 *Industrial Canada*, 3:9 (April 1903); *Financial Post*, 1 July 1916 and 8 January
    1910.

75 GBCA, 78–27, Associated Clothing Manufacturers, box 11, 'Arguments Pre-
    sented to the Board of Arbitration,' 23 April 1920; *Financial Post*, 16 July 1910;
    Industrial Canada, 16:10 (February 1916).

76 Sklar, *Corporate Reconstruction*, 57–68, discusses overproduction. On marginal
    utility and its popularization in Europe, see V. Walsh and H. Gram, *Classical
    and Neoclassical Theories of the General Equilibrium* (Oxford 1980), J.F. Henry,
    The Making of Neoclassical Economics (London 1990), and R.S. Howey, 'The
    Origins of Marginalism,' in R.D. Collison Black et al., *The Marginal Revolution
    in Economics: Interpretation and Evaluation* (Durham 1973), 23–38. See also
    Printer's Ink, 109:1 (2 October 1919).

77 R. Stanton, *A Legacy of Quality, J.M. Schneider, Inc.: A Centennial Celebration* (Kitchener 1989), 73; *Canadian Pharmaceutical Journal*, 41:8 (March 1908); *Printer's Ink*, 109:1 (2 October 1919); *Women's Home Companion* article reprinted in *Canadian Grocer*, 22:2 (10 January 1908).

78 *Printer's Ink*, 109:1 (2 October 1919); emphasis mine.

79 G. Porter and H. Livesay, *Merchants and Manufacturers* (Baltimore 1971), and 'Vertical Integration in American Manufacturing, 1899–1948,' *Journal of Economic History*, 29 (1969), 494–50; G. Gervais, 'Le Commerce de détail au Canada, 1870–1880,' *Revue d'histoire de l'Amérique française*, 33:4 (mars 1980), 540–3. For the importance of branding, see A.W. Frey, *Manufacturers' Product, Package and Price Policies* (New York 1940), 292–3. These changes were preceded by a gradual erosion of the wholesalers' credit function as manufacturers increasingly drew upon formal financial institutions and the stock market; see P.B. Trescott, *Financing American Enterprise: The Story of Commercial Banking* (New York 1963).

80 NAC, RG 33/18, vol. 21, 'Memorandum on Merchandising in Canada,' table XXII, 38; L.G. Reynolds, 'Some Notes on the Distributive Trades in Canada,' *Canadian Journal of Economics and Political Science*, 4:3 (August 1938), 540–1; *Canadian Grocer*, 39:15 (10 April 1925).

81 *Printer's Ink*, 106:10 (6 March 1919).

82 S. Ewen, *Captains of Consciousness* (New York 1976), 56–9; T.J. Lears, 'From Salvation to Self-Realization: Advertising and the Therapeutic Roots of the Consumer Culture 1880–1930,' in T.J. Lears and R.W. Fox, *The Culture of Consumption* (New York 1983), 1–38; R. Marchand, *Advertising the American Dream* (Berkeley 1985).

83 *Financial Post*, 28 March 1914; *Industrial Canada*, 32:1 (May 1921); *Financial Post*, 6 October 1922. For a more limited definition of overproduction, see Joseph Flavelle's speech in *Financial Post*, 4 February 1921: for Street's view, *Financial Post*, 10 October 1922.

84 *Men's Wear Review*, 17:7 (July 1927); *Furniture World*, 25:1 (January 1935); and NAC, RG 33/18, vol. 27, 'Copy of Memorandum Presented to the Rt. Hon R.B. Bennett by Warren K. Cook ... November 23rd 1933.'

85 *Financial Post*, 23 June 1922; *Shoe and Leather Journal*, 26:8 (16 April 1923); *Industrial Canada*, 37:1 (May 1936); *Canadian Business*, 10:7 (July 1937).

86 D.A. Hounshell, *From the American System to Mass Production* (Baltimore 1984), 305. National City Company newsletter quoted in *Financial Post*, 3 September 1926.

87 S. Fox, *The Mirror Makers* (New York 1984), 79.

88 *Canadian Grocer*, 22:3 (17 January 1908).

89 *Canadian Grocer*, 44:24 (4 December 1931) and 41:36 (7 September 1927).

CHAPTER 4 Progressive Retailing

1 *Canadian Grocer*, 14:32 (10 August 1900).
2 *Retail Merchants' Journal*, 1:3 (20 October 1903).
3 The basic works on this subject are A. Adlburgham, *Shops and Shopping, 1800–1914: Where and in What Manner the Well-Dressed English-Woman Bought her Clothes* (London 1964), and D. Davis, *Fairs, Shops and Supermarkets: A History of English Shopping* (Toronto 1966). An exceptional Canadian exploration of related themes is K. Walden, 'Speaking Modern: Language, Culture and Hegemony in Grocery Window Displays, 1887–1920,' *Canadian Historical Review* 70:3 (1989), 285–310.
4 B. Forster, 'Finding the Right Size: Markets and Competition in Mid- and Late-Nineteenth Century Ontario,' in R. Hall et al., eds., *Patterns of the Past: Interpreting Ontario's History* (Toronto 1988), 162–3; *Furniture World*, 8:2 (February 1918) and 22:2 (February 1932). Kelvinator used the catalogue-agency method with dealers in small towns; see NAC, Milton Rous Papers, vol. 1, file 32, M. Rous to Kelvinator, 5 April 1927.
5 *Furniture World*, 7:2 (February 1917); H.R. Yeandle, 'Sales Promotion in the Canadian Furniture Industry' (B Admin thesis, University of Western Ontario 1932), 69–72.
6 *Canadian Grocer*, 18:44 (30 October 1914); *Men's Wear Review*, 9:5 (May 1919); *Shoe and Leather Journal*, 25:3 (1 February 1911); *Furniture World*, 9:9 (September 1919).
7 *Men's Wear Review*, 13:4 (August 1923); *Canadian Grocer*, 37:41 (10 October 1913); *Western Retailer*, 25:8 (September 1938); *Canadian Grocer*, 27:4 (24 January 1913); *General Merchant of Canada*, 1:8 (5 August 1928); *Drug Merchandising*, 3:6 (8 February 1922).
8 F. Accum, *Treatise on Adulterations of Food and Culinary Poisons* (London 1820); J. Burnett, *Plenty and Want: A Social History of Diet in England* (London 1966), ch. 5.
9 For petitions from temperance organizations, see Canada, *Journals of the Senate*, 1873, 48, 67, 89, 90, 115, 124, and 141; also Canada, *House of Commons Debates*, 1884, 1132–6, 1246–50, 2390–8. The health inspectors found little evidence of purposeful adulteration, though the dominion analyst in Montreal did deplore the way both retailers and consumers diluted food with impure water. Tinned goods did, however, suffer many serious problems. Annual reports of the health inspectors can be found in the *Sessional Papers* from 1876 onward.
10 Canada, Royal Commission on Industrial Relations, 'Evidence,' vol. 2 (unpub. 1919), 2356.

11 National Council of Women of Canada, *Year Book, 1917–18* (Toronto 1918), 47; E. Forsey, *Trade Unions in Canada, 1812–1902* (Toronto 1982), 458; *Canadian Grocer*, 22:42 (16 October 1908) and 17:26 (10 July 1903).

12 *Canadian Grocer*, 17:24 (12 June 1903) and 4:25 (20 June 1890); D.T. Fraser and G. Porter, *Ontario Public School Health Book* (Toronto 1925), 152.

13 *Canadian Pharmaceutical Journal*, 45:10 (May 1912); *Canadian Grocer*, 24:1 (7 January 1910).

14 *Shoe and Leather Journal*, 39:4 (15 February 1916); *Calgary Herald*, 25 April 1959; *Canadian Grocer*, 34:44 (29 October 1920).

15 *Canadian Grocer*, 19:20 (12 May 1905).

16 Note Sam Peps's distribution of labour in the *Maritime Merchant*, 41:6 (15 September 1932).

17 *Shoe and Leather Journal*, 24:2 (February 1910); *Drug Merchandising*, 8:14 (6 July 1927); *Canadian Grocer*, 23:39 (24 September 1909).

18 AO, RG 22, Supreme Court of Ontario, Bankruptcy Office, 24:1409, R. Michael file, 'Cross Examination of R. Michael,' 3 March 1925; *Financial Post* 19 February 1926; F. Clark, 'An Analysis of the Causes and Results of Hand to Mouth Buying,' *Harvard Business Review*, 6 (1927–28), 394–400; *Canadian Grocer*, 36:43 (27 October 1922); *Men's Wear Review*, 15:3 (March 1925); L.S. Lyon, *Hand to Mouth Buying* (Washington 1929), ch. 22; *Canadian Grocer*, 14:18 (4 May 1900).

19 Calculated from RCUWO, Morrison Edwards Collection, 5351, purchase journal; 1926:37, and invoices, 1927:38; ibid., Cairncross and Lawrence Collection, purchase Books, February 1929–November 1933. See also SCO, Bankruptcy Office, 28:719, Nathan Fine file; 28:256, Frank Cochrane Henry file; 28:42, Alex Edward Packard file; 28:730, James Earl Mulholland file.

20 On traditional forms of borrowing, see C. Arsenburg and S.T. Kimball, *Family and Community in Ireland* (New York 1969), 344–5; A. Faure, 'The Grocery Trade in Nineteenth Century Paris,' in G. Crossick and H.-G. Haupt, eds., *Shopkeepers and Master Artisans in Nineteenth Century Europe* (London 1984), 168–70. For treatments of retail dependence on wholesale credit in Canada, see D. McCalla, *The Upper Canada Trade, 1834–1872: A Study of the Buchanans' Business* (Toronto 1979), 19–24 and 110–12 and G. Bevin, 'Aperçu sur le commerce et le crédit à Québec, 1820–1830,' *Revue d'histoire de l'Amérique française*, 36:4 (mars 1983), 541–53. See also J.W. Wingate and J.S. Friedlander, *The Management of Retail Buying* (Englewood Cliffs 1963), 279–301.

21 The figures offered here were determined on the basis of the most common discounts appearing in store ledgers. See, for example, AO, Marshall Stephens & Sons, letterbook, 1897–1905; WCA, Simon Armstrong, journal, 1868–79; WCA, Alexander Davidson, journal, 1880–1; WCA, Yeoman's Drug

Store, ledger 1898–1931; RCUWO, Morrison Edwards Collection, purchase journal 1926–37; J.L. Santink, *Timothy Eaton and the Rise of His Department Store* (Toronto 1990), 152. On credit terms, see *Le Prix courant*, 38:23 (5 juin 1925), and P. Nystrom, *The Economics of Retailing*, vol. I (New York 1930), 90–9. Laporte-Martin gave 10 days on grocery orders; see *Retailer*, 22:2 (February 1929).

22 RCUWO, Middlesex County Bankruptcy Records, box 1, file of H.M. Thomas, transcript of examination, May 1939; *Financial Post*, 16 (24 February 1922), see also M. Tebbutt, *Making Ends Meet: Pawnbroking and Working-Class Credit* (New York 1983), 151–73; PAA, Department of the Attorney General, J.F. Lymburn Ministerial Papers, box 4, file 128, A.J. Mackay to J.E. Brownlee, 24 November 1930.

23 *Canadian Grocer*, 33:13 (28 March 1919). For credit, see endnotes 7 and 8 for chapter 1 above.

24 For examples of contracts, see GAI, J.I. Case Company Papers, box 1, file 2, C. Sinclair contract with J.I. Case, 20 September 1935; box 1, file 5, various copies of bills of sale to secure notes and chattel mortgage agreements. This practice may well have developed during the interwar period: the Waterloo Manufacturing Co., a small machinery firm in Ontario obtained no security in the early twentieth century other than a lien on the machine itself; see S.L. Eadie, 'Threshing with Steam: The Threshing Industry in Southern Ontario, 1906–13' (BA thesis, Wilfrid Laurier University 1991), 25. An example of a store hiring its own customer was a piano company that took on a customer as a salesman and used his commission to pay off his debts; see GAI, Saskatoon Piano Company Papers, box 10, file 80.

25 WCA, Alexander Davidson, journal, 1880–1; RCUWO, Stepler Drug Store, customer account book, 1909–40; Canada, Select Standing Committee on Banking and Commerce, *Minutes of Proceedings and Evidence: Debts and Interest Rates* (Ottawa 1933), 29 and 195.

26 T.V. Dion, a Westmount grocer with an annual turnover in 1919 of $400,000, observed that his clientele 'required' service. Similarly, a butcher catering to 'the high class trade' in Rosedale, observed that if he eliminated credit and delivery, he would be forced to 'pull the blinds down tomorrow'; see Canada, Special Committee to Inquire into the Cost of Living, *Minutes of Proceedings and Evidence* (Ottawa 1920), 228–9, 243, and 251. The best discussion of urban credit in Canada is S. Taschereau, 'L'Arme favorite de l'épicier indépendant: éléments d'une histoire sociale du crédit (Montréal, 1920–1940),' *Journal of the Canadian Historical Association*, 1993, 265–92.

27 GAI, Williams Brothers Papers, box 1, circular to customers, n.d. [December 1930].

28 *Canadian Grocer*, 23:8 (19 February 1909) and 19:10 (10 March 1905).

29 Federated Council of Sales Finance Companies, 'Submission' to Canada, Royal Commission on Banking and Finance, *Submissions and Evidence*, vol. 37A (24 September 1962), 14–15; calculated from DBS, *Retail Merchandise Trade, 1930* (Ottawa 1933), table 6, and DBS, *Retail Merchandise Trade, 1940* (Ottawa 1944), table 9. The best general study is M.L. Olney, *Buy Now, Pay Later: Advertising, Credit and Consumer Durables in the 1920s* (Chapel Hill 1991), esp. ch. 4.

30 Canada, Royal Commission on Banking and Finance, *Report* (Ottawa 1965), 205–6. The percentages are taken from a real case: SCO, Bankruptcy Office, 28:357, Hardy Lusby Piano Co. Ltd. file, 'Affidavit of J.E. Day,' 16 July 1928; 'Minutes of Meeting of Creditors.' The complaining retailer was a piano dealer at his bankruptcy hearing; see ibid., 28:358, Ontario Piano and Music Co. Ltd., 'Minutes of meeting of creditors,' 21 August 1928; see also Royal Commission on Banking, 206–7.

31 DBS, *Finance Companies in Canada* (Ottawa 1941), 1–2; E.P. Neufeld, *The Financial System of Canada* (Toronto 1972), ch. 10 and appendix table B.

32 Canada, Standing Committee on Banking and Commerce, *Minutes of Proceedings and Evidence: Respecting Small Loans Companies*, vol. 5 (8 March 1938), 112–23, and vol. 1 (17 January 1938), 82; Standing Committee on Banking and Commerce, *Minutes of Proceedings and Evidence: 'Bill 58: An Act Respecting Central Finance Corporation and to Change Its Name to Household Finance'* vol. 2 (22 March 1937), 55–6, and vol. 3 (31 March 1937), 75.

33 *Census of Canada, 1941*, vol. 10 (Ottawa, 1944), table 6; *Census of Canada, 1931*, vol. 7 (Ottawa 1934), table 7.

34 About one retailer in twelve paid income tax in 1925, while one in twenty-five paid a corporation tax, see Financial Post, *Annual Statistical Review* (Toronto 1928), 175; Nystrom, *The Economics of Retailing*, vol. 2, 28–38.

35 *General Merchant of Canada*, 1:1 (5 January 1928); *Maritime Merchant*, 43:4 (16 August 1934).

36 Harvard's Bureau of Business Research began publishing composite financial information on American shoe stores in 1915 and steadily broadened its research. A list of contemporary statistical sources available for American retailing can be found in appendix C to H. Barger, *Distribution s Place in the American Economy since 1869*, rev. ed. (New York 1976). The Dominion Bureau of Statistics began to assemble annual statistics in 1933, but with the exception of the figures on chain retailing, they remained fragmentary before the war.

37 I am indebted to Carol Thomson for allowing me access to these important business documents: Thomson Furniture Company Financial Statements and

Reports, 1933–9; Rabnett, Lindey and Logan to The Thomson Furniture Company, 11 May 1933 and 10 June 1933; F.H. Rabnett & Co. to J.M. Thomas, 12 November 1935, 17 February 1937, 15 March 1935, and 19 December 1935 (copies in author's possession).

38 *Canadian Pharmaceutical Journal*, 60:2 (September 1926).

39 *Industrial Canada*, 28:12 (April 1927) and 29:4 (August 1928); *Marketing*, 29:3 (21 July 1928).

40 *Men's Wear Review*, 18:10 (October 1928); *Marketing*, 18:11 (2 June 1923); J.V. Coles, *The Consumer-Buyer and the Market* (New York 1938), ch. 9.

41 *Industrial Canada*, 28:12 (April 1927), 21:7 (November 1920), and 29:4 (August 1928); A.J. Brewster, *An Introduction to Retail Advertising* (New York 1927), ch. 21; V. Vinikas, 'Lustrums of the Cleanliness Institute, 1927–1932,' *Journal of Social History*, 22:4 (summer 1989), 613–30.

42 *Furniture World*, 10:11 (November 1920).

43 *Shoe and Leather Journal*, 26:7 (1 April 1912); *Furniture World*, 6:3 (March 1916); *Canadian Grocer*, 15:14 (5 April 1901); *Canadian Pharmaceutical Journal*, 52:8 (March 1919); *Canadian Grocer*, 17:19 (8 May 1903) and 14:3 (19 January 1900).

44 *Canadian Grocer*, 28:4 (23 January 1914); *Furniture World*, 6:5 (May 1916); Brewster, *An Introduction to Retail Advertising*, 41; W.S. Dygert, *Advertising: Principles and Practices* (New York 1936), 18; *Men's Wear Review*, 12:4 (April 1922) and 11:1 (January 1921).

45 *Le Prix courant*, 33:42 (16 octobre 1925); *Men's Wear Review*, 12:4 (April 1922); W.S. Hayward, *Chain Store: Its Management and Operation* (New York 1925), 8; S.R. Hall, *Retail Advertising and Selling* (New York 1924), 71; *Marketing*, 25:13 (25 June 1927).

46 Hall, *Retail Advertising*, 54; *BC Retailer*, 21:7 (July 1928). The maths used to justify this approach were often suspect; see *Canadian Grocer*, 31:17 (27 April 1917).

47 *Western Retailer*, 26:3 (March 1939).

48 *BC Retailer*, 13:3 (November 1921). Many smaller retailers, particularly those who pursued a turnover approach without accurate bookkeeping, soon came to realize the wisdom of Stewart's urging: see, for example, SCO, Bankruptcy Office, 24:143, 'Transcript of Examination of R.J. Carson,' 28–29 January 1924.

49 *Canadian Pharmaceutical Journal*, 59:4 (November 1925); *Drug Merchandising*, 13:5 (9 March 1932); *Men's Wear Review*, 20:2 (February 1930). Squibb discussed its advertising in *Canadian Pharmaceutical Journal*, 64:16 (15 April 1931).

50 NAC, Milton Rous Papers, box 1, file 23, B.A. Simon to M.E. Rous, 8 June 1926; ibid., box 2, file 2, 'Working Agreement between Kelvinator Dealers and Distributors'; *Refrigeration and Air Conditioning*, 4:11 (November 1938).

The activities of Imperial Tobacco are discussed in Canada, Special Committee on Price Spreads and Mass Buying, *Minutes of Proceedings and Evidence*, vol. 2 (Ottawa 1935), 1812–913.

51 *Financial Post*, 13 March 1925 and 10 July 1925; *Canadian Grocer*, 41:13 (24 June 1927). Figures on failures in hardware calculated from *Hardware and Metal*, May 1923-October 1928; W.J. Geldart, *For Want of a Nail: The Story of Cochrane-Dunlop Hardware Ltd*. [n.p., n.d.].

52 G.M. Lebhar, *Chain Stores in America, 1859–1962* (New York 1963), passim; for Liggett, see S. Merwin, *Rise and Fight Again* (New York 1935), and Canada, Royal Commission on Price Spreads, *Minutes of Proceedings and Evidence* (Ottawa 1934), 1302–5.

53 *Drug Merchandising: Pharmacy from 50 Years of Leadership* (Toronto 1969); *Canadian Grocer*, 41:9 (29 April 1927) and 45:9 (24 April 1931); Royal Commission on Price Spreads, 1310–11.

54 Special Committee to Inquire into the Cost of Living, 409; *Canadian Grocer*, 43:4 (15 February 1929) and 45:9 (24 April 1931).

55 *Retailer*, 22:1 (January 1929).

56 *Retailer*, 22:1 (January 1929); Special Committee to Inquire into the Cost of Living, 584–5; Royal Commission on Price Spreads, 1311 and 1069–71; Safeway Stores Inc Archive, 'The Company Moves into Canada,' typescript dated 2 June 1976.

57 RCUWO, W.L. Mara Papers, John Forsyth Ltd to W.L. Mara, n.d. [December 1923]; Comfort Kimona Manufacturing Company to W.L. Mara, 3 December 1928; interview with F.J. Gaca, December 1987.

58 Brewster, *An Introduction to Retail Advertising*, 41; E.B. Weiss, *How to Sell to and through Department Stores* (New York 1936), 30; *Globe* cited in Special Committee to Inquire into the Cost of Living, 419.

59 *Dry Goods Review*, 35:5 (May 1923); *Maritime Merchant*, 40:18 (3 March 1932).

60 *Census of Canada, 1931*, vol. 7, table 7, 64–9.

61 *Canadian Pharmaceutical Journal*, 35:7 (February 1902); calculations on starting capital from Ontario bankruptcy records.

62 NAC, RG 36/1, Food Board Records, R.J. McFall, 'Memo on Marketing,' [July 1919?]; *Canadian Grocer*, 18:46 (11 November 1904).

63 Canada, Unpublished Sessional Papers, 205, in NAC, RG 14 D 2, vol. 75, 'Annual Report of the Board of Commerce,' 1920, 2.

64 SCO, Bankruptcy Office, 24:1248, Adrien Pommier file, 'Examination of Adrien Pommier'; *Furniture World*, 8:7 (July 1913); *Canadian Grocer*, 29:2 (8 January 1915) and 27:2 (10 January 1913).

65 *BC Retailer*, 18:5 (January 1926); *Canadian Grocer*, 44:22 (24 October 1930); Special Committee to Inquire into the Cost of Living, 592–3, 270 and 280–1.

66 *Shoe and Leather Journal*, 26:19 (1 October 1912); *Canadian Grocer*, 30:30 (30 July 1916); *Shoe and Leather Journal*, 36:4 (15 February 1923) and 36:13 (1 July 1923).

67 *Canadian Grocer*, 42:15 (20 July 1928) and 32:8 (22 February 1918); *BC Retailer*, 13:6 (February 1922); *Shoe and Leather Journal*, 36:4 (15 February 1923); *Western Retailer*, 25:8 (September 1938).

CHAPTER 5 The Survival of the Fittest

1 A.R.M. Lower, *My First Seventy-Five Years* (Toronto 1967), 22–3; F. Bruser Maynard, *Raisins and Almonds* (Toronto 1972), 92 and 61.

2 *Shoe and Leather Journal*, 37:6 (15 March 1924).

3 *Men's Wear Review*, 17:3 (March 1927); *Shoe and Leather Journal*, 26:2 (5 January 1912); AO, RG 22, Supreme Court of Ontario, Bankruptcy Office, 28:64, W. Claude Ives file, affidavit of debtor, 17 September 1931.

4 SCO, Bankruptcy Office, 24:479, James Barter file, evidence and judgment in the matter of the authorized assignment of James Barter, 11 April 1923.

5 Canada, Special Committee on Price Spreads and Mass Buying, *Proceedings and Evidence*, vol. 1 (Ottawa 1935), 398; SCO, Bankruptcy Office, 28:329, Alex Zimmerman file, affidavit of the debtor, 24:143, R.J. Carson file, examination of the debtor, 28–29 January 1924; 28:82, Leo Danson file, examination of the debtor, 20 March 1928.

6 *Census of Canada, 1931* vol. 10, (Ottawa 1936), part 1, table 15; *Census of Canada, 1941* vol. 10, (Ottawa 1946), part 1, table 18.

7 *Census of Canada, 1931*, vol. 10, part 1, table 15, *Census of Canada, 1941*, vol. 10, part 1, table 18. For a more detailed analysis, see D. Monod, 'Ontario Retailers in the Early Twentieth Century: Dismantling the Social Bridge,' *Journal of the Canadian Historical Association*, 1993, 207–28.

8 Sample size and procedures followed are discussed in chapter 1, note 19, above.

9 Calculated from SCO, Bankruptcy Office records for 1924, 1928, 1932, and 1937.

10 SCO, Bankruptcy Office, 37:91, M. Kinkhammer file, examination of the debtor, 14 April 1937; 37:57, A. Bowers file; 37:203, J.E. Monteith file, examination of the debtor, 24 September 1937.

11 J. Benson, *Penny Capitalism: A Study of Nineteenth Century Working Class Entrepreneurs* (Dublin 1983), 129–32; J. Benson, *Entrepreneurialism in Canada: A History of 'Penny Capitalists'* (Lewiston 1990), 86–8; B.Bradbury, 'The Family Economy and Work in an Industrializing City: Montreal in the 1870s,' Canadian Historical Association, *Historical Papers* 1979, 90; D. Blackbourn, 'Between Resignation and Volatility: The German Petite Bourgeoisie in the

Nineteenth Century,' in G. Crossick and H.-G. Haupt, eds., *Shopkeepers and Master Artisans in Nineteenth Century Europe* (London 1984), 42.

12 SCO, Bankruptcy Office, 37:91, M. Kinkhammer file, examination of the debtor, 14 April 1937; 37:252, A. Kari file; 28:420, White's Cycle and Sports file, examination of A.E. White, 14 December 1928; 28:735, L.W. Brickenden file, examination of the debtor, 7 May 1929; *General Merchant of Canada*, 4:2 (10 February 1931).

13 *Dry Goods Review*, 10:7 (July 1900) and 12:1 (January 1902).

14 AO, Hiram Walker Collection, 20–17, Bartlett, MacDonald & Gow Ltd. Records, reel 1, D. Cameron to C. MacDonald, 9 January 1885; R.M. Ballantyne to Bartlett, MacDonald & Gow Ltd., 26 December 1922; partnership notices, 16 January 1877, 1 March 1887, and 5 February 1903; balance sheet, 21 February 1874; reel 17, ledger 1917–27, 'Expense Account'; reel 22, ledger 1927–31, 'Donations.'

15 Bartlett, MacDonald & Gow Ltd. Records, reel 23, 'Information filed pursuant to Instructions to Taxpayers Compiling Standards [*sic*] Profits Claims,' 17 March 1942; reel 22, ledger 1927–31, ledger account no. 75–6.

16 Bartlett, MacDonald & Gow Ltd. Records, reel 22, inventories, 1888–1940.

17 *Marketing*, 29:1 (23 June 1928); Bartlett, MacDonald & Gow Ltd. Records, reel 23, 'Information filed pursuant to Instructions to Taxpayers,' Sales Records, 1888–1912, sales records, 1913–40; reel 22, Company Ledger, 1917–27.

18 UBC, Special Collections, Hoffmeister Electric Co. Records, I:1, F.J. Groowe to R. Hoffmeister, 11 April 1919; J.J. Crossman to R. Hoffmeister, 19 November 1919; I:3, R. Hoffmeister to Paul & Paul Co., 8 March 1936; I:3, BC tax receipts, 1921; dominion income tax forms, 1923–32. GAI, Bertram F. Souch Papers, Alberta income tax receipts, 1931–40.

19 The exception here was 1932, when the average country store declaring bankruptcy in Ontario had been open for thirteen years. Throughout the twenties and later thirties, however, bankrupt country and city stores averaged roughly the same number of years in business. Calculated from SCO, Bankruptcy Office files for 1924, 1928, 1932, and 1937.

20 *Canadian Grocer*, 37:40 (5 October 1923); B. Emmett and J.E. Jeuck, *Catalogues and Counters: A History of Sears Roebuck* (Chicago 1950), 317–23; AO, T. Eaton Co. Papers, Early Notices, 1919–21, R.Y. Eaton to Department Heads, 16 September 1921.

21 *Census of Canada, 1931*, vol. 8, xvii–xviii; S. Davies, 'Marketing a Dream: Automobile Advertising in the 1920s' (paper presented to the Canadian Historical Association Conference, Winnipeg 1986), 27ff., 23; G.T. Bloomfield, '"I Can See a Car in the Crop": Motorization in Saskatchewan, 1906–1934,' *Saskatchewan History*, 37:1 (Winter 1984), 6–9; D.F. Davis, 'Dependent

Motorization: Canada and the Automobile in the 1930s,' *Journal of Canadian Studies*, 21:3 (fall 1986), 123–4; *General Merchant of Canada*, 1:1 (5 January 1928). For the varied impact of the automobile on shopping, see G.W. Mellis, 'Mobility of Commercial Services and Their Impact on the Strengths of Urban Communities in Saskatchewan' (MA thesis, University of Saskatchewan 1971), 7–14.

22 For Eaton's, see Special Committee on Price Spreads, vol. 2, 3053; for Simpson's, ibid., 2744. See also SAB, Department of the Provincial Secretary, Pse 6(d), H.S. Carswell, 'Memo Re. Henry Markham,' 33R 378–62, 30 September 1933; Pse 6(a), 'Memorandum Re. Rex vs. Neal Brothers ltd.'

23 Special Committee on Price Spreads, vol. 3, 3423 and 2965–6; *Le Prix courant*, 41:24 (15 juin 1928) and 44:9 (6 mars 1931); *Canadian Grocer*, 40:26 (15 January 1926); *Dry Goods Review*, 41:7 (July 1929); *Canadian Grocer*, 44:1 (3 January 1930); *Financial Post*, 11 September 1925 and 30 September 1927. In this experience, Eaton's anticipated and possibly served as a model for Sears; see A.D. Chandler Jr, *Strategy and Structure* (Cambridge 1976), 239. The most comprehensive account of a mail-order company's move into chain retailing is contained in Emmett and Jeuck, *Catalogues and Counters*, 196–244 and 338–57; see also J.C. Worthy, *Shaping an American Institution: Robert E. Wood and Sears, Roebuck* (Urbana 1984).

24 Special Committee on Price Spreads, vol. 3, 3070, 3174–6, 3420–3.

25 Much of expansion of the big departmentals came at the expense of the smaller department stores. In 1926 twenty-two of the latter in Ontario and the Maritimes merged to form the Canadian Department Stores, a voluntary pool. Unfortunately, the pool members had problems with financing, and in 1928 Eaton's was able to step in and purchase the entire chain for a lean $4.5 million. See *Canadian Grocer*, 40:25 (18 June 1926); *Dry Goods Review*, 39:6 (June 1927) and 40:4 (April 1928); *Canadian Grocer*, 42:2 (20 January 1928); *Financial Post*, 30 March 1928; HBCA, HBC Papers, 'Minutes of the Canadian Committee,' vol. 2, 28 April 1922; Special Committee on Price Spreads, 469 and 3069–70; Canada, Royal Commission on Price Spreads, *Report* (Ottawa 1935), 206. The problems of the department stores in the twenties have been widely reported: C. Fraser, 'Can the Small Merchant Compete with the Large Store,' *Harvard Business Review*, 3 (1924–5), 460–1; A.W. Zelomek, 'New Opportunities for Distribution,' *Journal of Retailing*, 25:2 (Summer 1949), 49–53; H. Barger, *Distribution's Place in the American Economy* (Princeton 1955), 58–60; R.M. Hower, *A History of Macy's of New York, 1853–1919* (Cambridge 1943), 390–1; C.G. Woodhouse, *The Big Store* (New York 1943), 65; H. Pasdermadjian, *The Department Store: Its Origin, Evolution and Economics* (London 1954), 34–5 and 54–60.

26 D. Monod, 'Bay Days: The Managerial Revolution and the Hudson's Bay
     Company Department Stores, 1912–1939,' Canadian Historical Association,
     Historical Papers, 1986, 173–96; and to put that study in proper context, see
     A.J. Ray, *The Canadian Fur Trade in the Industrial Age* (Toronto 1990).

27 The discussion of Simpson's which follows is based on: Special Committee
     on Price Spreads, vol. 2, 2745, 2750–7; vol. 3, 2828–49; HBCA, Robert Simpson
     Co. Ltd, Annual Reports, 1918–40; Simpson's Ltd, Annual Reports, 1925–40;
     Simpson's Ltd and Robert Simpson Co. Ltd, Profit and Loss Statements, vol.
     1, 1921–30; Comparative Summary of Net Earnings, vol. 2, 1931–4, vol. 3,
     1935–9, and vol. 4, 1939–40.

28 Reorganization redistributed some of this burden, as did selling off a couple
     of million in government bonds and a new $10 million stock issue, but Simp-
     son's continued to carry a heavy and at times onerous burden of debt. It was
     largely because the company managed to distribute some of that debt
     among its employees through a stock- and profit-sharing plan that certain
     politicians became upset with the owners in the mid-1930s. There is no evi-
     dence, however, that Simpson's was trying to saddle its workers with over-
     inflated and debt-burdened stock. Simpson's was a solid and profitable cor-
     poration which under normal circumstances would have had no problems
     managing its obligations. It was no more than unlucky timing that the com-
     pany chose to expand its stock-sharing plan rapidly just four months before
     the October 1929 crash. For more on the Simpson's sale, see Special Commit-
     tee on Price Spreads, vol. 2, 2777–803; and for a sympathetic discussion of
     Flavelle's involvement in the store: M. Bliss, *A Canadian Millionaire: The Life
     and Business Times of Sir Joseph Flavelle, Bart., 1858–1939* (Toronto 1978), 391–2
     and 443–5.

29 C.L. Burton, *A Sense of Urgency: Memoirs of a Canadian Merchant* (Toronto
     1952), 302–3; *General Merchant of Canada*, 3:1 (10 January 1930); R. Cassidy and
     H.M. Haas, 'Analyzing the Market of the Mail Order House Retail Stores,'
     Harvard Business Review, 13 (1934–35), 493–502.

30 HBCA, HBC Papers, Unclassed Dead Dossiers, G8, D.A. Stackpole, 'Aide
     Memoire: The Administrative System and Structure of the Hudson's Bay
     Company,' 1942, part C-10.

31 *Canadian Grocer*, 47:3 (10 February 1933); *Men's Wear Review*, 23:3 (April
     1933).

32 Special Committee on Price Spreads, vol. 3, 3325–6; AO, T. Eaton Company
     Papers, Incoming Notices, 1930, Advisory Board Recommendations, 6 March
     1930; Incoming Notices, 1931, Resolution of Directors' Meeting, 19 October
     1931; Incoming Notices, 1933, J.A. Livingstone to Heads of Departments, 6
     May 1933; Incoming Notices, 1935, Extract from Directors' Meeting, 11

March 1935; J.A. Livingstone, Resolution from Directors' Meeting to H.F. Switzer, 3 March 1935.

33 Of course, the department stores would enjoy a brief second childhood in the 1960s. Until then they would grow fitfully – Eaton's first expansion since the late twenties would not come until 1948, when the store acquired Spencer's – or they would try to unload some of their existing operations, as when Simpson's sold off part of its mail-order to Sear's (in 1953). It was the suburban mall of the 1960s that revitalized department store selling, though their frenetic expansion would again land them in serious difficulties when the 1980s brought an end to the good times.

34 Canada, Royal Commission on Price Spreads, *Minutes of Proceedings and Evidence* (Ottawa 1935), 811, 1140, and 681.

35 Royal Commission on Price Spreads, 864–6 and 2364.

36 Calculations based on annual statements in *Canadian Grocer*, 39:9 (27 February 1925); see ibid., 43:5 (1 March 1929), for the period 1920–4; and Royal Commission on Price Spreads, 777–80, for the years 1925–30; see also *Canadian Grocer*, 43:5 (1 March 1929) and 44:2 (17 January 1930).

37 J.L. McLennan, 'The Merger Movement in Canada since 1880' (MA thesis, Queen's University 1929), 64–74; J.C. Weldon, 'Consolidation in Canadian Industry, 1900–1948,' in L.A. Skeoch, ed., *Restrictive Trade Practices in Canada* (Toronto 1966), 228–79. For specific cases, see *Canadian Grocer*, 42:1 (6 January 1928); *Financial Post*, 11 March 1927; *Canadian Grocer*, 62:5 (2 March 1928); *Financial Post*, 30 June 1929; *Canadian Grocer*, 40:9 (26 April 1926); Safeway Stores, 'The Company Moves into Canada'; *Canadian Grocer*, 43:4 (15 February 1929); *Financial Post*, 27 April 1928; *Canadian Grocer*, 43:18 (30 August 1929). See also *Canadian Grocer*, 42:15 (20 July 1928); the *Financial Post*, 16 March 1928, makes a similar observation.

38 For Dominion, Royal Commission on Price Spreads, 770–8; for Loblaw's, ibid., 1154–8; for Tamblyn, ibid., 1252–5; for Woolworth's, ibid., 606–9. For a breakdown of costs, see ibid., statistical insert to face 2258.

39 For Dominion, see Royal Commission on Price Spreads, 777–80; for Carroll's, ibid., 941–6; for the A & P, ibid., 867–72; for Liggett's, ibid., 1306–9; for Metropolitan, ibid., 710–12.

40 Royal Commission on Price Spreads, 777–80, 812–16, 763, 717, and 1210–16. To be fair, tight wages did affect managers as well as workers: see ibid., 1329, 1979 and 2012; HBCA, Hudson's Bay Company Papers, Minutes of the Canadian Advisory Committee, vol. 14, 'Appendix to Minutes,' 28 August 1932; Royal Commission on Price Spreads, 2398.

41 Royal Commission on Price Spreads, 2410 and 2549.

42 Royal Commission on Price Spreads, 2131–47, 1849, and 784–5.

43 Royal Commission on Price Spreads, 1979–84.

44 Royal Commission on Price Spreads, 794, 606–9, 679, 991–6, 1140–1, 3706, 3709–10, and 4281.

45 Royal Commission on Price Spreads, 3706, 140–4, 2367; Special Committee on Price Spreads, 3168; E.B. Weiss, *How to Sell to and through Department Stores* (New York 1936), 137.

46 *Western Retailer*, 22:11 (November 1935).

47 *Men's Wear Review*, 21:1 (January 1931).

48 H. Lasswell, 'The Psychology of Hitlerism,' *Political Quarterly*, 4 (1933), 374.

CHAPTER 6 Resale Price Maintenance

1 As C.A. Curtis wrote in 1938, the demand for price maintenance encapsulated the Canadian retailer's 'reaction against a competitive system which may in the interests of society eliminate him.' In its denial of 'modern' competitive forces, price maintenance is thought to have revealed the independent traders' inability to compete and adapt to changing conditions and it demonstrated their intellectual parochialism. See C.A. Curtis, 'Resale Price Maintenance,' *Canadian Journal of Economics and Political Science*, 4:3 (August 1938), 356; L. Reynolds, *The Control of Competition in Canada* (Cambridge 1940), 127; J.M. Bliss, *A Living Profit* (Toronto 1978), 37–40. This view also informs M. Cox, 'The Transformation of Regulation: Private Property and the Problem of Government Control in Canada, 1919–1939' (PhD thesis, York University 1990). For more on rpm, see B.S. Yamey, *The Economics of Resale Price Maintenance* (London, 1954).

2 A.D. Chandler Jr, *The Visible Hand: The Managerial Revolution in American Business* (Cambridge 1977), 486.

3 *Canadian Pharmaceutical Journal*, 42:10 (May 1909).

4 *Dry Goods Review*, 9:1 (January 1899) and 9:5 (May 1899).

5 *Canadian Grocer*, 3:20 (17 May 1889), 14:29 (20 July 1900), and 23:41 (8 October 1909).

6 *Dry Goods Review*, 7:4 (April 1897); *Canadian Grocer*, 14:6 (9 July 1900) and 14:47 (23 November 1900).

7 *Canadian Grocer*, 14:3 (19 January 1900); *Canadian Pharmaceutical Journal*, 37:3 (October 1903).

8 *Dry Goods Review*, 12:1 (January 1902); *Canadian Grocer*, 16:37 (12 September 1902).

9 *Dry Goods Review*, 7:4 (April 1897); *Retail Merchant's Journal* 4:4 (April 1906).

10 *Dry Goods Review*, 7:3 (March 1897) and 7:7 (July 1897). *Canadian Grocer* ran five articles from *Scribner's* dealing with department stores between January

and May 1897. For the activities of the MRGA, see *Canadian Grocer*, 11:10 (5 March 1897), and for the Middleton bill, ibid., 11:14 (2 April 1897), 11:16 (16 April 1897), and 12:2 (14 January 1898).

11 The founding of the RMA was ignored by the trade press. The *Dry Goods Review* referred to it on only a couple of occasions in 1897 and never with approval (in particular, see 6:8 [August 1897]); neither the *Canadian Grocer* nor *Hardware and Metal* chose to mention the RMA's foundation. The membership estimate is a generous one: other retail organizations at the turn of the century were all small: the Vancouver Retail Grocers' Association had a dozen members, the BC Master Bakers' Association had thirteen, and the Toronto and Montreal Retail Grocers' Associations each had around sixty. The biggest organization seems to have been the Toronto Druggists Association, which numbered slightly over one hundred. The RMA was probably on the larger side: we do know that it had twenty-eight members sitting on its legislative committee, and by May 1898 it had five trade sections with twenty-five people on their combined executives.

12 *Dry Goods Review*, 8:3 (March 1898); for the TLC resolution, see *Canadian Grocer*, 11:16 (16 April 1897).

13 For Trowern's suit, see *Trader*, 21:5 (January 1900); *Retail Merchants' Journal*, 3:9 (September 1905); *Dry Goods Review*, 31:10 (October 1919).

14 *Canadian Grocer*, 18:34 (19 August 1904).

15 *Canadian Pharmaceutical Journal*, 38:9 (April 1905); *Canadian Grocer*, 44:7 (28 March 1930) and 30:38 (26 September 1916).

16 *Drug Merchandising: Pharmacy from 50 Years of Leadership* (Toronto 1969); *Canadian Pharmaceutical Journal*, 43:7 (February 1910).

17 *Canadian Pharmaceutical Journal*, 33:2 (September 1899).

18 *Canadian Pharmaceutical Journal*, 43:7 (February 1910) and 39:6 (January 1906). Ontario did not have a provincial association; instead, the OCP maintained thirteen separate divisional associations and guided the newly formed ORDA, see *Canadian Pharmaceutical Journal*, 37:8 (March 1904).

19 *Canadian Pharmaceutical Journal*, 36:9 (April 1903) and 47:1 (August 1913).

20 *Dry Goods Review*, 9:3 (March 1899); *Canadian Pharmaceutical Journal*, 34:1 (August 1900) and 33:6 (January 1900).

21 *Canadian Pharmaceutical Journal*, 34:11 (June 1901) and 35:10 (May 1902); *Retail Merchants' Journal*, 2:11 (November 1904).

22 *Canadian Pharmaceutical Journal*, 42:4 (November 1909).

23 *Canadian Pharmaceutical Journal*, 36:11 (June 1903), and 37:4 (November 1903); *Wampole & Co. v. F.E. Karn Ltd.*, *Ontario Law Reports*, 11 (1906), 621–23.

24 *Wampole & Co. v. F.E. Karn Ltd.*, 623.

25 In the grocery line, shop owners were already complaining that the first Elli-

man price-protected item, Shredded Wheat, gave too large a profit margin to wholesalers at the expense of the retailers; see *Canadian Grocer*, 19:20 (16 July 1905) and 16:37 (12 September 1902).

26 *Canadian Pharmaceutical Journal*, 38:8 (March 1904), 37:1 (August 1903), and 37:9 (April 1904).

27 *Canadian Pharmaceutical Journal*, 37:8 (March 1904), 37:9 (April 1904), 38:2 (September 1904), 38:8 (March 1905); and 39:3 (October 1905); *Wampole & Co. v. F.E. Karn Ltd.*, 624.

28 *Canadian Pharmaceutical Journal*, 39:5 (December 1905), 39:6 (January 1906), 39:7 (February 1906), 42:2 (September 1908), and 42:3 (October 1908).

29 *Canadian Pharmaceutical Journal*, 42:10 (May 1909), 39:6 (January 1906), 44:4 (November 1910), 45:7 (February 1912), and 42:11 (June 1909).

30 *Retail Merchants' Journal*, 5:2 (February 1907); *Furniture World and the Undertaker*, 2:3 (November 1912); *BC Retailer*, 11:2 (August 1920); *Canadian Pharmaceutical Journal*, 46:3 (October 1912).

31 *Canadian Grocer*, 23:41 (8 October 1909), 24:21 (27 May 1910), and 23:20 (14 May 1909); Canada, Select Committee on Agricultural Conditions, *Proceedings* (Ottawa 1924), 1041 (John McElroy, who made this statement, was an RMA member); *Shoe and Leather Journal*, 26:4 (15 February 1912).

32 *Canadian Pharmaceutical Journal*, 46:5 (December 1912); *Canadian Grocer*, 28:4 (23 January 1914), 27 (16 May 1913), and 29:40 (1 October 1915).

33 *Canadian Pharmaceutical Journal*, 47:4 (November 1913), 46:3 (October 1912), and 46:4 (November 1912)

34 Canada, House of Commons, *Journals*, vol. 22 (1888), 'Report of the Select Committee to Investigate and Report upon Alleged Combinations in Manufactures, Trade and Insurance in Canada,' 3–5; *Rex v. Beckett et al., Ontario Law Reports*, 20 (1910), 420–1.

35 Canada, Special Committee to Inquire into the Cost of Living, *Minutes of Proceedings and Evidence* (Ottawa 1920), 163; Canada, Board of Inquiry into the Cost of Living, *Report of the Board* (Ottawa 1915), 12–19.

36 J.A. Corry, 'The Growth of Government Activities in Canada, 1914–1921,' Canadian Historical Association, *Report*, 1940, 67–70; R.C. Brown and R. Cook, *Canada 1896–1921: A Nation Transformed* (Toronto 1981), 237–9. The quote is from NAC, RG 110 3, F.A. Acland to T. White, 22 May 1919. For the orders urging restraint, see B. Wilson, *Ontario and the First World War* (Toronto 1977), 124; NAC, RG 36/1, PC 25, 8 March 1918; PC 2959, 19 October 1917; PC 2190, 9 September 1917.

37 NAC, RG 36/1, J.R. McFall, 'Memorandum on Marketing,' July 1919.

38 NAC, RG 36/6, vol. 36, Opening session of the Board of Commerce, Toronto, 11–13 September 1919, 17–18.

39 NAC, RG 36/6, vol. 1, W.F. O'Connor to H.A. Robson, 21 October 1919.

40 T. Traves, *The State and Enterprise: Canadian Manufacturers and the Federal Government, 1917–1931* (Toronto 1979), ch. 4; K. Cruikshank, 'Taking the Bitter with the Sweet: Canadian Sugar Refiners and the Canadian State, 1878–1920' (unpublished paper presented to the Canadian Historical Association Conference, 1990); and M. Cox, 'Innovation Denied: The Board of Commerce of Canada and the Problem of Expert Authority, 1919–1920,' in P. Baskerville, ed., *Canadian Papers in Business History* (Victoria 1989), 189–212.

41 The WGA did protest sugar order no. 82, but only because it allowed the department stores to sell for less. Furthermore, as White noted, the petition read like a 'subsidiary request on behalf of the retailers, or perhaps not a request, but rather an expression of an opinion.' In short, not a strong protest. See NAC, RG 36 6, vol. 14, A.C. Pryke to W. White, 29 June 1920, and W. White to A.C. Pryke, 6 July 1920.

42 By 1920 most well-to-do retailers kept ledgers in which they entered their purchases and sales, but these records would have listed mostly expenditures and earnings by name of customer or supplier, not by product. Even those that did keep highly detailed accounts tended to group their stock by brand name (Kellogg's cereals, Rose ribbons, Hathaway shirts, Keystone brushes) and not by generalized product or price categories. This method of bookkeeping was perfectly appropriate to most businesses – retailers were able to calculate profits and losses by month and even in many cases by department – but it would not allow them to fill in the blanks on O'Connor's forms. What the board wanted to know was the mark-up on fifty specific items organized into price clusters, a demand that would have required most merchants to keep a new set of records (or at the very least to make a monthly stocktaking). Many manufacturers also opposed the questionnaires, as did Eaton's. NAC, RG 36/6, vol. 57–9 contain correspondence with retailers concerning the questionnaires. The RMA's lists are in vol. 59, as is the correspondence with R.G. Dun's, which also supplied lists. Retailers began to complain about the questionnaires in March 1920; the quote is from vol. 58, C. Bumside to Board of Commerce, 3 June 1920.

43 NAC, RG 36/6, vol. 14, H.C. Beckett to W.F. O'Connor, 10 January 1920, copy letter H.C. Beckett to E.M. Trowern, 2 January 1920; ibid., vol. 34, H.C. Beckett to G.D. Robertson, 20 January 1920; ibid., Board of Commerce Inquiry into the Wholesale Grocers' Association, 90–2.

44 On the guild/WGA, see Canada, House of Commons, *Journals*, 22 (1888), appendix 3, 3–29; *Rex v. Beckett et al., Ontario Law Reports*, 20 (1910), 401–32; Special Committee to Inquire into the Cost of Living, 393–402, 417–28; NAC, RG 36/6, vol. 34, CWGA, 'Canada's Board of Commerce: The Businessman's

Court,' 2 December 1919. O'Connor's opinion of the WGA was expressed in his judgment following an investigation into the association; see NAC, RG 36/6, vol. 24, Board of Commerce Inquiry into the Wholesale Grocers' Association of Canada, 888–91.

45 NAC, RG 36/6, vol. 34, C.C. Cooper to H.A. Robson, 10 February 1920, contains a complaint by a wholesaler (Macdonald Cooper Ltd) about the high mark-ups the association had imposed on the trade. O'Connor frequently rebuffed complaints against the WGA; see ibid., vol. 25, Wholesale Grocers' versus Dominion Canners Ltd, 19 February 1920; ibid., vol. 24, W.F. O'Connor to G. Keen, 6 February 1920, and W.F. O'Connor to M. Clow, 10 November 1919.

46 NAC, RG 36/6, vol. 47, Transcript of address to Mr Fitzpatrick by the Secretary of the Clothing Section of the RMA, 16 January 1920; *Men's Wear Review*, 9:12 (December 1919) and 10:1 (January 1920); NAC, RG 36/6, vol. 47, W.H. Blair to Chief Commissioner of the Board of Commerce, 25 February 1920.

47 NAC, RG 36/6, vol. 58 and 59 contain hundreds of protests against the board's questionnaires, as well as objections from two dozen RMA locals. See also ibid., 14–1, E.M. Trowern to W. White, 9 July 1920.

48 *Canadian Grocer*, 38:6 (8 February 1924).

49 *Canadian Grocer*, 35:7 (18 February 1921), 35:8 (25 February 1921), 35:15 (14 April 1921), and 36:26 (30 June 1922); *Attorney General for Ontario v. Canadian Wholesale Grocers' Association, Ontario Law Reports*, 53 (1923), 662; Cox, 'Innovation Denied,' 208.

50 NAC, RG 36/6, vol. 13, W. White, Memorandum for the Prime Minister, 29 July 1920; Special Committee to Inquire into the Cost of Living, 329; *Rex v. Beckett et al., Ontario Law Reports*, 20 (1910), 401.

51 NAC, RG 36/6, vol. 13, W. White, Memorandum for the Prime Minister, 29 July 1920.

52 House of Commons, *Debates*, 1923, 2520–1.

53 House of Commons, *Debates*, 1923, 2529, and 2521; *Financial Post*, 17 (11 May 1923); *Canadian Grocer*, 37:12 (23 March 1923).

54 *Canadian Grocer*, 36:17 (28 April 1922), 36:19 (12 May 1922).

55 *Canadian Grocer*, 39:5 (30 January 1925), 39:16 (17 April 1925), 39:33 (14 August 1925), and 41:23 (24 June 1927); *Financial Post*, 18 (20 June 1924), 19 (30 January 1925), (4 September 1925).

56 NAC, RG 36/6, vol. 34, E.M. Trowern to H.L. Drayton, 31 May 1920; *Canadian Grocer*, 34:21 (28 May 1920), 34:23 (4 June 1920), and 35:3 (21 January 1921); *Furniture World*, 10:10 (October 1920); *Men's Wear Review*, 32:6 (June 1920). Price deflation, not the RMA, was primarily responsible for the withdrawal of the unpopular tax.

57 *BC Retailer*, 12:1 (September 1921).

58 *BC Retailer*, 13:12 (August 1922); *Men's Wear Review*, 9:7 (July 1919) and 9:10 (October 1919).

59 *BC Retailer*, 16:10 (June 1923) and 17:6 (February 1924); *Druggists' Weekly*, 3:41 (1 November 1922) and 6:2 (21 January 1925).

60 *Druggists' Weekly*, 4:9 (28 February 1923) and 5:40 (1 October 1924); *Canadian Pharmaceutical Journal*, 58:8 (March 1925).

61 *Canadian Grocer*, 40:28 (23 July 1926); see also Crowder obituary in *Vancouver Province*, 31 May 1974.

62 In Ontario this move was undoubtedly partly a defensive measure. In the year prior to the affiliation, the druggists' section of the ORMA had grown from 50 to 700 members, while the ORDA had started to shrink. See *Druggists' Weekly*, 3:6 (8 February 1922) and 4:9 (28 February 1923); *Canadian Pharmaceutical Journal*, 55:10 (May 1922).

63 *Canadian Pharmaceutical Journal*, 56:4 (November 1922); on the British PATA, see ibid., 58:6 (January 1925) and 58:7 (February 1925); *Druggists' Weekly*, 1:19 (12 May 1920), 1:28 (14 July 1920), and 2:11 (16 March 1921).

64 *Canadian Pharmaceutical Journal*, 57:6 (January 1924) and 58:4 (November 1924); the CPhA's attacks on the RMA can be found in ibid., 55:2 (September 1921), 55:4 (November 1921), and 55:10 (May 1922).

65 *Canadian Pharmaceutical Journal*, 56:4 (November 1922), 56:9 (April 1923), and 57:1 (August 1923); *Druggists' Weekly*, 4:24 (13 June 1923) and 4:27 (4 July 1923). Twenty years before, the leaders of the CPhA remarked disparagingly that 'Mr. Glyn-Jones and commercial pharmacy have become almost synonymous terms in England' See *Canadian Pharmaceutical Journal*, 36:1 (August 1902).

66 *Druggists' Weekly*, 4:9 (28 February 1923), 4:24 (13 June 1924), and 4:27 (4 July 1924); *Canadian Pharmaceutical Journal*, 56:9 (April 1923), 57:1 (August 1923), and 58:8 (March 1925).

67 *Canadian Pharmaceutical Journal*, 58:10 (May 1925); *Druggists' Weekly*, 6:8 (15 April 1925); *Canadian Pharmaceutical Journal*, 58:11 (June 1925).

68 *Canadian Pharmaceutical Journal*, 58:12 (July 1925) and 59:3 (November 1925); *Drug Merchandising*, 6:11 (27 May 1925) and 6:15 (22 July 1925). The charge against the PATA was made by both George Tamblyn, in *Drug Merchandising*, 7:1 (6 January 1926), and by L.V. O'Connor, who authored the combines investigation report on the organization; see Canada, Department of Labour, 'Investigation into the Proprietary Articles Trading Association, Report of the Commissioner' (Ottawa 1927).

69 The reports of the investigations can be found in NAC, RG 110 vol. 72.

70 NAC, RG 110, vol. 72, 'Minutes of Joint Meeting of the Manufacturing,

Wholesale and Retail Druggists,' 29 May 1925; *Canadian Pharmaceutical Journal*, 59:11 (June 1926).

71 NAC, RG 110, vol. 72, 'Minutes of Joint Meeting of the Manufacturing, Wholesale and Retail Druggists,' 29 May 1925.

72 The largest stores generally did a smaller prescription business. For the midsized, estimates are based on a total gross profit of 34 per cent including prescriptions, estimating the dispensary trade at 15 per cent of the total. One small druggist in Saskatoon complained that PATA list prices were 20 per cent below what he had to charge; see NAC, RG 110, vol. 72, file 40, R.M. Pinder to J.G. Pearson, 21 December 1926. See also DBS, *Census of Trading Establishments, 1924* (Ottawa 1928), table 11. Reynolds, *The Control of Competition in Canada,* charges that PATA retail margins were 'unduly generous' and further suggests that 'there would probably have been a tendency, too, for these margins to increase with the passage of time.' The latter point is, of course, pure speculation, though it is significant that margins did not rise under the English PATA. As to the 'undue' generosity, we really need to put this issue in perspective. While the PATA affected margins, it did not raise prices in 90 per cent of cases. See PATA price lists in NAC, RG 110, vol. 12, 'List of PATA Articles: Minimum Retail and Minimum Wholesale Re-Selling Prices, 1927.'

73 NAC, RG 110, vol. 72, 'Minutes of Joint Meeting of the Manufacturing, Wholesale and Retail Druggists,' 29 May 1925. Smaller jobbers felt squeezed by the PATA's margins; see ibid., vol. 70, Bate and Bate Wholesale Drugs to Secretary of PATA, 9 September 1926, and vol. 72, R.M. Pinder to J.G. Pearson, 21 December 1926. Interestingly, the minimum retail prices on the PATA list were set according to the prices listed in the Eaton's mail-order catalogue; see ibid., vol. 71, W. Glyn-Jones to L.G. Henderson, 4 September 1926.

74 *Men's Wear Review,* 17:2 (February 1927); *Canadian Grocer,* 40:4 (22 January 1926).

75 *Canadian Grocer,* 40:6 (5 February 1926), 40:10 (5 March 1926), 40:13 (26 March 1926), and 40:19 (7 May 1926).

76 *Canadian Grocer,* 40:8 (5 February 1926), 40:10 (5 March 1926), 40:15 (16 April 1926), and 40:19 (7 May 1926).

77 *Canadian Grocer,* 40:12 (19 March 1926); *Marketing,* 22:9 (2 May 1925); *Drug Merchandising,* 8:10 (11 May 1927).

78 *Marketing,* 22:6 (21 March 1925); *Canadian Grocer,* 41:9 (29 April 1927) and 40:33 (1 October 1926); DBS, *Census of Merchandising, 1924,* table 7 and *Census of Canada, 1931* (Ottawa 1934), table 6B.

79 *Drug Merchandising,* 6:17 (19 August 1925) and 6:18 (2 September 1925). *Canadian Pharmaceutical Journal,* 59:8 (March 1926); *Drug Merchandising,* 8:13 (22 June 1927).

80 *Canadian Pharmaceutical Journal,* 59:8 (March 1926), 60:2 (September 1926), and 60:3 (October 1926); *Marketing,* 34:2 (23 January 1926).

81 Canada, Department of Labour, Investigation into the Proprietary Articles Trading Association, 'Interim Report' (Ottawa 1927), 14–17; *Drug Merchandising,* 8:5 (2 March 1927) and 8:8 (13 April 1927).

82 NAC, RG 110, vol. 70, 'Minutes of PATA Proceedings,' 11 February 1927.

83 *Drug Merchandising,* 8:5 (2 March 1927); *Canadian Pharmaceutical Journal,* 60:6 (January 1927), 60:7 (February 1927), and 60:9 (April 1927); *Drug Merchandising,* 8:8 (13 April 1927); *Canadian Pharmaceutical Journal,* 60:8 (March 1927), 61:8 (March 1927), and 61:1–4 (August–November 1927); *Drug Merchandising,* 8:21 (9 November 1927).

84 *Drug Merchandising,* 10:2 (16 January 1929) and 7:5 (1 August 1936); *Canadian Pharmaceutical Journal,* 66:7 (1 September 1933).

85 *Retailer,* 21:8 (August 1928) and 22:1 (January 1929); *Canadian Grocer,* 43:18 (30 August 1930). For the leadership crisis at the RMA, see *Dry Goods Review,* 40:10 (October 1928); *Retailer,* 23:11 (November 1930); and *Canadian Grocer,* 44:17 (15 August 1930).

86 *Drug Merchandising,* 10:18 (28 August 1929) and 9:18 (29 August 1928); *Canadian Pharmaceutical Journal,* 63:17 (1 May 1930), 63:23 (1 August 1930), and 63:10 (15 January 1930).

87 *Canadian Grocer,* 43:21 (11 October 1929), and *BC Retailer,* 20:3 (November 1927).

88 *Drug Merchandising,* 6:2 (21 January 1925), 8:8 (11 May 1927), and 6:8 (15 April 1925); *Canadian Pharmaceutical Journal,* 60:2 (September 1926).

89 *Canadian Pharmaceutical Journal,* 56:4 (November 1922); *Drug Merchandising,* 6:19 (16 September 1925) and 6:2 (21 January 1925); *Canadian Pharmaceutical Journal,* 58:2 (24 September 1924).

90 *Canadian Pharmaceutical Journal,* 38:2 (September 1904).

91 *Canadian Pharmaceutical Journal,* 38:2 (September 1904).

92 *Drug Merchandising,* 8:8 (11 May 1927) and 13:3 (10 February 1932).

93 *Canadian Pharmaceutical Journal,* 60:9 (April 1927), and *Drug Merchandising,* 6:9 (16 September 1925).

CHAPTER 7 The Politics of Folklore

1 The texts of R.B. Bennett's New Deal speeches were published as *The Premier Speaks to the People* (Ottawa 1935), sizeable excerpts can be found in J.R. Wilbur, *The Bennett New Deal: Fraud or Portent* (Toronto 1968). The *New York Times Magazine* article is cited in D.A. Hounshell, *From the American System to Mass Production* (Baltimore 1984), 322.

2 M.A. Ormsby, 'T. Dufferin Pattullo and the Little New Deal,' *Canadian Historical Review*, 40:4 (December 1962), 283; NAC, Paul Gouin Papers, vol. 9, E. Minville, 'Pourqoui de la petite industrie,' n.d.; and vol. 26, E. Minville's address to L'Association des marchands détaillants, in 'Raport officiel du 33ième congrès annuelle de la Province du Québec,' 9–10 septembre 1941; NAC, H.H. Stevens Papers, vol. 40, speech given in Grimsby, Ontario, n.d. [March 1934].

3 H.F. Quinn, *The Union Nationale* (Toronto 1979), 71; J.R. Wilbur, *H.H. Stevens* (Toronto 1977), 183. It is hardly surprising that John Irving, who believe that the Social Credit movement grew out of fear, status anxieties, and hero-worship, should have emphasized the support received from small-town business-people; see J.A. Irving, *The Social Credit Movement in Alberta* (Toronto 1959), 99, 334–3.

4 *Retailer*, 25:2 (February 1932).

5 *Retailer*, 23:10 (October 1930); CRHA, Minutes of the Retail Hardware and Stove Dealers' Association, Minutes of Directors' Meeting, 16 February 1931, and Minutes of 29th Annual Convention, 13–16 February 1934; *Retailer*, 25:4 (April 1932).

6 Calculated from *Canada Year Book, 1920* (Ottawa 1922), 329–35, *Canada Year Book, 1926* (Ottawa 1928), 390–5; and *Canada Year Book, 1932* (Ottawa 1934), 330–7.

7 Calculated from *Canada Year Book, 1932*, 330–7 and *Canada Year Book, 1936* (Ottawa 1938), 424–9. Changing consumption patterns were calculated from DBS, *Women's Factory Clothing Industry in Canada, 1929* (Ottawa 1930), and *Women's Factory Clothing Industry in Canada, 1933* (Ottawa 1934); DBS, *The Men's Furnishing Goods Industry in Canada, 1929* (Ottawa 1930), and *The Men's Furnishing Goods Industry in Canada, 1933* (Ottawa 1934); DBS, *Estimated Consumption of Meats, Dairy Products and Eggs, 1929* (Ottawa 1930), and *Estimated Consumption of Meats, Dairy Products and Eggs, 1933* (Ottawa 1934). Cotton underwear manufacturers began to experience difficulties in 1927–8; see *Monthly Commercial Letter Issued by the Bank of Commerce*, 153 (August 1928). For more on underwear, see E. Ewing, *Fashion in Underwear* (London 1971), 101, and W.H. Dooley, *Economics of Clothing and Textiles* (Boston 1934), 437–43.

8 NAC, RG 33/18, vol. 25, Swift Canada Co. Ltd to Moyer Brothers Ltd, 19 April 1934; *Canadian Woodworker and Furniture Manufacturing*, 35:7 (March 1935).

9 Calculated from *Canada Year Book, 1932*, 330–7, and *Canada Year Book, 1936* (Ottawa 1938), 424–9; *Census of Canada, 1931*, vol. 6 (Ottawa 1936), Table 13.

10 Calculated from *Canada Year Book, 1932*, 330–7, and *Canada Year Book, 1936*,

424–9. These figures do not provide for taxes, depreciation, payment on debt, and the like. For more on furniture, see J. Parr, *The Gender of Breadwinners* (Toronto 1990), 206–8.

11 Calculated from *Canada Year Book, 1932,* 330–7, and *Canada Year Book, 1936,* 424–9; F.R. Scott and H.M. Cassidy, *Labour Conditions in the Men's Clothing Industry* (Toronto 1935), 70.

12 *Dry Goods and Stylewear Review,* 45:9 (September 1933).

13 Canada, Special Committee on Price Spreads and Mass Buying, *Proceedings and Evidence,* vol. 2 (Ottawa 1934), 1939–40; NAC, RG 33/18, vol. 6, 'Copy of Memorandum Presented to the Right Honourable R.B. Bennett by Mr. Warren K. Cook ... November 3 1933'; NAC, Rg 33/18, vol. 6, Associated Clothing Manufacturers of the Province of Quebec, 'A Brief Summary of Conditions of the Clothing Industry of this Province'; Special Committee on Price Spreads, vol. 1, 91.

14 NAC, RG 33/18, vol. 6, 'Statement of Montreal Clothing Manufacturers' Association.'

15 Canada, Tariff Board, *Report of the Tariff Board in Reference 93: Furniture* (n.d. [1938?]); NAC, James Malcolm Papers, vol. 1, C.M. Bell to J. Malcolm, 1 February 1935 and Vol. 6, N.W. Tolmie to Alex Malcolm, 25 November 1931.

16 NAC, RG 33/18, vol. 137, Interview with M.L. Chalk, 26 April 1934; *Furniture World,* 23:3 (March 1933).

17 The druggists, for example, were solely interested in finding a way to legalize PATA-style organizations. Their interest in the passage of a national industrial recovery act derived from the fact that codification would have demanded changes to Canada's combines policy and these changes would have facilitated resale price maintenance. See *Canadian Pharmaceutical Journal,* 68:11 (1 February 1932), and *Drug Merchandising,* 15:9 (1 May 1934) and 15:18 (15 September 1934).

18 *Furniture World,* 25:1 (January 1935).

19 GBCA, Associated Clothing Manufacturers Inc. Papers, vol. 8/4 contains the association's first agreement with the Amalgamated Clothing Workers' Union; T.W. Learie discussed the organization's collapse in *Men's Wear Review,* 16:3 (March 1926). For context, see J. Naylor, *The New Democracy* (Toronto 1991), chs. 1 and 7; the quote is from GBCA, Associated Clothing Manufacturers Inc, box 11, 'Arguments presented to the Board of Arbitration,' 23 April 1920.

20 GBCA, Associated Clothing Manufacturers Inc., box 12/2, circular letters to retail dealers 24 January 1924 and 20 November 1922; *Men's Wear Review,* 16:3 (March 1926), 18:2 (February 1928), and 16:3 (March 1926); *Men's Wear Review,* 18:3 (March 1928) and 18:10 (October 1928).

21 *Men's Wear Review*, 20:2 (February 1930). During the Depression, the administration of direct relief for the unemployed in Ontario had been in the hands of the municipalities, but most places had followed a common system of distributing relief vouchers, which were redeemed at specified independent retail stores. See AO, RG 3/1, box 169, R.P. Sparks to J.D. Monteith, 16 February 1933; interview with F.J. Gaca, December 1988. For the Central Supply Warehouse, see AO, RG 3/1, box 169, R.P. Sparks to J.D. Monteith, 16 February 1933; T.W. Learie to G.S. Henry, 19 April 1933; Toronto *Globe*, 31 October 1932, 5 November 1932 and 30 November 1932; AO, RG 3/1 box 169, 'Memorandum Re Central Supply Warehouse'; *Men's Wear Merchandising*, 24:4 (August 1934); *Dry Goods and Stylewear Review*, 45:1 (January 1933) and 46:8 (August 1934).

22 NAC, RG 33/18, vol. 6, W. Cook, 'Short Stories,' 5–6.

23 GBCA, Associated Clothing Manufacturers Inc., box 1/1, W. Johnston to J.F. Marsh, 24 October 1934.

24 NAC, RG 33/18, vol. 6, Cook, 'Short Stories,' 6; *Men's Wear Review*, 23:8 (August 1933); *Dry Goods and Stylewear Review*, 45:9 (September 1933).

25 *Men's Wear Review*, 23:8 (August 1933).

26 *Dry Goods and Stylewear Review*, 46:9 (September 1934); *Furniture World*, 20:8 (August 1933), 20:10 (October 1933), 21:3 (March 1934), and 21:8 (August 1934); Parr, *Gender of Breadwinners*, 208–9.

27 *Industrial Canada*, 37:1 (May 1936). A more limited survey of 200 Quebec manufacturers in late 1932 found that only 7 per cent favouring the eight-hour day; see *Industrial Canada*, 33:9 (January 1933). Support for the idea of work reduction in the United States peaked in 1933; see B.K. Hunnicutt, 'Kellogg's Six-Hour Day: A Capitalist Vision of Liberation through Managed Work Reduction,' *Business History Review*, 66 (summer 1992), 489.

28 *Retailer*, 21:8 (August 1928).

29 One of Cook's letters can be found in SAB, Saskatchewan Retail Merchants' Association Papers, file 545, W.K. Cook to W.L. McQuarrie, 19 October 1933; see also *Retailer*, 26:8 (August 1933). For early retail attitudes to the New Deal, see *Retailer*, 26:11 (November 1933), and E. Hawley, *The New Deal and the Problem of Monopoly* (Princeton 1966), 83–84.

30 *Retailer*, 25:5 (May 1932); NAC, R.B. Bennett Papers, 275441–5, R. Webb to R.B. Bennett, 12 August 1934, and 277569, J.R. MacNicol to G. Perley, 8 April 1935.

31 *Men's Wear Merchandising*, 34:1 (February 1934); UTA, H.M. Cassidy Papers, box 64, J. Giroux to H.M. Cassidy, 16 March 1934.

32 NAC, H.H. Stevens Papers, vol. 22, W.K. Cook to H.H. Stevens, 10 August 1933; *Men's Wear Review*, 18:1 (January 1933). That Sparks and Learie were

involved is revealed by their comments in *Men's Wear Review*, 18:2 (February 1933). Sparks had first advised Stevens during the Customs' scandal of 1926: see Canada, *House of Commons Debates*, 1926, 4819; Stevens's own lack of interest in sweatshops prior to speaking with Sparks and Learie is shown by his response to questioning in the *House of Commons Debates*, 1932, 1325.

33 For more sympathetic portraits of Stevens, see Wilbur, *H.H. Stevens*, and L.A. Glassford, *Reaction & Reform: The Politics of the Conservative Party under R.B. Bennett* (Toronto 1992), 137–53. The quotes are from NAC, H.H. Stevens Papers, vol. 3, H.H. Stevens to R.J. Manion, 6 December 1929, and H.H. Stevens to R.B. Bennett, 7 November 1929: NAC, Charles Murphy Papers, C. Murphy to A.W. Robertson, 31 October 1934. O.H. Hill, *Canada's Salesman to the World: The Department of Trade and Commerce, 1892–1939* (Toronto 1977), ch. 20; NAC, R.B. Bennett Papers, 476050–3, R.B. Bennett to H.H. Stevens, 20 April 1934. For the Harbour Commission scandal, see R.B. Bennett Papers, 230802–1038.

34 A transcript of the speech 'Fair Trading or the Menace of Unfair or Unethical Trading Practices' can be found in box 110 of the Stevens Papers.

35 *Retailer*, 37:2 (February 1934); NAC, Charles Murphy Papers, box 26, C. Murphy to A.W. Robertson, 31 October 1934.

36 NAC, H.H. Stevens Papers, vol. 110, W.K. Cook to H.H. Stevens, 17 January 1934; *Men's Wear Merchandising*, 24:1 (February 1934); NAC, H.H. Stevens Papers, vol. 110, H.H. Stevens to J.B. Thomson, 22 January 1934.

37 R.B. Hanson, who succeeded Stevens as minister of trade and commerce, assured the House that 'we have no power, even were we so disposed, to set up a code similar to the NRA,' just moments after Stevens asserted that his aim was to 'get a code system.' See *House of Commons Debates*, 1934, 198–9 and 203.

38 Special Committee on Price Spreads, 125–6, 150, and 160.

39 This focus did not sit all that well with ordinary shopkeepers, and the *Retailer* was even led to question the attention being devoted to the departmentals and to wonder why the chains were not being similarly 'pilloried'; see *Retailer*, 27:3 (March 1934).

40 Special Committee on Price Spreads, 303; *Financial Post*, 3 March 1934; NAC, H.H. Stevens Papers, vol. 110, Speech to Conservative Study Club, 27 June 1934; NAC, W.L. Mackenzie King Papers, 172363, W.L. Mackenzie King to V. Massey, 7 August 1934.

41 *Men's Wear Merchandising*, 24:1 (February 1934); *Dry Goods and Stylewear Review*, 46:11 (November 1934) and 47:2 (15 February 1935).

42 NAC, H.H. Stevens Papers, vol. 40, H.H. Stevens to R. Messier, 26 May 1934;

vol. 98, H.H. Stevens to G. Hougham, 11 July 1934, and G. Hougham to H.H. Stevens, 23 July 1934.

43 *Dry Goods and Stylewear Review*, 46:5 (May 1934); NAC, H.H. Stevens papers, vol. 98, G.S. Hougham to H.H. Stevens, 23 July 1934; CRHA, ORHA, Minutes of Meetings, Minutes of Thirteenth Annual Convention, 12–15 February 1935, and Minutes of Directors' Meeting, 14 February 1935.

44 HBCA, Hudson's Bay Company Papers, RG 2, Series 7, file 524, A.Y. Little to P.A. Chester, 27 August 1931; *Canadian Grocer*, 45:1 (2 January 1931); *Maritime Merchant*, 42:20 (29 March 1934).

45 Canada, Royal Commission on Price Spreads, *Minutes of Proceedings and Evidence* (Ottawa 1935), 2066; NAC, RG 33/18, vol. 141, memorandum by J.G. Johnston concerning the Canadian Chain Store Association and attached by-laws, 24 February 1934; Royal Commission on Price Spreads, 2543 and 1905–24.

46 Royal Commission on Price Spreads, 3652.

47 NAC, R.B. Bennett Papers, 471474–6, J.L. Vaughan to R.C. Matthews, 30 May 1934. Burton did make up for the rest, denouncing Stevens and his associates (in one of his more colourful speeches) as just so many 'worms raising their heads to crawl about, leaving a slimy trail behind them that was putrefying and destroying the country'; see newspaper clippings cited in Wilbur, *H.H. Stevens*, 165. For Burton's view, see his *A Sense of Urgency: Memoirs of a Canadian Merchant* (Toronto 1952), 306–15.

48 HBCA, Hudson's Bay Company Papers, G 16, P.A. Chester, memo on meeting with J.E. Dodds of the T. Eaton Company, 8 September 1934; RG 2, series 7, file 524, 'Minutes of Store Managers' Conference' 7–10 January 1935; Royal Commission on Price Spreads, 1741–3.

49 NAC, H.H. Stevens Papers, vol. 41, speech to RMA Convention and unidentified press clipping, 5 November 1934; *Ottawa Journal* press clipping, 5 December 1934, vol. 110, Toronto *Globe* press clipping, 16 January 1934; Special Committee on Price Spreads, vol. 1, 394 and 768.

50 AO, T. Eaton Company Papers, 37–20, W.J. Abercrombie to D.S. McKellar, 11 January 1935.

51 NAC, H.H. Stevens Papers, vol. 125, Warren Cook to H.H. Stevens, 15 March 1935; R.B. Bennett Papers, 277564–5, J.R. MacNicol to Sir George Perley, 4 April 1935. The retailers' response was typically distressing. Stevens received about four hundred letters of support, but of these only eighteen came from RMA locals and an additional seventy-six were from individual shopkeepers. See NAC, H.H. Stevens Papers, vol. 127, 'Memorandum: Letters of Support,' 5 April 1935; ibid., vol. 41, Speech to RMA Convention, 5 November 1934.

52 W. Aitken, Lord Beaverbrook, *Friends: Sixty Years of Intimate Personal Relations with Richard Bedford Bennett* (London 1959), 89. The main difference between Stevens and the other reformers was that they mostly thought government spending, rather than regulatory control, was the best way of alleviating the Depression. The minister of railways, R.J. Manion, Bennett's brother-in-law William Herridge, and General McNaughton, the chief of staff, all thought recovery should be stimulated by massive public works spending on the construction of a St Lawrence seaway. See W.D. Herridge to R.B. Bennett, 16 January 1935, cited in Wilbur, *The Bennett New Deal*, 69; NAC, R.J. Manion Papers, box 9, W.D. Herridge to R.J. Manion, 22 March 1935. Tommy Church, the flamboyant ex-mayor of Toronto and a junior Conservative MP, wanted to create jobs and encourage investment by having the government purchase, level, and then rebuild the greater part of downtown Toronto; see *House of Commons Debates*, 1935, vol. 2, 1221–5. See also D. Forster and C. Read, 'The Politics of Opportunism: The New Deal Broadcasts,' *Canadian Historical Review*, 60:3 (1979), 329–35.

53 *House of Commons Debates*, 1935, 2668; unidentified letter to Stevens, cited in Wilbur, *H.H. Stevens*, 166.

54 The report was written by L.B. Pearson in collaboration with a group of Queen's University economists. The story of its creation can be traced through the correspondence in NAC, RG 33/18, vols. 150 and 138. See also *House of Commons Debates*, 1935, 1935, 3791–801.

55 A helpful memorandum on the implementation of the report can be found in GAI, R.B. Bennett Papers, vol. 2, file 37, marked 'Secret and Confidential.'

56 The *Maritime Merchant*, 63:23 (9 May 1935), described the NRA as 'unfair to consumers' and 'work[ing] against national recovery'; see also *Canadian Pharmaceutical Journal*, 68:17 (1 May 1935), and Hawley, *The New Deal and the Problem of Monopoly*, 67.

57 *Toronto Daily Star*, 7 June 1934; for manufacturer response to the Arcand Act, see GBCA, Associated Clothing Manufacturers Inc. Papers, box 1, file 1, W. Johnston to A. Kasman.

58 GBCA, Associated Clothing Manufacturers Inc. Papers, box 12 file 1, contains recommendations and activities of the Associated concerning the ISA; see also AO, RG 7, 1–3, T.W. Learie to D.A. Croll, 27 June 1935. For a survey, see M. Cox, 'The Limits of Reform: Industrial Regulation and Management Rights in Ontario, 1930–1937,' *Canadian Historical Review*, 68:4 (December 1987), 552–75. Furniture makers drew up their own 'code' in the summer of 1934, and it was this voluntary agreement that the ISA legalized and made binding; see *Furniture World*, 24:8 (August 1934), 25:1 (January 1935), and 25:7 (July–August 1935); AO, RG 7, 1–3, 'Statement of the Furniture Manufactur-

ers of Ontario Regarding the Industrial Standards Act,' June 1936, and J.A. Ferguson to D.A. Croll, 9 January 1936; Parr, *Gender of Breadwinners*, 220–4.

59 NAC, H.H. Stevens Papers, vol. 125, Platform of the Reconstruction Party, n.d.; *Financial Post*, 38 (20 July 1935).

60 A blow-by-blow account of the campaign may be found in Wilbur, *H.H. Stevens*, ch. 6.

61 *Dry Goods and Stylewear Review*, 47:8 (15 August 1935).

62 NAC, H.H. Stevens Papers, vol. 125, W. Cook to H.H. Stevens, 15 March 1935; PAA, Premiers' Papers, W. Aberhart, file 1101, A.C. Mackay to W. Aberhart, 26 September 1935; NAC, H.H. Stevens Papers, vol. 125a, B. Scott to H.H. Stevens, 7 August 1935; E.H. Crimp to J.H. Mitchell, 25 September 1935; *Retailer*, 37:7 (July 1935).

63 NAC, R.B. Bennett Papers, 602791–2, H.B. Scott to O.L. Spence, 5 August 1935. The role of small businessmen in the movement's local organization is treated in C.V. Carroll's fine thesis 'The Influence of H.H. Stevens and Reconstruction Party in Nova Scotia, 1934–1935' (MA thesis, University of New Brunswick 1972), 117–19. See also GAI, R.B. Bennett Papers, box 2, file 39, memo: 're important phase of differences between the Rt. Hon. R.B. Bennett and the Hon. H.H. Stevens,' n.d.; Wilbur, *H.H. Stevens*, 189–94.

64 While a full study of the 1935 election remains to be made, I took a sample of forty-six towns and cities and attempted to correlate voting in these places with the statistics on retailing in the 1941 census. I found no positive correlation between the number of stores in a place and the Reconstruction vote, nor did the vote change in any meaningful way according to total store turnovers or the size of the local retail sales force. I would not put too much faith in these findings: they represent a small sampling and they explore just three sets of variables. Furthermore, they cannot be taken to mean that retailers did not vote for Stevens: all that they show is that there does not seem to be a straightforward connection between the number or prominence of shopkeepers in an urban area and support for Stevens.

65 NAC, H.H. Stevens Papers, vol. 103, H.H. Stevens to M. Proskauer, 5 November 1935.

66 NAC, H.H. Stevens Papers, vol. 40, transcript of Grimsby speech, n.d. [March 1934]; vol. 41, transcript of speech to ORMA Convention, 5 November 1934; *New Outlook*, 2:4 (23 January 1935).

67 The first quotation is from a letter from an Asask retailer cited in D'A. Handy, 'Saskatchewan Merchants in the Great Depression: Regionalism and the Crusade Against Big Business,' *Saskatchewan History*, 43:1 (Winter 1991), 26. The other quotation are from letters found in NAC, H.H. Stevens Papers, vols. 93, 101, and 110 and in NAC, RG 33/18, vol. 4.

68 *Canadian Grocer*, 48:3 (9 February 1934); NAC, H.H. Stevens Papers, vol. 96, C.R. Kneider to H.H. Stevens, 11 April 1935; Royal Commission on Price Spreads, 22, 1782. On discounts, see Special Committee on Price Spreads, vol. 1, 395, 400–1, 433, 483, 511.

69 NAC, H.H. Stevens Papers, vol. 69, W.L. McQuarrie to H.H. Stevens, 18 May 1935; GAI, N.A. Farrow Papers, box 6, file 117, 'Minutes of Meeting of Retail Druggists' Association and the Retail Merchants' Association,' 25 February 1936.

70 *Maritime Merchant*, 42:20 (29 March 1934); *Drug Merchandising*, 15:12 (15 June 1934); *Western Retailer*, 36:3 (March 1939); *Maritime Merchant*, 43:15 (31 January 1935).

71 Special Committee on Price Spreads, vol. 1, 396, 328, and 352.

72 AO, T. Eaton Company Papers, 37–6, 'Memorandum Re Bill 79' (n.d.). Between 1935 and 1940, the Trade and Industry Commission followed up on 162 requests for investigations: see NAC, RG 36/12, vol. 1, Dominion Trade and Industry Commission, 'Report Forwarded to Finlay Sim,' 27 December 1940.

73 NAC, RG 36/12, vol. 4, J.W. Hams to G.H. Sedgewick, 29 June 1937; G.H. Sedgewick to Safeway Stores, 2 July 1937; L.W. Raley to G.H. Sedgewick, 29 July 1937; W.L. McQuarrie to G.H. Sedgewick, 18 September 1937 and 30 September 1937; G.H. Sedgewick to Star Department Store, 20 September 1937; G.H. Sedgewick to S.J. Hollis, 16 December 1937; *Western Retailer*, 25:1 (January 1938); NAC, RG 36/12, vol. 4, R. Hay to M.N. Campbell, 22 November 1939; *Retailer*, 30:12 (December 1937).

74 AO, T. Eaton Company Papers, vol. 5, 'Alberta Legislation,' Memo: Re Alberta Suggested Codes – Draft Toronto Statement, 10 December 1934; *Retailer*, 30:1 (January 1938); PABC, GR1222, 142.6, G.R. Matthews to T.D. Pattullo, 9 December 1937; A.P. Stade & Co. to T.D. Pattullo, 29 November 1937; G.R. Matthews to members of the Provincial Legislature, 30 November 1937; G.R. Matthews to T.D. Pattullo, 14 February 1936; *Canadian Grocer*, 52:6 (15 March 1938), 52:9 (1 May 1938), and 52:8 (15 April 1938). For Woodward's opposition, see *Retailer*, 31:6 (June 1938) and 31:12 (December 1938); PABC, GR1222, 156.6, G.R. Matthews to T.D. Pattullo, 19 May 1941. On the opposition of small, primarily Asian-owned stores, see *Canadian Grocer*, 53:10 (15 May 1939).

75 *Canadian Grocer*, 51:9 (20 April 1937); NAC, H.H. Stevens Papers, vol. 62, G. Hougham to H.H. Stevens, 2 April 1936. 'It is astonishing,' the *Maritime Merchant* observed soon after the election, 'that so many retailers are indifferent to the RMA and the facilities it affords for advancing their cause,' see *Maritime Merchant*, 64:3 (1 August 1935). See also *Western Retailer*, 23:6 (June 1936).

76 One insider suggested that Brownlee had been inspired by the report which
   F.R. Scott and H.M. Cassidy had prepared for the Associated Garment Man-
   ufacturers; see UTA, H.M. Cassidy Papers, vol. 63, W.D. King to H.M.
   Cassidy, 9 April 1935. See also PAA, Department of the Attorney General,
   J.F. Lymburn Ministerial Records, vol. 4, file 128, 'Resolutions of the Annual
   Convention of the Alberta Retail Merchants' Association,' March 1933, and
   ARMA, 'General Code of Regulations Applicable to all Branches of Retail
   Trade,' July 1934; PAA, Department of the Attorney General, R.A. Smith
   Papers, box 1, file 39, R.A. Smith to W.J. Major, 12 December 1934; *Canadian
   Grocer*, 48:8 (9 March 1934) and 48:8 (20 April 1934), *Dry Goods and Stylewear
   Review*, 66:4 (April 1934).
77 NAC, R.B. Bennett Papers, 475977–80, J.E. Brownlee to R.B. Bennett, 11 April
   1934, and 475981, R.Y. Eaton to R.B. Bennett, 12 April 1934; AO, T. Eaton
   Company Papers, vol. 5, 'Summary of telephone conversation between Mr.
   Loftus and Premier Brownlee,' 9 April 1934, and memorandum, 'Loss Leaders Year 1933,' 23 July 1934.
78 AO, T. Eaton Company Papers, vol. 9, memo, 'Re Suggested Code under
   Alberta Trade and Industry Act,' 10 December 1934. *Canadian Grocer* 48:26 (28
   December 1934); PAA, Department of The Attorney General, R.A. Smith
   Papers, box 1 file 39, R.A. Smith to W.J. Mayor, 12 December 1934.
79 Stevens met with Aberhart for discussions in Vancouver, and several joint
   conventions were held between Reconstruction and Social Credit riding
   associations. Unfortunately, the newly elected premier Aberhart needed a
   federal loan of $2 million by 10 September 1935 just to meet current accounts.
   Bennett provided the money, but for a price. As he informed one panicky
   Alberta Conservative, 'I do not think you need fear the amalgamation you
   mention. It will not take place. I have been talking to Mr. Aberhart on the
   telephone. The financial situation is desperate and he will have to come to us
   for assistance at once.' See NAC, R.B. Bennett Papers, 352330, J.S. Stewart to
   R.B. Bennett, 23 August 1935; 352373, W. Aberhart to R.B. Bennett, 4 September 1935; 352358, R.B. Bennett to J.S. Stewart, 3 September 1935; 352419, W.
   Aberhart to R.B. Bennett, 11 September 1935; 35242, R.B. Bennett to D. Elton,
   22 October 1935.
80 PAA, Premier's Papers: W. Aberhart, file 921a, 'Minutes of meeting of retail,
   wholesale and manufacturers' sections of the Edmonton Chamber of Commerce,' 10 January 1936; AO, T. Eaton Company Papers, vol. 5, clipping,
   Edmonton Journal, 16 March 1936; *Canadian Grocer*, 50:6 (20 March 1936);
   NAC, Canadian Manufacturers' Association Papers, box 90, memo on 'New
   Alberta Legislation,' 1936.
81 NAC, Canadian Manufacturers' Papers, box 90, memo: 'New Alberta Legis-

lation,' 1936; PAA, Alberta Attorney General's Papers, Civil Law Books, box A048, J.J. Frawley to W.D. King, 30 April 1938; GAI, Calgary Board of Trade Papers, box 1, file 5, press release, 'Despotism Triumphant,' n.d.; box 1, file 7, Edmonton Chamber of Commerce to W. Aberhart, 17 March 1937; GAI, Social Credit Party Papers, box 1, file 2, P.W. Abbott to E.C. Manning, 23 March 1936; HBCA, Hudson's Bay Company Papers, Minutes of the Canadian Committee, vol. 20, minutes of meeting, 30 April 1936; GAI, Calgary Board of Trade Papers, box 1, file 2, J.H. Hanna to J. Blue, 11 June 1936.

82 AO, T. Eaton Company Papers, W.H. Milner to H.G. Thomson, 13 April 1936; *Financial Post*, 11 April 1936; GAI, Calgary Board of Trade Papers, box 1, file 7, J.H. Hanna to W.L. Mackenzie King, 13 January 1938; L.A. Cavanaugh to J.H. Hanna, n.d. [1938].

83 SAB, Saskatchewan Retail Merchants Association, file 460, press clippings: *Regina Leader-Post*, 26 February 1936, *Edmonton Bulletin*, 26 February 1936, and *Regina Leader-Post*, 8 April 1936; GAI, N.A. Farrow Papers, box 6, file 116, Alberta RMA, 'Memorandum Re. Druggists Plan of Organizing and Operating a Provincial Trade Association,' 13 January 1937; PAA, Premiers' Papers, W. Aberhart, file 921B, P.L. Bourque to W. Aberhart, 19 December 1936; GAI, N.A. Farrow Papers, box 8, file 149, 'Minutes of Meeting of Advisory Committee,' 26 April 1939; PAA, Premiers' Papers, W. Aberhart, file 912A, 'Notes on a Consumers Co-operative Distributive System,' n.d.; F.R. Swann, 'Progressive Social Credit in Alberta, 1935–1940' (PhD thesis, University of Cincinnati 1971), 175–7; *Canadian Grocer*, 51:11 (28 May 1937).

84 C.F. Phillips, 'State Discriminatory Chain Store Taxation,' *Harvard Business Review*, 14 (1935), 348; T. Beckman and H. Nolen, *The Chain Store Problem* (New York 1938), 250–6; M. Lee, 'Anti-Chain Store Tax Legislation,' *Journal of Business of the University of Chicago*, 13 (July 1939), 1–80; *Canadian Grocer*, 44:11 (23 May 1930). AO, Premiers' Papers, G. Henry, box 139, 'Legislation: Assessment of Chain Stores,' n.d. [1932]; box 139, J.Z. Fraser to G. Henry, 11 June 1931; Box 143, 'Resolutions Submitted to the Hon. Prime Minister Geo. S. Henry from the Ontario Associated Boards of Trade and Chambers of Commerce,' 26 November 1931; *Canadian Grocer*, 47:5 (10 March 1933) and 47:6 (24 March 1933); *Le Devoir*, 25 janvier 1933 and 8 mars 1933; *Canadian Grocer*, 47:5 (10 March 1933); MMA, *Official Report of the Monthly Meeting of the City of Montreal*, 8 March 1933, and D 401.3, 'Taxation' file, press clipping, *Gazette*, 9 October 1934; *Le Devoir*, 11 janvier 1935.

85 *Canadian Grocer*, 52:10 (15 May 1938), *Le Devoir*, 28 février 1935; MMA, D 401.3, 'Taxation' file, press clipping, *Le Canada*, 1 mars 1935; *Canadian Grocer*, 50:8 (19 April 1935) and 50:13 (26 June 1935); MUA, Montreal Board of Trade

Papers, minute book, 6 February 1935–4 February 1942, enclosed letter, D.C. Abbott to Board of Trade, 24 March 1937. The QRMA, in the meantime, had voted in convention to ask the government for a law prohibiting any one business from owning more than three outlets; see clipping, *Gazette*, 19 August 1936.

86 MMA, D 401.1, 1935–7 file:, press clipping, *Gazette*, 10 January 1935; C. Houde, transcript of speech, 13 janvier 1935; *Le Devoir*, 24 janvier 1935; MMA, D 401.1, 1935–7 file, press clipping, *Gazette*, 23 January 1937. For a good survey of Montreal's tax plight, see T. Copp, 'Montreal's Municipal Government and the Crisis of the 1930s,' in A.F.J. Artibise and G.A. Stelter, eds., *The Usable Urban Past* (Toronto 1979), 112–29.

87 *Le Prix courant*, 51:5 (15 mai 1938); *Canadian Grocer*, 51:20 (1 October 1937), 53:3 (1 February 1939), and 51:20 (1 October 1937); *Le Prix courant*, 50:7 (15 juillet 1937). The royal commission was chaired by Eduard Montpetit. It should be noted that much the same thing was going on in Manitoba, where the Goldenburg Commission was established to investigate and rule against taxing the mass merchandisers. Unfortunately, that commission decided that higher taxes on Eaton's and the HBC were needed, placing the Legislature in the uncomfortable position of having to contradict its own commission when it voted against the taxes. See *Canadian Grocer*, 53:7 (1 April 1939) and 54:8 (15 April 1940); *Le Prix courant*, 52:6 (15 juin 1939).

88 AO, T. Eaton Company Papers, vol. 37–13, A.H. Grainger to H.F. McMullen, 12 April 1937, and A.N. Carter to A.H. Grainger, 12 April 1934.

A Closing Balance

1 Canada, Restrictive Trade Practices Commission, *Loss Leader Selling: Transcript of Evidence*, vol. 12 (Ottawa 1954), 2321–35. On Shelley Brothers, see Canada, Restrictive Trade Practices Commission, *Report of the Inquiry into Loss-Leader Selling* (Ottawa 1955), 55–6.

2 P. Joyce, *Visions of the People: Industrial England and the Question of Class, 1848–1914* (Cambridge 1991), 331.

3 M. Halbwachs, *The Collective Memory* (New York 1980), J. Fentree and C. Wickham, *Social Memory* (London 1992), and E. Tonkin, *Narrating Our Pasts: The Social Construction of Oral History* (Cambridge 1991) are excellent introductions. Among the best case-studies are L. Passerini, *Fascism and Popular Memory: The Cultural Experience of the Turin Working-Class* (Cambridge 1988), in which self-representations are the topic of ch. 1; P. Joutard, *Les Anciennes Combattants et la société française, 1914–1939* (Paris 1977); H. Russo, *The Vichy Syndrome: History and Memory in France since 1944* (Cambridge 1991); L.L.

Langer, *Holocaust Testimonies: The Ruins of Memory* (New Haven 1991); and F. Zonabend, *The Enduring Memory* (Manchester 1984).

4 The classic study is D. Schoenbaum, *Hitler's Social Revolution: Class and Status in Nazi Germany, 1933–1939* (New York 1966), ch. 4.

5 S. Ranulf, *Moral Indignation and Middle Class Psychology* (New York 1962), 43–6; S. Volkov, *The Rise of Popular Anti-modernism in Germany: The Urban Master Artisans, 1873–1896* (Princeton 1978), 302.

6 M.B. Miller, *The Bon Marché: Bourgeois Culture and the Department Store, 1869–1920* (Princeton 1981), 213–14. Emphasis added.

7 F. de Saussure, *Course in General Linguistics* (New York 1959), 74.

8 M. Sahlins, *Islands in History* (Chicago 1985), 153.

9 D. Hounshell, *From the American System to Mass Production* (Baltimore 1984), ch. 8; M. Orvell, *The Real Thing: Imitation and Authenticity in American Culture* (Chapel Hill 1989), part 3.

Index

Aberhart, William, 15, 286, 320, 330, 332

accounting. *See* bookkeeping

Accum, Frederick, 155–6

Achat chez nous, 92–3, 324, 336–7

Action française, 6

Action libérale nationale, 287

Adanac Stores, 182, 271–2

adaptation (*see also* mass-market culture), 13, 101, 150, 184–6, 190, 196, 204–5, 207–8, 210–11, 226–9, 241–2, 278, 281–2, 325–6, 341–3, 347

adulteration, 93, 155–7, 236

advertising, 13, 68, 147, 170, 198; cooperative, 265, 277, 279; false, 236–7, 323, 332; manufacturer-controlled, 29, 103, 141–3, 150, 171–2, 180, 183–4, 296; mass marketers and, 78, 119, 121, 127, 218, 222, 225–6, 236–7, 326–7

agency contracts, 153, 180, 181, 213

Amalgamated Clothing Workers' Union, 295, 298, 318

anti-Asian sentiment (*see also* nativism), 55, 92–5, 239, 264, 324

anti-monopolism, 12, 60, 132–5, 147, 235, 239, 252, 259, 286, 303, 305, 308, 311–12, 314, 322–4, 327

anti-Semitism (*see also* nativism), 4–5, 6, 8, 41, 91–4, 195, 324

appliance selling, 24, 153, 165–6, 180, 278, 294

Arcand Act, 318

Arnold Brothers stores, 221, 391 n48

artisans, 7, 22–3

Associated Clothing Manufacturers, 135, 293, 295–9, 302, 305–6, 319

associations (*see also* names of specific organizations), 8, 20, 27, 39, 76–7, 97–8, 199, 231–4, 246–7, 279–80, 282–3, 345; rivalries among, 241, 265, 278

Atlantic & Pacific stores, 125, 220–2, 225–6, 313, 337

automobiles, 111, 153, 165, 166, 207, 212–13, 294

bananas, 38

bankruptcy, 68–72, 187–8, 197–204, 302

Barter, James, 197–8

Bartlett, George, 206, 207

Bartlett, MacDonald and Gow, 206–9, 216
Bechhofer, Frank, 17
Beckett, H.C., 255–6
Beebe, L.W., 220
Bell, C.M., 294
Bennett, R.B., 286, 304–6, 313–14, 323, 331–2, 423 n79
Berger's Tailoring, 221, 296–7
Berkstresser, H.C., 313
biscuits, 111–12
Bliss, J. Michael, 7, 65
Board of Commerce, 188, 252–63, 301
book/stationery selling, 23, 46, 48, 278–9
bookkeeping, 21, 150, 168–70, 187–90, 204–5, 255, 268–9, 410 n42
boot and shoe selling, 20, 26, 46, 49, 64, 77, 135, 141, 151–3, 162, 196, 197, 247
boots and shoes, 111, 112, 117, 122, 135, 197
boycotts, 129, 134–5
Bradstreet Company, 162, 180
brand-name products, 29, 103, 140–1, 159, 161, 171–2, 183, 233–4, 240–1, 246, 248, 268, 295
Brandeis, Louis, 12–13
Brantford Washing Machine Company, 294
Brownlee, John, 330–1, 333
Bruser Maynard, Fredelle, 195
Bureau of Industries, 106–7, 385 n11
Burns, Jerry, 191
Burton, C.L., 216–17, 313
butchers, 20, 23, 28, 39, 46, 141, 151, 155, 157, 163
buy at home, 79, 248
buyer's strike, 135–7, 143, 147, 259

buying (see also manufacturing; wholesaling), 21–2, 202, 250–1, 270–1, 340–1; bulk, 121–2, 173, 177, 198, 225–6, 250–1, 293–4, 298–9, 305, 307–8; cooperative, 181–3, 240; direct, 103, 121, 141–2, 144, 153, 180, 185, 207, 240–3, 251, 261, 268, 270–1; discounts, 121–2, 225–6, 251, 256, 270–1, 307, 311, 323, 325–6, 332; hand-to-mouth, 136, 160–1, 177, 261; shipping, 153, 160, 270–1

Cairncross and Lawrence pharmacy, 160
Canadian Bank of Commerce, 137, 166
Canadian Chain Store Association, 223, 312, 336
Canadian Clothing Manufacturers Association, 295
Canadian Department Stores, 215, 217, 404 n25
Canadian Furniture Association, 58
Canadian Jewellers' Association, 309
Canadian Manufacturers' Association, 172, 174, 254–5, 258, 300–1, 333
Canadian Pharmaceutical Association, 77, 82–3, 88, 91, 244, 246, 248, 265–9, 277–9, 281, 302
canned food, 152, 157, 224, 292–3
Caplan, Ida and David, 48
Carlisle, C.H., 308
Carroll (William) stores, 124, 221, 225
cash selling, 21, 64–5, 114, 116–17, 150, 163–4, 167, 186
Cassidy, Harry M., 291, 307, 423 n76
catalogues. See mass merchandising

Central Finance Corporation. *See* Household Finance

Central Supply Warehouse, 297

chain stores. *See* mass merchandising

Charbonneau, L., 88

Charlton, E.P., 126

cheap goods, 65, 157, 234–5, 237, 259, 293–4

Chester, P.A., 313

Chinese (*see also* anti-Asian sentiment), 36, 38–42, 95, 375 n47

Civil Servants Association, 130

Clark, D.W., 271

Clawson, Mary Ann, 58

Claxton, Brooke, 336

clerks, 42, 63–4, 67, 74, 81, 88–90, 113–14, 123, 152, 158–9, 176, 205, 218, 223, 375 n45

clothiers, 20, 23–4, 26, 41, 46, 48, 89, 119, 126, 141, 153, 160–1, 165, 167, 177, 183–4, 197, 203, 206, 225, 257, 297

clothing, 23, 29, 105–6, 109, 112–14, 116–17, 127, 177, 197, 290, 294

cold storage, 134

Colgate-Palmolive Company, 249, 269, 277

Collective Agreement Extension Act. *See* Arcand Act

Combines Investigation Act: of 1910, 251, 256, 258, 260; of 1923, 259–61, 274–7, 316–17, 328

Comfort Kimona Manufacturing Company, 184

commercial travellers, 22, 70, 138

community, 62–3, 71–2, 78–9, 81, 116, 195, 207, 209, 279, 326–7

competition: price, 54–5, 86, 120–1, 123–4, 127, 135–6, 195–6, 198–9,

205–6, 212, 215, 218, 221, 236, 240, 271, 274, 280, 299, 302; service, 155, 177–9, 280–1; specialization and, 24–5, 30; unfair, 26–7, 32, 41–3, 66, 78, 85–6, 93, 231, 235–6, 238–9, 280, 325–7, 332

confectionery, 24, 46, 48, 142, 152

Consolidated Food Products, 221

consumer finance, 165–7

Consumer's League, 130, 134, 333

consumption (*see also* farmers; mass merchandising; middle class; women; working class): attitudes towards, 12–13, 44–5, 63–4, 71, 90, 112–17, 129, 131–2, 140–6, 177,; 233–6, 238–9, 252, 258–60, 297, 327; feminization of, 45, 63, 74, 90, 113–17, 119–20, 123–4, 134, 140, 157, 234, 238, 252, 281; growth of, 102–15, 128–37, 146–7

Cook, Warren K., 297–9, 302–10, 315, 318–19, 328, 330

Cook Clothing Company, 177

Cook County Business Man's Association, 236

Co-operative Commonwealth Federation, 207, 286, 321

cooperatives: consumer, 130, 133, 331; credit associations, 38–9, 164; voluntary pools, 150, 181–3, 191, 240–4, 248, 262, 268, 271–2, 278, 340

Copp, Terry, 110

cost of living (*see also* consumption), 103, 115, 129–30, 132–3, 143–4, 387 n19

Cost of Living Commission, 252–3

Cox, H.C., 215

Cox, Mark, 254

credit (*see also* cash selling; power

relations): abandonment of, 114, 150, 163–4, 166–7, 175, 186: instalment and hire purchase, 164–5, 296; rating, 47, 51, 161–2, 198; traditional, 21, 32, 64–5, 114, 161–3, 164–5; wholesale, 21–2, 38, 60, 70, 105, 138, 149, 161–2, 163–4, 168, 175, 177, 197–8, 202–3, 296

Criminal Code (section 498A), 251, 258, 260, 275, 316–17, 328

Crowder, J.T., 265, 267, 271–3, 275, 277–8, 280, 288, 302, 308, 375 n47

Davidson, William, 162

Davies (William) Company, 124, 221

deflation (*see also* mass production; overproduction), 104, 109, 110, 135–6, 138–40, 143–4, 172–3, 175, 201, 212, 264–5, 290–5, 296, 306; support for, 144–5, 172–3, 175–6, 252–3, 259–60, 296, 306, 348–9

Defoe, Daniel, 59

departmentalization, 150, 158, 169, 204

Desmarais, S.E., 278, 302

display, 28, 42, 63, 73, 81, 83, 85, 89, 115, 151–5, 157–8, 180, 186–7, 195, 265, 341–2; mass merchandisers and, 116–19, 281

Dominion grocery stores, 125, 220–5, 312–13, 337, 391 n48

Douglas, N.B., 267

Dowler's clothing stores, 124

Dreiser, Theodore, 116–17

Drug Trading Company (*see also* Druggists' Syndicate), 249, 269

druggists. *See* pharmacists

Druggists' Syndicate, 240–2, 244, 245, 256, 269

drugs, 140, 152, 233–4, 240–1, 248, 294

dry goods, 118, 151–2, 173

dry goods selling, 23, 26, 29, 41, 46–8, 151–2, 160, 173, 180–1, 184, 206–9

Dun (R.G.) & Company, 47, 50, 162, 199

Duplessis, Maurice, 6, 286, 330, 336–8

Dupuis Frères department store, 27, 118

Duquette, Charles, 329

Dysart, A.A., 330

early and Sunday closing, 27, 32, 42, 55–6, 85–6, 92–3

Eastern Townships Bank, 105

Eaton, R.Y., 120–1, 212, 305, 308, 331

Eaton, Timothy, 118, 119, 161

Eaton (T.) Company, 27, 54, 74, 88–9, 116, 118–23, 149, 154, 211–19, 237, 242–3, 293, 298, 312, 325, 331, 333, 375 n45, 389 n33

Eaton's groceterias, 215, 217, 314

Eby-Blain Company, 261

education and apprenticeship, 63–4, 82–3, 86, 141, 173, 178, 193, 241, 246, 248, 271, 283, 341, 381 n41

Edwards, F.A., 160

Elliman plan, 244–7, 249, 250

Elliott, Brian, 17

entrepreneurship, 10, 66, 99–101, 206–10

Épicerie Moderne Ltée, 272

Fair Trade League, 271–4, 276, 324

family, 30, 34, 38, 48–9, 74–5, 89–90, 94, 202–3

Farley, A.R., 278–9

farmers, 30, 64, 104, 108–9, 130, 162–3, 193; as consumers, 23–4, 71, 111–12, 212–13

fashion, 64, 112–14, 116–17, 197, 234, 293, 296

fixtures. *See* display

Flavelle, Joseph, 215, 308

flies, 155

Florence, Katherine and George, 50

food, 64, 104–7, 111–12, 125–6, 129–31, 140–1, 151–2, 156, 171–2, 252, 290

Forsyth Shirt Company, 183–4, 296

Franklin, Benjamin, 59

Freiman (A.J.) department store, 27, 274

fruiterers, 38, 40, 157

Fudger, H.H., 215

furniture and furnishings, 109, 111–13, 154, 234

Furniture Dealers' Association, 263

Furniture Manufacturers' Association, 295, 299–300, 306, 319

furniture selling, 26, 41, 49, 152–4, 160, 164–5, 170, 173, 225, 293–4, 299

Gascon, C.-A., 336

gendered work (*see also* clerks; power relations, male/female), 47–9, 73, 88–90, 114–15, 159

general merchants, 20, 21, 23–4, 26, 77, 83, 155, 160, 186, 195, 210, 212–13

Gibbard, G.E., 242–3

Gillard (W.H.) Company, 255, 261

Glyn-Jones, William, 267–70, 274–6, 280–1

Grassby, A.E., 306, 307, 309, 321

greengrocers. *See* Fruiterers

grocers, 20, 25, 26, 28, 30, 32, 34–5, 40–2, 49–50, 83, 85–6, 93, 104, 125–7, 141–2, 151–2, 158–9, 161, 167, 177–8, 181–3, 185–6, 191–2, 200–2, 221–2, 224–5, 234, 237, 261–2, 271–3, 277

Groulx, Lionel, 6

Gundy, J.H., 216

Hamilton, Richard, 57

Hamilton, Ruth, 88

hardware, 130

hardware selling, 24, 26, 28, 46, 152, 165, 181, 183, 203, 271, 302

Hargreaves, John, 235, 240–2, 244–5, 265, 269, 282–3

Harris, Stewart, 163

Hassall, Arthur Hill, 156

hawkers. *See* pedlars

Heinze, Andrew, 113

Henry, George, 335

hire purchase. *See* credit

Hoffmeister Electric, 209

Hofstadter, Richard, 8, 56

Holt, Herbert, 216

home delivery (*see also* parcel post), 117, 163, 223

Houde, Camillien, 336–7

Hougham, George, 62–3, 78–9, 86, 88, 186, 228, 264–5, 267, 288, 302, 306, 310, 314–15, 321, 326–30

Household Finance, 166–7

Hudon-Hébert-Chaput company, 262, 272

Hudson's Bay Company, 120, 124, 214–15, 217, 219, 311, 313, 331

Hughes, Everett, 6, 34, 41

hui, 38–9

Huston, B.T., 146

identification, shopkeepers' (*see also*

independence; legitimacy; profit;
respectability): class (*see also*
middle class; working class), 50,
81–96, 192–3, 279–81; ethnicity (*see
also* Chinese; Italians; Jews), 36–44,
69–70, 91–6, 100, 112–13, 188–9,
201–2, 204, 321, 375 n45; gender
(*see also* power relations,
male/female; women), 48–9, 51,
56, 73–6, 87–91, 281; limitations of,
72–6, 79–97, 231, 279–80, 310, 314,
322, 324, 345; symbols and, 56–68,
76–80, 97, 193–4, 282, 284, 322–4,
326–7, 343–5
Imperial Tobacco Company, 126, 180
independence, 59, 61–2, 70–1, 82,
101, 150, 191, 194–5, 282–3, 292,
343, 345
Industrial Standards Act, 318
inflation (*see also* consumption;
resale price maintenance), 105,
108, 110, 124–5, 129–33, 135, 175,
199, 211–12, 247, 252–3, 259; support for, 143–5, 138–9, 171–2,
176–9, 295, 300–1, 306, 348–9
Ing, Walter, 85
Ironside, Clayton, 83
Irving, John, 6
Italians, 36–7, 40–1, 188–9
Ives, Claude, 197

Jackson, R., 124
Japanese Shoe Repair Association, 39
Jenkins (H.M.) groceries, 158
jewellers, 20, 26, 28, 309
Jews (*see also* anti-Semitism), 36–7,
40, 42, 129, 188–9
Johnson, J.G., 223
Johnston, William, 296
Joyce, Patrick, 344

Kelvinator Company, 180
King, William Lyon Mackenzie, 134,
251, 308, 323, 329, 333, 349
Kinkhammer, Martin, 203
Kinnear, Thomas, 261
Kirkham's grocery stores, 221
Kneider, C.R., 325
Knox, S.H., 126
Kresge's variety stores, 126, 225

labour. *See* clerks
labour theory of value, 138, 145
Laporte Martin Ltée, 262, 272
Lasswell, Harold, 5, 7, 8, 12, 56,
228
Leader stores, 262, 271–2
Learie, Thomas W., 303, 305–6, 319
Legaré, P.T., 124
legitimacy (*see also* competition,
unfair), 56, 66, 80, 84–5, 90, 92–3,
96, 192–3, 231, 238–9, 280, 282–3,
345
Lesage, C.A., 156
Levine, David, 102
licensing, 27, 41, 55, 85–6, 193, 302,
325–6, 331, 333–4
Ligett (Louis K.) stores, 181, 222
Loblaw, T.P., 124, 226
Loblaw's grocery stores, 124–5,
220–5, 391 n48
Lord's Day Alliance (*see also* early
and Sunday closing), 42, 85, 92
loss-leaders, 120–1, 176–7, 198, 236,
313, 323, 326, 329, 331–3, 340
Lower, A.R.M., 195, 206
Lowney, Harold, 142
Lumbers (James) and Company, 182,
262, 272
Lyman (Arthur) company, 269, 271,
276

McCann, G.A., 233–4, 239, 241
McCraw, Thomas, 12–13
MacDonald, Colin, 206, 207
MacDonald's Consolidated, 191, 221, 262
McFall, J.R., 253
McGregor, F.A., 275–6
McKendrick, Neil, 102, 128
Mackintosh, W.A., 275
McLean, J.S., 148, 308
McQuarrie, W.L., 79, 325, 326, 328
McTaggart, E.R., 93
Mailloux and Parent grocery stores, 221
mail order. See mass merchandising
main-street shopkeeping (see also associations; identification; middle class; shopkeepers), 31–5, 38–9, 49–50, 81–4, 86, 150, 163, 168–70, 189–95, 205–10, 227–9, 238–40, 257, 268–70, 280–4, 310–11, 322, 325–6
Malcolm, James, 172–3
Mann, William, 6
Manning, Ernest, 333–4
manufacturing (see also mass production; buying, direct; power relations, supplier/retailer; regulation, manufacturers and; specific business and association names), 19–20, 22–3, 33, 132–3, 105–7, 109–10, 135–48, 150, 289–301, 319; attitudes to retailing, 141, 171–4, 176–80, 183–5, 248–9, 289; Depression's impact on, 290–5; industrial codes and, 298–300, 302, 307, 317–18; price-fixing and (see also inflation; resale price maintenance), 242–5, 251, 267–70, 273–7,

284; vertical integration and, 126, 233, 297, 294
Marland-Woolnough Company, 261
Martin stores, 221
Marx, Karl, 17–18, 292
mass-market culture (see also adaptation), 13, 15, 102–3, 114–15, 119–20, 123–4, 128, 145–9, 165–9, 174–5, 184–6, 190, 198, 232, 265, 342, 347–8; resistance to, 116, 233–6, 238, 241, 244
mass merchandising (see also advertising; buying, bulk; competition; consumption; loss-leaders; specific business names), 27, 47, 90, 109–10, 115, 149, 173, 177, 275; chains, 5, 124–7, 148, 195, 213, 215, 220–6, 270, 275, 280–1, 311–13, 336; consumers and, 90, 116–20, 123–6, 235–6, 311, 327; cultural goods and, 117, 119; departmentals, 27, 54, 116–24, 127, 135, 206, 213–20, 235, 305, 333; hostility to, 3, 27, 54–5, 78, 116, 118, 122, 196, 235–9, 264–5, 294, 308–9, 311, 314, 324, 329–30, 336; mail-order, 122–4, 211–13, 217, 314, 326; as model, 127–8, 149–50, 160, 167–8, 175, 284, 341
mass production (see also manufacturing), 22–3, 105, 294–5; critique of (see also inflation), 286–7, 295; ethos of (see also deflation), 144–5, 172–4, 232, 253, 259–60, 263, 275, 295–6, 300, 306, 349
Matthews, George, 329
Mayer, Arno, 56, 58
Merchants' Consolidated, 182, 183
mergers, 180–1, 215, 217, 221, 245, 261–2

Messier, Rossario, 320

Metropolitan Stores, 126, 222–3

middle class, 368 n5; consumption of (*see also* consumption), 40, 112, 117–19, 126, 130, 134, 157, 163; retailers as (*see also* identification, class; main-street shopkeeping), 32–5, 47, 191–2, 228–9

Middleton, J.T, 237

migration, 109, 110

Mill, John Stuart, 137

Mills, Charles, 213

Minville, Esdras, 287

Model Underwear Company, 294

modernization. *See* adaptation; professionalization

Moore, Tom, 307

Morgan (Henry) and Company, 27, 118

Murphy, C.A., 305

Murphy, Lucy Eldersveld, 73

Murphy's department store, 27, 119

Murray (W.A.) department store, 122

musical reproduction and instrument selling, 74, 111–13, 165–6, 277

mutual aid associations, 38–9, 41

Nash Tailoring Company, 297

National Cash Register Company, 169, 170

National Council of Women, 157

National Drug and Chemical Company, 245, 266, 269, 271

National Fair Trade Council, 306, 308–9, 313, 315, 317, 328

National Grocers Ltd, 261–2, 272

National Industrial Recovery Act, 288, 298–302, 307, 328

National Recovery Administration, 298, 303, 306–8, 315–17, 330

National Retail Trade Federation, 320

nativism (*see also* identification, ethnicity), 40–4, 71, 92–5, 189, 192, 239, 264, 324, 336–7

Neal Brothers grocery mail order, 213

New Deal, 315–16; in United States, 298–9

Nichols, G.B., 252

Noad's groceries, 221

Nord, Philip, 11–12

O'Connor, L.V., 276

O'Connor, W.F., 253–9

Ogilvy's department store, 27, 118

Ontario College of Pharmacy, 246, 277, 408 n18

Ontario Growers' Markets Council, 292

Ontario Retail Druggists' Association, 240–1, 263–5, 267, 278, 408 n18

Ontario Retail Hardware Association, 77, 83, 302, 310

Oriental Exclusion Act (*see also* anti-Asian sentiment), 95, 264

overhead costs, 69, 173, 175–6, 198, 208, 219, 222–5, 342–3

overproduction (*see also* mass production), 109–10, 136, 140, 143–5, 291–2, 299

Ozone Company (contract), 242–3, 245, 247, 249, 265, 273

packaging, 29, 140–1, 151–2, 155, 157, 159, 186, 224, 234

parcel post, 123

Parke Davis and Company, 243
Passerini, Luisa, 344
Pattullo, Thomas D., 320, 330
pedlars, 30–1, 38, 40, 55, 90, 213,
    302
Pentland, W.J., 125
Peps, Sam, 89, 128, 133
petite bourgeoisie: business history
    and, 9–10; concept of, 4, 14, 17, 56,
    287; mentality of, 4–13, 56–7,
    99–100, 228, 230, 232, 287, 346–7;
    politics and, 4–9, 230–1, 286–8,
    346; symbol of, 286–8, 302–3, 332,
    345–6; retailers as, 17–18, 99
Pharmacie Moderne, 88, 268, 329
pharmacists, 23, 24, 27–8, 74, 88, 91,
    127, 140, 155, 158–60, 181–2,
    209–10, 222, 240–50, 265–71,
    274–9, 280–4, 302; professional vs
    commercial, 82–3, 178, 233–4,
    240–1, 244, 246–7, 266–7, 269,
    278–9, 282–3
Phillip (A.O.) butcher shops, 221
Piggly Wiggly stores, 221
Piva, Michael, 110
Pollock, Nathan, 94
Pommier, Adrien, 189–90
populism, 8–9, 230
power relations, male/female (see
    also women), 45–6, 48, 73, 87–90;
    reform and (see also reform), 303,
    309, 327–8, 331–2, 334–5, 338–9;
    retailer/consumer (see also con-
    sumption), 14, 127–9; supplier/
    retailer (see also buying; credit),
    14, 121–2, 138, 141, 149–50,
    159–62, 163–9, 174–5, 177, 179–80,
    183–5, 190, 232, 244–5, 250–1,
    266–7, 269–70, 272, 284, 289,
    294–6, 341–3

price-fixing. See resale price main-
    tenance
price spreads inquiry, 306–13,
    315–17
professionalization, 82–4, 87–8,
    189–93, 202–5, 228–9, 231, 240–1,
    279–80, 282–3, 342
profit, 33–4, 68–9, 174–6, 190, 198,
    208–10, 215–19, 266–7, 289–91;
    price-fixing and, 244, 253–5, 257,
    270–1, 276, 413 n72; as symbol,
    65–6, 68–9, 82, 239;
profiteering, 133–6, 253, 255, 258
progress, 66, 192–4, 242, 282–3
Proprietary Articles Trading Associ-
    ation, 243–4, 266–79, 283–4, 288,
    299, 302, 314, 324, 329; British,
    266–7; membership in, 268
public health. See adulteration; dis-
    play; residence
Pure Food Stores, 221

Rabnett, F.H., 170
Randall and Johnston Clothing
    Company, 296–7
Raney, William E., 258, 261
Ranulf, Svend, 4, 8, 12, 56
Raynault, Adhémar, 336
Reconstruction Party, 15, 286,
    318–25, 327–8, 332, 423 n79
Red and White Stores (Ontario), 182,
    262
Red and White Stores (western), 272
reform: meaning of (see also regula-
    tion), 287–8, 322–4, 330
regulation (see also resale price
    maintenance), 12–13, 252–5,
    258–61, 303–4, 313, 315–17, 323,
    420 n52; manufacturers and,
    254–6, 258; shopkeepers and, 28,

95, 254, 263, 274–8, 301–3, 315, 319–39
resale price maintenance (*see also* inflation; manufacturing; power relations, supplier/retailer; profit; specific association names), 15, 79, 144, 172, 176–7, 179, 232–3, 242–5, 249, 251, 253–5, 257, 260, 266–78, 280, 299, 304–5, 307, 331
residence, 35, 47, 50, 87–8, 93, 107–8, 193, 206
respectability, 20, 59, 78, 80–1, 195, 209, 241, 283
Retail Grocers' Association, 27, 77, 237
Retail Merchants' Association, 41, 54, 62, 65–6, 77–96, 148, 164, 177, 186, 198, 232, 235, 237–9, 241–8, 256–8, 263–7, 271, 277–9, 282, 288, 301–3, 305–10, 313–15, 319–39, 340, 381 n41; membership in, 77, 86, 191, 207, 237–8, 246, 257–8, 263–4, 278, 313–14, 329–30, 412 n62
Rexall Drugs, 181–2, 268
Reynolds, Lloyd, 5, 270
Roebuck, A.J., 317, 318
Rolt, Richard, 59
Royal Commission on Price Spreads. *See* price spreads inquiry

Safeway Stores, 125, 183, 221, 329
Sahlins, Marshall, 347
St Laurent, Louis, 336
Saussure, Ferdinand de, 347
Savary, Jules, 59
Schneider, J.M., 140
Scoggie (W.H.) department store, 118, 122
Scott, F.R., 291, 423 n76
Scranton, Philip, 10

Sedgewick, G.H., 328–9
self-service, 158, 222
service (*see also* competition, service), 63–4, 119, 152
Shelley, A.A., 340
Shoe Dealers' Association, 135
Shoe Retailers' Association, 263
shoes. *See* boots and shoes
shoestring shopkeeping (*see also* identification; shopkeepers; working class), 30–6, 49–51, 85–6, 186–8, 200–4, 235, 270, 273, 342
shop assistants. *See* clerks
shopkeepers (*see also* main-street shopkeeping; shoestring shopkeeping; individual business and association names; specific activities; specific trades): affluence/income of (*see also* profit), 33–4, 68–9, 80–1, 84; business longevity among, 200–1; capital requirements of (*see also* credit), 187, 192, 197, 202–3; hostilities among (*see also* competition; nativism; power relations), 24–5, 27–8, 31–3, 38, 41–3, 55–6, 80, 85–95, 192, 280–1, 310, 319–20, 325; importance of class to (*see also* middle class; petite bourgeoisie; working class), 33–6, 50–1, 86, 100–1, 186–9; numbers and heterogeneity of, 19–20, 23–6, 30–3, 36–7, 45–6, 199–201, 227, 272–3, 343; predicted demise of (*see also* petite bourgeoisie), 5, 99–100, 127, 195–6, 210–11, 226–8, 230–1, 275, 296, 332, 346
shopping. *See* consumption
Simpson, Anne, 88
Simpson (Robert) Company, 27,

118–19, 122–3, 212–17, 219–20, 243,
   293, 298, 325, 405 n28
Sloan (John) and Company, 182
small shops. *See* shoestring
   shopkeeping
Small Stores Association, 92
Smith, Adam, 26
Smith, Morley, 313
Social Credit Party, 6, 286, 315, 321,
   332–5, 423 n79
Social Survey Commission, 113–14
Sommerville, Norman, 308
Souch, Bertram, 209–10
Sparks, Percy, 303, 305, 306, 308
specialization, 20–5, 138, 236
Spencer's department store, 27, 216
Squibb (E.R.) Company, 178, 277
Stanbury, R.B.J., 269, 279
standard of living. *See* cost of liv-
   ing; shopkeepers, affluence/
   income of
Steinberg's grocery stores, 337
Stepler's drug store, 162
Stevens, H.H., 15, 286–8, 303–9,
   311–24, 328, 330, 332–3, 335–6, 338
Stewart, T.J., 177
stock turn, 83, 169–71, 174–6, 190,
   202–3, 208–10, 215, 219
Stockdale, Frank, 76, 83
Stollery, Frank, 257
Stone, Ida, 49, 75
Stop and Shop stores, 223, 225
store size, 17, 117–18, 122, 152, 192
Street, O.D., 143
street trading. *See* display; pedlars
Superior Stores, 182–3, 191, 221,
   272
sweatshops, 291–3, 298–9, 302–3,
   305, 306–7, 314, 317, 323
Swift Canada Company, 290

Tamblyn (George) Company, 126,
   220, 270, 274–7
Tariff Board, 303–4
Taschereau, Alexandre, 317–18, 320,
   335–6
taxation, 79, 135, 168, 263, 288, 302,
   330, 335–8, 399 n34
Teco stores, 215
telephones, 117, 153, 160
temperance, 71, 156
Temple, William, 59
Tench, Charles, 21
Thomson, J.M., 170
Thrift Stores, 223, 224, 226, 337
Tinling, C.W., 266, 269
Tip Top Tailors, 126, 221, 297
toiletries, 111, 171–4
Tolmie, N.W., 294
tongs, 38–9
Trade and Industry Act, 321–2,
   334
Trade and Industry Commission,
   316–17, 328–9
Trades and Labor Congress, 130,
   134, 157, 237, 307
travelling salesmen. *See* commercial
   travellers
Tremble, John, 266
Trowern, E.M., 66, 78, 237, 244, 263,
   267
turnover. *See* stock turn

unemployment relief, 207, 297, 311,
   417 n21
Union Nationale, 287, 336–7
United Cigar Stores, 126
United Drug Company, 181–3
United Farmers of Alberta, 315,
   331–3
United Farmers of Ontario, 256

Vancouver Harbour Commission, 304–5
variety stores, 126, 222, 225
Victoria Independent Groceries, 182, 272
Volkov, Shulamit, 346
voluntary pools. *See* buying, cooperative; cooperatives: voluntary pools

Wampole (H.K.) Company, 243, 245
Watters, Henry, 54, 244
Weibe, Robert, 8
weights and measures, 157, 224, 312, 328, 332
Western Grocers' Company, 272
Whebby, A.S., 326
White, William, 258–9
Wholesale Druggists' Association, 243, 245, 248, 250, 267
Wholesale Grocers' Association, 251, 255–6, 261–2
Wholesale Grocers' Guild, 250–1
wholesaling (*see also* buying; cooperatives: voluntary pools; power relations, supplier/retailer; business and association names), 20–2, 29, 55, 109, 121–2, 138, 160, 198, 202; attitude to retailers, 147–8, 150, 171, 177–8, 180–1, 183–5; Board of Commerce and, 255–6; decline of, 141–2, 160–1, 180–1, 243, 245, 261–2, 284–5; price maintenance and, 243–5, 250–1, 266, 269–72

widows, 47, 49, 51, 90
women (*see also* power relations, male/female): clerks (*see also* gendered work), 89–90, 113–14, 159, 223; consumers (*see also* consumption, feminization of), 44, 90, 94, 106–7, 111, 117, 119–20, 128–9, 154–5, 157, 163; retailers (*see also* identification, gender; shoestring shopkeeping), 30, 34, 45–51, 75, 88–9, 100, 188, 201–2
Woodward's department store, 329
Woolworth, Frank W., 126
Woolworth's variety stores, 126, 220, 225
work, 59, 61, 81–2
working class (*see also* Trades and Labor Congress), 139, 235, 290–3, 297–9, 303, 306, 318, 321; background of retailers (*see also* identification, class; shoestring shopkeeping), 34–5, 188, 201–2, 205; consumers (*see also* consumption), 106, 110, 111–12, 129–30, 133, 143–4, 156–7, 163, 191, 297, 389 n33; housing, 106–8, 386 n14
Wyatt, J.H., 295

Yellow Dogs, 91, 281
York Trading Company, 122, 183, 256, 262, 272

Zola, Émile, 116–17